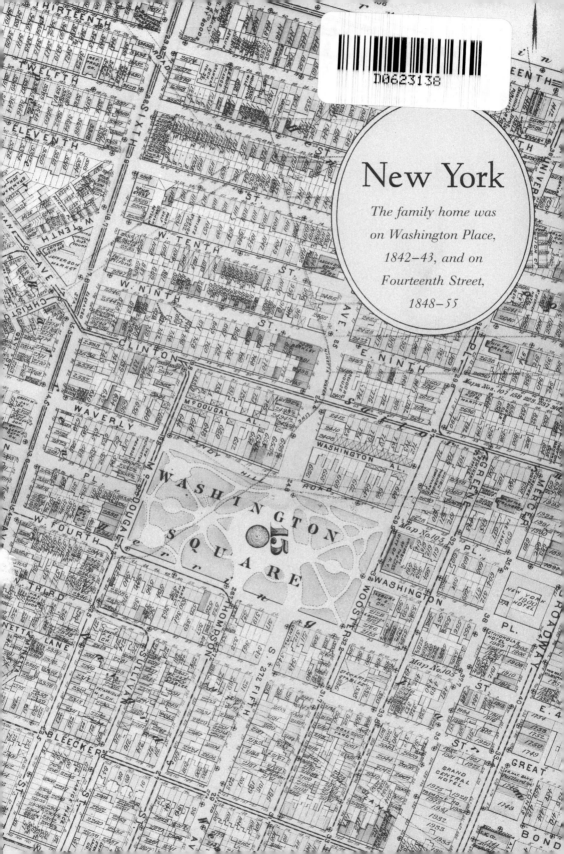

New York

The family home was on Washington Place, 1842–43, and on Fourteenth Street, 1848–55

1st Battlefield 1991

Other Books by R.W.B. Lewis

THE AMERICAN ADAM

THE PICARESQUE SAINT

TRIALS OF THE WORD

THE POETRY OF HART CRANE

EDITH WHARTON: A BIOGRAPHY

As Editor

MALRAUX: A COLLECTION OF ESSAYS

HERMAN MELVILLE: A READER

THE PRESENCE OF WALT WHITMAN

COLLECTED STORIES OF EDITH WHARTON

AMERICAN LITERATURE: THE MAKERS AND THE MAKING
(with Cleanth Brooks and Robert Penn Warren)

LETTERS OF EDITH WHARTON *(with Nancy Lewis)*

THE JAMESES

A Family Narrative

to us. The radiance of Harry's
visit has not faded yet & I come
upon gleams of it 3 or 4 times a day
in my farings to and fro, but it
has never a bit diminished the
lustre of far off shining Newport
all silver and blue & this heavenly
group below

(all being more or less failures, espe-
ially the two outside ones). The more
so as the above mentioned Harry could
in no wise satisfy my cravings to
know of the family and friends as he

THE
JAMESES

A Family Narrative

R.W. B. Lewis

ANDRE DEUTSCH

First published 1991 by André Deutsch Limited
105–106 Great Russell Street   London   WC1B 3LJ

British Library Cataloguing in Publication Data
Lewis, R.W.B.
The Jameses : a family narrative.
I. Title
929.20973

ISBN 0233987487

Published by arrangement with Farrar, Straus and Giroux, USA

Printed in the United States of America

For Judith McConnell and Sue Berger

Much more than kin, and much much more than kind

The aim of this book is to tell the story of a remarkable American family—as regards its literary and intellectual accomplishments, perhaps the most remarkable family the country has ever known—from its eighteenth-century Irish origins to the death of the novelist Henry James in 1916.

As the title indicates this is, in fact, a narrative, and not, for example, a series of textual commentaries. A great many texts are considered, and some of them gone into in a certain detail; it could hardly be otherwise with these extraordinarily productive and expressive writers. But the emphasis is in all cases on the personal and family aspects of the work in question, what it may reveal about the writer or suggest about a family predisposition; cumulatively, what it came variously to mean to be "Jamesian"—or, as William once put it, "a native of the James family." If such an emphasis can be limiting in one perspective—this or that dimension of a text may be slighted, even as numerous friends and associates are barely named or not named at all—it is obviously apposite to my purpose, and carries with it, I think, its own justification and reward. For to an exceptional degree the Jameses were family-minded, family-conscious; they talked and wrote and speculated about the whole phenomenon of family, their own and that in the American society at large.

To make my intention clearer, let me list the characters in the cast who are given more than passing mention: William James of Albany, the founder of the family's American branch, and his third wife, Catharine Barber James; each of their eight children, but especially Augustus, Edward, and Howard, and most of all the one who became Henry James, Sr.; that Henry and his wife, the former Mary Robertson Walsh, along with Mary's sister Catherine, "Aunt Kate"; each of the five children of Henry and Mary James—the philosopher William and his wife of more than thirty years, Alice Howe Gibbens; Henry, the novelist; Garth Wilkinson (Wilky) and Caroline Cary; Robertson (Bob) and Mary Holton; and Alice, the youngest of the progeny. Cousins, near and remote, come and go: Minny Temple, Kitty Prince, Bay Emmet; in-laws have their part to play; but the Jameses just listed occupy the center of the story. The ambition has been to trace the lives and personalities of those individuals, and not less to set forth the nourishing, bruising, and illuminating relationships among them. And this across a historically momentous century-and-a-half, extending—the Jameses, as I hope will become evident, would have appreciated this way of measuring the epoch—from the American Revolutionary War through the Civil War to the First World War.

The children of William, Wilky, and Bob make brief appearances in the later chapters. But I became increasingly struck by the desirability of knowing more about them. So, in a somewhat lengthy appendix, I have continued the family story through two, and in some instances three, generations beyond the more celebrated one.

Professional and personal acknowledgments may be found at the back of the book. But I cannot conclude this prefatory word without acknowledging my indispensable precursor, *The James Family*, by my former teacher F. O. Matthiessen, published in 1947. There are no footsteps I would more gladly follow.

R.W.B.L.

Bethany, Connecticut

GENEALOGICAL TABLES

WILLIAM JAMES OF ALBANY

b. Bailieborough, Ireland, son of William James and Susan McCartney; 1771;
d. Albany, N.Y., 1832

m. 1796 *(1st)*, Elizabeth Tillman,   *(twins)*
       1774–97   Robert, 1797–1821
                               William, 1797–1868

m. 1798 *(2nd)*, Mary Ann Connolly,   Ellen (King), 1800–23
       1779–1800

m. 1803 *(3rd)*, Catharine Barber,   Augustus, 1807–66
       1782–1859   Henry (Senior), 1811–82
                               Jennet (Jeanette) (Barker), 1814–43
                               John Barber, 1816–56
                               Edward, 1818–56
                               Catherine Margaret (Temple),
                                  1820–54
                               Ellen King (Van Buren), 1823–49
                               Howard, 1828–87
                               (two children died in infancy)

HENRY JAMES SENIOR

b. Albany, 1811; d. Boston, 1882

m. 1840, Mary Robertson Walsh, daughter of James Walsh and Elizabeth Robertson; b. New York City, 1810; d. Cambridge, Mass., 1882

William, 1842–1910
Henry, 1843–1916
Garth Wilkinson, 1845–83
Robertson, 1846–1910
Alice, 1850–92

WILLIAM JAMES

b. New York City, 1842; d. Chocorua, N.H., 1910

m. 1878, Alice Howe Gibbens, daughter of Daniel Lewis Gibbens and Eliza Putnam; b. Weymouth, Mass., 1849; d. Cambridge, 1922

Henry, 1879–1947
William, 1882–1961
Herman, 1884–85
Margaret Mary (Porter), 1887–1950
Alexander, 1890–1946

GARTH WILKINSON JAMES

b. New York City, 1845; d. Milwaukee, 1883

m. 1873, Caroline Eames Cary, daughter of Joseph Cary and Caroline Eames; b. Milwaukee, 1845; d. Milwaukee, 1931

Joseph Cary, 1874–1925
Alice (Edgar), 1875–1923

ROBERTSON JAMES

b. Albany, 1846; d. Concord, Mass., 1910

m. 1872, Mary Holton, daughter of Edward Holton and Lucinda Millard; b. Milwaukee, 1847; d. Concord, Mass., 1922

Edward Holton, 1873–1954
Mary Walsh (Vaux), 1875–1956

CONTENTS

Endpapers

FRONT: *Albany:* William James's home, 1813–32, was on North Pearl Street / *New York City:* The family home was on Washington Place, 1842–43, and on Fourteenth Street, 1848–55

BACK: *Newport:* The family lived on Kay Street, 1858–62, and on Spring Street, 1862–66 / *Cambridge:* The family home was on Quincy Street, 1866–82

Frontispiece

William James sketched six family members in a letter dated November 1861. Left to right, in "this heavenly group below": Alice, Aunt Kate, Father, Henry Junior, Mother, Bob

Following page 74

William James of Albany, 1820s
Catharine Barber James, about 1830
Henry James, Sr., as a young man
Alice James, about 1854
Henry Senior and Henry Junior, 1854
Henry James, age seventeen
William James in 1858
Henry James in 1862, by John La Farge
Mary Walsh James, about 1865
Henry James, Sr., about 1865
Catherine Walsh, "Aunt Kate," about 1860

For further information about these illustrations,
see *Picture Notes and Credits* on pages 643–48.

PART I

Generations

CHAPTER ONE

William James
of Ireland and Albany

THE CURKISH TOWNLANDER

The young Irishman who would be known, in this country, as William James of Albany came to America in 1789 at the age of eighteen. He brought with him, according to family legend, "a very small sum of money, a Latin grammar in which he had already made some progress at home, and a desire to visit the field of one of the revolutionary battles." It is a legend that invites us to trust it, for the three items mentioned, taken together and symbolically, suggest a good deal about the immigrant's background and interests.

This William James was born on his father's farm in Curkish, a townland belonging to Bailieborough, itself a spreading rural area fifty-odd miles northwest of Dublin in County Cavan.* He was the second of the three sons of yet another William James (1736–1822), whom we may refer to as the First William. The family habit, much deplored by the novelist Henry, of giving the names William and Henry to male offspring in every generation over two centuries has challenged many to find ways of distinguishing between the clustering namesakes.

---

* A later James put it out that the family lived in Ballyjamesduff, a tranquil and open-spaced village a dozen miles below Bailieborough. The mistake is understandable, but Ballyjamesduff, translated from the Gaelic, means "the Town [Bally] of Black James," and in context James is probably a first rather than a family name.

Bailieborough had been "planted" in the early seventeenth century by William Bailie, a Scotsman, as part of the larger plantation of northern Ireland; the British crown imported and settled increasing numbers of individuals and families, mostly English and mostly stout Anglicans, as landowners and rulers over the preponderantly Catholic population. (American readers may think of the "Plymouth Plantation" of roughly comparable purpose, in 1620s New England.) Bailie was granted about 8,000 acres, some of it swampy—*curkish* means "marsh" or "swamp"—but containing an abundance of arable land, sloping fields, gently rising hills, and picturesque green ridges. He built himself a castle on a high point in the region, and divided his holdings into "townlands"—that is, groups of as many as ten farms, all paying heavy rents to the lord of the castle. By the mid-eighteenth century, Bailieborough included about sixty such townlands. The First William, then, worked one of ten farms in one of threescore townlands. It is thought that his forebears came over to Ireland from Wales around 1700, though this cannot be proven.

William's farm, a gracefully slanted terrain of about twenty-five acres, lying just to the north and a little to the east of the present town of Bailieborough, produced oats and potatoes, and at this stage (the practice was later abandoned as too expensive) flax for the making of linen. It was not a particularly grim life: the countryside was colorful and varied, the land sufficiently fertile, the climate bearable and at times invigorating. The current resident of Bailieborough Castle was William Stewart, High Sheriff for County Cavan and a member of the relatively independent and short-lived Irish Parliament in Dublin. He was a man of parts, evidently; and it may be that his agent, McCartney by name, was a trifle less severe in collecting rents from this particular tenant than from others—the First William was married to the agent's daughter Susan (she was ten years younger than he, and outlived him by two years, dying in 1824). The agent's name was carried forward in the basic form of Cartney, first given to one of William's and Susan's many grandchildren.*

Even so, there were hardship and restriction. The Bailieborough Jameses were Presbyterians and as such were denied ownership of their farming acreage. A breakdown of the Irish population at the end of the eighteenth century shows the Presbyterians numbering about 900,000, double the number of the ruling class of Anglo-Irish, though

---

* The name is born today by a great-grandson of William James the philosopher. See Appendix B.

much less than a third of the number of Irish Catholics, whose figures ran well over 3 million. The Presbyterians supplied the small farmers and tradesmen, especially in the northeastern part of the country, where County Cavan was situated. The Anglo-Irish, of course, were the land-owners, the high officeholders, the magistrates, the churchmen. The Catholics constituted the peasantry; it can be supposed that the most strenuous labor on the First William's farm was done by Catholic tillagers.

But the Presbyterians suffered several of the restraints of their Catholic underlings. In the tangled history of Ireland before the Union of 1800, laws, whether promulgated in England or locally, came and went, and enforcement hardened and softened. Even so, it was gen-erally the case, as said, that Presbyterians were forbidden to own land; and they were not allowed to have *churches*, but only "meeting-places," and these only at a safe distance from a built-up area. Contamination by "dissenters"—a term that included a sprinkling of Methodists and that basically meant persons who would not make the politically ac-ceptable vow of churchly allegiance—was to be strongly resisted.

By a related policy, Catholics were absolutely forbidden any kind of education, and education for Presbyterians was anything but en-couraged; the vast majority of those outside the Anglo-Irish community were illiterate. Certain Calvinist ministers, however, bravely took it on themselves to instruct the young of their flock, some of them even admitting Catholic children to their informally organized but strictly run outdoor classes.

The First William, who appears to have been a person of some energy of vision, made the most of these slim educational possibilities. He so much honored the ministerial role in the townland life that he may even have urged his second son to enter the church; a marginal and perhaps less convincing bit of the later legend is that the boy fled Ireland to escape that destiny.

The training he received, in any event, involved careful practice in handwriting; William of Albany always rather prided himself, not without reason, on his elegant script. The boy was taught to read and to be at least mildly interested in reading; standard works of English literature, well thumbed, would crowd the shelves of the Albany home. He was firmly rehearsed by his teacher in the Westminster Catechism, with its antiphonal expression of orthodox Calvinist doctrine, and would so rehearse his own children in nightly sessions. And he made a start on classical study, beginning with the elements of Latin gram-mar; something he found rewarding enough to take the Latin volume with him, if only as a memento of home, on the voyage to America.

Young William's literary and religious instruction was obviously limited, but the subsequent verbal wizardry and cultivated play of mind of the American Jameses were not utterly unprepared for. They had an educational push behind them, an indistinct family tradition of intellectual betterment. William of Albany did not himself exercise any very graceful or animate prose style; the examples of his public discourse, which we shall look at, display a kind of unwarmed magniloquence. On the private side, one of his few extant letters, as we shall also see, shows him reduced to incoherent fury over his son's financial misconduct at college; but it also suggests a strangled eloquence of a sort that would flare to genuine rhetorical greatness in the extravagant invective of that same son, Henry James the Elder. It was he in turn who bequeathed to his children a passion for expressiveness—not only to the philosopher William and the novelist Henry, who in their diametrically opposite ways were among the great stylists of our literature, but also to Alice James, who in her letters and her diary became so adept at the cut and thrust of language; and even to the younger brothers, Wilky, who could at least write an ebullient letter, and Robertson, who was capable at times of a melancholy lyricism.

The rebellion of the American colonies against the mother country in the 1770s sent a confused tremble of excitement through the tenant farmers of northern Ireland. All across the country, indeed, daring and astute Irishmen in these years were seeking to establish their own form of political independence from England. British military defeats, particularly the decisive one at Saratoga in October 1777, seemed to hasten matters, for fearing loss of control in the New World, the British felt it strategically wise to fend off local rebellion by easing things in Ireland. (Other factors, among them the recruiting of Irish troops for the American war, were also at work.) Repressive laws were rescinded and rules modified; even the despised Catholics were given a few economic privileges. For the farmers, though, conditions remained uncertain at best; and the dream of independence would soon prove illusory. In the First William's household, Robert, the oldest son, stayed on dutifully at home and oversaw the tillaging of the Curkish farm alongside his father. But the second son, William—foreseeing no satisfactory future in Bailieborough (so one imagines) as he passed through his teens and toward his majority, and inspired by the triumphant outcome of the American war for freedom—packed his Latin grammar, pocketed his few coins, and departed for the newly created United States of America.

William James of Ireland and Albany

It is a fair guess that the battlefield young William was especially keen to visit was Saratoga, where General Burgoyne had been out-maneuvered and forced to surrender to the colonists in one of the pivotal battles of history (and where also, by a dim convergence of lines, the officer commanding the American artillery battalion was Major Ebenezer Stevens, the great-grandfather, as it turned out, of Edith Wharton, who would become so close a friend of the First William's great-grandson Henry James). It may even be hazarded that it was William's pilgrimage to Saratoga, if he ever made it, that led to his settling a few years later in the nearby village of Albany.

As to the "very small sum of money": the First William paid his landlord's agent in cash, and there could have been little money on hand to give the eighteen-year-old when he left home. By the time of his death forty-three years later, William James of Albany had ex-panded that small sum into one of the two or three largest fortunes in the young country.

THE MERCHANT OF ALBANY

The immigrant began his American career where his father left off: as a tradesman dealing in farm products and dry goods. We first hear of him in 1793—his whereabouts for the four years since his arrival in this country are not known—working in Albany as a clerk in what local lore referred to as "the old blue store" of a Mr. Robison. In 1795, he opened his own store, and two years after that he announced the open-ing of a second store "for the reception of country produce," and for that reason located in the dock area. By 1805, James was running at least five places of commerce in Albany, with another one in New York City, on John Street; and he had built himself a tobacco factory.

These were not inconspicuous events in an Albany that, in the waning years of the eighteenth century, was still a circumscribed little settlement. It liked to speak of itself as an "Ancient City"—it could be dated from 1664, when it was named for the Duke of Albany, the brother of Charles II, and it had been chartered in 1686—but by the late 1790s the population was hardly in excess of 3,500 persons, with a scattering of black slave servants. There was no doubt, though, that it was a place with a future. Its location, a visitor remarked as early as 1749, was "very advantageous with regard to trade"; that is, its standing at the confluence of the slim east-running Mohawk River and the mightier Hudson curving its way through the woodlands 140 miles southeast to New York City and the Atlantic.

Several developments around the turn of the century contributed to the expansion of Albany, and William James was associated with most of them. In 1797, Albany became the state capital of New York; turnpike roads (privately created, toll-collecting rural highways) sprang into being to connect the new political center with the rest of the state, and a certain sense of bustle and importance entered the town atmosphere. By the fall of 1803, the New York State Bank opened its doors in the handsome Renaissance-style building designed by Philip Hooker. James became a director of the bank soon after it began its large-scale business—it was capitalized at $460,000—and may have helped negotiate the $9,000 loan it made almost immediately to the Great Western Turnpike Company. And on a day in September 1807, Robert Fulton's sidewinder steamboat, the *Clermont*, docked at Albany after making the run upriver from Jersey City in about thirty hours (the trip by coach from New York took up to three days). Regular intercity steamboat service was quickly established, and commerce between the cities, which had long been considerable, now increased hugely. William James helped lead the way in shipping wheat, flax seeds, timber, and meat down to New York. Via his New York agent, James McBride, the Albany merchant paid out thousands of dollars annually for his own docking rights at the foot of Greenwich Village, and no few of the consignments received by McBride were shipped seaward aboard the *Dublin Packet* to the country of James's birth.

James's Irish origins, in fact, set him somewhat apart from the other members of the new breed of merchants who were beginning to dominate the town. The older breed, of course, had been of Dutch descent and were even Dutch-speaking: Van Rensselaers, Schuylers, Ten Eycks, Bleeckers, Ten Broecks, van Loons. The tiny society had formerly a Dutch look to it: husbands and wives could be seen smoking their pipes together companionably on the stoops of their solid houses. Things began to change after the end of the Revolutionary War, when large numbers of New Englanders started to move westward in search of new spaces and opportunities in the new nation, passing through Albany on their route. There was a sudden tidal wave of migration: it was said that on a single day in 1795, an Albany citizen counted over five hundred well-filled sleighs climbing the midtown slope and disappearing into the western distance. But a good many of these travelers chose to settle in Albany, and by about 1805 the Yankees in town outnumbered the Dutch, and English became the social language. It was from these New Englanders that the influential men of affairs in the early nineteenth century were mostly drawn: men named Townsend, Stewart, Spencer, Brown, Woodworth. William James of Ireland was something of an outsider; his social standing in Albany is suggested by his absence from the city directory for half a dozen years after it began in 1817.

As though determined to exploit this distinction, James further improved his fortunes through association, marital and commercial, with other Irish-American families in the region. His first wife, Elizabeth Tillman, who died in childbirth (1797) after giving her husband twin boys, was actually of German extraction, her grandfather having emigrated from Mannheim. But in 1798, James took as his bride Mary Ann Connolly, an Irish Catholic girl whose family seems to have originated in County Armagh, about halfway between County Cavan and Belfast to the north. There is some faint evidence that Mary Ann may have been the real love of William of Albany's life, if anyone was; but she, too, died in childbirth, at the age of twenty, and was buried in the Catholic cemetery in Mohawk, New York. Her father, Bernard Connolly, a second-generation American, was a well-to-do merchant with a 600-acre farm in Mohawk, some miles west of Albany, and her uncle Michael dealt extensively in New York land (in New York, he was the business partner of the now prospering Ebenezer Stevens). When Michael died intestate in 1799, Bernard, as his older brother, took over the sizable landholdings, and it was Bernard's son-in-law William James who arranged the settlement.

After letting three years go by, James, now thirty-two, married Catharine Barber, both of whose paternal grandparents, Patrick Barber and Jane Frazer, came from County Longford, which abuts County Cavan on its southern curve. Catharine Barber was of stronger stuff than her two predecessors; she bore her husband ten children, eight of whom survived, and outlived him by twenty-seven years, to become the figure her novelist grandson would remember dispensing hospitality with little soft sighs in the Albany home or reading a ladies' novel by candlelight. It was no small benefit to William James that his third wife's kinfolk owned and edited the Albany *Register*, the weekly newspaper in which James periodically announced some new venture in merchandising.

At the same time, James was becoming Americanized. The former visitor to a Revolutionary battlefield took evident pride in the exploits of his in-laws during the war: Major John Tillman, his first wife's grandfather, whose knowledge of German was put to good use, and several uncles of Catharine Barber, in particular Colonel Francis Barber, a dashing, romantic figure. As the evidence would show, James was an avid student of American history almost before it *was* history, and the most wholehearted American patriot of the clan. In August 1802, he was naturalized, in Albany, as a citizen of the United States.

On April 1, 1818, the *Register* carried a public notice by William James that he had "withdrawn from the superintendence of his commercial concerns, having relinquished that part of his business to his son who would conduct it in future, under the firm of Robert James & Co." Robert was one of the twin brothers born to James by Elizabeth Tillman, and he was just turning twenty-two when his father gave him this large responsibility. His tenure lasted only three years, until his death.

What the notice meant, in effect, was that William James would no longer devote his energy to his network of stores, to the buying and selling of grain, flour, flax, vegetables, and other commodities. That commercial part of his business would go forward, but it would be in the hands of others, his son in Albany, the efficient James McBride in New York City. James would always be on call in an emergency: when he received word one autumn evening (in 1827) that a fire had broken out down on the pier and was threatening a block of four of his stores, James hastened down to the riverfront and bailed water with a kind of fury, though to no avail, with the rest of the voluntary brigade.

But James's attention henceforth would be concentrated on matters more purely of finance, on profit-making investments. To some extent, James's career exemplified even as it contributed to the pattern of Albany's development (a pattern duplicated elsewhere in eastern America): from something like a barter economy to commercial and trade activities to the era of authentic capitalism. At the time of James's arrival in the upstate village, money was in such short supply that local firms were accepting payment in country produce and pelts. There followed a decade and more of steadily increasing trade, especially with New York, and then the age of banking made its start. Almost all the major banks of nineteenth-century Albany were founded during James's residence; and while continuing to serve as director of the State Bank, he became first vice president of the Albany Savings Bank when it opened in 1820.

In these official capacities, James saw to the granting of loans, the collection and the paying out of interest, the negotiation of mortgages, and the other various uses to which money could be put. At the same time, and relatedly, he entered the real-estate business on a truly enormous scale. Much of it had to do with land in and around Albany, but James McBride was kept busy assessing, mapping, and paying taxes on properties in New York, including a plot of land on the grounds of Columbia College. James acquired holdings all across the state, in Troy, Utica, Rochester, and Buffalo; and for a time, as we shall see, he was the virtual owner of the campus of Union College in Schenectady. James's financial strategy was carefully defined, as he would explain it in the will he drew up in 1832. Here (with the wordiness characteristic of that document) he empowered his trustees to invest incoming monies "in the purchase of real estate . . . or in loans, annuities or in any other safe and proper manner." But the trustees were enjoined

to bear in mind and keep steadily in view that my will and intention is, that investments shall from time to time be so made as that at the time appointed for the ultimate division of my estate, the same shall consist chiefly or altogether in real estate.

In the land-rich world of early-nineteenth-century America, no strategy could have been shrewder.

Perhaps James's most spectacular transaction came in May 1824, when he quite literally bought the village of Syracuse, far to the west of Albany. It was not much of a village, to be sure: 250 acres of marshes and fever-breeding swampland surrounded by vast stretches of forest, with three frame houses, a half-built red brick tavern, and a water mill, and about 250 villagers; so desolate a terrain that, in the still cherished words of a visitor in 1820, it was enough "to make an owl weep to fly over it." But it contained salt springs, as a Jesuit explorer was the first to discover; and by 1800, some 25,000 barrels of salt a year were being derived from raids upon the springs by a series of individual "squatters."

By a treaty with the Onondaga Indians toward the end of the eighteenth century, the state had acquired title to 10,000 acres of forest and swamp; they became the state-run Salt Springs Reservation. In 1804, the state had put up for auction the central 250 acres of the reservation, and they were bought for $650 by one Abraham Walton. By 1824, the Walton Tract, as it was called, had changed hands several times and its value had multiplied; it belonged at the moment to Henry Eckford, a Scottish-born shipbuilder, who had paid $22,500 for what was also beginning to be known as the village of Syracuse (it comprises the business section of the modern city). Eckford, who needed capital for his other ventures, was anxious to sell the village, and this was reported to William James by Moses De Witt Burnet, the unemployed husband of James's sister-in-law Margaret Barber. With Burnet as his agent, James bought Syracuse for $30,000.

The vast work of making the area suitable for living was done under the auspices of the newly formed Syracuse Company, of which William James, as president, held five-eighths of the shares, John and Isaiah Townsend two-eighths between them, and the trusty James McBride the final one-eighth. With Moses Burnet supervising the operations, the company, in the words of an observer, "stumped, drained, graded the tract, erected buildings, and continued to promote, build, improve and sell lots to others, often furnishing money for them to establish themselves." It was an archetypal capitalistic exercise. By 1830, the village had been carved up into about 320 lots, some of them being sold for $620 each, but many being deployed by James as profit-returning rentals.

James and his associates also acquired from Henry Eckford the Saratoga Salt Company, which was now producing 400,000 bushels of coarse salt a year from the springs within the village. As one index to the money value of this industry, it was estimated that, by 1846, $3,500,000 had been paid to the state from various companies in salt taxes. James was president of this company as well, and as such he performed as a sort of persuasive tyrant. It was said around town that "when old Billy James came to Syracuse, things went as *he* wished." An example often cited was that of the unhappy Moses Burnet, who became stricken with anxiety for his health amid the still poisonous terrain (which had indeed caused the death of an alarming number of workmen). He wrote James that he could on no consideration remain in Syracuse any longer. James came over from Albany and spent two days with Burnet inspecting the properties and the books. The reminiscent anecdote continues:

Near the close of the second day, they came to the old stone bridge, and stopped in the middle. Burnet repeated what he had written, with some collateral. Mr. James heard him with attention, and then said: "Mr. Burnet (as he always called him), *you must stay here!*" Then he walked immediately to the Syracuse House, and Burnet followed. They took a good whiff of old Holland gin, and sat down. In half an hour the canal packet came, and Mr. James started for home. Not another word was said about Burnet's going or staying.

[12

The atmosphere during the gin-whiffing sequence was no doubt affected by the fact that the darkly resplendent Syracuse House, where the two men were seated, was owned by Mr. James, as head of the company. A dozen years later, Burnet was still in the village, and is said to have barely stepped outside it.

"The rupture with my grandfather's tradition and attitude was complete," the novelist Henry James would contend. "We were never in a single case, I think, for two generations, guilty of a stroke of business." This was not strictly true: John Barber James, the novelist's uncle, was apparently a stockholder in two local railroads during his short life (he died in 1856); and another uncle, Augustus, succeeded his father, William, at least briefly, as co-director of the salt company. But Henry's basic point—the "sudden collective disconnectedness" of the later Jameses "from *the* American resource of those days," the resource of business—was accurate enough: enough, that is, to have been misleading. For the phenomena of money and business agitated the Jamesian mind, in the generations after the Albany grandfather, to a degree which it is difficult, or even impossible, to match elsewhere in our literary and intellectual history.

What these Jameses did was to displace the language and the motifs of the money world into other realms of discourse: into theology, philosophy, psychology, literature; and to entangle them with other urgencies of experience. Henry James, Sr., was particularly adept at the tactic of using the vocabulary of financial transactions, of mortgages and loans, debts and payments, to describe what for him was the grossly false Presbyterian version of the relation between man and God. Listen to him late in life, remarking on the Presbyterian teachings about salvation that had been distilled in him during childhood:

I cannot conceive any less wholesome or innocent occupation for the childish mind than to keep a debtor and creditor account with God . . . Nothing can be so fatal to the tender awe and reverence which should always sanctify the Divine name to the youthful mind and heart, as to put the child in a bargaining or huckstering attitude towards God, as was done by the current religious teaching of my early days . . . [The boy was instructed] to *transact* with God— on the basis of course of his revealed clemency in Christ—by the most profuse acknowledgments of indebtedness, and the most profuse promises of future payment . . . [but] I never stopped to ask myself how a being whose clemency to the sinner wears so flatly commercial an aspect,—being the fruit of an actual purchase, of a most literal and cogent *quid pro quo* duly in hand paid—could ever hope to awaken any spiritual love or confidence in the human breast . . .

Henry Senior's daughter, Alice, detecting a (for her) similarly offensive commercializing of religion in her last English years, picked up the paternal rhetoric and accused Protestant Christianity of imaging "a grasping deity" from whom redemption could be purchased "at a varying scale of prices." William James the philosopher took a more complicated view of the phenomenon: moving toward a definition of pragmatism in the 1906–7 lectures, he advanced the concept of "the cash value of ideas" in a way that seemed to value the cash as well as the ideas; and he was fascinated by an American figure like John D. Rockefeller and the extraordinary *energy* that enabled him to amass such boundless wealth. In the novels and stories of his brother Henry, money, while central and persistent, plays an even more ambiguous role.

Money is the inescapable fact in human experience, and the straining element in human relations, especially courtship and marital relations. In Henry Junior, the marketplace appears ever more insidiously as the marriage mart; a marriageable daughter is reified into a good investment, and by the time of James's "major phase" in the early 1900s, the involvement of marriage with financial gain or rescue has become nearly absolute. Money now takes on the aspect of *power*: Kate Croy, watching Milly Theale during the dinner party at Palazzo Barbaro in *The Wings of the Dove*, is struck by the impression emanating from the American girl of sheer wealth—"which was a power," she thinks, "which was a great power." Money in these moments rises to a metaphysical force. It is entirely fitting that in Henry James's late story "The Jolly Corner," decidedly one of his best, the James grandfather whose financial deeds and emphases had haunted his descendants for almost a century should return as a phantom figure, the materialized ghost of a business tycoon, and a presence whose "rage of personality" quite overwhelms the middle-aged dilettante who had sought him out in the old family home on Washington Place.

THE PATRIARCH

The thrice-married William James of Albany fathered a goodly number of children. The twin boys, Robert and William, had been born in 1797; and Mary Ann Connolly's daughter, Ellen, in 1800. The first surviving child of Catharine Barber was Augustus James, who was born in 1807 (there were two infants who did not last out a full year). Then there was the son named Henry, born on June 3, 1811. Catharine James presented her husband with six more children, three boys and three girls, over the next fourteen years.

In about 1813, the expanding family moved from a smaller to a larger house, this one on North Pearl Street, a main thoroughfare that ran diagonally away from the river. Here was the childhood home remembered by Henry James, Sr. (as he would be called after his son and namesake in the mid-1860s began to sign the name "Junior" to his stories and articles). It was a square frame stone structure, with library and other family rooms on the ground floor, and on the second floor innumerable bedrooms painted in a uniform yellowish white. Behind the house was a covered piazza with a swing, and a long garden sloping down to the stables—Mr. James kept a carriage and several horses—and a pigeon house, and with a view of the Hudson through the trees beyond. Some of these features, with others less factual, were attached to the Albany home of the Archers, in Henry Junior's *The Portrait of a Lady*.

In describing his childhood in the autobiographical fragment he wrote during his last years, Henry Senior spoke with surprising coolness and brevity about his siblings: "I have nothing to say of my brothers and sisters, who were seven in number, except that our relations proved always cordially affectionate." The remark partakes of the fictional aspect of the fragment, something we shall return to; the brothers and sisters who lived in the house on North Pearl Street were of course ten in number. But the remark also contributes to a larger rhetorical purpose: which was to present the family life in Albany as self-enclosed and sterile. "A certain lack of oxygen," James wrote, was characteristic of the American family atmosphere in general, and "our family . . . perfectly illustrated this common vice of contented isolation." The image would have been harder to maintain if James had acknowledged a bulging household of eleven children ranging (say, in 1821, when Henry was ten) from twenty-four years to a few months. As it was, James could warm to the theme that grew in importance to him with the passing of time: his Albany family had no "felt relation to the public life of the world . . . We contentedly lived the same life of stagnant isolation from the race which the great mass of our modern families live." But it was man's true destiny, James insisted, "to experience the broadest conceivable unity with his kind." The bar to that redemptive unity was what today is called the nuclear family, a phrase

Henry Senior came close to using: "the isolated family bond is the nucleus or citadel of this provisional civic economy"—that is, the then current and unsatisfactory state of affairs; "and practically, therefore, the interest of the isolated family is the chief obstacle still presented to the full evolution of human nature."

Henry Senior was not alone in his generation in his enlightened hostility to the nuclear family, but he was in a small and mostly un-attended minority.* Yet ironically enough, the family over which he came to preside, though anything but stagnant, had its own mode of isolated existence: through its affluence, its remoteness from the prac-tical or business world of America, its constant movement and geo-graphical relocation, its unique gifts of mind and imagination; and because of all that, through its immense self-enjoyment. Various social deprivations, Henry Junior was to believe, conspired to keep the family members, "collectively, so genially interested in almost nothing but each other." Whether this development was a matter for rejoicing, as Henry was inclined to suppose, is something for later reflection.

As to the actual family Henry Senior claimed to be looking back upon, he may have been somewhat unfair. At least, William of Albany's family consciousness extended beyond the immediate household. He should be credited with paying the passages from Dublin to New York of his nephews William and John James, the two older sons of his brother Robert, and with setting them up as a firm of merchants on South Street in New York City. He bequeathed John James the sum of $1,000 in his will, and paid out money at regular intervals to support the children of his in-laws. If only at this level of financial responsibility, a level where he operated best, William of Albany did evidently feel himself belonging to a larger clan. And it is hard to accept Henry Senior's implication that the only non-family persons ever to set foot in the family living room were clergymen—persons, moreover, Henry recalled, stressing the social sterility, who were dull, cautious, and deplorably unspiritual in their manners and conversation.

Still, William of Albany had a definitely patriarchal personality, though of a curious kind. He seems to have kept his public or business life and his family life separate, and would have regarded it as only proper to do so. Within the family, he appears to have been more an

* Stephen Pearl Andrews, an exceedingly astute freethinker on issues of social makeup and sexual relations, and an exact contemporary of Henry James, Sr., shared James's views. Part of the confusion in the public exchange between Andrews and Henry Senior in 1852 derived from a basic *agreement* on this topic. See below, p. 65 ff.

occasionally felt force than a presence. He was usually out all day, appearing only for the evening meal, where, at the head of the table, he must have made an imposing, if often a silent, figure. He led the children in prayers, and put them rigorously, every night he was at home, through their Presbyterian catechism. He might listen to them recite their lessons every so often, but he had no talent for parental intimacy.

If we inspect him in the early 1820s, we see a well-built, somewhat portly man; clean-shaven, with ruddy Irish good looks; cool, unfathomable black eyes, and a wig of matching color. There is about him an air of concentrated inwardness, as though he were meditating a particularly difficult but fruitful transaction. He comes down to us as driven, determined, and very well-ordered; humorless and unbending, with a coercively magnetic quality and very little charm.

The impression he made on his son Henry was by no means that of a harsh or irascible parent, but simply (it was Henry's word) an *indifferent* one. "I cannot recollect," Henry wrote, "that he ever questioned me about my out-of-door occupations, or about my companions, or showed any extreme solicitude about my standing in school." The father stayed clear of family affairs; the law of the house, in Henry Senior's phrase, was "freedom itself," though always "within the limits of religious decency." There is reason to wonder if William James could readily tell his children apart, at least the eight of them who were the offspring of Catharine Barber. And it is recorded that Mr. James once courteously informed a lady who was approaching the front steps of the house that Mrs. James was not at home, only to be told by the affronted lady that she *was* Mrs. James.

Only twice in the son Henry's experience was this impression of remoteness and indifference shattered, each time to incalculably influential effect. The first was in the summer of 1824, shortly after Henry's thirteenth birthday. At this stage of his young life, Henry was very much an out-of-doors boy. "I was never so happy at home as away from it," he wrote, and enjoyed nothing more than stealing down at dawn to watch the sun rise over the river and the woods. He was a sturdy, athletic youngster who liked every form of physical exercise: ball-playing, kite-flying, rabbit-hunting; "I lived," he recalled, "in every fibre of my body." He was also sociable by nature, and would regularly run over to the local shoemaker's shop to rendezvous with other lads his age and gossip with the two young men who worked the shop. The latter were knowledgeable types, in Henry's view, and the visits seemed to him (thinking back) to be an initiation into worldliness—the more so since he and his mates provided the artisans with edibles and bottles of wine surreptitiously lifted from their families' stores. This hearty, headlong mode of existence came to an abrupt end that summer afternoon.

With several other students at the Albany Academy, an excellent school (chartered in 1813) where Henry had been enrolled for some years, he had been in the habit of joining a young science teacher, Joseph Henry, to engage in the experimental flying of balloons. The balloon, made of the lightest material, probably muslin, was powered skyward by the heat of an affixed ball of tow, or hemp, soaked in turpentine and ignited. In the usual version of this oft-told incident, the thin cloth balloon eventually caught fire from the hemp and burned up, whereupon the wad itself fell to the ground, to be kicked about by the boys until extinguished.

On this particular afternoon, one of the balls, after hitting the earth, was accidentally booted through the upper window of a nearby stable. Henry James ran in at once, climbed into the hayloft, and began to stamp out the flames. By mischance, he had previously splashed some turpentine onto his pantaloons; his right trouser leg instantly took fire, and before he was rescued and carried out screaming, he had suffered terrible burns from foot to thigh.

During the agonizing bedridden months and years that followed, and after a "morbid process in the bone" had set in (so Henry described it), the adolescent boy underwent periodic surgery, needless to say without anaesthetic. There were at least two major acts of amputation; but as late as November 1827, his devoted thirteen-year-old sister Jennet, herself dangerously unwell, was writing a relative that Henry's leg seemed actually worse than the previous spring: "Instead of progressing it goes back and there is a greater space to heal now than there was before." By the time Henry was able to leave his bed and start hobbling about on crutches, he had lost his right leg to a point above the knee.

It was William James's reaction to his son's ordeal that lingered in Henry's memory. The father's agitation at the sight of the boy being cut into by the surgeon's knife was so extravagant that Catherine James was hard put to prevent her husband from making some sort of wild display, perhaps hurling himself upon the surgeon. The extremity of his father's tenderness and compassion, Henry would say, was such "as to give me an exalted sense of his affection," and for the moment, anyhow, obliterated the sense of paternal apathy.

The second paternal outburst occurred five years later, as we shall see.

During his protracted illness, Henry was also touched by the odd form of his mother's solicitude. In his autobiography, Henry Senior seems unable to settle his mind about his mother. He began his little account of her flatly enough: she "was a good wife and mother, nothing else—save, to be sure, a kindly friend and neighbor." In her neighborly capacity, Catharine James saw to the distribution of great quantities of beef, pork, and potatoes—supplied from Mr. James's provisions— to the needy poor of Albany during the winter. She had a number of distinguished Barber kinfolk, both military and juridical, but was curiously embarrassed by their fame and reluctant to talk about them. Indeed, her son remarked, as though making the discovery for the first time in his own old age, his mother "was the most democratic person by temperament I ever knew"; she "gravitated as a general thing into relations of the frankest sympathy with every one conventionally beneath her." Even as he wrote those lines in 1880, Henry Senior appeared unaware how frequently he had professed the same egalitarian attitude.

The clear and enduring image of maternal love came from the time of suffering, when constant watchfulness was needed. His mother would come nightly into his room sleepwalking, would cover his shoulders, adjust his pillows, and, still fast asleep, take her departure.

FILIAL REBELLION

In the fall of 1828, Henry entered Union College in Schenectady, a dozen miles north of Albany on the Mohawk River. Union, founded in the mid-1790s, was an academically flourishing institution, offering what was in that era the finest humanistic education in the country. Its achievements were largely due to the leadership of Eliphalet Nott, a man of extraordinary and varied abilities (his own specialty was moral philosophy, but he also took patents on thirty kinds of stoves and invented an anthracite-burning boiler for steamboats), who became president of the college in 1804, at the age of thirty-one, and who continued to guide its fortunes until his death in January 1866.

The college's admissions policy allowed Henry to enter the junior class. During his first year, he was set mostly to study classical writing, including the tragic dramas of Sophocles and Euripides, with a dose of political economy and natural philosophy. He spent much of his time, though, socializing with his fellow students, a friendly bunch who cheerfully assisted their crippled college mate across the campus and in and out of classrooms—until, later in the year, James acquired a wooden leg and began to hobble around on his own.

As his zest for life returned, young James began to indulge himself in ways that, before long, would enrage his father. He ran up bills all over town: at the bookstores, where he purchased volumes unrelated to his studies or any other proper purpose; at the tailor's, from whom he bought expensive bolts of cloth for gaudy new suits; at local taverns, where he could satisfy his appetite for oysters and his taste for "segars" (in one of these, he left a bill for the then colossal sum of sixty dollars). All these items Henry Junior charged to his father. In November of his senior year, he received a darkly minatory letter written, at his father's behest, by Archibald McIntyre, a financial underling of William James. "I consider you on the very verge of ruin," McIntyre wrote excitedly. He entreated the young man henceforth to follow his parents' instruction, to spend no more money without their approval. Some people, McIntyre wrote, considered Henry "already as lost, irretrievably lost"; but for himself, he could not believe anyone would witlessly throw away the material and social advantages given to Henry James—and thereby "become a loathing to himself and his best friends."

The letter had an effect opposite to the one intended. Within three weeks, Henry James had fled Union College, had gone to Boston, and had settled there—in his own mind, for keeps—in a new environment and a new way of life.

Henry James thus became what would be called a college dropout, and he was a classic representative of the breed. McIntyre's letter hinted at a conflict between Henry and his father about a career at law, William James demanding it, Henry resisting. But in Henry's departure, there were more strenuous motives at work.

In charging to his father his proliferating and frivolous expenses, Henry James was obviously making gestures of defiance against a parent who was virtually identified with money, with financial authority. (The earliest sinful act which Henry Senior would retrospectively admit to was filching small sums of money from the drawer of his father's dressing table, to pay off his account at the confectioner's shop. He recalled hesitating for a long time before dipping his hand into "the sacred deposit.") William James, when the several drafts were presented to him back in Albany, became incoherent with fury.

William James of Ireland and Albany

This was the second and, for Henry, the even more durably significant instance of the father's indifference giving way to passion. In a letter to McIntyre (as Henry was informed), William had spluttered that his son had "so debased himself as to leave his parents' house in the character of a swindler etc. etc.—details presented today—are the order which I enclose as a specimen of his progress in the arts of low vileness—and unblushing falsehood." Wrathfully detailing some of Henry's felonies, William predicted that the boy would be lodged "in a prison of some kind directly."

But the felt pressure of his father's power and influence was not restricted to Albany; it pervaded the very atmosphere of the college in which Henry was enrolled. William James was one of the two men who constituted Union's Board of Trustees, but more than that, the elder James held a mortgage on the entire campus.

The development was the end result of a long-unfolding academic and financial drama whose complications go beyond our narrative. The story begins in 1812, when President Nott decreed that substantial sums of money must be raised to pay for a new college campus, designed by Joseph Jacques Ranée, and featuring two classically styled buildings called North and South Colleges. In pursuit of the venture, Nott appeared before the state legislature in Albany and persuaded it by rhetorical arts amounting to witchcraft to institute a state-run lottery, from the proceeds of which Union's financial needs could be met. In April 1814, the legislature authorized "a Lottery for the Promotion of Literature and other purposes." Literary studies, that is, were singled out as the prime beneficiary of the monies, and the annual gambling event became known as the Literature Lottery.

From the first lottery, Union received $100,000 for the Ranée buildings, and another $100,000 for the library, for needy students, and to pay off current debts. Construction went ahead, expenses rose, the lottery was repeated. By 1823, however, the state government had grown sick of the whole business, and at this stage Eliphalet Nott stepped forward to propose that he himself, on behalf of the trustees of Union, take over the sole management of the affair. It was, says his biographer, "an offer unique in the history of education," and it was promptly accepted.

Handbills were printed up, receipts were collected, the prize money was distributed, and a percentage of the cash remaining was turned over to President Nott and the college fund. All contractual agreements were overseen by William James, a person Nott had trusted completely since the days when James was a parishioner of the First

Presbyterian Church in Albany during Nott's brief tenure there as minister, at the turn of the century. It was to James that Nott appealed in the winter of 1826 when disaster threatened.

"Lottery No. 3 for 1825" was under way, and it had advertised and guaranteed large sums of money for which there was nowhere near enough in the college fund to pay. In a matter of days, James had arranged a personal loan of $100,000. It was secured, according to the deed, "by the new college edifices and all the houses standing on the premises" of the new campus. An interest of 6½ percent was agreed upon. Union College was mortgaged to William James.

If Henry James was unaware of his father's large-scale intervention in Union College's financial doings before he arrived in Schenectady, he would soon have learned about it; for—and this element completed the situation Henry felt impelled to escape from—he was actually lodged, as an undergraduate, in the home of Eliphalet Nott, the college's president and his father's debtor. It can be added that Henry most likely found Nott himself a sympathetic person, engagingly liberal in temperament and policy. Nott often voiced skepticism about his ministerial colleagues. "Ministers, as a class," he said, "know less practically of human nature than any other class of men"; and he was learnedly tolerant of all Christian sects and denominations from Unitarians to Methodists to Calvinists to Roman Catholics—a theological broadmindedness that Henry James, Sr. (not entirely to his children's liking) would conspicuously emulate.

How Henry James, age eighteen and hampered by a wooden leg, made the journey across country to the city of Boston is not recorded. But he established himself in Boston without difficulty, finding a job with Francis Jenks, editor of the *Christian Examiner*, a Unitarian paper, and lodgings on the ground floor of the Jenkses' house on Hancock Street (years later James walked Henry Junior by the Hancock Street residence and remarked on it nostalgically). His assignment on the *Examiner*—it paid $200 a year plus board and room—was to check every quotation in the scholarly or theological volumes that came across Jenks's desk and to supply notices of new books. "My ambition is awakened," he wrote a friend at Union, in late January 1830.

He sampled sermons around the city, including those of Dr. William Ellery Channing, the frail, much loved Unitarian preacher at the Federal Street Church. James found Channing a "treat"; but everything in Boston was becoming a treat. "I have been introduced to some of the first society here," he bragged to his Union friend; he had been everywhere well received. Among the several delightful women James was encountering, as he reported, he was taken especially with the wife of the Reverend Alonzo Potter of St. Paul's Episcopal Church. Mrs. Potter, James said in a rush of candor, "is what Eve might have been before the Fall." His response to Mrs. Potter was heightened by the fact that she was the only daughter of Eliphalet Nott, and James felt obscurely resentful that she had had to change her name to Potter ("What a horrid name for *that* woman").

Nonetheless, before too many more weeks were out, Henry was persuaded to give up the Boston experiment and return to Union. He completed his senior year, and on the sweltering morning of July 18, 1830, he graduated from the college with some ninety-five classmates (Yale by comparison gave out seventy-one diplomas that summer, Harvard forty-eight, and Princeton twenty). Henry James's grades placed him twenty-fifth in the class, too low to make Phi Beta Kappa: results that could hardly have discomfited this least academic of men.

When the time came, around 1860, for Henry Senior's older sons to consider going to college, their father forcibly opposed the idea. He seemed, the younger Henry wrote, to feel "a great revulsion of spirit from that incurred experience in his own history." He saw his chosen seat of learning, "Union College, Schenectady, New York," Henry Junior recalled, "in I scarce know what light of associational or 'subjective' dislike." The son remembered that once, on an autumn day in their extreme youth, he and his brother William had made a pilgrimage to Union College, and "invoked . . . among its scattered shades, fairly vague to me now, the loyalty that our parent appeared to have dropped by the way."

The passage, from *Notes of a Son and Brother*, leaves it uncertain whether the story just rehearsed—William of Albany's financial lordship over Union and Henry Senior's subsequent flight from it—formed part of the James family lore. But a much earlier passage from *Daisy Miller* (1879) suggests that it well may have been, and preserved as a household joke.

At a hotel in Switzerland, early in the novella, the expatriate American Winterbourne is cautiously interrogating Daisy's brassy younger brother. The latter announces his own name, Randolph, and that of his sister. He goes on: "My father's name is Ezra B. Miller . . . My father ain't in Europe; my father's in a better place than Europe." Winterbourne supposes that this was the delicate way Randolph had been taught to say that his father had gone to his heavenly reward.

But the boy immediately adds: "My father's in Schenectady. He's got a big business. My father's rich, you bet."

DEATH OF A LEADING CITIZEN, 1832

On October 8, 1823, the first boat passed through the eastern portion of the Erie Canal, steaming along the Mohawk valley to Cohoes and down the Hudson to the tidewater at Albany. The great work, to provide an uninterrupted waterway from the Great Lakes to the Hudson, had been seven years in the making, and the boat's arrival touched off an exuberant celebration in the capital city. Salutes were fired, bells were rung, bands played martial music, and all the ships in the harbor were beflagged. William Bayard, chairman of the delegation from New York City, spoke briefly before the vast assembly, assuring it that "the canal will pour its fertilising stream into the bosom of your city, restore it to its wonted prosperity, and add another triumph to the patriotic efforts of its inhabitants." There arose in reply William James, chairman of the eight-man Committee of Citizens of Albany. He spoke at greater length, in a manner sonorous and turgid, and fervently patriotic.

It is the distinguishing attribute of man [he began] to be excited by what is grand, beautiful and sublime in nature, or what is great and beneficial in the combination of intellect and art. This principle of nature has congregated the immense number of citizens you now behold.

The canal, said James, was "a work that sheds additional lustre on the United States, bearing the stamp of the enterprising spirit and resolution which declared our independence." This thought led the immigrant from County Cavan to extol the blessings of New World freedom:

With the perpetual example of despotism and wretchedness in the old world before our eyes, we may look forward with a well founded hope that neither tyrannical aristocracies nor intriguing demagogues can ever succeed in corrupting our citizens, or blighting our liberties.

Then, for a moment, James lapsed into a personal tonality that had what might be called a Jamesian flavor to it. He confessed that he had not originally grasped the scope of the enterprise (although, in fact, he had signed a petition in 1816, with Archibald McIntyre, urging the legislature to vote for the building of the canal). But now: "I feel an indescribable emotion, something like a renewal of life, at partaking in the festivities of this day."

William James by 1823 had clearly won full acceptance in the city-world of Albany. He was recognized and honored; and his standing was further confirmed two years later when he was again chosen to head the Committee of Citizens at the ceremonial opening of the completed canal. The event took place on November 2, 1825, after the *Seneca Chief* had finished its 300-mile, eight-day journey from Buffalo and had come to rest at the newly built 4,000-foot pier of the huge basin in the Albany harbor. This time, in addition to guns, bells, and bands, there were long parades, the reading of prayers, and the recitation of a specially written ode, before Philip Hone greeted the Albany citizens on behalf of the New York committee.

The *Daily Advertiser*'s report on the occasion continued:

William James, chairman of the Committee of the Citizens of Albany, then delivered the following address, which for sound sense, strong ideas, and a clear and lucid exposition of the advantages that will result from the completion of our great works of internal improvements is worthy of high commendation. Mr. James became a resident of this city when it did not number half the population it now does. He has been untiring in his efforts to advance the interests of his place of abode, as well as to further this great work, which will pour inexhaustible and countless riches into the lap of the Ancient City.

James's oration, which must have taken an hour to deliver, touched alternatively upon the unexampled economic gains the canal would bring, and the greatness of the country in which such an accomplishment was possible. "We have reason," he declaimed, "to congratulate the Union on the successful completion of an enterprise, which, developing the resources and increasing the revenue and grandeur of this state, will embrace in its progress the prosperity and welfare of all." The canal, in his view, "reflects honor upon our nation, [and] increases and secures the moral and political happiness and comfort of our citizens." Later, he meditated upon America's unique and God-given fortune in invariably having the timely great man: in the not so distant past, there had been Patrick Henry and Samuel Adams, then the authors of *The Federalist Papers*, and now the indispensable man for the Erie Canal, De Witt Clinton.

In his later years, William James became as much respected in the city for his charitable activities and his participation in public life as for his financial exploits. He became trustee of the First Presbyterian

Church and chairman of the Albany Orphan Asylum; he was on every important civic committee and turned up at every important public event. He died on December 19, 1832, ten days short of his sixty-first birthday, during a cholera epidemic of vast proportions that swept in from the Far East and killed thousands in this country alone. In the quite fulsome local obituaries, his energetic good citizenship was memorialized as much as his accomplishments in commerce and real estate. The Albany *Daily Advertiser* said characteristically:

William James . . . had long occupied a conspicuous position among the merchants of the city, and as a liberal and enlightened citizen. Prosperous almost beyond parallel, his career exemplified how surely strong and practical intellect, with unremitted perseverance will be accompanied by success. Of unaffected manners, generous, hospitable, public-spirited, open ever to the claims of charity, prompt to participate in any enterprise of general utility or benevolence, Mr. James enjoyed, as he deserved, the sincere respect and esteem of his fellow citizens, and his loss was rightly considered as a public calamity.

Solemn and ponderous as the statement is, it offers a very fair summary of the man and his Albany career; and one senses that, in the writer's representative view, the late Mr. James was everything that a vigorous, generous, and intelligent man could be, except lovable.

About five months before his death, James drew up a lengthy Last Will and Testament which contained a farewell message, complex and orotund, to his family and associates. His wife's legacy was handled with dispatch; she received the entire property on North Pearl Street, including the horses and carriages and sleighs, and an annuity of $3,000. He turned next to the business, in effect, of cutting two of his sons, the half brothers William and Henry, out of the will once and for all. "To my son William," he gave and bequeathed an annuity of $2,000; and "to my son Henry" an annuity of $1,200. He made a point of insisting that these sums should *not* come out of the final disposition of the estate: the two sons were to have no part or share whatever in that process; the annuities should derive from ongoing "rents and profits."

Henry, of course, was being punished for his flamboyant malfeasance at Union College and his unauthorized departure from the institution. William, the child of Elizabeth Tillman (and twin of the late Robert), was being punished—so one gathers—for having entered the Presbyterian ministry against his father's wish. The elder James was ambivalent about the clergy: he liked having them over to the

William James of Ireland and Albany

North Pearl Street house after church on Sunday to sit (as it were) at his feet, and he enjoyed his relationship with the Reverend Eliphalet Nott; but despite the admiration of his own father for the breed, William James appears to have held ministers as such in secret contempt. His son William, in any event, stayed out of the paternal way while he pursued his ecclesiastical course. After graduating from Princeton College in 1816, he entered the Princeton Presbyterian Seminary. He was ordained by the Presbytery in Albany in 1820 and left at once for two years of study in Scotland. The Reverend William served as pastor of the Second Church in Rochester from 1825 to 1831, and was pastor of the First Church in Schenectady at the time of his father's death. During all this period the father's displeasure obviously remained unassuageable.

Mr. James, in his will, then appointed three trustees of the estate and was careful to explain why he did so. In view, he wrote

of the lamentable consequences which so frequently result to young persons brought up in affluence from coming at once into the possession of property, I have also determined that the trust shall continue, and that the final division of my estate shall not take place, until the youngest of my children and grand children living at the time of this my will and attaining the age of twenty-one years shall have attained that age.

Of the six grandchildren who were alive at the time (July 1832) "of this my will," the youngest, William Augustus, was just seven months old. If William of Albany's testamentary stipulations had been fully adhered to, the estate would not have been distributed until the end of December 1852.

The severe cautionary voice continued:

And in order to provide against accidental inequalities and diversities . . . but more especially with a view to discouraging prodigality and vice, and to furnish an incentive to economy and usefulness, I have further determined to invest my trustees with extensive discretionary powers in regard to the disposition of my property.

The trustees were Gideon Hawley, a legal advisor whom James had often called on; his son-in-law James King, husband of Ellen James, who had died at a tender age in 1823; and "my son Augustus James," the oldest child of Catherine Barber. One of the chief discretionary powers assigned the trustees was in the actual division of the estate.

William James stipulated "twelve equal shares," but he only specified eight and one-half of them: full shares to his sons Augustus, John Barber, Edward, and Howard; full shares to his daughters (all by his third wife) Jennet, Catharine, and Ellen, and to his granddaughter Mary Ann King; a half share to his grandson Robert. As regards the "remaining three and a half parts," James said, the trustees could allot them as they saw fit among any of those already designated as sharing "in the ultimate disposition of the estate"—that is, again pointedly, excluding the half brothers William and Henry.

And thereupon, the crucial rider:

If at the expiration of the period limited for the continuance of the trust, it shall satisfactorily appear to my trustees . . . that any one of those who would otherwise be entitled to share in such partition, leads a grossly immoral, idle or dishonorable life, such delinquent shall not be entitled to the share of my estate hereinafter provided for such person, but shall be considered as having forfeited the same either wholly or in part.

After that wordy threat of moral disinheritance, James seemed to draw himself together in the one passage that came from his (rather than his lawyer's) pen, as from his mind and heart:

And although the extensive and extraordinary power herein conferred of punishing idleness and vice and of rewarding virtue must from its nature be in a considerable degree discretionary and although its faithful exercise may prove to be a task at once responsible and painful, yet it is my full intention and earnest wish that it shall be carried into execution with rigid impartiality, sternness and inflexibility.

A few other items in the will are worthy of note. While rigorously forbidding his son William a share in the estate, the elder James made provision for William's daughter Anna McBride (named for the faithful agent), with an eventual and sizable outright bequest. And William of Albany's special affection for his second wife, Mary Ann Connolly, seems reflected in his assigning to Mary Ann's granddaughter and namesake Mary Ann King a full share in the estate. Finally, the trustees were enjoined "to make a full and particular inventory of the trust estate" within one month of William James's death and to file it with the Albany Surrogate Office.

The trustees accepted their appointment, but moved slowly in the matter of the inventory. They filed petition after petition asking for more time, citing the great size of the statewide property or the discovery of new holdings. It is obvious that they were stalling. The more they considered the moralistic provisions of James's will, the less easy they felt about seeking to enforce them; and it may be imagined that the amiable Augustus James had little stomach for overseeing the exclusion of his older and his younger brothers from shares in their father's estate. Augustus finally withdrew from the trusteeship; and on October 19, 1833, the other two trustees, Gideon Hawley and James King, filed a bill of complaint with the Court for the Trial of Impeachments and the Correction of Errors, declaring they considered it "improper and unsafe to execute many of the trusts contained in the said will, by reason of doubts that had arisen as to the true construction of many of its important parts."

On the July 25 following, William James and Henry James filed a cross bill of complaint, insisting in substance "that the trusts attempted to be created by the said last will and testament of the said William James, deceased, were in contravention to the statutes of this state, and therefore void, and that the estate and property of the said testator had passed to his heirs in law and next of kin, and praying full and adequate relief in the premises."

The brothers were legally in the right. The Court for the Trial of Impeachments and the Correction of Errors sustained their complaint in a decree handed down on December 30, 1836. The issue had to do, in the legal phrase, with "the power of Alienation": that is, the power to sell ("alienate") property or to give it away outright, as against merely renting. The state of New York had on its books (it remained there until about thirty years ago) a statute making it illegal to "suspend the power of alienation . . . for more than two lives in being." That portion of William James's will which sought to create a trust that would continue until the youngest of his grandchildren reached the age of twenty-one was in violation of the statute, and was therefore declared "illegal and void."

The court similarly reversed the moralistic provisions, though without actually naming them. After giving a series of rulings, it declared that "the trustees and executors" of the will had "no authority, power of trust, in and over the real or personal estate of the testator

William James, than such as in this decree is specified." And more generally: "So much of the decree of the Court of Chancery as is repugnant to or inconsistent with this decree, and as gives direction on any subject with respect to which directions are herein given . . . is hereby reversed."

William and Henry James were instructed to renounce the annuities given them in the original will. When they had done so, they were said by the court to be "entitled to their respective portions of the real and personal estate" of William James "in the same manner and to the same extent as his other heirs in law and next of kin."

The estate was divided into twelve equal parts. In addition to the (then) nine surviving children of William and Catherine Barber James, full shares were given to Mary Ann King and to Robert W. James and Lydia James, the latter two being the only surviving offspring of the deceased son Robert. When Henry was informed of his legacy, he is said to have murmured: "Leisured for life." And so he was.

At least one Albany newspaper, offering figures in support of the claim that William James had been "prosperous almost without parallel," ascribed to James a fortune of $3 million, and this is the value usually indicated. There is no way to translate such a figure with any kind of precision into terms meaningful in the late twentieth century. One could multiply, say, by twenty, and speak of an estate today of $60 million; but this does not begin to convey the image of one of the two or three richest men in the young country. James's fortune is in fact commonly said to have been, in the 1830s, second only to that of John Jacob Astor in New York State. Little wonder that money, for evil or good, in actuality and in metaphor, so gripped the Jamesian imagination.

As to Henry's share, his novelist son would recall himself and his siblings speculating about the matter: about what had become of "the admirable three millions," and what part of that romantic sum their father had inherited. The answers to their questions, Henry Junior implied, were never forthcoming; it was all a dark mystery. But the novelist was almost certainly being playfully disingenuous, as he so often was in his memoirs (one takes many of his reminiscences as literal only at one's peril). Henry Senior's leisuring legacy is conventionally calculated at $10,000 a year; and this figure receives indirect confirmation in the son's novella *Washington Square* (1881). That story, which in part is openly and even insistently autobiographical, turns on matters of money and inheritance, and amid all the talk about them the major recurring reference is to $10,000 a year. This is Mrs. Sloper's personal fortune, and it becomes the whole of her daughter Catherine's inheritance. It is Catherine's loss of the much larger sum from her father that causes the scoundrelly Morris Townsend, after vocally measuring the different possible legacies, to abandon her.

In the absence of bank and court records—the famous inventory has not survived—it is permissible to guess that Henry Senior's one-twelfth share of $3 million (or more) may have been closer to $12,500 a year than to $10,000. In any case, we may think of him as a man who in his twenty-seventh year began to live on an income that today would be in excess of $300,000 a year before taxes.

December 30, 1836, is the key date in this part of the family story: the moment when, as it would turn out, a major segment of American cultural history was determined by a statute unique to the state of New York. The court's statement moved on to the partition of the property "in and near" Syracuse, the chief source of the elder James's fortune. His five-eighths share in that property was ordered to be distributed by the trustees equally among the twelve heirs. It would be nine years, however, before the partition was fully completed, following a bill filed in September 1846 by Henry James and wife, John Barber James and wife, Moses Burnet, and Gideon Hawley. Syracuse House, the tavern, was sold to Augustus James, along with the mill which supplied water for it. But by this time Henry Senior had long been enjoying his princely income.

William of Albany's attempt to dictate the private conduct of his descendants, from beyond the grave and for two decades, was defeated in court, and as articulated in his will, it was ill-considered and singularly harsh in spirit. But James's apprehensions proved not ungrounded. The story of his house was for the most part a sorry one.

His progeny tended to die young; of the eleven who got beyond infancy, four died in their twenties, and three more were dead by the age of forty. Jennet James, who had been so worried about her brother Henry's maimed leg, was herself ailing most of her life and died after the birth of her second child (by William Barker) in her twenty-ninth year. Another sister, Catherine, contracted consumption in her thirty-third year from her stricken husband, Robert Temple; the two died within three months of each other. It was Catherine Temple's fifth child, Minny, whose death at the age of twenty-four (in 1870) was regarded by Henry James, Jr., as the turning point in his life. She was the original of the dying Milly Theale in *The Wings of the Dove*, and in the picture of Milly's forebears, we see the heirs of William James of Albany: an "extravagant, unregulated cluster . . . handsome dead cousins, lurid uncles, beautiful vanished aunts, persons all bust and curls."

Most of those who managed to live somewhat longer came to nothing, largely, as William James had feared, because of wealth bestowed early. Secure in their punctually delivered income, they tinkered with life; they trifled with sculpture or with music; they traveled abroad to no distinct purpose; in the words of Henry Junior, they hovered and vanished. Reaching back to his childhood memories, Henry Junior recalled the heavy sighs and headshakes that attended any mention of this or that relative in the hushed conversations of the clan. There may not have been instances of what William of Albany called a "grossly immoral . . . or dishonorable life"; but in Henry Junior's account there is a sufficiency of "prodigality," "vice," and "idleness," with acts of criminality he only hinted at. The "irresponsibles" is James's term for almost the lot of them, though he found a certain hazy charm enveloping the legend of their failures.

Augustus James, the nearest full brother of Henry Senior, was something of an exception. He accomplished little and left no mark. But there was a kind of sturdiness in this dapper, good-natured, undersized figure; he wore well, he was dependable, and at his estate Linwood in Rhinebeck, New York, with its river views and its gardens, he was always hospitable. Catherine Temple was taken in at Linwood in her last days, while her husband was succumbing over in Albany. Henry Senior—this was 1854 and James was forty-three—hurried up from New York to stand by during the event. He brought with him his eleven-year-old son Henry, who had thereby his first experience of death.

THE IRISH JAMESES

Toward the end of April 1837, almost immediately after coming into his inheritance, Henry Senior sailed from New York on the London packet *Westminster*, bound for Plymouth. He had just completed his second year at the Princeton Theological Seminary and had every intention of returning there in the autumn. But with his newfound wealth, he had designed for himself a four-month excursion in Great Britain, with a fairly long stay in London and a visit to his father's birthplace in County Cavan, Ireland. The latter plan has about it an air of intended reconciliation with a father whose threatened injustice had been wholly thwarted; almost, perhaps, an atonement for contemplating the ministerial profession which the father so opposed. At the same time, Henry Senior, alone in his generation of Jameses, had a genuine curiosity about the family origins, a pleased sense of the family's "Irishness," and a feeling of kinship with the Jameses across the seas. In the next generation, it may here be noted, Henry's daughter, Alice, would become the most passionately pro-Irish member of the entire tribe.

At the very start of the trip, the adventure was imperiled by an intrusion of American history—the financial panic of 1837, which caused enormous drains on state banks and led to a severe shortage of available cash: a particular problem for the traveling American, who needed letters of credit and bills of exchange for use overseas. It says a good deal for the soundness of William of Albany's investments that his son, in London, was able quite quickly to lay his hands on funds adequate for his needs. But it also says something for the Panic of 1837 that it elicited one of the only expressions of concern about money matters that the elder Henry James is known to have uttered.

James's first order of business in London was the acquisition of a right leg made of cork, to replace the awkward peg leg with which he had made do for a decade. The preparation of the new leg, begun in June, required a series of fittings and adjustments; but it was in place by some time in July, and James was able to stand and to move about in a far more graceful and comely manner. The cork limb also made possible what was to be one of James's favorite pastimes, which was to stroll through the busy streets of a city.

He had found lodgings with an accommodating English couple. Here in the last week of July he was joined by his former science tutor, Joseph Henry, who as a young man had presided over the calamitous experiment in balloon flying. Now a professor of natural philosophy at Princeton, where James had re-encountered him, Joseph Henry had won international recognition as a scientist with a special genius in the field of electronics, he having in fact anticipated Michael Faraday in the discovery of induced electrical currents. The tutor-pupil relationship between the two men had been succeeded by a warm and easy friendship (James had no qualms about offering and Joseph Henry none about accepting a gift of £250 for the purchase of scientific instruments). They differed on some things, including religious affiliation—Joseph Henry was just rejoining the Presbyterian Church, which Henry James was just about to quit. But they shared an alert sympathy for other human beings, and they were avid fellow seekers after truth. For Joseph Henry, the governing principle for human knowledge could be found in the domain of physical science; Henry James would discover that principle in his own brand of mystical theology.

It was Joseph Henry who, in letters back home, provided the most vivid account of what was really the star attraction of James's London ménage. This was his attendant, a black servant from Albany named Billy Taylor: a big man, handsome, steadily reliable, and (one judges) extremely entertaining, more than willing to clown it up whenever it was expected of him. The other servants in the house, Joseph Henry reported, made much of the first black American they had ever seen; he was invited to take all his meals with the English family, and the scientist surmised that if Billy Taylor had not been married—he had a wife back in Albany—he could have made his choice among a variety of young Englishwomen.

Henry James spent the better part of August 1837 in the town of Bailieborough. His aim, he told a friend, was to look up "an uncles family" and see if they were in want. The uncle in question was William of Albany's older brother Robert, the one who had stayed behind on the Curkish farm, and who had died in 1823. He left a widow and eleven children, a number of whom had followed their Uncle William to America, their passage being paid by him in two cases; three or four were still living in the Bailieborough neighborhood. Into this company there arrived Henry James, accompanied to the general astonishment and delight by Billy Taylor.

The Bailieborough experience became a favorite chapter in the James family folklore. Henry Senior's children in the early New York days—as the younger Henry would describe it in one of his finest feats of impressionistic re-creation—constantly begged their father to tell them again

in the winter afternoon firelight, of his most personal, most remembering and picture-recovering "story"; that of a visit paid by him about in his nineteenth year, as I make it out, to his Irish relatives, his father's nephews, nieces and cousins, with a younger brother or two perhaps, as I set the scene forth—which it conduced to our liveliest interest to see "Billy Taylor," the negro servant accompanying him from Albany, altogether rule from the point of view of effect. The dignity of this apparition indeed, I must parenthesise, would have yielded in general to the source of a glamour still more marked—the very air in which the young emissary would have moved as the son of his father and the representative of an American connection prodigious surely in its power to dazzle.

It was the enormous wealth, achieved in America by the former Bailieborough lad, that in Henry Junior's imagination constituted the "fairytale" that the friendly visitor could bring "his modest Irish kin" from the other side of the Atlantic. It was at this point in his narrative that the younger Henry spoke fancifully about the children puzzling over the precise amount of their father's legacy. But the whole arithmetical question, he went on, interested him only

through the brightly associated presumption that the Irish visit was made, to its extreme enlivening, in the character of a gilded youth, a youth gilded an inch thick and shining to effulgence on the scene not otherwise brilliant. Which image appeals to my filial fidelity—even though I hasten not to sacrifice the circle evoked, that for which I a trifle unassuredly figure a small town in county Cavan as forming an horizon, and which consisted, we used to delight to hear with every contributive circumstance, of the local lawyer, the doctor and the (let us hope—for we *did* hope) principal "merchant," whose conjoined hospitality appeared, as it was again agreeable to know, to have more than graced the occasion: the main definite pictorial touches that have lingered with me being that all the doors always stood open, with the vistas mostly raking the provision of whiskey on every table . . .

Bailieborough in 1837 was, as Henry Junior rightly if "unassuredly" said, a small town. It had been created as such, out of the vaguely defined rural territory, early in the nineteenth century by Colonel William Young, who had taken over the castle and the townlands from the Stewart family and who busied himself laying out a broad, down-sloping street, with a few side roads, and pressing the inhabitants into setting up rows of houses and shops and taverns, a post office, a market hall. The First William had died in 1822, at the venerable age of eighty-six. (His grave, a flat stone slab next to that of his wife, Susan, may still be found amid the shoulder-high weeds of the old Bailieborough cemetery.) His son Robert survived him by only a year. The Curkish farm was being run by Robert's son Henry, a near-contemporary (1803–73) of the visiting cousin, of identical name, from America.

Local records do not confirm Henry Junior's implication that there was a lawyer among the Bailieborough Jameses whose always open doors and kegs of whiskey were so pleasing an element in the father's oft-told story. But there was certainly a doctor: Robert James, M.D., the older brother of the farming Henry and the seventh child of the father for whom he was named. Dr. James's practice was thriving to the point where he could buy himself a house on the main street in town. The third generation in County Cavan, "the uncles family," was doing modestly well, as Henry Senior could see for himself.

In his recalling of the Bailieborough story, Henry Junior concluded by reverting to that part of it which always, in the telling, most enchanted the children:

the almost epic shape of black Billy Taylor carrying off at every juncture alike the laurel and the bay. He singularly appealed, it was clear, to the Irish imagination, performing in a manner never to disappoint it; his young master . . . had been all cordially acclaimed, but not least, it appeared, *because* so histrionically attended . . .

These passages, from *Notes of a Son and Brother* (1914), are worth quoting with almost all their asides and modifications, because they give so apt an example of Henry James drawing on the Irish connection for his own imaginative ends. What we have, all typically, is James's gathering recollection, late in life, of the children listening intently, fifty-five and sixty years earlier, to their father reminiscing on many a New York winter afternoon about an Irish adventure that had occurred a number of years before that. James's account is of that remembered adventure, but it is equally about the act of remembering, about picture-making and storytelling. It is perfectly in order, consequently, for James to get some of the facts wrong: Henry Senior was twenty-six, not nineteen; William of Albany was no longer alive, though the memoirist (in a sentence not included above) purports to think differently; there were no younger brothers on hand—John James, the third and last son of the First William, died, perhaps at sea, in 1813. Henry Junior is dissolving factuality in the interests of literary effect: the gilded youth shines yet more youthfully, and a younger brother or two are added "*as I set the scene forth.*" The Irish connection had, by 1914, been absorbed into the texture of Henry James's art of narrative, and there given a permanent memorial.

CHAPTER TWO

Henry James, Sr.:
The Endangering Self

THE TROUBLE WITH SEMINARIES

After marking time in Albany for several years following the death of
his father, Henry James, Sr., in the fall of 1835, had registered as a
first-year student in the Princeton Theological School. One reason for
the choice of orthodox Princeton—rather than, say, Yale, where the
"New Divinity men" were flourishing—was that his half brother William had preceded him there twenty years earlier; and another that
his tutor and friend, Joseph Henry, was on the scene as professor of
natural philosophy. The seminary experiment was, or turned out to be,
James's final visit to the world of conventional Calvinism in its American form.

By any standards, James was the most unorthodox of divinity students. He quietly delayed taking his place at the meal table until after
grace was said, and slipped away before the final prayer. He refused
to be drawn into any sort of doctrinal discussion. He baffled his brethren
by failing to show the slightest interest as to his whereabouts in the
afterlife; it was not his personal destiny, he would say, but the common
destiny of mankind that occupied his thoughts. He was a lively and
likable figure, clearly animated by a spirit of cordial fellowship; but
no one knew how to take him.

But here we must pause for a cautionary note. The description of
Henry James at Princeton comes from the "autobiographic sketch"

with which James was engaged at the time of his death; and in a complicated and artful way, that sketch is a work of fiction. It purports to be the memoirs of one Stephen Dewhurst, and to have been merely "edited" by Henry James, who supplies a lengthy and somewhat eerie preface.* In this, he tells how he had come to know Dewhurst at the seminary, how Dewhurst had won his discipleship by talking to him about the true nature of religion; how they left the seminary together, how their ways parted when Dewhurst took a position in the Treasury Department in Washington, and how, finally, Dewhurst on his death-bed (it is one of the fine old devices of Victorian melodramatic fiction) entrusted to James the personal document, which itself consisted of letters to the disciple. In the fragmentary memoirs that follow—they run to about thirty book pages—Dewhurst, in his own voice, gives an account of his childhood, of family and village life, the terrible accident, and early disturbances of conscience which we may take as more or less true to life. But he changes or distorts some of the actual Jamesian facts (he has himself growing up in Baltimore, and the accident becomes a gunshot in the arm). More important: in both the preface and the memoirs, Dewhurst is given religious and social ideas that—as we shall be observing—James himself did not arrive at for many a year after he left the seminary.

As to James's purpose in inventing the surrogate Dewhurst, it seems that after several tries James simply could not go ahead with a document that by nature was the expression of his personal self. He was, by every intellectual disposition, the radical opposite of the American literary Romantic who finds value in composing "advertisements for myself." He sought, rather, suppressions of himself; and in this case, he needed the guise of a fictitious alter ego. But it is also to be remarked that disguised autobiography grew into something of a family habit. William James, in *The Varieties of Religious Experience*, presented the most terrifying moment of his life in the form of a letter written to him by a fictive Frenchman, and Henry James began his own autobiography by identifying it as the story of the early life of his recently deceased brother William.

The fictionality of Dewhurst's memoir should be kept in mind as we consider the reasons adduced by his editor, Henry James, for Dewhurst's abandoning the seminary. It was the professionalizing of religion, James wrote, that disgusted him. He came to loathe the

---

* The title is: "Immortal Life: Illustrated in a Brief Autobiographic Sketch of the Late Stephen Dewhurst. Edited, with an Introduction, by Henry James."

"unconscious hypocrisy" which "seems to be inseparable from the religious *profession*." The average theological student became "personally mortgaged to an *institution*—that of the pulpit"; and the insisted-upon sanctity of that pulpit had a crushing effect upon the student's natural spiritual freedom. There was in the seminary, as one consequence, the same sort of self-serving isolation from the rest of the human world that James/Dewhurst discovered and deplored in the average American family.

An encounter in the summer of 1837—to go back to the real-life student—gave a decided spur to Henry Senior's religious thinking. During the fortnight that James and Joseph Henry were together in London in those months (before James went on to visit his Bailieborough kin), the former tutor introduced James to the great English scientist Michael Faraday. Forty-six years old, Faraday was lifetime professor of chemistry at the Royal Institution, to which he had been appointed by Sir Humphry Davy. Though Joseph Henry was in some respects Faraday's scientific equal, he revered the Englishman as the world's leading authority in electrical investigation. What immediately intrigued Henry James, however, was not Faraday's scientific accomplishments, much as he might honor them, but Faraday's association with a tiny, out-of-the-way religious sect dedicated to a mode of primitive Christianity and founded in the previous century by the Scottish-born Robert Sandeman. Faraday's parents had belonged to the Sandeman sect, and on turning thirty Faraday himself made a public confession of faith.

James could have known about Sandemanism from American witnesses, for Sandeman spent his last seven years in New England, setting up little communities of believers, and he had died in Danbury, Connecticut, in 1771. But the slim evidence suggests that James came to the cult in London by way of Joseph Henry and Michael Faraday. It was a timely meeting. Sandemanism arose out of a revolt against the institutionalized Presbyterian Church in Scotland; Henry James in 1837 was edging toward a withdrawal from the Presbyterian Church in America. Robert Sandeman dispensed with almost the entire ecclesiastical apparatus, especially (it was gratifying for James to learn) the professional clergy. The sect followed a variety of biblically based laws and rituals, none of which interested Henry James. But he was quickly drawn to such central ideas of Sandemanism as the prime importance of loving brotherhood and the common sharing of material goods.

He responded no less to the Sandemanian hatred of moral self-righteousness and to the conviction that Christ came into the world not to reward the highly moral, the Pharisees, but to redeem the hopelessly sinful. As early as 1767, a New England minister, gazing in consternation at the Sandemanian creed, declared that it presented Christ as displaying "the highest indignation against all virtue, and especially against those good works which are highly esteemed among men."

In the later family story, Henry Junior would recall the children's amusement, not unmixed with bewilderment, at their father's attitude toward morality. "He only cared for virtue," the son put it, "that was more or less ashamed of itself." And so "we had ever the amusement . . . of hearing morality, or moralism, as it was more invidiously worded, made hay of in the very interest of character and conduct; these things suffering much, it seemed, by their association with the conscience—that is, the *conscious* conscience—the very home of the literal, the haunt of so many pedantries." The elder James's earliest expression of this line of thinking was in his brief account of Sandemanism, written late in 1837. It is also the first instance we have of Henry Senior's uninhibitedly intemperate rhetoric:

The whole New Testament speaks aloud, that as to the matter of acceptance with God, there is no difference between one man and another; —no difference between the best accomplished gentleman and the most infamous scoundrel; —no difference between the most virtuous lady and the vilest prostitute; —no difference between the most revered judge, and the most odious criminal standing convicted before him, and receiving the just sentence of death from his mouth—in a word, no difference between the most fervent devotee, and the greatest ringleader in profaneness and excess.

That hammering sentence occurs in the unsigned two-page preface to James's American edition of Sandeman's *Letters on Thereon and Aspasia* (itself a 1757 rebuttal to a popular work of religious good cheer by an evangelical Anglican clergyman). As a statement of the radical moral equality of all individual human beings, it rivals the most forthright sounding of the theme eighteen years later in "Song of Myself" by the James family's favorite American poet, Walt Whitman: "This is the meal equally set, this the meat for natural hunger./It is for the wicked just the same as the righteous, I make appointments with all." No one who felt that way could be expected to remain within the confines of professional Calvinism.

James stopped over briefly in London after the Bailieborough reunion. On September 20, he embarked at Portsmouth on the *Ontario*, and arrived in New York on October 25. There was time for a hurried visit with his mother in Albany before he reported at Princeton. He delayed registering for the third year, and instead took to discussing the whole perplexing situation with a classmate. The latter's disaffection matched his own. The two young men made the decision to leave the seminary then and there, and leaped excitedly onto the first available coach for New York. That same November evening, the classmate introduced James to his family, ranged around the fire at 19 Washington Square.

ROMANCE ON WASHINGTON SQUARE

The classmate was named Hugh Walsh. He was the fifth of six children of the late James Walsh and Elizabeth Robertson Walsh; there were two older brothers, Alexander and John, and two older sisters, Mary Robertson and Catherine. Hugh, at twenty-one, was appreciably younger than Henry James and to a degree he was James's protégé. (Within the tangled skein of fiction that makes up the editor's preface to the Dewhurst memoirs, it seems that James, as the alleged impressionable young friend of Dewhurst, was assuming the role that Hugh Walsh had played vis-à-vis James in real life.) If he and James had hit it off so well at the seminary, it was partly because they came from similar mercantile and Presbyterian backgrounds, something which the two were now encouraging one another to break with.

Mrs. Walsh's father, Alexander Robertson, was of a Scottish line, coming to America around 1750 from Rannoch in Pertshire, and prospering in New York as a "Merchant." Henry Junior found him so listed in "a wee New York directory of the close of the century"; Henry could recall Robertson being spoken of as a person of "shining solidity," and of a legendary fortune no portion of which came down to any of the Jameses, despite the ensuing marriage tie. Alice James, who if anything outstripped her brother Henry as a collector of ancestral gossip, wrote in her diary that Alexander Robertson had returned to Scotland to take to himself a third wife, and that soon after she was established in New

York the bride had behaved so viciously toward one of her stepdaughters that she was shipped straight back to her native land.

In the same entry, Alice recorded what she had recently (1890) learned about the Irish side of her maternal ancestry—the first Hugh Walsh, who emigrated in 1764 from the village of Killyleagh in County Down, east of Belfast on the Irish coast; the Walshes had apparently been planted there from England at some earlier epoch. "Great-Grandfather Hugh Walsh," Alice wrote, "left Ireland, in a broken-hearted condition, in his youth because he was not allowed to marry a young lady, with whom he was in love." She continued, in her special vein of ironic romanticism and probably mixing fact with fancy: "He must have had some money, for he settled at Newburgh, on the Hudson and consoled himself by starting a Soap!! factory. He later took to building sloops. He married and named one of his daughters after his first flame." Soap factory or not, Hugh Walsh made a considerable fortune in Newburgh out of shipbuilding and river freight.

His oldest son, James, moved down to New York and had a successful career there as a cotton merchant. In 1806, he married Elizabeth Robertson; their second child, Mary, was born four years later. James Walsh died suddenly of apoplexy in 1820; but he left his widow and their six children reasonably well off and comfortably settled in the handsome house on the square.

In the earnest conversations that began to take place in the Walsh drawing room, it was clearly Henry James who set the pace. Inevitably, the talk turned to religion and religious affiliation. The Walshes were a devout churchgoing family, all of them members of the Murray Street Presbyterian Church, where the Reverend William James had preached for a time in the early 1820s. Henry James, seconded by Hugh Walsh, undertook to persuade the Walsh women that such membership was a mistake; that it was all wrong to think of the church as a *visible* entity to which one "belonged," and which dealt with tangible things, like the administration of the sacraments. The church, James was beginning to believe and to argue, was much rather an *inward* reality; in his later phrasing, "the actual life of God himself in human nature," a divine life-in-man which was not other than the spiritual and social welfare of mankind on earth.

The Walsh women listened with astonishment to their young guest's powerful and winning rhetoric, his disturbing yet oddly hypnotic harangues. The two sisters—Mary, twenty-seven, and Catherine, twenty-five—were so stirred that before long they took the momentous step of withdrawing from the Murray Street church. Elizabeth Walsh, the mother, glimmers for us as a silent attendant of these suasions; but she evidently gave tacit consent to her daughters' action.

Something else, though, was going on in addition to religious re-education, and it may be indicated by a line from *Richard III*, one of Henry Senior's favorite works of literature: "Was ever woman in this humour woo'd?" For that it was a courtship, with vibrant erotic un-dertones, is not to be doubted.

James would tell Emerson, who recorded it in his journal, that on his first meeting Mary Walsh, "the flesh said, It is for me, and the spirit said, It is for me." In matters of spirit, Mary quickly revealed her pliability and calm shrewdness; for the rest, if she was anything but a beauty, she was a full-bodied woman with a firm, composed face. But whatever James's spirit and flesh whispered to him, they did not hurry him into marriage. He seems, in fact, to have been experiencing dif-ficulty in fixing his marital sights. He was obviously attracted to Mary, but he also apparently felt the appeal of the younger Catharine; she was, we gather, more high-spirited and outspoken than her sister, more alert to those questions of society and history that were of rising im-portance for James; and she was almost equally captivated by the new friend. James's original emotional allegiance, it can be remembered, was to the brother Hugh Walsh, and it may be—the phenomenon is not unknown—that what James was seeking was an entirely new *fam-ily*: Hugh's family. In any event, it was not until July 28, 1840, that Henry James and Mary Robertson Walsh were wedded.

The marriage took place in the Walsh home on Washington Square, and it was a civil affair, presided over by the mayor of New York, Isaac Leggett Varian. All James's siblings were married by cler-gymen (the Reverend William officiating in several instances); but James's anti-clericalism forbade any ministerial presence. And as he would say of himself on his deathbed, he was a man "who has thought all his life, that the ceremonies attending birth, marriage and death were all damned nonsense."

One of Henry James, Jr.'s earliest short stories hints at a drama lying behind Henry Senior's choice of bride. This is "The Romance of Certain Old Clothes," published in February 1868. The story tells of the Willoughby family, residing some twenty miles from Boston in the mid-eighteenth century, a family consisting of the widowed Mrs. Willoughby, her son, Bernard, and her two daughters, Viola and Per-dita (the late Mr. Willoughby had been a lover of Shakespeare). Ber-nard goes to England to study at Oxford, and when he returns he brings with him a classmate, Arthur Lloyd. This gentleman is "a young man of reputable family," with a "handsome inheritance." He and Bernard Willoughby

were warm friends; they had crossed the ocean together, and the young American had lost no time in presenting him at his mother's house, where he had made quite as good an impression as that which he had received.

Lloyd, played up to by Bernard, discourses enchantingly for the benefit of the Willoughby women, gathered round the fire after tea in the little wainscoted parlor; they are charmed and beguiled, and both sisters fall in love with him. As for Lloyd, he found that "they were both very fine girls." He felt "a strong presentiment . . . that he was destined to marry one of them; yet he was unable to arrive at a preference."

Things remain in suspense for some months, until Lloyd makes his choice of the younger sister, Perdita. So far, the story rehearses Henry Senior's courtship days and his relation to the Walsh family almost step by step (though the children's ages have been shifted around). But at this stage the narrative tone changes. Perdita and Lloyd settle in Boston, and at the end of a year Perdita gives birth to a baby girl and dies soon afterward. On her deathbed she makes her husband promise that he will hold her rings and gowns in safekeeping for their daughter; Lloyd locks them up. After an interval he marries the other sister, Viola, "a devilish fine woman," in his opinion. It is not long before Viola is badgering her husband to give her Perdita's finery. Lloyd at last lets her have the key; Viola ascends in haste to the attic, and there she is found some hours later, lying dead on the floor in front of the open chest.

On her limbs was the stiffness of death, and on her face, in the fading light of the sun, the terror of something more than death. Her lips were parted in entreaty, in dismay, in agony; and on her bloodless brow and cheeks there glowed the marks of ten hideous wounds from two vengeful ghostly hands.

What is fascinating about this tale, in the present context, is not that it offers anything like a realistic portrait of the old triangular relation. For one thing, it is a ghost story, the first in a lifelong series of masterful exercises in this genre; and for another, it is a highly literary performance, with Hawthorne presiding over some of it and a clear echo of Poe's "Ligeia" (the dead first wife returning to destroy the second wife). But the massing of recognizable detail does suggest a muffled family tradition, as it were, about a silent emotional struggle between the two competing sisters; or at least Henry Junior conjecturing about that possibility. This is what gets fictionalized when Perdita, leaving the Willoughby house on her wedding day, espies her sister dressed in the bridal costume, standing in front of the mirror and gazing into it. The mirror, Perdita feels with a shudder, gives back "a hideous image of their old rivalry come to life again."

Henry James, Sr., was married, but he could hardly be said to have settled down. Over the next year and a half, James changed his and Mary's living place not less than five times. They spent some months with James's mother in the old Albany home. They took rooms in the expensive and showy Astor House in New York City. They rented a house at 5 Washington Square, not far from the Walshes. They returned to the Astor House, and here on January 11, 1842, their first child was born, and was named William, after his grandfather, great-grandfather, and uncle. At the same moment, Henry bought from his brother John Barber James, for the impressive sum of $18,000, a three-story brick house at 21 Washington Place, a quiet street that runs west from Broadway three blocks to the square. This was the first house of James's own; and here Henry Junior was born on April 15, 1843, just fifteen months younger—as he was given to remarking—than William. But soon the father was wondering aloud whether he might not be wise to find "a little nook in the country," perhaps in Connecticut. By October 1843, he had sold the New York house and was off with his wife and their two children for an indeterminate stay in Europe.

This to-and-fro mode of life reflected an uneasy, untargeted, inward condition, despite an outward show of self-possession. Externally, he gave a pleasing appearance: a well-turned-out young gentleman, tending a little toward stoutness, extremely fortunate in worldly goods, with a not ungraceful limp and a gift for lively and sometimes comically extravagant speech that was enhanced by an occasional stammer. He gave a sense of manliness, to use a word much invoked by him; and we may suppose him to have enjoyed a strong virile nature. In his memoirs, he lingered over the memory of how he had relieved the boredom of Sunday churchgoing, in his youthful days, by observing the "shapely maid" coming and going through the door of the house across the way; and how he liked to tease the "good-natured chambermaids" at home to the point where they threatened to smother him with hugs and kisses. The mature Henry James's attitude toward the heterosexual erotic relation, as expressed in his writings, was—to a degree unique in the known clan—at once candid and zestful.

But he suffered all the while from a profound self-distrust, a feeling that kept him constantly on edge and on the move. If the Dewhurst memoirs are to be trusted, the self-questioning began in childhood, and was aroused by his private image of God and of God's relation to the individual human being. The God to whom young Henry was introduced at home, at church, and in Sunday school was not at all a wrathful, vengeful figure. He had once been such a figure, but after Christ's intercession and atonement, God's "active enmity" dwindled to mere "chronic apathy or indifference." But Henry believed himself capable of converting the divine apathy "into a sentiment of acute personal hostility." This terrible experience (we are still following Dewhurst's memoirs) did not occur when he had stolen coins from his father's drawer or wine from his parents' cellar: these peccadilloes never kept him awake at night. What did make him conscious of "the spectral eye of God" upon him as he lay sleepless in bed was something else. It was always "some wanton ungenerous word or deed by which I had wounded the vital self-respect of another, or imposed upon him gratuitous personal suffering." It was turning on his sister Jennet with mocking derision, or roughly rejecting the plea of his brother John to join him in some sportive game. It was "when I remembered these things upon my bed, [that] the terrors of hell encompassed me, and I was fairly heartbroken with a dread of being estranged from God and all good men."

Some such moments may well have characterized Henry James's childhood. But it will not have escaped notice that the God who could be stirred from apathy to raging hostility bears no small resemblance to the paternal figure, William of Albany, whose eruption from congenital indifference to vindictive fury Henry could well remember from his Union College days. And when he tells us further, in the Dewhurst narrative, that the Sunday-school image of God's apathy always mingled in his soul with a contrary image, that of God's "ineffable love," we cannot but be reminded of his account only a few pages earlier of his father's usual remoteness giving way to an anguish of compassion during one of the surgical operations. But no simple derivation is to be asserted here. In the peculiar case of Henry James Senior, it is by no means obvious whether the paternal image retrospectively dictated the divine one, or whether the portrait of God, entertained by James, shaped the account of his father.

James, anyhow, was evidently able to subdue those terrors for a good many years, or to push them down into the recesses of his psyche. But by his own report, they re-emerged and intensified in the first years of his marriage. For now the "wanton ungenerous word or deed," the wounding of another's self-respect, involved a member of the family and household he had himself created. If, in the home on Washington Place, he gave his wife a sulky glance or spoke crossly to baby William or growled at the cook, he found himself "tumbling into an instant inward frenzy of alarm lest I should thereby have provoked God's personal malignity to me." (James's language as so often is hyperbolic and theologized; but the sense of inward writhing over a remembered cruelty or spitefulness to a fellow human is something familiar to many.) James prided himself on striving after moral excellence, and that very *pride* led to a feeling of horror within:

The more I strove to indue myself in actual righteousness, the wider gaped the jaws of hell within me; the fouler grew its fetid breath. A conviction of inward defilement so sheer took possession of me, that death seemed better than life.

James was also troubled about his role in life, but thought that he had found one through his meditations on the Bible. His study led him to suspect that the Book of Genesis was not intended as a literal account of the origins of the world and the human race, but rather a "mystical or symbolic record of the laws of God's *spiritual* creation and providence." In the terms of today's renewed debate on the issue, James opposed an allegorical to a "creationist" reading of Genesis, and wrote a series of lectures to that end, which he delivered before city audiences in 1842 and 1843.

The result was vaguely depressing. James came home one evening after his talk to write Emerson that his audience was falling away, and that he was clearly failing to interest the kind of religious-minded listener that he sought.

James for the moment was using Ralph Waldo Emerson as a sounding board. After attending the first of Emerson's lectures on "The Times," at the Library Society in New York on March 3, 1842, James sent him a spiritual love letter, expressing a desire "to talk familiarly with one who earnestly follows truth through whatever frowning ways she beckons him on," praising Emerson for an "erect attitude of mind . . . which in God's universe undauntedly seeks the worthiest tidings of God." He begged the New Englander to come visit the James home on Washington Place: "My occupations are all indoor, so that I am generally at home—always in the evenings." Emerson did so, and was quickly taken upstairs "to admire and give his blessing" (in the younger Henry's words) to the two-month-old William; a laying on of hands, as some would later think it to be. For his part, Emerson found Mr. James "the best apple on the tree thus far" in the world of New York. But James wanted more from Emerson than courtly cordiality. He wanted guidance.

"Here I am thirty-one years in life," he wrote, in the letter confessing disappointment over the lecture series, "ignorant in all outward science, but having patient habits of meditation which never know disgust or weariness." He was driven "to seek the *laws* of these appearances that swim round us in God's great museum." What should he do? Could not Emerson help him from the depths of his own inner wants? To these and subsequent appeals, Emerson remained silent. He had a dim but sufficient awareness—so later evidence would indicate—of the God-tormented soul that hid behind the questions, and knew himself incapable of offering a suggestion.

VASTATION AT WINDSOR, 1844

So, in the fall of 1843, the James family sailed to England, departing from New York on October 19 aboard *The Great Western*, a four-masted, paddlewheeler which made the run to Bristol in the good time of eighteen days. The party consisted of the two parents, Mary James's sister Catherine, the two boys, and a maid-servant Fanny, provided from the Albany household.

Writing to Emerson just before leaving, James had spoken of his mixed expectations for the trip: "How long I shall stay, and whether I shall gain what I go for specially, or something instead which I have not thought of, and all questions of that clap—I am of course in the dark about." He hoped to draw an essay from his lectures on Genesis, and he looked forward to meeting some of the intellectual folk in London, particularly Thomas Carlyle, to whom Emerson had supplied an introduction.

During three months in London, James was far more sociable than on the previous visit in the 1837 summer. He betook himself frequently to the home of Thomas and Jane Carlyle in Cheyne Walk, where, in addition to his host and hostess, he came to know John Stuart Mill, Tennyson, George Henry Lewes, and other men of intellect and imagination who made the Carlyle drawing room the scene of the best conversation in England. Looking back at these gatherings twenty-three years later, however, James would think that the participants, with some exceptions, were a discouraging lot—they were interested in ideas but with no concern for the consequences of ideas. "Take them all in all," he wrote, they "differed widely from Americans of the same type of thought. They had not half the seriousness of our men. Life to them began and ended in conversation, not in action." There in a single sentence bespeaking his own credo about *living* one's ideas, Henry Senior also formulated one of the tenets of his son William's philosophy of pragmatism, itself an unmistakably American doctrine. "What they had to say," James concluded, in a typical allusion, "was not a tenth so interesting as the talk you have in America with the person sitting next to you in the horse cars."

At the time of meeting, nonetheless, James regarded Carlyle as "the very best interpreter of spiritual philosophy which could be devised *for this age.*" So James had told Emerson earlier in the year, contending that Carlyle combined a hospitality to new ideas with a responsiveness to the old Calvinist principles. "You don't look upon Calvinism as a fact at all," James informed Emerson, "wherein you are to my mind philosophically infirm, and impaired as to your universality." To look upon Calvinism as a fact, for James, was to acknowledge the reality of human wickedness or selfishness as the first challenge in experience; the given, though not, happily, the permanent, condition of the individual. It was in this same letter that James made his pronouncement that "Jonathan Edwards *redivivus* in true blue would, after an honest study of the philosophy that has grown up since his day, make the best possible reconciler and critic of philosophy." It was an extraordinary statement for an American to make in 1843, and, of all people, to Ralph Waldo Emerson, whose immunity to the unsparing Edwardsian vision of human sinfulness and divine wrath (as in "Sinners in the Hands of an Angry God") was absolute.

For his part, Carlyle was much taken with the visiting young American, with his hesitancy of speech and his touches of humor. "James is a very good fellow, better and better as we see him more," he wrote Emerson. "Something shy and skittish in the man; but a brave heart intrinsically, with sound earnest sense, with plenty of insight and even humour. He confirms an observation of mine, which indeed I find is hundreds of years old, that a stammering man is never a worthless one."

James escorted the family over to France in mid-January 1844. The subsequent weeks in Paris were miserable: the weather was wretched, the lodgings were not of the best, and James was never comfortable in a non-English-language environment. It was with a lifting heart that he led the party back to England the last week in April.

After looking about for a few days, James found an ideal place for the summer. It was called Frogmore Cottage, and stood between the Great and Little Parks of Windsor (to the southwest of London), in the shadow of the royal castle. The cottage was surrounded by a well-trimmed hedge six feet high and two feet thick; there were trees and flowers in the courtyard, and fruit gardens ran along both sides of the house. To the rear, the Great Park stretched away for a dozen miles, its broad meadows dotted with oak trees; herds of cattle, deer, and sheep browsed across it, some of them straying up to graze directly beneath the cottage's nursery window—young Willy and Harry, their father thought fondly, could converse with them. The cottage itself fronted the entrance to the Little Park, whose pathways curved down to the banks of the Thames and the private gardens of Queen Victoria.

All this James reported in joyful detail to his mother, writing in the ground-floor study of Frogmore Cottage on May 1. The whole situation, he declared, punning happily on one of the opening lines of *Richard III*, gave every promise "of a 'glorious summer' to this son of New York." Nor, he insisted, was the rental an expensive one: the cottage cost four pounds, ten shillings a week, and the combined wages of a cook and chambermaid came to eight shillings. General living expenses were calculated at two pounds, and the total outlay could be reckoned at a maximum of forty dollars a week. Since James's personal income was in the neighborhood of $1,000 a month, the cost of Windsor living could not be called high.

Considering what was shortly to occur, James's high spirits and his sense of well-being should be stressed. The transition from gloomy Paris had been good for his morale, and James appears to have once again subdued that inner distress which had been besetting him somewhat earlier. He was physically well, and the family flourished; one-year-old Harry was patiently teething; Willy, two years and four months, had been a bit poorly but was now "on the mend" and "full of fun." James's study of Genesis was progressing famously; he really thought he was on the verge of contributing "a not insignificant mite to the sum of man's highest knowledge." The English weather was superb, and the grass as green as summer.

The letter of May 1 did, though, contain one curious note, tucked in amid the expression of contentment. James had raised a question about the date of the family's return to America, and confided that they might come back sooner than originally scheduled. He went on:

I confess to some potent feelings now and then dear Ma in your directions— "nursery" remembrances, and "little back room" remembrances come over me not infrequently which make Windsor Castle seem a great ghastly lie and its parks an endless sickness not to be endured a moment longer.

James was inclined to dismiss these potent memories of childhood days and maternal care in the Albany home; they were mere *"feelings,"* unrelated to his rational judgment.

The spring drifted enchantingly onward. And then, near the end of May, to Henry Senior sitting peacefully at the table after dinner, there came a terrible visitation.

His narrative of the event, in *Society the Redeemed Form of Man* (1879), begins with a reference to the essay on Genesis.

. . . I remember I felt especially hopeful in the prosecution of my task all the time I was at Windsor; my health was good, my spirits cheerful, and the pleasant scenery of the great Park and its neighborhood furnished us a constant temptation to long walks and drives.

One day, however, towards the close of May, having eaten a comfortable dinner, I remained sitting at the table after the family had dispersed, idly gazing at the embers in the grate, thinking of nothing, and feeling only the exhilaration incident to a good digestion, when suddenly—in a lightning-flash as it were—"fear came upon me, and trembling, which made all my bones to shake." To all appearance it was a perfectly insane and abject terror, without ostensible cause, and only to be accounted for, to my perplexed imagination, by some damnèd shape squatting invisible to me within the precincts of the room, and raying out from his fetid personality influences fatal to life. The thing had not lasted ten seconds before I felt myself a wreck; that is, reduced from a state of firm, vigorous, joyful manhood to one of almost helpless infancy. The only self-control I was capable of exerting was to keep my seat. I felt the greatest desire to run incontinently to the foot of the stairs and shout for help to my wife,—to run to the roadside even, and appeal to the public to protect me; but by an immense effort I controlled these frenzied impulses, and determined not to budge from my chair till I had recovered my lost self-possession. This purpose I held to for a good long hour, as I reckoned time, beat upon meanwhile by an ever-growing tempest of doubt, anxiety, and despair, with absolutely no relief from any truth I had ever encountered save a most pale and distant glimmer of the divine existence, when I resolved to abandon the vain struggle, and communicate without more ado what seemed my sudden burden of inmost, implacable unrest to my wife.

Now, to make a long story short, this ghastly condition of mind continued with me, with gradually lengthening intervals of relief, for two years . . .

All of Henry Senior's intellectual lifetime went into the wording of that account, which was, in fact, written only a few years before his death. We recognize in it emotionally charged words and phrases almost identical with those he had distributed among the other documents of his maturity where they dealt with moments of spiritual crisis: "insane and abject terror . . . fetid personality . . . frenzied impulses . . . tempest of doubt, anxiety, and despair." The event of May 1844 became for James, in a long retrospect, the paradigm of every significant experience he had undergone from childhood onward; yet it is not clear that he altogether understood it, or the whole of it.

One proceeds cautiously with such occult matters, and according to one's own leanings. The damnèd shape—a masculine phenomenon ("*his* fetid personality")—seems, then, to have been a presence conjured up by James as the source of the panic fear that had seized him. It may be taken, first of all, as one part of James's self in the horrified intuition or apprehension (for it was "invisible" to him) of another portion of himself. *This* is what he really was: not the righteous, virtue-seeking, family-loving man he had striven to be, but a nauseous, hateful, corrupted being that poisoned and destroyed everything he touched. At the same time, this was Henry James as he lay exposed to the spectral, all-perceiving eye of God. And finally—if this *was* an active element, it was one that James did not allow himself to acknowledge—the shape was the son in the outraged view of the father; a fulfillment of the father's furious prophecy, passed along by his surrogate years before, that he would "become a loathing to himself and his best friends."

Whatever the nature of the squatting horror, the effect upon James was utterly devastating. His vigorous and joyful manhood crumbled completely, and the person who had been having " 'nursery' remembrances" of late was reduced to a helpless infancy, feeling a wild desire to rush to his wife like a terrified child to its mother; until finally he did carry his burden of despair to the waiting presence of the calmly comforting Mary James. During the timeless period when he sat motionless, every belief he had previously held seemed "a ghastly lie" (to quote again from the letter to his mother); he found no relief of any kind, save for a thin, remote "glimmer of the divine existence."

After some days had passed, James felt able to bestir himself and consult several "eminent physicians," all of whom told him that he had simply overworked his brain in the exegetical labors on Genesis. They recommended the water cure at a resort they named. The treatment, which James dutifully took, was of no value, but while at the resort James became acquainted with a Mrs. Chichester, and she proved (as James would have said) a godsend.

The two met and talked frequently. One day, after listening to James recount the Windsor experience, Mrs. Chichester said: "It is, then, very much as I had ventured from two or three previous things you have said, to suspect: you are undergoing what Swedenborg calls a *vastation*; and though, naturally enough, you yourself are despondent or even despairing about the issue, I cannot help taking an altogether hopeful view of your prospects."

One wishes one knew more about Mrs. Chichester, with her oddly incantatory speech. She comes down to us like a figure remembered after many years by a character in a story by Henry James, Jr. The elder James tells us that she had died by the time he wrote about her, and that she had "rare qualities of mind and heart," and "a singular personal loveliness." James, anyhow, was quick to follow up on her diagnosis. He procured two of the less hefty volumes of Emanuel Swedenborg (*Divine Love and Wisdom* and *Divine Providence*) and began the long mental reconstruction which would culminate in his sublimely hopeful vision of the prospective destiny of mankind.

THE SAVING SECRET OF EMANUEL SWEDENBORG

In London, where he found the Swedenborg texts, James struck up what would be a long-standing friendship with J. J. Garth Wilkinson, an English physiologist and a leading exponent of Swedenborg's manifold writings, translating them from the Latin and editing them, with preliminary discourses that, according to Emerson, threw "all the contemporary philosophy of England into shade." James and Wilkinson saw much of one another, exchanged amiably argumentative letters on theological questions, and lent each other books. When Mary James gave birth to a third son in July 1845, he was named Garth Wilkinson.

There was nothing intellectually perverse in Henry James, on the nudge from Mrs. Chichester, turning to Swedenborg: in the mid-1840s, the Swedish mystic and his ideas were permeating the cultural atmosphere in both England and America. Emerson held forth on Swedenborg as *the* type of mystic in his lecture series on "representative men" in 1845–46; and although he had some harsh things to say about the man, especially about his stubbornly narrow Christian vision, he acknowledged him in the end to be "a colossal soul." In America, as

Sidney Ahlstrom has observed, Swedenborg's "influence was seen everywhere; in Transcendentalism and at Brook Farm, in spiritualism and the free love movement, in the craze for communitarian experiment, in faith healing, mesmerism, and a half-dozen medical cults; among great intellectuals, crude charlatans, and innumerable frontier quacks."

James found Swedenborg, as who would not, an exhausting writer (Emerson spoke of his "immense and sandy diffuseness"). Swedenborg (1688–1772) came to his mystical writings after a career as physician, engineer, mathematician, and economist, and as Assessor of the Board of Mines for King Charles XII of Sweden—"by whom," in Emerson's words, "he was much consulted and honored." It was a career that included inventions of genius, but it was not the best preparation for the lucid rendering of those transworldly experiences to which Swedenborg gave himself up at the age of fifty-one and recorded in thirty volumes. They were a series of visionary visits to heaven and hell, and conversations with such beings as he met there. On their basis, he reinterpreted a number of books of the Old and New Testaments as special kinds of allegories, complex and cryptic revelations about the true and the ultimate relation between God and humankind.

Henry Junior would remember that the Swedenborg volumes were a regular part of the family luggage on their travels in the 1850s, and that the family never felt settled until the books had been taken out and placed on the shelf (as a housewife might domesticate a hotel room by bringing out her favorite small vase). But whether the elder James really pored over the texts, early and late, is open to question. He turned up some entertaining and encouraging hints: for example, that the angels Swedenborg communed with were anything but angelic in the traditional sense, but very shabby beings, full of normal lusts and imperfections, and ascribing to God such good as might be in them. But James rarely addressed himself to Swedenborg without first disclaiming any particular doctrinal indebtedness. "I have not the least ambition to set myself up as Swedenborg's personal attorney," he wrote in *Society the Redeemed Form of Man*. He did not find Swedenborg at all fascinating, and thought him "at best an informer or reporter, though an egregiously intelligent one." Not a man of powerful or original thought, James concluded, but invaluable as a seer.

Swedenborg could be all things to all interested men. What Henry James derived from Swedenborg and made his own was *the radical menace of individual selfhood*. Continuing his narrative of the Windsor nightmare and its sequel, James declared that "the main philosophical obligation we owe to Swedenborg is in his clearly identifying the evil principle with selfhood." "Self-sufficiency," as he called it elsewhere and in a fit of clarity, was "the only evil known to the spiritual universe"; and this because it led to the "renunciation of God from the life"; it exerted a resistance to the influx of divine love.

Thinking back over his spiritual career prior to Windsor, James, with Swedenborg's help, saw that he had always assumed a quite independent Jamesian self that had sought to bargain, with an external and a potentially hostile deity, over the terms of salvation. This fatal misconception—about the very nature of God, and of God's true relation to man—arose from and confirmed an overweening self-conceit. Looked at theologically, this meant the exclusion of the divine presence from the human life. Looked at from a more purely human viewpoint, this meant all the symptoms of egotism to which man is prone: "opinionativeness" (James especially liked the word), dictatorial self-assurance, grasping selfishness, self-absorption; and by crucial consequence, it meant a disastrous separation from other human beings. Salvation required an exactly opposite course: the demolition of that hard center of self, the inflowing of divine love, and a union with all mankind through a common sharing in that love.*

This is what began to happen on that May evening at Windsor. His will, his "moral or voluntary power," simply collapsed: "thoroughly fagged out as it were with the formal, heartless, endless task of conciliating a stony-hearted Deity." More: he perceived the total falsity of that long-engaged-in task; he felt "a shuddering recoil from my conscious activity in that line . . . a loathing of the moral pretension itself as so much downright charlatanry." So it was that the self, the power of will, the energy of self-imposition—the damnèd shape in this perspective—was laid waste to.

When I sat down to dinner on that memorably chilly afternoon in Windsor, I felt [my faith in selfhood] serene and unweakened by the faintest breath of doubt; before I rose from the table, it had inwardly shrivelled to a cinder. One moment I devoutly thanked God for the inappreciable boon of selfhood; the next, that inappreciable boon seemed to me the one thing damnable on earth, seemed a literal nest of hell within my own entrails.

That total destruction of the damnable and damning self was what Mrs. Chichester, borrowing from Swedenborg, called a *vastation*: a

---

* Henry Senior would have cast a skeptical eye on the contemporary cliché about "finding yourself." He, like many a student in our day, had dropped out of college and set forth in search of himself. But after 1844, he would have insisted that what you must do is to lose yourself; and as to finding, it is others that one must find.

complete desolation of the ego. No more harrowing private experience can be imagined, and it is little wonder that in the months following James was psychically and physically immobilized. Going for a short walk was almost beyond his strength, and it took an enormous effort to sleep in a strange bed. Gazing out at the sheep in the park opposite, he would envy them "their deep unconsciousness of self, their innocence of all private personality and purpose, their intense moral incapacity." (In the phrasing of this 1879 memory, James is making skillful use of a passage from Whitman:

> I think I could turn and live with animals . . .
> They do not sweat and whine about their condition,
> They do not lie awake in the dark and weep for their sins,
> They do not make me sick discussing their duty to God . . .)

And yet this hideous condition was a necessary stage in the process of regeneration and redemption—so James would come slowly to believe and to accept. The empty place vacated by the self would be filled by the quickening presence of God.

With the passing of time, James sought to clarify, for himself and eventually for his readers, the second or redemptive stage in man's spiritual history. It was a social process, he would argue; a communal event. Human beings, in his developing view, *fell* individually, as single separate egos; but they were redeemed collectively, as members of the human race. We may glance ahead for a moment at James's adumbration of the theme in the volume of 1869 called *The Secret of Swedenborg*; a title that elicited from William Dean Howells the comment that it was a secret James had kept. The treatise does show James to be rhetorically struggling even more than usually. But one feels in it a passion of belief—as in the section from which the book's title is taken.

Here he was at pains to relate divinity to "man's common or natural want," to the deprivation and the desire in which "all men are absolutely one." By the same token, he denied any involvement of the deity with individual fulfillment, for in that sphere "every man is consciously divided from his neighbors." Speaking for his own destiny, and assuming the posture he would attribute to the fictive Dewhurst, James disclaimed any hope for divine favor "save in my social or redeemed natural aspect: i.e., as I stand morally identified with the vast community of men of whatever race or religion." To put it differently, it was God's *indiscriminate* love for the race that gave cause to hope for redemption. Here, he felt, was the Swedish visionary's final teaching.

Such, as I have been able to apprehend it, is the intellectual secret of Swedenborg; such the calm, translucent depths of meaning that underlie the tormented surface of explication he puts upon the spiritual sense of scripture.

Later in the same volume, James took off after the New Church, or Church of the New Jerusalem, founded in Swedenborg's name and propagating some of his principles. It had held its first American convention in 1817; by 1845, it numbered about 5,000 members in this country, some distinguished names among them. Henry Senior was not abandoning his whole-souled hostility to any mode of institutionalized religion, and his contempt for the New Church was expressed in the finest figurative language *The Secret of Swedenborg* has to offer. "The Swedenborgian sect," he wrote ". . . is only on the part of its movers a strike for higher wages"; that is, for greater popularity and publicity than other and older sects enjoyed. He warmed to the assault:

The sect of the *soi-disant* New Jerusalem . . . deliberately empties itself of all interest in the hallowed struggle . . . against established injustice and sanctified imposture, in order to concentrate its energy and prudence upon the washing and dressing, upon the larding and stuffing, upon the embalming and perfuming, of its own invincibly squalid little *corpus*. This Pharisaic spirit, the spirit of separatism or sect, is the identical spirit of hell . . . Let the reader, whatever else he may fairly or foolishly conclude against Swedenborg, acquit him point-blank of countenancing this abject ecclesiastical drivel.

In a witty inversion, James charged the New Church with a kind of parodic vastation—with emptying itself of all concern with the struggle for social justice, in its effort at self-puffery; as a result of which, in James's swift tropings, an institution which begins as a fat Christmas turkey, stuffed and larded, ends as a coffined corpse.

A CITY LIFE AND ''SOMETHING BETTER''

Recovering slowly from his breakdown, Henry Senior in the early days of 1845 was willing to risk another stay in Paris; an uneventful visit, with a belated sequel. A few years later, when Henry Junior unexpectedly described some urban scenes he had once glimpsed through a carriage window, it was realized that he was talking about the Place Vendôme and streets adjoining it in Paris that he had known only around the time of his second birthday.

The family was back in New York by the start of the summer, in time for the birth on July 21 of the infant boy named for Dr. Wilkinson. That autumn, the Jameses were in Albany for a prolonged stay with the widowed and hospitable Catherine Barber James in the old house on North Pearl Street. The place was overrun by members of the clan; two dozen uncles and aunts and cousins popping in and out, causing the sweet-tempered sixty-three-year-old Mrs. James to collapse into a chair every so often to catch her breath. The company of his mother was always good, in obscure ways, for Henry Senior; it served to straighten him out inwardly, if only for the moment. In December 1845, with something of his old vigor, James delivered a lecture to the Young Men's Association in Albany called "What Constitutes a State." When it was published the following year, it came in for high praise from *The Harbinger*, the official voice of the Brook Farm community.

After the turn of the year, James accompanied his brood back to New York to share quarters with his other family, the Walshes. For several years after the return to America, in fact, the Jameses led a commuting life between New York and Albany; and Willy and Harry grew used to the overnight trip on the paddle-wheel steamboat up and down the Hudson. The family happened to be in Albany when the fourth boy, Robertson (named for his maternal grandmother), was born on August 29, 1846. In New York once more, a year after that, James set up his expanding household in an apartment at 11 Fifth Avenue, at the northern edge of Washington Square. Finally, in April 1848, Henry Senior bought a more permanent home at 58 West Fourteenth Street, on the south side of that poplar-lined street, a long block west of Fifth Avenue, near the corner of Sixth.

It was a fairly comfortable place, with a new-style brownstone front, three stories and an attic, a library, a front parlor and a back parlor, and enough bedrooms to house a family of seven all told, including Catherine Walsh—now Aunt Kate in the family, and lodged on the third floor—and provide a guest room as needed. Henry and Mary James's fifth and last child and only daughter, Alice, was born in the West Fourteenth Street house on August 7, 1848. Henry Senior may seem to have overlooked that fact when, in a letter to Emerson the following summer, he spoke of his young ones as "four stout boys." The point of the reference, though, was that a new playroom was required for the boys because they had taken to importing "shocking bad manners from the street."

Indeed, as James continued to Emerson, he and Mary were pondering whether they should not go abroad with the children for a few years—to get away from the New York street life, to allow the children "to absorb French and German and get a better sensuous education than they are likely to get here." ("Sensuous" perhaps referred to the diverse appeal to the senses offered by Europe, but it was a curious adjective, since James was never very responsive to that appeal.) Emerson heard this proposal, he wrote in answer, "with some terror"; New York for him was only tolerable—only "amiable and intelligent"—so long as he knew Henry James was in it. The terror proved groundless. James did not take his family abroad again for another six years. The seven years' residence at 58 West Fourteenth Street was the longest stay together at the same address that the James family was ever to enjoy.

It was also the longest period of the elder James's intellectual concern with the nature of society, actual and possible, American and general. The social question was agitating men of good hope everywhere in these years, with the overthrow of the bourgeois monarchy in France—Gus and John James turned up on the New York doorstep one day to inform their brother Henry of the event; Henry Junior dated his "initiation into History" from those "rich words on my uncles' lips"—and the revolutionary fervor that spread across Europe in 1848. The evil conditions of American urban society were likewise visible to a New Yorker: as one result of the foreign upheavals, immigrants were pouring into the city, there to live in squalor. Henry Senior, to be sure, was more alert to what he saw as the inward drift of history—the working within it of divine energy—than to actual circumstances; and in this, he differed from his sister-in-law Catherine Walsh, who alone in the family responded with enthusiasm to the visit to America, in 1852, of the Hungarian patriot Lajos Kossuth. But poverty, misery, and inequity were always powerful issues for Henry James.

He was essentially an optimist, however, as regards the American social future, and had established his position in the 1845 Albany lecture, "What Constitutes a State." Here, in an astonishing peroration, he hailed as grand signs of human progress "our steamboats, our railroads, our magnetic telegraphs, which laugh to scorn the limitations of time and space." In these "gigantic throbbings," James declared, "dumb nature herself confesses the descent of that divine and universal spirit, which even now yearns to embrace all earth's offsprings in the bonds of a mutual knowledge and a mutual love." Hart Crane, celebrating the irradiation of the technological by the divine in his modernist epic *The Bridge*, would scarcely say it more ardently; though for quite another interpretation of the "gigantic throbbings," of the dazzling and terrible play of material forces in America, one must await the younger Henry James's chapter on "New York Revisited" in *The American Scene*.

Mary James caught her husband's philosophical and emotional attitude exactly in a letter from Albany to Mrs. Wilkinson in England, in late November 1846. She spoke of the pleasure she and Henry were taking in a little book by an acquaintance of theirs, Madame Gati de Gammon, and translated into English "by our dear friend Mrs. Chichester." The book, Mary said, laid out the vision of a future society from which poverty would be banished, "along with every motive to cruelty, injustice and oppression"; and thereafter, forms would be prepared "into which the divine love and mercy may flow without measure, and this earth become a paradise indeed." The epistolary language, one guesses, echoed remarks made by Henry James in asides uttered while he was reading Mme de Gammon's treatise aloud. But Mary added an observation in her own accent, at once devoted and amused: the book *had* to be prophetically true, but if it were not, then, "as my hopeful loving Henry says, something better must be."

It was to that "something better" that James addressed several lectures around the mid-century. In the summer of 1849, Emerson invited James to give a talk at the Town and Country Club of Boston, recently founded by Bronson Alcott and himself "for the study and diffusion of the Ideas and Tendencies proper to the nineteenth Century." James, after declaring himself quite unfit for the task, proposed a talk which would contrast "socialism," as an ideal possibility, and "civilization," as the way things currently were; than which nothing could be more relevant to the club's designated purpose. He expressed alarm at the thought of appearing before a Boston audience, one (he was sure) that would be made up largely of literary people. "There is nothing I dread so much as literary men," proclaimed the father of the most absolute literary personality in our history, "especially *our* literary men."

Catch them out of the range of mere personal gossip about authors and books, and ask them for honest sympathy with your sentiment or an honest repugnancy of it, and you will find the company of stage-drivers sweeter and more comforting to your soul.

But even here James could foresee a better situation: "It seems to me the authorial vocation will not be so reputable in the future as in the past." Men were beginning to live their ideas, he ventured, rather than to write about them. It was perhaps his least accurate prediction.

"Socialism and Civilization" was given in Boston on November 1, 1849. Reconsidering it and several of its companion pieces a few years later, James remarked to Emerson that his persisting aim was to convert himself "into an army of Goths and Huns, to overrun and destroy our existing sanctities, that the supernal splendours may at length become credible and even visible." That aim was reflected in the rhetorical movement of the discourses, which resembled rather the waves of an infantry assault, with enemy strongholds breached and flags triumphantly planted, than a logically unfolding argument. But James's way of phrasing his intention suggests a striking analogue with his personal experience and his hope. *Society* must undergo a vastation, a large-scale version of what the selfhood must experience, en route to its own rebirth in "supernal splendour." The social vastation had already begun in America, James announced in "Democracy and Its Uses" (winter 1851); American democracy was essentially a destructive not a creative force; its purpose was to overthrow "established institutions," to bring about "a dissolution or disorganization of the old forms." Brighter days would follow.

Throughout the talks of this period, we find a perceptible mix of the personal, the filial, and the paternal. The experience at Windsor provided the individual paradigm for social history. But in James's attack against "civilization," his father seems again to be the target: civilization's greatest blunder, James urged, was to look upon a crime against society, a theft of property, for example, as a sin against God; and its harsh institutional behavior followed from that confusion. Socialism would do away with that muddle by replacing "limited property" with "a property in universal nature and in all the affections and thoughts of humanity." James also drew upon his education as himself the father of boys. If society must run a course parallel to that of the ego, it might equally be likened to a growing boy. Ten-year-old Willy James, passing through a difficult stage, seems the source of Henry's elaborate figure for the "democratic" phase in a society's development—"the period of puberty in the race"; a time "in the history of the individual" that can be "extremely unhandsome." The boy expresses his sense of freedom "by rudeness towards his progenitors, calls his father the old man, and his mother, the old woman, and gives out, on every occasion, a suspicion that they have been over-estimated."

He "bullies the servants and his younger brothers," and gets into every sort of trouble. It is doubtful that William was ever quite so disagreeable a child, but a certain lordliness about him, a bullying bravado, is conveyed in his brother's reminiscences.

These talks on society, especially the Boston lecture, also, on a somewhat higher level, mingled visions taken from Swedenborg with the social planning of Charles Fourier, the French utopian thinker whose theories of "attractive industry" and perfectly organized communities, or "pholansteries," were having an important vogue in forward-looking American circles. As with Swedenborg, James both embraced and dissociated himself from Fourier, finding in him "many things to startle, many things perhaps to disgust"; but also attributing to him "glimpses . . . on every hand of God's ravishing harmonies yet to ensue on earth." It was a highly unusual reading of Fourier, as it were, a Swedenborgianized reading. But it partook of James's own glimpse of the harmonies, as in this characteristic concluding passage: "I look upon Democracy as heralding the moral perfection of man, as inaugurating the existence of perfectly just relations between man and man, and as consequently preparing the way for the reign of infinite love." Society and the individual, as we see, were to be simultaneously and identically redeemed. Society, in the title of Henry Senior's most compelling book, *was* "The Redeemed Form of Man."

Henry Senior's principal occupation in these mid-century years was lecturing, and the departure for the lecture hall of an evening was a recurring drama for the children, looking out from the front parlor windows, just before bedtime, onto West Fourteenth Street. Excitement was often added by the mother's last-minute anxiety that they were going off without the manuscript, and there were even times when the parents could be observed driving back to the house in a flurry to pick up the forgotten copy. Henry Junior would recall his father "at the door of the carriage and under the gusty street-lamp," produce the manuscript from his coattail pocket, "and shake it, for her ideal comfort, in the face of his companion."

The talks were collected in a volume of 1852 called *Lectures and Miscellanies.* One curious and, according to report, endearing feature of the talks, as of James's impromptu exchanges of opinion, was a contrast between a violence of verbal content and idea and a sweetness of presentation and manner. A related paradox was James's tendency to describe the nothingness of the self in robustly self-expressive language, as though the ego gathered all its force to denounce the ego.

Here in short was a towering personality who sought constantly in his public utterances to suppress the sheer authority of his presence. It seemed to enrage him that he could not wholly succeed. A friend of William James, writing soon after the father's death, commented that though the elder James, with his "immense temperament," could "score you black and blue" during a debate, one always felt that "the origin of the matter was his divine rage with *himself*"—a rage "at still being so dominated by his natural selfhood which would not be shaken off."

Life at 58 West Fourteenth Street and in its environs was varied and busy. Henry Senior liked to ride the horsecars up and down Sixth Avenue, not only because of the passing show, but (here he emulated his so "democratic" mother) because it brought him close to ordinary people—with whom, as we have heard, he felt more at ease than with literary and intellectual men. The companionship of the crowded horsecar, he was to say with comic earnestness, was the nearest thing to heaven on earth he had ever known.* Father would also take the older boys, Willy and Harry, one at a time for walks through the neighborhood, commenting on the sights as they strolled along Broadway, sometimes dropping in for a little treat at the home of Mrs. Walsh on Washington Square.

Incoming family visits were sources of pleasure: Albany uncles, Albany cousins, Grandmother James in her silk dress and gentle smile. A familiar sight was the arrival of the Reverend William, leaning out of the omnibus as it passed the Jameses' house to throw his nightgown and brushes onto the step and call out to the servant: "Tell Henry and Mary . . ." before the vehicle rumbled on over the cobbled roadway leaving the message unfinished. William, in his early fifties, had withdrawn from the active ministry and, with his restored legacy, was engaged in philanthropic enterprises. He was living in Albany with his wife, the former Marcia Lucretia Ames, and their three daughters, Anna McBride, Elizabeth Tillman, and Katharine Barber ("Kitty Prince," as she would become).

Literary people were made welcome, despite James's alleged aversion to them. Charles Dana, managing editor of the New York *Tribune*

---

* Talking once, to a correspondent, about Margaret Fuller, James declared her to be "a person of firm intellect and aspiration," but "a most uncomfortable neighbor, from the circumstances of her inordinate self-esteem. Omnibus drivers, and my splendid friend Darby the tailor, are sweet in comparison to that sort of pretension" (to Edmund Tweedy, February 24, 1852).

under Horace Greeley, came by for dinner on Saturdays. George Ripley, formerly of Brook Farm and now reviewing books for the *Tribune*,
was often on hand, as was the adventurous, tale-spinning Bayard Taylor. There were visitors from Boston, too, most of them urged on by
Emerson. Among them was Thoreau, in James's view a very strange
mixture of "mountainous inward self-esteem" and "harmless and
beautiful force of outward demeanor." (For Thoreau, Henry James
made "humanity seem more erect.") Bronson Alcott, the mystically
minded experimenter in children's education and communal life, was
in town occasionally. In Boston, Alcott had been greatly struck by James
and his lectures. "A voracious intellect," he wrote in his journal, "subtle, sinuous, clear, forcible and swift," and "a fearless sham-shower."
In New York, Alcott could himself be the object of Jamesian repartee.
Once, prodded too far by James, Alcott said to him: "You'll continue
a sinner to all eternity; you are damaged goods." A witness of the scene
remembered that Alcott then claimed to be "one with Pythagoras and
Jesus," one of a trio of sinless men. Mr. James pressed him: "You say
you and Jesus are one. Have you ever said 'I am the resurrection and
the life'?" Alcott replied that he had done so often. "Has anyone ever
believed you?" Alcott hereupon ended the conversation, muttering, "I
won't talk any more with you."

Above all, of course, there was Emerson, who came to stay in the
Jameses' solitary guest room—it earned the household title of "Mr.
Emerson's room"—when he was lecturing in or near the city. He would
stay at the Fourteenth Street house for several days at a time; if his
visit to New York was to be longer, he would put up at a hotel, but
only, as he once said, "that I may the more unblushingly spend the
whole day at your house." Henry Junior would re-create these occasions in his best atmospheric prose: Emerson, sitting between his parents, facing the fire in the back parlor at dusk, before the lamps had
been lit; "elegantly slim, benevolently aquiline, and commanding a
tone alien, beautifully alien, to any we heard roundabout." For young
Henry, it was the tone of Boston; to be in the presence of Emerson
was to be "in touch with the wonder of Boston." There were no rough
edges to the conversations with Emerson, as there could be with others;
simply an easy flow of (presumably) lofty-spirited talk.

Emerson did listen to James's settings-forth, and read at least some
of his written work, with an odd kind of admiration. "Emerson is here
lecturing," James wrote his friend Edmund Tweedy in February 1852.
". . . I see a good deal of him. He expresses himself much interested
in my ideas, only he thinks I am too far ahead. He read the proof of

one of my lectures the other day, now printing, and said many pleasant and apparently sincere things of it, only he would have it that I was (comparatively) 'a modern gentleman in the Saurian era.' " The phrase has the unmistakable Emersonian wit; but James felt Emerson to be too pessimistic about the possible regeneration of society in America, about "something better." And James continued to be bothered by Emerson's serene refusal to give him anything, intellectually, to catch hold of. Emerson was still at times what James had dubbed him a few years before: a "man without a handle."

James, seeking his own mental handle on the scheme of things, remained harnessed to his desk, and one opaque little volume followed another, with book reviews and letters to the newspapers in intervals between. *Moralism and Christianity*, which included the discourse on socialism (and with the two title terms conceived as in total opposition), appeared in 1850; *Lectures and Miscellanies* two years later. In 1854 there was a diatribe against the Swedenborgian New Church, on grounds obscurely announced in the title: *The Church of Christ Not an Ecclesiasticism*. Meanwhile, James had gotten embroiled in a public debate on the issues of marriage, divorce, and "free love," carried on in the pages of the New York *Tribune*; with the editor Greeley intervening every so often to blur the lines.

The other voice in the debate was that of Stephen Pearl Andrews, New York lawyer, Fourierite, and proponent of radical social and economic reform. For Andrews, as he was to say, Mr. James was "an astute and terribly searching and merciless, though not altogether a sound and reliable, critic of the old"; but cloudy and insubstantial, however high-minded, with regard to the future. The exchange began when James published in the *Tribune* a letter addressed to the New York *Observer* (but obviously unprintable there), replying to its attack upon him for his alleged hostility to the institution of marriage. James repeated his previously expressed opinion on the matter, a relatively enlightened one for its historic moment: that it was "not essential to the honor of marriage that two persons should be compelled to live together when they held the reciprocal relation of cat and dog, and that in that state of things divorce might profitably intervene." Andrews, following up in the *Tribune*, agreed with James thus far; and in fact, the two were in larger accord than either admitted or than their differing rhetorical strategies allowed.

Andrews savored James's "vigorous invective," as in his telling the *Observer*'s editor, whom he characterized as "a defeated trickster," that his paper enjoyed "an easy, good-natured audience, who do not care to scan too nicely the stagnant slipslop which your weekly ladles out to them." But Andrews, no doubt led astray by James's cavalier disregard for logic, persisted in seeing him as a champion of the self-sustaining family, and declaimed, as though arguing *against* James: "Who can foretell that isolated families may not come hereafter to be regarded as hot-beds of selfishness and narrow prejudice against the outside world, separating and destroying the unity of the human race . . . ?" The same thought could be found on many a page of the elder James, though usually with a theological twist: the unity of the human race, which the isolated family impeded, was a union in the divine being.

The two men differed on the question of free love, but amid such tortuous abstractions and modifications as to render the disagreement almost meaningless. Andrews was much more forthright—and as most would think today, more clearheaded—on the dilemma of women, and went into it far more thoroughly. "I ask for the complete emancipation and self-ownership of woman, simply as I ask the same for man," he told the *Tribune* at the close of a letter.

The great revealing difference of view came with Andrews's ex-altation of the individual, the sovereign self, and James's fear and hatred of selfhood. Andrews besought his readers to dismiss all "fears of the sovereignty of the individual. Cherish it rather as the glorious realisation of the golden age of the future." Henry James, Sr., of course, foresaw the golden age as the time when individual sovereignty would give way entirely to the communal life. He said so mildly, for him, in his response to Andrews's paean; but he pondered the problem more intently for another year or so, and in 1855 he brought out *The Nature of Evil*, in which he made his strongest statement about it.

The treatise in its immediate motivation was a rebuttal of the Reverend Henry Ward Beecher's claim that the Fall of Man had happened once and for all a long time ago, and was of no more than historic interest in the modern day. On the contrary, James wrote. He distinguished spiritual evil from both physical evil ("*which one suffers*") and moral evil ("*which one does*"). Spiritual evil was what one *is*, and it was truly and terribly present and active in the living moment. In the climactic passage, part of which was quoted from earlier, James held that "the conceit of one's finite endowments . . . is the origin of all the sin which afflicts humanity. This alone is spiritual evil, the only evil known to the spiritual universe, namely, self-sufficiency, and the consequent renunciation of God from the life."

Within the Jamesian context, this was cogent enough, though Andrews would have looked blankly at it. But try as he would, shifting about from subject to subject and from one rhetorical method to another, James's vision refused to work itself out. Each new effort, pursued with a surge of hope, led to fresh dissatisfaction; as it did in other aspects of his life in this time, the right school for the children, the right intellectual friend. By the close of spring 1855, James was once again ready for a change of setting, and booked cabins on the *Atlantic*, sailing to Liverpool on June 27. The New York life was over.

EDEN REMEMBERED

In Henry Junior's imaginatively shaped memoirs, the family's New York years took on an Edenesque quality. Early in his first autobiographical volume, James set himself to evoke "so far as I can the small warm dusky homogeneous New York world of the mid-century," and it was not long before he was recalling, on the part of his brother William and himself and within the aura of the day, "a general Eden-like consciousness." The allusion, suitably, was to the feeling experienced while the boys were consuming vast quantities of fruit—from the great heaps of fruit, of peaches and grapes and pears, deposited at the waterside piers and showing up on every street corner. But "what did the stacked boxes and baskets of our youth represent," James asked, "but the boundless fruitage of that more bucolic age of the American world . . . Where is that fruitage now, where in particular are the peaches *d'antan*?"

It was not only the infinitude of garden produce ("We ate everything in those days . . . as from stores that were infinite") that lent the Edenic air; it was also the absence of shadows in the neighborhood, of danger in the streets. Henry remembered knocking about Broadway with William, as a ten-year-old, in perfect freedom; and from this he inferred that "Broadway must have been then as one of the alleys of Eden, for any sinister contact or consequence involved for us." Within the context, Aunt Helen Wyckoff—a first cousin of Mary Walsh James, who lived with her family a block west of the Jameses—is portrayed as a person of "strong simplicity, that of an earlier, quieter world, a New York of better manners and better morals and homelier beliefs." Here though, in the picture of Aunt Helen, James is sliding imperceptibly from the childhood outlook to the foreboding irony of the grownup; for Helen Wyckoff Perkins, as she became, was a quietly tyrannical figure who kept her woolly-headed brother under wraps, allowing him but ten cents a day; and who never addressed her husband as anything but "Mr. Perkins," reducing him through her oppressive aloofness to a "nullity," a "zero," an absence.

So there could be ambiguous growths in the old urban garden, and this is made dramatically evident in the novella *Washington Square*. Or rather and better, it is precisely the invasion of an Eden-esque world by the sinister and the ambiguous that the novella manages to enact.

It was published in 1881, and the narrative continuously directs our gaze backward to an earlier time—to a time which, beginning with the first sentence, is made to seem very considerably earlier:

During a portion of the first half of the present century, and more particularly during the latter part of it, there flourished and practised in the city of New York a physician who enjoyed perhaps an exceptional share of the consideration which, in the United States, has always been bestowed upon distinguished members of the medical profession.

It is a skillful fusing of historical circumstantiality and fairy-tale vague-ness: once-upon-a-time, as it were, in the late 1840s. And from that moment forward, the author is uncommonly insistent on dates, on distances in time, on the relative ages of his characters.

Dr. Sloper was twenty-seven, we are told, when he married the wealthy and accomplished Miss Harrington in 1820; their daughter, Catherine, was born in 1825, or possibly 1826 (James, enjoying himself as one feels, is at once meticulous and a bit fuzzy in his arithmetic); and it was in 1847 or thereabouts that Catherine came to know Morris Townsend. Around 1843, Dr. Sloper moves his household uptown from a place near City Hall—"which saw its best days (from the social point of view) about 1820"—to Washington Square, which had become the ideal of "genteel retirement" in the mid-1830s. There are references to the standards of luxury "thirty years ago"—say, in 1850—and to architectural fashions "forty years ago."

The main action occurs in the late 1840s and early 1850s, the time of the James family residence at the head of Washington Square and then at 58 West Fourteenth Street. (The narrative aftermath, when the story has to "take a long stride," is set around 1863–64.)

Henry James, Sr.: The Endangering Self

The third section of the novella gives rise to a nostalgic evocation of the time and the place virtually unique in Henry James's fiction.

> I know not whether it is owing to the tenderness of early associations, but this portion of New York appears to many persons the most delectable. It has a kind of established repose which is not of frequent occurrence in other quarters of the long, shrill city; it has a riper, richer, more honorable look than any of the upper ramifications of the great longitudinal thoroughfare—the look of having had something of a social history. It was here, as you might have been informed on good authority, that you had come into a world which appeared to offer a variety of sources of interest; it was here that your grandmother lived, in venerable solitude, and dispensed a hospitality which commended itself alike to the infant imagination and the infant palate; it was here that you took your first walks abroad, following the nursery-maid with unequal step, and sniffing up the strange odor of the ailanthus-trees which at the time formed the principal umbrage of the Square, and diffused an aroma that you were not yet critical enough to dislike as it deserved; it was here, finally, that your first school, kept by a broad-bosomed, broad-based old lady with a ferule, who was always having tea in a blue cup, with a saucer that didn't match, enlarged the circle both of your observations and your sensations.

The passage modulates cunningly, as we see, from the "many persons" who might have a tenderness of associations with the Washington Square neighborhood to one particular person, "you," whose childhood was passed there and whose first cluster of enduring impressions (including those of a hospitable widowed grandmother) derived from it.

This lovingly detailed locale is the setting for the novella's developing drama, the always low-keyed and well-mannered but nonetheless brutal battle of egos between the implacably self-assured Dr. Sloper, his passively stubborn daughter, Catherine, and the engaging bounder Morris Townsend. But what is to be emphasized here is the relation *between* setting and action, and the nearly mythic dimension that relation adds to the story's meaning—and to the lost old world *d'antan*, of pre–Civil War New York.

It is the invasion of a singular Eden, the special Eden of Henry James: a world of childhood innocence and pleasure, of tender associations and clearer moralities; which yet, as represented by Washington Square, had a long, rich, decent social history. It is the invasion of this world by the hard facts of human nature and conduct; by greed, hypocrisy, cruelty, unbending vanity and selfishness, blind illusion. It is more simply the Jamesian version of the modern story, almost the

American story; the historical invasion of a simpler time by what James, in another work of autobiographical fiction, "The Jolly Corner," called "the money passion." It was what the boy who was born a step away from Washington Square and grew up nearby had to discover and find the means of portraying, as a mature literary artist committed to the world as it intractably is.

CHAPTER THREE

Overschooled Childhoods

A PROCESSION OF TEACHERS

Henry Senior was mentally returning to America even before the family took ship for Europe. On the eve of the June 27 (1855) sailing, James wrote his Boston banker friend Samuel Gray Ward (with whom he was arranging a letter of credit) that there was "a golden sunset in New York," and he could only hope that the family "might be sure of as golden sunrises on the other side. But America is the golden land now, and I feel it deeply as the hour of departure draws nigh." For the elder James, even at this time, America was a sort of other Eden, demi-Paradise; and when he was preparing to bring the family home for good five years later, in the summer of 1860, he wrote a kinsman that "America is 'the lost Paradise restored' to boys and girls both, and it is only our own paltry cowardice and absurd ducking to old world conventionalities, that hinder their realising it as such at once."

For the four boys at least—William, the oldest, was thirteen in 1855, and the youngest, Robertson, was almost nine—the shift from schooling in America to schooling in Europe was only another, if larger, stage in a perpetually changing educational experience. In the New York years, Henry Junior recalled, the brothers simply tumbled without stop out of one school and into another. He fictionalized a similar point in "The Jolly Corner," when he had Spencer Brydon return to New York after an absence of thirty-odd years, primarily to see again "his house on the jolly corner"—the one in which he had been born, and where "the holidays of his overschooled boyhood had been passed."

"Overschooled" is the right word for a process—Henry Junior called it a "procession"—whereby the older boys, Willy and Harry, were exposed to ten or more schools and a dozen or more chief teachers in the eight metropolitan years. The teachers' names flow poetically through Henry's recollections, except when he forgets one: as with a very large Russian lady who wore a very short cape. Meanwhile, we are introduced, sometimes at length, to Miss Sedgwick; Mrs. Wright (Lavinia D.); Mlle Delavigne, who represented France to the young Jameses; M. Maurice Vergnès, an easily irritated and bristling man whose school on lower Broadway swarmed with little homesick Mexicans and Cubans; Richard Puling Jenks, he of the sonorous syllables, a bald man with a goatee, under whose instruction the boys spent the year 1853–54. The broad-bosomed lady with the ferule who figured in the passage quoted earlier from *Washington Square* is evidently a fictive mixture of a Mrs. Daly and a Miss Rogers, teachers in a little red schoolhouse on Waverly Place where it abuts Washington Square.

The *Atlantic*, with the Jameses aboard, docked at Liverpool on July 8. The family party consisted of the seven Jameses, Aunt Kate (Mary's sister Catherine), and a fresh-complexioned, round-faced French maidservant named Annette Godefroi, originally from Metz (hence, in young Henry's punning Villonesque phrase, a "bonne Lorraine"). An Italian courier, Jean Nadali, was soon added, and Henry Senior began the process of maneuvering this sizable contingent through an unending series of European displacements.

After a few days in London, the group stopped briefly in Paris—time enough for some visits to the Louvre—and then made their way to Geneva; going by train to the end of the line in Lyons and proceeding onward into Switzerland in two hired carriages. On that long, bumpy drive, the twelve-year-old Henry, who had come down with malaria fever in England, was stretched out on a mattress-covered plank laid across the two seats of the carriage, and from this "absurdly cushioned state" he looked out—as he would never forget—on a village that contained a castle, a ruin, and a peasant woman working in a field; and "supremely, in that ecstatic vision," he would say, "was 'Europe,' sublime synthesis, expressed and guaranteed to me." The family settled in an old house near Geneva named Campagne Gerebsoff; William and Wilky went off to a school at nearby Châtelaine, the Pensionnat Roediger, where the rest of the family, including the convalescent Harry, visited on weekends.

This was supposed to be the goal of the entire undertaking: the family was going to Europe, Henry Senior had explained to Samuel Ward, in order "at last to place our dear boys at school in Switzerland." In open letters to the New York *Tribune*, James praised the living conditions in Geneva (no more than $10 a week for lodging) and enthused over the experimental Pensionnat Roediger for its playground and gymnastic facilities, the exemplary relations between teachers and students, and the large degree of freedom. Even so, he did not hesitate to transfer the boys, after a short spell, over to the much admired Institution Haccius, which specialized in languages and was hospitable to American pupils; and before two months were out, the father, in typically swift disenchantment, had given up altogether on Swiss schools as "over-rated," and had shepherded the company back through Paris to London.

He was of half a mind to take them all the way home to New York; but on the arrival in London and after an abundant and restorative October evening meal of cold roast beef, bread and cheese, and ale, at the Gloucester Hotel on Piccadilly, Henry Senior exclaimed with newly rising hopes, "There's nothing like it after all." London it was thus to be for the coming months and until the spring of 1856, when the elder James found it time to look for fresh educational pastures across the Channel, in France.

Throughout the London fall, the family occupied a small house near the Gloucester Hotel at the entrance to Berkeley Square; but at the start of December they had settled into a more spacious residence, with a large garden and a view of archery contests next door, partway down the sloping rural street called Marlborough Place in St. John's Wood. It was not far from the home of the parents' friends, the J. J. Garth Wilkinsons.

There were many and varied things to do in that early-Victorian London, but in later years the children held differing views about the value of it all. William denounced the London stay, and with it the next period spent in Paris, as "a poor and arid and lamentable time." They missed every opportunity for real education, William complained, and did nothing but walk about together, with their little high black hats and their gloves, staring at the December-gray street scenery, dawdling in front of shop windows, or going inside to buy watercolors and paintbrushes. Henry's reaction, according to his memoirs, was pointedly opposite:

It was just the fact of our having so walked and dawdled and dodged that made the charm of memory; in addition to which what could one have asked more than to be steeped in a medium so dense that whole elements of it, forms of amusements, interest and wonder, soaked through to some appreciative faculty and made one fail at the most of nothing but one's lessons?*

For Alice James, thinking back to that London winter, a moment that stood out involved the Christmas gift of a bonnet for her Swiss governess, Mlle Cusin. It had fallen to the seven-year-old Alice to instruct the milliner about the bonnet's design, which was intended to reconcile the aesthetic taste of London's Edgeware Road with that of the governess's native village. What emerged was a combination of "green shirred silk and pink roses"—"I can remember how my infant soul shivered, even then, at the sad crudity of its tone." But Alice shared with her brothers the excitement of Charles Kean's production, at the Princess Theatre, of Shakespeare's *Henry VIII*; for weeks afterward the children tried to make watercolor sketches of Queen Katharine's dream-vision (the white-robed figures dancing about her and doing her honor), and took turns marching about and reciting the last speech of Cardinal Wolsey ("naked to mine enemies"). Alice's infant soul also recorded the performance of Tom Taylor's mildly sophisticated new play, *Still Waters Run Deep*, and one particular line which went to her heart (though she would misquote it slightly): "My sister is a most remarkable woman!"

AUNT KATE

The enjoyment of *Henry VIII*, Alice recalled, "was somewhat obscured by the anguish of Aunt Kate's not being able to go"; as great a misery, she remembered thinking, as could be imagined. The remark testifies to the palpable presence on the family scene of Catherine Walsh during these European years—as she had been from the earliest days and as she would be, with various interruptions, until the deaths of her sister and her brother-in-law in 1882. She had been with the family in England through the epochal year 1844, and by now, as Henry Senior said to his mother, she was truly relishing the country. In the course

---

* "One's lessons" were with a young Scotsman, Robert Thompson; "a capital tutor," Henry Senior informed his mother. The younger Henry was delighted to learn, years afterward, that Thompson had gone on to run a school in Edinburgh, where one of his pupils was Robert Louis Stevenson.

(Above) William James of Albany, 1820s
(Below) Catharine Barber James, about 1830

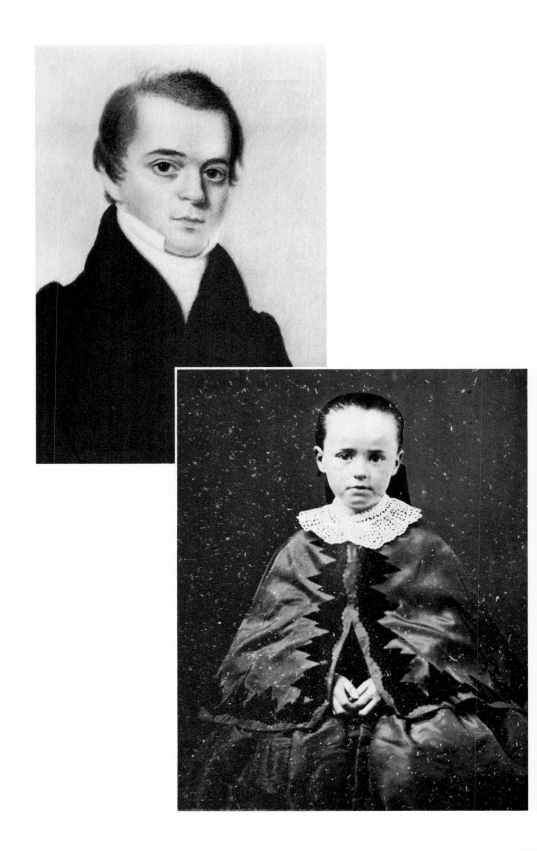

(Opposite, top) Henry James, Sr., as a young man
(Bottom) Alice James about 1854
(Above) Henry Senior and Henry Junior, 1854

(Opposite) Henry James in 1862, by John La Farge
(Above, top) Mary Walsh James, about 1865
(Bottom) Henry James, Sr., about 1865

Catherine Walsh, "Aunt Kate," about 1860

of the succeeding decade, she had, for her James nephews and niece, become virtually their *only* aunt, as regards the sense of close kinship. Aunt Kate was the one who most often escorted Willy and Harry down to the "torture chamber" on Wall Street of the dentist Dr. Parkhurst; while they were being attended to, she would go off to forage in the great ladies' shop, Stewart's, on Broadway at Chambers Street, a place whose wares were reputed to be irresistible to female customers.

Catherine Walsh was a more troubled personality than her older sister Mary. The two sisters resembled one another in height, bearing, and facial features, to judge from the available photographs; but Kate's face lacked the serene, faintly smiling, almost masklike composure of Mary's. Its mouth and eyes spoke of discontent, of failed or repressed hopes, perhaps of suffering. It seems more than possible that she fell in love with Henry Senior when he appeared at the Washington Square home, and this may explain what William James referred to later (in 1870) as "a sort of sub-antagonism" that had come to prevail "between her and father." She was given to ardent opinions about political developments. William tended to dismiss these latter as "intellectual foibles," and they may have been substitutes for other modes of satisfaction. At the same time, William, her favorite among the children, paid her his own kind of high compliment (if it was also a distinctly ambiguous one), when he observed "the total absence of any stagnant, lazy, sensual or selfish element in her, everything being so bright and clear with the energy of her active will."

Her relationship with Alice was changeable and not without pathos, as we shall be seeing: the one often reaching out, the other often seeking to evade. A recognition of this was implicit in Alice's comment, shortly after her aunt's death, that Aunt Kate had had but one *motif*, an "intense longing to absorb herself in a few individuals." It was a fair description; yet Catherine Walsh was anything but the conventional spinster aunt of the Victorian household. She was at once too vital and too enigmatic; and she was not in fact a spinster. On February 18, 1853, she had married Captain Charles H. Marshall in New York, the ceremony attended by the entire James family.

Marshall was sixty at the time of the marriage, a rich widower with several children, living a block away from the Jameses on Fourteenth Street, east of Fifth Avenue. He had made a fortune through his association with the Black Ball Line, as the commander of several of its ships, the first private vessels to make regular Atlantic crossings; and after 1834, as manager ashore of its extensive shipping concerns. The Black Ball Line contributed importantly to the growth of New

75   ]

York as a port city, and Captain Marshall was a highly regarded citizen.*

He began to press his attentions on the forty-year-old Catherine Walsh in the autumn of 1852, and soon after the turn of the year, Kate, in Henry Senior's rueful comment, "finally 'give out,' as they say in Rutland and Danbury . . . and has been doing an immense millinery and mantle making business ever since." Marshall was not Henry Senior's sort, being too committed to the shipshape life, rising at five, mustering the staff, taking note of the weather, inspecting the premises (in James's amused flow of nautical figures); but the brother-in-law wished the couple well. Aunt Kate would be sorely missed in the James family; and Henry Senior let his domestic and matrimonial imagery run rampant as he told his friend Tweedy:

Aunt Kate . . . has always been a most loving and provident husband to Mary, a most considerate and devoted wife to me, and an incomparable father and mother to our children. She has paid all the servants' wages over again by her invariable good humour and kindness, and been both sun and stars to us whenever our skies have been overcast by dread, or the night of any great sorrow has threatened to shut us in. God bless her in her new home, and make it as friendly to her as the old one!

The curious reference to "dread" suggests that Kate may have been of special comfort after the Windsor vastation. Catherine Marshall's new home, anyhow, turned out to be the opposite of friendly.

Their aunt's marriage was never mentioned in the James children's reminiscences; silence was allowed to fall upon the twenty-eight-month episode. By mid-June of 1855, Kate was back at 58 West Fourteenth Street, preparing to sail to England with the Jameses. In a letter to Emerson, Henry Senior voiced the opinion that Kate had made a "frightful mistake," and that marital life with Marshall had revealed a character "made of all the grinding littlenesses and coldnesses that are effectual in wearing out the human heart."

The old sea captain appeared in James's account as an example of that implacable selfhood he had just then been elaborating on in *The Nature of Evil*: the very enemy of the human, and by Jamesian implication of the divine. Marshall had a "spiritual isolation and iciness

---

* Jean Strouse, in *Alice James: A Biography* (1980), was the first to provide a full identification of Captain Marshall, and to piece together the story of his courtship and marriage to Catherine Walsh.

which left no green thing alive"; which "banished smiles and tears, laughter and all human sympathies to the opposite hemisphere." Kate, so James hinted, had been brought to the verge of spiritual and even actual death by the experience. But evidently Marshall himself had proposed a separation, and Kate fled in relief down Fourteenth Street to the familiar household, where, the elder James said, she was "our sweet and stainless 'Aunt Kate' again, the refuge of all hearts, and the solace of every weary hour." Writing from London a month later, Henry Senior stressed Kate's admirable performance on the Atlantic crossing, as a nurse to Mary and the children in their dire seasickness.

When her husband died in 1865, after quite honorable civilian work during the Civil War, Mrs. Catherine Walsh, as she now called herself, could read in the New York *Herald* that Captain Marshall had been "distinguished for his firmness, decision of character, persever-ance and manly independence." Whatever she thought of that, she probably agreed with the ensuing judgment that "like many men, who have from early life been engaged in nautical pursuits and accustomed to command only to be obeyed, he had an air of sternness about him that was somewhat repulsive to strangers." One may imagine what marriage to such a man could be like. In Catherine Walsh, though, Marshall took into his home not a timid and pliable young woman but a mature and traveled one with (as William said) an energy of active will—if also with a certain poignant and self-deluding hopefulness. The relationship must have been a disaster, and at several large re-moves it may be reflected in one of Henry Junior's fictional dramas about an aspiring and willful woman and a coldly self-centered older man.

FRENCH PASSAGES

The family crossed to France in June of 1856. Henry Senior's feelings about England, as they made ready to leave, were extremely cordial, though sharply observant as always. "There is no nobler ingredient going into the new humanity," he wrote Edmund Tweedy, "than that which comes out of these shy, sullen, honest men and these ill-drest, energetic, long-striding and unaffected women." From across the Channel and a distance of several months, however, James quite changed his mind. He had been reading Emerson's *English Traits*, published in August, and felt it to be misguided; the English, he now believed, did not deserve the lofty analysis Emerson accorded them.

Their qualities for good or for evil did not come "from any divine or diabolic depths whatever, but from most obvious and superficial causes." Still, he thought, they might be a cut above the French: "They do not lie, cheat, commit adultery and murder with half so much good will."

Adultery, with its consequences, was in fact on Henry Senior's mind at the moment, in the wake of his brother John Barber James's death at forty; and he went on, in the same letter to Tweedy, to reflect on that heartbreaking event. John James had for some time been caught up in an adulterous affair with a Mrs. Little, and was suffering acute pangs of conscience about it. On two occasions, when nearly prostrate with drink, he had spoken to Henry on the subject, extravagantly praising Mrs. Little's attractions but also declaring that her husband was equally dear to him.

Henry Senior interpreted the whole calamitous fraternal business by his own social theory, and carrying forward from the recent exchange with Stephen Pearl Andrews. "John had an enormous social instinct," he wrote Tweedy. "No one had a keener sense of human fellowship"; and although he loved Mrs. Little and was loved by her, he could not bear the thought of her husband being degraded by his, John's, action.

And this it was literally that killed him. He knew that the marriage was no marriage in God's light; he knew all the excuses that men are capable of making for such ties; he knew that the existing social order, or lack of order, was the great criminal in the case; but he could not justify himself in his own right, and whenever he was away from her for a few days, no longer sustained by the strength of her response, he rushed into gambling and drinking as if he wanted only to bring his life to the speediest possible end.

John James was reputed, in the family annals, to be the truly handsome member of the clan; one kinsman pronounced him the handsomest man he had ever seen. But his personal story, as it filtered down through the generations, had him gambling away his fortune and ultimately killing himself—as though an actual suicide rather than drinking himself to death, as his brother Henry implied. The latter, after referring sorrowfully to John's "youth and his beauty and his wit and his generosity," concluded his diagnosis by expressing doubt that what John had felt for Mrs. Little could be called love. For true love, he averred, *"knows no shame.* But I suspect that not one in a million now a days knows love from any actual experience. Lust, arising out

of unsatisfied sexual desire, is the only approximation of it they know."
A muted confessional tone may perhaps be heard in this final sentence.

Over the twelve months following the arrival in France, Henry
Senior led the family through four changes of habitation. In the first
Paris summer, the Jameses lived in a fine old house on the Champs-
Élysées, rented from an eccentric American. In September they moved
the short distance to an apartment on rue d'Angoulême (now rue de
la Boëtie), a narrow, dusky street busy with the varieties of Parisian
life. From the second-floor window, Henry Junior, already assuming
his alert spectatorial posture, could gaze down on a scene composed
of a bakery, a *"crémerie"* serving workmen and cabmen, all audibly
exchanging fierce opinions, the enclosure of an oyster lady, the cage-
like hut of a wood peddler. By the spring of 1857, the family was
installed in another apartment on the far side of Champs-Élysées, in
rue Montaigne; and at the start of summer, Henry Senior took the
entourage to the seashore, renting a house in Boulogne-sur-Mer at 20
rue Neuve Chaussée.

The three older brothers, during the 1856 autumn, had been tu-
tored by a M. Lerambert, a spare, pale, bespectacled type who found
the quick-thinking William a rewarding pupil, but for whom Henry
and Wilky (Henry was to maintain) were rather "a drag." Robertson
and Alice were in the care of a sympathetic governess, the smiling-
eyed Mlle Danse, who grew especially tender toward "l'ingénieux petit
Robertson," as she called him. After a sufficient testing of M. Lerambert, Henry Senior removed the boys from his instruction and placed
them in the Institution Fezandié on nearby rue Balzac. M. Fezandié,
a committed Fourierite, organized his school like a phalanstery and
accepted students of both sexes and all ages.

The continuing succession of tutors and schools and cities and
addresses was not due, in any but the slightest degree, to sheer mud-
dleheadedness on Henry Senior's part. It was due, rather, to a privately
held theory of education, and a passion of paternal love. The theoretical
principles had been enunciated in *The Nature of Evil* within the year:

I desire my child to become an upright man, a man in whom goodness shall
be induced not by mercenary motives as brute goodness is induced, but by
love for it or a sympathetic delight in it. And inasmuch as I know that this
character or disposition cannot be forcibly imposed upon him, but must be
freely assumed, I surround him as far as possible with an atmosphere of
freedom.

79   ]

The clearly masculine nature of the writer's child (Jean Strouse has underscored the point) was no slip of the mind; James's daughter was not to take part in the educational experiment. Women, in James's view, should not be exposed to formal education. He had said as much in an article on the " 'Woman's Movement' " in the March 1853 issue of *Putnam's Monthly*, where we read: "The very virtue of woman . . . disqualifies her for all didactic dignity. Learning and wisdom do not become her." It was unnecessary, even unseemly, for a woman to recite the Ten Commandments, since "her own pure pleasure" should "form the best outward law for man." Thus did Henry James, Sr., lend a certain rhetorical flourish to the conventional attitude of the American age toward female education.

In pursuit of his stated intention, Henry Senior regularly departed on journeys to this destination or that, hoping to find something—a school, a center of activity, a setting—which might serve to broaden the boys' outlooks, place them in touch with larger realities. No less regularly, the father would hurry back to the family ahead of schedule "with no account at all to give of the benefit aimed at" (Henry Junior would write), but instead a moving report on his misadventures at the terrible inns where he had been forced to stop, and the uncomprehending people he came up against.

Alice James had a similar affectionate memory of her father going away for a fortnight and returning after thirty-six hours, to pour out "the agonies of desolation thro' which he had come," while the five children pressed around him and Mother soothingly held his hand. Alice's first extant letter to Father, written from Geneva in the winter of 1860 after Father had taken himself for a stay in London, began: "We have had two dear letters from you, and find you are the same dear old good-for-nothing home-sick papa as ever."

"He reacted, he rebounded, in favour of the fireside," Henry Junior observed aptly; and if one of the father's images for ideal happiness was the horsecar, the other was the fireside. Between them, they communicated his two deepest impulses. The fireside was movable: it was wherever the family was gathered, in an apartment or a house or a hotel; in Geneva or London, in Paris or Boulogne. But the paternal love and concern which motivated the explorations of new environments also brought Henry Senior back, precipitately, to the family hearth.

The consequences for his offspring of Henry Senior's theory of schooling were long-ranging and diverse. Young William, as we have heard, dismissed virtually the whole European time as educationally worthless; and he remarked in an early letter that, when the family came back to Geneva in 1859, he was "a miserable home-bred, obscure little ignoramus." The suggestion was that he was still an ignoramus at age seventeen *because* he was home-bred, his education to that point being limited to tutors, family conversations, and walks with Henry. In fact, as he had slowly come to realize, William had for several years been engaged in a sort of educational tug-of-war with his father.

It had to do with vocation: in William's developing case, with an artistic as against a scientific calling. All the James children tried their hands, as most children do, at drawing and sketching; but William from an early age gave promise of genuine talent. In the Paris winter of 1857, the respected painter Léon Coigniet was so taken by some of William's drawings that he admitted the fourteen-year-old American boy into his atelier. William's interest in a possible artistic life was quickened by the experience, and he was beginning to show a dis-criminating enthusiasm for French painters, and especially for the dramatic and colorful canvases of Eugène Delacroix. But William had also displayed scientific promise, in experiments (sometimes as prac-tical jokes) with chemicals and electric batteries. Taking note of all this, Henry Senior, moving the family over to Boulogne-sur-Mer at the end of the 1857 academic season, enrolled the three older boys in the Collège Imperial there, and encouraged William to follow courses in science.

"Willy is very devoted to scientific pursuits," Henry Senior wrote his mother from Boulogne after three months' trial of the Collège Imperial (the latter being something like a top-flight high school). One of the boy's teachers had told Mr. James that William was "an ad-mirable student, and that all the advantages of a first-rate scientific education which Paris affords ought to be accorded him." Within days of this letter, Henry Senior did have the family back in Paris and reinstalled in the apartment on rue Montaigne. Presumably—the record is not clear about this—the elder James also settled William in some institute with a reputation for excellence in science. In December, however, financial troubles drove the family back to the more inex-pensive life in Boulogne, and the boys were again enrolled in the Collège.

At Christmas, William's gift was a microscope, which is said to have produced a more excited response than he had ever shown over a present. But his father professed himself far less concerned with William's intellectual than his "moral worth," as he told Mrs. James in Albany. He praised especially William's "perfectly generous and conciliatory demeanor towards his younger brothers, always disposed to help them and never to oppress." If William had been the model for the growing boy pictured in "Democracy and Its Uses," five years had made a striking if familiar difference.

In the summer of 1858, in any event, after the Collège had ended its term, Henry Senior took William and the family, not to Paris and science, but across the Atlantic to Newport, and for the two older boys a proximity at least to the studio of the painter William Morris Hunt.

THE PUPILS

Alice James, three decades afterward, expressed to William an opinion about the years of wandering even more hostile than her brother's. William at this time (1888) had just bought and refurbished a farmhouse in Chocorua, New Hampshire, for summer living. Do everything needed, Alice enjoined him, to *cling* to the new place, for the sake of the children. "What enrichment of mind and memory can children have without continuity and if they are torn up by the roots every little while as we were! Of all things don't make the mistake wh. brought about our rootless and accidental childhood." As for Europe, leave it until the children are old enough to have a real emotional response to it.

To be sure, Alice, at the end of the entire European experiment, was barely twelve years old, and was the one least considered when it came to decisions about where next to proceed. Within the family, her parents and Aunt Kate loved her and looked after her; William teased her and made her laugh; Wilky and Bob rode over her roughshod. Only Henry treated her as a fellow human being, something exemplified on an afternoon in the early summer of 1857, at Boulogne-sur-Mer.

With Harry, Wilky, and Bob, Alice had gone for midday dinner at the home of the new governess, Marie Boningue (the sophisticated Mlle Danse had been dismissed in mysterious and romantic circumstances). They had all been packed into a shabby *calèche*; and Alice remembered a long uncomfortable drive and "the anguish greater even than usual of Wilky's and Bob's heels grinding into my shins." After the meal, the children were

turned into the garden to play, a sandy or rather dusty expanse with nothing in it, as I remember, but two or three scrubby apple-trees, from one of which hung a swing. As time went on Wilky and Bob disappeared, not to my grief, and the Boningues. Harry was sitting in the swing and I came up and stood near by as the sun began to slant over the desolate expanse, as the dreary hrs., with that endlessness which they have for infancy, passed, when Harry suddenly exclaimed: "This might certainly be called pleasure under difficulties."

The moment, for Alice James, was a leap toward intellectual maturity. There came to her in a flash, she would remember, "the higher nature of this appeal to the mind, as compared to the rudimentary solicitations which usually produced my childish explosions of laughter." She was filled on the spot with deep self-congratulation, in that she "could not only perceive, but appreciate this subtlety, as if I had acquired a new sense, a sense whereby to measure intellectual things, wit as distinguished from giggling, for example."

The image of the adolescent Henry James conjured up by his sister was markedly true to life in the 1850s: he could usually find pleasure amid the material difficulties of the nomadic life. What he had always wanted, the memoirist decided, was "just to *be* somewhere—almost anywhere would do—and somehow receive an impression or an accession, feel a relation or a vibration." His parents, he felt, understood this very well, which was why they allowed him, even as a small boy, to wander alone at times through the New York streets. They knew he was anything but venturesome, and that—it was one of Henry James's choicest formulations—"the only form of riot or revel ever known to me would be that of the visiting mind." And so he walked and wandered, he dawdled and gaped, storing up impressions and vibrations; and as the years unfolded

in the streets of the great towns, in New York . . . and then for a while in London, in Paris, in Geneva, wherever it might be, he was to enjoy more than anything the so far from showy practice of wandering and dawdling and gaping.

For such a young person, change of setting was a recurring source of delight; and thus, for example, as to the abrupt departure from Geneva in the fall of 1855 and the passage back through Paris to London, he remembered himself feeling happily that "since one was all eyes and the world decidedly, at such a pace, all images," the journey simply "ministered to the panoramic."

Throughout Henry's account of that youthful time, the relationship with William provides a sinuous motif, one that is constantly surfacing only to go underground again. In the earliest remembered Albany days and the New York years, William was pictured as invariably far ahead of him: "as if he had gained such an advance of me in his sixteen months' [sic] experience of the world before mine began that I never for all the time of childhood and youth in the least caught up with him or overtook him. He was always round the corner and out of sight." They were never in the same schoolroom at the same time; and once, when Henry suggested he might accompany William on some expedition or other, William declined the gambit with the remark: "*I* play with boys who curse and swear!" Henry, who didn't know any boys like that, continued on his solitary saunterings.

Again unlike William, Henry was quite content with the company of his family, and in the absence of his older brother he turned for fellowship to the next younger one, Wilky, his junior by two years and a few months. In the first foreshortened stay in Geneva, the two became particularly close, and Henry found Wilky a distinctly warmer sibling than William—as the novelist conveys to us in the sly figure of having been "in the grateful . . . position of having one exposure, rather the northward, as it were, to the view of W.J., and the other, perhaps the more immediately sunned surface, to the genial glow of my junior." What Henry admired in Wilky, then and later, was "his successful sociability, his instinct for intercourse, his genius . . . for making friends."

As Henry observed him, Wilky was an assiduous explorer of personalities and a uniter of individuals; if William was often out of sight, the rotund, even tubby young Wilky was all over the place, but always coming back to introduce a new friend to his old friends. It was his only genius, Henry said; for in a family voracious in its reading and lust for knowledge, Wilky was notable for his aversion to the intellectual and literary. (The act of reading for him, in Henry's hyperbolic phrase, was inhuman and repugnant; in the father's view, Wilky was "more heart than head," though with some skill at languages.) But it was the example of Wilky that gave the watchful Henry the sharpening sense of two fundamentally different ways of taking life—Wilky's way and his:

one way of taking life was to go in for everything and everyone, which kept you abundantly occupied, and the other way was to be as occupied, quite as occupied, just with the sense and the image of it all . . .

Life might well be taken either way; but Henry would believe that, by his thirteenth year, he had understood his own occupation was to be not so much with direct experience as with the sense, the shaping image, of it.

It was in the Paris of 1856–57 that the older brothers began to become more fully aware of one another, and the lifelong fraternal relationship began to come into being. They took "long and beguiled walks" together, walking on wintry days down the Champs-Élysées and through the Tuileries to the Louvre. This was the winter when William was studying and practicing in the atelier of Léon Coigniet; and as the brothers roamed the galleries, William made pen-and-ink copies of woodcuts by Henri-Monnier, and imitations in charcoal and crayon of Delacroix, all the while lecturing Henry on the merits and probable durability of the recently past and present French artists.

Henry for the moment was (or adopted the pose of) the rapt and admiring pupil of William. But faithful to his personal impulse, he was also receiving impressions and hearing vibrations quite independent of William's discourses. Nowhere more so than in the Galerie d'Apollon in the Louvre. Crossing the threshold of the Galerie began to represent for the thirteen-year-old one of the crucial passages of his life: crossing the bridge, as he would put it, "over to Style." The Galerie introduced him to the splendid mystery of style, even as it spoke to him not only of "beauty and art and supreme design" but also of "history and fame and power." In that rich developing atmosphere, Henry had a sudden inkling, it would seem, of his own possible future fame and power; far-off glimpses that came back to him many decades later in what he called "the most appalling yet most admirable nightmare of my life."

In the climax of this dream-adventure Henry found himself pushing his way out of his bedroom and setting to flight a figure, a being, who only a moment before had been trying to force its way *into* the room. Henry pursued the fleeing visitant down a tremendous and glorious hall; a storm of thunder and lightning began to play through the windows to the right, and by the flashes it was revealed to Henry that the hall he was racing through was none other than the Galerie d'Apollon.

Later events in Henry's life story mingled and fused in this "dream of the Louvre." But one obvious identification of the fleeing figure, though far from the only one, is brother William; and in this regard, the late-in-life dream may have been a revivifying of Henry's youthful intuition that, in any rivalry between William and himself, he, Henry, would possess the power to triumph.

But to say even this much is apparently to belie Henry's recorded memory that in all his childhood and youth he never once "caught up with [William] or overtook him." We must remind ourselves once more, as we attend to Henry James's reminiscences, that we are in the presence of one of the masters of the art of fiction. Far more than the Dewhurst memoirs of Henry James, Sr., the younger Henry's autobiographical volumes are an extraordinary weave of the factual and the fictional. And within that weave, "William" and "Henry" (as F. O. Matthiessen remarked a long time ago) are semifictional characters, especially in the narrative up to about 1860. The persisting contrast, archetypically American and always amusedly emphasized, between the dawdler and gaper and the swift-moving resolute man of action: this reflects a novelistic or even a folkloristic symmetry. And in fact, as the case will show, it was Henry rather than William who moved swiftly and resolutely into his career. We may leave it, for now, that if the young Henry had the sense of ever running after William, he also had the prophetic feeling of passing him.

The career, meanwhile, began to take some dim form for Henry— so he thought to remember—on those Louvre visits. He sometimes visited by himself; and it was then that the characteristic future motifs and perspectives of his mature fiction seemed to rise and swirl in his imagination.

I had looked at pictures, looked and looked again, at the vast Veronese, at Murillo's moonborne Madonna . . . but I had also looked at France and looked at Europe, looked even at America as Europe itself might be conceived so to look, looked at history, as a still-felt past and a complacently personal future, at society, manners, type, characters, possibilities and prodigies and mysteries of fifty sorts . . .

In Boulogne, around the middle of the summer of 1857, Henry Junior came down with typhoid fever, that dangerous illness at one time so common with young Americans in Europe. From the vantage point of age, Henry would call it "the gravest illness of my life" and "an all but mortal attack." Henry Senior wrote his mother that the family had "trembled more than once for the issue." There was, fortunately, a good physician, an Irishman, in the village, and Aunt Kate again exercised her nursing skills. Harry was still convalescing when the Jameses returned to Paris and the rue Montaigne apartment in late October. And indeed, with his extraordinary alertness to the rituals of transition in his life story, Henry James would come to look upon the 1857 illness and the subsequent recovery as marking the "limit of my state of being a small boy"; and to think that, in slowly regaining his health, he had somehow been living "into a part of myself previously quite unvisited and now made accessible as by the sharp forcing of a closed door."*

Financial difficulty, as has been mentioned, caused the family to give up their residence in rue Montaigne and, before Christmas, to return to Boulogne-sur-Mer. The American economic collapse of 1857, almost as severe as the one that caught Henry Senior short in 1837, had led to falling stocks, bankrupt companies, and the calling in of loans. James cautioned his half brother William that he might have to ask the family to help out by making deposits in his name with Baring Brothers. He took the occasion to appraise the calamity (not without justice) in his personal language: "Was anything clearer than that these commercial disasters indicate the widest *social* disease in the community? The lack of the sentiment of brotherhood—the prevalence of self-seeking—this is the disease of the common mind as it is of the individual."

Even before the straitened circumstances, Mary James had been lamenting the costliness of life in Paris. The Jameses needed a large apartment or house—at least six bedrooms—and such lodgings were not easily come by. The French, Mary contended, built their homes only for small families. (Her theory was that the French kept their families small by sending the infants "away into the country to be nursed, where eight of ten died"; those that survived were placed in boarding schools.) An apartment sizable enough for the James family was likely to be frighteningly expensive: that on rue d'Angoulême, admittedly comfortable, had cost $2,200 a year, while the New York house brought in only $1,400.

During the second stay in Boulogne, through the winter and spring of 1858, the family lived in a house on Grande-Rue, the town's chief thoroughfare, which climbed steeply from mid-village to the venerable *haute ville* (old town). Henry Senior was growing fond of Boulogne, he said to his mother; it was a cheerful, bustling, picturesque place. Mary James was more contented yet. Their house, if not very elegant, rented for only 200 francs a month. Harry (still a bit wobbly) and Alice were at home, the others in school; and the entire expense of the

---

* The image eerily connects with that in the dream of the Louvre, set down not many pages earlier in *A Small Boy and Others*.

children's education, including Alice's dancing lessons and the tutors, was $40 a month.

Henry Junior's all but mortal attack and his parents' financial woes combined, under the pressure of memory, in one of James's finest novellas, "The Pupil" of 1891. This is the story of an intermittently penniless American family, the Moreens, who shift about from place to place in Europe according to financial need; of their second son, the precocious and sensitive Morgan, who understands his family precisely for the adventurers they are; and the troubled, concerned American, Pemberton, who becomes the boy's tutor. In Pemberton's recognition of the rare educational value for young Morgan of the "homebred" and wandering existence, Henry James makes an unequivocal pronouncement on the value that such an existence had had for him; as though still carrying on a debate with William about the matter.

Morgan, Pemberton reflects,

had the general quality of a child for whom life had not been simplified by school, a kind of homebred sensibility which might have been bad for himself but was charming for others, and a whole range of refinement and perception—little musical vibrations as taking as picked-up airs—begotten by wandering about Europe at the tail of his migratory tribe. This might not have been an education to recommend in advance, but its results with Morgan were as palpable as a fine texture.

For good measure, James has Pemberton accompany his pupil on walks in Paris which repeat those he had made with William, to the Louvre, to the Palais de Justice. Finally, the Moreens, reeling in some ultimate financial crisis (though living in luxurious quarters in "the most expensive city in Europe"), propose that Pemberton take Morgan away with him. In the ensuing excitement and confusion, Morgan has a mortal heart attack.

In his preface to "The Pupil" in the New York Edition, in the 1900s, James wrote that the Moreens, like himself, belonged to a romantic faraway time, "the classic years of the great Americano-European legend," a "golden age" for Americans abroad, one that lasted until about the middle of the nineteenth century. Mr. and Mrs. Moreen—whose "whole view of life . . . was speculative and rapacious and mean"—bear little if any resemblance to Mr. and Mrs. Henry James, those real-life participants in the golden age; though their flights and changes are a sort of parody of the Jamesian vicissitudes. But the parallels between Morgan and Henry Junior are striking, even as to age: Morgan goes from twelve to fifteen in the course of the narrative; Henry's age increased from twelve on the departure for Europe to fifteen by the end of the stay in Boulogne.

And if "The Pupil" ends with the death of Morgan Moreen, Henry Junior's first autobiographical volume, *A Small Boy and Others*, concludes in a dreamily dramatic manner with Henry, clutched by pain and terror, falling into unconsciousness. The memoirist recalls the sudden onset of the illness, recalls, too, the soft afternoon sounds of the Boulogne street coming through the window, and above all "the strange sense that something had begun that would make more difference to me, directly and indirectly, than anything had ever yet made." He remembers tumbling weakly out of bed and wavering over toward the bell just across the room.

The question of whether I really reached and rang it was to remain lost afterwards in the strong sick whirl of everything about me, under which I fell into a lapse of consciousness . . .

In a rundown on the children provided by Henry Senior for his mother in a letter from Boulogne, in which he spoke of Willy's scientific pursuits and said that Wilky was more heart than head, the father went on to remark about Harry that he was "not so fond of study, properly so-called, as of reading. He is a devourer of libraries and an immense writer of novels and dramas. He has considerable talent, but I am at a loss to know whether he will ever accomplish much."

The "libraries" consumed by Henry included a good deal of fiction: by Washington Irving, whom the boy had once met on an excursion with his father; Poe and Hawthorne; Charles Dickens in abundance (Dickens was always a special novelistic case for young James, as for many others); Thackeray, who had called on Henry Senior in the Fourteenth Street home, and had recently dined with the family in Paris, in the spring of 1857.* But if the father is to be believed and young Henry in Boulogne was busily writing both dramas *and* novels,

---

* On the first visit, Thackeray expressed astonishment over Henry's silver-buttoned jacket; to his English eyes, it made Henry look like a pageboy. During dinner in Paris (Henry recalled), he suddenly laid his hand on Alice's "little flounced person and exclaimed with ludicrous horror: 'Crinoline?—I was suspecting it! So young and so depraved!' "

then the period may have been as much a literary as a psychological turning point.

Prior to this, by his own confession, Henry's writing had been restricted to dramas, or at least scenes from dramas—each one completed by a picture illustrating the action. Addicted as he was from the outset to "fictive evocation," he could yet remember from his childhood days "no practice whatever of narrative prose . . . I cherished the 'scene.' " He had done so in particular since a moment in the early fifties, when, on a visit to his Uncle Augustus at Rhinebeck, he had heard his aunt addressing her recalcitrant daughter (who was protesting at being sent to bed): "Come now, my dear; don't make a scene—I *insist* on your not making a scene!" It was an instant of revelation: "Life at these intensities," he explained to himself, "clearly became 'scenes' "; but the great thing, the boy thought, was that "we could make them or not as we chose."

It would, though, be some forty years before Henry James, reconsidering his literary status in the mid-1890s, would elevate scene-making to the principal element in his own art of fiction.

The youngest brother—"l'ingénieux petit Robertson" for the doting governess, and Bob or Rob or Bobby to his father—was a lively, springy adolescent in the European epoch. Bob was "very clever and promising," his father said to Catherine James, and had "ten times the go-ahead of all the rest." But what was to stick in Bob's memory about Boulogne was that, on graduation day at the Collège Imperial, he and Wilky had failed to win any prizes. They were both given a beautiful book covered with gold figures; but the dominating image for Bob was the more successful scholars ascending the platform and kneeling at the mayor's feet to "receive crown or rosettes, or some symbol of merit which *we* did not get." The reminiscence occurred in an autobiographical fragment Bob wrote at the suggestion of his sister-in-law Mrs. William James, in the 1890s. Such an undertaking, he said to her, "would have to be the biography of broken fortunes," and he adduced the Boulogne story as a sign that "the luck had begun to break early!"*

But there were happy memories in that fragment, too, especially of the earlier days: his mother walking down Sixth Avenue to Washington Market with a basket on her arm, and Bob, age six, tagging

* Jane Maher took from this passage the title of her study of the lives of Bob and Wilky James, *Biography of Broken Fortunes* (1986).

after her and holding her shawl; Uncle William from Albany crying out, "Tell Henry and Mary . . ."; General Kossuth in a parade down Broadway; Thackeray carrying Bob on his shoulders. "It was a beautiful and splendid childhood for any child to have had, and I remember it all now as full of indulgence and light and color and hardly a craving unsatisfied."

NEWPORT, GENEVA, BONN: 1858–60

Mary James in a note to "dear Ma," appended to a filial letter from her husband, had confided that the elder Henry was secretly longing to return to America but that they would remain in France for reasons of economy and for the sake of the children. By the end of the spring of 1858 the family finances were in fairly good order and the parents thought it time to revisit the American scene.

They chose Newport, Rhode Island, partly perhaps because the New York home was still rented, and partly because of their great affection for the Newporters Edmund and Mary Tweedy, a generous-minded couple of independent means who had become the foster parents of Henry Senior's nieces (whom we shall shortly be meeting). The Jameses rented a house on Kay Street, up beyond the end of Bellevue Avenue. "We are settled very comfortably in Newport," James wrote a friend; and spoke approvingly about Mary at work removing inkspots from the boys' shirts and repairing rips in their trousers. The boys were enjoying their "recovered liberty," he said, and were boating and fishing and riding to their hearts' content.

What Newport came to mean to the James children—especially to William, Henry, and Alice—would emerge from later residence there, frequent shorter visits, retrospectives. But it would remain for them, primarily, the Newport they first experienced: pre–Civil War Newport, with the "shy sweetness" and strange, simple charm Henry Junior ascribed to it; its narrow upward-curving old streets, its peaceful tree-lined avenue; the ancient New England homes and taverns; Trinity Church, the resplendent white landmark visible from all directions, with its bell towers and its needle-like spire.

Newport was unmatched as the setting for ramblings, explorations, daylong outings. It provided, in Henry's later inventory, "a thousand delicate secret places . . . small, mild 'points' and promontories, far-away little lonely, sandy coves, rock-set, lily-sheeted ponds . . . a whole world that called out to the long afternoons of youth." Writing to his new friend Tom Perry from Geneva, in March 1860, Henry listed some of these, taking pleasure, as he said, in their very names: Lily Pond, stretching away from Ocean Avenue to the south; Spouting Rock, hanging over the Atlantic; Cherry Grove, through which, looking west onto the bay, you could see the lighthouse at the tip of Goat Island; Paradise Rock, on whose bulging brown expanse, overlooking the water on the eastward side, you could idle away many an hour, gaping and dreaming; and close by, Purgatory Chasm, a narrow cleft between the rock-sides, traversable by a tiny bridge.

It was on an early summer evening that the James children for the first time met a twelve-year-old boy named Thomas Sergeant Perry: a lad of impressive background (his mother descended from Benjamin Franklin, and his grandfather was Commodore Oliver Hazard Perry, the naval hero of the War of 1812), and an almost aggressive reader of books. Perry, who became the boys' lifelong friend (with periods of mutual annoyance and estrangement), thought in retrospect that even on that first evening the brothers displayed themselves in their characteristic ways. They went strolling along Cliff Walk, and on their way back to the James house, the sociable Wilky hung on to Tom Perry's arm "as if he had found an old friend after long absence." William, full of merriment, invented a game in which all joined amid much youthful chatter; except Henry, who relaxed on a window seat reading a life of the painter Constable.

With the coming of fall, the four boys were enrolled in the Berkeley Institute on Newport's own small Washington Square; a school named for the one-time Newport resident Bishop George Berkeley and headed by the Reverend William C. Leverett, curate of Trinity Church and an uninspiring teacher. Henry at least was politely bored, though with the others he managed to absorb something of classical literature. William, as usual, took more easily to his studies; but he was perhaps more enlivened by his visits to the studio of William Morris Hunt on Church Street, only a few minutes' walk from home. He was not yet a regular student of Hunt's, but the latter made him welcome and encouraged him in his sketching, as Henry Senior observed with a certain alarm. Another side of William, as Perry remembered it, was suggested by his bringing home a volume of Schopenhauer, to show the others a picture of the philosopher's "ugly mug," and read aloud examples of his "delightful pessimism" (William would not always consider it delightful).

Outside the school hours, it was an attractive life. But the elder James gradually succumbed to the congenital disappointment; and having vilified European schools and enthused in advance over American ones, in the France of 1858, he was saying despondently to Sam Ward at the tail end of summer 1859 that "I have grown so discouraged about the education of my children here . . . that I have come to the conclusion to retrace my steps to Europe, and keep them there a few years longer. My wife is completely of the same mind." The children, he feared, were in danger of acquiring those specifically American youthful vices of extravagance (i.e., with money) and insubordination. "I am a good patriot," he insisted, "but my patriotism is even livelier on the other side of the water." On October 8, the family sailed for Le Havre on the *Vanderbilt*—"Newport and the Newporters are surrounded with a halo, in my mind," Henry wrote Tom Perry from New York, a few hours before departure—and within a fortnight the family had settled for the year in Geneva.

Henry James's second volume of autobiography, *Notes of a Son and Brother*, opens with the family's arrival at the Hôtel de l'Écu in Geneva, and the view from the windows of their rooms of the Rhone River flowing swiftly beneath.* That view was one of the few happy impressions Henry carried away with him from the Geneva months, or so he would claim. William was a day student at the Geneva Academy, and the younger brothers were boarding at the *pensionnat* run by M. and Mme Maquelin, a little distance outside of town; but Henry was required to make his way daily to a dilapidated old stone house next to the prison in what he thought was the gloomiest part of the city, there to study mathematics and science. This was the Institution Rochette, which prepared students for the Polytechnical School in Zurich and similar places; and Henry was put there, he came to believe, because his parents "had simply said to themselves, in serious concern, that I read too many novels, or at least read them too attentively—*that* was the vice."

The diagnosis may have been correct: we shall soon be hearing the elder James saying very much the same thing about William's

---

* James thus passed over the second stay in Boulogne-sur-Mer and the entire 1858–59 period in Newport. He skipped the latter episode, he told his nephew and namesake Henry, because he felt overcome "by the sense of our poor father's impulsive journeyings to and fro and of the impression of aimless vacillation which the record might make upon the reader." But literary as well as filial piety was at work in these omissions. He also told Tom Perry (1914) that the reminiscences already contained "so many choppings and changes and interruptions and volatilities (on our parents' part, dear people)" that his treatment of it all was becoming literarily foolish. We have here a fine example of Henry James's fictive arrangement, as it were, of actual facts: the skippings are made in the interest of dramatic effect—the lapse into unconsciousness which brings the first volume to a close, the curtain rising on a large change of European scene in the second.

involvement with painting. Henry made a brief brave effort in the science classroom; but it was useless, and he gradually withdrew from the institution, "an obscure, a deeply hushed failure," according to his comedic memory, and by Easter of 1860, he had joined Willy at the academy and was following courses in French literature and anatomy. But this may have been another example of Henry finding pleasure amid difficulties. His several letters from Geneva show little resentment at being placed in the institution, though the other students, he said, were both unfriendly and uninteresting. And meanwhile, there were enjoyable tramps along the shores of Lake Geneva, and along roads lined with hedgerows and past the iron gates of handsome châteaus, with the snowy Alps glimmering on all sides.

Henry, too, was scribbling away in his spare moments; Wilky informed Perry that he had espied Harry at a table covered with "some poetical looking manuscripts," and with a "most authorlike" air. When Perry wrote to ask Henry what particular style he was developing, Henry answered: "To no style am I a stranger, there is none which has not been adorned by the magic of my touch"; and demonstrated by describing his waking up of a morning in extravagant mock-heroic rhetoric.

But it was William, eighteen years old in January 1860, who was clearly arriving at maturity. He was glowing with health, and seems to have been adept at everything he laid his hand to. We already make out in him what would become a hallmark of William James: a remarkable, almost a unique openness or accessibility to experience. As his brother would put it: "Whatever he played with or worked at entered at once into his intelligence, his talk, his humour." He was never more gregarious or popular. In the spring, William was taken into the Société de Zoffingue, a large Swiss organization that went in for brotherhood and beer; and one of the valued moments of the season for Henry was when he accompanied Willy on the three-day annual fête of the society in the mountains above Lausanne. There was an immense amount of drinking, singing, shouting, pipe-smoking, and clasping of hands. The carousing went on too long, in Henry's view, but he could enjoy William's social success.

Late in the winter, Henry Senior betook himself to Paris and then to London, for reasons unspecified. He managed for two long months to refrain from rejoining the family (though it was his repeated cry of anguished loneliness that inspired Alice's address to him as "dear old good-for-nothing home-sick papa"). For his absent father's benefit, William drew a verbal portrait of the rest of the family on a Sunday morning in their rooms at the Hôtel de l'Écu. "Mother does nothing but sit and cry for you. She refuses to associate with us and has one side of the room to herself. She and Aunt are now in Aunt's room. Wilky and Bobby, at home for the day, are at church. It is a hard gray day. H. is telling a story to Louis Osborne."*

There was no mention here of Alice, but William, in fact, at this time was being especially attentive to her in his arch-romantic manner. In another letter to Father, William told of a "sonnate" he had written in celebration of Alice, and which he had sung aloud before the assembled family.

> *The moon was mildly beaming*
> *Upon the summer sea,*
> *I lay entranced and dreaming*
> *My Alice sweet, of thee.*
> *Upon the sea-shore lying*
> *Upon the yellow sand*
> *The foaming waves replying*
> *I vowed to ask thy hand.*
> *I swore to ask thy hand, my love*
> *I vowed to ask thy hand.*
> *I wished to join myself to thee*
> *By matrimonial band.*

But the proud maiden in this Poesque ballad tells him he must never dare to hope for love from her. And so:

> *Your childlike form, your golden hair*
> *I never more may see.*
> *But goaded on by dire despair*
> *I'll drown within the sea.*

> *Adieu to love! adieu to life!*
> *Since I may not have thee,*
> *My Alice sweet, to be my wife,*
> *I'll drown me in the sea!*
> *I'll drown me in the sea, my love*
> *I'll drown—me in—the sea!*

* Louis Osborne was an attractive, ailing American boy staying with his family in the same hotel. William included with his letter a pencil drawing of young Osborne, in a large armchair, listening to Henry, who with raised finger is proceeding with his anecdote.

Alice took it all very coolly, William informed his father. But she may well also (as Jean Strouse has speculated) have been excited, confused, and embarrassed by the exhibition, and the image of herself as a female who could drive a man to his death.* Cool or not, Alice had learned to tease William back, and to adopt, as her best tactic with him, a bantering, chaffing tone.

The family went to Bonn, the Rhineland town in the shadow of the Venusberg, in July 1860. The immediate educational aim was the learning of German, now that the children had fairly well mastered French; and to this end, Henry and Wilky were placed with the family of Herr Dr. Humpert, professor of classics at the Bonn Gymnasium; and William with that of Herr Stromberg, of whom we know that he had a fair young wife who made pancakes and wrote tragedies. Bob James remained in Geneva with the Maquelins. The parents, Aunt Kate, and Alice were lodged in an imitation Gothic castle on the banks of the Rhine.

The longer intention was to spend the entire year in Germany, possibly in Frankfurt am Main, for further study of language and literature. But the family had scarcely settled in Bonn before William gathered his courage to confront Father about his state of mind. He felt so strongly the desire to make a try at a career in art that it would be wrong, he contended, to waste any more time or money on his scientific training. His keenest ambition was to go back to America as soon as possible, and to be enrolled in the Newport studio of William Morris Hunt.

The elder James was quite taken aback. As he acknowledged to Edmund Tweedy, he and Mary had decided to bring the family to Europe the year before exactly because William, in Newport, had shown too great an interest in art. In Henry Senior's agitation, even his punctuation was collapsing:

Willy felt we thought a little too much attraction to painting—as I supposed from the continuity to Mr. Hunt; let us break that up we said, at all events. I hoped his career would be a scientific one, as I thought and still think that the true bent of his genius was towards the acquisition of knowledge; and to give up this hope without a struggle, and allow him to tumble down into a mere painter, was impossible.

* Who can tell if this frothy "sonnate" might not have been lingering in Alice's mind many years afterward, when William's engagement and marriage drove his sister to image herself as drowning from despair? See below, p. 286.

Overschooled Childhoods

The parents, in Henry Junior's portraiture, made a practice "of liking for us after a gasp or two whatever we seemed to like"; and such was the case in the summer of 1860; though the elder James reiterated to Tweedy his belief in William's scientific calling and his hope that "the day may come when my calculation may be realised in this regard." He made reservations on the *Adriatic*, sailing from France on September 11, and then escorted Mary, Aunt Kate, and Alice down to Paris and the Hôtel des Trois Empereurs in the Place du Palais Royal, to await departure day.

As usual, Henry Senior put the best face on things. Really, he said to Tweedy, Willy's determination about art was providential, and for all the boys. He was glad they had made the second try in Europe: otherwise, they would always have a "misgiving that something was to be found here better than at home." As it was, prodded by William, they would go home "profoundly persuaded that no wilder hallucination exists at least in reference to boys who are destined to grow up into American men." It was only in America that "something better" was to be found; America was " 'the lost Paradise restored' to boys and girls both." Besides, intellectual development was not the main thing anyhow; and—here he invoked his principle about families opening out into society—it was time for the children to go back and make other friends.

They are none of them cut out for intellectual labors, and they are getting to an age, Harry and Wilky especially, when the heart craves a little wider expansion than is furnished it by the domestic affections. They want friends among their own sex, and sweethearts in the other; and my hope for their own salvation, temporal and spiritual, is that they may "go it strong" in both lines when they get home.

In a sort of postscript, and as though opening his eyes, of a sudden, to what the whole adventure must have been to his daughter, he added: "Our chief disappointment . . . on this side of the water has been in regard to Alice, who intellectually, socially, and physically has been at a great disadvantage compared with home."

With the American future assured, it was a summer of deepest contentment and fraternal closeness for the three boys: as William testified in a letter to his parents in Paris, on August 12. The three of them, he said, had gone off together after breakfast that Sunday morning, to a low wooded hill where they found a platform with a stone bench from which they had a view of the far-extending valley. They sat down, and Harry and Wilky each fell to perusing a copy of the magazine *Once a Week*, while he, Willy, made a leisurely sketch of the view. They wondered, among themselves, what the others in Paris were doing at that precise moment, 11:30, and conjured up a vision of them in their salon in the hotel:

Alice at the window with her eyes fixed on her novel, but eating some rich fruit that Father has just brought in for her from the Palais Royal, and the lovely Mother and Aunt in armchairs, their hands crossed in front of them, listening to Father, who walks up and down talking of the superiority of America to these countries after all, and how much better it is we should have done with them.

How the boys wished they could have been in that salon, to join in the conversation and partake of the fruit! "We got up from the seat with a heavy sigh, but in a way so fraternal, presenting such a sweet picture of brotherly unitedness and affections that it would have done you good to see us."

There is more than a hint of laughter behind that final image—William's epistolary prose at this time gleamed with the comic and the exaggerated—but the sentiment was sincere. Henry looked back on the summer of 1860 as an idyllic period, one in which he was most intimate with Wilky and most at ease with William. Wilky astonished him by his surging vitality and his ability in the class hour to talk all around the subject and never once engage it. He formed instant friendships with Dr. Humpert's other students, and on one occasion delicately dissuaded the son of the house, Theodor, from killing himself out of resentment for some parental mistreatment. William in turn reported that Harry and Wilky were getting on "in great harmony and enliven themselves occasionally by brotherly trials of strength." Sometimes William was visited by the other two while he was dressing in the morning; sometimes he walked over to call upon them—arriving in time to see Wilky fall out of bed in his sleep, and to denounce Harry, on waking, for not catching him.

Once the practical decision had been made that William would continue his artistic training in Newport, William could turn his attention to the theoretical basis of the issue: his father's whole attitude to art. He wrote Henry Senior from Bonn in mid-August: "I wish you would, as you promised, set down as clearly as you can on paper what your idea of the nature of art is, because I do not understand it fully, and should like to have it presented to me in a form that I might think over at my leisure." The matter was of highest importance to William, and his request for enlightenment was serious. But William's sense of fun was even in this context irrepressible, and his interest in Father's ideas led him, in the letter's next paragraph, to modulate into a parody of some of them.

Responding to what had apparently been a word of encouragement from Henry Senior about the children's moral development, William remarked: "Having such a father with us, how can we be other than in some measure worthy of him . . . I never value my parents (Father especially) so much as when I am away from them. At home I only see his faults and here he seems all perfection, and every night I wonder why I did not value them more when they were beside me." And then: "I beg darling old mother's forgiveness for the cruel and dastardly way in which I snub her, and Aunt Kate's for the impatience and violence I have always shown towards her. If ever I get back I will be perfectly sherry cobbler to both of them, and to the little Alice, too, for the harsh way in which I have treated her." Just so did Henry Senior chastise himself in print and (it may be supposed) in the family table talk for the cardinal sin of cruelty to a younger sister, mean-spiritedness to a brother, an angry gesture to his wife or to a servant.

Henry Senior's answer to William's letter has not survived, but from comments the father made elsewhere one can guess at it. About art, the elder James was characteristically perplexing. Art was or should be "the gush of God's life into every form of spontaneous speech and act," and by this definition the artist was the ideal, the universal man; Henry Senior was even willing to call him "the perfect or divine man." But whenever he said such things (as in *Moralism and Christianity* of 1850), he invariably hastened to add that by "artist" he did not mean actual practitioners, painters or poets or musicians. Actual artists were a sorry lot; the work they produced was crawling and sycophantic, adapted to the debased current standards of society: hence the father's dismay at the thought of William "tumbling down into a mere painter." To be an artist in William's sense, in short, was to betray the life of art in Father's sense.

Wilky James, for one, confessed, after reading Father's letter, that he was wholly unable to comprehend "father's artistico-metaphysical opinions." Henry made a mental note, for future expression, that rarely if ever before could parental opposition to a son's aesthetic career have been based on the notion that art was *too* respectable, rather than too little so.

Early in September, the three brothers made the long journey by train, in a first-class carriage, from Bonn to Paris, departing at mid-morning and falling into bed at the Hôtel des Trois Empereurs around midnight. The trip itself was a romantic adventure for the teenagers, with window visions of Cologne and Strasbourg, frequent stops when the passengers alighted to mill about the platform and clamor for warm food from passing venders; and, as companions in the boys' compartment, the several servants of a Madame la Marquise, who looked in and smiled at them all from time to time.

Rob came over from Switzerland to join the family. Wilky feigned great pleasure in an enlargement of company, after being "cooped up" with his older brothers all these months, and hearing nothing but their "commonplace table talk" and their quarreling. As to Henry Junior, his feelings during the last few days in Paris were so powerfully mixed that he was scarcely coherent about them in his memoirs. He was aware that his father had been terribly isolated, intellectually speaking, in Europe, and that he needed almost desperately to get back to his native milieu, thin as the latter might be for his purposes. Young Henry, too, was wary, as he wrote Tom Perry, of "this estrangement of American youngsters from the land of their birth." There was for him, also, the lure of Newport ("the place in America we all most care to live in"), and he strongly supported William's aim to work at his painting under Hunt.

But there all around him was Paris, was the Second Empire, was Europe. Henry hurried out of bed early each morning, while the others were still sleeping, to hang over the balcony outside their fifth-floor bedroom and stare down at the Place du Palais Royal and the New Louvre, and the rue de Rivoli already swarming with movement. His consciousness throbbed with premonitions of what the scene might mean to him at some future time. And so as the sailing date approached, he walked the Paris streets endlessly and haunted the galleries and arcades, storing up treasures of impressions that would keep him going until (as he remembered thinking) he "should somehow or other be able to scramble back."

PART II

Family Stories

CHAPTER FOUR

The Home Front

THE HOUSEHOLD ON KAY STREET

The family reached New York on a Monday morning in late September
(1860), after a tumultuous eleven-day crossing: bad weather, bad seas,
bad food, and bad service, according to the disgruntled Henry Senior.
By the following Sunday they were in Newport and occupying a house
at 13 Kay Street, at the head of Bull Street: a compact structure with
Gothic roofs and a little tower, a rustic lane with stables running alongside it. It served as the summer home of Colonel James McKaye, an
affable New York businessman, and the Jameses had in fact moved
into it for a number of months, from the winter onward, during the
previous Newport stay. McKaye's son Jim and William had become
very thick during that period; they were almost exactly the same age,
and at the time they shared an enthusiastic commitment to a career
in painting. As it turned out, Jim McKaye—as Steele MacKaye, dropping his first two names and respelling the last—would become famous
in the American theatrical world, as actor and playwright, and even
more as the inventor of special stage devices.

That friendship was renewed, as were others: with Tom or "Sargy"
Perry; and most propitiously for both William and Henry, with the
enormously gifted twenty-five-year-old John La Farge, whose first appearance as a student in Hunt's studio in the 1859 summer had caused
William to burst into exclamations about the amazing "new fellow":

"He knows everything. He has read everything. He has seen everything—paints everything. He's a marvel." The daily walks began again, along the cliffs, over to Paradise Rock and Purgatory Chasm; and— closer by and one of Henry's favorite places in the town—the richly stocked Redwood Library on upper Bellevue Avenue, superbly proportioned, invitingly graceful and quiet within, and already more than a century old.

Newport's hold on the family's affections increased steadily. There was not much in the way of year-round society among the older generation, but the locale was becoming popular as a summer resort, especially for New England families: that of Henry Senior's banker, Samuel Ward, and of others the young Jameses were slower to meet— Charles Eliot Norton, Longfellow, Julia Ward Howe. Newport could appeal to varying Jamesian predilections. For Henry Junior it was the one suitable place for persons, like themselves, who had been disjoined from the American setting by living for so long in Europe; in mysterious but appreciable ways it seemed to mediate between "Europe" and "America." But Newport also prided itself on belonging to the colony which first renounced allegiance to the British crown, having done so on May 4, 1776; which could gratify the elder James's established and young William's incipient Americanism.

William, Henry, and Alice set forth together of an autumn morning, walking a few blocks down Kay Street, across Bellevue Avenue and partway down Church Street. Here was the studio of William Morris Hunt, where Willy was taking up his art studies, with Harry tagging along to make his less determined artistic efforts. Here, too, was the small school run by Miss Rebecca Hunter and her widowed mother; Alice had attended it two years before, and now returned there. The school was remembered by one of Alice's classmates as a place of great refinement; and the obituary of Miss Hunter (after her apparent suicide in 1888) spoke of her training her pupils "in all the elevated thoughts, conduct, and duties of life." Alice's father seems to have been content with this regimen, though Alice, already something of an ironist, may have looked at it askance.

An equally characteristic side of Henry Senior was indicated by his disposal of the younger boys. Soon after the arrival in Newport, he and Mary accompanied Wilky and Bob by three-hour ferry and then carriage to Concord, Massachusetts, where the brothers were placed in the academy run by the enterprising Franklin B. Sanborn. (The school had been conducted in an earlier period by the Thoreau brothers, and had recently been reopened at Emerson's behest.) Sanborn had been associated with John Brown, whose ill-fated attack on the arsenal at Harpers Ferry, Virginia, had occurred the previous October and who had been hanged in December. On one occasion, Sanborn had fled to Canada, barely escaping the clutches of two U.S. marshals who had come to seize him in his own house, and he was still in danger of arrest. But the academy, under him, was earning a name for itself as a pioneering school, vocally abolitionist in sentiment and coeducational in makeup. Among the few boarding students in 1860 were two daughters of John Brown. Emerson's two daughters, Ellen and Edith, and his sixteen-year-old son, Edward, took classes there.

To his friend Mrs. Tappan, the elder James wrote that "I buried two of my children yesterday," leaving them at the school of "the famous Mr. Sanborn." (He did not add, as he might have, that Mr. Sanborn had for some years been an admirer of "Henry James's metaphysics," as expressed in *Putnam's Magazine*.) It had been a lovely fall day, with the maple, oak, and dogwood showing their colors; and James was pleased with the members of the small staff, especially the motherly Mrs. Clark, plain enough in outward features but "so tenderly feathered inwardly." The other teachers, by comparison, were so physically attractive that before the visit was over James had grown positively alarmed at the erotic temptations in store for his young ones.

"How it is going to be possible for my two boys to pursue their studies in the midst of that bewilderment I don't clearly see," he remarked to Mrs. Tappan. They went around to talk with Miss Waterman, a resident teacher, to express the hope that she would occasionally extinguish "any too lively spark she might see fall on the expectant tinder of my poor boys' bosoms." But Miss Waterman herself proved to be so delectable—"with round tender eyes, young, fair and womanly"—that James saw in her an additional danger. With only partially feigned consternation and carrying forward the incendiary figure so special for him, James claimed to anticipate a "general conflagration" which would end in "the total combustion of all that I hold dear on that spot." But his liberal spirit sought to rally itself by reflecting on the grand experiment in education the Sanborn school represented.

Leaving the academy, the Jameses drove over to the Emersons' house, where they found the front lawn smothered under fallen apples and pears. "The cordial Pan himself" was discovered in the midst of his household, ready with many soft exclamations of welcome. Age, the elder James thought, had just slightly dimmed Emerson's luster, but "an unmistakable breath of morning still encircles him, and the odour of primeval woods." So the visitors sat and consumed pears while Emerson discoursed with all his old eloquence, and Ellen and Edith sat quietly on stools in the chimney corner, hemming their handkerchiefs.

There was a last look-in at the academy and a mournful farewell to the boys. Sanborn gave the Jameses a tour of the coeducational living conditions, and during it Henry Senior experienced a vision not only of something better but so to say of something best: a "new world" where righteousness dwelled, preparing itself for his children and his children's children; and as he watched the two boys' eyes "drink in the mingled work and play of the inspiring scene," he could hardly keep from shouting out a *Nunc Dimittis*.

A friendship between the younger James boys and Edward Emerson grew apace, and Wilky and Bob were made free of the Emerson home. Thus it was that Wilky was present one afternoon when Emerson was chatting with an old friend and Harvard classmate George Partridge Bradford. Having come to know the James brothers, Emerson was curious about the sister: "And what sort of a girl is Alice?" he asked. Bradford replied somewhat stiffly: "She has a highly moral nature"; and at this Emerson, laughing, said: "How in the world does her father get on with her?" Wilky passed this on to Alice, who eventually jotted it down in her journal, pleased that Emerson had so perfectly understood her father's disrespect for the moral as against the religious nature.

Edward Emerson was in somewhat fragile condition that year, following a bout of typhoid fever, and the elder James thought the boy worked too hard at school. He was the more welcome when he came down to Newport with Wilky and Bob for the spring vacation in 1861. In a reminiscence of many decades later, Edward provided a telling and frequently quoted sketch of the James family in action:

"The adipose and affectionate Wilkie," as his father called him, would say something and be instantly corrected by the little cock-sparrow Bob, the youngest, but good-naturedly defend his statement, and then Henry (Junior) would emerge from his silence in defence of Wilkie. Then Bob would be more impertinently insistent, and Mr. James would advance as Moderator, and William, the eldest, join in. The voice of the Moderator presently would be drowned by the combatants and he soon came down vigorously into the arena, and when, in the excited argument, the dinner knives might not be absent from eagerly gesticulating hands, dear Mrs. James, more conventional, but bright as well as motherly, would look at me, laughingly reassuring, saying, "Don't be disturbed, Edward; they won't stab each other. This is usual when the boys come home." And the quiet little sister ate her dinner, smiling, close to the combatants.

It was here that the younger Emerson referred to the Irish element in the boys' mature and picturesque speech, and said that, even if they went astray in argument, "they saved themselves by wit."

In this scene, as sometimes elsewhere, one sees the Jameses acting themselves out in a family ensemble, each of the male figures taking up his prescribed role at the appointed moment—the affable Wilky starting the show, the brassy young Bob quickly rebutting, Henry brooding and then having his thoughtful say, William biding his time as the oldest son and coming in on cue; Father seeking to perform as play director, only to be shouted down with fond derision and forced to come into the skirmish as an equal; the final knife-waving climax. The two females, as well, give the impression of performing familiar parts as appreciative onlookers; Mother sedately non-participant, assured and reassuring; Alice a smiling, silent, attentive observer, keeping her counsel.

Early in the Newport autumn Henry Senior wrote to Edmund Tweedy, then in London with his wife, to announce the family's installation and to suggest that the Tweedys take the house next door on Kay Street, one of several belonging to the venerable Hazard clan; it would rent for $1,000 a year. The Tweedys arrived around the turn of the year, and with them were the four Temple girls.

The latter were the children of Catherine Margaret James, who was said to have been Henry Senior's favorite sister, and Colonel Robert Emmet Temple; there were two older brothers in addition. A darkly romantic aura hung over the Temples; there was a bad streak in them, according to one family source. Colonel Temple, a West Point graduate in the class of 1828, was briefly Adjutant General of the United States Army until, as it seems, he was implicated in an army scandal and was removed. His oldest son, Robert, was an intriguing scoundrel; "quite the most emphasised of all our wastrels," in Henry Junior's carefully chosen words: "the figure bristling most with every irregular accent that we were to find ourselves in any closeness of relation with." He had been sent to school in Scotland, where, surprisingly, he was converted to Roman Catholicism, and had wandered about Europe. He had a lively but wildly irregular mind, and expressed himself with gusto; we shall hear more of him, and of his postures and peccadilloes. His brother William Temple, always cordially received at Newport, was the most interesting of the Albany cousins for the young Jameses:

partly because he went first to Yale and then to Harvard, and partly because he was killed in battle at Chancellorsville.

The older Robert Temple and his wife, Catherine, died in 1854 within three months of each other; Henry Junior and his father, it may be remembered, were staying at Rhinebeck while Catherine was dying there. Meanwhile, Colonel Temple's older sister Mary had married Edmund Tweedy, after being courted by him assiduously in the Temple home on West Twelfth Street in New York. Mary had borne her husband three children (Henry Senior declared he had broken out champagne after the birth of the second child in August 1852), but all three had died of diphtheria in their infancy. By the time of their return to America and Newport, after a long sojourn in Europe, the Tweedys had arranged to take charge of the orphaned Temple girls: Katharine, seventeen; Mary, fifteen; Ellen, ten; and Henrietta. Mary Temple Tweedy was in her mid-fifties; and though she was in fact a cousin of sorts of the James children, she became from henceforth their "Aunt Mary."

Tom Perry noted in his diary on January 13, 1861, that he had that day in Newport been introduced by the Jameses to the Miss Temples; it was evidently at about that moment that they came to Newport under the Tweedys' wing and re-entered the life of the family. Among them, for William and Henry anyhow, Mary Temple, "Minny," was the one who "shone with the vividest lustre." Henry Junior evoked her with the tenderest and most admiring language at his command. She was possessed of "originality, vivacity, audacity, generosity"; she was spontaneous, and she was natural; she had beyond anyone the brothers had known "a felt interest in life." Minny Temple was indeed "the supreme case of a taste for life as life, as personal living." She was devoid of female earnestness, she was too unliteral and ironic for that. But she had "in her brief passage the enthusiasm of humanity—more, assuredly, than any charming girl who ever circled, and would fain have continued to circle, round a ballroom." She would be dead before her twenty-fifth birthday.

TRIALS OF ART

Even as William was starting to apply himself in the studio of William Morris Hunt, his father was surreptitiously asking Edmund Tweedy, by letter, to procure a "dissecting microscope" in one of the London stores—"Willy needs it and will be much obliged." But Willy had now diverted all his energies from science to art, presenting himself at

Church Street six mornings a week by ten o'clock and working ded-
icatedly for several hours, until Mrs. Hunt came in with a tray variously
laden with tea, wine, sandwiches, and Buckeye cakes. In the afternoons,
William often preferred to work out of doors, taking advantage of the
rare blend of Newport light and etching the shifting landscape and sea
views.

If it was a curious decision, in 1860, to come from France to
Newport in search of artistic training, the choice of William Hunt as
teacher was entirely plausible. Hunt was himself a mode of New England Parisian, having been born in Vermont, in 1824, and having
spent a decade in and near Paris as an apprentice painter. He came
first under the influence of Thomas Couture, a neoclassical painter of
some pictorial power with a restrained bent toward realism. But Hunt
grew disaffected from Couture's academic reverence for the past, and
by the late 1840s had discovered and allied himself with the new school
of Jean-François Millet, associated with the region of Barbizon, southeast of Paris. Hunt spent two years in Barbizon, dressing himself in a
peasant blouse and wooden shoes, and following Millet's lead in the
depiction of the attractions and miseries of life lived close to the soil.
After five more years in Paris, he came back to America, and in 1857
he settled with his young wife in Newport and began to function as a
teacher of painting—one of the first of that breed in the country.

Hunt's reputation, apart from being the one who introduced the
Barbizon School to America, began to be built on his distinction as a
painter of portraits (among others, of Chief Justice Lemuel Shaw,
Herman Melville's father-in-law). But he was an inspiring and invigorating teacher. Lean and muscular, with a high-bridged nose, glaring
eyes, and a long, luxuriant beard, Hunt possessed a personality that
was at once volatile, charming, and kind. He was endlessly free with
advice, suggestions, admonitions, some of which would have unmistakable cogency for William James: about the priority of feelings over
"duty" in painting ("Do as you feel—Hang duty"); about the sheer
importance of *doing* ("It's the doing of the thing that's important");
and especially about active as against passive observation (to the
wrongly inclined student: "Your eyes are windows through which you
receive impressions, keeping yourself as passive as warm wax, instead
of being active").

In the autumn of 1860, Hunt had only two full-time students
(Henry thought he recalled an earnest lady or two hovering and flitting),
William James and John La Farge. La Farge was married now to Tom
Perry's sister Margaret and, having passed through his own period of
vocational uncertainty (he had considered a legal career), was com-

mitted to the profession of art and was giving signs of immense potential. He served as a second *maître* for William and Henry James, a mediator between them and Hunt: not less because, as between Hunt's two French influences, La Farge was tending to favor the discredited Couture, even as he was characteristically fending off Hunt's pedagogical authority. For the young Jameses, at the same time, La Farge was Newport incarnate: he represented "Europe"—on the American scene, and he represented the American possibility in art. He had genuine French blood in his veins, his father having fled France during the Revolution; and although born and bred in New York City, he had spent stretches of time in Brittany, where he had a swarm of relatives, and in touring the museums in Europe.

La Farge and William worked close by one another of a morning in a studio on the second floor of the Church Street house; while Henry busied himself on the ground floor copying plaster casts—those of Hunt's sculptured figures, and of other sculptors past and present. But La Farge also took Henry with him on outings from time to time, and encouraged the seventeen-year-old's inadequate efforts with easel, palette, and canvas. Henry was to acknowledge a literary influence as well. He attributed his first acquaintance with *Revue des Deux Mondes*, with its sophisticated enchantments and news of the overseas cultural world, to La Farge. It was La Farge, the young man who (William had said) knew everything and had read everything, who drew Henry's attention to Browning, by showing the boy his illustrations of poems in *Men and Women*. Prosper Mérimée came into Henry's ken via La Farge; and so above all did the novels of Balzac.

There came a morning when Henry, giving over this attempt at cast-copying (Michelangelo's *The Captive* was the one he had worked at hardest), drifted upstairs to his brother's workplace. There he found his slender, red-headed, and much-liked young cousin Gus Barker, who was on a flying visit to Newport during a Harvard vacation, standing naked on a pedestal, modeling for William's pencil drawing of him.* It was Henry's first vision of a life model, and he remembered all his days how his personal artistic ambitions collapsed in an instant:

* Augustus Barker was the fifth and last child of the now long deceased Jennet James Barker, who had died giving birth to him in 1842. His aunt Anna Barker was married to Samuel Gray Ward. Henry Junior had a vivid recollection of visiting Gus Barker at his military school near Sing-Sing, and being taken on a tour of the state prison. A year after the incident here being recounted, Gus Barker enlisted in the New York Cavalry, where he became captain. On September 18, 1863, he was shot and killed by guerrillas near Kelly's Ford on the Rappahannock River in Virginia.

"so forced was I to recognise . . . that I might niggle for months over plaster casts and not come within miles of any such point of attack. The bravery of my brother's own in especial dazzled me out of every presumption." Then and there, Henry tells us, he put away his drawing pencil forever.

Henry James would seem, retrospectively, to give the late fall of 1860 as the time of clearly marked transition for him—from would-be painter to aspiring writer of fiction, comforted by the conviction, inculcated by John La Farge, that all the arts were essentially one. The process was certainly less coherent, less metaphorically exact than described; Henry, as we have conjectured, was probably scribbling bits of fiction for several years before the Newport season. But it was without question a long moment of decision, and one senses an air of relief, unmixed by regret, in Henry's no longer having to make a show of attempting something his brother did so demonstrably better.

William was indeed progressing well, under the shared tutelage of Hunt and La Farge. He was a superior draftsman, and while he took pleasure in dashing off sketches of his friends and family and had a nice flair for caricature, he was beginning to show real promise as a portrait painter. The oil portrait of Katharine Temple, the oldest of the sisters, is in every way—design and color, bend of head and slope of dark-clad back, intentness of facial expression—suggestive of burgeoning talent. The work was done at some time in early 1861, and within a month or so William had abandoned all plans for a career in art.

There has been a great deal of speculation about the causes and the implication of this seemingly sudden step. In Geneva, while looking forward to Newport, William had written a school friend, in French, that he would give the experiment with Hunt a year or two, to discover "whether I am suited to it or not. If not, it will be easy to withdraw. There is nothing on earth more deplorable than a bad artist."* The puzzle, of course, is that William was showing signs of becoming an extremely good artist.

Unlike Henry, William never composed a full-scale late-in-life autobiography in which he could, in thoughtful retrospect, trace his

---

* The original passage is somewhat tricky. In the final phrase, William's word for "bad" was *"méchant"* (rather than *"mauvais"*), which usually carried a moral connotation—as though, half echoing his father, William were speaking of the danger of becoming "a wretch of an artist." *"Déplorable,"* in addition, can mean "painful," or even "pain-inflicting." But it is hard to know how far William, by 1860, had mastered the nuances of French speech.

development through the formative years. The bulk of his correspondence does not really begin until the latter part of 1861; for the whole
previous era, we get at him through a scattering of letters, and through
the memories and assessments of his brother Henry and other family
members and friends like Tom Perry and Edward Emerson. We cannot
feel as intimate with the youthful William as—with proper provisos—
we do with Henry. In this matter of a career in art, we have, directly
from William, only stray bits of inconclusive evidence. He seems, for
example, to have remarked once to his son Billy, after the latter was
actually launched as a professional painter, that William Morris Hunt
had sought to dissuade him from going on with his apprenticeship on
the grounds that, in an America that did not value painters, the vocation
went unrewarded. So Billy James, perhaps half a century later, told
William's biographer, Gay Wilson Allen; but in a still later perspective,
this sounds more like a comment on Hunt himself, and the melancholy
which led to his apparent suicide (in 1879), than on William's decision.

In a footnote to the chapters on "Imagination" in *The Principles
of Psychology*, William offered the following: "I am myself a good
draughtsman, and have a very lively interest in pictures, statues, architecture and decoration, and a keen sensibility to artistic effects. But
I am an extremely poor visualizer, and find myself often unable to
reproduce in my mind's eye pictures which I have most carefully examined." It is an interesting disclosure; but it has to do primarily with
William's capacity not to paint pictures himself but to recall to his
inner eye the paintings of others.

Given Henry Senior's maneuvering at earlier moments, one may
well suspect some intensified paternal pressure to detach William from
art. It must be said, however, that there is no hard evidence at all to
support such a suspicion. Henry Junior, indeed, was altogether clear
in his own mind that Father's participation in William's career experiments was a consistent hostility to *any* final choice, as being in the
nature of things narrowing. Father was invariably uneasy, Henry recalled, in the presence of some particular successful filial activity, exactly because it "dispensed with any suggestion of an alternative. What
we were to do instead," Henry heard his father saying, "was just to *be*
something, something unconnected with specific doing, something free
and uncommitted, something finer in short than being *that*, whatever
it was, might consist of." Henry Senior fully apprehended William's
"other genius," for science, the younger Henry wrote; nonetheless, as
William in the years following moved on through chemistry, physiology, and medicine to psychology and philosophy, "*malaise* at every

turn characteristically betrayed itself, each of these surrenders being, by the measure of them in the parental imagination, so comparatively narrowing." In the same way, Henry's "surrender" to fiction writing was, the father would imply, unnecessarily restrictive.*

The reader today, amid our contemporary principles and prejudices, may of course find the young Henry's statement of the case rather bland; may feel that, however devoted Henry Senior was as a father, he seemed bent, through the years of uprooting, on manipulating and often frustrating his children, most of all his firstborn. Yet by almost any reckoning the long-range consequences for William of the paternal attitude were greatly beneficial. Through it all William, as F. O. Matthiessen has said, gained "flexibility and resilience, qualities without which modern man can scarcely exist." More: the experience led to William's perceiving flexibility and resilience as key ingredients of human thought and conduct. It led to a philosophy uniquely open to the pragmatics of life; to the *varieties* of human experience, religious and otherwise. It led to a mode of thinking, imagining, and expressing which habitually drew on art *and* chemistry, literature *and* electronics, religion *and* history; not to mention the different English, French, and German ways of organizing experience in language.

In the shorter run, however, the consequences were undeniably grave ones, though again it is not easy to sort out cause and effect. The first of the physical and psychic troubles that would plague William for years to come occurred in Newport at some time in 1861: nervous indigestion, to start with, and perhaps eye strain. The latter ailment could have ruled out any systematic attempt at painting, at least out-of-doors in the glinting Newport light; the former, with other aggravations, would in effect hinder William's settling on any career at all for a decade. As would gradually become apparent, the radiantly self-confident young figure of the Geneva gatherings had, within a year or so, turned into a troubled and, behind the engaging exterior, an uncertain individual. The changes of direction which had been so much to Henry's liking and benefit were serving, at last, to undermine in

---

* This view of Henry Senior's character and his role in William's vocational difficulties has been challenged, vigorously and at length, by Howard Feinstein in *Becoming William James* (1984). Professor Feinstein argues that, "despite his liberal protestations," the elder James "was determined to force William into science, no matter how strongly his son felt a painter's calling"; and that the father feigned a serious illness and threatened suicide to bring William to heel. The indictment is a powerful one, and in my view transects the historical reality at several major points. Finally, though, it seems to me a fascinating but fundamental misreading.

William any sense of his essential self. It was just this distraught individual, one may hazard, who decided not to go any longer to William Hunt's studio.

There is one other event that may have been a factor: the outbreak of hostilities between the Confederate States and the Union on April 12, 1861. Whether it bore directly on William's decision, it at least provided a dramatic context and occasion for making an important, even a crucial, change in his personal life.

THE ONSET, 1861

Those hostilities began, of course, when Southern batteries surrounding the Union outpost of Fort Sumter in the harbor at Charleston, South Carolina, opened a bombardment which forced the fort to surrender after thirty-six hours. On the fifteenth of the month, President Abraham Lincoln, who had been in office less than six weeks, issued a call for 75,000 volunteers to expand a Federal Army which at the time consisted of no more than 15,000 professional troops, most of them scattered about in remote military installations.

Two and a half months later, on the pleasant morning of July 4, Henry James, Sr., joined a procession of various companies, societies, and civic leaders making its way to Trinity Church, on Newport's Spring Street. There, after both Rhode Island and the nation had been saluted in patriotic song, prayers had been intoned, and the Declaration of Independence read aloud, the elder James delivered the annual Fourth of July address by invitation of the town's Committee of Arrangements. President Lincoln had called Congress into a special session, to begin that very day, and toward the close of his oration, peering down from the triple-decked wineglass pulpit at the packed congregation, James took notice of the fact. "How jealously should we watch the Congress today assembling in Washington!" And the "watchword" that he sent to the nation's capital was "We value the Republic so much, only because we value man more; that we value peace, prosperity and wealth not as ends, but as means to an end, which is justice truth and mercy."

James called his address "The Social Significance of Our Institutions," and it was his most spirited public performance. It opened with a diatribe against America's rich men, as a way of denying the prevalent assumption that what the country could be most proud of was the opportunity it offered for the acquisition of great wealth. Not so, James said. In Europe, wealth might be associated with refinement and the cultivation of the arts; but in America, "every one knows . . . how meagre and mean and creeping a race we permit our rich men to be." There was more of the same, with the ghost of James's father, the Albany millionaire—who said much the opposite at the opening of the Erie Canal—once again being flayed by the resentful and disapproving son.

What America *should* take pride in, James proposed, was its hospitality to all human beings of whatever condition. This was something Europeans could never understand—and he took off after the English literary class, "the purblind piddling mercenaries of literature, like Dickens," who scorned the native generosity in their stupid failure to see that what America honored was not so much individual *persons* but men; or rather, the manhood inherent in every man.

It was in that reverence for the commonly shared manhood, James would have it, that there could be located the true *social* significance of our institutions; for the term "social" (we have heard him saying so) had to do exactly with the sentiment of human brotherhood, of fellowship. Henry Senior then offered two homely and contrasting examples to convey his meaning. One came from the London winter of 1855–56, when James, as he told his closely attentive listeners, used to ride down to the city from St. John's Wood every morning in the omnibus, along with his immediate neighbors, men of business and professional men.

Very nice men, to use their own lingo, they were, for the most part; tidy, unpretending, irreproachable in dress and deportment; men in whose truth and honesty you would confide at a glance; and yet, after eight months' assiduous bosom solicitation of their hardened stolid visages, I never was favored with the slightest overture to human intercourse from one of them. I never once caught the eye of one of them.

To be sure, neither did his fellow passengers ever look at one another; at the slightest eye contact, James declared, "an instant film would surge up . . . just as a Newport fog suddenly surges up from the cold remorseless sea, and wrap the organ in the dullest, fishiest, most disheartening of stares." For a lover of omnibuses, it was very discouraging, and James concluded that the English were simply the worst-mannered people in Christendom.

The Newport *Mercury*, in its extensive coverage of the Trinity Church gathering, thought Mr. James's address to have been "a masterly production showing deep thought," but the language used about England and the English was "unnecessarily harsh."

For his second example, James went back to an earlier memory, when the family was living at the Astor House in New York. At table one evening, a hotel guest from Cape Cod, a complete stranger, asked Henry Senior if he might put the superfluous fat from his own plate onto that of Mr. James lest it be wasted. The *Mercury* reporter seemed bemused by the speaker's offering this anecdote as a gesture of Independence Day patriotism.

From this, James moved to the attack upon slavery, here offering views that the *Mercury* could only applaud and which were warmly received by the assembly. He emphasized to begin with that the Declaration did not claim that all men were *born* equal, which would be absurd: "for it is notorious that they are born under the greatest conceivable inequalities." What the Declaration said was that men are *created* equal: "That is, all are equal before God, or claim no superior merit one to another in his sight, being all alike dependent upon his power." A dozen years of socioreligious thinking along with a still-evolving theory of the phenomenon of divine creation led to his powerful statement.

What was it that had gone wrong since that inspired moment when the American people expressed itself in the Declaration of Independence? What had turned Americans "from an erect sincere hopeful and loving brotherhood of men intent upon universal aims, into a herd of greedy luxurious swine, into a band of unscrupulous political adventurers and sharpers?" It was slavery: *this* was the poison which had lurked in the American body politic from the outset. Of late years, James contended, the poison had pervaded the very heart of the American commonwealth: "until at last," he said, letting himself go in a crescendo of vituperation, "we find shameless God-forsaken men, holding high place in government, become so rabid with its virus as to mistake its slimy purulent ooze for the ruddy tide of life, and commend its foul and fetid miasm as the fragrant breath of assured health."

Inevitably, Henry Senior perceived some causes for hope. The great current crisis, he proposed, far from being some sort of terrible mischance, "as unprincipled politicians would represent it," was in fact a moment of grand transition in the national society, the native state of being: "from youth to manhood, from appearance to reality, from passing shadow to deathless substance." He saw in the future "an ever-widening sense of human unity . . . freer bonds of intercourse and fellowship." This was hardly the language of historians; but the elder James's brand of meta-historical poetry had carried him once again into the region where vast historical truths might at least be sought for.

In "the soft spring of '61," Henry Junior was to report, at the same time as the firing on Fort Sumter and Mr. Lincoln's first call for volunteers, he himself had suffered at Newport a physical mishap which was to bedevil him for an incalculable time to come. The evening accident occurred in the space of twenty minutes, during which, jammed into the acute angle between two high fences and working a rusty hand fire engine in order to play the hose on a "shabby conflagration," Henry gave himself "a horrid even if an obscure hurt." In the following summer, he went up to Boston with his father to be examined by a distinguished surgeon; the latter rather made light of the damage done, even pooh-poohing it; and there, wrote Henry, the "sad business" ended.

Leon Edel, in an exemplary act of scholarly investigation, has set most of the facts straight in this selective reminiscence. The conflagration occurred not in the spring but on the evening of October 28, 1861; it could hardly be called "shabby," being a raging fire that swept from the stable of Charles B. Tennant (in the Cliff Walk area, half a dozen blocks from the Jameses' house) some little distance to the stable of John West, destroying a carpenter's shop en route, razing one private home and endangering another. Young Henry James was apparently one of a number of volunteer fire fighters who pumped the several wells for all they were worth. As to the obscure hurt, Professor Edel marshals strong evidence that it was some species of back injury—"a slipped disc, a sacroiliac or muscular strain"—by which indeed Henry James would be plagued on and off for most of his life. The diagnosis has been contested; debate over this, the most famous injury in American literary history, seems not to be slackening.

The painful incident had an almost uncanny family aspect to it. Young Henry James may or may not have known about the nocturnal occasion when his grandfather feverishly worked the pumps on the Albany wharf in a dangerous and unsuccessful effort to save his shops from being gutted by fire. But his father's cork leg was a daily reminder of the catastrophe that befell Henry Senior when *he* attempted to put out a stable fire. Beyond that, Henry Junior, through powerful turns of rhetoric, associated his own mishap with the still greater and more consequential horror his father had experienced in the Windsor of 1844, and with the paternal doctrine that came out of it. And doing so, he simultaneously associated the hurt and the horror with the sufferings being undergone by other youths within the larger human family, on the Civil War battlefields.

What happened to him in those twenty terrible minutes, Henry wrote some fifty years later, "kept company . . . with my view of what was happening, with the question of what might still happen, to everyone about me, to the country at large: it so made of these marked disparities a single vast visitation." That phrase of course is a sort of stammering version (the younger Henry, like his father, had an intermittent attractive stammer) of the Swedenborgian term "vastation" (itself, as well, a spectral "visitation"). Much meditation on his personal nightmare, it can be remembered, had brought the elder James to his conviction about the primacy of the *social*: of the redemptive sentiment of human brotherhood. His son, similarly ruminating, arrived at a dramatist's version of the paternal motif:

One had the sense . . . of a huge comprehensive ache, and there were hours at which one could scarce have told whether it came most from one's own poor organism, still so young and so meant for better things, but which had suffered particular wrong, or from the enclosing social body, a body rent with a thousand wounds and that thus treated one to the honour of a sort of tragic fellowship.

In dating his injury at the very moment that the Civil War got under way, Henry James might seem to be explaining covertly why he had not leaped to arms at the presidential summons. But the tone throughout the section is much less that of guilt and self-exculpation than of regret that he, Henry James, had been able to participate only vicariously in the great national experience. And whatever else the misadventure brought about, it instilled in the younger Henry a deep feeling of kinship with the wounded life—in his fictional writings, with Ralph Touchett and Morgan Moreen and Milly Theale, and many another less conspicuous character.

GESTURES FROM HARVARD

As in the early stages of most large-scale modern wars, there was an aura of unreality, a mixture of the stagy and the dreamlike, during the first year of the war. On July 21, 1861, at Manassas, Virginia, twenty miles south of Washington, a large horde of civilians turned out with picnic hampers to watch the Northern infantry regiments engage the Confederate troops, expecting to cheer as the Northerners crossed Bull Run Creek, smashed through the enemy lines, and began the drive to Richmond and a swift end to the struggle. Instead of that, the Union forces were put to rout and the fleeing soldiers were chaotically tangled with the panic-stricken spectators as the latter tumbled into their carriages and made an undignified dash back to the federal capital. The savage battle at Shiloh, Tennessee, the following April of 1862—when the Union under General Grant won what it claimed as a major victory and lost thirteen thousand men—may be taken as the point at which the war became seen on both sides as deadly and long-enduring.

Life on the home front, however, was not quickly or visibly transformed. As late as the summer of 1862, when Ellen and Edith Emerson came to Newport to stay with the Jameses and make the long-delayed acquaintance of Alice James, they were put through leisurely and agreeable rituals of strolling along the cliffs, playing croquet, listening to the band, swimming ("the best time that I almost ever did have in the water," Ellen wrote home), observing the white-frocked ladies parading along Ocean Drive in their carriages. The Emerson girls went sailing in Bob James's little boat, the *Alice*, with Willy and "the real Alice," docking at the northerly village of Portsmouth, where they took their lunch near a pair of waterfalls. The chief novelty of the scene, and the only sign of the heroic and terrible events going on at a remote distance, was a military hospital which had been set up in Portsmouth Grove. Edith, Ellen, and fourteen-year-old Alice, with two other female companions, circled around the groups of convalescing soldiers (with their "good and interesting faces") for a protracted period, in the unfulfilled hope of starting up a conversation with some of them.

So it had been quite natural for William James to have been more absorbed in the question of his education than in the thought of military service—from which he was evidently exempted on medical grounds, in any case. In the early fall of 1861, William entered Lawrence Scientific School at Harvard. (Wilky was back at school in Concord. Rob, disaffected from Sanborn's institution, was at home in Newport, as were Henry and Alice.) The school had been founded a few years earlier by a substantial bequest from Abbot Lawrence, a wealthy textile manufacturer and Newport neighbor of the Jameses; by 1861, its stellar attraction was Louis Agassiz, the Swiss-born professor of zoology and geology, a flamboyant genius whose Museum of Zoology would become one of Harvard's chief centers of study. Students at Lawrence followed their particular scientific bent. William opted for chemistry, and with a dozen other students was placed under the direction of Charles W. Eliot, the new head of the chemistry laboratory, and the future president of the university. "I don't believe he is a *very* accomplished chemist," William said of Eliot in a letter to his mother.*

That attitude of skepticism, often wittily expressed, recurred in other communications to the family. Before many weeks were out, William was announcing his intention of completing the year in chemistry and then taking off for at least a semester at home.

The fact was, William was still at sixes and sevens, as the saying went, about his place in life. He had made a decision of sorts in coming to Lawrence, but he was not prepared to rejoice in it. If he retained doubts about the scientific career, he was even less captivated by the study of chemistry. In addition to this, and perhaps as a result of it, he was almost achingly homesick. In a September letter to Harry, he admitted that "I haven't for one minute had the feeling of being at home here." "Here" was Harvard, and it was also his lodgings with the Pascoe family in their home not far from the university campus. William's account of it made it seem gloomy; but he spoke more cheerily about Miss Upham's, at Oxford and Kirkland Streets, where he took his meals. He ate in a dark aristocratic dining room, he wrote, and a tall black-eyed Juno of a handmaid called out the abundant menu as the guests came to their seats. Miss Upham served up delicious pies and cakes, but there was "no well-stored pantry like that at good old 13 Kay Street." Among the other boarders was Francis J. Child of the Harvard English department, a fellow of considerable jest, and an able scholar of Spenser.

In the first weeks, William visited the post office several times a day, and in mentioning this to the family he drew two caricatures of himself: in the first, stalking to the P.O. with so hopeless a look on his college-boy face that women and children shied away as he passed; in the second, emerging with a letter and making such wildly happy gestures that a big crowd gathered about him and followed him to his lodgings. He spent the fall looking forward to Newport over Thanksgiving; but he passed Christmas (a spare holiday in the New England of the time, Harvard giving its students only a single day) in Cambridge.

---

* The remark would be partly echoed in a much-quoted comment by the philosopher Alfred North Whitehead, upon the appointment as president of Harvard of James Bryant Conant. A reporter asked Whitehead for his reaction and Whitehead could only lament: "A chemist! Imagine a *chemist* the president of Harvard!" "But, sir," the reporter said, "President Eliot was a chemist." "Yes," said Whitehead sadly, "but he was a very *bad* chemist."

The Home Front

December 25, that year, was a sharp cold day, with the temperature hovering near zero, snow threatening, and the streets covered with glare ice. William put in several hours sliding and slipping about town with his cousin Lily Barker (Gus Barker's sister), delivering presents to her friends, and in the afternoon he dropped off some small gifts of his own. Then, after Wilky made his appearance, having trudged over from Concord, William, sitting in front of the fire while the snow fell outside, wrote at length to the family:

Many times and bitterly to-day have I thought of home and lamented that I should have to be away at this merry Christmastide from my rare family; wondering, with Wilky, if they were missing us as we miss them . . . I see in vision those at home just going in to dinner; my aged, silvered Mother leaning on the arm of her stalwart yet flexible H., merry and garrulous as ever, my blushing Aunt with her old wild beauty still hanging about her, my modest Father with his rippling raven locks, the genial auld Rob and the mysterious Alice, all rise before me, a glorified throng; but two other forms, one tall, intellectual, swarthy, with curved nose and eagle eye, the other having breadth rather than depth, but a goodly morsel too, are wanting to complete the harmonious whole.

Henry Junior, who quoted the passage among a good many others from William's early Harvard days, in *Notes of a Son and Brother*, remarked on the "endless spontaneity of mind" that it displayed, and on William's delight in attributing to the family members features close to the opposite of their real ones. Father, for example, had no locks left to ripple, raven or otherwise; Mother, at fifty, was neither aged nor silvered; young Bob was going through a surly period; and as to Alice's "mystery," it "consisted all in the candour of her natural bloom, even if at the same time of her lively intelligence." By the same reckoning, Henry feared, the adjectives about him, "merry and garrulous," might mean that he struck William at times as mildly morose or anxiously mute. (In an earlier similar letter, William had referred to Henry's "babbling confidingness" of talk; no one, it may be supposed, babbled or confided less.*) William's self-portrait, in the letter, transforms a slender and slightly turned-up nose into an aquiline one, and in effect

* This pre-Thanksgiving letter is adorned with a sketch of the six Newport members of the family standing in a row with linked arms. The pleasant conceit of the drawing is that all of them have their heads covered: Father by a top hat, Mother and Aunt Kate by matronly bonnets, Henry with a pork-pie, Bob—who stands scowling to one side, hands plunged into his pockets—with a school cap, and Alice with what looks like a Russian fur hat, slanting leftward and twice as large as her little head.

restores to his face the short-lived mustache he had recently removed. Wilky's lack of depth, Henry implies, was an allusion to his mental powers; for the rest, Wilky's tubbiness was a family joke.

Family visits were the peak moments of the academic autumn. Wilky walked in periodically from the Sanborn school. "His plump corpusculus looks as always," William told the family; but concealed his pleasure in a series of mock-complaints. Wilky had been "nothing but disaster since he has been here, breaking down my good resolutions about eating, keeping me from any intellectual exercise, ruining my best hat," and so on. In December, William was "electrified by Robby's coming down on me today when I did not at all expect him." Even a chance encounter in a Boston theater with the Albany cousin Robert Temple was a welcome diversion. William found him more peculiar than ever, offering violently pro-slavery opinions and talking in the most extraordinary way about "the wickedness of human society." William would have liked to have seen more of him.

Perhaps the happiest occasion of the season, for William, was the arrival in November of his brother Harry. "The radiance of H.'s visit has not faded yet," William wrote afterward, "and I come upon gleams of it three or four times a day in my farings to and fro." He instantly slid into the teasing mood: "H. could in no wise satisfy my craving for knowledge of family and friends—he didn't seem to have been on speaking terms with anyone for some time past . . . He is a good soul, though, in his way."

William's letters and messages to his sister, Alice, from Cambridge, had (as Henry reread them) a special element of "affectionate pleasantry." A couple of weeks before Christmas, he asked the family to "tell Alice that I saw the Emerson girls and that they were perfectly wild, crazy, to have her come to Concord." Alice could divide a week between the Emersons, another family kin, and himself.

I would take splendid care of her, and would take most lofty pride in promenading the streets of Boston with her the observed of all observers for manly strength and beauty and for feminine grace and gentility.

The Emersons' invitation led to the first recorded instance when Alice James grew so excited by some prospect that she lost control of herself. Henry Senior told Emerson that he had encouraged "the palpitating Alice" to make the trip to Concord "at any expense of health," and at this she became wrought up to such a degree that it was all

Mary could do to calm her down and put her to bed. The visit was canceled. Henry Senior tried to comfort her by assorted conversational extravagances; but he feared, as he admitted, that "the tears still trickle in solitude." In the summer following, as we have seen, the Emerson girls came to Newport for a much enjoyed stay with Alice.

There was a similar but less devastating moment in March 1862, as we learn from William's letter of the period. "Charmante jeune fille, I find the Tappans [Boston friends of the family] *really* expected me to bring you to them and were much disappointed at my failure . . . I hope your neuralgia, or whatever you may believe the thing was, has gone and that you are back at school instead of languishing and lolling about the house." (William's way of addressing his sister did not always strike the right note, as it seems to do here.) He urged her to write him as often as she could; her letters did him more good, he vowed, than she could ever imagine.

Alice was a faithful enough correspondent, but in one of his sprightliest compositions William pretended that she never wrote a line, except to demand expensive presents. This letter is entirely in French, moving between the classic and the vernacular. "Est-ce-que tu songes jamais à moi comme moi je songe à toi?" it began; "—oh je crois bien que non!" Many times a day an image of her as an angel dressed in white comes to his ravished senses. "Eh, oua, oua, oua! c'est à faire mourir de douleur." He was miserable and unloved; *she* never wrote him, "La vaste mère me déteste, il n'y a que le frère qui me reste attaché, et lui par esprit d'opposition plus que par autre chose."*

At the start of the second term, William changed rooms from those of the depressing Pascoe family to that of the weird Sweetser household on Trowbridge Street. It was, he said, a family worthy of Dickens. Mr. Sweetser was a widower who sat all day in the bathroom clad in a dressing gown and smoking his pipe. His sister, Miss Sweetser, shook like an aspen whenever she was spoken to. The three Sweetser girls were given to gushing and to darting out of sight on William's appearance. The other guest was a woman who had gone out of her wits after her husband abandoned her and went to Cuba; the Sweetsers were tending to her. She had a marrow-chilling habit of lurking outside

---

* "Do you ever dream of me as I dream of you?—oh, I am sure not! . . . Oh, yeah, yeah, yeah, it's enough to make me die of grief." (*Oua* was a Swiss slang perversion of *Oui.*) "The large mother detests me, only my brother remains attached to me, and he more by spirit of opposition than anything else." The phrase *la vaste mère* puns romantically on *la vaste mer.*

the door of William's bedroom, whispering hoarsely, *"Gulielmo . . . Gulielmo."*

"Affectionate old papas like me," Henry Senior wrote a friend, seemingly in the summer of 1861, "are scudding all over the country to apprehend their patriotic offspring, and restore them to the harmless embraces of their mamas." As for himself, he had for several days been keeping "a firm grasp upon the coat tails of my Willy and Henry, who both vituperate me beyond measure because I won't let them go"— that is, to war. "The coats are a very staunch material, or the tails must have been off two days ago, the scamps pull so hard."

This latter statement is unconfirmed by any other source and, in fact, is distinctly implausible. William and Henry may conceivably have expressed a desire to join the Union Army, but it would have been a passing one, unmixed by vituperation and exaggerated by Father in order to bolster the image of manliness among the male siblings. The boys had also, no doubt, listened to their father set forth his position on the matter, as he explained it in the same letter:

The way I excuse my paternal interference to them is, to tell them, first, that no existing government, nor indeed any now possible government, is worth an honest human life and a clean one like theirs; especially if that government is likewise in danger of bringing back slavery again under our banner: than which consummation I would rather see chaos itself come again.

This was in keeping with the Fourth of July oration, which James had concluded by hurling the direst threats at Mr. Lincoln and Mr. Seward should they "make the least conceivable further concession to the obscene demon of slavery." The elder James was an ardent *theoretical* abolitionist, but not much of an activist for any cause.

There was another point to the fatherly counsel. "I tell them that no young American should put himself in the way of death, until he has realized something of the good of life; until he has found some charming conjugal Elizabeth or other to whisper his devotion to, and assume the task, if need be, of keeping his memory green." By this curious reasoning, only married Northerners would have gone to battle.

Henry Senior's stated policy may have provided intellectual comfort to the older boys, and especially to William as he wincingly saw one after another of his Harvard classmates drop out of college and join up. But the policy yielded with little struggle when it came to the younger brothers. On September 12, 1862, Wilky, seventeen years old, was not only permitted to enlist; one has the sense that he was paternally hustled when his father accompanied him to the recruiting station. He joined the 44th Massachusetts Regiment, then forming in Boston; while it was being put together, the recruits drilled twice a day on the Boston Common, where William could come in from Harvard to watch. Some fraction of Henry Senior's change of posture may perhaps have been due to the drastic change in the national and local atmosphere in the wake of the mutual slaughtering at Shiloh in April.

Ten months later, in mid-June 1863, Bob James, not yet seventeen, enlisted in the 55th Massachusetts Regiment, the second of two black regiments which had been recently formed in the state (Wilky, by this time, having transferred to the other black regiment, the 54th). It cost him a heartbreak, the elder James wrote Elizabeth Palmer Peabody, "to part with one so young on a service so hard." But he could not but "adore the great Providence which is thus lifting our young men out of indolence and vanity, into some free sympathy with His own deathless life . . . I seem never to have loved the dear boy before, now that he is clad with such an aureole of Divine beauty and innocence."

Behind those religious vapors, which show Henry Senior at his mentally least prehensile, there is the implication that Bob himself had been leading a vain and frivolous life; and so he had. But there had arrived in the family story the time when Wilky and Bob had become the leaders, the examples, the ones who were loved and missed. In a manner of speaking, they had become the older brothers.

CHAPTER FIVE

The Younger Brothers
in War and Peace

A NORTH CAROLINA CAMPAIGN

"To me, in my boyish fancy," Wilky James would tell a Milwaukee audience twenty years later, "going to the war seemed glorious indeed." In Company F of the 44th Massachusetts Infantry Regiment, lodged at Revere House in Boston, he found himself drilling alongside a batch of Harvard students, a contingent of hymn-singing Methodists, some tradespeople, and a few lawyers and architects. After a few weeks of this, he was, to his memory, "a strange youth in a strange land, equipped for battle, and eager for the start of my regiment to the seat of war." The start occurred on October 22 (1862), when the regiment departed by ship for the battle area, the elder James coming down to the Boston harbor to bid his son farewell. The 44th was transported to New Bern in east central North Carolina, at the mouth of the river Neuse, and within three days it came under fire.

After that first action, a mild set-to near New Bern, the regiment was subjected to a succession of long and hurried marches, heading generally westward amid continuing snow and rain; a ten-day campaign along the Neuse valley with the ultimate aim of destroying the strategically important railway bridge at Goldsboro. "We march 20 or 30 miles," Wilky wrote home, "and find the enemy entrenched in riflepits or hidden away in some out-of-the-way place; we send our artillery forward, and after a brisk skirmish ahead the foe is driven back into the woods, and we march on for 20 miles more to find the same luck." After dark, in the inclement North Carolina weather, the soldiers collected strips of rail fence and made fires. Wilky and the others sat near the blaze and made coffee in their tin dippers; the coffee and the hardtack being consumed, they spread out their rubber blankets and slept as soundly, Wilky declared, as any family in Christendom. At five in the morning, "the fearful reveillé" called them all to their feet; they brewed coffee and gulped it down, slung on their knapsacks, and went spanking down the road, as Wilky put it, "in one of Foster's regular old quicksteps." Major-General John G. Foster was the veteran commander of the Federal forces in North Carolina.* The sight of his headquarters campfires lighting up the sky four miles ahead, one chilly evening, was for Wilky James a most encouraging spectacle. "I assure you those miles were soon got over. I think Willy's artistic eye would have enjoyed the sight—it seemed so as if the world were on fire."

The soldiers of the 44th were an uncomplaining lot: the best-natured, General Foster said, of all his troops. The ever-gregarious Wilky James was altogether at home amid the comradeship and the enlivening danger: his peculiarly sociable nature had found the perfect situation in which to put into practice Henry Senior's views about human fellowship. Indeed, in his eighteenth year Wilky was markedly coming to himself as an individual and as a James; he was exercising *his* way of self-declaration, a way not shared and not even fully comprehended by any other member of the family. In some part of him, Wilky knew this, and it helps account for the remarkable tone of his letters home in the autumn of 1862 and the winter of 1863. With their vivacity and expressiveness, their steady good humor under most arduous circumstances, their richness of visual and physical detail, their sheer zest for life and living, they are, one might almost say, Wilky's contribution to the family's literary achievement.

The young man who had hitherto shown such an aversion to reading books could now be observed, on rest periods between marches, reading Victor Hugo's *Les Misérables* and returning more than once to the narrative account of the battle of Waterloo. There was a new assurance in Wilky's attitudes and judgments. Following "Divine Service" in the barracks one wintry Sunday morning, Wilky wrote the family about the chaplain's sermon, a diatribe against profanity. Hav-

* In this small campaign, General Foster had at his disposal 10,000 infantry, 40 pieces of artillery, and 640 cavalry.

ing delivered it, Wilky said, the chaplain sat down, "credulous being, thinking he had settled the question for ever." Colonel Frank Lee, the regimental leader, then arose. "I hope to God I have wounded no man's feelings by an oath," Wilky quoted him as saying; "if I have I humbly beg his pardon." Wilky heard himself saying afterward, in despite of the chaplain: "Let him swear to all eternity if he *is* that sort of man, and if profanity makes such, for goodness' sake let us all swear."

Wilky's interior fortitude was obviously reflected in his military performance; he was soon promoted to corporal and by mid-December was a sergeant. On December 14, he took part, with the regiment, in an engagement of some intensity near Kinston, about forty miles inland from New Bern. The 44th deployed in an open field, and Wilky's wing was ordered to move forward to support an artillery unit. On they went, with shells and bullets whizzing over their heads in what Wilky described as the longest half mile of his life. But when they charged down the field "in a manner creditable to any Waterloo legion," Wilky also felt it to be the greatest moment of his existence, and as if "all the devils of the Inferno" were milling about him.* The entire regiment had been seized with a kind of manic exuberance, and the air was filled with their yelling and howling. "So far I was alive and the thing had lasted perhaps 3 hours . . . I don't think Sergeant G.W. has ever known greater glee in all his born days."

That night the regiment went on a wild looting spree: "molasses, pork, butter, cheese and all sorts of different delicacies being foraged for"; houses entered and searched with no minimal show of civility; others "set on fire to show Kinston was our own." In a suddenly somber mood, Wilky remarked: "This is the ugly part of war. A too victorious army soon goes down." Luckily, the 44th had little time for "big demoralisation"; the very next day they marched seventeen miles to a spot near Whitehall, a small village on the Neuse, where the bloodiest episode in the small campaign took place.

The tactic in this instance had the regiment dashing down one field into another under heavy Confederate fire, then taking cover behind a rail fence on the riverbank, kneeling or lying prone, and firing at will till the early afternoon. There were eight killed and thirteen wounded in the fracas, but Wilky welcomed the encounter. The eruption of a fight meant a temporary end to marching and a chance to

---

* The Confederate force, under General N. G. Evans, consisted of not much more than 2,000 troops, from North Carolina and South Carolina units; but in the confusion, the Federal artillery fired on their own ranks.

throw down knapsacks. "I don't pretend I am eager to make friends with bullets," Wilky wrote, "but at Whitehall after marching some 20 miles, I was on this account really glad when I heard cannonading ahead and the column was halted and the fight began."

For the third day in a row, General Foster ordered the 44th into action (with four other regiments), at a point just below the village of Goldsboro, eighteen miles beyond Whitehall. The troops, under heavy fire, managed to destroy the railroad bridge across the Neuse. There was hard fighting for several days; but a huge Confederate reinforcement was rumored to be approaching, and General Foster withdrew all his units and returned by December 23 to New Bern.

At the year's end, Wilky, thoroughly battle-experienced, passed along to the folks on the home front his acquired wisdom about the character of men at war. "All we want is numbers!" he insisted. "*They* are the greatest help to the individual soldier on the battle-field. If he feels he has 30,000 men behind him pushing on steadily to back him he is in much more fighting trim than when away in the rear with 10,000 ahead of him fighting like madmen." And again: "Men will fight forever if they are well treated. Give them little marching and keep the wounded away from them, and they'll do anything." As for himself: "I am very well and in capital spirits, though now and then rather blue about home."

The 44th was quiescent for four months after the return to New Bern, and during this interval Lieutenant James, as he now was, served on the general staff at Hilton Head, South Carolina. The regiment's last serious action was in early April, but by that time Wilky was back in New England and enrolled in another unit. On March 23, 1863, Wilky and Cabot Russell, his closest friend, were transferred into the 54th Massachusetts Regiment. It was almost a dream come true. Wilky and Cabot had enlisted in the 44th on the same day in September 1862, and in early December Wilky was writing home about a new cavalry regiment being formed in Boston under the command of Cabot's cousin Charles Russell Lowell. "Now if we could only *both* get such a commission in that regiment . . ."*

---

* Colonel Charles Lowell's 2nd Cavalry Regiment began training at Camp Meigs, Massachusetts, in early January 1863, and was still there when the 54th was forming a month later. Lowell, also known as Beau Sabreur, was one of the most romantically dashing of Union officers; he had thirteen horses shot from under him before he was mortally wounded at Cedar Creek, Virginia, in October 1864. Henry James, Sr., wrote a noble letter of condolence to the widowed Mrs. Russell, and Henry Junior spoke of Lowell's "virtue and valor and death."

Cabot Russell—former Harvard student, eager and talkative, and with an air of running headlong into life—was a year older than Wilky. If the two youths did not get seconded to the cavalry outfit, they were assigned to something that in Wilky's view was more auspicious yet: the first black regiment, the 54th, recruited in a free state. A War Department order of mid-January 1863 had authorized Governor John Andrew of Massachusetts to raise volunteer companies of artillery and infantry which might "include persons of African descent." It was the climax of a long, hectic, and confused process.

THE BLACK REGIMENTS

Proposals for the recruitment and arming of black troops had been made even before the bombardment of Fort Sumter; after the outbreak of warfare, the idea was pressed more urgently. The leading voice, among many, was that of Frederick Douglass, the former Maryland slave who was now lecturing nationwide on emancipation and human rights, and editing his forthright Rochester (New York) journal *Douglass's Monthly*, which was read more attentively by the white American community than any other black periodical. In September he had declaimed in the *Monthly* in his clarion manner:

Let it be known that the American flag is the flag of freedom to all who will rally under it and defend it with their blood . . . Let colored troops from the North be enlisted and permitted to share the danger and honor of upholding the Government. Such a course would revive the languishing spirit of the North, and sickly over with pale cast of thought, the now proud and triumphant spirit of the armed slaveholding traitors of the South.

But that was decidedly a minority view in the year 1861, a view not shared by most of the press or by the administration of President Lincoln. The *National Intelligencer* in Washington spoke for the government when it stated without equivocation on October 8 that "the existing war has no direct relation to slavery. It is a war for the restoration of the Union under the existing Constitution." This being so, the arming of black men was at this stage, in the governmental view, quite out of the question. Abraham Lincoln *as President* was not an abolitionist, whatever his private feelings (they appear to have been mixed); he was a Unionist, as he was constitutionally required to be, and it was imperative to the Union cause to prevent the secession of the precariously loyal slaveholding border states: Maryland, Kentucky, and Missouri. The welcoming of fugitive black slaves and the enlisting of free blacks into the Northern Army could have been politically disastrous. So firm was Lincoln's resolve that when his Secretary of War, Simon Cameron, showed undue zeal in exhorting black recruitment, the President quietly removed him from the department.

Attitudes, both popular and official, began to shift, sluggishly, in the course of 1862. The war was going badly for the North, and major new sources of manpower needed to be tapped. It was grudgingly suggested that black soldiers might be allowed to do general duty in malarial areas, since, as was well known, they were less vulnerable than whites to infection. But the conflict began to be more clearly seen as very much involved with the institution of slavery as well as with the salvation of the Union. Congressional radicals mounted the attacks, and impatient individuals started taking action on their own. The audacious General David Hunter, then head of the Department of the South, declared in May 1862 that all the slaves in his department—in Georgia, Florida, and South Carolina—were free forthwith. Lincoln repudiated the order, but Hunter went ahead arming black troops until ordered to disband them in August.

Despite that, at almost the same time, Secretary of War Stanton authorized General Rufus Saxon—a West Pointer, and an even-tempered and diplomatic man—to raise a corps of volunteers in South Carolina that could include up to 5,000 persons, five regiments, of African descent. Editorial opinion in Washington and New York was profoundly skeptical. Was there any indication that blacks actually *wanted* to engage in fighting? "If Mr. Lincoln gives us the order to fight by the side of the negro, let us first find the negro who will stand by us." Saxon persevered, and in early November a company of the 1st South Carolina (black) volunteers was led on an excursion along the Georgia and Florida coasts. They drove back Confederate units, took some prisoners, destroyed a great deal of property, and came back with 150 slaves.

"It is admitted on all sides," Saxon wrote the Secretary, "that the negroes fought with a coolness and bravery that would have done credit to veteran soldiers . . . They seemed like men who were fighting to vindicate their manhood, and they did it well." Saxon capped this early triumph by the brilliant appointment, as colonel of the 1st South Carolina, of Thomas Wentworth Higginson, New England abolitionist, humanist, and man of letters (he was the puzzled but faithful sponsor of Emily Dickinson). On January 1, 1863, after a day of celebration in the regimental camp, a day of songs and prayers and speeches, Higginson wrote in his journal: "Just think of it!—the first day they had ever had a country, the first flag they had ever seen which promised anything to their people . . ."

What was being celebrated, of course, was the fruition of the Emancipation Proclamation issued by Abraham Lincoln the previous September. It had declared that upon the first of January following, "all persons held as slaves" in those areas where the people were in rebellion—that is the Confederate but not the border states—were to be "thenceforward and forever free." It also cautiously accepted the principle that blacks could be taken into the Union Army for garrison duty. The statement was carefully limited, but it had an immediate and explosive effect, political, military, social, and emotional. Before six months of 1863 were out, no less than thirty black regiments had been formed in the North, the first and—historically speaking—the foremost among them being the 54th of Massachusetts.

Almost at once upon receiving the authority, in mid-January, to raise a Massachusetts regiment of black volunteers, Governor John Andrew wrote to Francis G. Shaw, a New York financier, expressing the hope that the unit would be so organized as to provide "a model for all future colored regiments." Its officers, he said, should be "young men of military experience, of firm antislavery principles, ambitious, superior to a vulgar contempt for color, and having faith in the capacity of colored men for military prescription." It had occurred to him to offer the colonelcy to Mr. Shaw's son Robert, then serving with the 2nd Massachusetts Infantry, and he enclosed a letter to be forwarded to Captain Shaw offering him the commission. It was a shrewd choice: the presence, at the head of the unit, of Robert Gould Shaw, scion of several interrelating Boston families, would do much to muffle any white backlash against the enterprise.

Shaw was twenty-five at the time: slender ("lean as a compass-needle," in Robert Lowell's deft phrase), blue-eyed, with a curving mustache and a short tawny beard; a straightforward young man, dedicated to emancipation and with a cultivated love of music and literature—one senses in him a slight tension between his activist and his artistic natures. He had entered Harvard College in 1856, but left in 1859 to take up a position in a New York countinghouse, only to abandon that and enlist in the military. He was commissioned in the 2nd Massachusetts in late May 1861, and served with it through the battles of Cedar Mountain, Antietam, and Winchester, narrowly escaping death more than once.

The Younger Brothers in War and Peace

For a day or two, Shaw hesitated over Governor Andrew's invitation. He had grown attached to the 2nd Massachusetts; and besides, as William James was to say about him, he knew well enough that "in this new negro-soldier venture, loneliness was certain, ridicule inevitable, failure possible." But on February 6, he telegraphed his acceptance, and ten days later was in Boston.

The forming of the regiment was at first no easy matter. A regiment consisted of about 1,000 men, and there were in Massachusetts according to a recent census less than 2,000 free male blacks of military age. To judge from the usual percentage of *white* enlistment, this would mean only about 400 volunteers from the host state. Boston was able to furnish but a single company of the ten or eleven that were required. With recruitment lagging, a number of private citizens began to set up enlistment offices in Philadelphia, New Jersey, all across New York State, and as far west as Chicago. Stiff opposition, from insults and obscene threats to physical violence, was encountered at every turn; in Philadelphia, the location of the office had to be kept secret, and recruits were smuggled North one by one under cover of darkness. The undertaking was not eased by news of a Confederate order implying that all captured black soldiers would be summarily executed.

But then the numbers began to swell. There were four companies by the end of March, and in April recruits were pouring in at the rate of more than one hundred a week. Frederick Douglass was firing the entire Northeast with his summons to blacks to enlist in the 54th, announcing that the first two recruits from the state of New York were his sons Charles and Lewis; the latter was made sergeant major in April. Before May was far forward, the number of volunteers greatly exceeded the need. Wilky would remember that "we mustered our ten companies from the material which would have nearly organised two regiments"; and indeed, on May 12, a second black regiment, the 55th, started to form; Bob James would enter it the following month.

Wilky James knew most of the history just recounted; he had been living in and through it. When Governor Andrew applied to Colonel Lee, the hard-swearing commander of the 44th Massachusetts, to name three commissioned officers to complete the roster of the black regiment, he nominated Cabot Russell, G. W. James, and one other; and while a few of their fellow officers were sympathetic and even enthusiastic about the move, the youths, in Wilky's words, encountered "many sharp rebukes and more or less indignity"; something he thought should be recorded in "the annals of prejudice." But on their arrival at the 54th, Russell was made captain, and Wilky in lieu of the offered captaincy accepted an appointment as adjutant: the messenger-on-horseback of Colonel Shaw.

The regiment trained at Camp Meigs in Readville, a few miles south of Boston. Henry Junior, who was currently at the Harvard Law School, came out one morning for a visit. Wilky made a transforming impression on him. The younger brother's "state of juniority" gave way on the spot "to immensities of superior difference, immensities that were at the same time intensities, varieties, supremacies." All those plurals conveyed Henry's remembered astonishment that "this soft companion of my childhood should have such romantic chances." It was Wilky's native high spirits and sociability, Henry was inclined to think, that helped him rise so rapidly in his brief military career. But Henry seems not quite to have taken it in that those "romantic chances"—denied to Henry by circumstance—were the younger brother's reward for courage and skill.

It was a happy meeting in breezy spring air of Camp Meigs, with Wilky surrounded by "laughing, welcoming, sunburnt young men, who seemed mainly to bristle, through their welcome, with Boston genealogies." Of the twenty-nine officers, the great majority were in fact from Boston and nearby towns, no few of them from venerable New England lineage.* For the James brothers, there were other family aspects. Governor and Mrs. Andrew were social acquaintances of the Jameses; Wilky could claim to have known the governor well prior to the new undertaking, and to have honored him as being among the first to grasp the idea "that slavery was the basis of the southern cause," and that in the battle for freedom "the race most directly interested" should be allowed to take a hand. The brothers also knew—and Henry at least may have pondered this as an instance of odd cultural connecting—that their father had been in correspondence for some years with Mrs. Francis Shaw, the colonel's mother, on matters of theology, spiritual evil, Swedenborg, and the "lovely" Mrs. Chichester.

As for the troops, the surgeon-general at Camp Meigs, himself obviously a person of large humanity, reported on them with admiration and almost affection. They kept their barracks and kitchens spotlessly clean, he wrote; they were conspicuously neat in their attire

* No single officer was a black man. There was the strongest resistance in high places, up to the Secretary of War, against commissioning black soldiers. It was not until early 1865 that Sergeant Stephen A. Swails of the 54th, in the face of enormous pressure and after months of political give-and-take, was made second lieutenant. He was promoted to first lieutenant at the war's end, and two other black members of the regiment were commissioned at the same time.

and punctilious in military etiquette; they were buoyantly cheerful and given to bursts of hilarity. There was less drunkenness in the 54th, he observed, than in any regiment he had seen at Readville; he surmised that this may have been due to their not having been paid during the training period. The treatment of black troops with regard to pay, which we shall glance at later, was one of the scandals of the Civil War.

Departure date was set for May 28. On the eighteenth, there was a lengthy celebration, a sort of birthday party for the regiment, at Camp Meigs. At dawn ten days later, the 54th came up by train to Boston, filed out from the station, and marched across the city to the State House. All along the way, the sidewalks, windows, and balconies were crowded with spectators cheering and waving flags and handkerchiefs. As the troops passed the house of Wendell Phillips on Essex Street, his fellow abolitionist William Lloyd Garrison was espied on the balcony, fondling a bust of John Brown.

It was one of those stirring moments of united goodwill that strike on climactic occasions in American racial history. And like other such moments, it elicited an entirely opposite response. The marchers, Wilky said, were assailed by "prejudice of the rankest sort." Cheers alternated with groans; loud huzzahs and shouted reproaches sought to drown each other out as the 54th came down State Street. Amid the din, the regiment marched on to the Boston Common, where Colonel Shaw, on horseback, led the men in stately procession past the reviewing stand filled with civil figures and army officers, Governor Andrew at the center.

Around noon, the regiment marched from the Common down to Battery Wharf, lustily singing "The Battle Hymn of the Republic." Throngs still cheered them along, but at the wharves the rear of the column was attacked by Irish roughs, and a riot might have ensued had one hundred policemen not been on hand to quiet things down. The 54th boarded the steamer *De Molay*, and at four in the afternoon the regiment was on its way to South Carolina. Frederick Douglass, who had come on board to say goodbye to his sons and their companions, remained for a while and then returned to Boston on a tugboat.

FORT WAGNER AND ITS AFTERMATH

The sea voyage to Port Royal Island and Hilton Head, South Carolina, took six days. The 54th had scarcely disembarked before it was sent off on a plundering expedition eighty miles along the Georgia coast to

St. Simon's Island and then inland to Darien. This was a charming tree-shaded village, rich with storehouses and mills, perhaps a hundred plantation homes dotting the broad riverside street, several churches, a courthouse, a school. Colonel Montgomery—the fiercely combative commander of the brigade to which the 54th was temporarily attached—ordered the entire village burned to the ground, himself applying the torch to the last few buildings.

It was a "vain and inglorious" affair, to Wilky's mind; far from appeasing the black soldiers, it damaged their morale badly. Colonel Shaw was horrified, and said so in letters to Governor Andrew and to Charles Lowell (who had just become engaged to Shaw's sister); the 54th was quickly removed from Montgomery's command and sent to repair itself on the paradisiacal abandoned island of St. Simon's.

Two other developments outraged the regimental leader no less. One was a proposal, emanating from someone in Washington still hostile to the idea of Negro soldiers bearing firearms, that these troops be armed with pikes instead of muskets. The author of that suggestion, Shaw said, must have been looking "for a means of annihilating negro troops altogether." The second was the discovery, when the regiment's first payday arrived on June 30, that the black soldiers were not being paid at the same rate as the whites. When the regiment was being raised, Secretary Stanton had seemingly guaranteed that the black troops, like the whites, would receive $13 a month plus $3 for clothing. It now turned out that by a squalid legislative act the black volunteers were to be considered as laborers rather than soldiers and would receive $10 a month *minus* $3 for clothing. Shaw refused to accept the payroll as offered. Governor Andrew persuaded the Massachusetts legislature to make up the difference in pay for both the 54th and 55th; but this was rejected by the regimental spokesmen. By equal pay, they meant equal federal pay. Neither body of troops received any pay at all for almost eighteen months.

On July 9, the 54th moved up from Hilton Head to Folly Island, a narrow strip just south of the entrance to Charleston harbor. The whole area was thronged with troop transports, gunboats, and supply ships; a major effort to recapture Fort Sumter and seize the city of Charleston was in the making. The Union plan was to attack the city by way of Morris Island, another spit of land that began at the northern end of Folly Island and curved around into the harbor mouth. At its own northern tip was an immense Confederate earthwork known as Fort Wagner, and this would be the first main Federal objective. To disguise that intention, General Gilmore, in charge of the entire sizable force, ordered General Alfred A. Terry to mount a diversionary assault on the larger terrain of James Island, which formed part of the harbor itself, and might well seem the point of departure for the big attempt. Fort Johnson, at its head, stood directly across from Fort Sumter; its guns had fired the opening shots on the Union fortress.

The 54th played a central role in the fighting that ensued, which Wilky found enormously exhilarating. An eyewitness recalled Adjutant James riding hard along the line, "with cheery voice but unusually excited manner ordering the companies to form."* The attack began, but the Confederate counterattack was so brisk and well planned that, in the smoke and confusion, a number of Federal units found themselves isolated. (One of these was the company led by Cabot Russell, who almost had his head cut off by a Southern cavalry officer, before the latter was shot from his horse by a black soldier.) The 54th regrouped and held its ground against the fire long enough for the 10th Connecticut Regiment, which had been surrounded, to make its escape. A war correspondent, writing from Morris Island, said that

the boys of the 10th Connecticut could not help loving the men who saved them from destruction . . . Probably a thousand homes from Windsor to Fairfield have in letters been told the story how the dark-skinned heroes fought the good fight and covered with their own brave hearts the retreat of the brothers, sons and fathers of Connecticut.

Wilky was dispatched to General Terry with a report on the action, and came back with a message for Colonel Shaw: "Tell your colonel that I am exceedingly pleased with the conduct of your regiment. They have done all they could do." It was for Wilky an extraordinarily gratifying moment. With his fellows in the 54th, Wilky had been convinced that General Terry and, in fact, all white troops "abhorred our presence in the army," and would have preferred them anywhere but sharing the battleground. Now Adjutant James presented himself to the general to tell of the "heroic negro soldiers" who had won a battle victory "for the first time in the history of war." General Terry seemed to acknowledge as much.

The diversion worked perfectly; while it was taking place, all of Morris Island to within rifle distance of Fort Wagner was occupied

* The witness was Captain Luis Emilio of Salem, Massachusetts, whose long history of the 54th Massachusetts, *A Brave Black Regiment*, was published in 1891. Captain Emilio was himself cited after the battle of Fort Wagner as being exceeded in courage and gallantry only by Colonel Shaw.

and a number of guns and prisoners taken. The 54th was now itself ordered to report to General Strong on Morris Island, and they spent the night of the seventeenth getting there, in a raging thunderstorm and by means of a leaky longboat which could carry no more than thirty men at a time out to the transport steamer. The officers were given breakfast next morning, though there seem to have been no rations available for the men. Captain Russell, in the memory of the witness mentioned earlier, seemed as voluble and vivacious as ever, clearly ready for a scrap.

On the island, Colonel Shaw and his adjutant walked up to the front line, which had been established about 1,350 yards below the fort, and reported to General Strong. An attack on Fort Wagner, they were told, was to be made that evening. Aware of Colonel Shaw's lament when his regiment had been left out an action before, the general said: "You may lead the column if you say 'yes.' Your men, I know, are worn out, but do as you wish." The men indeed had been two nights without rest, had not been given rations for two days, and had been on the go since morning. But Shaw, his face brightening, turned to Wilky James and asked him to have the second-in-command, Lieutenant Colonel Hallowell, bring up the regiment. Wilky went off on his mission; the 54th arrived at six in the evening, only a little more than 600 strong, with the James Island casualties and men on sick leave.

Morris Island, as Wilky remembered it, was some three and a half miles long, and varied in width from perhaps 25 to 1,000 yards; it was a mere mass of sand heaps, some of them rising forty feet, with the Atlantic lashing its eastern side and marshes and swamps to the south and west. At the northwest extremity there reared Fort (or "Battery") Wagner, a towering, bulging mass of sand, earth, logs, and palm trees: "the strongest single earthwork in the history of warfare," in the opinion of the 54th regimental historian; Wilky called it a "Southern Gibraltar." A parapet enclosed an inner space, and there was a bombproof cellar big enough to contain 1,700 men. The fort mounted twenty guns of various calibers, including eight 30-pound cannons.

The fort, which had been attacked without success a week earlier, had been under bombardment since that morning, though, as Wilky remarked, it was virtually invulnerable to gun power. There had been counterfire from the earthwork and from Fort Sumter across the way. Late in the afternoon, the Confederate guns had fallen silent, and there followed an inexplicable but costly Federal delay—until the 54th led the charge at 7:45 p.m., with darkness falling rapidly.

The Younger Brothers in War and Peace

As the attack on Fort Wagner on July 18, 1863, went into legend over the years following, the survivors pooled and stretched their memories of every aspect of the event. It was remembered that a heavy sea fog began to drift in from the regiment's right flank. It was remembered that a black soldier, as a shell passed over, remarked casually: "I guess they kind of spec's we're coming." Colonel Shaw was recalled expressing a strong premonition that he would die in the assault, and giving letters and papers to a civilian friend to be handed on to his family. The officers recollected squeezing hands in the darkness and passing along the whispered last orders, while the colonel paced quietly up and down smoking a cigar.

"Move in quick time until within a hundred yards of the fort," Colonel Shaw instructed the men; "then double quick and charge." The regiment hastened in formation up to the line of trenches, two hundred yards in front of the fort, following their orders not to fire: the fort was to be taken by bayonet. The first wave of Confederate fire was passed through; Wilky waved his sword for another charge toward what was now a "living line of fire above us." The parapet seemed to erupt in a sheet of flame; and now men were shot down and falling on all sides. A shell suddenly tore Wilky's side, but in "the frenzy of excitement," he recalled, "it seemed a painless visitation." He continued to press forward, following the color guard, while every flash of fire showed the ground strewn with men of the regiment killed or wounded. Just beyond the trenches, Wilky was hit again, by a canister ball in his foot. As he wavered and reeled from the shock of the second wound, the ravaged column passed him by.

The color guard, a Haitian Negro (Wilky correctly remembered his name as Simmons), planted the flag in the southeast bastion of the fort, and clung to it until cut to pieces by rifle fire. Colonel Shaw gained the parapet and was urging the regiment forward when he fell dead of a bullet in his heart. In the next column, as they tried to scramble up the slope of the earthwork, Captain Cabot Russell and another officer were mortally wounded, though this was not known for several days. Lieutenant Colonel Hallowell was struck in the groin. When the final count was taken, considerably later, it was revealed that half the regiment had been wiped out in the attack. Fourteen of the twenty-four officers in the 54th were killed or wounded, and 256 of the 600 men (assuming that the one hundred men first reported missing were, in fact, dead). Later in the evening, other units renewed the assault and were no less savagely repulsed.

Colonel Shaw's body, stripped of everything except undervest and drawers, was dumped into a common trench with about fifty of the black troops: "Let him be buried with his niggers," the Confederate general was quoted as saying. This aroused a storm of anger in the North, but the chief vocal reaction to the event was almost awestruck admiration for the 54th, its officers and its men. "I saw them fight at Wagner," wrote the correspondent for the New York *Herald*, "as none but splendid soldiers, splendidly officered, could fight, dashing through shot and shell, grapes, canister and shrapnel, and showers of bullets, and when they got close enough, fighting with clubbed muskets, and retreating, when they did retreat, by command and with choice white troops for company." If the question of black valor and skill in action had not already been answered on James Island, it was answered once and for all at Fort Wagner. Looking back from a certain distance in time, the New York *Tribune* would say that the unfaltering performance of the 54th made possible the dispatch of 200,000 black troops subsequently, and cut short the war by a year.

It seems obvious that in this tragically ill-conceived attack, as famously elsewhere when another force of 600 charged into disaster, someone had blundered; Generals Gilmore and Strong in particular may have been guilty of gross miscalculation. But also as with the Light Brigade—though for more valid reasons—the attack assumed historical magnitude and the shape of story by passing into literature as extensively as any military event in the country's history.

Emerson wrote a poem to honor it in the October *Atlantic Monthly*. His young kinsman, Edward Bulkley Emerson, had reached the 54th just in time to take part in the fray, and acquitted himself ably; and Emerson could remember Mr. James's son Wilky from the boy's Concord days. The poem was named "Voluntaries" after the black volunteers, and it decried at some length the cowardly Northern figures who held back from any all-out effort to free the slaves. The nameless Colonel Shaw stands forth the more bravely:

> He who, in evil time,
> Warned by an inward voice,
> Heeds not the darkness and the dream . . .
> Peril around, all else appalling,
> Cannon in front and leaden rain.

The poem rarely rises above that earnestly felt level, but it did contain two lines that became favorites with the Jameses:

The Younger Brothers in War and Peace

So nigh is grandeur to our dust,
So near is God to man.

In August, James Russell Lowell wrote Colonel Shaw's mother that he had been "writing something about Robert, and if . . . it should turn out to be a poem I shall print it." The poem, "Memoriae Positum: R. G. Shaw," is overly solemn and verbally clotted (Lowell was rightly afraid he had made it "*obituary*"), but breaks into vividness at the moment of Shaw's death:

> *Right in the van,*
> *On the red rampart's slippery swell,*
> *With heart that beat a charge, he fell*
> *Foeward, as fits a man . . .*

The poem then dilates upon the meaning of such self-sacrifice for the rest of humanity.*

In the first days after the war's end, Governor John Andrew convened a committee in Boston to consider (so its mission said) the erection of a monument that might represent the patriotic devotion manifested in the war just concluded. It was decided that the work should picture the 54th Massachusetts in action, with Colonel Robert Shaw as the central figure. Twenty years passed before a sufficient fund was raised to commission Augustus St. Gaudens to execute the monument, and another thirteen before it could be unveiled. The lavish ceremony took place in the Boston Music Hall on May 31, 1897, and Professor William James of Harvard (considerably ill at ease, as he would later confess) gave the principal address.

Briefly evoking the scene on Morris Island that evening thirty-four years earlier, James raised the question: Why out of all the Massachusetts regiments, and the great engagements they had fought in, "this regiment of black men and its maiden battle,—a battle, moreover, which was lost—should be picked for such unusual commemoration?" The historic significance of an event, he suggested, is measured by the event's meaning, not by success or failure. Thermopylae was a defeat, but to the Greek imagination "it stood for the whole worth of the

---

* Among other poems dealing with Colonel Shaw and the 54th are those by Phoebe Cary, Thomas Bailey Aldrich, Richard Watson Gilder, Paul Lawrence Dunbar, Benjamin Brawley, Robert Underwood Johnson, and (in addition to the poem by Robert Lowell discussed below) John Berryman.

Grecian life." Bunker Hill was a defeat, but it conveyed a vast message about the willingness of the colonists to fight for their independence. So it was here: the war for the Union had "but one meaning in the eye of history," the abolition of the institution of slavery; and "nowhere was that meaning better symbolised and embodied" than in the first Northern black regiment. In then appraising the challenge of slavery, William drew upon some of his father's Fourth of July rhetoric: "By the end of the 'fifties our land lay sick and shaking with it like a traveller who has thrown himself down at night beside a pestilential swamp, and in the morning finds the fever through the marrow of his bones."

After sketching Shaw's character and tracing his career with no little grace and warmth, James, in his final minutes—in one perspective, they are the best part of his talk—turned to something of deepening importance to him: what would eventually be his theory about the moral equivalent of war. Man, he acknowledged, was and always would be "a fighting animal." What should be encouraged and kept alive, consequently, was not the wonderful but familiar courage shown by Robert Shaw as he led the troops into battle, but rather the lonelier courage he displayed in accepting the command of a black regiment. In times of peace, James remarked, this kind is called "civil courage"; and "the nation blest above all nations is the one in whom the civic genius of the people does the saving day by day, by acts without external picturesqueness . . ." War's moral equivalent is pointed to at the close of the address: "The civic genius of our people is its only bulwark."*

Sixty-three years after that memorializing moment, Robert Lowell, in a wintry season of the spirit but at the peak of his imaginative power, wrote another and exceedingly different salute to the Shaw monument and what it enacted. Lowell was an obscure kin of Cabot Russell, could feel himself related by marriage to Robert Shaw, and was no doubt

---

* Other essays, addresses, and prose discussions of Shaw and the 54th were written by Frederick Douglass, Thomas Wentworth Higginson, Oliver Wendell Holmes, Jr., Henry Lee Higginson, and Booker T. Washington. The most eloquent and heart-wrung response to Fort Wagner was privately recorded, and would not be known about for many years. This was the diary entry, a day or so after the attack, of Charlotte Forten, a heroically dedicated Northern black woman who had come down to Port Royal, South Carolina, in 1862 to teach black schoolchildren: "Tonight news comes, oh, so sad, so heart-sickening. It is too terrible, too terrible to write. We can only hope it may not all be true. That our noble, beautiful young Colonel is killed, and the regiment cut to pieces. I cannot, cannot believe it. And yet I know it may be so . . . There was an attack on Fort Wagner. The 54th put in advance; fought bravely, desperately, but was finally overpowered and driven back after getting into the Fort."

mindful of the verses by his great-uncle James Russell Lowell. "For the Union Dead" works out a pattern of relationships, in a series of ironic and somber contrasts and inversions. Borrowing the motto of the St. Gaudens memorial—*Relinquunt Omnia Servare Rem Publicam*—it observes the disappearance from the Boston scene (as from the American) not only of the *res publica* but of any sense or memory of those who once gave up everything to serve it. Contemporary construction work on a garage beneath the Boston Common threatens the memorial. Orange girders are bracing

> *the tingling Statehouse,*

> *shaking over the excavations, as it faces Colonel Shaw*
> *and his bell-cheeked Negro infantry*
> *on St. Gaudens' shaking Civil War relief,*
> *propped by a plank splint against the garage's earthquake.*

> *Two months after marching through Boston,*
> *half the regiment was dead;*
> *at the dedication,*
> *William James could almost hear the bronze Negroes breathe.*

> *Their monument sticks like a fishbone*
> *in the city's throat.*
> *Its Colonel is as lean*
> *As a compass-needle.*

The poem sets it down that

> *Shaw's father wanted no monument*
> *except the ditch,*
> *where his son's body was thrown*
> *and lost with his "niggers."*

(When Francis Shaw was offered the opportunity to recover Robert's body, he refused, preferring that it lie alongside those of the men he had led.) In its appraisal of the contemporary cultural moment (and in part for private reasons), "For the Union Dead" is a brilliantly bitter and scowling poem. But it is also an act which places Robert Lowell the poet, and to an extent that same moment, in living relationship

143]

with Robert Shaw and the 54th, with the legend of Fort Wagner, the genius of St. Gaudens, and the eloquence of William James.

Attention to the Fort Wagner story, of an imaginative or recreational sort, has not slackened. In his introduction to the thirtieth anniversary edition of *Invisible Man* in 1982, Ralph Ellison suggests further literary reverberations of the event. Going back to 1945 and the origins of the novel, which at the time was to deal with the question of racial identity in the context of war, Ellison recalled how there had popped into his mind, at a certain moment,

an incident from my college days when, opening a vat of Plasticine donated to an invalid sculptor friend by some Northern studio, I found unfolded within the oily mass a frieze of figures modeled after those depicted on St. Gaudens's monument to Colonel Shaw and his 54th Massachusetts Negro Regiment, a memorial which stands on the Boston Common. I had no idea as to why it should surface, but perhaps it was to remind me that since I was writing fiction and seeking vaguely for images of a black and white fraternity I would do well to recall that Henry James's brother Wilky had fought as an officer with those Negro soldiers, and that Colonel Shaw's body had been thrown into a ditch with those of his men. Perhaps it was also to remind me that war could, with art, be transformed into something deeper and more meaningful than its surface violence.

And early in 1990, there was released across the country a film called *Glory*, a powerfully dramatic account of the 54th Massachusetts from its formation through the heroic disaster at Fort Wagner.

WILKY COMES HOME

Wilky dragged himself with infinite effort away from the trench area toward the water, then crawled another 150 yards till he collapsed behind a ridge of sand. He expected to die where he lay, but a pair of ambulance men from the 54th happened to stumble by, carrying a stretcher. They paused long enough to place Wilky on it and began again to head for the rear. They had gone some distance when a random shot blew the head off one of the bearers; the stretcher fell to the ground, the second man vanished, and Wilky lost consciousness. He came to himself on the floor of a tent of the Sanitary Commission at the southern end of the island, and here, as he would tell his father, he had another ghastly experience. He remained there mostly comatose for twenty-four hours, when with a number of others he was taken by hospital transport to Port Royal.

It was here that he was discovered by Cabot Russell's father, who had been searching the battle area in vain for his son and was now persuaded that Cabot was dead. Coming upon the inert figure of his son's friend, Mr. Russell managed to get Wilky onto a stretcher and thence onto a boat for the 900-mile journey from South Carolina to New York and from New York to Newport. Wilky was carried unconscious inside the family home and set down there late on an afternoon near the end of July.

The memory of that twilight scene stayed in the mind of Wilky's brother Henry as clear "as some object presented in high relief against the evening sky of the west": the presence in their home of Cabot Russell's father sitting beside the stretcher, erect and dry-eyed, steady and gentle, in full awareness (Henry and the others knew) of the difference it would have made to him had it been his own son lying before him.

The Newport home to which Wilky was taken was not the house on Kay Street. In April 1862, Henry Senior had bought an old stone house belonging to a Captain Breeze, paying $6,000 for the building and furniture. The elder James preened himself to his brother Howard on acquiring the place for half its worth, predicting, in parodic emulation of his financier father, that such exploits would soon win him the presidency of the Newport bank. The new home was relatively far removed, oceanward, from the former one, standing at the corner of Spring Street (a major artery running parallel to Belmont) and Lee. Stone House, as it would be known, was big, solid, and comfortable; a square three-story structure to which Henry Senior, as he also boasted, was adding a one-story wing in the rear. James told a local friend, while idling away a three-hour boat trip to Providence, that he had not intended to continue living in Newport—there had been discussions of the family moving up to Boston or Cambridge—but that he had been invited to look at the cottage and could not resist it.

The entire family—except Bob, who was with his regiment on Folly Island—was waiting for the wounded son and brother. Henry Senior and Mary were there, trembling with concern and anxiety, as was Aunt Kate. William was on hand, in no very good health himself. He had, after all, completed the first year at the Lawrence Scientific School; but in the fall of 1862, his various ailments—they now included backaches, eyestrain, head pains—had grown measurably worse, and interacted with an increasing nervousness of temper. In January 1863, he had dropped out of the school, and had been living ever since with the family in Newport. Whatever his troubles, however, he was reading assiduously in literature, science, and philosophy, and expressing himself as articulately as ever on many a subject.

The younger Henry, that summer, had just come from a year in the Harvard Law School: the most unlikely episode of his young life. He took up legal studies, it would appear, out of some compulsion to *do* something; a need to be engaged in some mode or imitation of action seeming to loom for him, partly within the war atmosphere, partly perhaps through the example of his busy older brother. Henry lodged in Winthrop Square, but through the fall he took his meals with William at the dependable Miss Upham's, Henry adding his own sketches, for the family's benefit, of their hostess and the other guests. The fraternal bond was in some ways becoming tighter. Yet another reason for William's near-collapse and departure from Cambridge in January may well have been the amiably challenging daily company of his younger sibling. Henry, for his part, was surer than ever by the end of the law school experiment that what he wanted was a *literary* career; and in fact, the one fruit of the experience was an engaging little tale of the supernatural, "The Ghostly Rental" of 1876, in which the narrator is residing on the Harvard campus and studying theology at the Divinity School.

As for Alice, who was turning fifteen at the time of Wilky's return, she was rather withdrawing from life than trying to attach herself to it, as Henry had done. She occupied herself, when she could, sewing and rolling bandages for the Newport Women's Aid Society, which supplied 75,000 flannel shirts in a single year to the Quartermaster General in Washington. But she was otherwise inactive; William accused her, with loving mockery, of being "an idle and useless young female," who was not even going ahead with her studies. Perhaps she felt herself so, in the long American moment when history seemed to her a matter exclusively for men. But there were more particular reasons for a growing inwardness on Alice's part.

She was to look back upon the period—Newport during the war years—as one in which she thought to discover that her role in life was to be a silent one. "How I recall the low grey Newport sky in that winter of 62–3," she would write in her journal, "as I used to wander about over the cliffs, my young soul struggling out of its swaddling-clothes as the knowledge crystallized within me of what Life meant for me"—which was "to clothe oneself in neutral tints, walk by still waters, and possess one's soul in silence." She did not, of course, express her realization in language like that, as she walked along the cliffs; one can only guess at her actual thoughts. She had reached that moment of first awareness that she had within her a separate individual living self; the first phase of growing up (or emerging from "swaddling-clothes"). It is almost always poignant, but it was not unique with Alice. What was unique was her home environment: a father of vociferous public and private speech, a war hero for one brother, and two others exceedingly quick of tongue and agile of mind. Stillness, silence, and a sort of exterior colorlessness could easily seem the best posture for the time being.

But this, even then, was only one side of Alice. Another announced itself in the same journal passage, when she recalled the welling up within her of something special—the power, as we shall see, to *resist* the strains of life.

For many days after his arrival, Wilky lay passive in the bed, too weak even to turn himself on his pillow. Most of the time he dozed; William drew a charcoal sketch of his brother face down on the pillow, mouth open, sleeping. The side wound was not healing as it should, and the doctor decided to cut it open to remove the matter that had collected in it. The other wound had been caused by a small bullet which had lodged in the foot for many days and could be taken out only by slicing down through the foot and pulling it out at the sole.

Sometimes Wilky would cry out for Cabot Russell, for Colonel Shaw and his other lost comrades. Once, he sat up and broke out into a fevered speech to his father, which Henry Senior transcribed and, it would seem, paraphrased without complete accuracy:

"Ah father, it is easy preaching faith in God's care, but one night it was hard to practice it. I woke up lying in the sand under my tent, and slowly recalled all that had happened, my wounds, my fall, the two men that tried to drag me to the rear, their fall one after the other, my feeble crawling to the ambulance— when memory slept, and I here woke to find myself apparently forgotten of all the world, and sick and faint for loss of blood. As I lay ignorant of all that had happened meanwhile and wondering whether I should ever see my home again, a groan beside me arrested my attention, and turning my head I discerned by the dim camp a poor Ohio man with his jaw shot away, who finding that I was near to him and unable to move, crept over on me and deluged me with his blood. At that I felt—"

"Here he stopped too full to proceed," Henry Senior told his correspondent, "and I suppose he was going to say, that then he felt how
hard it was to hope in God."

The doctors predicted it would take a year at least for Wilky to
recover; but this opinion was kept from the invalid, who was soon
talking about rejoining his regiment in the autumn. It was not that he
was pining to go back into battle; rather, he was eager to serve again
in what he regarded as the great anti-slavery crusade.* "He is the best
abolitionist you ever saw," William wrote his cousin Kitty Prince in
September, "and makes a common one, as we are, feel very small and
shabby." Wilky, on whom the teachings of Frank Sanborn had obviously rubbed off, was the most committed and active abolitionist in
the James family. Henry Senior's stance on that cause remained
trenchantly theoretical; William, in the 1860s, was generally distracted
from public turmoils; Henry, though personally and fraternally disturbed, tended to size up the drama *as* drama; Bob, while currently a
military participant, had almost nothing to say about abolition. Alice,
in her quiet way, was probably closer in spirit to Wilky on the issues—
slavery, the human sacrifices required, the figure of Abraham Lincoln—than any of the others.

Henry Senior, writing to a friend, put Wilky's special and personal
position very well: "He is vastly attached to the negro-soldier cause;
believes (I think) that the world existed for it; and is sure that enormous
results are coming out of it." Meditating this and almost visibly shaking

---

* While Wilky was convalescing, Louisa May Alcott sent him an afghan (a multicolored crocheted coverlet), with a poem inscribed "to GWJ . . . after being wounded
at Wagner."

> In the lost age of lance and shield
>   Maids wrought on banner, scarf and glove
> Emblems of chivalry and love
> When valiant young knights took the field.
>
> Our age brings back romance and strife,
>   Both wearing a far nobler guise;
>   Now liberty, not love, the prize
> Sought in the tournament of life . . .
>
> Lie lightly on the loyal breast
>   Our many-colored woman's shield;
>   Warmth, sleep, and happy visions yield;
> For he who dares has earned his rest.

Louisa May was, of course, the daughter (then thirty-one) of Henry Senior's friendly
disputant Bronson Alcott. She had been writing sketches, poems, and stories for some
years. Her first novel, *Moods*, would be published in 1864.

his head, Henry Senior continued: "I could hardly have supposed he might be educated so suddenly up to manhood altogether as he appears to have been." In "the negro-soldier cause," Wilky had found the spring of his own personality.

William, back at Harvard, was informed in September that " 'Wilky was improving daily.' I hope he is, poor fellow," William went on. "His wound is a very large and bad one and he will be confined to his bed a long while. He bears it like a man." The autumn passed into winter and 1863 into 1864. At the end of January in the new year, Wilky, out of bed but limping heavily, resigned his commission in the 54th Massachusetts.

BOB JAMES IN THE FIELD

The youngest of the brothers began his Civil War career not long before Wilky almost came to the end of his. Bob James had enlisted in the 55th Massachusetts Black Regiment and was drilling at Camp Meigs by the middle of June, when Henry paid a second visit to Readville to see him there. Bob was only sixteen when he signed up (he probably lied about this), but he was tall for his age and strongly built. The family learned that, on the basis of his performance during the training period, he had been commissioned second lieutenant.

The 55th followed its predecessor south, departing on July 21, and by the first days of August (just after Wilky, stretcher-borne, reached Newport) it was established, 1,000 strong, at the northern end of Folly Island, just outside the Charleston harbor. For the rest of the summer and long into the fall, the regiment was kept at heavy fatigue duty on the adjacent Morris Island, digging trenches, cutting and hauling logs, mounting cannons, carrying ammunition for an anticipated renewed assault on Fort Wagner. Bob professed to enjoy the experience: building an earthwork while rebel shells buzzed over them and around them until officers and men scuttled to the trenches "like so many land-crabs in distress." Others in the regiment found the work less entertaining: one officer spoke accusingly about black units being continuously ordered by brigade headquarters "to lay out camps, pitch tents, dig wells etc. for white regiments who had lain idle until the work was finished for them." Colonel Hallowell, who had moved over from the 54th to take charge of the 55th, was eventually instructed from above to disregard future fatigue assignments.

The tedium was broken at last in early February 1864, when part of the 55th, Bob James among it, was taken by General Truman Seymour on a sortie into northern Florida, where Jacksonville was occupied with scarcely a skirmish. The regiment was left behind as garrison in Jacksonville, however, when Seymour's troops marched inward toward Lake City, encountered an unexpectedly large Confederate force, and suffered close to 2,000 casualties. At the same instant, Bob was visited by his own calamity: from standing on guard in the February heat, he suffered sunstroke, so grievous that he was recommended for discharge. Instead, he applied for and was given general staff duty—probably at Hilton Head—and this was his occupation for the better part of six months.

But Bob had entered an unhappy frame of mind, and in letters home he talked of quitting the army (on medical grounds) and coming back to Newport. His father argued strenuously against any such course, appealing to Bob's "manhood" to resist the temptation. He would not be home a month, Henry Senior said, using language he had deployed at the time of Bob's enlistment, before he would again be sunk in "all the ennui and idleness of old times." In follow-up letters, the elder James, who had been declaiming everywhere about *Wilky's* amazing "manhood," denounced Bob's impulse to resign as "passing effeminacy" and "an unmanly project." "I conjure you to be a man," he told Bob on August 31, "and force yourself like a man to do your whole duty."

Henry Senior's words could not but have made a bad condition worse. Even as a fledgling, Bob had worshipped his father, expressing that reverence in the familiar way of striving to please and sometimes managing to vex and worry. But he always felt restive and inferior in the presence of the intellectually and artistically gifted William and Henry; as one sign of this, he had more than once in the Newport years threatened to run away from home. Now he was invited to pay homage to the manliness of the heroic Wilky.

He, Bob, had hurried off to war in order to assert his personal maturity, his individual identity within the family. But his experience was sadly unlike that of Wilky. Indeed, the distinction between the younger brothers, here and later, is to be stressed, since all too often they have been regarded as virtually indistinguishable, as leading almost identical and equally dismal and defeated lives. In the war chapter of those lives, Bob James, unlike Wilky, had seen almost no serious action, had passed his time mainly with fatigue and garrison duty, and instead of honorable wounds had been felled by sunstroke. Nor did the young dropout from the abolitionist school in Concord find any moral or psychological sustenance in the slavery issue.

The Younger Brothers in War and Peace

As a result of all this, and contributing further to his poor state of mind, Bob appears to have been misbehaving somewhat at Hilton Head. A certain tone in recent letters, Father observed, "suggests to me, my dear Bob, that your conduct may not have been irreproachable of late in your own eyes, and that the softer feelings which are now germinating in your bosom are merely the effort which your better nature is making to restore you to self-respect." He proceeded to offer Bob some extremely opaque advice about "our moral life" being "dependent at every moment" upon a balance of good and evil in the spiritual world.

It is not readily apparent what immoralities a seventeen-year-old officer could have been getting up to in Hilton Head, South Carolina, in the summer of 1864. From various innuendoes, one surmises a good deal of drinking—there was not, perhaps, very much else to do—and an amount of whoring; in one meaning of "manliness," a fondness for liquor and women, Bob outstripped all the males in the family. Henry Senior reverted to the matter in a loving and artfully designed letter of September 15. He was replying to what was evidently a lament on Bob's part about his own moral lapses as compared with the straightforward goodness of his three brothers:

My darling Bobbins:

Your letter of the 2nd has just come in, and I lose no time in telling you how full of comfort it is in that you are looking at things so seriously. Don't be troubled; you were never so well off as you are now when your opinion of yourself is at the lowest. Certainly you were never so near and dear to your father's & mother's heart as you are at this moment. Be very sure of that.

Our three boys at home, as you say, are very good boys, and we appreciate their goodness very highly; but don't you remember the parable of the Prodigal Son, how the fatted calf is killed, and music and dancing inaugurated, not to celebrate the virtue that never falters, but that which having faltered, picks itself up again? . . . It is only the repentant bosom that is really softened to the access of the highest things, and there is nothing accordingly so full of hope and joy to me as to see my children giving way to humiliation. You mistake if you suppose any of the boys have a perfectly good conscience; they all sin and all repent just as you do; though their sins perhaps being of not so conventional or public a quality as yours, their repentance is not quite so profound.

The elder James closed by exhorting the boy to open himself to God's perfect love, and sent "bushels full pressed down" of human love from all the family.

151   ]

It was Henry Senior's special kind of epistle. Bob could have recognized in it the committed paternal belief in the inestimable value of self-disaffection and have taken comfort; it even made him, via the father's upside-down moral vision, curiously superior to the boys back home. But opportunities for "public sinning" were coming to an end. At some time in September, Bob transferred to the 10th Army Corps in Virginia, in time to take part in the attack of September 29 on Fort Gilmer, one of the defense points of Richmond.

Soon after that, Bob was back with the 55th Massachusetts. He arrived, as it seems, at the moment the black troops were being paid for the first time since they were mustered in, seventeen months before. It was a remarkable occasion: no noisy celebration; only a few short speeches and some singing. Almost the first thing the men did (such is the record) was to pay back the loans given them by the officers over the period, and to discharge their debts to the provisioner who had carried them on credit for all the months.

Bob may have been present in the 55th's costly effort, in late November, to cut the Charleston-Savannah railroad at Honey Hill. But the most enjoyable action of the war for Lieutenant James took place in early February 1865. The 55th had by this time returned to the Charleston harbor area, and Bob was aide-de-camp to the recently brevetted General Hartwell, the officer he most admired among all he served under. As pressure on Charleston mounted, the 55th was ordered to break through the rebel picket lines on Brimball's Causeway, at the lower end of James Island. Bob was given a chance to prove himself, and he seized it with a kind of fierce joy.

"It was when the line wavered," he wrote home, "and I saw Gen'l Hartwell's horse on my right rear up with a shell exploding under him that I rammed my spurs into my own beast, who, maddened with pain, carried me on through the line, throwing men down, and over the Rebel works some distance ahead of our troops." For this exploit, Bob was given a battlefield promotion to captain. A fortnight later, the 55th entered the evacuated Charleston, and in March Wilky and Bob James were reunited on the outskirts of the city.

WITNESSING THE END

Wilky had gone through a long convalescence. It was not until the first days of December 1864 that he could be recommissioned first lieutenant and rejoin the 54th on Morris Island. Shortly afterward, a portion of the regiment was assigned to a division moving inward toward

Pocotaligo, where it would meet the forces of General Sherman. It was wretched swampy country; when required to proceed on foot, Wilky told a friend, he found himself knee-deep in mud and slush. As the newly appointed aide to the brigade commander, however, he was mostly on horseback, and reported with pride to the family that he was "in excellent condition in regard to my wounds." He had ridden twenty-six miles the day before without feeling any the worse for it; his foot was "bully."

Savannah fell to Sherman on December 10. At word of this, all fifteen regiments in Wilky's division lined up and roared their enthusiasm in unison. But the Confederate General Hardee, whom Wilky respected as a cunning old fox, managed to escape with his army intact; Wilky's unit took off in pursuit. There followed a series of skirmishes, in one of which the section of the 54th was "whipped," and from all of which the Union force suffered heavy casualties. During a lull in the fighting, Wilky and the brigade adjutant went forward to the enemy lines with a flag of truce to pass on letters from Confederate soldiers who had been taken prisoner.

On a reconnaissance in later January, Wilky was thrown from his horse and partially redamaged his foot. He was immediately transferred to the headquarters of the Department of the South at Hilton Head, and made aide-de-camp to his old chief, General Gillmore. His new duties, which he found not without interest, had him shuttling up and down the departmental area from South Carolina to Florida. Wilky was with General Gillmore on a gunboat outside Charleston harbor on the morning of February 20, when the general, looking through his field glass, observed the Stars and Stripes flying above the city's town hall. Charleston had been abandoned that very day, and had been entered by elements of the 55th black regiment. Wilky accompanied General Gillmore to Fort Sumter, an utter mass of ruins, and helped raise the colors there. "It was without exception the proudest moment of my life," he wrote Alice.

There was a more formal ceremony some days later, when, with Secretary of the Navy Gideon Wells, a number of other "notables," and several Northern ladies looking on, General Robert Anderson (who had commanded the fort when it was first bombarded) raised the flag. There was to be a big "shindy" that night; Wilky only wished the family could join in it. But as to the military outcome, Wilky felt at once thrilled and desolate:

I never go to Sumter without the deepest exhilaration—so many scenes come to my mind. It's the centre of the nest, and for one to *be* there is to feel that the whole game is up. These people have always insisted that there the last gun should be fired. But the suffering and desolation of this land is the worst feature of the whole thing. If you could see what they are reduced to you couldn't help being touched. The best people are in utter penury; they look like the poorest of the poor and they talk like them also. They are deeply demoralised, in fact degraded.

"Can't H. come down and pay us a visit of 2 or 3 weeks?" Wilky ended. "I can get him a War Dept. pass approved by General Gillmore." H. was unable to accept the invitation. H., in fact, was happily busy at his writing desk. His first work of fiction, a short story called "A Tragedy of Error," had appeared the year before; the first of his Civil War tales, "The Story of a Year," was about to be published in *The Atlantic Monthly*. Henry was also writing unsigned reviews for the same periodical; his literary life was under way.

By this time, Wilky had caught up with his brother Bob, whom he found ensconced on the veranda of a pleasant country cottage outside of Charleston, puffing on his pipe in the company of General Hartwell. Each officer expressed privately to Wilky his high regard for the other. They seemed wonderfully comfortable, Wilky thought, and to be taking life easy, as well they should after their march of 180 miles through South Carolina.

With the war's end—effectively, on April 9, 1865, with Robert E. Lee's surrender at Appomattox Court House—abolition of slavery was accomplished; but Wilky James's fervor about the whole matter had not abated. In a letter home, he described a discourse by South Carolina's Governor Aiken, a "gradual Emancipationist" who said that President Lincoln's worst act was his sweeping Proclamation. Before that, everyone in the state was ready to come back into the Union on a system of gradual liberation of blacks; Lincoln's pronouncement had "driven them to madness." There was nothing to such talk, in Wilky's opinion; the Southerners had had five months' warning before the Proclamation went into effect, plenty of time to return to the fold. Wilky drove the governor home, and on the way was subjected to a tirade about the ingratitude of the Negroes. Aiken could not conceive "how the creatures he has treated with such extraordinary kindness and taken such care of should all be willing to leave him." Aiken declared himself (Wilky could not realize how grotesque the claim was) to have been "the first man in the South to introduce religion among the blacks"; and his plantation of 600 Negroes had been "a model of civilisation and peace."

On another occasion, Wilky listened to a conversation between former Senator Yurlee of Florida, a strong early secessionist, and Secretary of the Treasury Salmon P. Chase. The latter, in Wilky's view, was not a brilliant man, but he was a person of moral depth who was committed to human freedom. The senator, on the contrary, gave vent to "the wildest religious cant" to prove that God never intended black people to be free. Wilky, more his father's son than ever, was astonished that men like Yurlee, so attentive to the Lord's will, should be so convinced that it worked exclusively for their own ignoble ends. "Between religious and political knavishness," he concluded in a sudden rush of impatience, these "rascally leaders" had deceived both themselves and their Southern fellows.

All the more was Wilky affected to the quick of his nature when the news filtered down to South Carolina that Abraham Lincoln had been assassinated on April 15. Writing his father on April 27, Wilky struggled to find meaning, to make out something providential in the event.

My darling father: my heart is overflowing tonight with mingled sorrow and hope at the frightful calamity which has stricken the magnanimous people of the North. I have never felt in all my born days before the same sentiment of grief and consternation that tonight almost completely possesses my soul. The effect of poor Lincoln's death has given a life-long lesson to those who watch it, and the effect that his death has made upon the army is truly very touching. Every man feels that his own well being has been trampled on, that his own honor has been violated.

He and the other officers had been holding meetings and collecting subscriptions for a monument to be built immediately; "and I hope," he added in a nice turn of phrase, "that his memory may in some degree impersonate himself for a little while longer."

Wilky was sure that his father could "see something a great deal higher than I do in this murder." Striving to adopt the elder James's visionary reading of history, Wilky arrived at the theory that God's "wise Providence" had taken from the Southern sinners "a too pure-minded and clement judge," one who would never "give the hell to these men" that they deserved; and had put over them "a less worthy" but more timely arbiter. It was midnight as Wilky wrote, and as he made ready to turn in, he found himself—it was an odd, unknowing parallel with his brother Henry—associating the national tragedy with the time of his own wounding: "I feel for you and mother tonight the same feeling that I did when you were nursing me in my bed in the summer of 1863."

Henry Junior, in his memoirs, recalled how the people of Boston—those he mingled with as he came down from Beacon Hill to the Common in the early hours of April 15 (a day which he was ashamed to admit was his own birthday)—also, as it were, could see "something higher" in the death of Lincoln. He remembered the "huge general gasp" that filled the streets "like a great earth-shudder"; people stared at each other and not a word was spoken. The silence, he felt, was "part of the lift and the swell," for tragedy, if "of a pure enough strain and a high enough connection," imparted to the human attendants the sense of an enlargement of life. The collective feeling, Henry wrote, "was of a sadness too noble not somehow to inspire, and it was truly in the air that, whatever we had as a nation produced or failed to produce, we could at least gather round this perfection of a classic woe."

In May, Wilky James, now a captain, was sent on the last military mission—cruising up and down the Florida coast from St. Augustine to Key West, with a special detail in search of Jefferson Davis. The quest continued for a week or so, until it was learned that Davis had been captured in southern Georgia on May 10, by the 4th Michigan Cavalry. Wilky had a glimpse of the fallen Confederate leader when he passed through Hilton Head en route to Fort Monroe, Virginia. Davis made a strong and not unfavorable impression, but Wilky thought the man unaware of the generally violent feelings about him, especially in the wake of Lincoln's assassination.

THE WAR'S LONG SHADOW

William James, as we have heard, felt that his own abolitionist stance was "small and shabby" as compared with that of his brother Wilky. The phrase bespoke his guilt at not having taken any active part in the great national conflict; at not having proven his manhood by the confrontation of mortal danger as Wilky (and of course others of William's acquaintance, like Captain Wendell Holmes) so conspicuously had done. The immediate consequences for William, in the 1860s, will be considered in the next chapter. But the effects of the war years upon

William's intellectual life and actual behavior were to be very long-lasting indeed.

Here we can only marshal a few exemplary quotations to suggest how William drew upon his own and the family's war experience and failed experience to arrive at some of his most characteristic ideas. Talking about the will in *The Principles of Psychology* (1890) and the need betimes to face up to "sinister and dreadful" objects, William's rhetoric rises to the statement that in the kind of man that does so, in "the heroic man," the world "finds . . . its worthy match and mate." In "Is Life Worth Living?," published with other addresses in *The Will to Believe* (1897), James virtually identified living itself with a constant standing up to danger: "It is only by risking our persons from one hour to another that we live at all."

The case would be put even more directly, and entertainingly, in "What Makes a Life Significant?"—one of the "talks to teachers and students" which James brought together in book form in 1899. He there described a week spent at a model village on Lake Chautauqua, New York, a place perfectly organized and without flaw or blot. On the trip back east, he said, he told himself that what he found unbearable about the Chautauqua life was exactly the absence of "the element of precipitousness, of strength and strenuousness, intensity and danger." As early as a book review in 1875, he would advance the belief that the *mental* or "theoretic" life should be as adventurous in its way as the practical life; and this Jamesian idea would be given a kind of epic expression, as we shall be seeing, in the last of the lectures on pragmatism delivered in New York in 1907.

Henry Junior was immensely intrigued by the extent to which the family had been involved in the most convulsive and tragic epoch in the nation's history; and he says so, implicitly, time and again in *Notes of a Son and Brother*—always with a subdued air of ironic amusement, as though conscious as well of the family's settled reputation for being entirely divorced from the great public crises and the burning public issues of its era. The inveterate collector of impressions tells us that more impressions swarmed back to him from the war years than from any other source. He lighted particularly on the moment when he went out to Readville to see Wilky with the 54th Massachusetts. "The whole situation was more wound up and girded then," he wrote; and "the formation of negro regiments affected us as a tremendous War measure"; a measure, he goes on at once to say, "that was at the end of a few months most pointedly to touch ourselves."

Henry's physical proximity to the war consisted of those visits to Camp Meigs and a pilgrimage, in August 1861, to the military convalescent camp at Portsmouth Grove, where Alice James would come with the Emerson girls the following summer. Then there was the long hot day in July 1863 when the Battle of Gettysburg was under way, and the family, with some New York cousins, moved about the garden of the Newport home, almost as though they could hear the sounds of battle,

restlessly strolling, sitting, neither daring quite to move nor quite to rest, quite to go in nor quite to stay out, actually *listened* together, in their almost ignobly safe stillness, as to the boom of far-away guns. This *was*, as it were, the War— the War palpably in Pennsylvania.

Before the figures of those who had fallen in battle, Henry felt, or came to feel, a becoming humbleness. They seemed to him to have the power of "facing us out, quite blandly ignoring us, looking through or straight over us at something they partake of together but that we mayn't pretend to know." This was the locus of Henry's immediate and his long-range response: regret—not guilt—at having failed to acquire the knowledge of combat, violence, death. In talking of his younger brothers and their letters from the front, he put it more personally: that the effect of them coalesced into "the single sense of what I missed, compared to what the authors of our bulletins gained, in wondrous opportunity of vision, that is *appreciation of the thing seen*— there being clearly such a lot of this, and all of it, by my conviction, portentous and prodigious." It was patently the literary practitioner not less than the envious brother who was talking.

The thing he *had* seen and appreciated, needless to say, was the home front. If he could not indulge his taste (which was very real in him) for the portentous and prodigious in fictions of massed and uniformed heroics, he could tell about the war from the perspective of those who stayed at home. This he did in three long short stories between 1865 and 1868.

Each of the tales involves a wounded or wasted Union officer, and the clearest recollection of Wilky James is in the picture of Lieutenant Ford in "The Story of a Year," gravely wounded at Rappahannock, being carried back unconscious from Virginia to his New England home, "borne up to the door on his stretcher, with his mother stalking beside him rigid with grief." "The Story of a Year" turns mainly on the reactions over the slowly passing year of Lizzie Crowe, Jack Ford's fiancée, to sitting at home and making an existence out of letters from the field. She finally admits that she finds Jack's letters boring, and to being herself quite tired of the war; though since she is described for us as shallow, her sentiments are not perhaps to be confused with those of the Newport Jameses. By the plot's end, anyhow, Jack has died of his wounds, and Lizzie is about to marry her civilian suitor.

The Civil War is at best incidental to "Poor Richard" (published over three issues of *The Atlantic* in 1867). The novella is more interesting to the Jamesian for its foreshadowing of *The Portrait of a Lady*: a spirited, wealthy, and handsome young woman, Gertrude Whittaker, and her three suitors—one a taciturn, well-born gentleman; one a scoundrel after her property; one a pugnacious, forthspoken Yankee. Gertrude is in love with the gentleman, Edward Severn; but the two are kept apart by a mean-spirited trick, and she agrees to marry the conniving Major Lutrell. When poor Richard, the Yankee (here anticipating Ralph Touchett in *The Portrait*), tells her that her friends will be dismayed by her choice, Gertrude replies in the accent of Isabel Archer: "My friends are very kind, but I marry to suit myself." As it happens, she marries no one, and goes instead to live in Florence. But before that, in an outburst to Lutrell, she has given expression to what the home front meant to women:

War is an infamy, Major, though it is your trade . . . It's a miserable business for those who stay at home, and do the thinking and the—the *missing*. It's a miserable business for women; it makes us more spiteful than ever.

"A Most Extraordinary Case," which ran in the April 1868 *Atlantic*, is the best of Henry James's early tales, and a story in which we can see his imagination fixing on several of the motifs and postures and methods that he would develop over the next decade and later. Even the title is suggestive, for James was beginning to be drawn to the special, the extractable situation in human experience; particularly if the "case" spoke in some manner to his sense of his own condition. Colonel Ferdinand Mason, who is discovered, in the spring of 1865, lying weak and feverish in a New York hotel room, is the first of James's "wounded" characters with whom he clearly affiliates. One has the impression of an intimacy, almost an understanding, between the war-wasted Union officer and the author with his wrenched back.

They might also seem to share a certain stance in life, that of the inactive observer. Mason is rescued by his generous-minded aunt, Maria Mason, and taken to her comfortable home on the Hudson to recuperate; as he slowly does so, he finds himself regarding the life around him as a charming spectacle, "a spectacle which he watched with the indolence of an invalid." He becomes so attracted to Mrs. Mason's niece Caroline that he decides to make the effort to get well, and tells the brisk young doctor who has been tending him, Horace Knight, that he now has "a positive wish to recover." There then occurs what would be a recognizably Jamesian moment: when Mason, hidden in the shadows, observes Caroline and Dr. Knight bending toward one another at the piano; and soon after Mason is informed that they are engaged. He sinks under the blow, gives up, and soon dies; "the most extraordinary case I ever heard of," says Dr. Knight.

But Mason on these occasions is not altogether a surrogate for Henry James, or more generally for the writer of fiction standing apart from the human scene in order to examine it. He also represents, in part at least, James's fear (in 1868) that to be a writer was to be *merely* a passive observer, uninvolved with the actions of life—a fear James was to experience and dramatize recurringly, as he would get beyond it and even resolve it. Similarly with the figure and role of Horace Knight. It is true that William James at this time was in the Harvard Medical School, shortly to become a doctor; and one might think to detect in "A Most Extraordinary Case" a reflected sibling rivalry and Henry's apprehension of somehow being defeated by his older brother. But what we have in fact, I venture, is not the actual fear of being bested by William but—it is not quite the same thing—the imagining of what it would be like to entertain such a fear.

Looking ahead: on Henry, too, the war cast a far shadow. *The Bostonians* (1886) acts itself out within a palpably post–Civil War atmosphere, and one of its finest scenes takes place in Memorial Hall at Harvard, where Basil Ransom is showing Verena Tarrant the tablets naming those Harvard men who died on both sides in the conflict— Robert Shaw and Cabot Russell, though they are not mentioned, among them. Six years later, in a reverberant ghost story called "Owen Wingrave," Henry James, somewhat in the style of William this time, tested the value of military traditions and the mystery of human valor. In *The American Scene* (1907), finally, ruminating on his visits to Richmond and Charleston, he let loose a burst of what feels like long pent-up rhetoric, in assailing "the old Southern idea—the hugest fallacy, as it hovered there to one's backward, one's ranging vision, for which hundreds of thousands of men had ever laid down their lives"; the "immense, grotesque defeated project . . . of a vast Slave State."

The Younger Brothers in War and Peace

The war resonated strangely and deeply for Alice James. In her journal, which is the chief *document* by which we know her, there are only a few overt allusions: as to "the freeing of millions of human beings from bondage," for example; and to "poor old, tragic Lincoln." But what she would have characterized as the war on slavery, with her own family's special contributions to it, bred in her a certain cast of mind about public affairs. We recognize it in some of her reactions to British governmental conduct in her English years. But it operated most powerfully, as will be apparent, in her championing of the Irish cause in the late 1880s and early 1890s, and in her ardent feeling for the political and moral kinship between the struggle for home rule and the war for emancipation.

THE FLORIDA ENTERPRISE: 1866–67

Captain Wilky James was mustered out of the service in Boston on August 20, 1865, and Captain Bob James a month later. Their father had relocated the family home again, moving, in May 1864, to a three-story red brick house at 13 Ashburton Place, in the Beacon Hill section of Boston. Henry Senior had increasingly felt the need for intellectual companionship, or at least stimulating intellectual opposition, and had enjoyed his sessions, on visits to the city, at the Saturday Club, where he could exchange views with Emerson; his banker and fellow Swedenborgian, Samuel Gray Ward; and among others, James T. Fields, founder and editor of *The Atlantic Monthly* (the elder James also kept up a sprightly correspondence with Mrs. Annie Fields, to whom he once described Emerson as "the divinely pompous rose of the philosophic garden"). Mary James was anxious to bring the family close together, which meant shifting up from Newport in the direction of Cambridge. She so told her oldest son, who expressed pleasure at the thought of leaving Newport: "because I am tired of the place itself"; and he agreed with his mother about the necessity of "the whole family being near the arena of the future activity of us young men." William recommended Cambridge, as an attractive place, though Brookline or Longwood would do. Henry Senior chose Boston as the best temporary compromise.

William now made Ashburton Place his home, commuting from there to the Harvard Medical School, which he had entered in the first days of 1864. When Wilky and Bob re-entered civilian life, however, William was away, having withdrawn from school to join a zoological expedition to Brazil, under the direction of Professor Louis Agassiz. Henry Junior was very much in residence, occupying a room on the third floor, writing steadily; it was here that he wrote "The Story of a Year" and the first of his book reviews.*

Their sister was making a diffident trial of the larger world she had been holding back from. She was attending a school in downtown Boston run by a pretty, birdlike lady, Miss Clapp, and was making friends with some of the other students. The most cherished of these was Fanny (Frances Rollins) Morse, two years younger than Alice and the first person outside the family, so far as one can tell, to whom Alice James wrote a letter. "I feel myself to be a more respectable human being when I consider that I have you for a friend," she confided one evening while simultaneously doing up her hair for the night. "And I have you, haven't I, notwithstanding all my sins?" Alice was finding her own style of expression, at once self-mocking and self-doubting; and turning a little outward toward female company.

Bob James was feeling nervy and at loose ends, the recognizable condition of many another American army officer after demanding war service. Wilky, for his part, was casting about eagerly for some way to carry forward in peacetime his efforts on behalf of the country's black people. Governor John Andrew for the second time created the opportunity, or drew attention to one, when in the fall of 1865 he raised a subscription of $35,000 to organize the American Land Company and Agency, with the aim of sending Northerners down into the South to buy and run cotton plantations with freed blacks as the main labor force.

The process had begun while the war was still being waged, with adventurous civilians settling in the Mississippi Valley and the South Carolina Sea Islands. After the war, veterans came in a flood. The number of Northern planters in the six Southern states affected—South Carolina, Georgia, Florida, Alabama, Mississippi, and Louisiana—may have risen as high as 35,000 in the first year or so. About 40 percent of the total, and much more than that in the Southeastern states, came from New England, including a fair number of former officers in the 54th and 55th Massachusetts Regiments.

---

* Henry's first unsigned review was a piece on Nassau W. Senior's *Essays on Fiction*, for the *North American Review* in October 1864. He found the volume—a group of essays on five British novelists—a bitter disappointment, the author having nothing to say about "the nature and principles" of the subject professedly being treated. But James took the occasion to discuss the merits of Sir Walter Scott at some length.

The Younger Brothers in War and Peace

The overwhelming motive for nine out of ten of the planters was financial. Word came North of enormous profits to be made almost overnight from the venture. Southern land was selling for next to nothing, the price of cotton was soaring to $2.50 a pound, and black labor was cheap and thought to be docile. About the black workers' energy and skill, even Northern "liberals" had mixed expectations, half hopeful and half skeptical. But among the well-disposed there was also a concern that the ex-slave field hands would be exploited only to be abandoned. "The ignorant Blacks," said the New York *Tribune*, should not suppose that "a Yankee, *because* a Yankee, is necessarily their friend." New Englanders of all types, including the very worst, would invade the South like locusts, "getting hold of abandoned or confiscated plantations and hiring laborers right and left"; they would grow their cotton, corn, rice, and sugar, would sell it as fast as possible, and then "run away with the proceeds, leaving the negroes in rags and foodless." So it was in large part. Even the agents of the Freedmen's Bureau, set up in March 1865 to help former slaves become free laborers, were said to be lining their pockets handsomely.

But there were some few honorable exceptions. Harriet Beecher Stowe gave $10,000 to a cotton-raising undertaking in Florida for her alcoholic son Frederick, not only because she believed the work "might straighten Fred out," but also because, as she said, "I have had for many years a longing to be more immediately doing Christ's work on earth"; to that end, she hoped actively to assist "that poor people whose cause I have tried to plead." Henry Lee Higginson, a younger cousin of Colonel Higginson and a friend of both Wilky and William James (he would later become William's financial advisor), bought a plantation in Louisiana primarily, as he emphasized, to ease the transition of the black slaves to freedom.* Wilky James and, for a period, his brother Bob were comparably motivated, though proceeding under the idiosyncratic paternal influence.

In early February 1866, the brothers joined five other onetime Union officers in purchasing 3,100 acres of land in Alachua County, in north central Florida, some miles above Gainesville. At $4.50 an acre, the transaction cost about $15,000, payable over three years; of this, the elder James was prepared to contribute some $4,300 for his two sons' share. On the suggestion of one member of the group, Colonel Henry Scott, the apprentice planters named the area Gordon, after

---

* Henry Higginson's brother Francis Lee served with Wilky in the 54th Massachusetts.

Scott's brother-in-law General George Gordon, former commander of the 2nd Massachusetts, in which the then Captain Shaw had served. The intention was to plant 250 acres of cotton, each of which, in Wilky's wildly optimistic calculation, would produce 150 pounds of cotton, and another 100 acres of corn. Other portions of the land were to be rented at $75 a year per acre.

Wilky, at least, was seized with the highest ambition and declared himself in the healthiest of conditions. He had "systematized" his duties, he told his father near the end of March, and never had he been able to reason about his life "more clearly and with less difficulty than I do now." They had thirty black field workers and a total company of seventy persons. With the establishment of a post office at Gordon, of which Wilky was made postmaster in June, and the appointment of another associate as justice of the peace, there had come into being a genuine little community—"a community of thrifty, loyal, and prosperous Floridians."

It was Wilky's homespun, postwar version of the Fourierite community his father had been envisioning for many years, and of which he himself had had a taste during his stint in the Institution Fezandié in Paris; with the crucial new element of the black participants. These were living up to the best expectations, Wilky said, and in the face of predictions by the local white population (an ignorant, rude, and lawless breed, by Wilky's estimate) that no one could possibly keep them together for as long as a week. In two months' time, Wilky reported on April 7, they had accomplished an immense amount. "Our seed has all been planted, our corn came up a week ago, and our cotton made its appearance yesterday and is doing well." He and the others, Wilky said with firm pride, had "fully vindicated the principle we started on, that the freed negro under decent and just treatment can be worked to profit by employer and employee."

The planters set up a school in Gordon for about fifty white and black children, in a tiny schoolhouse Wilky built with his own hands. He asked the elder James for books, slates, and pencils, and also for some Bibles which Father could get from the Bible Society. "We want to give our negros an insight into eternity as well," Wilky wrote, revealing himself not less unknowing than the governor of South Carolina about the ex-slaves' already richly religious nature and manner of expression.

One episode in the 1866 summer which much encouraged Wilky and Bob involved a black laborer of theirs named Simon, who had served in a black regiment and was of a thorny disposition. Simon was accused by a white overseer of stealing the latter's pistol. He was brought to trial, defended by Colonel Scott, and eventually declared not guilty by the white jury. The brothers thought this a wonderful blow for human progress, and Bob wrote about the case in an open letter of October 30 to the Boston *Daily Advertiser*, in an account of "the experience of seven Massachusetts men who have bought and successfully cultivated plantations" in Gordon.

Bob was in fine fettle at this stage of the venture: "remarkably lively and well," Wilky wrote Henry Senior, and "willing to work hard." In a letter written on his twenty-first birthday, July 21, Wilky admitted that Bob had his "small eccentricities"—this was a reference to the brother's drinking—but "he has so much good sense and manliness . . . that you don't feel [them] at all." Bob could not, though, get along with the third key figure, the conscientious but small-minded Colonel Scott; and at the end of July he moved over to Boston Place, a new property of 1,000 acres west of Gordon that Wilky had recently bought.

His enthusiasm for the cotton enterprise was undiminished. In his letter to the *Daily Advertiser*, he sought to allay the fears of those Northerners who hesitated to risk money in Southern planting because of alleged assaults by whites "upon negroes and loyal men," and because of the much rumored "rascality and indolence of the negroes." About the black laborers, Bob asserted that "with judicious management, and with a certain amount of indulgence" (Bob had none of Wilky's evangelical rhetoric), "they can be profitably worked." The white neighbors, he said, had been invariably civil; and it was in this connection that he told the story of Simon and the pistol.

One of the readers of that letter was John Murray Forbes of Boston, a financier of sizable accomplishments—he had amassed a fortune from the China trade, several Midwestern railways, and a New England cotton mill—and a man of principle devoted to keeping the Southern states within the still unstable Union. He was a friend of the James family; Henry Senior had written Emerson one of his wittily mystical letters of congratulations when Edith Emerson became engaged to Forbes's son William, and the elder James seems to have shown Forbes Wilky's letters from Florida. Under the stimulus of Bob James's newspaper communication, Forbes, with his associates, now invited the James brothers to come to Boston to discuss the Gordon possibilities, and sent several representatives to Florida to look things over.

One of them wrote back that Forbes's company should strive to "make Gordon, or some other place, a nucleus of sufficient importance to exert a positive influence in the state." Another reported in March

1867 that the colony in Gordon was "in a thriving condition," though experiencing some difficulty in recruiting a sufficient number of hands. "They have an excellent location and good land," he wrote, and the opportunities for persons of small means seemed admirable. "Colonel Scott and Captain James will rent to any Northern farmers such amounts of lands as they may want with house."

From the point of view of Bob James, the seeming intervention of John Murray Forbes provided the moment of largest promise and excitement in the Gordon affair. But difficulties were simultaneously setting in, among them the one mentioned by Forbes's agent. Bob and Scott had toured South Carolina and Georgia in search of field workers, and had returned after three weeks without any. "He and I sit in our room this chilly night together," Wilky wrote on February 1, almost exactly a year after the brothers' arrival in Florida, "thinking more than ever of our dearest family in Cambridge, and wishing that the same roof was to cover us all again tonight. Bob feels despondent of course, but I have made a vow not to feel so." Remarking on further bad news—that the price for Gordon cotton had sunk to fifty cents a pound, half of what factors were getting elsewhere—Wilky then made an unerring assessment of his personal nature as contrasted with his brother's:

I feel discouraged of course, but as I said before I have an instinctively implicit faith in accomplishing all possibilities. I wish Bob had more of it, but on the whole I wish I had less of it. As I grow older I get more and more shy of my own capacity.

In August of the same year, Forbes put an end to his role in the Florida schemes, feeling he had spent enough money on them. This had an additional dispiriting effect upon Bob. Wilky reported in July that "Bob is alternately elated and depressed, and leaves me to do most of the enthusiastic." Wilky went on doing the enthusiastic, however doggedly; but after another three months Bob gave up and went back home.

He brought no joy to the James household. Bob "is perfectly wretched at home," Mary James wrote William, who was now in Germany, "and makes us all very uncomfortable." She was sure that Bob had been "a sore trial" to Wilky "on account of his temperament" (again, his drinking habits). After a short interval, the parents had "fitted him out as before and bade him Godspeed": this time to Iowa, where John Murray Forbes had found him a job as timekeeper in the

Burlington station of the Chicago, Burlington and Quincy Railroad. It was a return visit, since Bob had worked briefly at the Iowa outpost after his discharge from the army. During the earlier stint, Bob had been lonely and discontented, and had pleaded to be allowed to come home and study architecture. It was a request made clearly in emulation of William's fling at an artistic career, but it met with little sympathy. Mother's response to Bob had been that he might possess a certain talent but he tended to exaggerate it, and would in any case never stick it out for the necessary three years; should he do so, he would never make much money in the profession. He would be better advised to join Wilky in Florida: which he shortly did. Coming back to Burlington in 1867, two years later, Bob had given up any serious thought of the artistic life.

He had allowed the Florida effort twenty months. Wilky would stay with it three years more, through misadventures, seasons of optimisms and disappointments, and challenges to "the principle I professed when I was a soldier in the field"—"the faith of my father," as he also called it.

CHAPTER SIX

William James
and the Moral Business

THE CHOICE OF VOCATION

Writing to his mother in the fall of 1863, from his comfortable little room in Cambridge, William had said that he felt "very much the importance of making soon a final choice of my business in life." He had come of age at the start of the year, and the moment of decision was upon him. But a son of Henry James, Sr., was scarcely trained and encouraged to make a final choice about any matter. In the case of the firstborn, who had fallen prey to special afflictions and disorders, it would be close to a decade before a decision with a semblance of finality would be reached.

When he came back from Newport to the Lawrence Scientific School in Cambridge at the start of the 1863–64 academic season, after half a year of "vegetating," William turned from chemistry to comparative anatomy, and his outlook brightened at once. His teacher was Professor Jeffries Wyman, a modest and genial man, little known outside of Harvard because he published so infrequently; but in William James's maturing opinion a great scientist and the finest teacher he ever knew.

"I have a filial feeling toward Wyman already," William told his sister barely a fortnight into the new term. The phrase was more than playful: William could recognize in Professor Wyman human and pedagogical qualities akin to his father's but also appreciably different.

William James and the Moral Business

There was in particular a concern that younger persons be given a maximum amount of intellectual freedom: yet a freedom *focused*, with Wyman, in a concrete scientific area, and linked to aesthetic and humanistic interests. William was to recall that students of Wyman could be led "unawares into taking dogmatic liberties, which soon resulted in ignominious collapse before his quiet wisdom." To an important extent, Professor William James, the expert classroom performer, can be seen as an academic son of Jeffries Wyman. And meanwhile, since comparative anatomy was regarded as preparatory for medical school, the course helped William sharpen his sense of the alternatives that faced him.

William listed four of these in a letter to Kitty Prince: "Natural History, Medicine, Printing, Beggary." The question of earning an adequate income, implied in the final joking alternative, was not yet a pressing one for William; but it would be so before long, and he warned his mother that he might—should he stick to a nonpaying scientific profession—have to "drain away at your property for a few years more." A career in printing seems for the moment to have been a real possibility; it was, William advised his mother, an honorable and attractive business. The previous autumn, when the elder James was in Boston, William made the rounds with him in search of a printer for the father's new volume, *Substance and Shadow*. William told Alice, with a little surge of pride, that between his father, himself, and the printer, "one of the prettiest books of modern times will be produced— plain, unadorned, but severely handsome." Entering the printer's trade thus shaped up for William as in some way entering into a professional relation with his father. It should be recorded, though, that when *Substance and Shadow* was about to appear, William, in the privacy of his startled family, designed a woodcut for its cover that showed a man flogging a dead horse. Father is said to have been much amused.

The fundamental choice for William came to lie between scientific study and medicine. This much was clear in late 1863, and Henry Junior, thinking back, felt that their father had after all been justified in his conviction that William's bent was toward the acquisition of knowledge: toward some mode of the scientific. *Pure* science was the more dignified and appealing, but there was the economic issue. It did seem hard "on Mrs. W.J.," William said to his mother, ". . . to ask her to share an empty purse and a cold hearth." Continuing in the same vein to Kitty Prince, William admitted that medicine would undoubtedly pay, "but how much drudgery and of what an unpleasant kind is there!"

Still, he was inclined to vote for it. As to a specialty, he rather thought that "of all departments of Medicine, that to which Dr. Prince devotes himself is . . . the most interesting." Kitty's husband, Dr. William Henry Prince, was superintendent of the State Hospital for the Insane in Northampton, Massachusetts, and William yearned to visit the asylum. He was beginning to cast a clinical eye on insane persons, an alertness quickened by the female guest at the Sweetser family's home who used to hover near William's bedroom door gasping out his name in Italian. But there were family sources for William's interest.

Marcia Ames James, the wife of the Reverend William James (Henry Senior's older half brother), had gradually gone mad. Her condition had in some manner been concealed from her husband for a considerable period of time. Aunt Kate passed along to the younger generation a memory of her distraught in-law, Reverend William, pacing agitatedly up and down in the living room of Henry Senior's home (probably Cambridge) and exclaiming, "Everybody in New York knew it but I," and, "There was nobody who would *tell* me!"

Katharine James Prince, young William's cousin Kitty, was the child of this pair. In her twenties, she developed symptoms of derangement severe enough for her to be placed under Dr. Prince's care at Northampton. By the time she was seemingly cured and released, doctor and patient had formed a deep attachment and were married. But there were to be periodic lapses; Kitty Prince would spend much of her life in an asylum, and be "let out," according to family lore, only "during lucid intervals." She lived into her mid-fifties, and in her later years Cousin William, now a budding psychologist, was able to help look after her; while William's wife, Alice, solicitously spent hours at a time in her company. Kitty Prince was slight and dark and pretty; she would sometimes visit the William James home on Garden Street in Cambridge, and her second cousin, the youngest Henry, would remember her as a "shy, faint, quiet little lady."

Before the year 1863 was out, William had committed himself to medicine, and instantly expressed doubts, even cynicism, about the decision. "I embraced the medical profession a couple of months ago," he wrote a friend in February 1864. "My first impressions are that there is much humbug therein, and that, with the exception of surgery, in which something positive is sometimes accomplished, a doctor does more by the moral effect of his presence on the patient and family, than by anything else. He also extracts money from them." William James's opinion of the American medical world appears to have been widely shared in the 1860s, even by some of those—Dr. Oliver Wendell

Holmes, for example—who practiced within it. William was prepared to be ashamed in advance if he should achieve worldly well-being in medicine (so he informed his mother) only by some sacrifice of his "higher nature."

A great deal was at stake in these ruminations. William, as he fumbled about among the options, was not merely looking for a good paying job or even for a "profession" in the developing meaning of that phenomenon. Almost three years after he had given up on a career in art, he was still seeking to determine his very role in life, the human space he might most rewardingly and usefully occupy, his potential identity as a self and a James. "The worst of this matter," he confided to his cousin Kitty, "is that everyone must more or less act with insufficient knowledge—'go it blind,' as they say." And always, one must assume, he could hear his father's voice cautioning against a premature settling and narrowing of identity, a too rapid retreat from an openness to universal being.

WITHDRAWAL TO BRAZIL

William put in a satisfactory but uninspiring year at the Harvard School of Medicine, concentrating on physiology and continuing his anatomical study with Wyman. In the spring of 1864 (to repeat), the James family moved up from Newport to a new home on Ashburton Place in Boston, and William went to live there. But by the winter of 1865, he was making ready to drop out of medical school for a prolonged absence.

Louis Agassiz, the Swiss-born naturalist who had come to this country in 1846 after distinguished scientific achievement in Europe, had been appointed professor of zoology at Harvard two years later at the age of forty-one. He exerted an immediate and enormous impact upon Harvard and the American scientific community in general; a university museum bearing his name had been opened, and William James was only one of the very many who thronged to his dynamic lectures. In March 1865, the news circulated that Professor Agassiz and his wife, the former Elizabeth Cabot Cary, were organizing an expedition to Brazil, with the purpose of netting and classifying the many hitherto unknown species of fish which Agassiz believed could be found there—he was first of all an ichthyologist, and his earliest scientific works were extremely well-informed studies of Brazilian and then of Central European fish. It was also reported on the Harvard campus that the Agassizes were willing to take on several young men as assistants, if they could pay their way. One of the first to sign up was Tom Ward, a good friend of William James and the son of Henry Senior's banker, Samuel Gray Ward.

The promised companionship of Tom Ward helped William decide to join the expedition. He hesitated, however, to ask his parents for the passage money: his Harvard expenditures, restrained as they might seem, had been a lingering source of edginess between William and his mother. (Given Henry Senior's unworldly nature, it was Mother who had accepted the task of prodding the children about their finances; which may help to account for William's lifelong money-mindedness.) But Aunt Kate came through with most of the $600 which Professor Agassiz had assured William was all a twelve-month trip would cost. The expedition sailed from New York on March 31 aboard the crack Pacific Company liner *Colorado*, a ship bound for Rio de Janeiro and then for San Francisco. Thanks to Samuel Ward, who guided the company's financial affairs, Agassiz and his associates—there were now six assistants—were traveling free of charge.

William was obviously excited by what he took to be a romantic prospect, but we can make out other motivations. On the morning of April 2, after listening to a sermon by a regular paying passenger, Bishop Alonzo Potter (the same cleric whom Henry Senior had come to know and whose wife he had aspired after in Boston thirty-five years earlier), the group went out onto the deck, where their attention was seized by a thick drifting dark cloud on the coastal side. It was smoke billowing up from the center of Richmond, Virginia, set afire by Confederate troops fleeing the capital city, by gangs of looters, and by men who had broken out of prison. For William, it was a dramatic and a symbolic moment. The war was coming to an end; his warrior brothers—both of them, as William presumably knew, in the neighborhood of the Charleston harbor, past which the *Colorado* was about to steam—would soon be returning home. It was a suitable hour for William to be departing on a journey to South America, which was also by his own calculation (as we shall see) a journey in search of himself.

The Brazilian experience, which for William James lasted almost eleven months from port to port, was a preview of the recurring and the overarching rhythm of William's life in the decade of the sixties—particularly in the violent swings between wretchedness and ebullience. The *Colorado* was off the coast of the Carolinas when it ran into trade winds that, in William's words, far from being "gentle zephyrs," were "hideous moist gales that whiten all the waves with foam." He fell desperately seasick, with "that kind of seasickness," Mrs. Agassiz wrote worriedly in her diary, "that makes the head giddy and heavy." On April 21, as the ship was approaching Rio de Janeiro, William wrote his parents about what he had been through:

You cannot conceive how pleasant it is to feel that tomorrow we shall lie in smooth water at Rio and the horrors of this voyage will be over. O the vile Sea! the damned Deep! No one has a right to write about the "nature of Evil," or to have any opinion about evil, who has not been at sea. The awful slough of despond into which you are there plunged furnishes too profound an experience not to be a fruitful one. I cannot yet say what the fruit is in my case, but I am sure some day of an accession of wisdom from it. My sickness did not take an actively nauseous form after the first night and second morning; but for twelve mortal days I was, body and soul, in a more indescribably hopeless, homeless and friendless state than I ever want to be in again.

The parody of the elder James's vastation talk is evident enough, and the general teasing of the parent-author of *The Nature of Evil*. The string of hyperbolically desolate adjectives is likewise akin to William's cartoon of himself approaching the Cambridge post office with a stricken face; it is always important, in reading the William James of these years, to take note of the comic or the wry as it interpenetrates the miserable or the desperate. But it had been a fearful ordeal, in all seriousness, and contributed its effect to what followed only two weeks later.

William found the harbor at Rio, with the looming mountains, as spectacularly beautiful as other visitors have done; only Shakespeare, he said, could have devised words for it. The day after arrival, with eight others of the company, William took a boat to shore and explored the town: "The day of my life," he wrote his parents, "on which I had the most outward enjoyment." He was struck by the Negroes and Negresses—"which words," he said, "I perceive we don't know the meaning of with us." The men wore white linen drawers and short skirts over them; the women wore huge turbans and walked with "a peculiar rolling gait that I have never seen any approach to elsewhere." The Brazilians themselves were civil and well dressed, though communication with them was limited (but "that's their lookout," William remarked). The visit ended with "the best dinner I ever eat."

Yet for all his pleasure in the exotic surroundings, William felt displaced from the warmth and stimulus he was used to back home;

except for Tom Ward, his "fellow 'savans' " seemed an uninteresting crew. He saluted by name all those at Ashburton Place, and said about the two absent brothers: "I have felt more sympathy with Bob and Wilk than ever, from the fact of my isolated circumstances being more like theirs than the life I have led hitherto." And, before closing: "I think Father is the *wisest* of all men whom I know."

Expeditions into the interior began in early May, but for the time being young James was left at Rio with the task of setting up a marine laboratory. He had been at this no more than a few days when he came down with a high fever and was rushed to a hospital, where the Brazilian doctors diagnosed smallpox. Agassiz, after examining William on his return, was of the opinion that his assistant had been hit rather by varioloid, a lesser disease that resembles variola, or smallpox. Whatever it was, William lay quarantined for nearly three weeks, abysmally depressed and scared, and with his eyes so inflamed and painful that he actually feared total loss of sight.

By June 3, he was up and about, but determined to stay on in his hospital room another week or so before returning to his Rio quarters: "I need a soft bed instead of a hammock, and an arm-chair instead of a trunk to sit upon for some days yet." From this room he wrote Henry Senior a long, self-searching letter.

His sight was restored, and he was heartened to learn (what was true) that his face would not be marked in any permanent way by the disease. But he had decided, after a great deal of thought, to give up the expedition and come home on the first possible boat. His signing on had been a mistake to start with—"and a pretty expensive one both for you, dear old Father, and for the dear generous old Aunt Kate." The cost, should he stay, would be triple the amount Agassiz had indicated. But more than that, he was temperamentally unfitted for so demanding an enterprise. He recalled saying to himself before leaving Boston: "W.J., in this excursion you will learn to know yourself and your resources somewhat more intimately than you do now, and will come back with your character considerably evolved and established." His prophecy had been fulfilled sooner and differently than he had anticipated:

I am now certain that my forte is not to go on exploring expeditions. I have no inward spur goading me forwards on that line, as I have on several speculative lines. I am convinced now, for good, that I am cut out for a speculative rather than an active life,—I speak now only of my *quality*; as for my *quantity*,

William James and the Moral Business

I became convinced some time ago and reconciled to the notion, that I was one of the very lightest of featherweights.

On the steamer from New York, William went on, he had been reading an account of the travels of Alexander von Humboldt, the enormously acclaimed German nobleman (he was once said to be the most famous man in Europe after Napoleon Bonaparte) who had journeyed almost two thousand miles across South America and ten thousand miles across Russia, and had virtually founded the science of meteorology. (Louis Agassiz had written articles about him.) In his own idiom, William was "illuminated" by the book, and saw in a flash where his personal course lay. When such men as Humboldt were "provided to do the work of traveling, exploring, and observing for humanity," what business had novices like William James "to pant after them and toilsomely try to serve as their substitutes?"

Men's activities are occupied in two ways: in grappling with external circumstances, and in striving to set things at one in their own topsy-turvy mind . . .

William felt himself unequipped for activity in either fashion. Further:

The grit and energy of some men are called forth by the resistance of the world. But as for myself, I seem to have no spirit whatever of that kind, no pride which makes me ashamed to say, "I can't do that."

These were painful utterances to make to a father who set such store by manliness, and in the wake of fraternal examples of vigorous "grappling with external circumstances." But although William James here set himself down unequivocally as "speculative" rather than "active"—and indeed as an intellectual lightweight who lacked the courage or the will to face up to the world's resistance—he had, without realizing it, already settled the *terms* of his internal debate. His long-delayed resolution of that anguished private dialectic would largely realign the language evoked to his father halfway through his twenty-fifth year.

Three months later he was again writing his father, but from north central Brazil and in a radically altered mood: "I feel like an entirely new being. Everything revives within and without." William, with the group, had made the slow interminable journey up and around the Brazilian coast to Belém (or Pará, as it was then called) on a small dirty steamer, intending to catch a boat for New York from the Belém seaport. But he was persuaded to stay with the expedition a little longer, and accompanied the party on a riverboat, the *Icamiaba*, running inland 350 miles to Santarém on the Amazon River, by which time William was enjoying the forest scenery so much that he could not tear himself away. At Santarém, William and two others were sent off by Professor Agassiz on a 300-mile canoe trip westward up the Amazon to Manáos to gather fresh specimens and preserve them in alcohol.

William was elated at having survived this adventure, and having even displayed an amount of "grit": he returned with hands scarred, feet darkly sunburnt, and head shaven (as he told his sister). His good feeling was due as well to a deepening appreciation of Louis Agassiz. At the start of the trip, William had been condescending about the expedition leader. He was flattered to be included in the company and thought Agassiz could be fascinating at times, but in William's view, the professor was childlike in spirit and talked a great deal of rubbish. William took offense at Agassiz's implacable refusal to give any hearing to the theories of Charles Darwin as set forth in *The Origin of Species* six years earlier. Agassiz, the son of a Swiss Protestant pastor who was himself descended from a long line of evangelists, held firmly that all biological species were from God, and were immutable and rigidly separate divine creations; Darwin's theory about mutation and survival was for Agassiz not only scientifically wrong but sacrilegious.* In this regard, William James honored Jeffries Wyman's willingness to keep an open if a recoiling mind about Darwinian doctrine. But Agassiz's devoted mastery of scientific *fact* gradually won William's esteem and finally his affection. He wrote the elder James from Manáos:

No one sees farther into a generalization than his own knowledge of details extends, and you have a greater feeling of weight and solidity about the movement of Agassiz's mind, owing to the continual presence of this great background of special facts, than about the mind of any other man I know.

William's morale was strong enough now for him quite to relish Agassiz's pitching into him for his "loose and superficial way of thinking." "James, you are *totally* uneducated," Agassiz told him impa-

* Bishop Potter's first Sunday sermon at sea had enjoined his listeners, in William's derisive paraphrase, to "give up our pet theories of transmutation, spontaneous generation, etc., and seek in nature what God has put there rather than try to put there some system which our imagination has devised, etc., etc. (*Vide* Agassiz, *passim*.) The good old Prof. was melted to tears, and wepped profusely."

tiently one morning, after William had advanced some large and infirmly grounded hypothesis. But on a moonlit August evening, as the *Icamiaba* chugged up the Amazon and the travelers swung in their hammocks on deck, Agassiz turned and whispered: "James, are you awake?" and continued: "*I* cannot sleep; I am too happy; I keep thinking of these glorious plans." In a memorial talk at Harvard in December 1896, William James reminded those present that Agassiz usually named his occupation simply as that of "teacher," and gave an image of Agassiz's teaching: "He always said: 'There, you see you have a definite problem; go and look and find the answer yourself.' His severity in this line was a living rebuke to all abstractionists." Another academic parent had joined William's ancestry.

William went on a series of smaller and larger river journeys out of Manáos through the fall of 1865, sometimes as far as the Peruvian border. But as winter approached, he grew homesick for his native seasonal environment and wrote slyly to his parents—with a particular smiling nod toward his father—that he "longed for a good, black, sour, sleety, sloshy winter's day on Washington Street. Oh, the bliss of standing on such a day half way between Roxbury and Boston and having all the horse-cars pass you full! It will be splendid to get home in midwinter and revel in the cold."

Get home in midwinter he did. With Tom Ward, whose intelligence and energy he was admiring more and more, William found passage out of Belém just after Christmas. In the early days of February 1866, both young men were back in Boston with their families.

FAMILY FAILINGS

Soon after his return, William wrote Wilky, who with Bob James was just organizing the purchase of acreage in northern Florida for their cotton plantation, to give him several varieties of news. President Johnson had made a drunken speech. The government had suppressed the Richmond *Examiner*. Elly Van Buren (the daughter of Henry Senior's long dead sister Ellen, who had married the son of former President Martin Van Buren) had been by, seeming rather affected and superficial. Minny Temple and her sisters were arriving in a day or so. Their ineffable older brother Robert Temple had been convicted of forging a check in New York and sentenced to a year's hard labor on Bedloe's Island. He, Willy, had been seeing something of Ellen Hooper: "by far the nicest girl to me in all Boston."* He was working with Professor Agassiz's son Alex every morning down at the docks, repacking the barrels of fish sent up from Brazil. Brother Bob reported himself "disgusted" with the Florida business, but was not downhearted and sent home "long and admirably written letters . . . He is decidedly the letter writer of the family." As for those at home:

I think Harry much improved, he is a noble fellow—so delicate and honorable and true—and Alice has got to be a very nice girl. But everyone else seems about the same.

For Henry, the year of William's absence had been a memorable one. The previous spring, of 1865, was to assume dramatic shape for him; he would always associate the end of the war, the "Northern triumph" which brought back hordes of "bronzed mature faces" to crowd the local scene, with William's romantic adventuring in Brazil. Both events, he was to say, provided further lessons for him in how to deal with "borrowed experience"; he followed William's doings in South America with the same "mild divinatory rage" with which he had followed "the military fortune of my younger brothers." All of it taught him the strange matter, perhaps the necessity (he also called it the "fun") of "living by my imagination." For while his brothers were soldiering and exploring, Henry was writing and publishing; and he confessed in his memoirs an "admiring tenderness" toward his first stories "for their holding up their stiff little heads in such a bustle of life and traffic of affairs." Contributing to his sense of himself as an imaginative onlooker was an August 1865 visit to North Conway, New Hampshire, where the Temple girls were summering. Henry drove up by coach with Wendell Holmes, recently a lieutenant colonel, and Wendell's friend, the bearded John Chipman Gray, recently judge advocate on the staff at Hilton Head. This "interesting pair," paying lively court to Minny Temple, "the heroine" of the party, possessed "a quantity of common fine experience," Henry reflected, ". . . of a sort that I had no acquisition whatever to match."

It is not clear from which direction Harry had "much improved," as William claimed to think in the winter of 1866. His detectable physical improvement had dated from William's departure the previous March; but his back, which had caused him little discomfort during

* Ellen Sturgis Hooper, the eighteen-year-old sister of "Clover" Hooper, who would marry Henry Adams, was the future wife of Ephraim Gurney.

the interval, began to bother him again upon William's re-entry at Ashburton Place. It grew worse. That spring, the elder James took a six months' rental of a cottage in Swampscott, on Massachusetts Bay, forty minutes by train northward from Boston; and in Henry James's notebooks years later was a reminiscence of lying on his bed in Swampscott reading George Eliot's *Felix Holt* (about which he was to write a piece for E. L. Godkin's recently founded *The Nation*) and feeling "miserably stricken by my poor broken, all but unbearable, and unsurvivable *back*."

William remained in Boston till midsummer, living in a rented room in Bowdoin Street and working as an intern at the Massachusetts General Hospital, a stint that would count toward his Harvard medical degree. He went up to Swampscott on weekends, and wrote Wilky that the setting of sea and shorelines was wonderful, and reported Mother and Father to be more "happy and sympathetic" than he had ever seen them. Harry, Alice, and he, William said, seemed "aged and solemn owls beside them." After the uplift of a family visit, the daily round at the hospital was discouraging, and William was soon again feeling at loose ends. To Tom Ward, who had taken a job with his father's New York banking firm, Baring Brothers, and who was feeling even more wrongly stationed, William in June wrote a small essay on the rhythm of the individual life.

Tom, as he often did, had expressed admiration for William's natural serenity, and William began by remarking that "I am less quiet than you suppose." With the talent for self-observation that all the Jameses possessed—the ability simultaneously to experience and to study one's self experiencing—William drew from his own ups and downs, his exertions and exhaustions, a general human image. "Every man's life," he deposed, "continuously oscillates." Pursuing the thought: "Each man's constitution limits him to a certain amount of emotion and action," so that "if he insists on going on under a higher pressure than normal for three months . . . he will pay for it by passing the next three months below par." He was, meanwhile, reading the *Meditations* of Marcus Aurelius, and trying, without much success, to see how his individual will might be harmonized, in the Aurelian manner, with "nature's will," whereby he might be serving *some* purpose in the scheme of things even without knowing it. This was a curious mélange of personal intellectual impulse and fatherly mysticism, characteristic of William at this stage; but with it he was inching closer to a decisive formulation of the dilemma of his being.

179]

William was back at the medical school in the fall, taking up his studies with scant enthusiasm, especially since it was becoming plain to him that he had no desire to enter the profession after graduation. "It comes to me," wrote Henry James in a fine understatement, "that the purpose of practising medicine had at no season been flagrant in him, and he was in fact, his hospital connection once over, never to practise for a day."

In early November (1866), the Jameses moved from Boston to Cambridge, where Henry Senior had leased a house at 20 Quincy Street. It belonged to Louis Thies, a former curator of prints at Harvard who had gone to live in Germany temporarily; and the choice was the end of an eight months' search for a suitable new home. This one served the family needs so well that the elder James bought the house in 1870, and he and Mary would live out their days together there. No. 20 stood at the crest of Quincy Street, where it sloped down toward the river; across the way was the home of the president of Harvard, and the Yard lay nearby. It was a good square house, in the memory of a family friend, with the best fence in Cambridge for children to walk on.

Even as the family was settling at Quincy Street, Alice James was telling her friend Fanny Morse of "my sad fate for the winter." She was shortly to go to New York, under the wing of Aunt Kate, for a protracted stay—six months, as it turned out—at the home (on Broadway near Thirty-fifth Street) and in the care of an orthopedic surgeon, Dr. Charles Fayette Taylor. "Is it not dreadful? . . . I don't know what will become of me, but I suppose I will survive it, at any rate, I must try to." Alice, now eighteen, was almost as deft as her brother William at communicating her suffering and her fear, and making mock of them.

The symptoms of Alice's condition at this time are not recorded. They probably included nausea, loss of weight, fits of tears and depression, excitability leading to collapse and fainting; an assortment of troubles that a few years later would be called "hysteria," the term devised by the neurologist S. Weir Mitchell (from the Greek word for womb, *hystera*) for otherwise unnamed female maladies. To some degree, it seems they took their rise with Alice—as they did with other women of Alice James's class, age, and background—in a conflicting interplay of bodily, emotional, and social factors. In a general way, we see the vulnerability of such a woman within the erotic-antierotic atmosphere of the American social culture in the late 1860s: in the formulae of Jean Strouse (who has surveyed the historical terrain most astutely), amid "the conflicting claims of sexuality and suppression, of the human body at war with 'civilized' Victorian society."

Traces of such conflicts can indeed be found in the later journal and letters of Alice James. In her maturity, she was decidedly puritanical, even as she was, at the same time, alert to the often diverting phenomenon of sexuality and to the sexual abuse (in England, as she would think, the hideous and scandalous abuse) of women. But one must be tentative about equating life in the James family household with American Victorian life at large. The elder James, whatever his views on female education, was, as has been suggested, more uninhibited about the matter of eros—even if his remarks might be enveloped in Swedenborgian cloudiness—than most persons of his time. Mary James remains as inscrutable in this regard as in others; but the New York–born woman seems to have been more or less devoid of New England repressiveness and hypocrisy on the sexual side. She was incomparably the healthiest member of the family. William paid her an ambiguous tribute in a mid-November letter to Alice (at Dr. Taylor's), saying that Mother was "doing any amount of work . . . putting up cornices and raking out the garret-room like a little buffalo," to get the new house in order. Mary herself, writing to the absent William the following June, and after giving him "a full account of our invalids," added that "the poor old Mater wears well I am happy to say; strong in the back, strong in the nerves, and strong in the eyes so far, and equal to her day." It was a calculated piece of boasting: declaring herself fit in exactly those areas where William was suffering the most; but it was a faithful evaluation.

From Alice's point of view, even so, the challenges to identity and spiritual freedom—those challenges that were deeply at work in her collapsed state—did come from the family, from family forces and attitudes, rather (or more) than from the social conventions of the age. Familial pressures, however loving the parental and the sibling intentions, had only intensified with the years. Alice's sometimes overpowering father adored her and paid a kind of courtly love to her in letters to New York, but he had not changed his view that woman was man's absolute inferior in passion, intellect, and strength. Her older brother lavished compliments and was capable of adopting a sappily erotic posture to her; but he was a man of such dazzling brilliance of mind and expression that Alice could insinuate, quirkily, that William had taken to himself some of the intellect that was rightfully *hers*. Signing herself once "your loving *idiotoid* sister," she remarked that her "having so little mind may account for your having so much."

Her mother was dutifully attentive, and did not take Alice's ailments lightly; but she was showing signs of possessing a limited fund
of patience with young female weaknesses, especially when they were
undiagnosable. On this count, as it might be said, Aunt Kate took up
the slack. The steadiest family relationship for Alice in these years
continued to be with her brother Henry, the one who understood, in
his later saying, that "in our family group, girls seemed scarcely to
have had a chance." Henry was appreciative, fraternally friendly, and
witty—his literary gift was starting to declare itself—but he was never
as exciting or disturbing as Father or Willy.

The latter, addressing Alice on Christmas morning, 1866, displayed again his relish for extravagance of statement:

Alas that at this jocund time we shd. be separated. That we shd. come down
each one morose & silent to his separate breakfast & have nothing to say to
each other of a pleasant nature after the mechanical & forced salutation of
the day. Whereas if Aunt Kate were here with her buoyant nature & thou who
art always so overflowing with good humour & merriment in the early morning,
things wd. be widely different. The quip, the krank, the merry joke, the flash
of poetry, the tinge of pathos, the gleam of love would all be there.

Given the usual thrust of William's humor, it may be supposed that
Alice tended to be silent and huddled in the early morning. (*Krank*—
rather than "crank," as in Milton's "quips and cranks and wanton
wiles"—is the German word for "sick.") In the same "jocund time,"
Henry Junior reported that the Temple girls were in Cambridge and
that the Jameses and Temples sobbed and tore their hair together at
Alice's absence. He also recommended that Alice read a new story by
Mr. Howells ("who lives here, and is a very nice gentleman") and Dr.
Holmes's novel *The Guardian Angel*.

In New York, Dr. Taylor's treatment—it seems to have included
rest, massage, and a series of large meals (Alice was said by a cousin
to be "looking as fat as butter")—was doing some good; or so her
parents thought after coming down for a visit in February. William
passed along to Alice a parental account of her that was "well fitted
to tranquillize anxiety & annul pity but not to kindle enthusiasm or
excite envy." Charles Taylor, in Jean Strouse's sketch of him, emerges
as a physician whose widely accepted opinions about women can appall
in the present day: "While education in men makes them self-con-
trolling," "for women [it] seems to produce the contrary effect . . . Give

me the little woman who has not been 'educated' too much, and whose only ambition is to be a good wife and mother . . . Such women are capable of being the mothers of men." But he did recognize that women suffering from "hysteria" were experiencing genuine pain and needed to be ministered to, if also scolded judiciously, rather than to be clapped in the attic or into an asylum.

William's reference to envy, above, was an allusion to himself, as one prepared to be envious of any person in good health. His back was hurting so much that on his rounds in the medical school he could hardly bend over. He was also finding "the humdrumness" of his life "very tiresome," as he said to Alice in a letter which urged her to find him some "spirited & romantic creature whom I can fall in love with in a desperate fashion." As spring approached, William was conversing with his parents about pulling out of Harvard and going to Germany for a year, to take mineral baths for his back, to learn the language, to attend scientific lectures. The sailing date was set for April 16 (1867), on the *Great Eastern*.

It had been decided that Alice would stay on in New York with Aunt Kate, under Dr. Taylor's care, until the first of May. Her brother William would be gone before she returned to Cambridge, her mother informed her, and hurried to forestall any cry of disappointment: "There is no wisdom in indulging your selfish regrets in the matter, but accept cheerfully the fact, that life is made up of changes and separations from those we love."

BAD TIMES IN GERMANY

The luxurious *Great Eastern* carried William to Liverpool. He crossed the Channel, lingered for a few days in Paris, where he wandered the remembered streets and saw a play by Alexander Dumas *fils*, and journeyed across Germany to Dresden, there to settle into rooms waiting for him at a *pension* on Christianstrasse run by the amiable Frau Spangenberg. He spent his Dresden days, through the spring and much of the summer, walking and reading and studying German. He also made observant note of the various nationals among the other guests in the *pension*—Americans, English, French, Germans—and in letters home drew cogent contrasts of manners which anticipated his brother's first fictional achievements in this mode. But by mid-August his back was hurting so badly that, on the advice of a Dresden physician, William took a train for Teplitz, in what was called Bohemia—now Teplice, just across the Czech border from Dresden—to try the thermal baths there. The treatment sapped his strength and did little to improve his back. William enjoyed the setting, and liked having breakfast in the park served by a little maid who reminded him of Henrietta Temple, while a band played music somewhere. But after a fortnight, he gave up and went north by train to Berlin, with the expressed hope of following some lectures at the university. He arrived on September 4 and engaged a room near the lecture halls on Mittelstrasse.

William stayed in Berlin four months, until just after the turn of the year 1868. His health, on arrival, was worse than when he left Cambridge, and that was very bad indeed; so bad, he wrote Tom Ward, that for a long time he had concealed his condition from the family and even now had not told "Alice and the boys," but only his parents and Harry. The latter deserved to know, as one who had long been "interesting" because of a bad back. "It is evidently a family peculiarity," William added—Bob was currently afflicted by it, too. But William's lame back could almost be called the least of his troubles. He was suffering as well through the 1867 autumn from frequent headaches and severe eyestrain, from insomnia, from what he described to his father (on September 5) as "chronic gastritis of frightful virulence and obstinacy," and, as a general consequence, from spells of utter weariness.

His psychic state, in his own view of it, was deplorable; but it should be stressed as before that he did have a view of it—he was never more self-watchful. We have the sense, during the German period, of William's "psychologist" self (in its earliest stage) standing aside to watch and take notes on his smitten self; and it is the less surprising that in a November letter to Tom Ward he remarked: "It seems to me that perhaps the time has come for psychology to begin to be a science," adding that German scientists had made some studies in the relation between the nerves and the consciousness. He could, thus, explain to his father that the confinement to his room and the inability to engage in social life were making him irritable and tremulous to a degree never before experienced. To Tom Ward, no doubt reflecting on Henry Senior's dark view of the ego, he generalized that "sickness and solitude make a man a mere lump of egotism without eyes or ears for anything external." He repeated as much to Wendell Holmes—"A tedious egotism seems to be the only mental plant that flourishes in sickness and solitude"—and went on to suggest a fundamental distinction drawn from considering himself and his brother Henry. He admired Harry's pluck more and more, for Harry appeared positively to derive stimulus from his physical difficulties, while he, William, seemed simply to relapse into "crass indolence." *Pain* was a definite spur; however intense, he said, it was "light and life" compared to a condition, like his, where sheer "hibernation" was "the ideal of conduct."

There was intellectual and rhetorical vitality in these pronouncements, but they were addressed to a profound desperation of spirit. There is, in fact, no doubt that steadily over the year 1867, and intermittently for several years thereafter, William lived with the thought of suicide. The combination of persisting physical agony, vocational indecision, and (as cause and consequence) deep self-dislike brought him close to putting an end to himself. "All last winter," William confessed to Tom Ward, referring to the first months of 1867, ". . . I was on the continual verge of suicide"; and this at a moment when Tom was referring to him as a man "of calm and clockwork feelings." He told his father in strict confidence and putting a literary face on it that during the Dresden summer "thoughts of the pistol, the dagger and the bowl began to usurp an unduly large part of my attention." This was why he had gone over to Teplitz, and he was sure Father would think the expense of that trip justified.

Months later, in May 1868, when he was again in Dresden, William made a try at defining his "present condition" to Wendell Holmes in general philosophical terms: "What reason can you give for continuing to live? What ground allege why the thread of your days should not be snapped *now*?" William's existential posture was akin to that of Albert Camus nine decades afterward, when the French writer began his essay "The Myth of Sisyphus" with the remark: "There is but one truly philosophical problem and that is suicide." William answered his questions somewhat vaguely, by his own admission, though in retrospect we can see him aiming in the (for him) right direction: at certain times, his clutch on life was due to "a dogged desire to assert myself"; at others, "the undetermined hope of making *some* nick, however minute, in the pile which humanity is fashioning."

William was not, to be sure, encased in unchanging despondency. After appraising himself to Wendell Holmes as " 'a mere wreck,' bodily" and as suffering from a "deadness of spirit," William insisted that his mental makeup was not as gloomy as that implied, and that he could always experience "moments of keen enjoyment." He was finding pleasure, for one thing, in the German language: a remarkable instrument, he said, which permitted one to change one's mind as the sentence went forward, by tossing in modifiers and invented nouns. (This was an instinctively pragmatic sense of language: verbal forms as testing and even begetting ideas.) Wilky, his brother thought, would find German congenial, for it was "the native tongue of all Wilky-isms"—of sentences that began without quite knowing where they were headed.

The city of Berlin appealed to him for its home-like quality. In Dresden, it had always seemed to be afternoon, and made him think of Grandmother's autumnal old house in Albany. But Berlin was American in looks: by which (he told Henry) he meant that the streets were all at right angles and the houses uniformly bleak and unsettled-looking—as though, like American houses, they were still in the state of *becoming*. There was a sort of colorlessness to the visible exteriors; and as to the creative spirit, it was an entirely practical one. The restaurants were not bad, but the waiters were "insolent and disobliging," and he longed for "the honest, florid and ornate ministers" at Boston's Parker House. Henry, as we shall see, was not taken in for a moment by any of this.

Following his brother's lead, William was reading a good deal of French fiction in the fall of 1867. He listed and labeled several of his favorites for Henry: "Mrs. Sand, the fresh, the bright, the free; the somewhat shrill but doughty Balzac . . . Théophile Gautier the good, the golden-mouthed . . . the peerless Erckmann-Chatrian," and Diderot of the animal spirits. He also looked into some German stories, and in late September sent Henry a "notice"—for possible onward routing—of Hermann Grimm's novel *Unüberwindliche Mächte* [*Invincible Powers*]: a bit too idealistic, William opined ("Father would scout him for his arrant moralism"), but distinguished for its imagination and eloquence. The review was mere taskwork, William said; he wrote it for lack of something better to do. "Style is not my forte," he declared, and one hears a trace of pride in the remark; ". . . to strike the mean between pomposity and vulgar familiarity is indeed difficult." Henry sent the piece on to Godkin at *The Nation*, and it was published there in the November 28 issue: William James's first appearance in print. It earned him $10.

Not long after, following an introduction from Emerson, William was invited to dinner by Hermann Grimm, who was unaware that the young American had done a review of his book. At this festive affair, Grimm wore a multicolored coat which, William said to Alice, had probably been bequeathed to him by his father and uncle, the brothers Grimm, who had written the famous fairy tales. Among the guests was a Herr Professor, a soft fat man with black hair who overflowed with information about "everything knowable and unknowable." William received the unusual and striking impression that the man's learning was an integral part of his nature: as against the American situation where a person's "intellectual occupation always has something of a put-on character." The professor talked and laughed incessantly, took a short nap at the table after dinner, and awoke to hurl himself into a debate with Grimm about the identity of Homer. William did not catch his name; it was W. C. Dilthey, professor of philosophy at Basel, and about to emerge as one of the great minds of later nineteenth-century Germany.

William's solitude was more lastingly alleviated by the arrival in October of T. S. Perry to share the Berlin lodgings: the family's old friend "Sargy" from Newport days, in his second year of postgraduate French and German literary study and readying himself for an appointment at Harvard. William could enjoy his friendly presence and share his pursuit of German into the new year. As to female companionship, William, in Dresden, had literally looked at it from afar: peering through a telescope from his room on Christianstrasse at the young girls in a boarding school across the street, among them a ravishing Jewish female. From Berlin, William notified Alice about an actress he had met, of Bohemian origin, "with whom I am in love." On hearing this news, Mary James, in her literalist way, immediately began to worry aloud that William would marry the woman. But William, in this his twenty-seventh year, was as remote as could be from any such undertaking.

We are given a clue to William's stance on the question of marriage, and the heterosexual relation in general, by his message of advice to Tom Ward in January 1868. Tom had grown interested in a young New York lady and wondered if he should marry her; he supplied William with details and asked for counsel. William, acknowledging in an ironic parenthesis his own inexperience, suggested that if Tom had the slightest doubt about his feelings, or if he saw any fault or taint, "any macula *whatever*" in the young female, he should drop the affair at once. "Damn it, Tom," he said, "a little fleck, hardly visible to the naked eye at first in the being of a girl we are attracted to, ends by growing, when we are bound to her in any way, bigger than the whole world, so that it mixes with everything and nauseates it for our enjoyment." It is a surprisingly violent image, even if with a basis of psychological or subjective truth: a female flaw enlarging, through intimacy, to surpass in size and to sicken the entire cosmos. Henry

Senior's discourses, public and private, about extremes of marital discord are audible in the background; but it is also possible to speculate whether William was feeling touched by nausea in his own sexual nature. Perhaps there was something about womankind that at least temporarily repelled him; and perhaps, relatedly, he was experiencing a sense of disgust at what appears (the evidence is skimpy) to have been a hard-to-overcome habit of self-abuse. The physical nausea he kept mentioning might, obviously, be compounded by such sensations.

Whatever his feelings about marriage, William's love for his family, and for the idea of family, was stronger than ever. "The longer I live," he told Alice in a bonny letter of mid-November, "the more inclined am I to value the domestic affections." In a pleasurable mood of nostalgia, he pictured his "youthful-hearted though bald-headed father . . . telling touching horse-car anecdotes" and "serene Harry dealing his snubs around." He was glad Bob was with them (the family and Mary James in particular, it may be recalled, were far less than glad), and trusted that Aunt Kate's leg had improved. Re-evoking the rhetorical spirit of earlier times, he charged Henry Senior—"author of Substance & Shadder, etc."—to procure him a certain book, and vowed that there would be "thorns upon his side, and lumps in his mashed potatoes, until he do it."

In the winter of 1868, while Wilky was battling various elements in Florida and Bob was with the railroad company in Wisconsin, William wrote the latter that he felt ashamed "to stand in [their] presence . . . without having earned a cent." Wilky and Bob, William said to his father, "are still the working ones of the family"—adding, as though by afterthought and in brackets, "(Harry too, though!)." Harry, in fact, had been working hard and earning a creditable income: $800 during the whole of William's absence in Germany, from nine stories in *The Atlantic Monthly* and the *Galaxy*, and from articles and reviews in *The Nation*.

Partly, it may be surmised, out of smothered envy and to counter a sense of guilt, William, writing from Bad Teplitz in March, offered Henry a somewhat testy critique of his last two stories. They showed "a certain neatness and airy grace of touch which is characteristic of your productions," but the material, as in earlier tales, had been *"thin"*; there was a felt "want of blood." This charge was a bit odd as applied to "The Romance of Certain Old Clothes" (February 1868), which, we remember, ends with Arthur Lloyd's second wife lying dead on the floor with "ten hideous wounds" on her cheeks and brow "from two vengeful ghostly hands." As to the other tale, "The Story of a Masterpiece" (January–February 1868)—it has to do with a wealthy New York widower who has his fiancée's portrait painted by her former lover—the central motif is exactly the distinction between achieving "the real" in art and achieving "the brutal."

As he so often would be with Henry's work, William was perceptive without being altogether appreciative; and this he acknowledged in a follow-up letter to Harry in April. He apologized for the "law-giving tone" of the earlier comment. "I hope it did not hurt you in any way, or mislead you as to the opinion I may have of you as a whole, for I feel as if you were one of the two or three sole intellectual and moral companions I have." Having read "A Most Extraordinary Case" in the April *Atlantic*, he conveyed to Henry a better understanding of his literary purpose: which was to "give an impression like that we often get of people in life. Their orbits come out of space and lay themselves for a short time along of ours, and then off they whirl again into the unknown." Henry, he now saw, shrank on principle from trying to give full expression to his characters' feelings, from attempting "to drag them all reeking and dripping and raw upon the stage." William had been showing forth his personal feelings more or less reeking and raw upon the pages of his correspondence all year; and he approved the practice in literature. But again, William put his finger on the story's theme in the act of questioning its value; for "A Most Extraordinary Case" describes the withholding of raw emotions, those of Colonel Mason, to the point of extinction.

Henry made no reply to William's foray into family literary criticism; he could rest content for the moment with the proposition in Godkin's *The Nation* that "within the somewhat narrow limits to which he confines himself, Mr. James is the best writer of short stories in America." But several months before, he had sent William a salvo after receiving his brother's review of the Grimm novel, along with his disavowal of the whole literary business and the picture of cheerless homelike Berlin. He hoped William would try his hand again at reviewing:

I assure you it is quite worth your while. I see you scoffing from the top of your arid philosophical dust-heap and commission T. S. Perry to tell you (in his own inimitable way) that you are a d——d fool. I very much enjoy your Berlin letters. Don't try to make out that America and Germany are identical and that it is as good to be here as there. It can't be done. Only let me go to Berlin and I will say as much. Life here in Cambridge—or in this house, at least, is about as lively as the inner sepulchre.

Henry's image of the tomb-like atmosphere at 20 Quincy Street had some justification; the household had for some time been no very cheerful place. Wilky, up from Florida for a stay, had passed most of his time in bed with chills and fever. Alice, on a visit to Fanny Morse in Brookline, had fallen so ill that her mother had driven out to bring her home by carriage. It was "one of her old attacks," Mary had written William, "and a very bad one. She will have dear child to live with the extremest care." Aunt Kate, called down to New York on Walsh family affairs, was less of a resource than usual. Henry Senior, struggling to bring the intractable *Secret of Swedenborg* to completion, seems rather withdrawn from the family life in this period. And Henry himself was physically disabled, or so he said. His back had improved instantly upon William's departure, as he made plain. "I have felt quite strong since you sailed," he had written William in May; ". . . essentially better since you left." But as the autumn set in, he was declaring his back to be as bad as ever, and foresaw "a very long row to hoe before I am fit for anything—for either work or play." With regard to his work, stories of impressive size by Henry James, Jr., were about to appear at the rate of one a month through the summer of 1868; but the brothers, rivals in so much else, were also rival invalids.

EXCHANGES WITH FATHER

A chief event of William's fifteen months in Germany was a continuing debate with his father, not always wholly conscious and sometimes at one or two removes. Astute observer as he was coming to be, William recognized that, with his constant "indigestion and blueness," what he was passing through was a crisis of identity, though he did not use that more modern phrase; and there occasionally welled up in him a resentment at having been subjected to Father's theory of education, which trained him in nothing and prepared him for nothing. Educationally speaking, he told Tom Ward, "the greater part of the last ten years had been worse than wasted." He felt this with special bitterness when he attempted to follow several series of lectures at the University of Berlin, in particular one by a Professor Du Bois–Raymond on physiology, with implications for the study of psychology. If only, William lamented, he had been forcibly *drilled* in mathematics, chemistry, physics, and so on. But at another time, he could hold with some warmth that the great mistake of his own past life had been "an impatience with *results*," an American characteristic, as he thought; and asserted with bland filial forgetfulness that if only someone had cautioned him against reaching too rapidly for results, it would have been a large benefit to him.

On several matters, William met his father directly. One was the "world-wide gulf" William found Henry Senior putting "between 'Head' and 'Heart,' " between thought and emotion; "to me," William wrote, anticipating his later theory of knowledge, "they are inextricably entangled together." Another was the philosophical issue of creation, to which he devoted several letters from Berlin. William James, who even as a fledgling thinker had no great respect for exactitude of terms, was flabbergasted by his father's spongy illogicality. "I cannot logically understand *your* theory" of creation, William complained. Creation for the elder James seemed, as William groped with it, to involve something called an *alienation* from the creator, the result of which was phenomenal nature; but the process appeared at the same time to be "the descent of the creator into nature." How could this be? "These are points on which I have never understood your position," William wound up, "and they will doubtless make you smile at my stupidity; but I cannot help it."

Henry Senior, dimly aware that these were gestures of communion from a disturbed and fear-ridden son, did his best to answer. As to the act of creation, the father wrote: "You mean I don't explain it *physically*, for I have done nothing else but explain it *metaphysically*." This was true. From the New York lectures on Genesis onward, and especially in *Christianity and the Logic of Creation*, written while he was living with the family in Paris in 1857, James had argued repeatedly that creation was not an event that had occurred once and for all in some determinable place and time, like the American Revolution. It was a never-ending process whereby God *gives being* to already *existent* human creatures. "By saying that God creates them," James instructed his son, "we mean that He who is infinite Love and wisdom constitutes their spiritual and invisible being." The Book of Genesis, he added, reiterating his old formula, "is a purely symbolic or pictorial statement of the truth, without the slightest value as history"; and if indeed one should take it as history, it becomes at once puerile nonsense.*

Before what he would call his father's "metaphysical letter"

---

* The elder James's theory of creation, as worked out, was an interesting mix of Aristotle, whom James did not know, and modern existentialism, which was long after his time. A central principle, as indicated above, was that *existence* preceded *being* (solely with humans; animals, tellingly, had existence only, without true being). Another was that Nature was the author, or mother, of existence; and that God was the author, or father, of being. In all procreative activity, James wrote elsewhere, the father is generative, and the mother simply productive; the father gives life or soul, the mother existence or body. This metaphysical sexism has an exceedingly ancient and honorable ancestry.

reached him, William had written again about his sense of things. His own state of being, he said, was "wholly skeptical," but he was not without hope that he might somewhere find firm mental ground: "and it may be where you stand, if I ever fully understand you." Meanwhile, William went on, "I want you to feel how thoroughly is my personal sympathy with you, and how great is my delight in much that I do understand of what you think." The sympathy took on a sudden intensity:

You live in such mental isolation that I cannot help often feeling bitterly at the thought that you must see in even your own children strangers to what you consider the best part of yourself . . . [But] you can feel sure of the fullest and heartiest *respect* I feel for any living person.

A good deal more of William's mental and moral condition and of his relation to Henry Senior was revealed in a discursive letter to Tom Ward from Berlin in early January 1868. Tom had quit his father's bank to try his hand at scientific study, but had abandoned science and returned to banking. William expressed a fellow feeling for this behavior. He wished that Tom had stuck to science; but then, apparently unconscious that he was pronouncing a sort of down-to-earth version of paternal doctrine, he remarked that "I really don't think it so *all*-important what our occupation is, so long as we do respectably and keep a clean bosom. Whatever we are *not* doing is pretty sure to come to us at intervals, in the midst of our toil, and fill us with pungent regrets that it is lost to us."

To his former shipmate, who was feeling bored and listless, William proposed "a new gospel of cheer." "Remember when old December's darkness is everywhere about you," he said, "that the world is really in every minutest point as full of life as in the most joyous morning you ever lived through; that the sun is whanging down, and the waves dancing, and the gulls skimming down at the mouth of the Amazon, for instance, as freshly as in the first morning of creation."

But William had far more substantial fare than that to offer. What served *him* in moments of darkest doubt, he said, was "the thought of my having a will, and of my belonging to a brotherhood of men possessed of a capacity for pleasure and pain of different kinds." William was here beginning to make a crucial intellectual turn; but there was an impediment yet to be gotten by. When he spoke forthrightly about having a will, he was affirming himself as against his father's doctrine of self-surrender. But when he allied himself to the brotherhood of men, he was embracing Henry Senior's humanitarian vision. The two concepts were yoked by a kind of theoretical violence when William declared his readiness to give up any idea of "final causes," since "we can, by our will, make the enjoyment of our brothers stand us in the stead of a final cause."

It was a position in which William sought at once to reject and to accept the father's teaching, to follow his father and to break with him. And it was the more difficult to maintain because, as William was quick to acknowledge, any genuine engagement with the human fraternity was nearly impossible. "We long for sympathy," he continued to Tom Ward, "for a purely *personal* communication, first with the soul of the world, and then with the soul of our fellows." But most men would have to confess "that they are perfectly isolated from the soul of the world"—that strange mystical Marcus Aurelian entity—and much worse, "that the closest human love incloses a potential germ of estrangement or hatred." William would give candid specifics to this perception in a letter to Wendell Holmes a few months later: "With Harry and my Dad I have a perfect sympathy 'personally,' but Harry's orbit and mine coincide but part-way, and Father's and mine hardly at all, except in general feelings of philanthropy in which we both indulge."

How then, finally, might an individual enter into a true relation with his "brothers"? By adding something to "the welfare of the race": a work of art, a new moral insight, a patent medicine, a piece of machinery. In so doing, one would affect the lives of other individuals— and hence be "in *real* relation with them"—even if one's name was forever unknown. So it has always been, William maintained, and thereupon launched into a hymn of praise for the deeds of men across the ages, a passage distinctively Emersonian in its prose rhythm and brilliant inconsequence:

Our predecessors . . . have made us what we are. Every thought you now have and every act and intention owes its complexion to the acts of your dead and living brothers. *Everything* we know and are is through men. We have no revelation but through man. Every sentiment that warms your gizzard, every brave act that ever made your pulse bound and your nostril open to a confident breath was a man's act. However mean a man may be, man is *the best we know* . . .

Toward the end of May 1868, William drew up a summary for Tom Ward of his comings and goings, including two more visits to the baths of Teplitz, since giving up on Berlin five months before. In January, he had decided that life in Berlin was damaging to his back and so had quit his university studies and escaped to Teplitz. After "eight mortal sick weeks cooped up in a house in a Bohemian village," he had gone to Dresden for a month "and got as well as I was before leaving Berlin, then went back to Teplitz to risk a mild course, and finally have been here again"—in Dresden—"for two weeks." No doubt William intended the effect produced: that of weary circling, of the bleak repetitiveness traditionally associated with the experience of hell. What chiefly characterized him, he told Ward, echoing the latter's self-portrait, was "dissatisfaction and general listlessness and skepticism."

At Frau Spangenberg's in Dresden one evening, there occurred what William described to Tom Ward as a crisis of feelings. Another of the guests was a Miss Havens from New York, a nice little woman in her late twenties; she was a prey to her nerves, William said, but her mind was in good order and she had a real genius for music. When Miss Havens played the piano and two other guests sang, the sheer beauty of the music stirred in William a sudden glimmer of immense and vital possibility; and in the same instant, as he wrote in his diary, he felt an "unspeakable disgust" with himself and "the dead drifting of my own life for some time past . . . Oh God! an end to the idle, idiotic sinking into *Vorstellungen* [representations] disproportionate to the object. Every good experience ought to be interpreted in practice." And after a pause: "Keep sinewy all the while,—and work at present with a mystical belief in the reality, interpreted somehow, of humanity."

Nothing William James wrote in this epoch was a more suggestive linking of personal inclination and paternal legacy: the longing for a clear identity and sense of direction; the impatience with aimless and disconnected play of mind; the sharing in the father's dedication to humanity; the reassertion of the will, implicit in the word "ought" and in the injunction to "keep sinewy"; even a foretaste of the pragmatic method—in the phrase "interpreted in practice," the last word should obviously be underscored.

During his last weeks in Germany, William came upon unexpected cultural allies in his long-drawn-out conceptual struggle with the elder James: Goethe and the ancient Greeks. William had known Goethe before, but he now realized that the great German writer's appeal was as the supreme poet of the actual in opposition to the abstract. "He *is* a perfect born *collector*, as much as Agassiz," William enthused to Tom Ward, "and he does hate to lose *anything* in creation." The Greek poets and dramatists, upon a rereading, offered him a vision of the essential rightness of the natural realm: "This world in so far forth as it stood was good to them. Evil was synonymous with perishability." With remarkable prescience, William contrasted this sublime simplicity with the mordant skepticism and the addiction to irony and ambiguity of the modern temper. He cited an example. For the modern, "the justness of the just man" was not a final fact, as it had been for the Greeks, but something susceptible to the charge of self-righteousness or vainglory and made to seem more subtly evil than normal *lack* of justness.

The diagnosis, for all its generality, related to Henry Senior's congenital distrust of any expression of the natural self, and William was quite aware of it. It was in good part because of his father's example, William told Tom Ward, as well perhaps of his own tendencies, that he had grown up with "a very non-optimistic view of nature . . . But of late the sturdy realism of Goethe and the obdurate beauty and charm of the Greeks have shaken my complexion more than anything else."

In late June, William went to Heidelberg with the notion of spending the summer there attending lectures by Hermann von Helmholtz, the distinguished investigator into the physiology of vision. He was back in Dresden within a week, having found the university coming to the end of its term and the surrounding terrain unsuitable for the limited exercise of which he was capable. By mid-August he was trying the publicized baths at Divonne in the French Savoie, having stopped off in Geneva on the way, where he sought with scant success to locate the old family residences and schools of 1859–60. The treatment at Divonne was another failure, though William enjoyed practicing his French. He went to Paris in October for a stay with Henry Bowditch, a fellow medical student and future professor at Harvard. On October 29, he wrote Tom Ward: "I am coming home to get well. This vagabond life is not the thing for me." He was sailing from Brest on November 7 in the *Ville de Paris*, and if Tom could be on the New York wharf when the ship arrived, "you may help me as well as make glad my heart at the sight of you."

HALLUCINATIONS ON QUINCY STREET

Though William knew from his parents that Alice had gone through a miserable period in the spring of 1867, he had little idea how bad it had been. He kept hearing that Alice was "delicate," and once or twice that she was "prostrated" for a few hours: he wrote his sister to say that he was exceedingly sorry at the news, but was sure she would "soon grow out of it." For her benefit he drew one of his fantasy portraits, this one of a "noble stranger" seen wandering the streets of Dresden and overheard occasionally to mutter the mysterious words "Alice . . . beloved child." In a subsequent letter he enjoined Alice to "keep a stiff upper lip & snap your fingers at fate . . . and your sickness will wear itself out as it almost always does."* In accord with the general opinion of the day, William took Alice's delicacy as adding to her attraction; indeed, along with "moral untaintedness"—that lack of taint or "macula" of which William had spoken to Tom Ward—as exemplary of what was best in young American women.† He rejoiced as well in the "total absence" in them "of that worldly wisdom, or rather that muscular ability and joy to cope with all the commercial and material details of life which characterizes her european sister." In the perspective of the late twentieth century, that sentence could stand as a paradigm of what is regarded as male chauvinism (though the faintest trace of irony may be detectable); but if Alice resented it, she was feeling too fragile to respond.

What William did not realize, at any event, was that Alice's "muscular ability" to cope with anything had collapsed early in the spring of 1868. She had been showing danger signals for several weeks; her parents had to rule out any social visiting on her part as too "trying." Her nervous turns began to occur with increasing frequency in the first days of April, and were brought on (Mary James wrote Wilky) by the slightest exertion. "It is a case of genuine hysteria for which no cause as yet can be discovered. It is a most distressing form of illness, and the most difficult to reach, because so little is known about it." This was accurate and informed reporting; but the rest of the mother's analysis reflected a wishful incomprehension: Alice's mind was untouched by the disturbance; she did not dread the attacks in advance,

---

* This is William's version of what was becoming known as "Mind-cure." In *The Varieties of Religious Experience*, he would locate "the doctrinal sources of Mind-cure," for which he always had a certain respect, in the four Gospels, "Emersonianism or New England transcendentalism," Berkleyan idealism, spiritism, and Hinduism. "The leaders in this faith," he said, "have had an intuitive belief in the all-saving power of healthy-minded attitudes as such [and] in the conquering efficacy of courage, hope, and trust."

† "Delicate," Jean Strouse observes (*Alice James*, p. 100), "was the way middle-class Victorian young ladies were supposed to be. With its range of meanings, from refined, sensitive, subtle, and gentle to sickly and frail, the word *delicate* described the mid-Victorian ideal of beauty: a graceful languor, pallor, and vulnerability—even to the point of illness—were seen as enhancing the female form."

was "perfectly happy when they are over," and was patient and affectionate throughout.

Something close to the exact opposite of these comforting conditions had, in fact, obtained during what would be revealed as one of the two or three worst breakdowns of Alice James's life. She gave an account of it in her journal entry for October 26, 1890, writing in South Kensington, London. It began with a reference to an article by William in *Scribner's*: "The Hidden Self," a commentary in the main on some recent studies of "hysterical somnabulists" by Pierre Janet, professor of philosophy at Le Havre. Janet's thesis was that one human being could contain different "personages," and that under special circumstances "the total possible consciousness may be split into parts which co-exist, but mutually ignore one another." He gave examples of a "split-off," partial and "buried self" which would "come to the surface and drive out the other self."

Alice was impressed by William's paraphrasing remark that "an hysteric woman abandons part of her consciousness because she is too weak nervously to hold it all together." "Abandons," she thought, was just the right word—

altho' I have never unfortunately been able to abandon my consciousness and get five minutes' rest. I have passed thro' an infinite succession of conscious abandonments and in looking back now I see how it began in my childhood, altho' I wasn't conscious of the necessity until '67 or '68 when I broke down first, acutely, and had violent turns of hysteria. As I lay prostrate after the storm with my mind luminous and active and susceptible of the clearest, strongest impressions, I saw so distinctly that it was a fight simply between my body and my will, a battle in which the former was to be triumphant to the end. Owing to some physical weakness, excess of nervous susceptibility, the moral power *pauses*, as it were for a moment, and refuses to maintain muscular sanity, worn out with the strain of its constabulary functions. As I used to sit immovable reading in the library with waves of violent inclination suddenly invading my muscles taking some one of their myriad forms such as throwing myself out of the window, or knocking off the head of the benignant pater as he sat with his silver locks, writing at his table, it used to seem to me that the only difference between me and the insane was that I had not only all the horrors and suffering of insanity but the duties of doctor, nurse, and straitjacket imposed upon me, too. Conceive of never being without the sense that if you let yourself go for a moment your mechanism will fall into pie and that at some given moment you must abandon it all, let the dykes break and the flood sweep in, acknowledging yourself abjectly impotent before the immutable laws. When all one's moral and natural stock in trade is a temperament forbidding the abandonment of an inch or the relaxation of a muscle, 'tis a neverending fight. When the fancy took me of a morning at school to *study* my lessons by way of variety instead of shirking or wriggling thro' the most impossible sensations of upheaval, violent revolt in my head overtook me so that I had to "abandon" my brain, as it were. So it has always been, anything that sticks of itself is free to do so, but conscious and continuous cerebration is an impossible exercise and from just behind the eyes my head feels like a dense jungle into which no ray of light has ever penetrated. So, with the rest, you abandon the pit of your stomach, the palms of your hands, the soles of your feet, and refuse to keep them sane when you find in turn one moral impression after another producing despair in the one, terror in the other, anxiety in the third and so on until life becomes one long flight from remote suggestion and complicated eluding of the multifold traps set for your undoing.

Amid the extraordinary density and energy of metaphor in that extended passage, we can observe, with other things, that Alice like William posits the *will*—which she also calls "the moral power" and the policing agent—as the only element that seeks to resist and even control the enemy: in her case, the wild surge of her physical being (with its infirmities and longings) to tear itself apart. But she recalls being grimly confident that the will would always be the loser. The "waves of violent inclination" that then possessed her were, so to say, enormously intensified versions of William's more intellectualized impulses: to kill herself, or to kill her benignant father as he sat nearby scribbling away in the library at Quincy Street. At such moments, in her heightened recollection, she seemed to herself far worse off than, say, her aunt Marcia James or cousin Kitty Prince: she not only suffered fits of lost sanity but had to restrain and minister to her deranged self. She was alone in her field of desolation and terror.

Any effort at serious and sustained *thinking*, at school or elsewhere, then and later, she remembered, would bring on terrible sensations of upheaval and revolt in her head, until she had to "abandon" her brain. This may of course be read as abandoning any attempt to compete with her older brothers on a cerebral level; but in the family fashion, Alice James—at least in her 1890 journal—won an imaginative victory of her own in the very language by which she re-enacted her defeat. She had already used the odd and interesting phrase "muscular sanity." Now, in the passage's climax, she attributed rising *in*sanity to the parts of her body which have been let go along with her brain and her will: until the pit of her stomach is maddened by despair, the palms of her hands by terror, the soles of her feet by anxiety. The imagery is superbly grotesque, phantasmagorical, beyond anything Henry James contrived in the eeriest of his supernatural tales. Yet these hallucinatory invasions—of mind by body, of body by mind—are utterly and instantly recognizable.

Alice was in a subdued state by the time William reached home in late November; her hysterical "turns" had diminished, but she still needed to be protected. William, needless to say, was anything but buoyant; and Henry spoke of recurring back pains and of his desire to seek an improvement in health by getting away to Europe. It was in regard to this time that Lilla Cabot, the daughter of a well-known Boston surgeon and (in 1874) the wife of Tom Perry, gave her contemptuous and often quoted sketch of family life at the Jameses'. The Quincy Street home was stiff and stupid, she said, its "poky banality" ruled over by Mrs. James. Mr. James, whom Miss Cabot found delightful, came and went, limpingly, but he "never really seemed to 'belong' to his wife or Miss Walsh, large stupid-looking ladies, or to his clever but coldly self-absorbed daughter."* Henry successfully made his escape at the first convenient moment, which was mid-February 1869, on the S.S. *China*, bound for Liverpool. On the way to New York, he stopped off at Pelham to see Minny Temple, who was staying there with her married sister. Minny, too, had been very ill, more so than Henry knew; but the two did not talk of it, discussing instead a plan to meet in Rome the following year.

William, meanwhile, was preparing for his medical-school examinations, though with minimal effort. From Germany in May 1868, at a moment of almost total demoralization ("what with sickness and weakness from these baths, and general disgust at my prospects"), he had written Henry Bowditch that he had let his medical study slide altogether and had forgotten all he had ever learned about disease and treatment. Now, seven months later, he told Bowditch that the slightest physical exercise and even the slightest "mental labor" had an immediate harmful effect upon him. He compiled a routine medical thesis about the impact of "cold" upon the human body, drawing solely on

* Alice James voiced a matching opinion of Lilla Cabot after the latter's marriage to Sargy Perry. The new Mrs. Perry's intellectual vanity might be bearable, Alice told Sara Sedgwick: "but now that she rams her moral perfections down your throat it's a little more than my imperfect digestion can stand." Lilla Perry a number of years later developed into a painter of distinction and charm, working under the particular influence of Monet.

books at hand, with no new experiment or research. He was getting himself up for the oral examinations, he said, by going back through "the old medical textbooks," but taking only "small doses daily, so as not to get too *interested* and so fall into *study*—a poor business." Alice, with her taxing experience of trying "to *study* my lessons" and her awareness that serious effort of any kind almost did her in, would have agreed.

A development of long-range importance for William James was causing a flurry at this time in Cambridge and Boston: the selection of the new president of Harvard. On May 21, the corporation and trustees confirmed the appointment of Charles W. Eliot. In the elder James's judgment, Eliot was "a man of the grossest lack of tact." William partially agreed about his former chemistry teacher, but saw some good points: for all Eliot's "meddlesomeness" and grudge-bearing habit, William said to Bowditch, "his ideas seem good and his economic powers first-rate." There were, besides, no other acceptable candidates.

One month later, William presented himself for his oral ordeals, not altogether sure by his own mental arithmetic whether or not—with a year's absence from the school in Brazil and another eighteen months in Germany and France—he had actually fulfilled the required three years of medical study. He was examined in anatomy by Dr. Oliver Wendell Holmes, sometime dean (1847–53) of the medical school, novelist, poet, and wit, and one of the elder James's favorite Boston figures. (Alice recalled her father saying that Holmes "was worth all the men" in the Saturday Club.) The doctor asked the candidate a single question, and when William answered correctly, Holmes, according to a local tradition, said: "That's enough! If you know *that*, you must know everything. Now tell me—how is your dear old father?"

After receiving his medical degree in late June, William set himself to vegetate for a year, as he had vowed to do. (Henry, to whom his brother's program was reported, wrote from London that "I thoroughly agree with you that to exonerate your mind in the manner you speak of will of itself conduce to your recovery.") He went with the family to Pomfret, in northeastern Connecticut, for a summer stay in a farmhouse pleasantly surrounded by trees. He spent long hours lying in the hammock reading; his mother thought that he rested too much (as she told Harry), and, though improved, he was still in a "morbid state"—by which she seems to have meant that William indulged his feelings of sickness more than necessary. William contended that he was incapable of serious study and had to stifle any desire for it. But "study" is a flexible word in the Jamesian context. A surviving notebook lists the titles at least glanced into by William in the last six months of 1869. It is a staggering collection of philosophical and literary texts in several languages: treatises of Henry Senior mingling with those of Spencer, Comte, Kant, Fichte, Mill, and others; the poetry of Browning with works by Balzac, George Sand, Dumas *fils*, Leopardi, and so on.

Darkness began to close in at the start of the winter. On December 21, he confessed in his journal to being unfitted by "Nature and life . . . for any affectionate relations with other individuals," and that he recognized more than ever the limits of his personal faculties. Humanly estranged and incapable, he expressed again a tired acceptance of a spectator's role in life: "I may not study, make or enjoy—but . . . I can find some real life in the mere respect for other forms of life as they pass, even if I can never embrace them as a whole or incorporate them with myself."

Around January 10, 1870, William suffered a "dorsal collapse," in his phrase, evidently more severe than anything he had yet known. After three weeks of agony, compounded by other sources of depression, he wrote in his diary that he had arrived at the moment of crisis. "Today, I about touched bottom, and perceive plainly that I must face the choice with open eyes: shall I *frankly* throw the moral business overboard, as one unsuited to my innate aptitudes, or shall I follow it, and it alone, making everything else merely stuff for it?"

"The moral business" was William's way, under the influence of Henry Senior, of referring to the whole question of the active will— Alice, we recall, spoke of it as "the moral power"—and the affirming ego; at this phase of the story, we can virtually equate will and ego and identity and even manhood in William's mental workings. The elder James, in William's idiom, had decisively thrown the moral business overboard after the vastation at Windsor—had decreed the "absolute decease of my moral or voluntary power," and the surrender of his being to the vitalizing love of God. William did indeed perceive the choice for him as plain as could be: should he follow the example of his father and give up once and for all any attempt to energize and exert his will; or, quite the contrary, should he make the active will the very center of his life's effort, with all else contributory to that? He went on, in the same February 1 entry, to say that he had not hitherto given any real trial to "the moral interest," but had deployed it chiefly to hold in check certain bad habits, tendencies to "moral degradation" (another allusion, probably, to auto-erotism). Now perhaps his "moral life" might become more active.

201]

There was a slight stir of possibility in the final lines, but it did not endure. Within a matter of days, as it seems, William James descended to his own vastation. He would give a first-person memoir of the episode in the sixth of his lectures on "the varieties of religious experience" at Edinburgh in 1901; and though it occurred in fact in William's second-floor dressing room on Quincy Street, it purported to be conveyed to Professor James by a French correspondent. The general subject of the lecture was "the sick soul," and the particular topic at the moment was "religious melancholy," of which John Bunyan and Tolstoy had already served as examples. "The worst kind of melancholy," James asserted, "is that which takes the form of panic fear." He pretended to be translating freely from the French:

Whilst in this state of philosophic pessimism and general depression of spirits about my prospects, I went one evening into a dressing-room in the twilight to procure some article that was there; when suddenly there fell upon me without warning, just as if it came out of the darkness, a horrible fear of my own existence. Simultaneously there arose in my mind the image of an epileptic patient whom I had seen in the asylum, a black-haired youth with greenish skin, entirely idiotic, who used to sit all day on one of the benches, or rather shelves against the wall, with his knees drawn up against his chin, and the coarse gray undershirt, which was his only garment, drawn over them inclosing his entire figure. He sat there like a sort of sculptured Egyptian cat or Peruvian mummy, moving nothing but his black eyes and looking absolutely non-human. This image and my fear entered into a species of combination with each other. *That shape am I*, I felt, potentially. Nothing that I possess can defend me against that fate, if the hour for it should strike for me as it struck for him. There was such a horror of him, and such a perception of my own merely momentary discrepancy from him, that it was as if something hitherto solid within my breast gave way entirely, and I became a mass of quivering fear.

After this experience, the reminiscence continued:

The universe was changed for me altogether. I awoke morning after morning with a horrible dread at the pit of my stomach, and with a sense of the insecurity of life that I never knew before, and that I have never felt since. It was like a revelation; and although the immediate feelings passed away, the experience has made me sympathetic with the morbid feelings of others ever since. It gradually faded, but for months I was unable to go into the dark alone.

In general I dreaded to be left alone. I remember wondering how other people could live, how I myself had ever lived, so unconscious of the pit of insecurity beneath the surface of life. My mother in particular, a very cheerful person, seemed to me a perfect paradox in her unconsciousness of danger, which you may well believe I was very careful not to disturb by revelations of my own state of mind. I have always thought that this experience of melancholy of mine had a religious bearing.

The lecturer said he wrote the correspondent asking him to explain those last words, and the reply was:

I mean that the fear was so invasive and powerful that if I had not clung to the scripture-texts like "The eternal God is my refuge," etc., "Come unto me, all ye that labor and are heavy-laden," etc., "I am the resurrection and the life," etc., I think I should have grown really insane.

Like Alice James's retrospective account of her 1868 breakdown, William's narrative of hallucination was a highly charged literary composition. He himself drew the parallel with his father's recollected nightmare: "For another case of fear equally sudden," he remarked in a footnote, "see HENRY JAMES: *Society the Redeemed Form of Man*, Boston, 1879." The family similarities are very notable: the lightning suddenness of the invading panic; the total collapse of the self— Henry Senior, after ten seconds, felt himself "a wreck; that is, reduced from a state of firm, vigorous, joyful manhood to one of almost helpless infancy," and William, feeling the core of his being give way, became "a mass of quivering fear." The two men, father and son, sought to ward off insanity by vaguely thinking of "the divine existence" or by invoking New Testament phrases; and both, looking back, marveled at having managed to live (Henry Senior to age thirty-three, William to twenty-nine) in such unawareness of the horror that could beset them.

But the differences are no less arresting. The father, living domestically in the attractive surroundings of Windsor, had been in a particularly hopeful frame of mind; William, in darkened Quincy Street, was burdened by philosophical pessimism and deeply depressed about his career. For the elder James, the basic metaphor had been theological or meta-human: a damnèd shape raying out deadly influences from a fetid personality. With William, it had been medical and psychological: an epileptic idiot whom William appears to have seen on a visit to Dr. Prince's asylum in Northampton. (As has been remarked, Henry Junior's comparable nightmare took place no less appropriately in a great art gallery.)

In an especially revealing distinction, Henry Senior only half consciously recognized the squatting presence as a repressed part of himself; it was the heart of the terror for William that he recognized the immobilized mindless figure as his potential self—what his dead drifting and paralyzing despair could bring him to. And we notice, too, that while Henry Senior, giving up the struggle to hold himself together, had stumbled off to communicate his weight of unrest to Mary James, William was careful not to distress that same person—his cheerful, "healthy-minded" mother—by telling her of his condition.

THE RESISTANT EGO

William may be imagined just beginning to climb out of the lowest depths of despond when, on March 9 (1870), he received the news that Minny Temple had died the previous day at her sister's home in Pelham. The cousins had been together in November, when Minny came up to spend some days at Quincy Street, and again in early December, when she made a feverish round of visits in Cambridge. No more than anyone else had William been aware that the twenty-three-year-old girl was dying of tuberculosis of the lung, and when told of her death he was too stunned for speech. In his diary he drew a three-sided emblem, presumably a tombstone, and within it wrote: "March 9 / MT / 1870." Perhaps he felt that silence could be his only greeting to this intrusion of actual death, and of so vibrant a creature, into a world, for him, already shadowed over by the sickly.

The great turn came on April 29, and it was spurred by a reading of the second in a series of philosophical *essais* by the French neo-Kantian Charles Renouvier. (William had first come across his work in Paris two years before.) The diary entry for April 29 must be given in full: it is an image of the mind in its straining and swerving, and needs to complete itself without break.

I think that yesterday was a crisis in my life. I finished the first part of Renouvier's second "Essais" and see no reason why his definition of Free Will—"the sustaining of a thought *because I choose to* when I might have other thoughts"—need be the definition of an illusion. At any rate, I will assume for the present—until next year—that it is no illusion. My first act of free will shall be to believe in free will. For the remainder of the year, I will abstain from the mere speculation and contemplative Grübelei in which my nature takes most delight, and voluntarily cultivate the feeling of moral freedom, by reading books favorable to it, as well as by acting. After the first of January, my callow skin being somewhat fledged, I may perhaps return to metaphysical study and skepticism without danger to my powers of action. For the present then remember: care little for speculation; much for the *form* of my action; recollect that only when habits of order are formed can we advance to really interesting fields of action—and consequently accumulate grain on grain of willful choice like a very miser; never forgetting how one link dropped undoes an indefinite number. *Principiis obsta*—To-day has furnished the exceptionally passionate initiative which Bain posits as needful for the acquisition of habits. I will see to the sequel. Not in maxims, not in *Anschauungen*, but in accumulated *acts* of thought lies salvation. *Passer outre.* Hitherto, when I have felt like taking a free initiative, like daring to act originally, without carefully waiting for contemplation of the external world to determine all for me, suicide seemed the most manly form to put my daring into; now, I will go a step further with my will, not only act with it, but believe as well; believe in my individual reality and creative power. My belief, to be sure, *can't* be optimistic—but I will posit life (the real, the good) in the self-governing *resistance* of the ego to the world. Life shall [be built in] doing and suffering and creating.*

An incalculable amount of William James is present or implicit in that entry: his mental and psychic life in the years just past, his intellectual stance in the years ahead. As background: the disempowering skepticism into which he had sunk in the German period, and the sense that suicide was the only action available to the impotent will. Now he reached the conviction, with the help of Renouvier, that freedom of the will—"moral freedom"—is a *mental affair*: a matter of choosing what to think about and even more what to believe in. It followed logically that as an initial act of his free will he could choose to believe in free will. His course lay before him: to acquire the habit of strong mental activity, for in habitual "*acts* of thought" lay his salvation. (The seeds of the chapter on habit in *The Principles of Psychology* and of the doctrine contained in the essay on "The Will to Believe" are evident here.)

What was being rejected, clearly and with a kind of hopeful firm-

---

* Some notations. *Grübelei*: an abbreviated or slang form of *Grübeleien*, from the verb *grübeln*—to scratch about on the surface of things, as animals do. James's idiomatic use of the term might be translated "mental rummagings."

Bain: Alexander Bain, British psychologist, whose book *The Senses and the Intellect* William also picked up in Paris in 1868.

Principiis obsta: "Resist beginnings"—a phrase of Ovidian origin (*Remedia Amoris*).

Anschauungen: observings or contemplations ("lookings out").

ness, was the role of passive onlooker which William had felt was the most his nature fitted him for: a posture first adopted in Brazil, and returned to regularly thereafter. All "mere speculation," all passive pronouncements (maxims, for example) are set aside in favor of thoughts conceived as actions: and it is to be noted that in what James himself called an "exceptionally passionate initiative," "action," or words related to it, recur no less than eight times. William James was to elaborate on the theme of "*acts* of thought" some years later in disputing Herbert Spencer's "spectator theory of knowledge," a theory which for a long season had been William's as well. "The knower is not simply a mirror floating with no foot-hold anywhere," he would maintain, "and passively reflecting an order that he comes upon and finds simply existing. The knower is an actor . . . Mental interests, hypotheses, postulates, so far as they are bases for human action—action which to a great extent transforms the world—help to *make* the truth which they declare."*

The notion—thus far only germinating in William's mind—of thought not only discovering but helping to shape truth led him to speak of his intellect as a "creative power," and of the life he was prepared to choose as built on "doing and suffering and creating." It was a sober declaration, still tentative and probing, and made in full consciousness of the tragic potential in experience. It was also a position that finally, after much struggle and pain, reversed that of his father. Far from suppressing the self as the seat of spiritual evil, William formally and vigorously gave his commitment to "the self-governing *resistance* of the ego to the world."

* Henry Junior, as we have seen, was concerned with the comparable question—of the artist as actor, and art as a mode of making—as early as his story "A Most Extraordinary Case." He had, in fact, arrived at fresh formulations of the matter a few months before William's April 30 entry, as will be described in the chapter following.

[206

CHAPTER SEVEN

Henry James
in the Early 1870s

THE DESCENT INTO ITALY

Henry's initial reaction to dark, wintry London was to feel homesick: "abjectly, fatally homesick"; and confessing this to his mother (in early March 1869), he said that he had come to sympathize with Father's habit—when the family was wandering "all over this blasted Europe"—of starting out on a journey only to hurry back to the family the next day. But a week later he was able to assure Alice that he was having the time of his life in London, and that "I haven't felt better in I don't know when," even after a strenuous day that began with breakfast at the Nortons' and ended at dinner with William Morris and his two nieces. "My experiment is turning out a perfect success," he wrote William on March 19, from his lodgings on Half Moon Street, off Piccadilly; and, rubbing it in a little, he declared that the strenuous socializing was a main reason for it.

During the weeks in London, Henry was sponsored on many an outing by Charles Eliot Norton, of staunch New England and Unitarian heritage, who at forty-two was soon to become professor of fine arts at Harvard (solicited thereto by his cousin President Eliot) and widely respected for his cultivated articles in the *North American Review* and *The Nation*, of both of which he had been co-editor. Henry warmed and cooled toward Norton's companionship and his increasingly moralistic views on art (Charles, Henry remarked to the family, takes art so *hard*). He felt more at ease with Norton's younger sister Grace, a widely read student of Montaigne. It was Grace Norton who, on a Sunday afternoon in May, took Henry to a house in Regent's Park to call on Mrs. G. W. Lewes, George Eliot; the high point in a period which included visits with John Ruskin, Charles Darwin, and Dante Gabriel Rossetti, with others already named.

In a review of *Middlemarch* in 1873, Henry James was to say that "George Eliot seems to us among English romancers to stand alone," and that *Middlemarch* "sets a limit, we think, to the development of the old-fashioned English novel"; his own relation to her achievement would be one way to track his career. In 1869, he already felt reverential, and indebted, to the author of *The Mill on the Floss* and *Silas Marner*. He came away from the Sunday meeting almost literally enchanted. "She is magnificently ugly—deliciously hideous," he wrote Henry Senior next day; but "in this vast ugliness resides a most powerful beauty which, in a very few minutes, steals forth and charms the mind, so that you end as I ended, in falling in love with her." Yes, he said, behold him really in love with "this great horse-faced bluestocking." Trying to locate the source of the charm, Henry suggested "a mingled sagacity and sweetness . . . a great feminine dignity and character . . . a hundred conflicting shades of consciousness and simpleness—shyness and frankness—graciousness and remote indifference." But the visit had to be cut short when Mrs. Lewes's twenty-four-year-old second stepson collapsed onto the floor with an attack of agonizing pain in his spine.

Henry's back, he was pleased to report, was giving him almost no pain for the moment, but he was suffering intermittently from digestive trouble. In April, he betook himself to Malvern, north and west of London in the hills of Worcestershire, and a therapeutic retreat run by a Dr. Raynor. The regime had Henry alternating between baths, meals, and brisk walks, and did him some good. He stopped over in Oxford on the way back to London; and lingering in the courtyard of Magdalen amid the evening dimness, he thought that his heart "would crack with the fulness of satisfied desire." The whole place, he said, gave him a deeper sense of English life than anything yet experienced. There were a few more days in London before Henry crossed the Channel to Boulogne, paused briefly in Paris, and then went on to Switzerland and a hotel-*pension* at Glion, above Montreux and the Lake of Geneva.

The aim of the European venture had all along been Italy, and Henry had been mentally and physically preparing himself for the plunge. What he especially needed before taking it, he seems to have understood, was to pull himself into psychic shape by connecting his present being with that younger self of the European school years twelve and fourteen years earlier; and he had begun to do so from the moment he set foot in London. He had the illusion, he wrote Alice, of having lived long in the "murky metropolis," and: "I actually believe that this feeling is owing to the singular permanence of the impressions of childhood, to which my present experience joins itself on, without a broken link in the chain of sensation."

He tested those childhood impressions again in Boulogne, which seemed to him exactly the same as in the dusty summer of 1857, except that it was smaller than he recalled. Paris struck him as changed for the worse, full of "flare and glare"—"the reflection of torrid asphalt and limestone by day and the feverish currents of gaslight by night"; but it did his soul good to stroll again through the galleries of the Louvre.

In Switzerland, where he passed most of the summer, he could look down from his perch at Glion to Montreux directly below, and, along the lakeside, to Vevey and Lausanne; behind the promontory in the western distance, as he knew, lay the city of Geneva, in and near which he and his brothers had been so variously schooled. By the end of August, he felt ready to make his entrance into Italy: an event that, in his telling of it, was highly ceremonial, as well it might be. Henry was the first member of the James family ever to undertake it.

One final chore remained before his departure: a reckoning up of his expenses to date. There had been some emanations from Quincy Street, including a questioning letter from Willy, to the effect that he was spending rather too much money. On May 10, Henry had written his father in anguish: "To have you think that I am extravagant with these truly sacred funds sickens me to the heart." All told, in eleven weeks in England, he would have spent no more than £120 (600 American dollars of the time), including sums for the considerable purchase of clothing. Henry preferred to make his financial reports to his father, and when Mary James replied to his letter with mild and unusual remonstrance, Henry was startled into an eloquent defense of his conduct.

He had come abroad, he explained, with the idea that travel, frequent changes of setting—not a single change, say from Cambridge to Paris—and new associations would be the best cure for a condition of health which, in the three or four months before sailing, had completely prevented him from reading or writing ("Willy can tell you").

The winter in Italy would by no means be, as his mother had called it, a "recreation"; it would be "an occasion not only of physical regeneration, but of serious culture too (culture of the kind which alone I have now at twenty-six any time left for)." The physical improvement and the cultural enrichment would permit him thereafter to work, to write and publish and earn money; the whole thing was a sound investment.

To this, Mary James, writing from Pomfret in late July, replied with a gush of maternal emotion:

Your letter last evening opens the deepest fountains in my soul, and my bosom seems as if it would burst with its burden of love and tenderness. If you were only here for an hour, and we could talk over this subject of expense, I could, I know, exorcise all those demons of anxiety and conscientiousness that possess you, and leave [you] free as air to enjoy to the full all that surrounds you, and drink in health of body and mind in following out your own safe and innocent attractions.

She positively commanded him to "throw away prudence" and think only of his own comfort and pleasure. Nothing could be better for him than Italy in the winter. "You dear reasonable over-conscientious soul! Take the fullest liberty and enjoyment your tastes and inclinations crave, and we will promise heartily to foot the bill."

Mary drew a portrait of summer life in the Connecticut hills that almost caused Henry, as he would say, to "go leaping home in the simple spirit of childhood." It was an Arcadian existence, Mother said, passed mostly under the pines. The weather was warm and fresh; and on the day of writing, while she and Alice had their books and their sewing, and Father exchanged weighty opinions with a friend, Willy had been lying in the hammock with a volume of Browning in his hands, and Lizzie Boott sat nearby sketching at her easel.* Mary could hear Willy and Lizzie murmuring together about art and literature. She thought that Willy might be falling in love with the girl, and that his "susceptible heart may be coming to the rescue of his back." Which

* Elizabeth Boott, with her father, Francis Boott, a composer of sorts, was also staying in the same rustic boardinghouse in Pomfret that summer. She had spent most of her young life in Europe, chiefly in a villa on the Bellosguardo slope outside of Florence. She had arrived in Newport recently, and had quickly become a good friend of Minny Temple. Lizzie Boott was to be one of Henry James's most cherished women friends, and would figure in his fiction as the source for Pansy Osmond.

reminded her: "You know Father used to say of you, that if you would only fall in love it would be the making of you."

Henry began his descent into Italy around August 21. After Glion, he had gone up into the Bernese Oberland and on to Lucerne, where he hoped in vain to catch up with Aunt Kate, somewhere in Switzerland touring with a friend. Henry took the steamer down Lake Lucerne to Fluelen, at its southeastern tip, and from there, bulky knapsack on his back, he walked down to Hospenthal on the St. Gotthard Pass, a two-day trip. Here he veered west in the direction of the Simplon Pass, but partway up the Grimsel his legs gave out and he indulged himself in a diligence for the six-hour journey to the village of Brig, spread out below the snow-covered crags that guard the Simplon Pass to the south. The next morning he arose at four-thirty and, having hired someone to carry his knapsack, started across the pass. It was the pleasantest day he had known in Switzerland: superb weather, views clear and unclouded, his strength restored "with interest" (Alice was the recipient of his colorful travelogue); and above all, "the sense of going down into Italy—the delight of seeing the north melt slowly into the south—of seeing Italy gradually crop up in bits and vaguely latently betray itself." By evening, after a thirty-mile mountain clamber, he came to the Italian frontier village of Isella, lying narrowly between the sharply rising mountainsides; it was the scene, two years later, of Henry's adventurous little tale "At Isella."

Fatigued as he was, he was up at dawn to catch the public stage-coach down to Domodossola and Lake Maggiore. "I had a ride of six hours to Baveno on the shore of the Lake. Down, down—on, on into Italy we went—a rapturous progress thro' a wild luxuriance of corn and olives and figs and mulberries and chestnuts and frescoed villages . . ." In making that memorable descent from the Simplon, in Leon Edel's phrasing, it was as if Henry "walked into his future." So acutely and ritualistically did Henry himself feel this that, after a day of boating around the perfumed and terraced Borromean Islands on Lake Maggiore, he decided to walk back into Switzerland and make the descent a second time. He trudged northeastward and crossed up and out of Italy by the Bernardine Pass ("a lovely pass" but "an awful grind"). He spent a day resting, and reading Harriet Beecher Stowe's *Old Town Folks*, which he had come upon by chance, then made his way to the village and the precipitous, windswept pass of Splügen, and cautiously down to Chiavenna. He was again in Italy. A lake steamer next day, August 31, transported him to Cadenabbia, on the western side of Lake Como, opposite Bellagio. In its general appearance, Henry mused to Alice, Como did not strike him as superior to the finest Swiss lakes that he had seen: "But it's when you come to the details—the swarming shimmering prodigality of the landscape—that you stand convinced and enchanted before Italy and summer."

APPROACHES TO AN IDEAL SELF

On this first exploration of Italy, Henry spent some four and a half months. He rode down from Como to Milan to collect the luggage he had sent on there, and then proceeded across northern Italy, stopping at Brescia, Verona, and Vicenza en route to Venice. He allowed himself ten days in Venice: it was "quite the Venice of one's dreams," he wrote John La Farge, "but it remains strangely the Venice of dreams, more than of any appreciable reality."

Coming down from Venice to Florence, he succeeded in transforming "Padua, Ferrara, Bologna and Parma from names into places," as he informed Alice on October 6, writing her from the Hôtel de l'Europe, near the Carraia bridge in Florence. His response to Florence was mixed. It was not "a particularly cheerful city," he said in a sharp-eyed report to his mother; "its aspect—thanks to the narrowness of many of the streets and the vast cyclopean structure of many of the buildings—is rather gloomy than otherwise." His digestion was acting up, and his small hotel apartment was so frigid that he had to warm his fingers with a candle. Even so, before long, and after walking back and forth along the elevated connecting corridor between the Uffizi and the Pitti Palace, he was saying that if he should ever feel like living in Italy for a time, this was the place he would choose. It had abundant vitality, was full of varieties of foreigners, had an unsurpassed collection of art treasures, and on all sides wonderful walks out into the soft, encircling Tuscan hills.

But Rome, which he reached on October 28, drove all before it. "At last—for the first time—I live!" he exulted to William. "It beats everything: it leaves the Rome of your fancy—your education—nowhere. It makes Venice—Florence—Oxford—London—seem like little cities of pasteboard. I went reeling and moaning thro' the streets, in a fever of enjoyment." In the course of the single day of arrival, and after an all-night journey by carriage through steady rain from Florence, Henry traversed almost the whole of the ancient city, catching glimpses of the Forum, the Colosseum ("stupendissimo"), the Campidoglio (the equestrian statue of Marcus Aurelius especially caught his fancy), the

Pantheon, St. Peter's, the Castel Sant' Angelo (he carried Stendhal's *Chartreuse de Parme* in his pocket), and a series of minor piazzas and monuments.

What was most marked during this whole Italian autumn was Henry's developing insight into Italian art of the fourteenth, fifteenth, and sixteenth centuries. Or more accurately, into Italian artists; for what struck him after a morning in the Doge's Palace and the Accademia in Venice, he told William, was that he had not "half so much been seeing paintings as *painters*." There was a recognizable touch of John Ruskin and Charles Norton in the saying, and more so when Henry went on to argue about Tintoretto, whom he regarded as unquestionably the greatest of the Venetian painters, that "he ends by becoming an immense perpetual moral presence." But Henry also brought his own sensibility as a writer and critic of fiction to bear on the pictorial texts. Tintoretto's greatness, he speculated, lay in his habitually conceiving "his subject as an *actual scene* . . . wrenched out of life and history"; as in his *Annunciation*, which Henry described graphically: "To the right sits the Virgin, starting back from her angelic visitant with magnificent surprise and terror. The Angel swoops down into the picture, leading a swarm of cherubs, not as in most cases where the subject is treated, as if he had come to pay her a pretty compliment but with a fury characteristic of his tremendous message."

Illuminating contrasts began to proliferate in Henry's observing and meditating mind. As against the terrible narrative force of which Tintoretto was capable, the beauty of Paolo Veronese, as seen in the large canvases in the Accademia, came from "the perfect unity and placidity of his talent. There is not a whit of struggle, nor fever, nor longing for the unobtainable, simply a glorious sense of the look of things." In Padua, Henry was staggered by the extraordinary quality— which he recognized on the spot—of the several dozen frescoes by Giotto adorning the walls of the Scrovegni Chapel: scenes from the lives of the Virgin and of Christ, and of the Last Judgment. He had always assumed, Henry wrote Alice, that Giotto had been merely the favorite of the sentimentalists in criticism. "But he is a real complete painter of the very strongest sort. In one respect he has never been surpassed—in the faculty of telling a story—the mastery of dramatic presentation."

And then, in these early-fourteenth-century frescoes, Italian art seemed to Henry to "tremble and thrill with a presentiment of its immense career—for the next two hundred years." Henry's tone throughout was youthfully self-assured ("*Cet âge est sans pitié*," Henry would say some years later, looking back on such earlier judgments), but in his assessment of Giotto and other "primitives" he was fifty years ahead of American popular taste; for despite the efforts of James Jackson Jarvis, begun as early as the 1860s, the Pre-Renaissance Italian masters would not be accepted in America until around 1920. In the 1870s, Americans tended to honor the sixteenth-century Bolognese artists. But in Bologna, when he paused there, Henry James became conscious of the exact reversal of the spectacle he had witnessed at Padua: "art having played itself out and living on memories, precepts, and ambitions—Guido, Domenichino, the Carracci etc."

In these diverse judgments, Henry was clearly testing and measuring himself as an apprentice *literary* artist. Was his talent essentially placid and harmonious, or did he welcome struggle and the need to strain beyond his given grasp? Was he placed by historical circumstances at the end of a literary development with little to feed on but memories of past achievements; or was a new age, maybe a long one, of high accomplishment in the offing? Did *he* possess a genuine faculty for storytelling and for dramatic presentation? The whole matter came to a temporary climax in the fundamental distinction that Henry drew, in Rome, between the artistic character of Raphael and that of Michelangelo.

In Florence, Henry had come to regard Michelangelo's tombs in the Basilica of San Lorenzo for the two later and lesser Medici, Giuliano and Lorenzo, as forming "the most impressive work of art in the world." He found "the warrior with the cavernous visage"—the helmeted Lorenzo—to be "absolutely terrible"; and, in a perception that has never been bettered, saw the figure shedding "an amount of inarticulate sorrow sufficient to infest the Universe." The paintings of Raphael in the Uffizi were likewise works of genius, but of an entirely different order. Raphael was unique: an example of "genius pure and simple, unalloyed and unmodified by the struggles of development and the teachings of experience." The singular charm of his art, Henry said to his mother, was due to his seeing the world as "clear, tranquil and serene . . . You don't in the least feel about his figures as about many others—M. Angelo's especially—that they *might* have been ugly."

But after further visual study of the two artists in Rome, Henry hardened what had been a fairly genial opposition—like that between Tintoretto and Veronese—into a sort of absolute of the creative spirit. He brooded over Raphael's frescoes in the Vatican *stanze*—*The School of Athens* among them—and a couple of days after Christmas he passed on his verdict to William. "I have found after much fumbling and worrying—much of the deepest enjoyment and of equal dissatisfaction—the secret of his incontestable thinness and weakness. He was incapable of energy of statement." And it was finally "this energy—positiveness—courage,—call it what you will" that was the "fundamental, primordial quality in the supremely superior genius. Alone it makes the real man of action in art and disjoins him effectually from the critic."

After standing in almost uncontrollable excitement that very morning before Michelangelo's statue of Moses, at San Pietro in Vincoli, Henry felt sure that "Michel Angelo's greatness lay above all in the fact that he *was* this man of action"—probably the supreme instance in human history, considering what Henry conjectured was Michelangelo's "temptation . . . to be otherwise." For what was overpowering about Moses was "the eloquence with which it tells the tale of the author's passionate abjuration of the inaction of fancy and contemplation."*

Henry James was here defining his ideal self, and rejecting the part of him that might be tempted to accept the role of spectator. He was giving voice to his nascent belief that creativity involved risk, struggle, courage, adventure: in short, action. In his later formula, a work of art, literary or otherwise, constituted a "braving of difficulties," or it was nothing. The letter from Rome advancing these aesthetic notions probably reached his brother William, in Cambridge, in the middle of January 1870—a fortnight or so, perhaps, before William's nightmare vision of the epileptic idiot. There is no way of determining how much of Henry's sizing up of things clung to William's mind. But we can observe that when William began to fight up out of the darkness in the early spring, he took a stance provocatively similar to Henry's: a declared abstention "from the mere speculation and contemplative *Grübelei* in which my nature takes most delight," and a commitment to the active exercise of his will, and to being, as it were, the real man of action in thought.

Henry's return journey from Rome to London was made by train and channel steamer. From the Charing Cross Hotel, he again totted up his expenses and calculated that he had spent about £400 during

---

* This is a brilliant reading of the sculpture. In the strenuous twist of his body and the sharp turn of his head, Moses seems to have only seconds before decided to shake off a period of brooding passivity; and Henry James detects in that posture the *artist's* renunciation of the contemplative role.

his year abroad. This was, in fact, a sizable chunk, possibly a fifth, of his father's income, and Henry knew it. But he made the point (it will be familiar to other lovers of travel) that while he could perfectly well do without all kinds of things, those things he did want to have and do were not likely to be cheap.

He went back to Malvern in mid-February and to Dr. Raynor's establishment. He had had a wretched spell of indigestion and constipation during the last part of his stay in Florence; but wise medical advice from Willy and some pills prescribed by a Florentine doctor had done wonders. The visit to Malvern was mainly a safety precaution. He wrote William proudly that he was walking twelve miles a day, and spoke with surging confidence of his literary plans and ambitions. Florence, he was sure, would figure in them; the city had really entered his life, and was destined to operate there, he prophesied, "as a motive, a prompter, an inspirer of some sort."

It was at Malvern on March 26, 1870, that Henry learned from his mother that Minny Temple—"dear bright little Minny," in Mother's words, and Henry blessed her for them—had died in Pelham, at age twenty-four, of tuberculosis of the lung. The letter Henry immediately wrote and dispatched alternated between efforts to catch hold in language of his cousin's matchless but evanescent qualities and a recurring realization of "the hard truth that she is *dead*—silent—absent forever." He became sensible, he said, "how her image . . . operated in my mind as a gentle incentive to action and enterprise." To William three days later, he spoke of Minny as a sort of ultimate paradigm of the human possibility. "I feel," he said, "as if a very fair portion of my sense of the reach and quality and capacity of human nature rested upon my experience of her character." He had not actually been in love with her: "and yet I had the great satisfaction that I enjoyed *pleasing* her almost as much as if I had been." The saddest of his reflections, as he thought and wrote about Minny, was "of the gradual change and reversal of our relations: I slowly crawling from weakness and inaction and suffering into strength and health and hope: she sinking out of brightness and youth into decline and death."*

Henry, grateful for having been spared the sight of Minny's suffering, declared himself "perfectly satisfied . . . to have her translated from this changing realm of fact to the steady realm of thought." There,

---

* Leon Edel, at the close of *The Untried Years*, points to two little-known tales by Henry James, "Longstaff's Marriage" (1878) and "Maud-Evelyn" (1890), as being sinister and ghostly versions of the phenomenon here described by Henry.

he predicted, "she may bloom into a beauty more radiant than our dull eyes will avail to contemplate." This of course was what did happen, after Minny Temple re-entered Henry's mind and fiction-making imagination in the 1890s and reappeared as Milly Theale, whose early death spurs the denouement in *The Wings of the Dove* in 1902. Henry brought to an end his autobiographical volume *Notes of a Son and Brother* in 1914 by reference to that novel, after devoting the last forty pages to Minny, her life, her recorded words, her death. John Chipman Gray, by now a longtime professor of law at Harvard, had at some earlier date given Henry a bundle of letters Minny had written Gray from January 1869 to February 1870, just before her death; and while having them transcribed into his manuscript (before, apparently, destroying them), Henry allowed the letters to set astir memories going far back to the Newport days, to North Conway in the summer, to meetings and impressions and echoing exclamations.

Even Henry's last picture of her, carried away from his farewell visit to Minny at Pelham, before sailing for England, had gained a kind of permanent radiance: Minny gliding with swift grace about the old-style parlor, talking eagerly, eyes glowing, tossing her head back in the familiar way and opening her mouth in musical bursts of laughter that disclosed her large shining teeth. In several of the letters to Gray, Minny spoke of Willy James, saying in an early one: "He is one of the very few people in this world that I love. He has the largest heart as well as the largest head . . ."* In her next to last letter, near the end of January 1870, she said that "Willy James sometimes tells me to behave like a man and a gentleman if I wish to outwit fate." She perfectly took the spirit of the odd injunction. "What a *real* person he is!"

As his reminiscence completes itself, and with it the volume of autobiography, Henry coalesces the two figures, Minny and Milly. "Death, at the last, was dreadful to her; she would have given anything to live"—he could have been speaking about either young woman— "and the image of this, which was long to remain with me, appeared so of the essence of tragedy that I was in the far-off aftertime to seek to lay the ghost by wrapping it . . . in the beauty and dignity of art." Then, fading backward in memory from 1914 through the writing of *The Wings of the Dove* in 1902 to that moment in 1870, and speaking

---

* Henry sent this on to William, who was visibly moved. "Few spirits have been more free than hers," he wrote back. Minny had "no analogue in all my subsequent experience of people."

as well for his brother, Henry put a period to it all: "We felt it together as the end of our youth."

THE CAMBRIDGE SCENE
AND THE WRITING OF FICTION

Henry had a rendezvous in London with Aunt Kate, and they made the ten-day crossing on the *Scotia* together, reaching Quincy Street on May 10 in unseasonably warm weather. Gazing out from his open bedroom window, and writing to Grace Norton (herself in Siena for a long stay), Henry Tuscanized the Harvard scene: "Opposite thro' the thin trees I see the scarlet walls of the president's *palazzo*. Beyond, the noble grey mass—the lovely outlines, of the library: and above this the soaring *campanile* of the wooden church on the *piazza*." From a distance, he added, there came the sweet tinkle of horsecars. He could announce his family as being well, his parents particularly so. Alice seemed "quite an altered person" in strength and activity, and William's condition inspired him with hope (Henry had evidently been given some limited account of the crisis William had been passing through). His older medical brother, meanwhile, after a careful examination, declared Harry to be in excellent condition and (this to Bob James) his constipation no longer a serious problem.

Henry lost little time inserting himself into the Cambridge social and literary life, such as it was. He saw something of the Sedgwick clan—the oldest of them, Susan, was married to Charles Eliot Norton and in Italy with her husband; but the younger sisters were still in the nearby Kirkland Street home, Theodora—"a most delightful young lady"—and Sara, now Alice James's closest friend; along with the brother Arthur, a lawyer and editor. With Clover Hooper and Lizzie Boott, Henry went to lunch at Shady Hill, the attractive estate of the absent Nortons, a few minutes walk from Quincy Street. James Russell Lowell, Harvard professor and prolific essayist and poet, was occasionally in view; the benign Mr. Longfellow showed on the horizon. William Dean Howells, newly established editor of *The Atlantic Monthly*—"monarch absolute" of that periodical, Henry would say some months later—was giving a series of lectures on Italian literature at Harvard in the spring of 1870, and Henry went to hear them, listening with his eyes closed and dreaming of Florence. In a second letter to Grace Norton, Henry made mention of a new name: "Do you know Henry Adams? . . . He has just been appointed professor of

History in College, and is I believe a youth of genius and enthusiasm—or at least of talent and energy."

After a summer spent partly at Saratoga, with successive fortnights at Pomfret—"the lovely—the *quasi* Italian!"—and at Newport, Henry said guiltily to Miss Norton that he was doing no work of consequence and hardly knew when he might expect to. In fact, three new stories, substantial enough to run, between them, through five issues of the magazines in which they appeared, would be published that fall and in the spring and summer of 1871. (*Watch and Ward*, which was technically Henry James's first novel but which he would later disavow, would also be serialized over six months in 1871.*) All three tales came out of Henry's European *Wanderjahr*, and the first of them, "Travelling Companions," is little more than a rehearsal of Henry's trip from Milan through Verona and Vicenza to Venice and down through Padua to Florence; with those admirable passages on Tintoretto and the Giotto chapel in Padua lifted almost intact from letters home.

The third story, "At Isella," Henry forwarded to Grace Norton soon after its appearance in the August 1871 *Galaxy* (the rather short-lived, 1866–78, New York rival of *The Atlantic Monthly*, which featured Whitman and Mark Twain as well as Henry James). It resulted from a "vague desire to reproduce a remembered impression and mood of mine." The plot turns on a young American who comes down from Lucerne over the Simplon Pass to have his first view of Italy; about half the narrative is given to a colorful rewriting of Henry's letter to Alice about his own epic descent. At the frontier village of Isella, he comes upon a comely Italian *marchesina* who is fleeing her brutish husband to join her ailing lover in Geneva. The American, stirred by her plight, provides her with the carriage fare to Geneva, and she makes her escape just before her *sposo* arrives in pursuit. It was the kind of romantic adventure Henry had daydreamed of having: an experience in keeping with his high feelings about coming into Italy.

Much the most ambitious of the new stories was "A Passionate Pilgrim" (*The Atlantic*, March–April 1871), and it may have been too ambitious for its own literary good. The narrator, barely arrived in London, encounters a fellow American, a sickly and penniless person named Clement Searle—another in Henry James's extending line of moribund lead characters—who thinks he has a claim on the property of the English Searle family. The narrator escorts him to Lockley Park (Lock*leigh* is the name of Lord Warburton's estate in *The Portrait of*

* See below, pp. 239–40.

a Lady), where they are greeted kindly by the timid Miss Searle but are raged at and derided by the brother, Richard Searle. The Americans repair to Oxford, where Searle goes into his final decline. Miss Searle comes to his deathbed with the news that her brother has been killed in a hunting accident. Had Searle lived, he could have married Miss Searle and inherited the property.

Around this slender anecdote there swirl themes that would be developed in many a later story, novella, and novel: the sources and confusions of identity; ghosts, doubles, and opposites; the intimate connection between truly living and truly loving; the contradictions inherent in an American's passionate devotion to the old country. From his current personal life and even more from the psychic troubles of his brother William, Henry derives what is, or wants to be, the main focus of interest: the vicissitudes of the human will and of individual effort. Clement Searle sees himself, accurately, as one who has merely drifted all his life, wholly lacking in "will and purpose and direction." In Oxford, he makes the acquaintance of an English counterpart, an aging down-at-the-heels Oxford graduate, and when the latter complains of his bad luck, Searle reads him a lecture: "My friend, you're a failure! Be judged! Don't talk about chances . . . It lies neither in one's chance or one's start to make a success . . . It lies in one's own will! You and I, sir, have had none."

Henry thought well enough of "A Passionate Pilgrim" to make it the title story in his first collection of tales in 1875; and despite its cluttered quality, it was, in fact, his best narrative performance to date, an early fulfillment of the process by which Henry had been gathering and straightening himself as a fiction writer. His mother, in a letter from Pomfret the previous summer, had pictured Alice sitting under the trees with Mr. Gray discussing "Harry's stories," and had voiced her opinion that the most recent one, "Gabrielle de Bergerac," was his best. Henry, after thanking Mother and Alice for their compliments, said that the work now struck him as thin and watery, especially "as regards its treatment of the Past." (The story purports to be the narrative by an aged French refugee and former nobleman of certain melodramatic events that occurred in France before the Revolution.) Having seen something of the past with his own eyes, Henry had gained a sense "of what a grim old deathly reality it was," and an awareness that, to cope with it, you needed a firmer command than he had of historical facts. The present and the immediate future now seemed to him the better and truer province of fiction. Henry would not cease entirely to deal with the past, but he would do so, as will be noted, in special and strategically artful ways.

Contemporary history at this time assumed the form of the Franco-Prussian War, which had erupted two months after Henry's return to Cambridge. Henry watched it with the keenness of one who had recently watched the American Civil War from a distance, and conveyed to Grace Norton the James family's strong sentiment in favor of the Germans. The war, he wrote, had effected "a prodigious unmasking of French depravity and folly"; and the official French utterances, wrote this future devotee of Paris, struck him as those of "barbarians and madmen." The virtues of Germany, he felt, shone forth by contrast; and here we may postulate the influence of William, who would have been Germany's spokesman at Quincy Street. But Henry was also in the first flush of his infatuation with Italy; and he admitted to Grace that he took satisfaction from the fact that "while France and Germany, those great pretentious countries, were fiercely cutting each other's throats, the lovely country of my heart was Italianizing Rome with barely a gunshot." The capital of the newly united Italy was being transferred from Florence to Rome in September 1870, and Henry dared hope that with its withdrawal "the Florence of old" might be recovered and a stop be put to "the rank modernization" visited on it since 1865 by the governmental presence.

Another matter with a historical dimension was of greater personal urgency for Henry, and had been since he pondered the course of Italian art in Padua and Bologna. Where did American literature stand at the start of the 1870s, and where did he, Henry James, stand within it? He was not altogether pleased by William's admiration for Hawthorne and the form in which it was expressed. William, earlier in the year, had read *The House of the Seven Gables* for the first time, and called it "a great symphony": he rejoiced that Hawthorne was an American, and added that it tickled his "national feeling not a little to note the resemblance of Hawthorne's style to yours and Howells's." The fact, he went on, that with all the available English models Harry and Howells should "involuntarily have imitated (as it were) this American" seemed to William to point up the existence of "some real American mental quality." To this, Henry, from Malvern, had replied minimally that he was glad William was liking Hawthorne, but that he meant "to write as good a novel one of these days (perhaps) as the House of the Seven Gables." Henry's curiously ungenerous remarks about Hawthorne in a review two years later can be set against this exchange.

The question of Henry's contemporary, Howells, was no less complicated. Henry had taken to the affable and energetic Ohio-born writer from the moment he came to Boston in 1866, at the age of twenty-nine, to join the staff of *The Atlantic Monthly*, and the two had engaged in endless walks and talks together. Henry was gratified by Howells's strong editorial support of his work, and enjoyed Howells's writings as being "really American." But that, Henry was sometimes prone to suggest, was just the trouble with them. About Howells's first novel, *Their Wedding Journey* (1872), Henry said to Grace Norton that it was "a somewhat melancholy spectacle"—Howells's "charming style and refined intentions are so poorly and meagrely served by our American atmosphere"; what could be duller than an American journey?*

But Henry was troubled by a suspicion that Howells possessed a gift he was not quite capable of appreciating; and he kept giving his friend literary honor with one hand and taking it back with another. Howells's collected sketches from *The Atlantic*, Henry opined to Charles Norton in early 1871, belonged "by the wondrous cunning of their manner, to very good literature," and yet Howells was perhaps fatally limited by his native subject matter—which would yield its secret, Henry was beginning to think, "only to a really *grasping* imagination. This I think Howells lacks. (Of course, *I* don't.)" Still, Howells was a bright spot in the local society, and for Henry, there were not many others; there was a kind of staleness in his repeated allusions to the Sedgwicks and to Lowell and Longfellow (the latter, Henry remarked pointedly after an evening with him, "is not quite a Tintoretto of verse").

"Our dear detestable common Cambridge" was Henry's title for it on returning to town at the end of the 1870 summer. During the summer following, he discovered modest pleasures in rambling the hills of Waltham and Arlington, and reclining on the wooded slopes to take in the view of "the great blue plain of Boston and its bluer copes of ocean." With the family away at Scarborough Beach in Maine, Henry occupied the house alone, until the arrival of Wilky James. The younger brother had finally given up on the Florida affair, and was thinking of following Bob to Milwaukee; but at the moment he was, imaginably, full of talk about the long railroad trip he had made to California, in a private Pullman car and in the company of Emerson, John Murray Forbes, and a number of others.

---

* Theodore Dreiser, for personal and literary reasons, would find the novelized journey "one fine piece of work; not a sentimental passage in it, quarrels from beginning to end, just the way it would be, don't you know, really beautiful and true."

Henry James in the Early 1870s

But Cambridge was a representative part of the larger American setting, as to which Henry was torn by contrary responses. He was indeed in this time caught up in a network of ambivalences, interrelated and interacting, of which the dominant symbols were "America" and "Europe." While still abroad, he had inveighed against American tourists for their "stingy, grudging, defiant, attitude towards everything European," and pronounced them ugly in voice and feature. Even then, though, he allowed Americans to be a people of character and vigor and "intellectual stuff." After he had been home for six months he found himself liking America to a degree that astonished and moved him. His next stay in Europe would be a long one, he conjectured to Charles Norton, and he did not want to be haunted, when hearing some American sound on the other side of the Atlantic, by the "fantasy of thankless ignorance and neglect of my native land."

By midwinter of 1872, Henry was achieving the kind of poise—as regards the besetting question of the two worlds—that was prerequisite for him as a writer. Acknowledging to Norton an almost morbid desire to hurry over to the other side, he paused to acknowledge his exaggeration of European merit. "It's the same world there after all and Italy isn't the absolute any more than Massachusetts. It's a complex fate, being an American, and one of the responsibilities it entails is fighting against a superstitious valuation of Europe." Willy would have agreed so wholeheartedly that he could almost have written the sentences.

On May 11, 1872, two years virtually to the day since his reappearance at home, Henry took ship for England, this time as the companion and shepherd of his sister and Aunt Kate. In a newsy letter to Elizabeth Boott in Tuscany, a few months before, Henry had given the latest word on the younger children: Bob had spent a week with the family; Wilky was pursuing "his Western work" (thinking of which made Henry count his blessings at not being "lodged in one of the innermost circles of the Inferno—in Wisconsin," even if he were momentarily stuck in Cambridge); and Alice had gone for a week "with Mrs. Walsh, to New York." The chief purpose of the trip, Henry thought, was "to buy a 'party-dress'—though her parties are rare." The implied pathos may have been overdone. Alice was evincing enough vitality, anyhow, to brave her own first experiment of Europe after a dozen years.

223]

THE FAMILY COURIER

She would remember it as an act of courage, of surmounting a terrible *"funk"* that she felt, suddenly, on the eve of embarkation. Alice had been both impressed and demoralized by Henry's letters about the great Italian masters, and wondered nervously if she should even "know what to *do* with the pictures" she would be confronting. Imagine therefore, she wrote in her journal, "the bliss of finding that I too was a 'sensitive,' and . . . that a Botticelli said an infinity of things to me—and this in a flash of mutual recognition, after the years of toil in trying to establish some sort of relation, either of speech or silence, with the Botticelli of Boston." According to her brother, who hovered nearby with approval and delight, she established a relation with astonishing ease. Alice's undertaking, he wrote their parents from Oxford in early June, "has already proved a most distinct and brilliant success. She enjoys, admires, appreciates and observes to the utmost possible extent."

Alice began to thrive, Henry said, from the moment the party landed at Liverpool and made the little journey over to Chester, to settle in for a week at the agreeable Queen Hotel. In the sitting room of their suite, Henry drew an ink sketch of Alice fronting a large bow window and hunched over a table to write a letter home; able to gaze out onto an elegant, richly green garden; and looking oddly younger than her nearly twenty-four years. Aunt Kate, Henry hinted, was not particularly relishing the trip on her own count, and had come mainly to be of help to Alice. As for himself, Henry, who bragged that he had not missed a single meal on the "boisterous" Atlantic crossing, was finding Chester an exceptionally fine old place, with its ancient wall that circled the town, its English-style porticos, and its total lack of modern conveniences. He would shortly write an article about Chester for *The Nation*, and would send Lambert Strether wandering through its streets in the opening of *The Ambassadors*.

Curbing his impatience, Henry escorted the ladies to London by gentle stages, with periodic days out for rest. Alice was rather oppressed by the vast metropolis with its "great seething multitude," and was inclined to scorn the English for having produced only one superior painter (she seems to have meant Turner). Paris, which the threesome reached on June 26, was much more to her taste; and indeed she took to the Parisian life, the meals and the wine, the sightseeing and the dressmaking, with such intensity—and said so in letters back home with so much avidity—that her parents grew positively alarmed. Henry assured them that Alice, in Paris, "displayed more gaiety, more elasticity, more genuine youthful animal spirits than I have ever seen in her." But her mother sent signals about self-restraint, which were muffled by joking references to the "cerebral derangement" Alice must have suffered in crossing the Channel, and Father worried that she was fatiguing herself dangerously. Willy perhaps gave her the sagest advice for once: "Let your mind go to sleep and lead a mere life of the senses. Forget your conscience and religion, which will return tenfold better for it when you are home again by my side."

These Paris days were certainly, for Alice, her ripest experience thus far of that "sensuous education" that Henry Senior had once said was uniquely available in Europe. But after a surprisingly short time, Henry made the strange decision that the three of them should leave the city and go to Geneva, where they stopped at the old Hôtel de l'Ecu of childhood memory. He feared, so he said, that Alice would be affected by the extreme heat of Paris in summer, and that she would be better off on a Swiss lake and in the mountain air. In fact, after a month of traveling eastward across Switzerland from Geneva to Thusis—by way of Bern, Interlaken, Lucerne, and Andermatt—Alice underwent the only nervous collapse in this period. Henry, giving a cautious report and reversing his earlier judgment, blamed the incident on Alice's being overstimulated by the "stiff mountain air." There were, though, additional sources for the ten-day attack.

Lizzie and Francis Boott joined the party at Villeneuve, outside Geneva; and while even Henry, who liked them, felt the constant presence of the pair conduced to nervous exhaustion (especially since Francis Boott insisted on addressing him as "Mr." and could rarely be made to laugh), Alice was plainly put off by the proximity of an accomplished young female rival for attention. "It makes some difference in Alice's buoyancy," Henry admitted, "whether she is the centre of a body of three members or of six." Beyond that, Alice had made plain her preference for Paris, and to be snatched away into the Alps was, to her frail sensibility, in some sort a denial of her.

"Alice's own impulse and curiosity," Henry was brought to acknowledge, "is almost altogether towards cities, monuments, and the *human picturesque*, of which she has seen, during her lifetime, so little." (The same impulse would work in Milly Theale, abandoning Switzerland for London, in *The Wings of the Dove*, on the grounds that, though she was all for scenery, "she wanted it human.") Remarking that they would skip the lakes in northern Italy, Henry said: "Alice would give a lake for a city any day," and that if she could be guided through *all* the cities of Europe her "invalidism" would be practically cured.

There were four days in a Venice swarming with mosquitoes, and then up through the South Tyrol en route back to Paris, where they arrived in mid-September. Alice fairly fell upon the city, walking about (Henry said, using a word of special import for himself and William) "with unabated elasticity," shopping frenetically, plunging from monument to monument. Part of the human picturesque in Paris was composed of Americans: Uncle Edmund and Aunt Mary Tweedy, staying at the same hotel as the James party; Mr. and Mrs. James Russell Lowell; Chauncy Wright, an intellectually stimulating friend of William; Charles Norton, whose entourage lacked his wife, Susan (she had died in childbirth in January).

Alice and Aunt Kate had a few days in London, with Henry, before they sailed for America on October 15. The city again struck Alice as crowded and charmless, though Henry did his best to make it attractive for her. Throughout the six months' jaunt, Henry, according to Aunt Kate, had been quite remarkably attentive and thoughtful. "He *forgets* nothing," Kate wrote her sister Mary, "and his care and consideration for Alice is unceasing." If Mary could see how Henry folded and stowed away the shawls and rugs, the parasols and umbrellas, after every outing, tears would flow from her eyes. On his side, Henry sensed his aunt's impatience to get back to Cambridge, but insisted that "her devotion to Alice has been *immeasurable*, and has been everything in seconding the benefit of our travels."

Henry estimated that by the time he saw Alice on board ship, he would have spent about $2,400 of the "paternal bounty" on the European trip. It was an impressive amount, but the family, on inspecting Alice after her return, was quick to agree that it had all been worthwhile. William declared at once that the experience had been "a great thing" for Alice in every way, and that there was no end to her lively chatter about people and places. As the weeks passed, however, Mary James was giving familiar words of warning. Alice continued to seem much stronger than before she had left, Mother wrote Henry in December; but the life in Cambridge offered her so few distractions that Alice might be forced to fall back "upon her books," an eventuality her mother obviously considered alarming.

Before summer's end, Henry had made a firm resolution, as he put it, to try his luck at remaining abroad. "I feel as if my salvation, intellectually and literarily, depended upon it," he informed his parents from Bolzano. He had had a spell of poor health; but "my improvement is going on now at so very rapid a ratio that I feel an almost unbounded confidence in my power to do and dare. In short, I am really well, and am confident of being able to work quite enough to support myself in affluence." The move toward Europe was also a clearly marked stage in Henry's gradual withdrawal from the family—as the environment in which he might most readily flourish, not only as a writer, but as a human individual. His "salvation" lay elsewhere.

After his sister and aunt had departed, Henry went back to Paris, where he put in the remainder of the autumn. It was at this time that he began to strike up a friendship with James Russell Lowell: "a furious intimacy" was his mildly sardonic phrase for it, to his father; Henry thought the fifty-six-year-old poet friendly and entertaining, but shallow in his opinions. Going to dine with Lowell on a Sunday, Henry encountered Emerson staying in the hotel, and two days later the pair of them walked through the Louvre together. Emerson's presence had as always "a sovereign amenity," Henry told Norton; though his perception of art was not very keen.* By Christmas Day, Henry was lodged on the Via Gregoriana in Rome.

He settled down with a kind of reverence, and in a month was saying to Alice that Rome "quietly, profoundly, intensely delights and satisfies"; it was "monstrously amiable." Part of the pleasure was social: Henry entered almost immediately into the most hectic social existence he had yet known. He had complained to William that he had not met any Frenchmen in Paris, and it cannot be said that he met many Italians in Rome. But there was an abundance of Americans; every afternoon Henry passed carriageloads of people he knew in the Corso. There were those who came briefly and went on, like Henry Adams and his wife of half a year (the "Clover Adamses," Henry called them). There were more permanent residents, like the Tweedys and the Bootts—Henry got along famously with the latter in the absence of Alice, and took to horseback riding with Lizzie in the Campagna for two hours at a time, his first such exercise in years. In this category, too, and longtime friends-to-be, were Sarah Wister of Philadelphia, daughter of the great and popular actress Fanny Kemble, and "the terrific Kemble herself," by whose "splendid handsomeness of eye, nostril and mouth" Henry was smitten at a small supper party. And

---

* Emerson and his daughter Ellen were on a long trip to help him recover from the shock and distress of the fire which had burned down his Concord home. Henry had heard about the disaster from his mother, in a letter received in Switzerland.

finally there were the Roman Americans, like the household of William Wetmore Story, a sculptor of wide renown, in Palazzo Barberini; and that of Luther Terry, painter of large solemn religious pictures, in the Piazza dei Santi Apostoli (Mrs. Terry was the sister of Julia Ward Howe, whose "Battle Hymn of the Republic" was still resoundingly in fashion).

For all his busy and happy socializing, Henry was hard at work; though, as usual, he complained that amid the distractions of Rome he was getting little done. He had been in print intermittently for some eight years; but we will not be far wrong if we date his arrival as a professional literary man in this five months' stay on his own in Via Gregoriana—near the end of which he celebrated his thirtieth birthday. He contributed a stream of articles to *The Nation*, several of which were garbled by the typesetters ("pavements," for example, coming out as "garments"), and he sent articles and short stories to *The Atlantic Monthly* via his father, who gave tireless service as editor, proofreader, and agent. For Tom Perry at the *North Atlantic Review*, Henry wrote a longish appreciation of Théophile Gautier; and one of the most brilliant of his earlier pieces was an article on George Eliot's *Middlemarch* for the *Galaxy*. William had written to say that he was "aghast" at the novel's "intellectual power." Henry thought this too strong, the kind of thing one says about Shakespeare; but certainly, he allowed to Grace Norton, "a marvellous *mind* throbs in every page of *Middlemarch*. It raises the standard of what is to be expected of women—(by your leave!). We know all about the female heart; but apparently there is a female brain, too." The paternal opinion was being conspicuously revised in the younger generation.

The most telling work of the months in Rome was a short story, "The Madonna of the Future," in which an art-loving American, in Florence, comes to know an elderly countryman, Theobald, who is possessed by the dream of painting the quintessence of all Madonnas. It is gradually revealed that Theobald is the pathetic victim of a complete illusion: after twenty years, his canvas remains blank, and the allegedly beautiful female whom he had befriended and who was to serve as his model is simply a rather coarse old woman, though a good enough soul. When he is made to face up to the reality, Theobald, in the manner of Jamesian protagonists, confesses his failure—his inability to "act" or to "dare"—and sickens and dies.

It is possible that, in describing Theobald and his nonexistent painting, Henry had remotely in mind his sometimes ineffectual-seeming father and the book he had never (yet) quite managed to write.

What was much more palpably on his mind, however, was the continuing question of art and the American practitioner. Strolling together out of Piazza Signoria and along the Arno—the Florentine setting is vividly done—Theobald and the narrator address the problem. "We are the disinherited of Art!" Theobald exclaims. "We are condemned to be superficial! . . . The soil of American perception is a poor little barren artificial deposit." To this the narrator answers firmly: "Nothing is so idle as to talk about our want of nutritive soil, of opportunity, of inspiration, and all the rest of it. The worthy part is to do something fine! There is no law in our glorious Constitution against that. Invent, create, achieve!" Thus, the two Henrys arguing with each other; or a trifle more accurately, the Henry of 1873, in the person of the narrator, rebutting the self of a few years earlier.

"My appetite for domestic tidings is getting sharp," Henry observed to Alice in early February, adding that he was sorry to hear she had been suffering from headaches. His sister did experience some mysterious physical and psychological backslidings during the winter months: "Poor child!" Mother lamented to Henry, "*why* is it that she has gone back so? Can there be any thing in the climate to account for it?" On the whole, though, Alice was in fairly good form, busy in several activities, riding horseback, and (shortly) taking pleasure in the new phaeton—a four-wheeled open carriage, drawn by two horses—purchased for her by her father. "She always holds the reins," Aunt Kate remarked.

The parents, both of them entering their sixties, continued to be in good health and full of affection. The previous summer, when Alice was still abroad with Henry and Kate, Mary James had drawn an idyllic, if sentimental, portrait of Father and "the delight he takes in hearing from and writing to you; his entire freedom from all kinds of responsibility; no little girl to manage and inspect him, no one but his docile wife to make much of him and be made much of by him . . ." The news about the younger brothers as of the winter of 1873 was varied. Both were working in Milwaukee as clerks with the Milwaukee and St. Paul Railway, though Bob was being transferred to the outpost at Prairie du Chien on the far western side of the state. The previous November Bob had married a Miss Holton; after the bridal couple had spent a week with the family in Cambridge, Henry Senior told Harry that Bob's "little dame" was a person of no " 'innards' " whatever, but was "altogether in her senses," a condition Father approved, since it would help her to rescue Bob from his fits of moodiness and suspicion.

229   ]

Wilky was undergoing some unspecified difficulties—he must learn to stand on his own feet, Mother wrote cryptically in January—and he, too, was preparing to marry a Milwaukee girl, a Miss Cary, whom Mary James disliked.

"The most fearful thing in letters from home," Henry complained to his father, in begging for more precise information about Wilky's *inamorata*, "is to be told that some one else has told us all about such and such a matter." It would be some time before the various fraternal shifts and alliances could be sorted out for the self-exiled Henry.

THE ANGEL AND THE DEMON:
REUNION IN TUSCANY

The news about William in the spring of 1873 was at once more detailed and more complicated. During the first half of Henry's two-year sojourn at Quincy Street, William (as his brother could observe) had mostly been biding his time, as regards scientific or philosophic study. His private commitment to active thinking, of which he perhaps gave Henry some inkling, remained theoretical; serious intellectual effort continued to disturb and fatigue him. As before, he was devouring novels, essays, biographies, poems at a rate that Alice, at least, found nearly incredible, especially since Willy seemed never to miss anything of importance in any text. But he spoke of himself dispiritedly. Explaining to Bowditch that he did not feel up to a conference with Jeffries Wyman, recently returned from Florida at the end of 1870, William said that the best he could do was to read newspapers and books: "Thought is tabooed, and you can imagine that conversation with Wyman should only intensify the sense of my degradation."

He took a step toward the world of science in the spring of 1871 by enrolling in a series of lectures at Harvard on "Optical Phenomena and the Eye": "the first mingling in the business of life which I have done since my return home." In September, he began to use Bowditch's laboratory at the medical school for some experiments of his own. A few months later, he completed an unsigned review for *The Nation* of Hippolyte Taine's *On Intelligence*, his first publication of any kind in three years and one which, brief though it was, offered a first airing of his philosophical interests. (Henry, who read it in Paris, professed to admire the piece, little as he understood it.) But the marked change in William's external fortunes came in the summer of 1872, when President Eliot appointed him instructor in physiology at Harvard, to offer a course which would begin the following January. The course would be coupled with that by an anatomist, Timothy Dwight, and the salary would be $600 a year. William was in Scarborough when the word reached him, and his delight in it found expression in the picture he gave Henry of his coastal surroundings: "The steady, heavy roaring of the turf comes through the open windows, borne by the delicious salt breeze over the great bank of stooping willows, field and fence . . . The broad sky and sea are whanging with the mellow light."

To his family, as the year 1872 drew to a close, William seemed to be in better health than in years; and from Paris, Henry exulted in the expatiations by Aunt Kate and Alice on "the remarkable salubrity" of his brother's appearance. Soon after the turn of the year, William began his teaching, lecturing on physiology three times a week at eleven in the morning. He was much stimulated, he wrote Henry, by the intellectual challenge of the enterprise, how to get his "matter" across to the students; and not less by the practical problem, which he grasped from the first moment he ascended the platform—"how to govern them, stir them up, not bore them, yet make them work etc."

His father held forth to Harry, in a March letter, on William's classroom success and his state of being. "The students (fifty-seven)," he wrote (there were actually forty-five), "are elated with their luck in having such a professor, and next year he will have no doubt a larger class still, attracted by his fame." William had come to him the other afternoon, Henry Senior went on, and after pacing up and down animatedly for a time, he exclaimed: " 'Dear me! What a difference there is between me now and me last spring this time: then so hypochondriacal' (he used that word, though perhaps in substantive form) 'and now feeling my mind so cleared up and restored to sanity. It is the difference between death and life.' " The engagement with live human beings in the classroom represented for William (who said as much to Henry) an escape at last from the prison of his mind and those philosophical broodings to which, despite himself, he was still addicted.

He was also and significantly clarifying the mental maneuvers that had temporarily liberated him in the spring of 1870. When the elder James asked him how he accounted for the great change, William replied: the reading of Renouvier and especially "his vindication of the freedom of the will"; the reading of Wordsworth; and, related to both writers, a giving up of "the notion that all mental disorder is required to have a physical basis." This notion had become quite untrue to him, Henry Senior wrote. William now "saw that the mind did act irrespectively of material coercion, and could be dealt with therefore at

231   ]

first-hand, and this was health to his bones." That last characteristic paternal remark was peculiarly felicitous: for William, though still acknowledging the impact of body on mind, was now ready to affirm both the genuine independence of the mind—and hence its susceptibility, as it were, to self-policing—*and* the mind's reverse impact upon the body.

The semester was barely half over when President Eliot, conscious of young James's rapidly growing reputation, offered William "the whole department"—that is, the two courses in physiology and anatomy—for the following year. William instantly went into a tailspin, and over the next four months changed his mind about the presidential invitation half a dozen times. He oscillated between alternatives in a manner reminiscent of a decade before, aware that at the heart of it all was the old question of intellectual energy and determination.

His first response to Eliot was that he had "resolved to fight it out in the line of mental science"—to devote himself full-time to the study and teaching of philosophy, and the psychological dimension of it. Three days later, he went around to the president's office to say he would accept the appointment in physiology and anatomy, and would stay in that department. Philosophical activity in any long run, he had again come despondently to feel, was not suitable for him. The building of comprehensive concepts, he wrote Henry, was simply beyond his strength; and besides, "to make the *form* of all possible thought the prevailing *matter* of one's thought breeds hypochondria." Thinking about thinking depressed him terribly; he needed "some stable reality to lean upon," and the concrete facts of biological science supplied it. Moreover: the philosopher as such, so William was making it out, never counted on something in beneficent nature to get him through the bad times; the philosopher made combat with his own purely intellectual weapons, by the active play of his individual mind—exactly as William himself had begun to do in the spring of 1870, but felt disempowered from doing now.

A month later, he was wondering whether he would be up to teaching anything at all in the year ahead. He knew his classes were popular, but the pedagogical effort was almost abnormally exciting to him: "a feverish sort of erethism" was William's more technical phrase. He recognized that his symptoms resembled those of his sister, in the rhythm of excitement, exhaustion, collapse, though he did not suffer the extended attacks undergone by Alice. Within the household, he watched her more attentively than ever. Each sign of improvement in Alice encouraged him, he told his mother, since he judged "her weak, nervous condition" to be very like his own.

Henry James in the Early 1870s

Mary James was finding it hard to be patient with her oldest son; or perhaps one excessively nervous child at a time was enough for her. "Morbid" was her recurring word for him. She remarked, with a curious lack of approval, that William had "a morbid sympathy" for any form of privation or trouble. Last evening, she wrote Henry in early summer, William suddenly began to lament that the kitchen held only one armchair for three servants. Mother soothingly promised to add two more.

To Henry, his mother made little effort to conceal her favoritism. In September, after praising Henry's "dear courageous hopeful heart," she said that Willy was "still very *morbid*," and "much more given than he used to be to talk about himself." She went on: "If dear Henry you could only have imparted to him a few grains of your own blessed hopefulness he would have been well long ago." William certainly did not see this letter, and Henry would not have mentioned it; but the atmosphere in Quincy Street was unmistakable, especially to anyone as alert as William James. Even from across the water, the shadow of his healthier, professionally and financially prospering younger brother must have loomed large indeed.

Its presence can be sensed in William's self-reproachful remarks. In September, William notified Eliot that he could not accept reappointment at Harvard for 1873–74, and had decided to go abroad for the winter. When he had broached this possibility to Henry earlier, Henry had proposed Rome as the most nourishing place to stay, and had spoken of the many hospitable people to drop in on and the villas and churches to sit around in. The vision conjured up was not precisely what William intended, but he thanked Henry for his advice—while hoping earnestly he would not have to verify it: "as such a step would be about equivalent to desperation of any continuous professional development, and would leave my future quite adrift again." He felt wretched, too, at the thought of his travels being an expense to their father, when Bob and Wilky were in such financial need. But after further weeks of vacillation, William gave up, and in October booked passage for Liverpool. He immediately felt better and began to talk to the family about taking courses of study in Florence or Heidelberg.

Henry had left Rome in May, had paused briefly in Perugia (where, at the inn, he ran into William's Berlin host, Hermann Grimm, with his wife "drinking their tea with a great reverberation," and seeming most amiable), and had gone up to Florence. He looked kindly upon the Tuscan city, but thought that Rome "had murdered her" with its myriad enticements, and after a few weeks moved on to Switzerland

233]

and a little later to Bad Homburg in Germany. It was mid-October before he returned to Italy and the Hôtel de l'Europe on the Florentine Arno, where he settled down to wait for his brother.

In a reckoning up, Henry calculated to his father that he had drawn about $500 for living expenses in the previous four months, while arranging for writing fees of $600 to be forwarded to the elder James. In an earlier accounting from Rome, Henry had showed an equally favorable balance: $575 drawn out over five months, and $740 paid in. Even those cheering figures were a bit misleading, for throughout the Roman period Henry had a number of articles and stories accepted but not yet printed or paid for. Henry was producing so much and so fast that American magazines could scarcely accommodate him. In the spring and summer of 1873, Henry sent off a barrage of articles to four different periodicals—on Rome, Siena, Homburg, the writings of Turgenev, unsigned notices and reviews; and a number of shorter and longer works of fiction. Nothing was too slight to escape the transforming pressure of his pen. Referring to a piece about horseback riding in the Roman Campagna, Henry said (to Mrs. Wister): "I had to make up for small riding by big writing. But what's the use of writing at all, unless imaginatively? Unless one's vision can lend something to a thing, there's small reason in proceeding to proclaim one has seen it."

In Bad Homburg, Henry completed "Madame de Mauves," his most substantial and shapely deployment to date of what was emerging inevitably as "the international theme" in his fiction. The theme is built into the story through a young American with the melancholy name of Longmore, who, in the Paris suburb of St.-Germain-en-Laye, observes with varying emotions the deteriorating marriage between a young New England woman, Euphemia Cleve, and the dissolute Baron de Mauves. But it is not quite the drama of New World innocence and virtue versus European immorality and corruption: the son of Henry James the Elder was unlikely to present anything so elementary. The American-born baroness, indeed, embodies much of what the James children had been taught to regard with deep suspicion: "I have nothing on earth but a conscience," she explains to Longmore. In the outcome, her puritanic rigidity baffles and frustrates her husband until he blows his brains out. Longmore, another of James's male figures who think about taking part in the human drama but never do, holds back from asking the widow for her hand. His chiefest feeling for her, he realizes, is not desire but *awe*.

"The Angel sleeps in number 39 hard by," William wrote Alice from the Hôtel de l'Europe in Florence at midnight on October 29,

(Above) William James, age nineteen
(Below, left) William James at Newport, about 1863
(Right) William James, about 1862

Dine by Milly Faulds for Frank Lincoln
1859

HERE I AMD SOAROW SIT

letters. Never before did I know
what mystic depths of rapture lay
concealed within that familiar word.
Never did the same being look so different, as I going in and coming
out of the P.O. if I bring a letter
with me. Gloomily, with despair
written on my leaden brow I stalk
the street along towards the P.O.
women, children and students involuntarily shrinking against the wall
as I pass. - Thus
But when I come
out with a letter an
immense concourse
of people
attends
to my lodging
attracted
by my
gestures
and look.

(Left) William at the P.O. *(Below)*
From a playlet by William James
about meeting Emerson at a boot-
black stand; 1864

(Opposite, top) The Wizard: sketch by
William James, 1859. *(Bottom) Here I
and Sorrow Sit*: sketch by William
James, early 1860s

The Foreboding Meeting
or
The Artist's Fate.
Drama
Dram. Personae.
Sage of Concord
W. J.
Scene
Parker's boot blacking
establishment

Enter W. J.
W. J. I say, boy, just give my boots
a lick.
          x x x x
Enter. S of C.

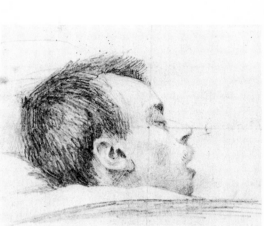

(Opposite, top, left) Garth Wilkinson James, September 1862. (Right) Garth Wilkinson James in uniform, 1863. (Bottom) Robertson James in Newport, April 1862. (Above, left) Adjutant James and Lt.-Col. Hallowell, July 1863. (Above, right) Wilky James recovering from his wounds, sketched by William. (Right) William James in Brazil, June 1865

(Right) Alice James in 1870. *(Below)* Alice James in a sketch by Henry, May 1872

(Left) Minny Temple, 1869.
(Below) Henry James, 1863–64

William James in 1869

"all unwitting that I, the Demon (or perhaps you have already begun in your talks to distinguish me from him as the Archangel), am here at last. I wouldn't for worlds disturb this his last independent slumber." William had hurried through London and Paris ("terribly monotonous-looking"), and had made a twenty-two-hour train ride to Turin, followed by a twelve-hour trip amid pouring rain to Florence.

"Angel" had been an epithet bestowed upon Henry in his younger days, seemingly by his mother. William normally invoked it with a certain derision, and here, as we see, he suggests that he himself might be taken as an angel of a higher order. His first report on Henry, to his parents on November 9, was a typical blend of the serious and the joshing. "First—of the angel," he wrote. "He is wholly unchanged. No balder than when he quit; his teeth of a yellowish tinge . . . his beard very rich and glossy" (due, William understood, to a substance called Brilliantine). His clothes and shoes were in good condition, and he had just stolen from William a pair of excellent garters. "The 'little affectations' of which Mother spoke I have not noticed," William continued, in a rare clue that Henry did not go uncriticized in the maternal conversation. "He probably fears me and keeps them concealed."

The angel then gave way to the ogre, in one of William's most sportive passages. "He speaks Italian with wonderful fluency and skill as it seems to me; accompanying his words with many stampings of the foot, shakings of the head and rollings of the eye sideways, terribly upon the awestruck native whom he addresses. His manner with the natives generally is very severe."

In this epoch of new and requickened initiatives for the James children, it was the first time the older brothers had been together in Europe since 1860, when, with Wilky, they went from Geneva to Bonn for a German summer. While they were still, possibly, reminiscing about that moment, there arrived a letter from Henry Senior with the double report that Wilky and Miss Cary had gotten married, and that in the same week Mrs. Bob James had given birth to a baby boy. Neither of the older Jameses had much good to say about Wilky's wife: a young lady with no conversational ability at all, Father said, with a strain of obstinacy and no pull on the affections. William, speaking for Henry as well, expressed regret at the lack of enthusiasm for Miss Cary, but rejoiced unrestrainedly over the other news. It was, he said, a grand occasion in the family story: "the 3rd generation of the J. family is in full swing! We are uncles, grandmothers, aunts etc., all drawing our subsistence as such from that one worm-like being in Wisconsin."

William's visit was also his first experience of Italy; and in effect it was to *Henry's* Italy that he was being exposed, in guided Florentine tours of the Uffizi and the Pitti, in strolls up to San Miniato and Bellosguardo, in excursions to Fiesole and the high-perched village of Vincigliata. In all situations, Henry was the translator and interpreter. At the hotel, the brothers congregated in Henry's spacious room, with its windows looking south across the river and the fireplace before which Willy was wont to sit and write letters to the family. William could observe Henry at his morning's work each day; and he would have been made privy to the literary news Henry was sending home: a check for $75 for "From a Roman Notebook"; the dispatch of a bundle of articles on Florence to the recently formed and well-paying magazine, the *Independent* of New York; the arduous revision of the essay on Turgenev (it was on the German text of *King Lear of the Steppes*, and Henry Senior, a warm admirer of the Russian novelist, had urged a number of changes); an inquiry from Howells about Henry collecting the best of his stories into a volume, and Henry's parallel proposal to bring together his travel articles (they would appear as *Transatlantic Sketches* in 1875).

Despite all this, William, as the days went by and to every outward appearance, grew steadily stronger in health, spirit, and humor. Henry's comments reflected the process. They were at first restrained and judicious. "He varies a good deal at different times," Henry wrote in November. William faithfully explored the galleries and churches, but he was often tired. A fortnight later: "I value greatly *his* impressions; they are always so lively and original and sagacious that it is a real profit to me to *receuillir* them." That somewhat patronizing note quite vanished from the later communications.

The brothers went down to Rome at the end of November, and Henry observed with pleasure that Willy was enjoying "all the melancholy of antiquity under a constant protest . . . His talk as you may imagine, on all things, is most rich and vivacious. My own more sluggish perceptions can hardly keep pace with it." Henry meant at least half of what he said: in his "Florentine Notes," he offered abundant examples of shrewd and lively talk attributed to an "inveterate companion" or to "W." And Henry would have been amused and encouraged by William's chaffing remarks (to Alice) about Henry's new addiction to wine, and his tendency to tremble with rage if the waiter were slow in bringing it.

But William was undergoing other and darker interior events that Henry could scarcely have guessed at. On the journey down from Florence, William had been appalled by the sight of the hill towns, and said so to his father: "They make one realise how man's life is based historically on sheer force and will and fight." It may have been that tense familiar vision, always both stirring and fearful for William, that brought about an experience, during a visit with Henry to the Colosseum one night, that verged on a "vastation." It was, startlingly, more like his father's nightmare at Windsor than his own in Cambridge.

When we entered the mighty colosseum walls and stood in its mysterious midst with that cold sinister half moon and hardly a star in the deep blue sky—it was all so strange and I must say inhuman and horrible that it felt like a nightmare. Again would I have liked to hear the great curses which you would have spoken. Anti-Christian as I generally am I actually derived a deep comfort from the big black cross that had been planted on that blood-stained soil.

If Harry had not been there with him, William concluded, he would have fled "howling" from the place. It seems not to have occurred to William that Henry's commanding presence, in just that instant of their lives and their relationship, might have contributed to the psychic ordeal. Henry himself, standing at his ease by William's side, had no inkling of his brother's near-collapse and spoke affably to Father of Willy's special pleasure in a "moonlight walk to the Forum and the Colisseum."

But gradually, subtly, in the rhythm of their days, the earliest of the fraternal relationships crept back into being. The change was related to illnesses. William had a mild brush with that form of malaria known as Roman fever (perhaps contracted in the swampy Colosseum: Daisy Miller would pick it up there, and die from it). To escape a worse attack, he went hurriedly back to Florence, Henry carried along in his wake. In Florence, Henry came down with something that sent him to bed for ten days; the symptoms were fever and racking pains in the head. Henry described it as "a strange and mysterious visitation"; and continuing in what might be called the coded family language, he said: "Willy has simply been a ministering angel," who had nursed and tended him throughout "with inexpressible devotion," not to say medical skill.

What the episode portended for Henry, he told the family, was that Willy was not only "most vigorous and brilliant," but that "he seems *entirely* the Willy of our younger years again"; the superior and radiant Willy, one gathers, of Geneva and Paris. And also perhaps the Willy who used to lay down the law: in the letter's next sentence Henry said he had been revising his plans about the future and that, more or less accepting William's view of the case, he had "pretty well made up my mind to return home during the coming spring." When the brothers separated in early February (1874) and William went to Venice and the north to join the Tweedys in Dresden, Henry began to say that he actually felt better *since* his sickness than before it. It was oddly put, but Henry seems to have been confusedly expressing a certain relief at William's departure. Indeed, the "visitation" may well, though only in some indeterminate way, have resulted from Henry's sense of being crowded by his renewedly dazzling brother. It even seems likely that the Florentine period with William would play its part, a great many years later, in Henry's own nightmare or near-vastation that "the dream of the Louvre," as it is called, was also in part a memory of Palazzo Pitti.* But there is also no doubt—for contrary impulses flowed and always would flow between these two—that one outcome of the Italian months together was an increased mutual appreciation, a sort of affectionate watchfulness that could be essentially helpful for both.

PIAZZA SANTA MARIA NOVELLA

A sign of this with William, soon after his return to Cambridge around the middle of March, was his firm declaration to Henry: "I'm in a permanent path." He welcomed any gossip Henry might have about Florence, but he himself now felt toward the city as he did "towards the old Albany of our childhood, with afternoon shadows of trees etc." He, Willy, by implication, had put away things childish and European. "All my moments here," he could admit, "are inferior to those in Italy, but they are part of a long plan which is good, so they content me

---

* The Louvre dream was described in Chapter 3 above: Henry's late-in-life "nightmare" (his word) of arduously putting to flight some invading figure and pursuing him down the hall of the Galerie d'Apollon. One obvious identification of the invader is his brother William.

In "Florentine Notes" of 1874, Henry tells of walking through Palazzo Pitti with "W——," his "inveterate companion," and quotes William expressing the wish to gaze at length "down through the open door at that retreating vista of gilded, deserted, haunted chambers." The scene stirred and frightened him, William indicated, though he couldn't say why. Henry suggested to his readers that the fear arose from an awareness of the "ghostly presence" of struggles and desperations and dreams over the centuries.

For Henry at least, the moment in Palazzo Pitti seems to have provided a lasting but muffled association between a vista of haunted chambers and a sense of brotherly pressure.

more than the Italian ones which only existed in themselves." He was ready to begin a professional American career.

For Henry, hard at work again in Florence, the fruit of the time with William was to launch himself at last on a full-length novel. It was spurred by a letter from Josiah Holland, editor of the new periodical *Scribner's Monthly* (and himself a prolific author of popular fiction), proposing that Mr. James write a novel for it. Henry conferred by mail with Howells. "To write a novel I incline and have long been inclining," he observed on March 10, "but I feel as if there were a definite understanding between us that if I do so, the *Atlantic* should have the offer of it." After brooding a little, Henry hit upon $1,200 as the sum he would ask for what he conceived as a twelve-part narrative. The elder James was the negotiating agent, as he had been for his son in other instances, and in April he received a note from Howells agreeing to the terms and accepting the novel as a serial to begin in January 1875.

Henry's words suggest that he regarded the new undertaking as his first attempt at the novel form. Howells may have thought this curious, since *The Atlantic* had brought out a novel by Henry James, Jr., in five installments from August through December 1871. It was called *Watch and Ward*, and Henry thought well of it at the time: "Something slight," he told Charles Norton, "but I have tried to make a work of art." By 1875 he had pretty much disavowed the work, and though he saw to its publication in book form (for copyright reasons) in 1878, he made no allusion to it in his later backward glances over his career.

Flawed and, so to say, aesthetically thoughtless though it may be, *Watch and Ward* is not without its attractions, both literary and biographical. It tells of Roger Lambert, a genteel Bostonian—though we are not sure that the setting is Boston until, halfway through, we find ourselves on Washington Street—who adopts a twelve-year-old girl under rankly melodramatic circumstances. Nora, the ward, grows to young womanhood with the years; and Roger (himself growing "bald" and "corpulent," in partial image of his creator) performs the Jamesian role of the watcher. He hopes, needless to say, that in due course Nora will consent to marry him. But two other suitors make their appearance: Roger's cousin Hubert Lawrence, a light-minded clerical gentleman, and Nora's cousin George Fenton, a scoundrel of sorts. The tripling of suitors, first occurring in the tale "Poor Richard," it may be noted, would be handled most adroitly in *The Portrait of a Lady*, which in other respects brings to fruition matters introduced in *Watch and Ward*.

Family elements abound in this apprentice novel, which is itself concerned at every turn with family relations, with parents and off-spring and adoptive children and cousins. The narrative sends Roger to Rio de Janeiro and on to Lima; and Fenton—in a fictive echo, as we shall see, of Bob James—thinks of seeking his fortune in Texas. Far more striking are the moments in which Roger is contrasted with each of the other courtiers, in ways plainly derived from relationships in the James family home. Hubert and Roger, we are informed, "had been much together in early life and had formed an intimacy strangely compounded of harmony and discord. Utterly unlike in temper and tone, they neither thought nor felt nor acted together on a single point . . . but each, nevertheless, seemed to find in the other a welcome counterpart and complement to his own personality." Surveying George Fenton and Roger, Nora finds that "Fenton represented to her fancy that great collective manhood of which Roger was not. He had an irresistible air of action, alertness, and purpose. Poor Roger, beside him, was·most prosaically passive."

But it is Roger who wins Nora's hand, after certain implausible plot maneuverings which leave Fenton thoroughly discredited. Thus the seemingly passive figure wins a complete victory over the alleged man of action and purpose. Roger triumphs, we may say, exactly be-cause he has been not only so dedicated but so assiduously *active* a watcher. "Do they know her," he cries to his friend Mrs. Keith, "have they watched her as I have done? What are their months to my years, their vows to my acts?"

It is to be admitted that the male-female relationship is sometimes expressed in disconcerting language, as when Roger dreams of play-fully forcing apart "the petals of the young girl's nature" to make it ready to "receive his own sowing"; or when Nora, wanting to borrow a key to wind her watch, discovers that Roger's key won't fit, while Hubert's needed "some rather intimate fumbling" before it could be adjusted to "Nora's diminutive time-piece." Edel wonders whether James did not write those passages with tongue-in-cheek. Perhaps he did: elsewhere in *Watch and Ward*, amid whatever misfirings, there is a clear self-consciousness about the nature and the importance of the psychological and familial themes. The presence of such embarrass-ments, even so, may be the reason for James disowning the work.

Roderick Hudson, as the novel would eventually be called, would forever be associated for Henry James with Piazza Santa Maria Novella, the Florentine square facing the fifteenth-century cathedral of the same name, with its almost incomparably elegant façade by Leon Battista Alberti. Henry took an apartment there in April, on the second floor of a house at the corner of Via della Scala: a large, high-ceilinged, charmingly shabby sitting room; two bedrooms (he invited Alice to lodge herself in the "guest chamber"); a scullery and a china closet. Santa Maria Novella had always been Henry's favorite piazza in Florence; now he could enjoy it to the full, looking out through the slits of shutters, closed against the glare, at the dusty and "ever-romantic" quadrangle; at the rococo obelisk in the unpaved center, and along the side, in the shade, the rows of horsecabs, with the drivers sprawled asleep in them.

In the spring and early summer of 1874, Henry came to love Florence as never before: it seemed to him, he told Howells, like a familiar literary masterpiece that one reads and rereads with constant pleasure. He had located a French restaurant nearby on Via Rondinelli which (he made Willy's mouth water at the news) had lobsters and truffles in the window and was an excellent place to dine. When it was too hot to stroll in the piazza, he could sit in the cathedral, which he described as divinely cool and picturesque. But it was a solitary kind of existence: Henry told his mother in June that he had dined out only twice since Christmas.

There was in Florence nothing resembling the American colony in Rome. The Lowells came to town as usual, and Henry had desultory gatherings with some rather pathetic people named Lombard. But Henry seems to have been only dimly aware of the English residents in Florence (studious observers of the Tuscan scene like Janet Ross and Violet Paget, for example, or the various members of the Trollope clan); and he made notably little effort to cultivate, or be cultivated by, the Florentines themselves. As to the latter, he had remarked with an air of bafflement to Grace Norton, in January, that "I have been nearly a year in Italy and have hardly spoken to an Italian creature save washerwomen and waiters." He admitted this might be his fault, but pointed out that even so ardent a lover of the whole Italian scene as he could not find any "easy initiation into what lies behind it."

Other American Italophiles have felt so since; but in the case of Henry James there was a social opportunity he refused to grasp. He had been given an introduction to Karl Hillebrand, a much admired German scholar of literature and philosophy (William had had some correspondence with him), who made his home on Lungarno Nuovo (now Amerigo Vespucci), five minutes' walk from Henry's piazza. "Hillebrand offers me the *entrée* of *any* Italian society *au choix*," Henry told his parents with apparent glee in late February; he went to dinner at Hillebrand's at least once and visited on a couple of other occasions. But he found Hillebrand less and less *simpatico*—he was an "unmistakeable snob," Henry explained to William. He did go, on Hillebrand's proffered invitation, to a ball in the Cascine, where he saw "a concentration of the élite of Florentine society," but otherwise Henry took no advantage of the social opening.

He communed with his mother about the general problem: where might he live, in Europe, if he should choose to stay on for another year? Florence was too empty, socially, for him; and he could not face what he feared would be "a year of British solitude." What he desired more than anything else, he said, and what would do him the most good, humanly and as a writer, "is a *régal* of intelligent and suggestive society, especially male. But I don't know how or where to find it. It exists, I suppose, in Paris and London, but I can't get at it."

Here spoke the incipient social novelist who was still in search of a society. For Henry, as for his father (and by inheritance from his father), the word "social" was beginning to take on a "splendid meaning"; but also like his father, if on the literary rather than the theological level, Henry was profoundly dissatisfied—for his own needs and aspirations—with any actual society he had thus far encountered; though he sought to conceal the fact by lamenting that the available society was not cordial enough to *him*. It was indeed the subtly estranging effect of his family upbringing that had brought him to such a pass; but that same upbringing would give him his abiding theme—the "otherness" of the human situation.

Henry had already made up his mind, as it happened, to come home at the end of that 1874 summer. The issue between the two worlds, old and new, continued to loom large for him; but for the moment he thought to resolve it on practical grounds. Henry foresaw that life at home (as he wrote his mother) would be less agreeable and less conducive to good literary work than life in Europe. But he could peddle his wares there, in America, more easily and rapidly, and he could cease being a financial drain on his parents.

One version of his case had been put to him by William, in the same letter which announced Willy's "permanent path," and which also spoke of a dinner at Mrs. Tappan's where no one said a word except Dr. Holmes, and Emerson displayed a "refined idiocy of . . . manner" which seemed nearly an affectation. The Cambridge folk in general, Willy said, struck him as provincial, as excessively quiet and prudent, sly and cerebral; and this brought him to the subject of Harry's return. Here was his brother's dilemma:

The congeniality of Europe, on the one hand, plus the difficulty of making an entire living out of original writing and its abnormality as a matter of mental hygiene . . . on the other hand, the dreariness of American conditions of life plus a mechanical, routine occupation possibly to be obtained, which from day to day is *done* when 'tis done, mixed up with the writing into which you distill your essence.

The allusion to "abnormality" reflected William's view that a life wholly devoted to writing was so deficient in the active principle as to be bad for psychic health. So it would have been for William; and Henry, too, in a corner of his mind, had a lurking dread of the same possibility. For the rest, the suggestion that Henry should get some sort of job back home, and do his real work on the side, had no appeal for Henry whatever; it admittedly staggers the hindsight imagination, but it was not altogether farfetched at the time. In any event, Willy's appraisal helped Henry clarify his thinking, and he asked Mother to tell Willy so—shrinking, evidently, from the task of sorting over these questions with his not wholly perceptive brother. He would give America and Cambridge another try, but he emphatically made no commitment for the long future.

In June, the Tuscan heat drove him to a mountainside inn above Lake Como, and after an uncomfortable week there he continued north to the Black Forest. At Baden-Baden, he put in a very dull stay, but he scribbled away busily every morning. He was largely satisfied with the ongoing novel, and worried only that it might possibly be too analytical and psychological.

A LAST NEW YORK WINTER AND A FIRST NOVEL

When he turned up at 20 Quincy Street in September, after a slow westward passage on the *Atlas*, Henry seemed to his mother to resemble "a robust young Briton," with his newly purchased English tweed and the sunburn acquired at sea. She thought he was well pleased to be home, and trusted he would come more and more to feel—she wrote Bob James in Wisconsin—"that it is much better to live near his family and with his own countrymen, than to lead the recluse life he so strongly tended to live abroad." The last phrases suggest that Mother had cut through Henry's protestations to discern an actual evasion of social companionship, and Henry spoke in a similar vein to his brother Bob after a month's stay in Cambridge: "Home seems very pleasant after the lonely shiftless migratory life that I have been leading these two years." The weather had been glorious in the New England autumn; he had seen nothing in Europe to equal it. But he did not close without modifying these sentiments: "I confess I have become very much Europeanized in feeling, and I mean to keep a firm hold of the old world in some way or other."

The family he returned to was, for once, on a fairly even keel. Henry Senior was reading and meditating, and hobnobbing with his friends in Boston; Mary James kept the household peaceably. William had resumed his teaching, and was offering an ambitious course that dealt comparatively with anatomy and physiology, plus a portion of biology and anthropology. Alice, still experiencing the afterglow of her European venture, passed much of her time watching—with a mixture of enjoyment, wistfulness, and derision—the courtship doings of her acquaintances. In Wisconsin, the next generation of Jameses had made its appearance. Bob James and his wife, Mary, we recall, had produced an infant son, Edward, the year before; and Wilky and his bride of twelve months, Caroline Cary ("Sister Carrie," as William called her), became parents of an offspring named Joseph Cary.

Over the fall of 1874, Henry did little except press ahead with his novel. There was an evening or two with Longfellow, and Henry loaned the poet some volumes of Turgenev, containing, he said, the best short stories ever written. Otherwise, he kept to his desk, though even so, by the start of winter, with the serial due to begin in *The Atlantic* in a fortnight, it was not yet completed—a fact that, looking back long afterward, would cause Henry to "live over again, and quite with wonderment and tenderness, so intimate an experience of difficulty and delay."

Soon after Christmas, Henry bundled up his manuscript and his notes and transferred himself down to New York, where he found two rooms at 111 East Twenty-fifth Street, between Lexington and Park Avenues. (Basil Ransom, in *The Bostonians*, would be placed in a seedier section of the same neighborhood.) It was another move of double import. In part it was an escape from the family, from an existence surrounded and invaded by the family loved ones, and, in particular, from the proximity of a still somewhat excitable and wobbly older brother. It was also a move *toward* the literary marketplace.

During the six months he spent in New York, Henry published

articles at the rate of two a week in the periodicals open to him. He wrote on English, French, and American subjects; on Emerson, Cooper, Ellery Channing, on Taine and Masson; on a book about an antislavery expedition to Central Africa, and another about American communistic societies; about the New York theater, which he thought uninspired, and about several art exhibitions (for future reference, we note his reserved praise of an American painter named Frank Duveneck). Some of this was plainly journalistic hackwork, but most of it was of a singularly high order.

An article on Tennyson's poetic drama drew admiring words from the influential E. C. Stedman; and in grateful reply, Henry admitted to being an outsider when it came to poetry—"I know poets and poetry only as an irredeemable proser!" This was entirely accurate. Henry James would become perhaps his country's most distinguished man of letters; but insofar as the designation means excellence in all the forms of literature, he fell short of it: he was not even a *failed* poet. In his critical discussions of poetry, moreover, Henry James was expressive but unsurprising. Indeed, William James had a warmer appreciation of poetry—Whitman, Leopardi, and Goethe were among his much-read favorites—and drew upon it more in his writing.

Henry returned to the city of his birth and childhood, he said at first, with a real relish, but before long he was disliking it: "*Hideous,*" he told a friend, was "the most amiable word" he could apply to it. He was in another ungregarious mood, and the city had no capacity to talk to him (as it would so loudly thirty years later). By July, he was again at Quincy Street, settling plans for an indefinitely prolonged stay abroad.

His professional fortunes continued on the rise. *A Passionate Pilgrim*, containing the title story and other tales of Americans in Europe, was published by Houghton Osgood and Company on January 31, 1875. William Dean Howells led the not inconsiderable critical applause, declaring unguardedly that in richness of expression and splendor of literary performance, "we may compare him with the greatest, and find none greater than he." "If kindness could kill," Henry wrote by way of thanks, "I should be safely out of the way of ever challenging your ingenuity again." *Transatlantic Sketches*, the brilliant articles Henry had written on his travels, was brought out by J. R. Osgood and Company on April 29, with Henry Senior paying the costs of publication. The press was even more complimentary than it was about the short stories, and Father was soon reimbursed. And still a third volume by Henry James, Jr., was coming out in monthly installments in *The Atlantic.**

Roderick Hudson is the story of a gifted young sculptor who is idling away his life in Northampton, Massachusetts, when he is discovered there by a somewhat older devotee of the arts, Rowland Mallett. (One suspects some buried reason for the confusing similarity of names between artist and patron, as though we were being referred to a single personality split in two for narrative purposes.) Mallet takes Roderick to Rome and sets him up in a studio. The youth makes an auspicious start on a career, until he falls under the spell of the distractingly beautiful Christina Light, the daughter of a raffish American adventuress and (though she is said not to know it) a *cavaliere* from Ancona. Christina ambiguously encourages the sculptor's pursuit of her, but under a variety of pressures she is constrained to marry Prince Casamassima, an immensely wealthy Neapolitan nobleman. Roderick Hudson's creative energy deserts him completely; he degenerates morally and psychologically, and finally plunges to his death from an Alpine cliff.

Reconsidering the novel in 1909, Henry pointed to several flaws, among them the too rapid pace of Roderick's downfall (to which we can add the characters' habit of making speeches at each other rather than engaging in the give-and-take of dialogue). But he felt forgiving about such matters, since the real subject of the book, he contended, was not the sculptor's adventures but rather Rowland Mallet's "view and experience of him." "The centre of interest throughout *Roderick*," he held, "is in Rowland Mallet's consciousness, and the drama is the very drama of that consciousness." This is pure late-Jamesian talk.

The protagonist, once again, is thus the watcher, one of Henry James's surrogates (to repeat) for the literary artist—but here as elsewhere, an unreliable surrogate, so to speak; not what James was, but the mere onlooker he feared of being. What Mallet observes, himself sometimes unobserved, is a young man of almost limitless talent who is self-obsessed and petulant, with a frailty of will and a suicidal drive. It might be seen as a distorted image of William James, greatly gifted, at one time an aspiring and promising artist, with his charm and his complaining, his collapses of will and his self-destructive impulse. This would be William at his worst, or as viewed by his mother when her

* Henry's literary earnings in 1875 most likely ran beyond $3,000, the figure he himself mentioned frequently to his parents as necessary for the life he wanted to lead—in Europe.

sympathy had run out. "He looks *very well*," Mother had written about Willy in March 1874, "but says he had looked better—the trouble with him is that he *must express* every fluctuation of feeling, and especially every unfavorable symptom, without reference to the effect upon those about him."

A central element in the narrative, obviously, is the tension between the creative life and the emotional and erotic life. This was conceivably on Henry James's mind at the time of writing, if only because of intermittent nudging by his mother. The previous May, Mary James had held forth at some length about Henry's Florentine existence, and how his fine "intellectual and aesthetic life" needed to be completed by a more satisfying life of the "affections." Her solution was clear: "You would make dear Harry according to my estimate the most loving and loveable and happiest of husbands. I wish I could see you in a favorable attitude of heart towards the divine institution of marriage." To this Henry replied good-humoredly that if his mother would supply "the 'inclination' " as well as the wife and the fortune, he would take them all. He had manifestly no slightest inclination to marry; but he could imagine such a compulsion, as he could imagine a life role as spectator, and in *Roderick Hudson* he traced the disastrous consequences that could ensue for an artist embroiled in an emotional liaison.

In the 1909 preface to the novel, Henry James indicated satisfaction at his rounding out of the story. A major novelistic principle was at work here, as he made evident in a sonorous sentence: "Really, universally, relations stop nowhere, and the exquisite problem of the artist is eternally but to draw, by a geometry of his own, the circle within which they shall happily *appear* to do so." But in the same preface, Henry willingly acknowledged an exception of sorts to the principle laid down. The reader may, by the author's geometry, be diverted from wondering what will become, say, of Mary Garland, Roderick's fiancée from Northampton, or of Rowland Mallet; but who can fail to speculate about the future life of Christina Light?

The vibrant contradictions in the young woman—of temperament, Italo-American attitudes, moral sense, resolve—give her a vitality palpably in excess of her fictive companions. She bursts through the antithesis designed for her: that of the corrupted and corrupting European versus Mary Garland's bravely innocent rustic American. Henry James put it more technically: the multiplicity of creative touches that went into Christina's portraiture "produced even more life than the subject required, and that life, in other conditions, in some other prime relation, would still have somehow to be spent." It would be so spent, of course, in the novel of 1886, *The Princess Casamassima.*

Making ready for his sojourn abroad, Henry arranged with White-law Reid, editor of the New York *Tribune*, to be the Paris correspondent for that newspaper and to contribute three or four articles a month on things Parisian (exclusive of the political), for a fee of $20 per piece, which Henry considered small. He also persuaded *The Atlantic* to pay him in advance the $400 for the last four installments of *Roderick Hudson*, and worked frantically into mid-October on the proofs of the novel.

On October 20, Henry bade farewell to the family at Quincy Street, pocketed a letter of credit from his father, had breakfast with Howells (Harry James, Howells would tell a friend, had "gone abroad again not to return, I fancy, even for visits"), and embarked for Liverpool on the *Bothnia*. Twelve days later, he addressed the entire family from Story's Hotel in London, just off Piccadilly: "Dear People all—I take possession of the old world—I inhale it—I appropriate it!" With his ritualizing sensibility, he knew himself again to be on the threshold of some great experience.

PART III

Joinings and Departures

CHAPTER EIGHT

Marriage Ventures

MARY HOLTON

By November 1875, Bob James had been living and working, variously, in Wisconsin for more than seven years. He had gone out to Iowa in the fall of 1867, it may be recalled, to take up a lowly job as timekeeper with the Burlington depot of the Chicago, Burlington and Quincy Railroad. As before, a few months in this remote location were enough. Early in 1868, Bob quit the post and moved to Milwaukee, where he soon found employment as a clerk in the auditor's office of the Milwaukee and St. Paul Railway. It was anything but uplifting work, and the social life of Milwaukee, as Bob began to experience it, was dull. But he managed to stay put, more or less, for a surprisingly long stretch of time.

For a moment during that period it seemed possible that Bob might pull out and betake himself to Texas, where, according to Mother, he was in line for a position as treasurer and secretary of a railroad in Galveston. It would pay $1,500 a year and had a future. Henry, writing to his sister from Florence, spoke of hearing from Bob Temple that the latter had run into *their* Bob in New York, where he was " 'negotiating' " the subject. It was Bob himself who broke off the negotiation, perhaps because Texas appeared to him even farther away from the family home than Wisconsin. But in fact Bob had little interest, then or later, in bettering his status as a railroad man. The only profession he can be said to have hankered after, and this but fitfully, was in art. And what occupied him in his young manhood, more than jobs or careers, was the satisfying of his private urgings.

Bob was not quite twenty-two when he arrived in the steadily growing Wisconsin city. He was slender and fairly tall, held himself erect in a soldierly manner, and dressed fashionably. His finely chiseled face resembled that of his brother William, and like William he sported a mustache. But he continued to be set apart from his siblings by the intensity of his erotic nature—or, as one might say in a different perspective, by the normality of that nature—and by the conflict within him of sexual impulse and filial religiosity. More than anything else, these phenomena provided the motifs of Bob's early Milwaukee years.

His eye was caught at once by the "pretty and nice" daughter of the family with whom he was lodging. Nothing came of that, but in the year after a visit back home in the summer of 1868, Bob became secretly engaged, as it seems, to one of his cousins, Kitty by name. It is a tantalizingly murky episode in the family saga. The only real sources of information about it are two letters from William to Bob, the first in November 1869. Since William here alluded to a "consanguinous union," it has been supposed not only that the young woman *was* a cousin but that she was Kitty Temple, the older sister of the beloved Minny. But Kitty Temple had married Richard Emmet in September 1868; and indeed, she had given birth to a baby boy in July 1869. The Kitty in question was almost certainly Catherine Barber Van Buren, the daughter of Henry Senior's sister Ellen, who had married Smith Van Buren (the President's son) and had died thirty years before. Kitty Van Buren was the same age as Bob James.*

In his November 1869 letter, William expressed strong opposition to the marriage, less because the partners to it were cousins than because both suffered, as William did, from the James clan's "dorsal infirmity." Having just returned from his physically and psychically unhappy time in Germany, William was inclined to think that "the greater part of the whole evil of this wicked world is the result of infirm health," and that the worst thing one could do was to generate "unhealthy offspring." He, William, intended never to marry, and since "this dorsal thing" was something in the blood, Bob (he implied) should make the same vow."

Two months later, and almost by way of commenting on this fraternal lecture, Bob reported to William on his assorted troubles of

* See Jane Maher, *Biography of Broken Fortunes.*

body and mind: back pains, bad digestion, depression, constipation, and nocturnal emissions. They added up, we can surmise, to a state of extreme nervous tension, in some way related to sexual frustration. William's advice was an interesting mixture of the modern and the medieval: iron, limited exercise, and, as one observer has put it, "painting the back with coats of iodine until the skin peeled off" (a mode, as it were, of self-flagellation), plus sheer willpower.

But William fully understood Bob's special difficulty, given the younger brother's known temperament, and in another letter besought him to have an openly announced engagement or none at all. "These nondescript conditions, neither fish, flesh or fowl, are impracticable on every ground. Ruinous to peace of mind, preventive of forming other lifelong ties, and certainly dangerous to chastity, for what man, or woman either, could with certainty answer for her or himself, in rarely snatched and passionate interviews?" William added a note of condolence over Father's failure to sympathize with Bob's dilemma: "his religious optimism," William remarked about Henry Senior, "has I think a tendency to make him think too lightly of anyone's temporal troubles, even to neglecting to look closely into them at all."

The engagement, whatever it had amounted to, apparently came to an end at some time in 1870. It seems to have been in late 1871 that Bob James came to know Mary Lucinda Holton, the eldest daughter of one of Milwaukee's most prominent citizens. By the summer of 1872, they were formally engaged to be married.

Mary's father, Edward Dwight Holton, was fifty-seven years old in 1872. His career to that point had been as exemplary of its historical time and place as that of William James of Albany, with which indeed it had more than a little in common. Holton was born in 1815 in a homestead in Lancaster, New Hampshire, originally acquired by his grandfather Timothy Dwight Holton, a product of the Connecticut valley who was said (like so many others) to have been a warm friend of George Washington. At the age of twenty, young Holton made his way to Buffalo, New York, where he worked for several years in a shipping and forwarding company. The lad purchased goods for himself from time to time, and in 1838 he loaded them onto a covered wagon and journeyed to Wisconsin, of which he had read stirring descriptions in a book by Timothy Flint. Milwaukee, with its population of 1,500, struck him as discouragingly desolate; but he rented a frame building in the village for $75 a year and, with the supplies he had transported from Buffalo, set himself up as a dry-goods merchant.

After eight profitable years of this, Holton in the developing Amer-

ican pattern sold his store and moved on to land speculation and banking. He founded the Farmers' and Millers' Bank in Milwaukee and
served for a decade as its president; after which, in 1863, he organized
and became president of the First National Bank. He was very fond
of money, a local historian said of him, and in the accumulation of it
was uncommonly successful. So much so, in fact, that in 1867 he retired
from banking and devoted himself to managing his extensive real-
estate holdings and to raising thoroughbred horses on his Highland
Home farm outside of town. At the moment Bob James began to court
his daughter, however, Holton was about to re-enter the financial fray,
having cannily observed the great increase in demands for insurance
coverage following the Chicago fire. For the next few years, he would
act as vice president of the Northwestern National Insurance Company.

With these and other involvements, Holton had all along been
one of the busiest and most conspicuous citizens in the generation that
created the city of Milwaukee, and that also included the somewhat
older Solomon Juneau, Byron Kilbourn, and Alexander Mitchell. He
was one of the founders of the Milwaukee Board of Trade; took part
in the building of churches and schoolhouses, and pushed the matter
of reforming the school system; had a hand in devising a city charter
and in improving the harbor facilities; helped raise an endowment of
$475,000 and himself contributed $37,000 for what became the Milwaukee Female College. The achievement for which he would most
be remembered, however, was the building of railroad lines across the
state, several shorter ones being absorbed into the Milwaukee and
Mississippi, which ran from Lake Michigan to Prairie du Chien on
the great river. Holton, in a public discourse in 1858, referred to it as
"the great pioneer road of the city and the state"; and, indulging his
relish for money figures, recalled helping to persuade the city to put
forward $234,000 in bonds for original construction, and calculated
that by 1858 $25 million had been spent on railways, which added
$65 million to the wealth of the city. In the 1860s, the Milwaukee and
St. Paul Railway became the parent company, taking in most of the
other Wisconsin lines as subsidiaries. Holton was no longer formally
associated with the company when Bob James took a job there in the
auditor's office, but the presence of the former tycoon must have been
inescapable.

In the years before the war, Holton had been a truly dedicated
abolitionist and Free Soil advocate. He was among the organizers of
the Republican Party in Wisconsin as the party of abolition, and worked
so energetically with the Free-Soilers in Kansas, to whom he supplied

money and arms, that they named the town of Holton after him. In 1853, he ran unsuccessfully for governor as the Free Soil candidate. He managed a term in the state assembly a few years later; but Holton's main political accomplishment was getting himself elected sheriff of Milwaukee County—a feat that was acknowledged at the time to be surprising, since Holton had a statewide reputation as a strict and crusading teetotaler. In the cause of temperance, said a contemporary observer, Holton was a very Samson; against what he regarded as the greatest curse of the human race, he was utterly firm and fearless. Bob James, who undoubtedly honored his future father-in-law's championing of freedom for black slaves, may well have squirmed a little over his relentless hostility to drinking.

The Edward Holton that Bob was coming to know was a man of slightly less than medium height, with a large head, a florid complexion, and a goatee. He was of a nervous and impatient temperament; he spoke in loud, distinct tones, with a strong, twangy New England accent. Holton was tireless in his concern for the betterment of others, was always confident (according to the observer just mentioned) that he knew wherein that betterment lay, and insisted on being at the head of anything he was connected with. A street was named for him in Milwaukee while he was still in the prime of life, but few public figures aroused more animosity.

In 1845, Edward Holton married Lucinda Millard, originally from Michigan and a cousin of former President Millard Fillmore. Their first child, Mary, was born two years later. Two other daughters followed in due course.

The wedding of Mary Holton and Bob James was set for November 1872. The engagement itself had barely been announced when Wilky arrived in town. The Florida enterprise had ended in failure verging on disaster; and after a period of travel and a stay in Cambridge, Wilky was determined to try his own fortune in Milwaukee, where he could also enjoy the undemanding companionship and the assistance of his younger brother. Bob's fiancée introduced Wilky to her friend and former schoolmate Caroline Cary—"Carrie" to her intimates—and the two seem to have immediately fallen in love.

The family message system was at work. Both the young Milwaukee women evidently wrote about themselves to Mrs. James, back in Cambridge; and Mother communicated her speculations about them to Alice (herself in Switzerland with Harry). Neither of the girls was "at all intellectual," in her judgment. Of the two, Miss Cary seemed the more capable of strong affection, but the other was clearly far the more practical. Indeed, thought Mother, "little Mary" could easily manage a household for both couples together: "She would be equal to any emergency, so great a little power is she."

Mary Holton was in fact a "little" person physically; Father would even say that she was more attractive sitting than standing, being so short of stature. She was a pretty, round-faced creature, with a stocky build of soft outline. If not intellectual, she was at least a graduate of the Milwaukee Female College, which her father had helped to launch and of which her mother was a trustee. Mrs. James's attribution to her of great practical vigor was probably based on the conviction that Mary Holton was in every way her father's daughter. But in the outcome, Mary Holton James does not strike one as a particularly managing individual.

She does, though, seem to have exerted a lively sexual appeal, of a sort both to arouse Bob James and to worry him. With the wedding still half a year off, Bob found himself again given to nightly ejaculations, and was simultaneously seized with the fear of impotence. He unburdened his mind of this to William, who (in late June) sought to assuage him. Bob's case, he wrote, was, as described, nothing to be alarmed about; the emissions, should they continue despite medical treatment (iron and iodine), would certainly cease "when sexual intercourse begins regularly." Nor should Bob be "in the least degree anxious about impotence. That is an effect of a totally different class of cases from yours, and moreover very uncommon." William ended: "I love you my dear old Bob, more than words can express."

But Bob's troubles were not so easily gotten over, nor were they by any means purely physical. The elder Jameses came out to Milwaukee in August; they met and took a liking to Miss Holton, though, for a reason to be guessed at, they were not introduced to Miss Cary. But what belatedly impressed Henry Senior about the little visit—so forcibly that he wrote Bob about it on the railroad journey to Boston— was Bob's openly expressed desire to live anywhere but in Milwaukee, and by implication in the neighborhood of Edward Holton. "I forgot to ask you," Father said, ". . . why under the sun you didn't think of coming home at once?" Bob's response has not survived, but it seems to have indicated a restlessness of spirit that would not be cured by the home atmosphere. What it amounted to, Father wrote in his next letter, was that Bob was "passing through a crisis in your spiritual history known as rejuvenation." Henry Senior may well have been right, within his own vocabulary. Bob was undoubtedly undergoing— or seeking to undergo—a spiritual experience of radical import.

Marriage Ventures

In a letter of late October, Bob gave a lyrical accounting of the experience, and located its origin in talks with his father in Milwaukee: talks in which Henry Senior obviously set forth again his vision of the transformation scene to come.

The short time you stayed here has left its print deep in my memory, and at quiet moments—of which I have many—the truth you gave me then strikes up through every other insufficient thought and makes this world sweet and the goodness of the world-to-be almost a present thing.

Every time he turned a page in a book by his father, or by Swedenborg, Bob went on,

some glorious intonation of the love and wisdom of God and our great destiny flashes up like some dazzling sunlight in the bottom of the sea. Already there are two or three priceless thoughts which will walk with me like sweet companions on the path of life. Every day they abide more deeply in my memory, come to mind more quickly, grow more real, are more facts than ideas.

Bob's great regret was that he could not, or dared not, mention "this speechless bliss" to his Mary. Once or twice he had tried to talk about it with her, but could see that she listened only out of courtesy.

I never knew a mind that questioned less than hers. But perhaps this glory, this new light which bathes the world at break of day and shines through every hour till night comes, will fall upon her by and bye.

The Holton family journal, which had been kept faithfully for thirty years, had the following entry on November 18, 1872:

Mary was married to Robertson James at half past eleven this morning. The day was very pleasant and the house made cheerful with beautiful flowers and handsome presents. She was married in her travelling dress of navy blue with no ornaments but a few natural flowers. About fifty guests were present. The ceremony was performed by Rev. Mr. Ladd in a simple and beautiful manner.

Immediately after that perhaps surprisingly limited gathering in the Holton home on Milwaukee Avenue, the couple boarded an eastbound train. They spent a week with the Jameses in Cambridge. Henry Senior reported at length on the visit to Harry, who was just settling in Rome. The letter at first glance shows Father at his most exuberantly contradictory, even incoherent; but a closer look reveals a good deal of the odd paternal wisdom.

There was true affection on both sides, Henry Senior thought, and "the providence which has knit the tie is I think palpable even to sense." He went on to explain this opinion. Bob was "the most subjective and self-conscious of creatures, sensitive, shy, suspicious, moody, cloudy, rainy, freezing if need be." As to the wife, she "has absolutely no 'innards,' but is altogether in her senses, so that her influence over Bob *must* be to rescue him from his natural tendencies." In the terms of elder-Jamesian doctrine, this meant that Bob was still immersed in selfhood, with its attendant qualities; while the new Mary James was so devoid of self-awareness, so lacking in any interior life, that in her very superficiality she could rescue her husband from his natural state.

Bob's wife, Henry Senior went on, was all on the outside: "a little creature you like to pet. Alice caresses her all the while as she would a child; Willy was charmed by her." But she took such attentions as simply her due; she was "a peer of all the world," and had not the slightest notion "of a life beyond the senses." This boded well for the marriage, Father believed; and the rest of the family, if not exactly satisfied, was "encouraged, hopeful, delighted." But it was Bob himself, just because of his troubled condition, who showed promise of that authentic human development that the father always hoped for in others. In a second rush of conflicting adjectives, Henry Senior described Bob as "grim, self-inverted, thoughtful, speculative, religious, manly." He struck the family as being caught up in "a very profound mental experience"; and Father rather thought that Willy's intellectual beliefs had been deepened by conversations with his brother.

Shortly after the couple returned to Milwaukee, Bob was transferred to the Milwaukee and St. Paul station at Prairie du Chien on the far western side of the state. He was given charge of the outpost and, Aunt Kate wrote elatedly to Henry, would receive a salary of $1,800, with an additional fee coming from a river steamer which connected with the railroad at that point. (Aunt Kate had once visited the area and remembered the Mississippi making a lovely bend below Prairie du Chien.) It was a strenuous job. "We have been filling two ice houses," Bob wrote his father in late January 1873, "and at other times the work is out of doors"; but he felt "like a giant and full of health." Bob had to rise at five o'clock every morning, Mother informed Henry, and kept at it till nine in the evening. But he seemed blissfully happy.

And so he did. Writing his mother in the first days of the new year, Bob said that Mr. Holton had pressed him to take the position (not adding that going to Prairie du Chien got him out of Milwaukee and a goodly distance from his father-in-law), and that Mary was quite willing to make the change. "We both feel launched now upon the sea of life," he rhapsodized; and though there might be bad weather ahead, "we have such an asylum of love and hope to dwell in, that where or how we live is a matter of small account." Aunt Kate, quoting to Henry from this letter to her sister, remarked that "Bob's long lane has at last come to its turning point."

For her nephew in Rome, Aunt Kate then gave some of the latest news. Willy's first lecture at Harvard had been a great success. John Gray was engaged to Nina Mason. She, Kate, was in New York staying with cousin Helen Wyckoff and attending a series of good talks about France and Germany. Smith Van Buren was reputed to have been placed in an insane asylum because of "softening of the brain."

SISTER CARRIE

Wilky, as has been said, stayed on in Florida some three years after Bob left—though that statistic is misleading: about a year and a half more of continued effort, some long visits in Cambridge, and the better part of a year trying to bail out of the financial mess.

In the absence of his brother, Wilky found himself feeling "pretty lonesome and secluded," he wrote the family in April 1868. A visit from his old schoolmate Edward Emerson had brightened the scene, but in its wake Wilky was overcome by home-yearning:

[I] often think of you and Mother and all the family with intense longing, and wonder whether the day will soon come when I can with honor and satisfaction to myself, and with profit to the family, live once more in your midst free from all the many smallnesses and wretchednesses arising out of this chaotic condition of southern society: where I can get sympathy and instruction in what pertains to all things heady and hearty, by turning to my father, and a constant example of joy and affection and saintliness, by turning to my mother in all things that pertain to holy living, and holy thinking, the constant fellowship of such minds as Aunt Kate's, Harry's and Alice's (especially the latter), and this all by merely asking for it.

No clearer cry from the heart—for family sustenance—exists in the James annals; nor one which better mixed eloquence and emotion, and even a trace of wit ("heady and hearty"). Bob and Willy, of course, were excluded from the particularized litany of devotion, the one being in Wisconsin, the other in Germany.

During the later months of that year, 1868, Wilky's belief in the moral and social aspects of his venture began to erode. Two years earlier he had expressed a kind of angry confidence in the cause of black development. White society, he had said to William, had made "immense backwards strides . . . since the surrender"; and a Union man in the South was now "despised and hunted down by everyone save the negro." But he was sure about what must be done.

Equal suffrage based on educational qualification to every man white and black should be forced now on the south. Ten years from now, they will thank us for it; they talk about a war of races now if such a policy were adopted. 10 years from now the negro will demand it and their beloved theory of a war of races will be forced upon them.

But by the fall of 1868, the local situation, as Wilky saw it, had deteriorated to the point where he was far less sure of things.

The day before the election in November 1868, a party of five white men rode up to a Negro cabin on land adjoining Wilky's and murdered the occupant. "They shot at him through the cracks of his house and tore down his roof, threw a light-wood knot of fire into his room, and tried to smoke him out. He came out finally exhausted to deliver himself up and they put 8 holes through his body with their rifles." Wilky thought this horrifying incident might be a rare one (in the South at large, as has been determined, it was anything but rare). But he learned from the overseer at Gordon that a body of armed men "were prowling nightly around the plantation to take his life, that these threats were openly made and that at any moment he might be killed."

For Wilky, it was suddenly a state of siege. He wrote the elder James in mid-November:

I have been rebaptized in the faith of my father of late, and it has come about through trouble and anguish. The fact is, affairs here have assumed such a change, that I no longer feel that safety which I once felt, and to tell the plain truth I feel that at any moment, I may be called upon to give up my life for the faith of the principles I professed when I was a soldier in the field.

His few white friends had turned against him. One of them called on Wilky to announce that "hereafter I am his enemy. He had recently learned that I was an officer of the 54th Mass. and that hereafter all our intercourse must cease." If such a man, a person of intelligence and cultivation, with "one of the warmest hearts I ever knew," could hold such a view, then, commented Wilky, "all I can say is, that it becomes me to stand as firmly as I did in 1863 and to give up everything else in so doing."

He was far from quitting; and he repeated the claim that he had been "rebaptized in my faith": rededicated to the vision, inherited from his father, of just and humane society, and with the consolation that "if all goes with me, my example if it is a worthy one remains behind to attest to the strength of my convictions." The treachery of his Southern friends did not in the slightest affect his opinion about "these detestable and mistakeable Carpetbag governments"; in fact, he saw the two phenomena as interrelated. But by the end of the year, Wilky had pretty much lost heart in any sort of social possibility. On New Year's Eve, he sat alone, with rain pelting outside, and communed with his parents. He was wishing fervently, he said, that he had "in my staunch body, full of strength and health, half the delicate and moral force which either one of your afflicted brethren and inmates of Quincy Street possess." It was an apt allusion: each of his several brethren and at least one of the Quincy Street inmates were afflicted with ailments; but all of them, Wilky thought humbly, possessed a *moral* force which he had need of.

He needed it to help him rise from a condition of deep disenchantment, not only with the white folks in the county, but with the black people as well. "White men and negroes alike, whether they come from Massachusetts or South Carolina, are all bent upon getting the best of each other . . . Politically and privately, all men, with but few exceptions down here, are working for but one object, namely, that of cheating every one else in order to add a few dollars to their own possessions." "All men": it was as though Wilky had finally arrived at the primary or root principle in his father's pattern of faith: that the real and universal original sin was selfishness; the only true spiritual evil a form of greed.

On the material side, matters were hardly less discouraging, though for another half year Wilky resolutely put the best face on it. Torrential rains and a plague of caterpillars had done severe damage to the main plantation, but with another advance of $5,000 from Henry Senior, Wilky had purchased a tract of land twenty miles north of that property, which he called Serenola (a name that his brother Henry applauded) and soon came to love. "The most magnificent plantation in Florida," he enthused to Father. "It is really fit for you and Mother and Alice and all to live on, and a winter here you would enjoy exceedingly." At the end of April 1869, he wrote Alice in all cheeriness that "everything is looking remarkably well. I never had before so little trouble with my niggers, nor my crops so clean. I defy the caterpillars to injure me much this year."

A month later he was in his old room at Quincy Street, resting from his labors. But at the end of August he received word from his cotton brokers, Savage and Haile, that another visitation of caterpillars had wreaked havoc with the fields, to the degree that there was no point in his coming back down for the time being. This, in effect, was the end of the Florida adventure for Wilky. He went back South to spend the year of 1870 seeking to negotiate the sale of his lands, with only limited results. Jane Maher, by inspecting land records, has determined that Wilky did transfer one-half interest in 1,000 acres of land to one William R. Robeson (would someone, Henry begged in March 1870, please let him know "*who and what* is William Robeson") for $8,000. Wilky also, according to the records, sold two parcels of land outright for a total of $2,500, but the Jameses (including Aunt Kate who had invested a little of her income) owned several portions of land even after Wilky moved. The whole story, in retrospect, fades into a hopeless tangle of ill-considered purchases, loans, mortgages, unpaid accounts, defaultings. Within the family saga, the episode is a parody of the career of William James of Albany; and in some dim part of himself, Wilky may, in fact, have been hoping to take his place in the clan, not only by renewing his battlefield courage, but by being the first James in two generations to have a fling at "business."

After idling a few months at home in the early part of 1871, Wilky accepted an invitation to join a party traveling to California by train. It was organized by John Murray Forbes, chiefly to provide change and a much needed rest for Ralph Waldo Emerson, who was exhausted almost to the point of breakdown from the strain of delivering sixteen lectures at Harvard (on "the Natural History of the Intellect") and of a variety of university obligations. Mr. and Mrs. John Forbes headed the group, which also included their son William and his wife, Ellen Emerson Forbes, their daughter Alice, and James B. Thayer, a remote kin-by-marriage of Emerson, who would write a rather bland account of the trip (*A Western Journey with Mr. Emerson*, 1884). Garth Wilkinson James was presumably asked as welcome company for Edward Emerson, but the latter had to cancel out because of sudden illness—later diagnosed as varioloid, that dangerous but pseudo-smallpox with which William James had been stricken in Rio de Janeiro.

The several contingents from Boston forgathered in April at the station in Chicago, where they boarded a private car, the *Huron*, lent to Forbes for the occasion by his friend George Pullman. The travelers were carried westward in decided luxury (the well-stocked kitchen, Pullman boasted, could supply as good a dinner as the Parker House in Boston), crossing the Missouri River by ferry at Council Bluffs, passing through Omaha, climbing up and over the Rocky Mountains. After a pause in Ogden, Utah, and a side trip to Salt Lake City, they made the 900-mile trip nonstop to San Francisco, which they reached on April 21. It had the makings of an exceedingly rich experience, with phenomena at every turn—flowers and birds, giant trees, antelopes and elks and gophers—that almost no one in the party had ever laid eyes on before. California itself could cast a permanent spell: "There is an awe & terror lying over the new garden," Emerson wrote his wife, Lidian; ". . . I should think no young man would come back from it." But young Wilky James seems never to have written a line home about it.

He may be imagined sunk in the deepest depression over the Florida failure, and temporarily at least consumed by guilt about it. Wilky was, in addition, not very fit physically, nor had he been in Florida, for all his brave words about his "staunch body" with its "strength and health." He had never fully recovered from the wound to his foot at Fort Wagner, and he had contracted a bad case of malaria more than once in summer dampness. But his characteristic hopefulness seems to have been on the rise again before the California trip was done. He left the party in Iowa on the return journey, to look into the possibility of a railroad job at Burlington, as Bob had suggested. He spent a number of weeks with Bob and Mary in their Milwaukee home, and wrote his parents a letter about work possibilities in that city that Father said was "encouraging," though in so general a way that "we can't as yet see clearly *how* encouraging it may be."

Henry Senior took the occasion to offer some fairly stern if affectionate paternal advice to the son who had mismanaged his financial affairs so badly in Florida: "Your manhood is going to be tasked in this new (or *any* new) occupation, my dear boy, a little differently from what it has been hitherto." Wilky must henceforth earn his own way in life, and in circumstances quite new to him. Father had no doubt

263]

whatever that Wilky's manhood would "stand the test," and he feared only the congenital American desire to grow rich quickly: an impulse, Father said, "which leads young men to become disgusted with such employments as they have, and which are barely remunerative, to seek wealth by speculation; or else tempts them to misuse funds belonging to other people." Wilky had never succumbed to the latter temptation, Father hastened to say, but the former one would try him hard. "If you hold out there, you are safe for ever." He concluded with special messages of love from all back home: Mother, Willy, Harry, and Alice.

Of those named, only Harry was on hand when Wilky got to Quincy Street in July. The others, with Father and Aunt Kate, and with Bob, who had come East for a visit, were at Scarborough Beach in Maine, staying at an inn called Atlantic House. (Wendell Holmes, the Bootts, and the Sedgwicks were among other Cambridge folk who were putting up in the area.) This was the summer when Henry was discovering the pleasures of roaming the hills around Cambridge, while overseeing the first installments in *The Atlantic* of his novel *Watch and Ward*. It may be supposed that Wilky, after a time, went on up to Scarborough: the main purpose of the trip was to say goodbye to the family before heading into what was likely to be a long separation. By the end of the year, Wilky was settled in Milwaukee, as a clerk in the office of the Milwaukee and St. Paul Railway—side by side, perhaps, with Bob, who presumably found him the job—and with lodging at 643 Astor Street.

The Miss Caroline Cary to whom Wilky was introduced by her old friend and classmate Mary Holton was twenty-seven years old in 1872, the same age as Wilky. She was light-haired, almost blond, Wilky told Fanny Morse in the summer of that year as the relationship was growing apace, and perhaps less intellectual than Miss Holton. Mother, hearing vague rumors about the young woman, wrote Wilky in some perturbation, asking for detailed information about her. Wilky replied defensively that he would have told Mother all about Miss Cary if he had been given time; as it was, the love which filled his bosom for "this pure lovely girl" was so deep and so strange that he was at a loss to analyze it rationally.

He continued, not altogether coherently: "We are different in disposition and temperament, as different as we can be. She is exceedingly reserved and unimpassioned and never betrays an emotion or feeling on any subject scarcely, but the outward lack of it is only the sign of an inward fullness which cannot be computed." She had lost her mother at an early age (Wilky put it at eight years old, but, in fact, Carrie had been thirteen), and for many years she had been the head of her father's house, the cement which held the whole family together (there were three younger brothers, two of them at home). Her father worshipped her, Wilky said, and would undoubtedly insist on living with the couple after they were married. Wilky then gave a thumbnail sketch of Carrie's father, describing him as good, simple, and straight-forward, but also as "rather cold and undemonstrative," with no oc-cupation except that of sitting on the front porch, reading the papers and checking the thermometer.

Joseph Cary, as Wilky observed, was one of the first settlers of Milwaukee, coming there from his home village of Litchfield, in Oneida County, New York (near Utica), in 1836 at the age of twenty-nine. He set himself up at once as a merchant tailor and clothier; Edward Holton, opening his dry-goods store two years later, found the firm of Cary and Taylor well established in a wooden building on East Water Street. In that same year, 1840, Cary married Caroline Eames, originally of New Hartford, New York. Their first child, Caroline Eames Cary, was born in 1845. After her mother's death in 1858, young Carrie was sent by her father to a school in New York City for several years: her first glimpse of a world outside of Milwaukee.

His contemporaries recalled Joseph Cary as a kind and generous man, utterly punctilious, and a person of absolute integrity. They re-membered his slow thoughtful way of moving and his soft musical voice. Cary was reticent to an extreme, held no public office or trust, and belonged to no association. But his tailoring trade flourished. Like Holton and other Milwaukee businessmen and tradespeople, Cary in-vested his profits in real estate, doing so with such acumen that he was able to retire completely in 1853, at the still young age of forty-six. He spent his days thereafter "managing his property," in the then cus-tomary phrase; rarely straying from his first and only home in Mil-waukee at the corner of Oneida and Jefferson; and, in his mid-sixties, to be usually found, as Wilky said, on the piazza, reading the papers and fiddling with the window blinds.

The elder Jameses, during their visit to Milwaukee in August of 1872, did not meet Mr. Cary or his daughter. Wilky, writing to Alice and Henry soon afterward, remarked that the visit had been a great success, and that Mother and Father "saw Mary Holton but they did not see Miss Cary." His explanation was studiedly disingenuous: "At that time I did not know myself what was in store for me, and of course very little was said to them about the matter, except inferentially by my friends." Wilky must have sensed his mother's instinctive if ground-less hostility toward his chosen bride-to-be, and thus saw to it that they did not meet one another. In the same letter, he made an oblique acknowledgment of the true state of things by telling Alice that her family role was about to expand, to become "that of standing before Bob and myself in a sort of double sisterhood," as sister to her new sisters-in-law. He had never felt closer to Alice, he said.

Shortly after New Year's, 1873, Wilky came home for a few days. Aunt Kate thought he looked quite well, but was depressed (she wrote Henry) "with monotonous work in a close office." In the spring, how-ever, he was transferred to the station at Watertown, a westward run of an hour and a half from Milwaukee. His duties there as assistant paymaster had him on the road three or four days a week distributing wages; not very enlivening work, Mother remarked to Henry, but at least it kept him out of doors. Wilky was brought back to the Milwaukee office in September, with a promotion and an increase in salary. It now seemed possible for him to set a marriage date.

Mary James, while not actually obstructing the event, was vocal in her doubts about it. She had already spoken to Harry about "a crisis in Wilky's life," in that he was "brought face to face for the first time with the fact that he has got to stand on his feet, and provide for himself, and that too under the deepest sense of his own infirmities and temp-tations." The words referred to Wilky's demonstrated financial inep-titude, about which Mother spoke in the same hushed voice that she used about Bob's drinking habits. With regard to Caroline Cary, Mrs. James, for Henry's benefit, described her as coarse-looking, in a pho-tograph, and wearing an unattractive black dress. "I am afraid she is not a strong helpful woman," she added, in another letter, "and does not keep up his courage." Her view brightened a little when she heard that Mr. Cary had turned over to Carrie the house at Oneida and Jefferson, "all comfortably and fully furnished." It later transpired that Carrie's brothers raised such a storm about the proposed gift that Mr. Cary changed his mind.

Wilky had counted on the property to ease his economic situation, according to Mother. But Carrie appeared to have a certain income of her own, and the young couple decided to go ahead with their plans. The marriage took place in the Cary home on November 12, 1873. Bob came over from Prairie du Chien to participate in the festivities and wrote a jocular account of the day for the family in Cambridge ("I saw three men packing Wilky's valise, and two more exploring his quarters for his bridal suspenders at the last minute"). What Bob did not say was that he had left his own wife about to give birth to their first child. "Wilkie married and Bob goes to wedding," Mary Holton James wrote resentfully in her diary on November 12. Bob, in fact, returned home in time for the birth, but Mary was slow to forgive him.

Wilky and Carrie journeyed immediately to Cambridge. The elder Jameses gave a large evening party for the pair, with sixty guests, including a number of Wilky's old friends. "A beautiful entertainment truly," Father wrote to the two older brothers, who were enjoying their reunion in Florence. "Such flowers! Such meats and drinks!" But Henry Senior's portrait of his second daughter-in-law was undisguisedly negative. "Your sister Carrie is a somewhat plain young lady," he began, "of less than your mother's height, fair complexion, light brown hair, very slender person, self-possessed, even nonchalant." She was most stylishly dressed, and wore two diamond pendants worth five thousand dollars (by Father's astonished calculation) and jewelry amounting to "a thousand or two" more on her fingers.

She had "no conversation either in *esse* or in *posse*," and had, he thought, "a good disposition I should think where every thing goes smoothly, but an extremely firm not to say obstinate will when things go against it." Father found Carrie "in every way inoffensive . . . as to any *positive* tendencies and yet does not in the least conciliate your affections or your prognostications." He could not for the life of him imagine why Wilky had ever fallen in love with Carrie. "He *is* in love apparently," Henry Senior believed, and hoped that Wilky had no suspicion of the parental attitude. "We are assiduous to hide our feelings of course, and put on a mask of gaiety when we are at bottom of the gravest." Mary James, whose opinion of Carrie was even more severe, also pointed to the one consolation in the affair: that Wilky "seemed to have no shadow of misgiving himself, about his having drawn a prize."

There was what seemed to be happier news to convey about Wilky a few months later. According to his mother, he was about to leave his railroad job and "to enter a business for the making of iron chains and bolts." The business had been started by a young man, John Whaling, son of "one of the kings of the Milwaukee and St. Paul Railway," and because of that connection profitable contracts were in the making. Wilky had told the family about it on a recent visit, explaining that he had borrowed $5,000 the year before and invested it in young Whaling's enterprise. Mother was cautiously hopeful. "Wilky is so sanguine that one can place no reliance upon his judgement," she wrote Henry, ". . . but he has to do the routine work which will make things much safer."

Mrs. James had not perhaps been listening very carefully. The firm was called the Milwaukee Bridge and Iron Works, and consisted (so its advertisement ran) of "engineers, bridge builders, and contractors. Iron work for bridges of all kinds, piers, trestles, roofs, turn-tables and general iron construction." It may have been started by John Whaling, but the key figure in 1874 was Leon Soulerin, a civil engineer, with Garth Wilkinson James as partner and accountant. The $5,000 had been borrowed by Wilky from Joseph Cary, with a portion of the Florida holdings as collateral. The firm was not a large one, but it was Soulerin, James & Co. that, on the basis of designs by Soulerin, built the North Street aqueduct bridge across the Milwaukee River to carry the main pipe through which water would flow into the city's reservoir (capacity: 21 million gallons). Water was first pumped through the Soulerin-James installation on December 23, 1874.

THE TROUBLED COURTSHIP OF WILLIAM JAMES

It was in the mid-1870s that William James began audibly to find his own philosophical voice. At Harvard, he was still teaching physiology and anatomy in various combinations, but his attention was veering toward the relation between physiology and psychology, between the oddities of the body and those of the mind; and in the fall of 1875 he offered a course on that subject in the graduate program being established by President Eliot. (For the purposes of the seminar, William set up the first psychological laboratory in America.) In the following year, when he offered a similar course for undergraduates, he was promoted to assistant professor, after two and a half years of actual service in the university; he was given a salary of $1,200 a year, with the promise of an increase to $2,000 in 1877.* These were gratifying

* These were not inadequate salary figures, according to the parsimonious standards of the Harvard president. Eliot prided himself on raising the salary of full professors, in 1869, from $2,400 a year plus a probable but not certain additional grant of $600 to $4,000 a year. But as late as 1889, the maximum salary for a full professor was $4,500 a year, and that of an assistant professor $3,000. Matters were not much better a decade later; Eliot's niggardliness in this regard had a depressing effect on academic salaries across the land. These figures, it may be noted, were supplied by William James's son Henry in the latter's life of Charles William Eliot in 1930. The younger Henry evidently felt that it was unbecoming to discuss the matter of faculty salaries openly, and only addressed the subject in any detail in his second volume in a footnote.

developments—William in his mid-thirties was at last standing on his own—but they were less important for the ongoing career than the review essays that were appearing over his name.

William had published a good many notices and articles in the preceding years, all of them reflecting an elastic mind and a talent for expression, but none perhaps of true lasting value. (The most suggestive was a comment in 1869 on E. Sargent's *Planchette*, which shows William already fascinated, as was his father, by the phenomenon of spiritualism, and wishing the spiritualists would make a more plausible presentation of themselves.) What is striking about the new writings is a sinuous continuity of intellectual theme and a controlled personal urgency.

In an 1875 review of *Problems of Life and Mind* by the English philosopher G. H. Lewes (by whose "wife," George Eliot, Henry had been so enchanted), William picked up on some of the principles he had painfully arrived at during his nightmare period in 1870, especially the voluntary nature of belief. Lewes, he said, approvingly, had moved beyond the currently popular skepticism, as all serious thinkers ultimately must: for "at a certain point most of us get tired of the [skeptical] game, resolve to stop, and assuming something for true, pass on to a life of action based on that." Men should be as adventurous in their thought, James proposed, as in their worldly affairs. "In practical life we despise a man who will risk nothing, even more than one who will heed nothing." Might not the same be said about the theoretic life? He took a step further along this line, a year later, in a comparative discussion of books by Alexander Bain and Charles Renouvier. Here he praised his French associate's insistence on the freedom of the will as against what he regarded as Bain's capricious determinism. Even a skeptical attitude (this was a subtle thrust) is a free choice: "Doubt itself is an active state, one of voluntary inhibition or suspense."

Elsewhere he returned to the issue, which had intermittently obsessed him, of pessimism versus optimism as the proper outlook for a man of sense. Commenting on a German study of pessimism, a work which he found both temperate and witty, William James refused to accept Schopenhauer's all-embracing gloom. "Practically considered," he argued, "optimism is just as true as pessimism . . . The existence of Walt Whitman confounds a Schopenhauer quite as thoroughly as the existence of a Leopardi refutes a Dr. Pangloss." (Professor James's Harvard colleagues probably caught the reference to Voltaire, but not many of them would have known the tragic and beautiful poetry of Giacomo Leopardi.) Pursuing this theme in a discussion of Ernest Renan's *Dialogues et Fragments Philosophiques* in *The Nation*, William grew surprisingly vitriolic. It was, he said, a work of "dandified despair"; it evinced a "boneless fear" of the modern egalitarian spirit, and was an example of "insincerity and foppishness." The uncharacteristic harshness of tone seems to have been a response to Henry James's enthusiasm for Renan, with whom he had dined in Paris. Henry declared the French historian's table talk to be "exquisite for urbanity, fineness and wit," and it was he who sent William the *Dialogues*. Pouncing on the volume, William discerned in it an exaggerated version of everything that (as he was telling his brother at the time) he most feared about Henry: priggishness, fussy self-regard, and a disdainful—by implication, an anti-American—elitism.*

It was in the midst of such versatile productivity and turns of mind on William's part that there occurred an event that became a cherished item in the family memory. On a certain evening in the winter of 1876, Henry Senior came back to Quincy Street from a meeting of the Radical Club in Boston, sat down in front of the fire, and told the others—Mary, William, and Alice—that he had just encountered William's future wife. He had exchanged only a few words with her, but enough to discover that she was an unusual and impressive young woman, and that she was a teacher in Miss Sanger's School for Girls in the city. William, apparently undisturbed that his father was picking his wife for him, went to the next session of the Radical Club, and there was introduced to the person in question, a Miss Alice Howe Gibbens. The following morning, William, who had once announced to his brother Bob his determination never to marry, wrote Bob's wife, Mary, that he had the evening before come upon "the future Mrs. W.J."

She was twenty-seven, sturdily built, and of middle height, brown-haired and dark-eyed, with an intentness of expression that could change easily into friendly brightness. On that very first evening, she proved quick and open in conversation, and William was charmed by the warm timbre of her voice. She was not without a sense of humor; and indeed, one of her early acts, as a relationship began to form, was to send her intriguing new friend a copy of a satirical poem, in imitation

---

* Another moment in the continuing subterranean exchange between the two brothers was provided by George Eliot's *Daniel Deronda* (1876). Henry, in letters home, had been uttering frequent if ambiguous words of praise for the novel. William, reviewing G. H. Lewes's *Physical Basis of Mind* in 1877, went impishly out of his way to say: "Not, indeed, since reading *Daniel Deronda* have we been so annoyed by a writer's redundancy, have we found ourselves so persistently seized by the button and moralized to when we were most impatient for the story to move along and for the author to effect something with his materials."

of Poe's "The Raven," about a group of lofty-minded individuals at the Radical Club.

Alice's mother, Elizabeth ("Eliza") Putnam Webb, was of genteel New England background, a woman of delicate and vulnerable disposition. The father was Daniel Lewis Gibbens, Jr., of Boston. (His grandfather perhaps emigrated from Ireland around 1780; his father, who began his career as a grocer in Boston, was a prominent member of the Chauncey Place Church.) Gibbens was trained to be a physician, and was admitted to the Medical Society in 1847 at the age of twenty-three; but he had no inclination to practice, even if he liked to be addressed as "Doctor." He was a roving, intemperate man; in his early married years he was given to violent bouts of drinking, followed by such deep depression that his wife, in alarm, hid his razor and his pistol from him.

In 1856, when Alice was seven, Dr. Gibbens transplanted the family—it also included five-year-old Mary Sherwin, and another daughter, Margaret Merrill, was soon to be born—from New England to California, where he had a try at ranching, at Los Altos in the Santa Clara valley. This effort came to nothing, though the endearment of the flat widening landscape would palpitate within the oldest child's memory, especially on much later visits of her own to the West Coast. By the summer of 1859, the Gibbenses were again in the Boston area, the mother and daughters living in Weymouth, the father in Boston. Gibbens was at best an intermittent provider; but in his unsettled way he felt an attachment to the family, and wrote affectionate evasive letters to his "dear children." He was possessed as well of a certain literary taste and religious curiosity; in his commonplace book, he quoted from the Old Testament, St. Augustine, Milton ("The mind is its own place . . ."), Tennyson, *Adam Bede* ("Think what it is, not to hate anything but sin"), and Whittier ("For of all sad words of tongue or pen, / The saddest are these: 'It might have been!' ").

In November 1862, Gibbens went down to New Orleans to serve as assistant to T.C.A. Dexter, a Boston friend who was state treasurer in the military government of the city. He was then taken on as secretary to a succession of federal officers who performed as "Acting Mayors" of New Orleans, two of whom, on Executive Department stationery, spoke in the highest terms of Gibbens's sound judgment, patience, "kind and decorous demeanor," and the "honest discharge" of his duties. In May 1865, he transferred to Mobile, Alabama, and went to work as assistant to his friend Dexter, now supervising special agent of the Treasury Department in Mobile, the agent responsible for collecting cotton confiscated from the defeated Confederate authorities.

Calamity followed, as Gibbens got caught up in the spreading scandal related to the vast cotton dealings. In early November 1865, Agent Dexter was charged with stealing more than 3,000 bales of cotton, and with accepting a $25,000 bribe for arranging the appointment, as subagent, of one John Garner. Daniel Gibbens was not charged, but rumors were flying about his involvement in the crimes, and witnesses were said to be ready to swear that Gibbens had pocketed the $25,000. At eight in the morning on Sunday, December 3, Gibbens committed suicide in his lodgings by cutting his throat with a razor.*

Alice Gibbens, in Weymouth, had learned to her excitement that her father planned to come North at Christmas time and make a home for the family near Boston. But before mid-December, Eliza Gibbens was informed by telegram that Daniel Gibbens's body, embalmed, would be delivered next day to the Boston railroad station. She collapsed completely, and was incapacitated for months to come.

It was Alice, now sixteen, who took charge of the household, running it as best she could on her mother's income of $1,800 a year. In 1868, probably at Alice's urging, the family went to live in Germany, first in Heidelberg, then in Dresden (following William James there by a year or so) and Berlin. They spent 1872–73 in Florence, where all unknowingly they may have passed Henry James, sallying forth along the Arno from his Hôtel de l'Europe. The family was back in America at the end of 1873, living in Boston, and Alice had found a position in Miss Sanger's school.

Alice began almost at once to attend the Radical Club, which met regularly in the handsomely adorned parlor of the home, on Chestnut Street in Boston, of the Reverend and Mrs. John T. Sargent. It had been founded in 1867 by Mrs. Sargent ("our pretty hostess," in the words of one member), to meet "the growing desire of certain ministers and laymen for larger liberty of faith, fellowship and communion." Talks were given by Emerson, Dr. Holmes, Whittier, Julia Ward Howe, W. H. Channing, Christopher Cranch, Henry James, Sr., among others; and they ranged beyond customary ministerial concerns into topics in literature and music, the nature of tragedy and of comedy, evolution, the North American Indians. Mark Twain was once in attendance, claiming a special interest when the discussion turned to metempsy-

---

* See Appendix A, "The Strange Death of Daniel Gibbens."

chosis ("that doctrine accounts for me"); and the former abolitionists Wendell Phillips and William Lloyd Garrison showed up. Henry Senior lectured on the Creator as infinite good and the Creature as utmost conceivable evil (Dr. Holmes, asked to comment, begged leave to study the text at his leisure); and another time explained how marriage transformed the selfish heart into the social heart.

During the first couple of years at the Radical Club sessions, Alice Gibbens did not happen to run into the elder James. One person she did come to know, perhaps at her first meeting, was John Greenleaf Whittier. The friendship that followed meant a great deal to the Quaker poet, now in his late sixties: "I am very thankful for the good Providence that brought about our acquaintance," he wrote "my dear friend Alice Gibbens" on Christmas Day, 1875; "it has been a comfort and a refreshing to me." On a summer 1874 visit to Whittier's home in Amesbury, Massachusetts, with her mother and sister, Alice presented her host with a glass of the wine brewed by the Benedictine monks at La Certosa (an abbey south of Florence—Alice had acquired the wine during her Tuscan stay the year before). In reply, Whittier gave Alice his new volume of poetry, *Hazel Blossoms*. On another occasion, he sent her leaves from the brookside at Amesbury, and expressed concern that "thee are getting tired with thy school labours."

After an evening together in the winter of 1875, Whittier wrote to say how he had enjoyed their talk about "eternal hope and suffering." He was interested in particular, he said, in Alice's account of Swedenborg, and the Swedish mystic's hint about the final extinction of evil. Thinking about this, Whittier had written some lines he sent along to his young friend: a poem of eleven two-line verses called "The Two Angels." In it, God summons the angels Pity and Love and sends them forth to quench the "wail of woe and sin" in hell. Downward they fly.

> *The way was strange, the flight was long, at last the angels came*
> *Where swung the lost and nether world, red-wrapped in penal flame.*

Pity drops a tear at the spectacle, Love smiles upon it.

> *And lo! that tear of pity quenched the flame wherein it fell,*
> *And with the sunshine of that smile, hope entered into hell.*

Considering the evasions and postponements that lay ahead in his courtship, William James bespoke himself at first with admirable rapidity and forthrightness. In the summer of 1876, and writing from Keene Valley in the Adirondacks of upstate New York—a region to which he was becoming addicted—William said that "seven weeks of insomnia and reflecting on the matter" moved him to make this "premature declaration," even though it was nothing short of a crime to startle her so. "To state promptly the whole matter: I am in love, *und zwar* (—forgive me—) with yourself. My duty in my own mind is clear. It is to win your hand." He begged her to let him know if there was any "absolutely irrevocable obstacle" to such a consummation; for if so, he would set about eradicating his feelings, with a sense of gratitude that the suspense was over. But even if there was not, she need feel no pressure about reaching a decision. He allowed himself to suppose, William said, that she felt some sympathy for him; but he was constrained to issue a warning: "I can furnish you with undreamed of arguments *against* accepting any offer I can make." She was coming to Keene Valley; William was moving over to Lake Placid. If Miss Gibbens would write him there, she could give the letter to the stage driver, who would hand it on to the driver of the Saranac coach. There followed glowing summer days together that Alice Gibbens at least would look back upon with sadness a year later.

Alice proved more than willing to attend to the expressive and intellectually omnivorous Harvard teacher, though unaware that Mr. James's father was so keen on the match that he offered to augment William's salary in order to make it possible. (Father's enthusiasm was no doubt the greater in view of his prospective daughter-in-law's penchant for Swedenborg. It would be almost like having a theological spy in his son's household.) She was an independent spirit, moreover, valuably toughened by experience, and was not shy about being frequently in her suitor's company. And so, as the autumn of the year went forward, they walked and talked on the Boston Common, they went driving together, they sat side by side at public lectures. In a bit of wordplay borrowed from Fichte, William told her of his new motto: "*Glückwürdigkeit*"—being worthy of happiness—rather than "*Glückseligkeit*," a simple feeling of happiness. They conversed till late hours about religion, with William apologizing the next day for having done too much of the talking. Belonging to no church himself (a condition, as he could have said, that his father had seen to), he was curious about the Congregational Church, of which Alice was a faithful member, and the religious doctrines she had espoused.

As time went on, however, William seemed oddly bent on undermining his case. There were moments of bravado, as when (in November 1876) he could say: "You sitting self-contained and self-supported at a distance, not needing me, will have one day to recognize me, to respect me . . ."* But he also took pains to furnish his loved one with those "arguments *against* accepting" him, of which he had spoken months before. Presumably, he dilated upon the history of his uncertain health and unsettled nerves, his occasional loss of energy, his instability. He alternated between appeals for help and staunch disavowals of his need. "Do not apprehend from anything I say in the preceding lines," he wrote in late November, ". . . that I am getting unstable or that I again shall be a mendicant at your hands."

On a deeper level, William was suffering from a genuine anxiety, essentially intellectual but nonetheless disturbing for being so. His feelings for Alice Gibbens intensified his awareness of his potential weakness, and that very awareness seemed to hamper his highest intellectual ambition. The latter was provisionally defined in a letter from Newport, during the Easter holiday in 1877, where he said that "the only single use for which my life was given me" was "the *acting* for the deepest, widest most general good I can see and feel." It was mental action—what he was wont to call "acts of thought"—that William was still somewhat confusedly talking about; and he told Alice in the same letter that he would rather postpone their marriage forever than "abdicate" that life mission. The grandeur of the mission and William's sometimes overpowering conviction that he was accomplishing it were conveyed in a follow-up letter from Newport, in which, rising to a kind of Whitmanian fervor, he exulted in his sense that he was "giving the moral universe a shove ahead; that I am baffling the powers of night; that I belong to the morning and the flowing tides of health and strength and good . . . It elevates one's soul to feel that on the puny stage of his personality bits of the *Absolute* drama are being enacted, and that his will can score an indefeasible gain for the good." But it was unclear where, in this exuberant battle against darkness, William's emotional, not to say his erotic, longings might be allowed their play.

At this stage, William was brought down to earth, so to say, by the intervention of a friend of Miss Gibbens, a Miss Kate Hillard, who proposed that the two women go to England in the forthcoming summer, apparently so that Alice could get over her infatuation with Professor James. William was not resentful: the other woman, he said, did

* This particular fragment breaks off at that point. Many of William's courtship letters exist only in Alice Gibbens's transcription.

not realize that "the affair is so serious between us"; the trip to England might not be a bad idea. To this Alice replied in her clearheaded way that she and William should put an end to concealment by becoming formally and publicly engaged. The suggestion set off one of those fits of oscillation and indecision which had plagued him for a decade and a half.

"My friend, my sister," he wrote Alice on April 23, "I am bowed down with this solemn happiness . . . I feel as if henceforth nothing ill can come to me. I have reached my goal." Even so, he hurried on to say, they should not yet engage themselves. Any decision should be postponed till after the English trip; and "you must go to England." He foresaw a long engagement, in any case: why make it still longer? That was on a Monday evening. On Tuesday morning, William was accusing himself to Alice of "pedantic folly" in urging her to go to England. In his sudden new happiness, he said, he had had the foolish idea of encouraging her to flirt with other young men, as though to test the strength of her commitment. On the contrary, they should see as much as possible of each other at home during the summer; and what she could tell Miss Hillard was that William had proposed but that she could not bring herself to accept him—yet.

A week had not passed before William was once more changing his position. He simply could not trust himself, he now said, to believe in Alice's readiness to yield to him. His whole sense of "the human type" was "shocked at the thought of a being like you countenancing one like me. You *ought* not to be willing to do it." She really must not make any decision about their relationship until she had carefully considered every other possibility; and this could well take many years. So after all, maybe, considering everything, she *should* go to England.

Alice appears to have been given pause by this performance, though her reactions are not recorded. But whatever she said or did had the effect of steadying down William's overwrought spirit for a time; by the end of May he could say that he was no longer possessed of doubts, though he was so sleepless from excitement that he needed to take a week off. He administered an end-of-term examination in psychology at Harvard, stiffening the backbone of a student who threatened suicide if he did not pass the course; took the train to Fall River and the boat to Newport; slept beautifully and awoke to a health-giving day of walking and sailing.

From Newport, William wrote Alice a long, chatty, easy-tempered letter in the form of a four-day diary. He was reading exams and perusing a life of Byron; he was sleeping and exercising. A letter from

Alice arrived: *his* name in *her* hand made his heart leap, and he was glad to learn from it that she had been visited by John Greenleaf Whittier—he hoped to know Whittier through her, and they could read his poems together. His brother Bob would be there tomorrow (June 3); William looked forward to the visit, but admitted that he always felt anxiety where Bob was concerned: "He's so eccentric." (Bob showed up on schedule, and William confided to him the whole state of affairs between himself and Miss Gibbens.) Alice, temporarily exhausted perhaps by the courtship drama, argued in the letter that, after William's return, they should communicate by letter and not see each other for a time. William replied with lordly good humor that this recommendation was on the amusing side. "Don't think . . . that you shall escape the future rides which it is your doom to take with me."

Back at Quincy Street on June 7, William addressed to Alice what amounted to a major statement about his own nature—his very posture in the world of experience—and about the relevance of that posture to their emotional relationship. He began:

I have often thought that the best way to define a man's character, would be to seek out the particular mental or moral attitude in which, when it came upon him, he felt himself most deeply and intensely active and alive. At such moments there is a voice inside which speaks & says *"This is the real me!"* . . .

Now, as best he could describe it, he went on,

this characteristic attitude in me always involves an element of active tension, of holding my own as it were *trusting* outward things to perform their part so as to make it a full harmony, but without any *guarantee* that they will. Make it a guarantee—and the attitude immediately becomes to my consciousness stagnant and stingless. Take away the guarantee, and I feel (provided I am *überhaupt* in vigorous condition) a sort of deep enthusiastic bliss, of bitter willingness to do and suffer anything, which translates itself physically by a kind of stinging pain inside of my breastbone (don't smile at this—it is an essential element of the whole thing!) and which, although it is a mere mood or emotion to which I can give no form in words, authenticates itself to me as the deepest principle of all active & theoretic determination which I possess.

It was the fullest expression William had yet given to his vision of the need to accept risk in life, of that stance of mental daring he had alluded to in his review of G. H. Lewes's book and earlier in the privacy of his journal. His increased clarity and conviction in the matter came

277]

almost directly from observing himself in relation to Alice Gibbens. "Last fall and last winter what pangs of joy it sometimes gave me to let you go! to feel that in acquiescing in your unstained, unharnessed freedom I was also asserting my deepest self, and cooperating with the whole generous life of things!"

To put their relation at risk, in those earlier months, had given him that familiar and pleasurable stinging pain. Recently, though, he went on, there had been two successive stages in *his* sense of the situation: that is, of the relation between his attitude-to-life as described (the felt necessity of tension) and his "habitual feelings" for Alice. In the depth of his happiness at being recognized and accepted by her, he found himself craving to "own you more and more." But such a desire for ownership was exactly an emotion he felt bound to resist; and as tenderness welled up within him, he found himself saying, "If she is mine she must be called on to make *no* sacrifice whatever which I can avert. I must cut loose from all my past thoughts if she once endows me with herself." His "feelings" had triumphed over his "attitude"; and in the instant he became aware of this, he heard within him a "still small voice," a "sad warning voice," that "called me a traitor."

He had spoken to Alice forty-eight hours before about this silent accusing voice; but now, on this seventh of June, he had grown radiantly certain that the two dimensions were fusing. "For the past hours I have been feeling so strongly *both* impulses, the loyalty to you and the loyalty to the wider Not-me (the willingness to serve the universe), that I have said we *must* all three come to accord." He had a recollection of having written something about his "attitude" at an earlier date. (He was probably thinking of the journal entry in April 1870 when he first posited "life (the real, the good) in the self-governing *resistance* of the ego to the world.") He looked for the passage without success; but he did come upon a lengthy private discourse called *Optimism and Pessimism*, which, he said, "was written many years ago when I was going through the pessimistic period" (and which, we may suppose, had returned to his mind when he was writing about German philosophical pessimism and decrying Renan's dandified despair).

But Alice had been seized with the direst misgivings. She felt, apparently, that she had been made part of some bizarre triangle, with "the universe" as the prodigious rival for William's affections. In a recent conversation, William had "boasted" (in his own abjectly apologetic paraphrase) that "in certain contingencies 'I should not scruple to sacrifice you.' " His later protestations—that he was feeling both the basic impulses at once, and that "we *must* all three come to accord"—

did not sufficiently comfort her. Their possible marriage, she seems to have told William, was being subordinated to the working out of his "doctrines." "Do not speak of my 'doctrines,' " William wrote her agitatedly in July; "—they are only provisional perceptions of the facts of life—I feel from henceforward how much more you know of marriage and all that is cognate to it than I have ever known or perhaps ever shall know."

When Alice declared her intention to go to Canada with her sister for the summer, William besought her to come back instead to Keene Valley; and if she still thought that "our separation for some time the healthiest thing," he would take his vacation somewhere else. But Alice had more in mind than a temporary separation, as William was gradually made to realize. "I must begin *de novo* now," he acknowledged in early August, "if I'm to begin at all, with no promises at the outset." Alice did go up into the province of Quebec with her sister Margaret, and William, in the Adirondacks, was left to contemplate his behavior. After a considerable silence, and addressing her again as "My dear Miss Gibbens," William wrote Alice on August 24: "Little by little time will perhaps give me something to think about but my own unspeakable impotence and culpability, and the outrages which they wrought upon your thrice divine being."

"Impotence" was a curious word for what had been an outward display of male arrogance, the threat to "sacrifice" Alice, which William now repudiated with self-loathing. What William was referring to, one gathers, was his spineless refusal to take action toward their marriage, his retreat into the realm of ideas. For him, as William explained more than once, "impotence" meant a weakness or an absence of will. One may also perhaps allow a hidden-away sexual implication.* After castigating himself further anyhow, William renewed his appeal that Alice make a visit to the valley. She had already expressed reluctance to come back to the haunts where she had been so happy the previous summer; and William, quoting Dante's Francesca, urged that she make no decision based on "*ricordarsi del tempo felice*." He personally, William added, was glad that "Keene Valley and Lake Placid have become part of the secular scenery of the world for me, and I am free hereafter to enjoy them."

Alice stayed on in Canada, and returned to Boston directly from

* William also, of course, used the word "impotence" to refer to sexual incapacity, as in his correspondence with his brother Bob. And although that sense of it was not consciously being invoked in the August 1877 letter, it does seem obvious that during much of the courtship period William was suffering from a sexual flinch, and hence from an impulse to postpone the marital relation as long as possible.

Montreal. The two met and exchanged civilities on September 23, and the next day William wrote Miss Gibbens that she had seemed pale— perhaps it was only a cold—but he trusted that Canada had at least satisfied her "moral needs." "You will not expect to see me often, will you?" he asked humbly. "But you will think of me as always truly yours Wm James." To Bob James in Wisconsin, William said as though in a whisper: "The affair I confided to you at Newport is fallen through. I charge you to breathe no word of it *ever* to anyone. The family knows nothing of it yet, and must not hereafter. It is a painful business, but she is an angel incarnate."

A WEDDING IN BOSTON

On William's side, the courtship doggedly started up again over the autumn months of 1877 and into the winter of 1878. There are no letters until late in this period. William may have become more wary about setting down his thoughts on paper; or it may be that Alice Gibbens, who would be the curator of the courtship correspondence, chose for some reason not to keep the communications by either party.

There is no question, though, that William was sorting himself out in a manner that boded well for his and for their shared future. One extant sign of this is the fragment of a letter written by him on Sunday, February 24, and transcribed by Alice "from a letter she destroyed."

To me such decisions seem acts by which we are *voting* what sort of universe this shall intimately be, and by our vote creating or helping to create "behind the veil" the order we desire. On the one hand, I despise a Universe in which an individual shall not be willing to suffer and even inflict some evil for the sake of the Law of general decency and sanity; but on the other hand I no less refuse to belong to a Universe which should exact such sacrifices as the violent breaking of such love and faith as ours has been in each other.

It is the first discoverable use by William of the democratic figure: strong individual preference as helping to shape the way things in general are to be. He casts two negative votes, both bearing on the relationship with Alice Gibbens: against a universe in which either should be exempted from suffering caused by the other; *and* against a universe which would wrench them asunder, for all their love and faith in one another.

The letter was written from Baltimore, where James, on the invitation of President Daniel Coit Gilman of the recently founded Johns Hopkins University, was giving a series of ten lectures on "The Brain and the Mind." The main drive of the discourses was to distinguish between the *brain*, as a physical mechanism responding more or less automatically to the horde of outside stimuli, and the *mind*, which might better be called "consciousness" or "the mental life," quite a different entity and composed of swarms of interacting ideas and feelings, choices and aversions, hopes and terrors. The elaborated distinction was epochal both for the speaker and for the history of thought in America. It was devised, of course, as a rebuttal to those materialists, Herbert Spencer and others, whose theory of mind as automaton was gaining a decided ascendancy in American intellectual circles.

James's older Harvard colleague, the watchful, gossipy, and learned professor of English, Francis Child, was lecturing at Johns Hopkins in the same weeks; and after observing James close at hand, he wrote J. R. Lowell, then American ambassador to England, that William "was sleepless and restless, and, as it turned out, not because the lectures troubled him, but because his fate was in the scales and Miss Alice Gibbens would not say the word he wanted." What Child could not realize was that the very content of James's brilliantly successful lectures was to an important degree being colored and designed by his feelings about Miss Gibbens.

The series came to a rousing climax with another avowal of the authentic and separate creative energy of the mind in all its rich complexity:

I, for one, as a scientific man and a practical man alike, deny utterly that science compels me to believe that my conscience is an *ignis fatuus* [unreliable guide] or outcast, and I trust that you too, after the evidence of this evening, will go away strengthened in the natural faith that your delights and sorrows, your loves and hates, your aspirations and efforts are real combatants in life's arena, and not impotent, paralytic spectators of the game.

The passage is redolent with family and personal allusions: the implied inversion of Father's view of conscience as obstructive to the divine life in man; the military metaphor—William's rhetorical equivalent of the actual warfare his younger brothers had participated in; the notion of impotence carried over from his self-accusing letter to Alice Gibbens, and of paralysis from his nightmare vision of himself as a motionless idiot.

In a long review of Spencer's *Definition of the Mind as Correspondence*, later in the year, William James formulated the whole matter even more richly—especially the relation, within the mind, of feeling and thought, and the image of the mind as *active*. He denounced Spencer's definition as reducing all mental life to the phenomenon of cognition, omitting "all sentiments, all aesthetic impulses, all religious emotions and personal affections," and beyond those, all emotional *choices*. "How much of our mental life . . . involves preferences or repugnances on our part." In fact, James argued, pushing hard along his now clearly perceived course, it is feeling that determines the nature and the direction of thought. "Interests which we bring with us, and simply posit or take our stand upon, are the very flour out of which our mental dough is kneaded . . . Not a cognition occurs but feeling is there to comment on it, to stamp it as of greater or lesser worth." In an article of the 1890s, and referring back to the Spencer review, James put the case in the strongest terms: "The conceiving or theorizing faculty . . . functions *exclusively for the sake of ends* that . . . are set by our emotional and practical subjectivity."

Thus, out of his deep concern over the relation between his intellectual aspirations and his desire for Alice Gibbens (his two loyalties) did William James construct a *Weltanschauung* wherein intellect was at the service of emotion. The review of Spencer's *Definition* rose to a peroration which was plainly an enlargement on the letter to Alice of the previous February:

The knower is not simply a mirror floating with no foot-hold anywhere, and passively reflecting an order that he comes upon and finds simply existing. The knower is an actor, and co-efficient of the truth on one side, whilst on the other he registers the truth which he helps to create. Mental interests, hypotheses, postulates, so far as they are bases for human action—action which to a great extent transforms the world—help to *make* the truth which they declare. In other words, there belongs to the mind, from its birth upwards, a spontaneity, a vote.

"The knower is an actor . . . [who] registers the truth which he helps to create. Mental interests . . . help to *make* the truth which they declare." William was here envisioning an ideal self no less distinctly than Henry had done, prefiguring himself in Michelangelo, the man of action in art.

The next scrap in William's handwriting that Alice Gibbens retained, cut off from the rest of the letter, was a passionate cry of renunciation. "I renounce you! Let the eternal tides bear you where they will! In the end they'll bear you round to where I wait for you. I'll feed on death now, but I'll buy the right to eternal life by it. If there is a life of any sort after this, there in sight of God and man I will lay my hand upon you and say 'she's mine,' and you will yield."

There was something strangely exultant in the outburst (as though an otherworldly vision of Emily Dickinson had been re-expressed in the thundering rhetoric of an Ahab*). In its fervor of tone, it chimed with a paragraph added twenty hours later on the other side of the page: "O friend of my soul how could you write the note which has thrown me into such a frenzy? Which has been like the touch of red hot coal to gunpowder. Here in the dead bowels of the night, I concentrate myself afresh. I will not abdicate." And at the foot of the page: "If so, Amen! Amen my own Alice Gibbens, now and forever mine."

These fragments are undated, but they can be assigned to late April or early May. On May 8, 1878, William, on the last of the extant snippets, wrote: "Oh! divine, blessed Alice! If you might say yes!" Below that is a notation, not in Alice's hand but probably in that of the firstborn child of the union, Henry: "They became engaged, definitely, on May 10, 1878."

There was general rejoicing at the event throughout the James and Gibbens clans. The elder James had been eagerly promoting the match from the outset; and Mary James can be imagined breathing a sigh of relief at William's domestic settlement and its obviously healthful effect upon him. Mrs. Gibbens openly adored her son-in-law-to-be; and William could find in Eliza Gibbens a maternal figure whom he could not only love but cherish and support; a more satisfying filial responsibility than he had been accustomed to.

The younger Henry received the first word from William in late May at the Reform Club in London, and he answered at once. He had been expecting just such news, Henry said; not that he knew anything about Miss Gibbens, only "a slight mention a year ago, in a letter of mother's, which had never been repeated." (The Quincy Street contingent had remained strategically silent about the affair.) "The wish, perhaps," Henry went on, "was father to the thought. I had long wished to see you married; I believe almost as much in matrimony for most other people as I believe in it little for myself—which is saying a good deal." (Henry perhaps hoped William would show their mother that

---

* William James was capable of Melvillian grandiloquence—for example, here and there in the notes on *Optimism and Pessimism* which he had forwarded to Alice Gibbens. There is no evidence that Melville was known to any member of the James family, and more's the pity, as F. O. Matthiessen once remarked.

last sentence, so that she might not seize the occasion once again to press him toward the altar.) "What you say of Miss Gibbens . . . inflames my imagination and crowns my wishes . . . Give her then my cordial—my already fraternal—benediction."

But it was Wilky James, writing Miss Gibbens from Milwaukee, who made the most searchingly sympathetic appraisal of the development. His brother Bob, despite William's prohibition, had evidently confided to Wilky something of the ups and downs of the relationship. William's engagement, Wilky said, "is the greatest event by far that has ever taken place in the history of a family in which events of a startling nature have not been infrequent." He found it peculiarly interesting: "because in its nature (dating from the origins of his affection for you, his conflict with its attending emotions) there must have been presented to the world, 'behind the scenes' of course, the most sincere struggle for attaining a rightful end, without any semblance of suffering inflicted upon any human being." Suffering there had been on both sides, as we know; but Wilky's intuition was none the less exact. To William, he declared himself so carried away with excitement and enthusiasm that he felt like going out and blowing up the North Chicago Rolling Company (where he was currently employed and about which he had no good feelings) or setting fire to the city.

Then, growing more serious: "I can imagine . . . no greater good to befall you than a love of this kind." He anticipated for William an experience like his own, though his personal need had been more extreme than William's: "I should have been by this time deep down in Hell, if it had not been for my wife." William, his brother continued, had other qualities and features of character "which would save you *any way.*" And in a singularly shrewd insight, he added: "But you have an intellectual force to your being, which must be very much helped and softened by the influence of love and all that it brings with it. —Your loving brother, Garth W. James."

The wedding was set for the second week in July. At the start of that month William went to the Adirondacks, to stay in the Keene Valley cottage, or shanty, of Dr. James Putnam, a Boston and Harvard friend (and already, at thirty-two, recognized as a pioneer in the study of nervous diseases), and his sister Lizzie. After a happily exhausting day climbing through the woods to the top of a waterfall and a hearty dinner, William sat in the still sunlit front room; and while another guest read to Jim Putnam and the ladies from W. H. Mallock's *The New Republic* (a spirited satire of 1877 on English literary and intellectual folk), William addressed himself to Alice: "I have thought of you incessantly—of your dear true heart, of your trusting soul, and O Alice of all the sad moments I have given them. Oh might I blot out all in the past that I *cannot cannot* remember and which yet refuses to be forgot." He was *sure* that she would never more "feel any chasm between us. I can't help saying this here darling because it has been so corroding my mind." But this, he said, should be the last of it; and he went on to ask how many things Alice had bought for her trousseau.

In a follow-up letter the next morning, William reported with glee that Jim Putnam had offered the bridal couple the use of his cottage for six or eight weeks. This would be their honeymoon home, and far more attractive than the " 'hanging round' sort of honeymoon" they would otherwise have spent in a hotel in the White Mountains.

William James, age thirty-six, and Alice Howe Gibbens, age twenty-nine, were married on July 10, in the home of Alice's eighty-one-year-old grandmother at 153 Boylston Street in Boston, the Reverend Rufus Ellis presiding. A small gathering of relatives and friends attended the ceremony. The couple left soon afterward, taking a late-afternoon train to New York City, where they spent the night at the Windsor Hotel on Fifth Avenue. The next day they traveled by the Hudson River line north to Saratoga, passing their second night there at the Grand Union; amid the later blur of memory, William would recall a vast enclosed court, with a marble floor, elm trees, and electric lights. On the twelfth they reached Keene Valley, and there began, in William's phrase, their "sad-sweet honeymoon summer."

What Wilky James regarded as an event of historic magnitude, William's thirty-year-old sister, Alice, seems to have found personally devastating. Less than a fortnight after the formally announced engagement, Alice was said by her mother (in a letter to Bob) to be having "a nervous breakdown of a very serious character—an aggravated occurrence of her old trouble"; it had started a few weeks earlier. She rallied a bit in June, and Mary James could tell Bob that her "periods of depression and feeling of inability to meet life" had become less frequent, and that between attacks she was quite cheerful and "like herself." She was able to go out driving for an hour and a half in the phaeton which Father had given her two years before.

But after the July wedding, Alice fell apart completely, and for months thereafter, Henry Senior said to the youngest brother, she was more than half the time "on the verge of insanity and suicide." It was during this period that father and daughter held a long conversation on the nature and propriety of suicide, as the elder James would record.*

No one in the family had any particular explanation for the onslaught. Mary James's description—"an aggravated occurrence of her old trouble"—was the accepted version. One or two commentators have hazarded the guess that the collapse was due to Alice's sense that her new sister-in-law disliked her. Alice may well have entertained such a thought, but it had little if any basis in fact. On her side, when she was slowly recovering in late November, Alice spoke to her friend Fanny Morse of "the great joy that has been brought into life by William's marriage." It was, she said then, "a happiness which grows day by day as we get to know our dear Alice better. How William can have been so fortunate a man, we cannot any of us understand, and he himself less than the rest of us." One can hear the faint fond derision about her brother, but what she says about his wife sounds more than merely conventional.

It was, though, a truly terrible stretch of time for Alice James, probably the worst she was ever to undergo; and she has left us a fascinatingly cryptic allusion to it. In February 1892, not long before the death she knew to be upon her, Alice communed in her diary about the future state of her soul, an element which she described as a "poor, shabby, old thing." She continued: "The fact is, I have been dead so long and it has been simply such a grim shoving of the hours behind me as I faced a ceaseless possible horror, since that hideous summer of '78, when I went down to the deep sea, its dark waters closed over me and I knew neither hope nor peace."

What she was remembering, it seems possible to say (Jean Strouse has written effectively about this), was her feeling about the (for her) terrible loss of William from the family life. It opened up unbearable vistas for her. Her brother Henry was firmly ensconced in London; a short, infrequent visit from him was the most that could be hoped for. She had never felt much warmth for Wilky and Bob, though there had been a rapprochement at the moment of their marriages; in any case, in the unlocatable northern Midwest, they were farther away, psychologically, than Henry. Aunt Kate was occasionally on hand, but her home was now in New York. Alice's parents were in their late sixties and showing signs of infirmity: how long would they last? This was one of the times, as Alice would recall, when, while her mother and father watched over her through the pain-racked nights, she would cry out to them repeatedly "to know what would become of me when I

* See below, pp. 320–21.

lost them." So the departure of William, even though, as it happened, simply to nearby Harvard Street, signified not only the wrenching away of that warming, teasing, electrifying daily presence, but the end of the family and of her life within it. This was the possible horror that she saw stretching out ceaselessly before her that summer: a life-in-death of unending solitude, without hope and without peace.

The year of his marriage, 1878, was the most telling year, intellectually, of William James's life thus far. In addition to the essay-review of Spencer's definition of mind and the lectures at Johns Hopkins (which provided James's definition of mind), there was an article written in French by James on "Quelques Considerations sur la Méthode Subjective," which Charles Renouvier, editor of the *Critique Philosophique*, where it appeared, called "*très remarquable*," and by an author who did the periodical honor. The issue that James laid down, at the start of the article, was whether (in translation) "one has the right to reject a theory apparently confirmed by a very considerable number of objective facts solely because it does not respond to our interior preferences." James's answer, needless to say, was a resounding "yes."

Another work of importance composed in the same year was a fifty-page disquisition on "the sentiment of rationality"—James must have been the only thinker of consequence in America who would juxtapose just those two terms—which, according to the author's note, was the first chapter of a work on the psychological motives "which lead men to philosophise." Taken together, these several writings (Jacques Barzun has made the point) comprise the basis for almost the whole range of William James's later and dazzlingly original intellectual vision.

In all of this, Alice Gibbens did more than lend affection and support, though as time went along she was indispensable in that way, too. At once self-effacing and tough-spirited, intelligent and understanding but rarely intrusive, calmly and steadily loving, erotically wifely and composedly maternal, she was close to the ideal of a philosopher's spouse—certainly of a man of genius, irrepressible humor, puritanical wincing, and nervous excitability like William James. But Alice Gibbens also had her key part to play in William James's intellectual coming-together, as we have seen. To repeat, and as distinctly as may be: William clarified his ideas and sharpened his expression of them by meditating and worrying over their changing relationship, and by acting out his part in their emotional drama.

Professor Francis Child was uncommonly acute, or else he spoke more wisely than he knew, when he noted to Lowell that even on his honeymoon William had begun work on "a Manual of Psychology," and that this phenomenon could be explained by the fact that "they are both writing it." The manual had been commissioned by Henry Holt and Company in New York, as a textbook in Holt's American Science series; William had signed the contract in June. Holt, aware that James was emerging as a forceful and prolific writer of wide reputation, asked if the manuscript might be ready in a year, but William, pleading other engagements and sometimes precarious health, thought it would take until the fall of 1880. It would, in fact, be a dozen years before *The Principles of Psychology* appeared, an immeasurably larger and more abundant work than William originally intended. But as though to confirm Child's allegation, William wrote his academic friend from Keene Valley in late August, alluding cheerily to his wife's studious immersion in deterministic psychology—the letter being dictated by the husband and written by the hand of the wife. The invitation to the Childs to visit the honeymoon couple was reiterated, and the letter closed with "your always doting (W. and A.) J."

CHAPTER NINE

Henry James
and *les siens*

THE AMERICAN IN PARIS

It was not until five days after his brother's wedding that Henry learned from Mother the date scheduled for the ceremony. "As I was divorced from you by an untimely fate on this unique occasion," he wrote William on July 15 from the Reform Club, "let me at least repair the injury by giving you . . . a tender bridal benediction." The reference to having been "divorced" was little more than fraternal fooling; but it is true that the whole phenomenon and hence the vocabulary of marriage—courtship, marriage, the failed marriage, the marriage that doesn't come off, the devious matter of divorce—had been tugging hard at Henry's imagination. It was of course a Victorian literary commonplace; but for personal as well as literary reasons, it had become a major concern for Henry James. Marriage had been the central element in the plotting of *The American* in 1876, the first fruit of Henry's settlement in Europe, and it would be no less so in *The Portrait of a Lady*, which, in 1882, brought this first six-year stay abroad triumphantly to a climax.

After only a week in London near the end of 1875, Henry had crossed the Channel and made his way to Paris. Here he took a snug fourth-floor apartment on the rue de Luxembourg (now rue Cambon), which ran from rue de Rivoli to the Boulevard des Capucines. Its makeup answered Henry's felt need, not simply for lodgings, but for a personal home of sorts, a place to live and to work: a parlor looking east, two bedrooms, an antechamber which could serve as a dining room, and a kitchen with a woodpile and an array of copper casseroles. There were, he said, mirrors and clocks and curtains and lamps and candlesticks in abundance; and the *portier* gave him "all conceivable service" for thirty francs a month.

Within these eminently congenial surroundings and in the very center of the great city, Henry began to lead a most manifold existence. His literary energy was unflagging. He sent off the first of his fortnightly letters to the *Tribune* ("Paris Revisited"), and other articles and notices flowed across to Godkin at *The Nation*. He was already at work on a new novel, and on December 1 he wrote F. P. Church of the *Galaxy* that he assumed Church would publish it without delay in that magazine. "The title of the thing is *The American*." He also had in mind a couple of short stories, minor efforts as it turned out and published the next spring in *Scribner's Monthly*. Nor should one forget his prolific and eloquent correspondence. "I remember no period at which letter-writing . . . has taken up more of my time," he told his mother, who had chided him for writing home (particularly her) so rarely. His long letters from the rue de Luxembourg in 1875–76, especially those which give portraits of Turgenev, Flaubert, and others, have their visible place in Henry James's literary achievement.

If he had been laggard in seizing social opportunities in Florence, he was quick off the mark in Paris. A letter from Godkin elicited introductions—among others and in short order—to an Orleanist duc, a deaf but gracious " 'chatty' " princesse, an obese but cultivated and beguiling sixty-year-old marquise. Henry also dined with the historian Ernest Renan and his wife; and it was his praise of Renan's conversation as urbane and witty that in part caused William James to castigate the Frenchman's *Dialogues* as an example of "insincerity and foppishness," of "dandified despair."

Henry was simultaneously coming to know the more purely literary scene in Paris, having been escorted into it by Ivan Sergeyevich Turgenev. One of Henry's first acts in Paris was to put himself in touch with "the great Muscovite novelist," as he wrote Aunt Kate; and upon Turgenev's cordial reply, he went to call upon the writer in rue de Douai in Montmartre, where Turgenev occupied an ambiguous position in the household of the operatic star Pauline Viardot and her husband. It was the start of one of the most nourishing human and literary relationships in Henry's experience. On this first occasion, Henry thought the Russian "a magnificent creature"; physically huge and broad, but very simple and friendly, "his whole aspect and temperament of a larger and manlier kind than I have ever yet encountered in a scribbler."

The older Russian and the younger American writer were in each other's company frequently in the months that followed. One rainy afternoon, Henry went to visit with Turgenev at the latter's request, he being too ill to come round to rue de Luxembourg; and Turgenev talked unforgettably, for Henry, about his own writing. "He had never *invented* anything or any one," Henry quoted him as saying. "Everything in his stories comes from some figure he has seen." (Henry would recall this discourse in his early-1900s preface to *The Portrait of a Lady*.) Less enjoyable was one of Mme Viardot's interminable Sunday musicals, where poor Turgenev was observed "acting charades of the most extravagant description, dressed out in old shawls and masks, going on all fours etc." Henry struggled in vain to imagine such a spectacle back home, with Longfellow or Lowell or Charles Norton engaged in comparable antics.

On a Sunday in December, Turgenev took his young friend to the Faubourg St.-Honoré to meet Gustave Flaubert. The French writer, who greeted his visitors in a long dressing gown, impressed Henry powerfully: "a great, stout, handsome, simple, kindly, elderly fellow," he wrote his father, ". . . with a serious, sober face, a big moustache, and a mottled red complexion." Turgenev had called him a *naïf*; and Henry was touched by Flaubert's embarrassment in having to cope with a stranger and an American. Henry had already expressed his admiration for *Madame Bovary* in a *Galaxy* article, where he had little favorable to say about Flaubert's other novels; now he warmed completely to the man.

Of the other "young realists" whom Henry met at various Sunday receptions, he thought Alphonse Daudet "a brilliant talker and *raconteur*," but an irritating writer. Edmond de Goncourt was the very type of French *gentilhomme*; Zola was a very common fellow. It was being rumored that Zola's *L'Assommoir* would be removed from the magazine in which it was running because of readers' protest against its scandalous nature.

Something about the Parisian literary circuit, however, began to put Henry James off, and in the late spring of 1876 he offered Howells a self-distancing appraisal: "I have seen almost nothing of the literary fraternity, and there are fifty reasons why I should not become intimate

with them. I don't like their wares, and they don't like any others"—
Henry had noticed how the writers at Flaubert's tended to blackguard
their rivals. "Tourguéneff is worth the whole heap of them, and yet he
himself swallows them down in a manner that excites my extreme
wonder." But even there, Henry interrupted the letter to hurry over
for a farewell call on Flaubert, who was leaving the city. "*He* is a very
fine old fellow [Flaubert was fifty-four], and the most interesting man
and strongest artist of his circle." When he had time to absorb it all,
later in London, Henry would realize that for the better part of a year
he had been enjoying the kind of male society he had earlier longed
for, and the company of writers whose lively and searching talk about
their art, and indeed their craft, could be of inestimable benefit for his
own.

Mother, who had been showing Henry the sterner side of her
nature, took him severely to task early in the new year (1876) for "living
extravagantly." He was particularly culpable, she seems to have indicated, at a time when Father's income was curtailed due to a decline
in Syracuse real-estate values; and when Bob—who had given up his
railroad job and was now trying to run a farm in Prairie du Chien—
needed frequent assistance. Under the circumstances, Henry's "drafts
of money had been excessive and inconvenient." Henry fairly groveled
in apologies and explanations: he hadn't *really* been extravagant,
though he would have been especially careful had he known the family's financial facts; the last draft was not only for the two months but
for the foreseeable future; in any case, there had been a mistake in
accounting.

There had also been a misunderstanding with the *Galaxy* about
the serialization of the new novel. Henry had been assuming that the
Galaxy was to start running *The American* in the May issue, and he
had firmly demanded $150 for each of its projected nine parts. When
Church, the magazine's editor, began to bumble and procrastinate,
Henry brought him up short. "These then are my terms," he told him
in March, "—$150 a number—to commence in *May*—and failing this
to send the copy instantly to Cambridge," to Mr. James at Quincy
Street. This is, in fact, what happened; and the elder James promptly
turned the manuscript over to Howells, who had been lobbying to get
it for *The Atlantic*. Howells, after examining the manuscript, begged
Henry to divide the story into twelve rather than nine installments; and
Henry, agreeing to do so, remarked that when he had encountered
Zola, pale-looking on the staircase outside Flaubert's apartment, he

had "saluted him with the flourish natural to a contributor who has just been invited to make his novel last longer yet."

Howells was able to begin *The American* in the June 1876 *Atlantic*; but two months after that, the *Tribune* letters had come to a halt, and with them the modest income they had been bringing. In August, Whitelaw Reid wrote to say that Mr. James's letters were rather "too good" for newspaper readers; could he not make them more "newsy" and gossipy, and less literary? Henry replied that he was not able to write in any different manner. "If my letters have been 'too good' I am honestly afraid they are the poorest I can do, especially for the money! I had better, therefore, suspend them altogether."

The letter was written in a blend of dry amusement and an open contempt for the state of literacy in American newspapers. Two decades later, Henry James would compose a story, "The Next Time," at once comical and contemptuous, about a gifted novelist who tries hard to bring forth saleably bad works of fiction, only to discover his incapacity, as the narrative puts it, to make a sow's ear out of a silk purse.

The idea for *The American*, as James was to recall it, came to him while he was seated in an American horsecar (probably in Boston): the situation of a compatriot, in another country and an aristocratic society, suffering some grievous wrong "at the hands of persons pretending to represent the highest possible civilisation and to be of an order in every way superior to his own." The idea came back to life in Paris, James said, when that "many-tinted medium by the Seine" suddenly and clearly offered him everything needed to make the conception concrete. Rereading the novel in the 1900s, James remembered interrupting the writing of it to hang over the window bar of his workroom to catch a glimpse of the troop of cavalry as it charged down the rue de Luxembourg each morning. The novel, indeed, had to fight for its life against the insidious lure of the Paris spectacle.

The American became the story of a wealthy retired American businessman, Christopher Newman, who comes to Paris and there entertains the hope of marrying Claire de Cintré, the widowed daughter of the Marquise de Bellegarde, *grande dame* of an ancient aristocratic family in the Faubourg St.-Germain. After some equivocating, the Bellegarde family disdainfully rejects Newman's suit: and this, James said, looking back with an air of surprised discovery, was what made the narrative a *romance* rather than a fictional rendering of reality.

Romance, in the definition he then drew up (in the preface to the work in the New York Edition), gives "experience disengaged . . . exempt from the conditions that we usually know to attach to it." *The American*, as a prime example, was "uncontrolled by our general sense of 'the way things happen.' " What would have happened in particular, in the case of Christopher Newman, James had come to realize, is that the Bellegardes "would positively have jumped . . . at my rich and easy American, and not have 'minded' in the least any drawback." From our vantage point, we may see *The American* as a conspicuous moment in the development from the special Jamesian mode of romance to the special Jamesian mode of realism.

It is an interesting, even fascinating, mixture in other respects: a brilliant comedy of manners, encased in the most unblushing melodrama, with a denouement of tragic import. The comedy consists largely of the social and conversational collisions between Newman (whose name adds a touch of allegory to the blend) and the Bellegardes, as the latter weigh the hateful prospect of admitting an American tradesman into the clan. The melodrama centers on Count Valentin, Claire's sympathetic and witty brother, who encourages Newman's courtship but himself gets entangled in an affair and is forced into a duel and fatally wounded; in his death throes, he puts Newman on the track of a terrible family secret. When Newman learns that Claire's engagement to him has been broken off, he ferrets out the secret; and in a device that outdoes the darkest revelations of Victorian fiction, the truth emerges that the fearsome old marquise had murdered her husband.

Newman thus has a weapon with which he could gain revenge by bringing the family down in scandal and disgrace; but he withholds it. Claire de Cintré has been shut up in a convent, and in our last view of him Newman is standing outside the building gazing at it with pain and frustration. Howells was dismayed by this literal closure and urged Henry to reconsider. The very request, Henry answered, set him trembling. Marriage between Mme de Cintré and Newman would have been unthinkable; the whole point of the ending was the concept of Newman's *losing* the young woman, while not striking back at "the insolent foreigner" who had wronged him. But if one can share Henry James's skepticism about marriage—or an enduring marriage—between a Midwestern American millionaire and an 1870s product of the Faubourg, one might also feel that the denouement devised, Claire's immurement, was strangely cruel. Yet perhaps the combination of the convent walls and the implacable wall of French Catholicism represented the only obstacle that Christopher Newman's American

[294

sweep and dash could not possibly overcome; and in this regard, the plot device is entirely sensible.

After more than a century *The American* holds its place among the best of James's novels, deserving of the accolades that first greeted it. The achievement is due in part to the greater distance between author and protagonist than obtained in *Roderick Hudson*. The surprisingly complicated Newman—he is "frigid and yet friendly," Henry writes, ". . . shrewd yet credulous"; a mixture of "innocence and experience," at once (we are disposed to add) high-minded and money-minded—has a fine independence of being. There is also another and well-realized kind of distance, the untraversable one between a Newman and a Bellegarde. In a searching remark to Howells, Henry said: "We are each the product of circumstances and there are tall stone walls which fatally divide us."

He was talking about the novel's ending; and also about the human condition, and about himself. In Paris, as the year 1876 went forward, Henry felt increasingly shut away from genuine nourishing social intercourse. He had not come to know the social gentry in the Faubourg St.-Germain, and on the whole thought he didn't want to. With the literary community, as we have seen, he felt uncomfortable: its inveterate carnality made him somewhat squeamish (by the same token, he would feel more at home with the decorous hypocrisy of the British). He saw all too much of the small American "set," and found it deadly boring; though he did enjoy a series of meetings with William's eccentric friend Charles Sanders Peirce, the physicist and logician who was pursuing his studies in Paris and did not of course belong to the American set or any other. Peirce led a life of "insupportable loneliness," in Henry's account of him; but he was "a very good fellow—when he is not in ill-humour." Apart from Peirce and some visits to the Comédie Française, there was little, for James in Paris, to please or stimulate. The social novelist in search of society had again grown disaffected; he foresaw, as he would say, that in Paris he would be "an eternal outsider."

At a certain moment, accordingly, Henry heard himself saying: "Go to; I will try London." He could never quite remember what brought him to the decision, but rather thought it had been a letter from William in which his brother said: "Why don't you?—That must be the place." London *was* the place, as it turned out; but what Henry could not have anticipated was that the lesson of the place would be the particular kind of outsider he was, all profitably, destined to be.

Daisy Miller AND THE CHOICE OF LOCATION

In the second week of December, Henry wrote Alice from his newly found and "excellent" lodging at 3 Bolton Street in London, on the northeast corner of Piccadilly; and spoke with relish about his first breakfast there: tea, eggs, bacon, and the tasty English loaf. But he was also admitting to Howells that he knew very few people in the city; and on a drizzly, sleety, foggy Christmas Eve, though he made a brave show of things to his mother ("My spirits were never higher. I take very kindly indeed to London"), he could not conceal his loneliness and uncertainty. But Mary James's answering letter of concern had not even reached him before Henry's life had been "transmuted," in his word, and at such a pace that he hurried to get some of it down before he forgot.

"I am beginning to 'go out,'" he told his mother at the end of January 1877, and proceeded to give a listing of recent social engagements that left the Quincy Street household gasping, and Alice in particular agog for further detail. At one banquet, he met Andrew Lang, essayist and translator of Homer; at another, Sir William Power, K.C.B. and a son of the famous Irish actor Tyrone Power. At dinner in the home of George W. Smalley, European correspondent for the *Tribune* and an amiable sycophant, Henry fell in with Robert Browning; John Motley, the American historian; James Froude, the English historian; and Edward Pierrepont, the American minister to England. "What strikes me here," he said to Mother, as his social gazette drew to a close, "is that everyone is someone or something—represents something—has, in some degree or other, an historical identity."

Henry had brought with him a few introductions, from Henry Adams and others, but he used them sparingly. The London that had kept him at arm's length on previous visits now showered invitations on the rising American author. Lord Houghton—Adams's friend Richard Monckton Milnes—had Henry almost at once for one of his famous breakfasts; a word from Lord Houghton went far in the making of a career, Adams was to say, but "an invitation to his breakfast table went farther." Henry took to him without reservation: "He has breakfasted me, dined me, conversazioned me, absolutely caressed me," Henry informed Adams as he prepared to go to another morning repast at his lordship's, "and I have seen, under his wing, a great variety of interesting and remarkable people." Later there would be Sunday

[296

breakfasts at the "queer little house" in Chelsea, on the river, of the American-born painter James Whistler—Henry claimed to think that Whistler painted abominably, but he liked his tomatoes and buckwheat cakes and his guests.

There were invitations to country houses; Henry spent several days with the Gaskells (the husband was another friend of Adams) at Wenlock Abbey in Shropshire, and drew a scintillating sketch of the awkward and engaging Catherine Gaskell worthy to be deployed (though it never was) in one of his novels. John Motley arranged for James to have guest privileges at the Athenaeum Club on Pall Mall; from its "beautiful great library" in February, Henry wrote his father (to be passed along to William) that Herbert Spencer was asleep nearby; and he liked to say later that he napped next to Spencer each afternoon. Less than eighteen months after settling in London, Henry was elected a member for life of the Reform Club, also on Pall Mall. It took the average Briton sixteen years to be admitted to the elitist institution, according to Henry. His election, he told Alice, had "doubled my 'selfhood,' as Father would say"; and to Father himself he declared *"J'y suis, j'y reste*—forever and a day," adding that he had perforce drawn £42 on his letter of credit to pay his club dues.

At moments, Henry sought to deprecate the social whirl, insofar as it involved him. In a joint letter to his father and his sister in May 1877, he quoted Sara Sedgwick—now married to William Darwin, the banker son of Charles Darwin, and living in England—as reporting his family to be laboring "under the impression that I 'go out immensely' in London . . . Disabuse yourself of this: I lead a very quiet life." One had to dine somewhere, he pointed out; and went on to speak of a festive dinner in honor of George Du Maurier, cartoonist of *Punch*, and another banquet at Lady Goldsmidt's, "a very nice, kindly elderly childless Jewess, cultivated, friend of George Eliot etc. who is of colossal fortune and gives banquets to match in a sort of country house in the Regent's Park."

But the fact was, the more Henry was welcomed and made much of within the higher reaches of English society—this was perhaps the saving paradox—the more conscious he became that he was an outsider; and the more he accepted and even insisted upon that identity. During the summer of 1877 when, as he said, he was sorting through the impressions received over the previous winter and spring, he remarked to Grace Norton that he had taken a great fancy to London as a place, but that, though he had met and talked with a great number of people, he had "become familiar with almost none." He had arrived at an important self-recognition, and he formulated it with exactitude: he was "a good deal more of a cosmopolitan (thanks to that combination of the continent and the U.S.A. which has formed my lot) than the average Briton of culture; and to be—to have become by force of circumstances—a cosmopolitan, is of necessity to be a good deal alone."

In this judgment, Henry was not talking out of mere vanity. William James would give voice to a comparable insight a few years later, in Germany, as we shall see; and both brothers were taking note that a certain kind of literate American tended to be broader in his interests and perhaps his cultural awareness than the average educated but nationally focused European. It is, of course, entirely a matter of degree: no member of the James family, with the occasional and marginal exception of William, saw beyond a horizon formed by "the western world." (It goes without saying that the less literate kind of American has always been capable of an invincible narrowness of view.) Henry, in any case, attributed his own mental largeness, by implication, to his father's theory and practice of upbringing. Thus belatedly did that paternal policy once again prove its value.

By the end of 1877, Henry was saying to Grace Norton, during a short stay in Paris, that he was on his way "to London whither I find I gravitate as towards the place in the world in which, on the whole, I feel most at home." He had, in other words, at long last made his choice of location; and it compared, in the length of time taken to reach it and the variety of alternatives considered, with William's long-delayed choice of calling. He had made his trial of Cambridge and New York, of Florence and Rome and Paris—as William had been trying art and science, medicine and psychology—and now London, once and for all, was to be his home. But he brought to London—its society, its literary milieu, its intellectual habits, its culinary standards—what he himself called a cosmopolitanism, and what his father would have rejoiced to call a universality of outlook. He had determined his role in his chosen habitat: it would be "that of an observer in a place where there is most in the world to observe." The location, the breadth of view, the perceived role: these, combined, would be the making of him as a writer.

As Henry's decision began to be apparent in Quincy Street, William made one last effort to bring his brother back to America. It was his duty, William declared, to re-establish himself in his native land; and if he needed a great urban capital for his literary welfare, he should live and write in Washington. "I think there is much in that," said

Henry, who of course thought nothing of the sort; but he remarked firmly that he expected "to spend many a year in London." As for his literary requirements: "If one will take what comes, one is by no means cut off from getting American impressions here." He knew what he was about, he added; he always kept his eyes on the country of his birth.

In support of those calm contentions, Henry might have cited the story taken a month earlier for *Cornhill Magazine* by Leslie Stephen— *Daisy Miller.*

At other moments, he could be gripped with an excitement of self-confidence, revealing it with a sort of smiling pride to members of his family. To his mother, in February 1878, Henry said that she could look forward to a fund of reflected glory—"of which latter article I propose to furnish myself with a very considerable amount. It is time I should rend the veil from the ferocious ambition which has always *couvé* beneath a tranquil exterior," and "which enabled me to support unrecorded physical misery in my younger years." To William in January he had written: "If I keep along here patiently for a certain time I rather think I shall become a (sufficiently) great man."

The literary dialogue with his older brother had not slackened. Henry had long realized that his father had little interest in the art of fiction, the writing of novels; and for all he knew, the elder James still believed, as he had once said to the editor of *Scribner's*, that his son's "critical faculty is the dominant feature of his intellectual organisation." Mary James and Alice were devoted and unquestioning admirers of his work. But William—in addition to the concealed darts he threw at Henry in the guise of published comments on Renan or George Eliot's *Daniel Deronda*—had for many a year been visiting upon his younger sibling one cautionary or adverse comment after another. Several of those remarks seem to have gathered in Henry's mind in the spring of 1878, when he was writing *Daisy Miller.*

As far back as 1870, William had expressed himself with particular harshness about "Guest's Confession," a story written at Quincy Street. This unappetizing tale has to do with the vindictive behavior of an older brother—a morbidly self-concerned medical man—toward the prospective father-in-law of the younger brother; and William could properly have taken offense at the remote caricature of himself. What he objected to instead, however, were two phrases in the narrative, one in French and one rather precious. "Of the people who experience a personal dislike so to speak of your stories," William said, "the most

I think will be repelled by the element which gets expression in these two phrases, something cold, thin-blooded and priggish suddenly popping in and freezing the genial current." He then went on, as he customarily did, to praise Henry's sense of beauty and to insist on the pleasure Henry's stories gave him.

The travel articles Henry wrote during and after the European tour with Alice and Aunt Kate were, William admitted with some surprise, being very favorably received. For himself, William thought them overrefined, and suggested that a bigger dose of human interest might "agreeably speckle the columns." Henry's style in general, he ventured, "ran a little more to *curliness* than suited the average mind." It was as apt a word as one could deploy to identify Henry's inveterate indirectness and prolixity. Indeed, although William's manner could be overbearing and smacked betimes of an unearned expertise (which did not quite hide a simple dash of envy), his critical perceptions were often extremely acute; and if Henry fended them off with varying rhetorical strategies, he took them privately to heart.

He meditated a good deal over William's response to his *Tribune* letters from Paris. "Keep watch and ward," William wrote, pointedly invoking the title of Henry's repudiated novel, "lest in your style you become too Parisian and lose your hold on the pulse of the great American public, to which after all you must pander for support." If *Daisy Miller* was for its author a major test of his abilities, and a resolute statement of artistic identity, it was in part because, on one level, it was a response to these brotherly challenges.

The opening phases of *Daisy Miller* are dotted with small and mainly superficial family notations. Winterbourne, the young American expatriate through whose clouded vision the story comes to us, is first espied sitting in the garden of an inn in the Swiss town of Vevey; his fixed placed of residence, we are told, is Geneva, and he had "an old attachment for the little metropolis of Calvinism," having been "put to school there as a boy," and having "afterwards gone to college there." When the ten-year-old Randolph Miller appears, Winterbourne reflects that he had himself been brought to Europe at about the same age (Henry James had actually been twelve). There follows shortly the private family joke mentioned earlier, when Randolph, having said that his father wasn't in Europe but in a better place than Europe, adds—to the relief of Winterbourne, who had thought the boy was referring to heaven—"My father's in Schenectady. He's got a big business. My father's rich, you bet." There may even be another mild reminiscence of the earlier William James, or rather of his wife, in the allusion to Mrs. Miller's habit of treating her servants as friends.

But when Daisy Miller steps onto the scene, the narrative tone at once deepens in seriousness. Charmed and puzzled by her (Winterbourne had never heard a young American girl say, as Daisy does, that "I have always had a great deal of gentlemen's society"), Winterbourne says about himself almost exactly what William James had warned his younger brother *against*. "He felt that he had lived at Geneva so long that he had lost a good deal; he had become dishabituated to the American tone." When Winterbourne agrees to accompany Miss Miller to the Castle de Chillon, his aunt Mrs. Costello, the very type of snobbish American female in Europe, admonishes him: "You have lived too long out of the country. You will be sure to make some great mistake. You are too innocent."

Daisy moves on with her family to Rome, where she is at first taken into the American colony, but where she is also reputed to be running around with some undesirable Roman characters, in particular a young man with a big mustache. When Winterbourne turns up and seeks to remonstrate with Daisy about her behavior, she exclaims, giving a hard laugh, "I never heard anything so stiff!" She repeats the word "stiff" on several subsequent occasions: it is her upstate New York version of the term "priggish" that William had applied to the style and atmosphere of Henry's short stories, and by extension perhaps to Henry himself.

It is sufficiently clear, by this time, that Winterbourne is a walking embodiment of some of the charges leveled at Henry by William. What people disliked in Henry's writing, William had said, was "something cold, thin-blooded and priggish suddenly . . . freezing the genial current." In a belated testing of that contention, Henry projected a young American who has long been absent from his native country and whose name is Winterbourne: and who, in enactment of that name, is palpably limited by a certain wintriness of nature, a coldness and thin-bloodedness; a priggishness which tends to freeze a natural impulse toward geniality. There is no doubting the planted suggestiveness of Winterbourne's name in a story that flanks him with a girl named Daisy and a young Roman (Daisy's chevalier) named Giovanelli, which adds the notion of "little" to the Italian word for youth, *giovane*.

The wintry and prematurely old side of Winterbourne's character quite defeats the better side when he comes upon Daisy and Giovanelli exploring the Colosseum by night. For some moments, in the familiar

Jamesian tableau, he observes the two of them unobserved, convinced—since a nice girl would never pay such an unchaperoned night-
time visit—that Daisy was "a young lady whom a gentleman need no
longer be at pains to respect." Daisy (to the grief of untold numbers
of readers) catches a fever in the Colosseum miasma and dies soon
thereafter, though not before sending Winterbourne a message which
he understands, too late, to mean that she would have appreciated his
esteem.

Winterbourne and Giovanelli meet in the Protestant cemetery
where the girl lies buried beneath the April daisies. "She was the most
beautiful young lady I ever saw," says poor Giovanelli, ". . . and she
was the most innocent." Winterbourne is ready to accept the description. In his last words to his aunt, before returning to Geneva, he says:
"You were right in that remark that you made last summer. I was
booked to make a mistake. I have lived too long in foreign parts." But
Winterbourne, of course, means the exact opposite of what Mrs. Costello had meant.

Henry James's achievement in this endlessly appealing and literarily brilliant tale is of several kinds. Here what may be stressed is
Henry's success, as we might say, in outwitting his older brother. He
did so by bringing into being an American female figure, so wondrously
true to her species as well as so touchingly alive, that demonstrates
beyond all question Henry's mastery of the American subject, his hold
on the American pulse. No less remarkably, Henry makes this figure—
enchanting, headstrong, vulnerable, ignorant, profoundly innocent—
known to us through the eyes of a character who possesses all the traits
that William worried about Henry possessing, and who never really
sees her. The delineation of Winterbourne was Henry's triumph over
the Winterbournism William attributed to him. The portrait of Daisy
was Henry's testimony that he had not, after all, lived too long in foreign
parts, and that he was not endangering his literary career by settling
in England.

"AS AN ARTIST AND AS A BACHELOR"

Daisy Miller, which appeared in the June and July 1878 issues of
Cornhill Magazine and in book form a few months later, was a stunning
success on both sides of the Atlantic. Henry exploited the situation by

bringing out a number of his writings—*The American* and some short stories among them—that had not previously appeared in England. His income increased gratifyingly, and his social life almost beyond reckoning. To his family, Henry sent periodic disclaimers about the social doings; but in early June 1879, he informed Grace Norton that he had dined out 107 times during the winter just passed—a figure he upped to 140 in a later communication to an American associate in London. Trying as he often did to enliven Alice's days by an account of the social whirl, he confessed he could not easily sort things out: "The dinners . . . fall into a sort of shimmering muddle in one's memory." Walking home from the nightly dinner party, he said elsewhere, he tended to forget where he had been by the time he turned the corner. This whole affair—Henry James's and London's siege of one another—reached its peak in 1878–79.

Henry consorted as before with the writers and artists of the teeming mid-Victorian age—Browning ("loud, sound, normal, hearty"), Tennyson ("less agreeable than his works"), Trollope (entertaining and likable), Arnold ("I know [him] very well and like him much," Henry told Tom Perry), Meredith, Pater, Whistler, Millais; with political personalities, like the energetically talkative John Bright; with editors and publishers, bishops and "bishopesses," dukes and duchesses. He organized smaller gatherings of his own—one, memorably, in June 1879, for the visiting Turgenev, at the Reform Club; he spent weekends at large country estates in Cornwall (where he listened to "the music of an Atlantic gale") and Devon; and at the several homes of Lord Rosebery, the immeasurably wealthy breeder of champion racehorses and future Prime Minister of England.

He seemed to turn up everywhere and to be welcomed everywhere. London society was reading his stories and articles, however casually, and wanted to know him; or it had been intrigued by meeting him, and hurried to read his stories. He was the best of company: good-looking, if balding and a bit portly (at thirty-six); with a soft beard and keen watchful eyes; well tailored and with very fine manners; and a delightful conversationalist—the one thing Henry James never could do in conversation, an admiring acquaintance recalled, was to be commonplace. But if Henry James was greatly and patently enjoying this crowded time, he also managed on the whole to keep his ironic balance. So much is evident from his novella of 1883, *The Siege of London*, in which the much-divorced Mrs. Headway, the former Nancy Beck of the American Southwest, conquers English aristocratic society chiefly by making it roar with appreciative laughter at her comical way of talking; and marries a baronet, to the horror of his mother, the dowager Lady Demesne.*

And then, of course, Henry James was a bachelor, likely to be socially available and temperamentally ready to make the most of his condition. "For one who takes it as I take it," he wrote in his notebook in 1881, "London is on the whole the most possible form of life. I take it as an artist and as a bachelor; as one who has the passion of observation and whose business is the study of human life."

His bachelorhood continued to prey upon his mother's mind, though she rarely mentioned it anymore. She did allude hesitantly, in a letter of October 1880, to a rumor that Henry had gotten engaged to some young lady or other. This report, her son said in his usual vein, was "a slight mistake"; he was not just then making "any matrimonial arrangements," though he was aware of the rumors and of the many well-wishers who "think that I should be 'so much happier' if I would only marry." Henry took a special pleasure in friendships with spinsters and widows, as it were, the older the better. One of his favorite people in late 1870s London was the venerable and imperious Mrs. Anne Benson Procter, who could, from her richly stored memory, draw anecdotes of Keats and Shelley, Byron and Coleridge and Landor (a resource, as a window onto "the visitable past," when Henry was writing *The Aspern Papers*). Though she had entered her eighties, Henry confidently expected (he told his mother) to hear that their engagement had been announced.

But to Grace Norton the following month, Henry pondered the matter in a more thoughtful tone of voice. Miss Norton had disclosed to Henry a vision she entertained of him as a husband; and to this, Henry said that peering ahead into his imaginable future, he couldn't "discern the particular figure which you seem to have *entrevue*." He was unlikely ever to marry, he wrote; and at the risk of sounding "dismally theoretic," he spelled out his reasons.

One's attitude toward marriage is a part—the most characteristic part, doubtless—of one's general attitude toward life. Now I don't want to calumniate my attitude toward life; but I am bound to say that if I were to marry I should be guilty in my own eyes of an inconsistency—I should pretend to think just a little better of life than I really do.

---

* In the conventional view of the American observer in the tale, Mrs. Headway is definitely not respectable; and is in fact all the "bad" things said about Daisy Miller. *The Siege of London* is among other things a parody or inversion of that earlier story, as it is a parody of James's London life.

Henry's deployment of "attitudes" in that passage—with its tantalizing affinity to William's use of the term in *his* musings about marriage versus *Weltanschauung*—could serve as a critical touchstone for the marital behavior of Henry's fictional creations. In the graceful dance patterns of *The Europeans*—a novel that Henry called "a sketch" and that ran in *The Atlantic* through the summer of 1878—it is Robert Acton's hardened suspicion about the motives of others that immunizes him to the overtures of the American-born Baroness Eugenia, and leaves him to go dryly on his bachelor way, while others are contentedly altar-bound. In *The Europeans*, Henry James worked a double reversal of his established form: changing geographical direction, he brought European manners to America and New England, in the person of Eugenia and her artist brother Felix; and, Acton apart, he ended the tale with a positive scurry of marriages. "The offhand marrying . . . was *commandé*," he said to Lizzie Boott with a touch of grumpiness; after Howells's distress over the bleak conclusion of *The American*, James had promised "distinct matrimony" to end the new work, but felt that he had been maneuvered into violating his life-attitude.

Henry thought that Lizzie's favorable comments on *The Europeans* "showed the highest discrimination." Far otherwise was what must have been a harsh critique by William, bearing (it seems) upon an alleged triviality of subject and a form that failed to please. Henry studied his brother's letter for a painful hour in the Devonshire Club on St. James's, and straightened himself to reply. "I am beginning to hold up my head a little," he wrote, especially since he felt he could estimate the book as justly as need be and was aware of "its extreme slightness" (overaware, one may perhaps think today). But: "I think you take these things too rigidly and unimaginatively—too much as if an artistic experiment were a piece of conduct, to which one's life were somehow committed." This was well said. William, in his mind's workings, was moving toward those emphases on habituated conduct and the once-and-for-allness of moral commitment that he would elaborate in *The Principles of Psychology*, and Henry was speaking for the flexible imagination.

An education in readership was in progress for Henry. As his popularity rose, resistance to his work began predictably to be expressed in different quarters. When his tale "An International Episode" appeared in late 1879, Henry was pleased to hear from his mother that William and his wife thought highly of it, but had to report a certain recoil from the story by English readers. The narrative introduces the wealthy and amiable Lord Lambeth to New York and Newport, where he pays court to an American girl, Bessie Alden. Bessie later travels to England to see his lordship in his native milieu, and here she is treated with cold aristocratic vulgarity by his duchess mother and her friend the Countess of Pimlico. It was the presentation of the English ladies that aroused the resentment of the London readers. "It is an entirely new sensation for them (the people here)," Henry said to his mother, "to be (at all delicately) *ironized* or satirized, from the American"—as against the Dickensian or Trollopian—"point of view." To another reviewer, a Mrs. F. H. Hill, who objected to what she took to be Mr. James's general view of English manners in the persons of the duchess and the countess, Mr. James set about trying to explain the facts of the creative life. The two ladies were in no way "a resumé of my view of English manners"; they were "a picture of a special case": two well-bred women who for family reasons were determined to be as uncivil as possible to the little known American girl. Then came a formulation in which, one feels, Henry James was finally recognizing his artistic bent as well as describing it:

One may make figures and figures without intending generalizations—generalizations of which I have a horror. I make a couple of English ladies doing a disagreeable thing . . . and forthwith I find myself responsible for a representation of English manners! Nothing is my *last word* about anything—I am interminably supersubtle and analytic . . .

Henry was still reflecting on the thinness of the English reader's skin when he was given a demonstration that the American reader's skin was a good deal thinner. In the early fall of 1879, he completed a "critical essay" on Nathaniel Hawthorne for the English Men of Letters series edited by John Morley of Macmillan. It appeared toward the end of the year; and when it reached the elder Jameses, they were delighted with it, though Mary James wrote Henry that he had been "very bold" to have "braved the wrath of the Boston critics." Henry was not conscious of any special audacity; he thought the tone of the book gentle and good-natured. But Mother was right: the essay drew forth a storm of abuse from reviewers of all kinds.

The recurring complaint, sometimes shrill in utterance, was that James had been condescending to Hawthorne and to the New England, in effect the America, of his time. As the worst example of an alleged Anglophile snobbery, critics quoted from James's discourse on "the negative side of the spectacle on which Hawthorne looked out." Remarking that "one might enumerate the items of high civilization, as it exists in other countries, which are absent from the texture of American life," James provided what would be an oft-quoted catalogue of what was missing in America: "No State . . . no sovereign . . . no court . . . no church, no clergy, no army, no diplomatic service . . . no cathedrals, nor abbeys, nor little Norman churches," and all the way to no Eton or Harrow, no Epsom or Ascot.

America admittedly did not have an Established Church, as in England; but the Protestant Church and Protestant ministers had been a conspicuous feature of the national landscape from the beginning (as no one knew better than Hawthorne). Cathedrals were still in the future, but there was talk of the same in the late 1870s (work on the Cathedral of St. John the Divine in New York began in 1891). For the rest, the country most obviously did have an army and a diplomatic service; it had its own fine private schools of long vintage, and seasonal horse races had been major events in the Belmont Park area for two hundred years and in Kentucky since the 1860s. It might have been hoped that readers would detect the vein of parody that ran through the indictment. But the passage was subjected to a series of humorless diatribes; and after some months of it, Henry wrote Tom Perry: "The whole episode projects a lurid light upon the state of American 'culture' . . . Whatever might have been my own evidence for calling American taste 'provincial,' my successors at least will have no excuse for not doing it."

Hawthorne is a minor masterpiece of its kind. It is alive with telling observations about the American as compared with the French or English social life; about the generation of Emerson and Margaret Fuller before the Civil War; about each of Hawthorne's major writings (recalling, from his eighth year, the little shudder with which people alluded to *The Scarlet Letter* when it first appeared), about the inferiority of allegory as a genre. And yet the critics were right, if mostly for the wrong reasons, to detect in the book a studied though muted deprecation of Hawthorne.

Henry James's ambivalence toward his precursor had been more openly disclosed in a (then) little noticed review, written for *The Nation* in early 1872, of Hawthorne's French and Italian Notebooks. The volumes, he said, "show us one of the gentlest, lightest, and most leisurely of observers, strolling at his ease among foreign sights in blessed intellectual irresponsibility, and weaving his chance impressions into a tissue as smooth as fireside gossip." In Henry's image,

Hawthorne, in Paris and Rome, could be seen "bending a puzzled, ineffective gaze at things, full of a mild genial desire to apprehend and penetrate."* In summary: "We seem to see him strolling through churches and galleries as the last pure American—attesting by his shy responses to dark canvasses and cold marble his loyalty to a simpler and less encumbered civilization."

James could praise Hawthorne's writings in all unreserved sincerity; he could single out for special honor Hawthorne's concern for "the deeper psychology," and his "catlike ability" to see in the spiritual dark. All that pertained to the writer in prewar New England. But in Europe, Hawthorne stood revealed as intellectually incompetent, shy and ignorant, weaving mere chance impressions into mere gossip, locked into a simpler past. Now he, Henry James, was of the later generation, at his ease in churches and galleries and on the social scene of Europe, the astute observer forging a literary career out of vigorously collected impressions of Americans in France and Italy and England. Hawthorne could be canonized as the last pure American; Henry James was foremost among the new and more complex and cosmopolitan breed. Thus has it so often been (as Harold Bloom has brought us to realize) with a writer's literary ancestry no less than with his actual progenitors. James could be equally doubled-voiced about George Eliot, his other unmistakable forebear; while about Balzac, who posed no real threat to his sense of self, he had almost nothing but good to say.

The most bizarre performance by Henry James over this stretch of time was the shortish novel *Confidence*, begun in the fall of 1878 and completed the following summer. It tells of two young Americans, Gordon Wright and Bernard Longueville, who become differently involved with an American girl, Angela Vivian, in Siena and then in

---

* Robert Lowell picked up on the image, as he did not infrequently with both Henry and William James—it is one of the happiest instances of continuity and variation in our literature—in his poem "Hawthorne" of 1964:

> *Leave him alone for a moment or two,*
> *and you'll see him with his head*
> *bent down, brooding, brooding,*
> *eyes fixed on some chip,*
> *some stone, some common plant,*
> *the commonest thing,*
> *as if it were the clue.*
> *The disturbed eyes rise,*
> *furtive, foiled, dissatisfied . . .*

Baden-Baden. Gordon proposes, is turned down, and goes off in a pique to marry another girl, Blanche Evers. Bernard, who had thought himself to dislike Angela, discovers that he is deeply in love with her. Angela is responsive, and they are engaged; at which point Gordon turns up in a frenzy to say that he still loves Angela, that his marriage was a mistake, and that he will divorce Blanche if Angela will have him. But Angela deftly patches everything up, reunites the estranged pair, and joins in wedlock with Bernard.

The storyline is implausible to the verge of inanity; but beyond that, one gains the unsettling impression, as one reads along, that the three main characters are talking, alluding, reacting within a different, a darker and more melodramatic plot than the one we are given—only to discover that this is exactly the case.

According to the original notebook sketch of the tale (November 1878), the spurned lover disposes of his wife by murdering her, the appalled heroine breaks with her fiancé and enters a convent, and the two male friends are left indissolubly bound by the homicidal secret. Another curiosity is that in the original the name Longueville is given to the rejected suitor and wife-killer, while the object of shared pursuit is named Bianca—the latter name, Gallicized, being eventually given to the other young woman. *Confidence* (which has some merit as the title of the *other* story) is not accomplished enough to warrant prolonged analysis; it evidently managed to struggle only partway out of the murky depths. But we may perhaps assume that the radical change of plot and the shifting about of names reflected a grave if momentary indecision on Henry James's part, possibly about how his "attitudes" were holding up. At the same time, the original outline suggested James's continuing taste for violence and melodrama.

What is also to be remarked about *Confidence* is that the writing of it was done between early forays into what became *The Portrait of a Lady*. In a letter to William in July 1878, months before *Confidence* was even thought of, Henry told his recently married brother: "The 'great novel' you ask about is only begun . . . It is the history of an *Americana*—a feminine counterpart to Newman." Nine months later, in the midst of writing *Confidence*, he spoke hopefully to William about "the big novel"; he planned to get to work on it immediately. In the summer of 1879, he remarked to Howells that short novels like *The Europeans* and *Confidence* did not satisfy him: "I must try and seek a larger success . . . in doing something on a larger scale than I have yet done. I am greatly in need of it—of the larger success."

It was not until the end of March 1880 that James felt able to return to what was still only a fragment, though one endowed with a title: *The Portrait of a Lady*. He had left London and its hectic socializing, and had come by way of Paris, Turin, and Bologna to Florence. "Florence was divine, as usual," he would write in his notebook, "and I was a great deal with the Bootts. At that exquisite Bellosguardo at the Hôtel de l'Arno, in a room in that deep recess, in the front, I began the *Portrait of a Lady*—that is, I took up, and worked over, an old beginning, made long before."* He went on: "I returned to London to meet William, who came out in the early part of June, and spent a month with me in Bolton St., before going to the continent."

THE BROTHERS IN LONDON/
WILLIAM ON THE CONTINENT

William reached London, in fact, a little after the middle of June, and Henry was able to put at his disposal a suite of rooms on the floor below his own apartment on Bolton Street. To Henry, who had not seen his brother for five years, William seemed, at first, little changed. "All his vivacity and brilliancy of mind," Henry wrote Father, were "undimmed." But William was very tired from lack of sleep, and was both physically and psychologically out of sorts.

It had been a wearing year. William's teaching schedule took most of his time: a small graduate seminar on "Physiological Psychology" in the fall of 1879, undergraduate classes on Renouvier and Spencer (this had thirty students), plus a weekly lecture on physiology. These academic enterprises had been going along well enough; but for William, his household circumstances left much to be desired.

William and Alice had taken furnished rooms at 387 Harvard Street after their marriage; not far from the family home on Quincy Street, and at a distance that provided sister Alice, rallying from the 1878 breakdown and the long period of depression, with a "delightful little stroll at dusk" for a visit. A son, named Henry for his proud grandfather, was born to the couple on May 18, 1879. William did not take very readily to the experience of paternity: the child's needs and his wailing made it almost impossible for William to work in the

---

* Henry is here using the word "Bellosguardo" in its literal meaning: not as the name of the hilly Florentine section where the Bootts lived, but simply as "beautiful outlook." Henry's hotel room looked down directly on the Arno and the Ponte Vecchio.

crowded home quarters, and he resented Alice's attention to the infant. There were sharp exchanges between husband and wife—irascible on William's part, spirited on Alice's—that then and later served oddly to solidify rather than impair the relationship. The textbook on psychology, William lamented to a friend, was "hanging fire awfully." Like Henry in his apprentice years, William tended to exaggerate his inability to get ahead with his writing; in 1879–80, he produced several essays and unsigned reviews that would find their place in the *Principles*. But he did feel confined and distracted, and as early as the summer of 1879 a pattern began to be established when William betook himself to a lodge at Oak Hill on the coast of Maine for a brief season of freedom and refreshment.

He was instantly visited by the tenderest feelings for those he had left behind. He felt his wife especially near to him, he wrote her from Oak Hill in the latter part of August; and there came to him a sudden image of "last summer," when on their honeymoon they had stumbled together up the hill in Keene Valley and she had "laughed with dilating nostrils at me! When shall I again kiss those nostrils?" As to their three-and-a-half-month-old child, whom William had taken to calling Embry (for Embryonic), "I have a daily growing love for the dear little boy. Ah! Alice! I will to eternity do all I can for him."

It was a restorative interval. William lounged at his leisure under the trees, working on a review of Spencer's *Data of Ethics* and dipping occasionally into a mystery novel by Gaboriau. He went swordfishing, without result; and on one particular evening, while the other guests were gathered in the parlor singing songs from *Pinafore*, William wandered out to lie on a ledge and watch "the moonlight shooting its stitches o'er the waves, and hearing the sea crushing and sobbing among the black seaweed-covered rocks below." He was glad to be by himself; in distinction from his sister, William often enjoyed natural scenery divested of the human.

The following February (1880), there was an enforced break in William's home and academic routine when the parents received an alarming report from Wilky about Bob's condition and William went out to investigate. It appeared that Bob was drinking more heavily than ever, and there was even—so Mother wrote Henry, in London—some question about his sanity. William stopped off in Chicago on the way to Milwaukee and consulted with a local nerve specialist named Dr. Jewell, who, William told his wife, "advised taking B. east, even if for asylum treatment there." A telegram from Wilky addressed to William at the Palmer House read: SITUATION UNCHANGED.

Things had not gone well with Bob James. For a year or so after he moved to Prairie du Chien with Mary and their infant son, Edward ("Ned"), it appeared that Aunt Kate's optimism—about this promising turn in Bob's life—might be justified. But just after a second child, Mary Walsh, was born, in August 1875, Bob quit his job with the Milwaukee and St. Paul Railway, bought himself a farm of undetermined acreage, and set himself to working it. It was another effort toward emancipation from Edward Holton, who, almost as though pursuing his son-in-law, turned up periodically in Prairie du Chien to give a public talk on the evils of drink and to promote the temperance movement. The farming venture came to nothing; by the spring of 1877, Mary was back in Milwaukee with the children, staying with her father. Bob soon followed.

He next secured an appointment as City Editor of the Milwaukee *News*, and in 1878, with three others, Bob acquired a partnership in the newspaper. For a brief moment, the outlook must have seemed hopeful, but the *News* was a commercial failure (due in part, it would seem, to editorial ineptitude), and in the fall of 1879, it was sold at auction. By this time, Bob had been given a job, listed as "temporary," auditing the books of the Milwaukee, Lake Shore and Western Railroad, a small outfit that ran 158 miles to Clintonville.

Something in his interior being—his moral being, William would have said—seemed to have sagged fatally; and perhaps, as his sister would have added, there was not much there to begin with. Such flimsy ambition as he may once have possessed had now evaporated, and he had taken to heavy and prolonged drinking. Upon examining him, however, William found that Bob's mental condition was by no means as desperate as had been feared, though he let drop a hint to his wife that the younger brother had been indulging in extramarital activity. But there was, as always, something winning about Bob, a lingering sweetness of sensibility (Henry was in agreement about this quality), an aura of gifts unused and promise unfulfilled. What William recommended was "a medical change of environment," in the form of a visit back home. Bob evidently seized on the excuse to get away.

Wilky had fared no better of late, though, as William could testify, he bore his misfortune more calmly. The marriage with Carrie Cary was in most respects a happy one; Wilky was proud of his wife and, as Henry put it, spoke insistently of her "conjugal and domestic virtues." Two children had been born to them: a son, Joseph Cary (referred to by the second name) in the first week of October 1874, and a daughter, Alice, on December 24, 1875. ("We have had one good present," Alice James wrote Annie Ashburner on the day after Christmas that year, "in the shape of a little niece . . . making the fourth grandchild.") But his participation in the Bridge and Iron Works proved too much for him after three years, and in 1877 he took a post as bookkeeper in the North Chicago Rolling Mill Company, a sizable Milwaukee smelting plant. Wilky hated the job, of which he gave dismal accounts to the family. He put up with it for a year, until he managed to gain an appointment as cashier and deputy collector for the Internal Revenue Service in the Milwaukee Customs House. There he was laboring when William arrived.

While Bob was suffering from a failure of will, Wilky was plagued by sheer physical disability. The old war wound in his foot had begun to ache intolerably, and he was showing the first symptoms of a rheumatic heart. His finances as well were in bad disarray. Wilky's father-in-law, Joseph Cary, died (at age seventy-two) a month after William's visit, and it was hoped by the family that this would mean some easement in Wilky's financial situation. It would soon be revealed, however, that the situation was beyond all saving. Yet Wilky retained the qualities that had endeared him to his older brothers from childhood on. He was "eminently social in his nature," a friendly observer said about him; he was "gentle and kindly and without guile." He was nothing of a writer, said the same observer, but Wilky James had "the literary tastes and aptitudes of his family"; he was a rare conversationalist, and enthralled his acquaintances with reminiscent anecdotes about Emerson and others, and his own upbringing in Geneva and France. Captain James, as he was usually called—the war which was his physical ruin was also the source of his honored public identity—was one of the best-liked people in the Milwaukee community.

How much of all this William was able to gather on his three-day visit is not clear. What is marked is the intensity of his personal reaction after viewing the two Milwaukee households: an outburst of love for his wife, a passionate appreciation of her. He gave voice to this in a letter written to her on the New York Central train as it thundered eastward from Chicago. He had a new sense of Alice's "preciousness, her capacity, her depth and profundity of judgment" (though not, he added, teasing, in matters of medicine). He had a new awareness of "her physical, moral and mental beauty . . . her passionate and headlong loveliness, her unaffected modesty, her golden truth." William found himself cherishing an image of Alice's "frowning brow with starlike orbs pouring their fire beneath."

In April, William spent a day in Baltimore talking with D. C. Gilman, president of Johns Hopkins University (where he had lectured two years before), about an appointment in philosophy there. William had a good feeling about Gilman—"in philosophical intelligence," he wrote Alice, he was "worth a dozen Eliots"—and the proposed terms, as to salary and teaching, sounded reasonable. William understood that one could get a good house for as little as $500 a year, and a good cook for $10 a month. At the same time, William was at odds with the chairman of the Harvard philosophy department, George Herbert Palmer, both as to Palmer's philosophical orientation—his "priggish English Hegelianism" ("priggish" again meaning bloodless, in this case excessively abstract)—and his handling of departmental affairs. William thought him "an extraordinarily able man," but said that "associating with him is like being in a dentist's chair the whole while."* Despite these considerations, William did not long pursue the Johns Hopkins possibility; and in fact, in that spring of 1880, he was drawing up plans to build a house on his father's property on Quincy Street.

Still, as the term came to a close, William felt the need of a temporary change, if not a permanent one, and a longing for the company of philosophers other than his Harvard colleagues. Mrs. Gibbens had bought a house at 18 Garden Street, not far from the entrance to Harvard Yard, for herself and her daughter Margaret; and she now suggested that, since the lease was due to run out on the furnished rooms, Alice and little Harry move in with her, leaving William free to travel. William sailed for Liverpool on June 6.

The summer that followed, in London and on the Continent, was characterized by an ebb and flow of feeling about Alice, even as it was punctuated by insomnia recurring and disappearing. On the train from Chicago, William had apostrophized his wife's "passionate and headlong loveliness"; but in the first days at sea, he confessed to a sense of torpidity and said he could not get enthusiastic about her or anything else. A little later, as his ship steamed past the Irish coast, he found Alice constantly in his thoughts. "It is," he said, "the queerest renovation of my old lovesick days." After his arrival in London, he went about all day, William recorded, overcome by "a kind of paroxysmal

* Palmer, in turn, would look back on William James as having been "corrupted by kindness" in his relations with students. Palmer's long retrospective comment on James (quoted in Allen, pp. 195–96) was for the most part shrewd and fairminded.

sense of you and worship of you, body and soul—rehearsing incessantly experiences we had had together." His letter of June 22 reflected another large shift of mood. He was afflicted by feelings of guilt. What a burden he had been to her all along! His whole business in life henceforth was "to be your husband well." Now she seemed to him "unapproachable . . . as you used to during those two winters of non-intercourse! You have the same 'wraith' to me," he said as she did then; no longer solid, but "insubstantial, trembling, and with a sort of passive crimson radiance . . . keeping me off."

In Bolton Street, meanwhile, the two brothers, at once affectionate and wary, gave intermittent expression (in letters home) to what might be called a professional misapprehension of each other. Henry was immensely stimulated by William's company and conversation, but as day followed day he thought William tended too much to "descant upon his sensations." Writing to their mother in the maternal idiom, he said: "Even at best there remains more of nervousness and disability about him than I had supposed, and I can't get rid of the feeling that he takes himself, and his nerves, and his physical condition, too hard and too consciously." No more than other members of the family could Henry realize that William, the psychologist-physician, was using himself as an object of study; holding forth on his symptoms (no doubt repetitiously and at too great length) exactly as he was so carefully charting his emotional course for Alice.

On his side, William was grateful for Henry's generosity: Harry, he said, insisted on paying his lodging, his cabs, and his dinners whenever they dined together. "He is a good kindly creature," William told Alice unemphatically, "whom I am glad to be with"; and he was happy that Henry was set to do a volume on Dickens in the same series that contained *Hawthorne*—"it would be a splendid counterpart and vindication" of that work. (This book never got written.) William could see that Henry's literary dedication was prodigious, but in his estimation, Henry's existence was a self-centered one. This was the import of William's letter to Henry Senior in July.

One of his strolls had taken him to St. John's Wood, where the family had lived in a rented house through the winter and spring of 1856. Examining that old scene, William wrote Father in a rare moment of open filial admiration, brought him to contrast "the life you led there with that which Henry is now leading in Bolton Street, [and] it made me feel how few things you laid claim to and how entirely at that time your lives were given up to us." William was disposed to exonerate himself a little from Henry's mode of extreme selfhood: his parental condition, he wrote, made him better able to escape the "ego-tistic standpoint" than he could before.

Henry's social life also bothered William, and baffled him. Re-marking on it, William gave the elder James a judgment on his brother in which insight vied with blindness. "I think as he grows older that he is better suited by superficial contact with things at a great many points than by a deeper one at a few points. The way he worked at paying visits and going to dinners and parties was surprising to me, especially as he was all the time cursing them for so frustrating his work." William quite missed the histrionic tone in Henry's curses; and, while accurately noting Henry's exaggerated respect for the social cal-endar, failed to understand that the social visiting was an actual di-mension of the literary task (William's repetition of the word "work" accidentally hit on this), the important preliminary collecting of impres-sions and anecdotes.

But William's dictum about different kinds of "contact with things" made an apt, if not wholly intended, distinction between the man of letters and the man of intellect, the novelist and the philosopher. In fairness to the fraternal story, however, two emendations are in order: Henry was rarely superficial in his relation to the world of ex-perience, and no one was less limited than William in the number of things with which his far-darting mind sought contact.

Among these phenomena, during the weeks in London, were sev-eral English intellectuals. Andrew Lang, Henry's friend, had William to lunch to meet Herbert Spencer, who quoted Mark Twain and smiled a lot; William thought the conversation had been very trivial. He found himself more than once in the presence of G. Croom Robertson, pro-fessor of philosophy at University College, London, and editor of the periodical *Mind*, which had carried William James's article on "The Perception of Reality" some years earlier. Professor James was evi-dently induced to talk about the article on "the perception of space" which had been occupying him for many months (and which had entered whimsically into the marital discourse: what he liked, William had told Alice in the February letter, was "her enthusiasm for 'Space'—the space I occupy"). Robertson asked to have it for *Mind* and William wrote Father to send it on.*

On a late June afternoon, William went for a walk with Alexander

* "The Perception of Space" was not printed in *Mind* until 1887. By this time, it had grown enormously in size; in the *Principles* it would provide a chapter of 150 pages, taken by some readers (among them, Jacques Barzun) to be the most powerful and brilliant section of the entire treatise.

Bain, whose work William admired and disputed with. Bain was a talkative little man, William reported, who discussed "in an utterly dogmatic and charmless way." There was "no atmosphere to his mind." But the figure William took most to his mind and heart was Shadworth H. Hodgson, a non-academic philosopher in his late forties, a widower who lived in a rooming house and devoted himself to his voluminous writings (William would quote from them, especially *Time and Space*, frequently and at length in the *Principles*).

If, as might be argued, the London intellectuals played for William a role not dissimilar to that of the Paris novelists for Henry, then Hodgson may be said to have become William's Turgenev. William found him shy and silent on a first encounter (William himself being a bit nervous), but amiable and charming, though still bashful, at lunch in his rooming house, and given to telling anecdotes and laughing till he choked. What made William's mental pulse quicken was Hodgson's contention that Charles Renouvier, though he disagreed with the Frenchman's theory of free will, was "the most important philosophical writer of our time. You can't think," William wrote Alice, "how it pleaseth me to have this evidence that I have not been a fool in sticking so to R."

William crossed to Holland on July 11, taking a Channel steamer from Queensborough. He passed through Amsterdam and Antwerp into Germany, and from Cologne came down the Rhine by boat. He felt exhilarated, and far better than when he arrived in London. The river scene he found lovely beyond description: the air was "whanging with light," he said, in one of his favorite synaesthetic images, and "the hills and villages and castles spread out as in a picture." In Heidelberg he caught up as planned with Stanley Hall, a former Harvard associate for whom William had a particular liking. Hall had taught English at Harvard for a year or two, but his graduate degree was in psychology and he was showing exceptional promise in that area. Like William James, Hall had studied in Germany, but unlike William, he had explored not only the world of ideas but the world of Eros, discovering through two successive and passionate liaisons capacities in himself (as he wrote in his autobiography) "hitherto unusually dormant and repressed and [that] thus made life seem richer and more meaningful." He had returned to Germany in 1878, to continue his studies in psychology and presumably his erotic education.

In three days together, the two men—Hall was two years the younger—spent almost forty hours in talk. They strolled the old city

317]

and climbed slowly up the Heiligenberg slopes at Nauheim (a walk known in fact as *Philosophenweg*). They discussed "general philosophical tendencies," in William's report to Alice; in a vivaciously joking letter to Henry Bowditch, William claimed that he and Hall had been "carrying on the highest and most instructive conversation," which makes one suspect that they may also have touched discreetly on aspects of sexual experience. William wound up thinking Hall a "*herrlicher Mensch*" (a magnificent man) and hoped fervently that he, Hall, would be given the appointment at Johns Hopkins, as shortly he was.

William thereafter went down into Switzerland, journeying in a leisurely manner through Basel to Lucerne, by coach to Interlaken, and on to Grindelwald. Here, on July 28, he underwent a crisis of spirit of such intensity that, in his account of it to Alice, he described it as a "moral thunderstorm."

Despite his references in Holland and Germany to renewed good health, extreme alternations of mood had persisted, with William's sense of Alice invariably implicated in them. On the evening of the twenty-eighth at the inn in Grindelwald, William was in one of his lowest states. He was irritable because his itinerary for the next days would not clarify itself. He had grown angry at some English people seated near him at supper. He was helplessly enraged at the trouble his eyes were giving him, making it impossible to read for more than an hour at most.

He lay awake for a long time, he wrote Alice, "and my rage finally vented itself on myself for my unmanliness. I had a great crisis as I lay in bed. You know that I have only *cried* thrice [in] our marriage. But I did it again this time and it was gorgeous." William's narrative continued:

A sort of moral revolution poured through me; I seemed to have been rolling down hill and now to be beginning to mount again, and this dear sacred Switzerland whose mountains, trees & grass and waters are so pure, so good, and as it seemed to me so *honest*, so absolutely honest, all got mixed up into my mood, and in one torrent of adoration for them, for you, and for virtue, I rose towards the window to look out at the scene. Over the right-hand near mountain the milky way rose, sloping slightly towards the left, with big stars burning in it and the smaller ones scattered all about, and with my first glance at it I actually wept aloud, for I thought it was *you*, so like was it unto the expression of your face—your starry eyes and the soft shading of your mouth.

Henry James *and* les siens

Dropping into a somewhat lighter tone, William went on:

Dearest, I'm afraid you'll think I've gone crazy, and I certainly hope you won't read this aloud at the Petersham dinner table [Alice and the boy were spending the month in Petersham, Massachusetts], for they will be sure of it. I am not crazy at all, only I had one of those moral thunderstorms that go all through you and give you such relief.

It was, as William recognized, an experience, essentially mystical and profoundly joyous in nature, of an absolute totality of being; an apocalyptic version, if one may risk the phrase, of the 1870 vastation. It also involved a sudden recapturing by William of that adolescent time in this same Grindelwald, when he was at a peak of radiant good health and spirits.

I felt ten years younger the next morning although I'd slept so little and Nature, God & Man all seemed fused together into one Life as they used to 15 or 20 years ago,—as I drove out on the coachman's box along the Grindelwald road.

William finished with a detailed tracing of his travels on foot through the mountains, climbing one morning to the top of the Grimsel—which Henry had tried to do and failed in 1869—where he took lunch at a hospice before running all the way down the other side to a place calling itself Rhone Glacier Hotel; here, in one of the little bedrooms, as the afternoon waned, he was writing the letter. On August 3, after breakfasting at Thusis, he crossed the Splügen Pass on foot and took a stage down to Bellagio.

He spent an hour at Villa Serbelloni on a hillside above town, gazing down at the two arms of Lake Como; then took the steamer to Como and went on to Milan. He crossed Switzerland again, this time pausing in Geneva to stroll about his old schoolboy haunts and feeling that this part of his past was "deader than any doornail." At a health resort named Uriage-les-Bains, near Grenoble, William had a day with Charles Renouvier and his talented disciple François Pillon, time at least for a rapid exchange of philosophical views and intentions. He had a week in London before sailing aboard the *Parthia* on the twenty-fifth. From Bolton Street he wrote Alice: "My rich, my gentle, my solid, my deep, my rare, my crimson and purple and blue wife. I feel your nature best in the language of colours." He was off to keep an appointment with Charles Darwin and was in a vivacious mood. He was beginning to understand, he said, why Harry loved London so much.

THE SISTER IN THE ADIRONDACKS

During the Bolton Street conversations, it may be imagined, William gave Henry the latest word, not only about the younger brothers, but about figures outside the immediate family. He probably confirmed the unlikely story that Minny Temple's brother, the scapegrace Robert, had become a tender of sheep on some farm or other. "Was there ever a more exquisite turn of fate," Henry had written on first hearing of this, "than his being in a *pastoral* capacity?" Their uncle Howard James, last heard of shut up in a Maryland asylum for inebriates, had become a traveling book salesman: his "plausible personality," Henry observed, ought to stand him in good stead.

About their sister, Alice, William could speak with positive encouragement. She was venturing forth with some frequency on excursions through New England, accompanied and cared for by her invaluable friend Katharine Loring.

The year 1878, from the April breakdown onward, had been "hideous," as Alice herself was to say. Through the summer and into the fall, she had been—so Henry Senior wrote Bob in mid-September—"half the time, indeed more than half, on the verge of insanity and suicide"; family nerves were stretched to the snapping point.

One day, in a relatively calmer state, Alice engaged her father in a discussion of suicide, her thoughts veering in that direction, as her fevered mind had done a decade earlier. She quite understood, Father told Bob, that "her frightful nervousness" was simply "a part of our trouble as a race, struggling to get free," and that when she groaned with anguish it was in the conviction that every one else felt the same mortal burden—of sickness, pain, and suffering—that she did.

When I was telling her that this persuasion grows out of a diabolic influx into the human mind from the spiritual world, to which something in her temperament rendered her peculiarly susceptible, and that we should all feel grateful to her for so stoutly resisting the persuasion, and fighting against it, she laughed at the idea of her not succumbing to it, "though she must confess that she hated it with all [her] heart," and then asked me whether I thought that suicide, to which at times she felt very strongly tempted, was a sin. I told her that I thought it was not a sin except where it was wanton, as when a person from a mere love of pleasurable excitement indulged in drink or opium to the utter degradation of her faculties, and often to the ruin of the human form in him; but that it was absurd to think it sinful when one was driven to it in order to escape bitter suffering, from spiritual influx, as in her case, or from some loathsome form of disease, as in others. I told her so far as I was concerned she had my full permission to end her life whenever she pleased; only I hoped that if ever she felt like doing that sort of justice to her circumstances, she would do it in a perfectly gentle way in order not to distress her friends.

In response to all this, Father continued, Alice

remarked that she was very thankful to me, but she felt that now she could perceive it to be her *right* to dispose of her own body when life had become intolerable, she could never do it: that when she had felt tempted to it, it was with a view to break bonds, or assert her freedom, but that now I had given her freedom to do in the premises what she pleased, she was more than content to stay by my side, and battle in concert with me against the evil that is in the world. I don't fear suicide much since this conversation, though she often tells me that she is strongly tempted still.

Henry James the Elder was not the only intellectualizing father to dissolve some passionate impulse on the part of an offspring by *approving* it in coolly abstract philosophical terms. Alice's response was almost certainly not couched in the language ascribed to her (especially as to battling in concert against evil); but one senses in it, even so, an ebbing of personal desire in the matter, as though the contemplated act had been deprived in advance of any kind of bitter gratification. The paternal strategy obviously worked, and partly, it can be surmised, because Alice on her side felt the genuine emotional concern behind her father's weightily judicious sermon. It remains to be said, though, that no more curious exchange between father and daughter, on such a subject, can have taken place in that American era outside of the James family.

Alice made no quick recovery. Not three days went by, Henry Senior said, but his daughter had a breakdown of some sort; and it was not until the end of November that Alice could take up her correspondence and say to Fanny Morse that she was beginning to behave herself better. Throughout the ordeal, her physical sufferings were less terrible than her mental state. "My patience, courage & self-control," she told Fanny, "all seemed to leave me like a flash & I was left high and dry." She went on with sad irony: "For a young woman who not only likes to manage herself but the rest of the world too, such a moral prostration taxed my common sense a good deal. But, I suppose I needed the lesson greatly."

Having gained back a little of her "moral" power (her Jamesian courage of will), she was inclined to speak critically of her old Cambridge friend Sara Sedgwick. Despite what Alice regarded as an excellent "matrimonial venture" in her marriage to William Darwin, Sara, on a recent visit to introduce her husband, had managed to look forlorn and in private had expressed to Alice an unhappiness about her English environment. "I cannot . . . forgive her," Alice said to Fanny, "for not being able to make some enthusiastic expression about her delightful husband, for how is existence possible unless we resolutely make the most of all our blessings." As an exercise in this stout New England attitude, Alice, in the same letter, spoke in the most admiring and affectionate manner of her new sister-in-law. "She is a truly lovely being so sweet and gentle & then with so much intelligence besides. I do not believe there ever was a marriage that gave so much satisfaction as this, to one side of a house at any rate."

As Alice James turned thirty, the blessing she was beginning most to count was Katharine Peabody Loring. It was Miss Loring who had supervised Miss James in the Society to Encourage Studies at Home in 1875; but the closer relation between the two young women (Katharine was by one year the younger) had its start when Katharine helped to care for Alice during the early stages of the 1878 crisis. The family was swift to appreciate her. Henry wrote William on May 1 that Mother had told him "all about" the new friend, "whose strength of wind and limb, to say nothing of her nobler qualities, must make her a valuable addition to the Quincy circle." Henry delighted in the thought of her, and asked William to say as much to Alice.

Katharine was the oldest of the four children of Caleb William Loring, a lawyer and president of the Plymouth Cordage Company, and Elizabeth Peabody. There were two younger brothers, William and Augustus, both skilled in the legal profession, and a younger sister, Louisa, quite beautiful, socially talented, frequently ailing. Louisa's demands on her sister's attention, which tended to be imperious, were to conflict with those of Alice James and hence to affect the latter's fortunes in years to come.

The family home was on a twenty-five-acre farm on the Massachusetts coast at Prides Crossing, in the Beverly Farms area; and here the Loring sisters ran the house for their now widowed father and the two brothers. Katharine also kept busy, and usefully so, with the Society to Encourage Studies at Home (the society would have 1,000 students in 1882), the Saturday Morning Club in Boston (where not only Henry James but, in 1887, Robertson James gave talks), and the Harvard Annex, so called, founded in 1879 and later named Radcliffe College. In photographs of Katharine Loring, we see a straight-backed woman, with a calm and resolute face, eyes glinting behind a pince-nez, and the faintest hint of humor to relieve the plainness and the air of no-nonsense.

On July 1, 1879, spurred on and accompanied by Miss Loring, Alice made a trial of her physical capacities by a foray into the Adirondacks. It turned out to be a singularly uncomfortable and at one moment a frightening experience, but it was one which gave enduring solidity to the friendship. Their place of refuge was what Alice called "William's panacea for all earthly ills, the Putnam shanty": that is, the lean-to in the depths of the woods at some little distance from the village of Keene Valley, New York, where William and his Alice had spent their honeymoon. It was at this time still owned by the Jameses' friend Jim Putnam and his brother Charles; later William James and Henry Bowditch would buy into it. In one of her most colorful epistolary narratives, Alice assured Sara Darwin that the shanty lacked "nothing in the way of discomfort" and that after a fortnight she had found that "the bosom of nature was just about as much of a humbug as I always knew it was."

In order to bathe, Katharine and Alice had to step from stone to stone across the lively brook; after which they sat on sharp-edged rocks listening to the "babbling water" and being bitten by mosquitoes. At night, Katharine slid a rubber blanket between Alice's "fair form" and the log floor: "thereby putting a cruel barrier between me and all the dear little crawlers I had come so far to feed and who would no doubt have found me as delectable and succulent a feast as did their winged brethren."

The only romance in the situation, Alice remarked, was in the evening when the two of them sat by their bonfire with the woods all around them and no one within a mile—

save some lively cows who in the middle of the night with that unreasonableness characteristic of their sex would charge the shanty with their horns driving K. to her revolver and me under the bed.

Soon, however, a "male protector" appeared in the form of Dr. Charles Putnam, who came over to spend the day with them before, with "unexpected propriety," betaking himself to Beede House for the night.

The letter is such a tissue of parody and hyperbole, and of insistent sexual innuendo, that it is hard to sort out the actual from the invented. But clearly Dr. Putnam—who is portrayed as having a pious mouth, "virtuous spectacles," and a "general maiden-aunt like . . . figure"— appears as no slightest sexual threat to "two virgins of thirty summers living alone in the woods"; even as he is made to seem the least dependable of protectors by comparison with the doughty Katharine Loring. The latter point is made emphatic:

I wish you could know Katharine Loring, she is a most wonderful being. She has all the mere brute superiority which distinguishes man from woman combined with all the distinctively feminine virtues. There is nothing she cannot do from hewing wood & drawing water to driving run-away horses & educating all the women of North America.

A couple of months later, Alice returned to the theme and the accolade. "I was a good deal knocked up the first of the summer," she wrote Fanny Morse, "by a crazy expedition to the Adirondacks"; and still could not get around very much. But she was consoled for all disappointments "by the revelation of Katharine Loring's virtues whose depths I had thought I had sounded long ago but I found I had only stirred the surface thereof. She is a phenomenal being and no one knows what she has been and done for me these trying months I have been through." The two friends had just spent a happy ten days at Cotuit on the Massachusetts coast. Beckoned onward by Katharine Loring, whose instinctive understanding of Alice's needs was indeed remarkable, Alice made a series of trips across New England in the summer of 1880, while the family looked on in disbelief. In May 1881, Katharine and Alice sailed to England.

They spent four months there, the easygoing tour being interrupted briefly when Alice came down with a fit of nerves while visiting at Kew with Katharine's uncle Asa Gray (an eminent Harvard botanist who had married Caleb Loring's sister Jane) and his wife. The event was described to the family as accidental, perhaps a last manifestation of the old malady. In view of later events, we are likely to agree with Jean Strouse that the incident was, rather, the first item in a pattern of response, whereby Alice took to her bed as a way of expressing displeasure at having to share Katharine Loring with anyone else.

Henry James, returning to England in mid-July after a long and productive stay in Venice, met his sister and Katharine at the Star and

Garter in Richmond. Alice wrote Mary Holton James that Henry, re-encountered after six years, was "the same delightful kind creature of old." To their mother, Henry said that Alice seemed "rather weaker in body than I expected, but stronger in spirits, cheerfulness, &c.," and full of "animation, vivacity, gladness to see me, wit, grace, gayety." Alice and Katharine moved up to London and took rooms on Clarges Street, near to Henry's apartment. "Delightful to me is London at that time," Henry inscribed in his notebook. "Delightful to me, too, it was to see how *she* enjoyed it—how interesting was the impression of the huge, mild city. London is mild then; that is the word."

The warmth of feeling between brother and sister was palpable, but Alice made it clear that she had far less need of fraternal support than she had on the European trip in 1872. "Alice and Miss L. are very independent of me," Henry wrote home in August; "—& A. indeed seems so extraordinarily fond of Miss L. that a third person is rather a superfluous appendage." After being excused from seeing the two off on their return voyage from Liverpool in late September, Henry observed with a faint petulance that he had been made to feel "a fifth wheel to their coach." But Henry, turning an interested, and on the whole a grateful and a musing, eye on Katharine Loring, held to his opinion that she was a blessing beyond compare for Alice, and the best companion his sister could possibly have found.

THE LARGER SUCCESS

Henry departed for America a few weeks after his sister, arriving in New York on the first of November and going straight up to Cambridge. After three weeks in the Quincy Street household, he removed himself to the distanced privacy of the Brunswick Hotel in Boston. On the twenty-fifth, he sat down in his hotel room and began to set forth, in a notebook purchased in London, a long, retrospective account of the vicissitudes of his personal and creative life since he had left the country in 1875.

"Here I am back in America," he wrote, ". . . after six years of absence." He felt he was wise to have come. "I needed to see again *les miens*, to revive my relations with them, and my sense of the consequences that those relations entail. Such relations, such consequences, are a part of one's life, and the best life, the most complete, is the one that takes full account of such things. One can only do this by seeing one's people from time to time, by being with them, by entering into their lives." It was a statement of the family credo *about* the importance of family. But if three weeks had sufficed for the closest kind of intimacy with *les siens*, it was because, as Henry had written Mrs. Alice earlier in the year, "one wishes to be morally united to one's family; but after a certain age, one doesn't want to be materially united—at least, too closely." William had just then given up the notion of building a home on the father's Quincy Street property, and Henry supported the decision. "If I were he," he wrote his sister-in-law, "I would hire a neat house, at Cambridge, at a sufficient distance from Quincy Street to make of the two dwellings two distinct and unamalgamated homes." William was in the process of doing something very like that.

Henry had not taken a room at the Brunswick in order to get ahead with any particular work-in-progress—he had nothing of major import at hand—but rather to think back over his career to date. He reminded himself (and, as it were, some other imagined presence or future reader) of each step he had taken since the farewell breakfast with Howells in 1875: the year in Paris, the shift to London, the variety of his London life and the growing sense that London, for all its drawbacks, was "on the whole the most possible form of life" for him; the literary efforts undertaken. Coming toward the present, Henry lived again through the unforgettably gratifying four months he had spent in Venice the previous spring, when, fleeing the London hubbub, he had come on to Venice carrying with him the half-finished manuscript of *The Portrait of a Lady*.

He had taken rooms on the Riva degli Schiavoni, the broad walkway that goes eastward from the Doge's Palace flanking the water, at No. 4161 on the fifth floor. "The view from my windows was *una bellezza*," Henry told his notebook; "the far-shining lagoon, the pink walls of San Giorgio, the downward curve of the River, the distant islands, the movement of the quay, the gondolas in profile." He recorded the daily round of his life in Venice with loving detail: breakfast each morning at Florian's café, under the arcade of Piazza San Marco; wandering about studying the street life and looking at pictures; a "real breakfast" at noon in the Caffè Quadri, across San Marco square from Florian's; then back to his room to work until five or six o'clock.

As James would recall in still another evocation of this long moment—in his preface to *The Portrait* in the New York Edition—the Venetian vista (like that of Paris when he was writing *The American*) was almost too beguiling. He was constantly driven to the windows in "the fruitless fidget of composition," mentally searching for some proper phrase, some "happy twist" of his subject, only to feel pulled away from his creative task by the spectacle beneath: "the waterside life . . . the large color-spots of the balconied houses . . . the repeated undulation of the little humped-back bridges." Little wonder that, in that same preface, James pictured the act of novel-writing itself in the image of a man standing at a window (unmistakably Italian) looking out. "The house of fiction," he said in one of his most well-wrought accounts of the creative process, "has . . . not one window, but a million." They might all be dissimilar in shape and size; but—

they have this mark of their own that at each of them stands a figure with a pair of eyes, or at least with a field-instrument, insuring to the person making use of it an impression distinct from every other . . . The spreading field, the human scene is the "choice of subject;" the pierced aperture, either broad or balconied or slit-like and low-browed, is the "literary form;" but they are, singly or together, as nothing without the posted presence of the watcher— without, in other words, the consciousness of the artist.

In that Venetian spring of 1881, Henry seemed to understand that some immense circuit had completed itself, something that had begun much further back than 1875. As though to celebrate the fact, he had, on leaving Venice, reversed the epochal journey south (the descent into Italy) he had made in the summer of 1869, going directly to Cadenabbia on Lake Como, and from there north through Chiavenna, up across the Splügen Pass and over the mountainous terrain to Lucerne. The memories of his "old Swiss days" revived with an intensity that surprised him, and he carried them back with him to England and his sister, Alice.

Writing all this down in his Boston notebook, Henry was led to contemplate the whole shape of his life—to *shape* that shape, one might say—from young manhood onward. A visit from Wilky James, coming from the West to spend Christmas with the family, aided the effort, for Henry had not seen his younger brother in more than a decade. "The long interval of years drops away," he wrote, "and the edges of the chasm 'piece together' again, after a fashion. The feeling of that younger time comes back to me in which I sat here scribbling, dreaming, planning, gazing out upon the world in which my fortune was to seek, and suffering tortures from my damnable state of health."

The piecing together continued until the younger aspiring Henry and the current accomplished Henry were joined together. It was a classic instant of connecting up, of self-reunion, an act which no one performed more often or with a keener sense of the ritualistic than Henry James, unless it was his brother William.

What comes back to me freely, delightfully, is the vision of those untried years. Never did a poor fellow have more; never was an ingenuous youth more passionately and yet more patiently eager for what life might bring. Now that life has brought something, brought a measurable part of what I dreamed of then, it is touching enough to look back. I knew at least what I wanted then—to see something of the world. I have seen a good deal of it, and I look at the past in the light of this knowledge. What strikes me is the definiteness, the unerringness of those longings. I wanted to do very much what I have done, and success, if I may say so, now stretches back a tender hand to its younger brother, desire.

For the time being, at least, Henry James's selves were at one with each other. Rarely has a writer so clearly grasped the experience, or—especially in this closing figure of the fraternal handclasp—expressed it with such vibrancy.

The occasion for these ruminations, for the long pause to survey his life's history, was of course the completion of *The Portrait of a Lady*, which, by the time Henry finished it in June, had already been running for nine months in *Macmillan's Magazine* and for eight months in *The Atlantic Monthly*. The final installments of the novel had just appeared in the Boston periodical when Henry made the notebook entry just quoted.

He knew that, whatever the critical response or the sales, he had, in *The Portrait*, achieved that "larger success" of which he had spoken to Howells in the summer of 1879. He knew as well that, in order to do so, he had drawn upon the full range of his experiences, his acquired knowledge, his literary resources. In the childhood of Isabel Archer there is the Albany of Henry James's childhood, the big square old house with the many second-floor rooms painted a uniform yellowish white; the back porch with the swing, the garden sloping down to the stables, the peach orchard; and the gentle old grandmother who sighed a good deal and was endlessly hospitable. Isabel's "deplorably convivial father" has his Jamesian antecedent in Henry's unhappy Uncle John, who gambled away his fortune and destroyed himself for love of a married woman. Like young Henry James, Isabel has made three Atlantic crossings before she has passed her adolescence, and has been in and out of a series of schools and attended by a succession of governesses (one of them, like the Jameses' London *bonne*, is from Neu-châtel, and re-enacts the delightful scandal associated with Mlle Augustine Danse). Isabel flourishes amid this unorthodox educational program, and in the manner of her creator feels that it has provided her with large and liberal opportunities.

In these repetitions and renewals, Henry James is doing much more than transferring his personal memories to the fictive life of his heroine. He is moving Isabel Archer through the significant processes of his own life—essentially his imaginative and creative life, with its excitements and apprehensions, its anxieties and rewards. The novel is itself a large-scale effort at connecting up, and in it James is affirming by and through the devices of his narrative what the literary artist can be and do.

The phase is worth following. Isabel, when the narrator comes to sketching her, after her arrival at the English country seat, Garden-court, of her uncle Daniel Touchett, is presented as having "an immense curiosity about life"; she is a collector of impressions and is "constantly staring and wondering"—a nice version of Henry's re-membered habit of dawdling and gaping. Her sense of some high destiny in store for her leads her to reject the wealthy and agreeable Lord Warburton (an upper-class "radical" of the sort Henry James had been rubbing elbows with); and afterward she is smitten with a fear like that undergone by Henry in the wake of William's criticism. Was she, she asks herself, "a cold, hard priggish person?" In Isabel Archer's case, the adjectives referred to a possibly excessive fastidi-ousness on the sexual side, but that quality is an analogue for the cast of mind—a sort of fussy evasiveness—that William had declared his brother prone to.

Isabel's destiny, as we know, takes the form of Gilbert Osmond, the widowed and dilettantish American expatriate who lives with his fifteen-year-old daughter, Pansy, in "an ancient villa crowning an olive-muffled hill outside the Roman gate of Florence." This is Villa Castellani (or Mercedes) in Bellosguardo, which Francis Boott had occupied with his daughter, Lizzie, since 1857, and where Henry had visited over a number of years (its first fictional appearance was in *Roderick Hudson*). Osmond has nothing in common with Francis Boott, for whom, William James was to say (in a memorial tribute), the ad-jectives "honest," "sturdy," and "faithful" were the ones that rose when anyone thought about him. But there is an affecting cousinship between Pansy and Lizzie, in their unformed prettiness, their filial docility, their slender artistic leanings.

In his preface to *The Portrait*, James proposed that in choosing so "slight" a personality as Isabel Archer for his central character, he had given an example of a "deep difficulty braved," it being exactly the *métier* of "the really addicted artist" to establish and then to overcome the deepest possible difficulties. He saluted himself for taking one further risk: that of making this underexperienced provincial his point of view. " 'Place the center of the subject in the young woman's own consciousness,' I said to myself, 'and you get as interesting and beautiful a difficulty as you could wish.' " The climax and triumph of this daring experiment, James felt, was Isabel's "meditative vigil" in Chapter 42. He thought it, with reason, the best thing in the book. It is in fact one of the best things ever written by an American novelist; and in it, the process of personal reunion here being traced comes to fulfillment.

Isabel is married by now, though her situation is an increasingly painful one; and she is living with her husband in a Roman palazzo. Returning to the palazzo one winter afternoon, she is about to enter the drawing room when something makes her pause on the threshold. It is the sight of Osmond and the latter's mysterious friend Mme Merle, and what brings her up short is not that they have been engaged in friendly conversation but rather that Mme Merle is standing and Gilbert Osmond is seated, leaning back in his chair and looking up. It makes, for Isabel, an impression; as it makes for the reader the most striking instance to date of the Jamesian tactic of the unobserved observer: "Their relative positions, their absorbed mutual gaze, struck her as something detected."*

Later that evening, following an interview with her husband during which Osmond has treated her with cold dislike, Isabel sits on in the salon, alone and motionless, until long after the fire has gone out. She is reviewing her whole situation, plumbing it to its depths: the true discovered nature of her husband, the true history of their relationship. She recognizes now Osmond's faculty "for making everything wither that he touched . . . It was as if he had had the evil eye; as if his presence were a blight." Looking back at the bright hopes she had brought to their marriage, she sees that Osmond "deliberately, almost malignantly, had put the lights out one by one." As the hours go forward, Isabel recalls the moment when she had first intuited the terrible design of her life with Osmond, and which only now can she put into words:

* Readers today may be reminded that such a posture—the man seated, the woman standing—used to suggest a rather extreme degree of intimacy.

She could live it over again, the incredulous terror with which she had taken the measure of her dwelling. Between those four walls she had lived ever since; they were to surround her for the rest of her life. It was the house of darkness, the house of dumbness, the house of suffocation. Osmond's beautiful mind gave it neither light nor air; Osmond's beautiful mind indeed seemed to peep down from a small high window and mock at her . . . It was something appalling. Under all his culture, his cleverness, his amenity, under his good-nature, his facility, his knowledge of life, his egotism lay hidden like a serpent in a bank of flowers.

What he had accomplished in the chapter, James would say, was not only to represent Isabel as "motionlessly *seeing*," but to do so in such a way as to make "the still lucidity of her act as 'interesting' as the surprise of a caravan or the identification of a pirate" in a conventional adventure story. Her seeing, in short, was an action, a dramatic taking-hold. A similar notion is planted within the long sequence itself, when the narrator tells us that the misery Isabel was exploring was "an active condition; it was not a chill, a stupor, a despair; it was a passion of thought, of speculation, of response to every pressure." Isabel is not merely looking about her and taking note of the appalling facts. To a serious degree she is *making* the human realities, by the active play of her imagination, by the force and hard beauty of her interior metaphorical language. The withering touch, the extinction of lights, the house of suffocation, the beautiful mind peeping down from a small high window (a peculiarly chilling image), the serpent in the flowers: these and a host of organically related figures come together not so much to attest to the truth as to beget it.

Isabel Archer, so long an observer, so long given to staring and wondering, has become an actor: exactly in Henry James's sense of the literary artist as actor. In *The Portrait of a Lady*, James succeeded in forging an extraordinarily rich impression of life; but what seems to have excited him even more was that he placed as the source of it a young person who at the crucial moment performed like an artist, like himself.

What should be added is that the character finally realized in Isabel's shaping imagery, Gilbert Osmond, is cast in the elder James's concept of evil. He is selfhood incarnate, the embodiment of that egotism which Henry Senior regarded as the unpardonable spiritual sin. It is in this character that he displays what might otherwise be puzzling: an utter emptiness at the core. Human selfishness, William James would say in reviewing his father's ideas, was the product of the primal void; and for all his capacity to manipulate and to wound, we feel in Osmond an essential nothingness; even as we observe an odd social crudity, as it were a nothingness of manners. Isabel, after journeying to England and the deathbed of her cousin Ralph, will return to Rome and her loveless marriage, if only to be of service to poor Pansy. But for all the bleakness in store, she is able, as she tells herself, to entertain the fitful feeling that "life would be her business for some time to come." There again she spoke for Henry James.

CHAPTER TEN

Deaths in the Family,
1882

THE DEATH OF THE MOTHER

The household at Quincy Street, around the middle of January 1882, consisted of four family members. Henry James, Sr., and Mary James were visibly aging, at seventy and seventy-one respectively; William had warned the younger Henry that their parents had become frail, and to Henry, arriving from England, his mother seemed worn and shrunken. Alice, still experiencing the psychic uplift of her trip abroad with Katharine Loring, struck everyone as in stronger health and spirits than for years. Bob James had drifted in from the Midwest a few days after Christmas. He was at loose ends; he had separated from his wife, and had left Mary and the two children (nine-year-old Ned and seven-year-old Mary) under the paternal wing in Milwaukee; he had not tried to hold a job in over a year, and seemed deprived of any purpose in life. Henry had sent him $250 to pay for his trip East, though thus far Bob had not spent it. "An equal sum is at your disposal as often as you need it," Henry promised in a late-January letter.

William, with his Alice and their two-and-a-half-year-old Harry, were living in the cramped quarters on Louisberg Square in Boston which they had rented, for lack of better, after William's return from the European summer in 1880; but he was about to follow Henry's advice and take a house in Cambridge at a discreet distance from Quincy Street. Alice and the boy often accompanied William on the horsecar to Cambridge, to spend the day with Grandfather. William had been named assistant professor of philosophy in the autumn of 1880, though given his mix of academic offerings, the departmental designation did not perhaps mean very much. As Jacques Barzun has put it: "William was successively: assistant professor of physiology after teaching psychology for two years; assistant professor of philosophy after undertaking to write *The Principles of Psychology* and establishing the first psychological laboratory in the country; and full professor of philosophy five years before the *Psychology* appeared." Already in 1882, William James was manifesting his skill at evading any precise professional designation, heedful (it would seem) of the father's warning against narrowness.

Wilky had been in and out. Henry had sent him what Wilky, adding a fraternal benediction, called a "princely gift" of money. In the same letter, Wilky let it be known that he was on crutches that day (November 11, 1881), "stiffened with an attack of rheumatism in my foot-wound." He counted on some pills by the new James family physician, Dr. Beach, to relieve the pain. After contemplating his mounting indebtedness, Wilky decided to indulge himself in the holiday season and used Henry's present to buy himself train tickets to Boston and back. He spent ten days at the Cambridge home. Henry, not having seen his younger brother in more than a decade, thought him "wonderfully unchanged for a man with whom life has not gone easy." But the lively, cultivated, chaffing atmosphere of Quincy Street left Wilky glumly dissatisfied with his Milwaukee situation when he got back to it in early January. Writing to John Chipman Gray, he voiced the hope that before long he might move with his family to Boston or New York. "Every year of this western life grows more and more intolerable to me . . . the dreary commonplaceness of its social life is unspeakably demoralising."

Henry had gone down to Washington for an indefinite stay soon after the turn of the year, and found two sunny rooms at the Metropolitan Club on 15th Street. He spent much of his time, as he said to an English correspondent, with "our good little friends the Henry Adamses, whose extremely agreeable house"—at 1607 H Street—"may be said to be one of the features of Washington." Through Adams, he met Senator James G. Blaine, who invited James to a "big and gorgeous banquet" in honor of President Arthur. Henry rather enjoyed himself with the robust and genial President. Arthur, who was originally from Albany, confided that he had been an intimate friend of Johnny James—the nephew of William of Albany who had come from Ireland with his brother to America in 1816 through their uncle's generosity—and that Johnny had committed suicide, he, Arthur, attending the deathbed. There was also talk of Smith Van Buren, the son of another Albany-born President and also connected, by marriage, to a James.*

At the start of the last week in January, Mary James came down with what was designated bronchial asthma. Bob informed Henry, but indicated that Mother was in good hands and making a recovery. On Sunday, January 29, Henry wrote his mother a letter of love and comfort, hoping, as he said, that the worst of the illness was over. That evening, as he was dressing for dinner, a telegram arrived from William's Alice: YOUR MOTHER EXCEEDINGLY ILL. COME AT ONCE. In fact, as twilight was falling that wintry afternoon, and with her husband and daughter sitting by her bed, Mary James had suffered a heart seizure and quite swiftly and peaceably had died.

Poor train connections kept Henry from reaching Boston until Tuesday morning, but he learned on his way through New York that his mother was dead. The next day, February 1, Wilky arrived, and with William present, the four brothers were together for the first time in fifteen years—and as it turned out, for the last time in their lives. Later that morning, James Freeman Clark, Unitarian minister and writer on liberal religious themes, read from the Scriptures in a brief service at the Quincy Street house; by the family's request, there was no eulogy of Mary James. The funeral party then moved across town, between high banks of snow and under a gleaming blue sky, to the Cambridge cemetery, where the brothers carried their mother's coffin to a temporary vault near the river.

Bob James felt the religious strain in his nature—it was the most intense of any of the children's—touched and quickened by the experience. The secret of his parents' union was a religious one, he wrote his wife in Milwaukee, referring back to the moment, more than forty years before, when Mary Walsh resigned from the Presbyterian Church and in effect abjured her Calvinist beliefs under the persuasions of her suitor. His mother's passing was not an occasion for great grief, Bob continued. "We have been all educated by father to feel that death was the only reality and that life was simply an experimental thing." Mother's departure was taken as "an orderly transition." Neither he

---

* After the death of Ellen James, Smith Van Buren had married a Henrietta Irving, leaving her a widow in the 1870s. Later in the year 1882, Henry described her with genealogical relish (to William's wife) as "Mrs. Van Buren, the widow of the husband of one of our deceased aunts."

nor Father nor Alice had shed a tear that Sunday evening; but Bob thought that the other boys when they came "were very much shocked, Harry especially who had a passionate childlike devotion to her." Bob's emotions were concentrated on his father. For the last few nights, Bob had been sleeping in his mother's bed, next to Father's, and the two had been having "quite happy talks . . . about Mother's nearness and about our pride in her." A purpose in life had been accorded him, Bob declared: to keep close to his father and dispel as much as he could the loneliness in which Father would remain. "The last two weeks of my life have been the happiest I have known."

There is scant evidence of William's reaction to his mother's death. His son Henry, in the introduction to his father's letters, said that "William James spoke of her very seldom after her death, but then always with a sort of tender reverence that he vouchsafed to no one else." Such hurts and discords as there had been seemed to have receded fairly quickly to the back of William's mind. Writing to his wife from Vienna in the fall of the year, William launched into a prose poem about the "old wrinkled peasant women" he had seen in Germany, "striding like men through the streets, dragging their carts or lugging their baskets." Their poor ravaged faces and their bodies "dried up with ceaseless toil" made him weep. They incarnated for him the mystery, the burden, the unthinking selflessness of women. "The Mothers! The Mothers! Ye are all one! Yes, Alice dear, what I love in you is only what these blessed creatures have; and I'm glad and proud, when I think of my own dear Mother with tears running down my face, to know that she is one with these." The passage rings strangely, especially coming as it does at the end of a long letter about Viennese speech, a visit to the opera, a stroll along the Ringstrasse, an identification between his present self and the troubled "youth of 1867" in Dresden and Berlin (we will come back to this). It is in any case almost William's only recorded word about Mary James's death.

For both Henry and his sister, Alice, their mother figured then and later exactly *as* a mother, though in different imaging from William's: as a nearly sublime paradigm of the species. Alice would say in her diary that Mary James had become "a beautiful illumined memory, the essence of divine maternity." And Henry, writing E. L. Godkin, a frequent visitor to the family home, said: "You knew my mother and you know what she was to us—the sweetest, gentlest, most natural embodiment of maternity—and our protecting spirit, our household genius."

Henry elaborated on that last phrase in his notebook entry on February 9: "She was our life, she was the house, she was the keystone of the arch. She held us all together, and without her we are scattered reeds." Wilky offered the same testimony in more concrete terms when he told Fanny Morse, in a letter of early March, that with his mother's death "I lose the regular correspondence, which for years she unstintingly devoted to her sons; it was, I gather, a very vital link [that is, between all the sons], the habit of receiving almost a letter a week from home." "She was patience, she was wisdom, she was exquisite maternity," Henry went on in his notebook. "Her sweetness, her mildness, her great natural beneficence were unspeakable."

Literary analysts in our time have trained themselves to be severely skeptical of such marks of filial devotion, and to dig hard for hints of buried animosity, of covert fear and resentment. In the present case, we have Leon Edel's representative contention that for all Henry James's incantatory eloquence about love and loss, wisdom and beneficence, "on a deeper level of feeling, which he inevitably concealed from himself, he must have seen his mother as she was, not as he imagined and wanted her to be." What she was, in fact, as Edel sees her, was a woman who was in no small degree responsible for the strains and contradictions—in some filial cases (the younger brothers and Alice) destructive ones—that darkened the family life. The main evidence for this view is the series of mothers in Henry James's fiction: "strong, determined, demanding, grasping women" like Mrs. Touchett, or Mrs. Gereth in *The Spoils of Poynton*, or Mrs. Newsome in *The Ambassadors*. It is in these portraits that Henry's true feelings about his mother get expressed.

The adjectives quoted are well chosen for the fictional women named, and Edel's argument may be a useful corrective of the younger Jameses' sentimentalizing memory. It should be said, beyond that, that Henry James seems to have been only minimally aware of his mother's occasional closed-heartedness toward his sister, as when Mother forbade Alice to indulge in any "selfish regrets" over William's departure for Europe in 1867; and Alice, with the passing years, seems to have forgotten or discounted such moments. At the same time, evidence drawn from the fiction is precarious; it is doubtful whether Henry James's villainous and self-serving *fathers*—Gilbert Osmond, Selah Tarrant (*The Bostonians*), Lionel Croy (*The Wings of the Dove*)—suggest Henry's true but repressed feeling about Henry Senior. But these are admittedly intricate issues, for which the eye of the biographical observer—affected as it must be not only by the latter's experience but by what William James would call his view of the universe—counts inevitably for a very great deal.

The only aspect of Henry James's devotional language that might give this observer pause is, if it can be said without irreverence, that it almost seems to describe not Mary James but the Blessed Virgin Mary. But that, too, may not have been altogether accidental: the mother, that essence of divine maternity, as Alice called her, did appear to some of her children as a godlike creature—though only, as we shall learn, of the special, home-conceived James variety.

But about Mary James, there is a bit more evidence yet to consider.

Within days of the funeral, Henry again withdrew a little from the family, establishing himself this time in ugly but comfortable rooms (his words) at 102 Mount Vernon Street in Boston, near the center of town. He settled into a pleasant enough routine. Each morning he walked down across Boston Common to take his breakfast at the Parker House, then back to his lodgings, where he would sit writing till the late afternoon. At the day's end, he usually went on foot to Cambridge, following the route he would depict in *The Bostonians*: over "the long low bridge that crawled, on its staggering posts, across the Charles," and passing "the desolate suburban horizons" on his way to the more attractive section of Quincy Street. He dined quietly with Father and Alice, and walked back into town by starlight. "I got in this way plenty of exercise," Henry said half a year later, in casual reference to the daily eight-mile round trip.

He looked back on it as "a simple, serious wholesome time." His mother's death, he felt, had left behind "a soft beneficent hush," in which the three of them, and William and his Alice when they were visiting, lived for several months. With the coming of spring, Henry could see that his father was taking hold of life again, with something of his old intellectual zest. He could also see his sister showing conspicuous energy and skill in running the household. The mother's death, as Aunt Kate said to Bob's wife, seemed "to have brought new life to Alice." She obviously felt liberated to the point of rebirth and, perhaps for the first time, felt that she was genuinely needed by someone else, rather than herself being in pitiful need of support. She rose to the challenge with a kind of gratitude. Henry felt free to return to the London home for which, as he had been telling his English friends, he had been positively sickening. The others encouraged him to do so, and on May 10 he sailed from New York on the *Gallia*.

While Henry was still in New York waiting to embark, Henry Senior wrote him a long letter to be delivered in London. He had gone the day before, he said, to see William, who had been ill. Willy came down from his bedroom "*dancing* to greet me," and they had a "capital talk" about Renouvier and others. On his way back, the elder James had encountered his grandchild Harry in the company of the boy's Aunt Margaret Gibbens, aboard a Park Square horsecar. The whole outing put him in an exceptionally tender family mood, something, as he wrote on, that he focused particularly on his second son. "All my children have been very good and sweet from their infancy, and I have been very proud of you and Willy. But I can't help feeling that you are the one that has cost us the least trouble, and given us always the most delight. Especially do I mind Mother's perfect joy in you the last few months of her life, and your perfect sweetness to her." That special maternal love, Father believed, was part of his own legacy from Mary James. "I feel that I have fallen heir to all dear mother's fondness for you, as well as my proper own, and bid you accordingly a distinctly widowed farewell." As one might say, he loved all the children equally, but he was especially devoted to Willy and Harry, and with the mother's love for Harry added to his own, his heart was now filled most of all with love for the never difficult second son.

But Henry Senior had more to say about "that blessed mother," what she had meant to him and how he longed to rejoin her.

She was not to me "a liberal education," intellectually speaking, as some one has said about his wife, but she really did arouse my heart, early in our married life, from its selfish torpor, and so enabled me to become a man. And this she did altogether unconsciously, without the most cursory thought of doing so, but solely by the presentation of her womanly sweetness and purity, which she herself had no recognition of. The sum of it all is, that I would sooner rejoin her in her modesty, and find my eternal lot in association with her, than have the gift of a noisy delirious world!

The elder James, in his own idiom (recall his talk at the Radical Club), had been taken out of his enslaving selfhood and transformed into a social being, in effect redeemed, by the unconscious influence of his non-intellectual wife.

This image of Mary James may not be dismissed as a mystico-fictional construct. It seems an expression at once of unbounded husbandly devotion and (to the contemporary view) perfectly assured husbandly sexism. But indeed, in her very human but sometimes startling inconsistencies (of public demeanor and maternal attitudes, for example), Mary James invited contradictory verdicts. Witness the harshness of Lilla Cabot; and much more recently, the suggestively witty phrase of Jean Strouse about Mother: "tyrannical selflessness."

It was not long after this letter was dispatched that Henry Senior and Alice gave up the Quincy Street home where they had lived for eighteen years and, following the direction of the younger Henry, took over a small house at 131 Mount Vernon Street, at the foot of the hill and facing the river. It was not only that the Cambridge residence was too large for them, especially since Mrs. William politely resisted any suggestion that the William Jameses move in with them there. It was also a matter of convenience. Henry Senior had been journeying to Boston almost daily to visit his beloved bookstores; he was never happy if kept from those stimulating premises for long, but Alice felt he was growing too old and feeble for such excursions. Mount Vernon Street was in the heart of the bookstore district. Another attraction was Francis Boott, who, with Lizzie, was staying for the moment at 470 Mount Vernon Street, partway up the slope.

At the start of July, with the weather becoming uncomfortably hot, Alice took her father to a cottage she was having built at Manchester-by-the-Sea. She had bought the property for $4,000 (probably advanced by Father) at some earlier date. The site appealed to Alice as being only a few miles along the Massachusetts coast beyond the Lorings' home at Prides Crossing; it was situated on a small peninsula across from Manchester Harbor and faced out toward the Atlantic. Alice showed unexpected astuteness and authority in overseeing the construction (as Father had done with the stone house in Newport, and as Spencer Brydon, emulating both of them in Henry's tale, would do with the New York property in "The Jolly Corner"). It was another index of her current vitality; and though crews of painters and paperhangers were at work throughout the house when father and daughter arrived and pump water was in short supply, Alice declared herself (to Mary Holton James) delighted with the place and sure "the little house" would be "quite perfect" when completed.

Henry had gone up to inspect it just before sailing and gave it his seal of approval. The landscape was a bit scraggy, he thought, but the cottage was pretty, the sea washed up close to the veranda, there was an atmosphere of restfulness, airiness, and peace, and there were charming inland drives. The house was a three-story, gabled affair, shingled, with casement windows; a long, narrow pier ran out into the water, and a horse and carriage were lodged in the stable. That first summer, the Henry Adamses, along with the Higginson and Harland families, were close by, thus completing that kind of humanized landscape that Alice always preferred.

WILLIAM TAKES A SABBATICAL

On June 17, Mrs. Alice gave birth to a second son, William—"Billy," for the most part, thereafter; and the event produced in his father, as before, a strong inclination to escape the confines of a household largely given over to infant care. William had declared his attitude in such a matter the previous September, after he and Alice had spent a particularly intimate fortnight in Keene Valley and Alice had gone back to Cambridge. His letter of September 18 began with a sort of amorous rhyming: "My love, my life, my bride, my wife," and continued with almost overt sexual intensity: "I never knew till the last few days how deeply I love thee. Under all the incrustations of age and custom, all the prosaic accretions of keeping house and tending baby together, I find that the volcanic fires of youth still burn unaltered and need but the touch of a short separation, sweeping away the superficial aches, to lay bare the glowing heat beneath." Keene Valley was virtually deserted by now, and amid the "sabbath stillness and loveliness of the valley," William felt a sweet melancholy creep over him. He thought back to their past together, his and Alice's, especially in the fateful spring of 1878. "Darling," he wrote, "at bottom, our relation is exactly what it was in those days, as rare, as metaphysical, as tragic—and we will live up to it forevermore." Now, in the summer of 1882, there were two babies to tend to (Harry, in fact, was just three years old), and William felt a strong need for another separation.

He left for New York immediately after Billy's birth. During a week there, the sight of the Windsor Hotel reminded him of their first honeymoon night, and of "that free young maid, who looked steadfastly into the future uncertainties & chose to trust me & take them all rather than be safe and free." (Here as elsewhere, William's "doctrine"—in this case, about risk as basic to the good life—interacted with his sense of the marital experience.) He spent ten days away from Cambridge in July, several of them at Manchester-by-the-Sea, and several more at Tanglewood, Massachusetts, where, as he told Alice, he met and fell in love with Emma Lazarus: "a poetess, a magaziness, & a Jewess

. . . She told me my works had converted her from pessimism to optimism!"*

But these short removals were not sufficing. William had become sleepless and irascible again, and a longer stretch on his own seemed called for. A few months earlier, William had at last taken the step of buying a home for his family, an attractive house but quite a small one at 18 Appian Way in Cambridge, an easy walk from Harvard Yard. It seemed for the moment imprisoning. Alice, in her staunch and loving way, seconded William's plan to arrange a year's leave of absence from Harvard and to go abroad. The Appian Way house was rented; Alice and the children moved in with her mother at nearby Garden Street ("I don't exactly understand in what house you are living," Henry wrote his sister-in-law in October); and in the first days of September, William sailed from Quebec aboard the *Parisia* for England.†

The ship was still passing along the St. Lawrence River when William wrote Alice to say how much he had been thinking of her "heroic motherhood," and of what she "went through in June, & of how little credit I gave you for it." But the strongest image he carried with him, he said, was of her "delicate stately womanhood," when, clad in a black dress and bonnet, she accompanied him to Young's Restaurant on the day of his departure, and on to the depot where he took the train for Quebec.

Henry met William at London's Euston Station, and was there greeted by a fraternal outburst that became a nugget in the family collection. "My!—how cramped and inferior England seems!" William is purported to have said, on this occasion or several occasions. "After all, it's poor old Europe, just as it used to be in our dreary boyhood! America may be raw and shrill, but I could never live with this as you do . . . It was a mistake to come over!" The rhetoric does not sound

* Emma Lazarus, born in 1849 of a wealthy and devoted Jewish family in New York, was the author that same year 1882 of *Songs of a Semite*. For compelling cultural reasons, her work—that of a woman passionately concerned with racial persecution and injustice—has drawn more attention recently than earlier; though Emerson was a sponsor of sorts, and she dedicated a volume of verse to him. Her sonnet "The New Colossus" was written in 1883, and its lines inscribed on the pedestal of the Statue of Liberty: ". . . Give me your tired, your poor,/Your huddled masses yearning to breathe free." Emma Lazarus's collected *Poems* appeared in 1889, two years after her death.

† He also arranged for Josiah Royce to be his part-time replacement at Harvard. The twenty-seven-year-old Royce had come to James's attention as a promising figure in philosophy, though at the time he was teaching English at the University of California in Berkeley.

much like William James, and in fact William's son Henry pieced the speech together from his memory of family talk; but the sentiments are an exaggeration of the familiar. The image of Uncle Henry's reaction to such periodic explosions seems more in keeping: "He usually ended by hurrying William onward—anywhere—within the day if possible—and remained alone to ejaculate, to exclaim and to expatiate for weeks on the rude and exciting cyclone that had burst upon him and passed by."

William hurried himself away in this instance, leaving for the Continent after a token visit with Henry, and heading directly for Cologne and then Nuremberg. "I like the look of things in Germany very much so far," he wrote Alice on a postcard. "My old feeling comes back quite vividly." He recalled the "loneliness and *langweile*" he had had to endure in Germany fifteen years before, and contrasted it with his current family environment. But in Vienna, looking back at the previous week in Nuremberg, he found that "the strangest identification of myself with the youth of 1867 in Dresden and Berlin" was taking place within him. Much the same problems—of physical disability and psychological disquiet—needed to be faced, he said, in much the same way, chiefly with patience.

At the same time, he was conscious of another kind of connection, between "the actual present of our married life" and his entire acquaintance with Alice Gibbens from the first moment of meeting. "I feel your existence woven into mine with every breath I take, dear"; and this felt union, he implied, would sustain him and carry him through. He was sure that his working capacity would gradually improve, and he knew how best to profit from his year abroad: "to make a moral task of it." It was in this context that William penned the hymn to the moral beauty of mothers, including his own mother and the mother of his children.

By October 3, William was in Venice, declaring it to be "absurdly shabby," with signs everywhere of "irremediable decay," but saying that he was "perfectly enamored" with the city. He knew little Italian, and was the more delighted when the sweet-voiced chambermaid remarked, about his stammering efforts, " '*Il signore parla discretamente.*' Discreetly!!" he exclaimed. "Could the grace of compliment go farther? as if there were voluntary reserve about it on my part." (Professor James misconstrued the word: *discretamente*, with one *e*, actually means "not badly.") There was, meanwhile, a certain amount of easygoing social intercourse.

In a restaurant one day, William encountered Mrs. Van Buren;

hearing his voice, she had thought he was Henry. He called on the friendly Mrs. Bronson at Ca'Alvisi, where Henry had visited the year before; and on Daniel and Ariana Curtis, whom Henry also knew slightly, at Palazzo Barbaro, across the bridge from the Accademia, and "a house the like of which for colossal dimensions and general grand style I have never entered." At lunch with the Curtises and their son Ralph, William met the son's friend John Singer Sargent, just becoming recognized as a painter of great promise. His picture of "a Spanish woman dancing, tumbling over backwards amid a swirl of petticoats" made a sensation in the salon the previous year, William said, but he personally preferred Sargent's more recent sketches of Venetian life.

William also had a good deal to say about the daughter of an Italian lady in his *pensione*, with whom he had fallen in love; they had many grammar-school talks. "Dear," he said at the end of this, "you will get used to these enthusiasms of mine and like them"; it was flattering to *her* that he was responsive to female attraction elsewhere. After, perhaps, brooding on this for a day or two, William reverted to their fortnight together at Keene Valley in the 1881 summer. "What a tower, a refuge, a prop, a harbor, a cushion, a home, a melody, a perfume, a vital breath you were to me." He was shivering with desire to see her, to hear and touch her, he wrote Alice in a follow-up letter, and wondered how he could last for eight more months.

Toward the end of October, William put Venice and Italy behind him without regret, glad to be re-entering the Germanic world, "a land of sternness and morality," as he said to Alice. A twenty-four-hour train ride brought him to Prague; and here, after strolling across the great suspension bridge over the Elbe, he pronounced it a "grand city." Italy, he opined, possessed nothing but charm; and he struggled to find the right words for "the peculiar quality that good German things have, of depth, solidity, picturesqueness, magnitude and homely goodness combined."

In Prague, William was enlivened and intellectually cheered by meeting and talking with Ewald Hering, professor of physiology, and Ernst Mach, physicist and "genius of all trades." But the high point was many hours of walking and conversing with the psychologist Carl Stumpf, who was already making a name for himself with a study of "space-perception" from which William James had been learning and which he would put to his own use. Stumpf was "pale and anxious-looking," as William portrayed him, but also "clear-headed and just-minded." The two became fast friends. Throughout these gatherings, what restored William's faith in himself and his native academy, and no doubt helped account for his sudden burst of good health, was his discovery that he had "a more *cosmopolitan* knowledge of modern philosophic literature" than any of the professors he had met on these travels. (Even so, Henry, in London, had found himself to be "a good deal more of a cosmopolitan . . . than the average Briton of culture.") The French and German psychologists and philosophers didn't know each other's work, and the Italians didn't know anybody.

In Berlin, William had several particularly stimulating sessions with the professors. "Good square-chested talks again," he wrote Alice, "which I couldn't help contrasting with the whining tones of our students." But after pausing in Leipzig and Cologne, and spending some time in Liège in the hospitable home of a Belgian professor of philosophy, William grew undefensively proud of Harvard. He was, he told Alice, readier than when he had left Cambridge "to believe that it is one of the chosen places of the earth. Certainly the instruction and facilities at our university are on the whole superior to anything I have seen."

American academics, he said, were not a whit more isolated than those in Europe. "In all Belgium, there seem to be but two genuine philosophers . . . and I really believe that in my way I have a wider view of the field than anyone I've seen (I count out, of course, my ignorance of ancient authors)." William's expanding intellectual patriotism stopped short at the professorial voice at home: the "abominable, infamous and infra-human voices and way of talking." William, whose own voice was somewhat high-pitched, proposed establishing a German-style club in Cambridge where the members would be trained to talk more sonorously.

These first months of William's sabbatical were essentially preparatory: exemption from all university duties and family involvements, complete change of scene and exposure to new varieties of impressions, a survey of the relevant intellectual terrain, bracing conversations with his philosophical fellows. In the third week of November, William went on to Paris, ravenous, as he said, to begin work on the *Psychology*.

At the Grand Hotel, he found some sixteen letters awaiting him, including six from his wife and one from Harry, who had been staying in the same hotel and had left the city for London twenty-four hours earlier. (Henry had spent much of the fall wandering through the provinces of France, exploring castles and ruins and old walled towns; the outcome of the venture would be *A Little Tour in France* in 1885.) His sister, Alice, was reported to have had some kind of relapse and to be hemorrhaging; William suggested that she undergo a uterine examination in search of the cause. The spate of family news, both good and bad, made him feel "fearfully homesick," and he wondered if he might not go back to Cambridge and, if need be, take a room near the Garden Street house and visit with his wife several hours a day.

The homesickness was already subsiding when William received a cable from his Alice saying that the elder James was failing rapidly. He went at once to London, to join Henry in Bolton Street. On December 10, a cable arrived for the two brothers: BRAIN SOFTENING POSSIBLY LIVE MONTHS ALL INSIST WILLIAM SHALL NOT COME. It was decided that Henry would take the first possible boat for New York, and he did, in fact, sail from Liverpool on the *Werra* two days later. William was ready to abandon his sabbatical and leave for home if it would do any good. "I wanted to get to see [Father] if possible before the end," he wrote his wife as Henry was preparing to leave, "and to let him see me and get a rag of pleasure from the thought that I had come." But Alice's telegrams suggested the "possibility of his not recognizing me or caring and if so I would rather not see him but have my last memory of him as I bade him good-bye at Manchester."

THE LAST DAYS OF HENRY SENIOR

Alice James and her father had stayed on in the Manchester cottage through September. On the first of August, Mary Holton James arrived with the two children for a fortnight's visit. (Her estranged husband was bunking with his brother in London.) Alice's sympathies had remained steadfastly with her sister-in-law in the marital falling-out, as her mother's had been. Recalling that fact, Alice had written the younger Mary a few months before that "I can never hope to be half the help to you that she was, but you must remember that I have a perfect understanding of all your troubles." Alice expressed herself as filled with wonder and admiration at Mary's sweetness and patience in these difficult years, and the August visit served to strengthen her feelings.

Bob James himself appeared in the second week of September. His commitment to hold close to his father, to help alleviate the elder James's loneliness, had not lasted very long; but this appears to have been due less to a lack of staying power than to Bob's awareness that Alice had taken control of the household and that he was being shunted aside. He had gone off on a lengthy trip to Egypt, followed by a storm-tossed voyage to the Azores, and made his way to London. He had a few days with Henry, then drifted off to Wales; came back to London, accompanied Henry—and William Dean Howells, who was in town for the summer and whom Bob admired—to a literary lunch or two, and took his departure for America, where he showed up, to no very hospitable welcome, at his sister's cottage.

He stayed a week, went sailing and fishing, and did some drinking. In talks with his father, he said that the main source of friction with Mary was that she never sided with him in his criticism of Edward Holton; as Henry Senior put it, that "she showed a strange indifference to his manhood." The elder James's opinion of Holton was even more vehement than Bob's. After Holton and his wife had spent a couple of days at Quincy Street in the summer of 1881, Father had written William that, though Mrs. Holton was "a very sweet good woman," she had "the most empty-hearted coxcomb of a husband that ever woman had." Holton was no more than "an animated town-clock." He did nothing but orate and gesticulate, waving his hands like a windmill; and by the second evening, knowing he had made an ass of himself (Father said), he left.

But during the Manchester visit, Henry Senior sought to be conciliatory. He told Bob of a letter he had received from Mr. Holton earlier in the summer that spoke nicely of his son-in-law; and he quoted Mary as insisting that Bob was mistaken "in charging ill will and prejudice to her father." So Bob, in Father's account to the younger Henry, decided to return to Milwaukee and make it up, if possible, with his wife. "How long it will last of course, no one can tell," Alice in turn wrote Henry, "but we must be thankful for the present respite." She thought Mary would be happy about the change, but she was never more scathing about the youngest brother: "Poor boy! his vices and his virtues, his joys and his agonies are all equally superficial, he seems to be without any interior at all." Henry James would put the case in a kindlier way when he offered the opinion that Bob was "an extraordinary instance of a man's nature constituting his profession, his whole stock in trade."

Alice described the life at Manchester as very quiet: "Father and I being neither of us strong enough to go about much or see much company." Henry Senior arose early each morning, between five and six, and wrote at his desk until one. His undertaking was a theological text, *Spiritual Creation*, which he hoped Osgood (who had published several of Henry Junior's novels) would bring out in the fall. By the start of October, he was ready to exchange the seaside for the city, and the two moved back to Mount Vernon Street, Katharine Loring supervising the transition and hiring a parlormaid for the house (she soon proved to be too religiously inclined for father and daughter and was let go). Alice's own state of mind was disclosed to Fanny Morse: "The last seven months have brought such changes in so many ways and to me so many new responsibilities that I feel at times that I may not be equal to them, but I find I am from day to day and I try to keep in mind as much as possible the invaluable thought that one has only to live one day at a time and that all the vague terrors of the future vanish as the future at every moment becomes the present." It was a gallant statement, and an accurate self-appraisal, even if the writer of it sounded exceedingly tired.

Father went out every few days to see Mrs. Alice and his grandchildren at Garden Street, and reported to William that they were a joy and a delight. Mrs. Alice helped him up and down the stairs. In November, Wilky came East to consult a Boston heart specialist. Enlarged heart valves were diagnosed, according to Father, who understood that with care Wilky should live a long while. He had never seen Wilky "so sweet and good natured," though he ate so much one day— a big lunch, lobster salad at the Parker House, high tea at home—that he had a nearly fatal attack of indigestion.

In the third week of November, Henry Senior suddenly began to loosen that grip on life he had exerted so hardily since Mary James's death. He declined steadily in strength of body and force of mind. At the first symptoms, Alice's nerve gave way, and she took to her bed for a ten-day period. Dr. Henry Beach, after investigation, declared rheumatic gout to be the cause of the breakdown, and promised that his pills (of which he was a convinced dispenser) would soon cure her. Aunt Kate, ready as always, entrained in haste from New York to see to the household.

The elder James had evidently settled on his course: he was starving himself to death. It took no small effort to quench that vital fire— "It is weary work this dying," someone heard the old man say. On December 2, now growing weaker daily, Henry Senior underwent two successive fainting spells. Alice, who had partly recovered, again collapsed. "She thought he was dying, and I did too," Aunt Kate told Henry Junior, adding that "the faithful Katharine" was by Alice's side and would stay there.

The last sayings of Henry James the Elder were recorded and preserved in the family annals as though those of a holy man. He was asked what funeral arrangements he would prefer, and made a discourse that Aunt Kate transcribed. Say to the minister, he declared,

that here is a man who has always believed in the only true spiritual life, a direct intercourse with God—and who leaves it as his dying wish that men should know and understand that all the Ceremonies usually observed in births, marriages and funerals are nonsense and untrue.

In his daughter's saltier memory, Father had dismissed all religious ceremonies as "*damned* nonsense," rearing up in bed as he did so. He could become dangerously excitable in those final days, angrily refusing to be fed and crying out against "this disgusting world." But for the most part, he was content to let his life ebb away as, to his vision, the spiritual world opened for him. "He has distinctly made up his mind not to live," Mrs. Alice told William. "His will to die" was "unshaken," she wrote on December 11. He was "impatient to go."

He made his will, with the help of Joseph Warner, the solemn lawyer-husband of Alice's friend Margaret Storer. For the rest, he lay facing the bedroom window, which he insisted be left uncurtained. Once, he complained to his daughter that his pulse kept going. "Never mind, Father," Alice replied. "The old pulse will stop soon." On Sunday evening, December 17, Alice withdrew to her room, unable to face the death throes of her father and what they would mean to her. William's Alice and Katharine Loring were in attendance for her. In Father's bedroom, Aunt Kate and a nurse were sitting by. The next morning, Monday, Aunt Kate heard Henry Senior murmur: "Oh, I have such good boys—*such* good boys!" His voice had thickened, but she made out the phrase "my Mary" being uttered repeatedly. A little before 3 p.m. he said clearly and with great joy: "There is my Mary," and died.

The younger Henry disembarked in New York at noon on Thursday. Letters from Aunt Kate and Alice were waiting for him on the dock, that from his sister giving the exact time when "Darling father's weary longings were all happily ended." About herself, she went on, "I have no terrors for the future for I know I shall have strength to meet all that is in store for me, with a heartfull of love and counting the minutes till you get here." The funeral was scheduled for Thursday, and, in fact, had taken place in the Cambridge cemetery as Henry's ship was entering the harbor.

Bob James, in from Milwaukee for three days, met Henry at the

Boston station. Wilky was too ill to travel. Alice had climbed out of bed for the funeral, but had retreated to it immediately afterward; on Friday, Katharine bundled her up and carried her away to Beverly. On December 26, Henry wrote William that he himself was confined to bed with frightful head pains, and Aunt Kate, the only other occupant of the Mount Vernon Street house, was sitting alone downstairs—"not only without a Christmas dinner but without any dinner, as she doesn't eat according to her wont!" He gave William a detailed and even a comforting account ("He prayed and longed to die") of their father's departure from life.

On December 14, William had written Father a letter of farewell from the London lodgings. It has taken its place as one of the supreme texts in the family story.

Darling old Father,—

Two letters, one from my Alice last night, and one from Aunt Kate to Harry just now, have somewhat dispelled the mystery in which the telegrams left your condition; and although their news is several days earlier than the telegrams, I am free to suppose that the latter report only an aggravation of the symptoms the letters describe. It is far more agreeable to think of this than of some dreadful unknown and sudden malady.

We have been so long accustomed to the hypothesis of your being taken away from us, especially during the past ten months, that the thought that this may be your last illness conveys no very sudden shock. You are old enough, you've given your message to the world in many ways and will not be forgotten, you are here left alone, and on the other side, let us hope and pray, dear, dear old Mother is waiting for you to join her. If you go, it will not be an inharmonious thing. Only, if you are still in possession of your normal consciousness, I should like to see you once again before we part. I stayed here only in obedience to the last telegram, and am waiting now for Harry—who knows the exact state of my mind, and who will know yours—to telegraph again what I shall do. Meanwhile, my blessed old Father, I scribble this line (which may reach you though I should come too late), just to tell you how full of the tenderest memories and feelings about you my heart has for the last few days been filled. In that mysterious gulf of the past into which the present soon will fall and go back and back, yours is still for me the central figure. All my intellectual life I derive from you; and though we have often seemed at odds in the expression thereof, I'm sure there's a harmony somewhere, and that our strivings will combine. What my debt to you is goes beyond all my power of estimating,—so early, so penetrating and so constant has been the influence. You need be in no anxiety about your literary remains. I will see them well taken care of, and that your words shall not suffer for being concealed. At Paris I heard that Milsand, whose name you may remember in the "Revue des Deux Mondes" and elsewhere, was an admirer of the "Secret of Swedenborg," and Hodgson told me your last book had deeply impressed him. So will it be; especially, I think, if a collection of extracts from your various writings were published, after the manner of the extracts from Carlyle, Ruskin, & Co. I have long thought such a volume would be the best monument to you.—As for us; we shall live on each in his way,—feeling somewhat unprotected, old as we are, for the absence of the parental bosoms as a refuge, but holding fast together in that common sacred memory. We will stand by each other and by Alice, try to transmit the torch in our offspring as you did in us, and when the time comes for being gathered in, I pray we may, if not all, some at least, be as ripe as you. As for myself, I know what trouble I've given you at various times through my peculiarities; and as my own boys grow up, I shall learn more and more of the kind of trial you had to overcome in superintending the development of a creature different from yourself, for whom you felt responsible. I say this merely to show how my *sympathy* with you is likely to grow much livelier, rather than to fade—and not for the sake of regrets.—As for the other side, and Mother, and our all possibly meeting, I *can't* say anything. More than ever at this moment do I feel that if that *were* true, all would be solved and justified. And it comes strangely over me in bidding you good-bye how a life is but a day and expresses mainly but a single note. It is so much like the act of bidding an ordinary good-night. Good-night, my sacred old Father! If I don't see you again—Farewell! a blessed farewell! Your

William

Henry went out to the Cambridge cemetery on the morning of New Year's Eve and, standing by the father's grave, read aloud William's letter—"which I am sure," he said to his brother, "he heard somewhere out of the depths of the still, bright winter air. He lies extraordinarily close to Mother, and as I stood there and looked at this last expression of so many years of mortal union, it was difficult not to believe that they were not united again in some consciousness of my belief." That last phrase may perhaps be translated: in some trans-worldly domain of consciousness that I myself believe to exist.

On his way back from the cemetery, Henry stopped off to see Mrs. Alice and the recently born baby, the new life of the Jameses and "a most loving little mortal." He also called on Francis Child, the professor of English who was more stricken by Henry Senior's death than anyone outside the family. William, Henry noted, seemed in his letter of December 20, just received, to be thinking of coming home ("I hardly know what to decide about staying or returning," William had written). *"Don't for the world think of this, I beseech you."* There was nothing to be done just yet about Father's will. He, Henry, was going out to Wisconsin to see the younger brothers, and would give William a report after that trip. "Aunt Kate is still here. Make the most of London."

MEASURING THE LOSS

William had passed anxious and uncertain days in London since Henry's departure. "My condition is a curious one," he wrote his Alice from the Reform Club on December 15; "immersed in the smoky fog;— heir to the luxury of Harry's rooms & Club, expecting every moment to hear of Father's death, and of consequently an entirely new segment of life to begin." Feelings of guilt were beginning to well up. "I have been stingy and grudging in the open acknowledgement of all he's been for me—I know not what freezing has come over me often in his presence, so that my admiration of him I let all see but himself." Perhaps in the last moments, Alice could make Father feel this. "I wrote a letter to him yesterday, but it was not nearly warm enough."

Thoughts of Father and of his robustness of expression aroused William, a few days later, to an outburst of vituperation quite worthy of the elder James. He had been to dinner at the Wilkinsons', and there came in afterward a fellow Swedenborg scholar bearing a work allegedly derived from the Swedish mystic: "the most infernal Swedenburgling, Swedenburfling, Swedenbungling bore I ever met in my life, bringing the animal strength of the elephant, the insensibility of the rhinoceros, the learning of the German, & the intelligence of the jackass to converge upon the sole end of boring you."

Before that letter was mailed, however, William heard the news through an aristocratic friend, a Lady Rose, who drove up to say that she had just seen the newspaper notice of the death of Henry James, Sr. William added a hurried word to his letter and dispatched it. That evening he sat down to review, for his wife's benefit, the design of his father's life. He let his mind wander back over so much of that life as the children had been told by the reminiscing parent and the part they themselves could recall: the boyhood in Albany, the financier father and the brothers and sisters—"with their passions and turbulent histories"; the childhood accident and the amputation; "his college days and ramblings, his theological throes, his engagement and marriage and fatherhood, his finding more and more of the truths he finally settled down in"; then, the years of the old house in New York "and all the men I used to see there"; and "the quieter motion down the later years of life in Newport, Boston and Cambridge, with his friends and correspondents about him, and his books more and more easily brought forth." What would remain for himself, William said, was "the humor, the good spirits, the faith in the divine, and"—here he attributed to Henry Senior what his Alice would recognize as one of his own most cherished principles—"the sense of his right to have a say about the deepest reasons of the universe." How different was that figure from "the cool, dry thin-edged men who now abound."

William saw at once that Henry Senior's "literary remains" must be collected and published, and he committed himself to the task. As he pondered it in the waning December days, it was borne in upon him as never before that the theistic, the God-affirming, principle was at the center of everything his father had thought and written. In this he seemed unique: Father alone in his time, William told Alice, "conceived of theism in an entirely radical and consequent way." He was smitten by another pang of filial remorse. "How insensible I must have seemed to him, I sometimes get a glimpse of in the way these other men appear to me. The men of the Stephen and Robertson lot here are so atheistical, & shut out even from any play of the imagination on the religious side. My blank silence to so many of Father's conversational openings must have seemed to him so hard, so blind."

Leslie Stephen and Croom Robertson were members of the so-called Scratch Eight, an occasional gathering of intellectuals with whom William James had been consorting, and whose members also included Edmund Gurney and Henry Sidgwick, co-founders the previous February of the Society for Psychical Research; Frederick Pollock, professor of law at University College; and the always sympathetic if intellectually elusive Shadworth Hodgson. William found their company mind-stirring, and in February would try out on them a newly written portion of the *Psychology* on the difference between thought and feeling. But it was just by contemplating what he now took to be a severe limitation in them that William began to clarify several related things: his father's philosophical position, its special place in the Anglo-American culture of the day, and his own intellectual needs and purposes, some of these, as he was already dimly envisaging, of a long-range nature.

He turned again to Alice, in much the way he had during the courtship days. He asked of her a "new intellectualization" of an old function. "You must not leave me till I understand a little more of the meaning and value of religion in Father's sense, in the mental life and destiny of man . . . My friends leave it altogether out. I as his son (if for no other reason) must help it to its rights in his eyes, and for that reason I must learn to interpret it aright as I have never done, and you must help me."

William worked sporadically for a year and a half on what became *The Literary Remains of the Late Henry James*, finishing it in a rush in early August 1884, after what he described to Alice as "a wonderful solemn kind of week with poor old Father's ghost, deep into whose intimacy I have wrought." The "remains" included the autobiographical fragment, the unfinished essay called *Spiritual Creation*, and *Recollections of Carlyle*. William supplied a long introduction weaving together key passages from the father's major writings—through the most powerful and enduring of them, *Society the Redeemed Form of Man* in 1879—with a good deal of interpretive comment. The commentary offers the spectacle of the most lucid philosopher in American intellectual history expounding the salient ideas and the vision of our least communicative thinker.

Henry James, Sr., appears in these pages as "a religious prophet and genius, if ever prophet and genius there was"; a passionate and driven theologian, a God-intoxicated man who was born unluckily into an age that distrusted any kind of theological system-making and that tolerated, at most, only a vague and apologetic manner of religious expression. The wonder was that, with no discernible influence upon the religious thought of his day and with no more than a handful of loyal and like-minded correspondents, Mr. James kept steadily at his work and remained "serene and active to the last." He was in part sustained, William said, by a nearly unparalleled energy of rhetorical statement, a style which "to its great dignity of cadence and full and homely vocabulary, united a sort of inward palpitating human quality, gracious and tender, precise, fierce, scornful, humorous by turns." It was a style that recalled "the rich vascular temperament of the old English masters, rather than that of an American of to-day."

William's review of Father's ideas passed in particular through the two great stages of what he called "the creative drama as pictured by Mr. James." In the first or formative stage, God, through intercourse with the ancestral void, produces what is best termed Nature: that is, humanity in its *natural* form, subject to a desperate falsity of selfhood and the evil of spiritual pride. It needed to be stressed that the "other parent" of Nature was a nothingness, a *"positively yawning emptiness,"* a total negation. The selfishness of the individual human beings who constitute Nature was thus not other than "the trail of the serpent over creation, the coming to life of the ancestral void." Hence it was that individuals unredeemed and self-imprisoned revealed an utter hollowness at the core (an insight used to fine fictional advantage, we recall, by Henry Junior in his portrait of Gilbert Osmond, and later of John Marcher in *The Beast in the Jungle*).

There followed the second stage, the slow patient continuing movement of redemption. Here the divine love floods and purifies the separate selves and draws them together into a perfect harmony. Society is the name bestowed by Mr. James upon that harmony: that is, upon humanity in its *redeemed* form. William James located the two stages as successive moments in the grand myth of history:

The facts of our nature with every man in it blinded with pride and jealousy, and stiffened in exclusiveness and self-seeking, are one thing,—that thing whose destinies Church and State are invoked to control, and whose tragic and discordant history we partly know. Those very same facts, after conscience and religion have played their part, and undermined the illusion of the self, so that men acknowledge their life to come from God, and love each other as God loves, having no exclusive private cares, will form the kingdom of heaven on earth, the regenerate social order which none of us yet know.

We note the role of "conscience and religion" in the cosmic plan: not finalities, but acting rather as psychic destroyers of the resistant self, and so freeing the ground for what was really important, the influx of divine power. As to the kingdom of heaven on earth, the elder James never did supply details, his son admitted. The more or less concrete hopes of such a society entertained by the elder James in his Fourierite years, in the late 1840s and early 1850s, had faded with time, and he had become content to "cast the whole burden upon God." But that Henry Senior was a redeemed man, an exemplar of the visionary union, William had no doubt. "He lived and breathed," William said in a turn of phrase that reversed a paramount conviction of the age, "as one who knew he had not made himself, but was the work of a power that let him live from one moment to the next, and could do with him what it pleased."

William's family membership made him peculiarly alert to the personal basis of his father's mystical philosophy. He quoted Henry Senior's assertion (in *The Secret of Swedenborg*) that "self-conceit and self-reproach, pride and penitence" make up the alternating sicknesses—"the fever and the chill"—of "our moral and religious experience": that is, of the whole human story before it gives way to the divine. His father, William wrote, seemed to have an unusually lively and long-drawn-out visitation of that double malady; and indeed "his philosophy . . . is but the statement of his cure." At this point, William put before the reader several autobiographical passages, central among them Henry Senior's account of his vastation at Windsor in 1844 and the "cure" that was begun under the guidance of Mrs. Chichester.

The quoted paternal pages and the filial commentary, as one reads on, seem to become more and more in tune with each other: or better, to arrive at a contrapuntal relation. There was occurring in the very enactment of the editorial task what William had predicted: "I'm sure there's a harmony somewhere, and that our strivings will combine." The combining is evident in the vivacity of respect accorded the fatherly vision, and the full acceptance of the religious component in any appraisal of the human condition. The basic themes of *The Varieties of Religious Experience*, in fact, rise into view in the closing paragraphs of the introduction, where "healthy-mindedness" is set over against "the *morbid* view." There is the confident sense of the power of will, on the one hand, and the sick feeling of impotence on the other. There is, one might say, the son on the one hand and the father on the other; but though William does not relinquish that commitment to "the resisting ego" which he had struggled toward in the nightmare days, he acknowledges (out of his memory of those days) the reality and the truth of the other state of being.

Speaking of what he was to call "the sick soul"—here a person " 'all sicklied o'er' with the sense of weakness"—William declares: "Well, we are all *potentially* such sick men. The sanest and best of us are of one clay with lunatics and prison-mates." His father's self-effacing vision and his own voluntarism are perceived as at once intellectually incompatible and humanly companionable. As to making a choice between them, William appealed to the dispute-settling method he would make the groundwork of *Pragmatism*, an appeal to "the umpire of practice." What one should ask, he said, is which of the two tendencies was "on the whole the most serviceable to man's life, taking the latter in the largest way." The controlling dialectic, the array of embattled terms for charting the universe, was his father's; the mode of resolution was William's. "All my intellectual life I derive from you."

William put it a little differently in answering a letter (of February 1885) from Shadworth Hodgson, thanking William for the *Literary Remains* and alluding to the elder James's "deep and true insight into the moral and spiritual nature and wants and faiths and aspirations of man." "Anything responsive about my poor old father's writing falls most gratefully upon my heart," William wrote back. "For I fear he found *me* pretty unresponsive during his lifetime; and that through my means any post-mortem response should come seems a sort of atonement." It was an atonement, William's words make one realize, in one of its root meanings of at-one-ment; William was at peace with his father. "He was the humanest and most genial being in his impulses whom I have ever personally known, and had a bigness and power of nature that everybody felt."

Henry James, after receiving two copies of the *Literary Remains* in the last days of December 1884, wrote William from London that the work had given him "great filial and fraternal joy." His brother's introduction seemed to him "admirable, perfect," and the extracts included in it made Henry realize as he had not hitherto "how intensely original and personal" Father's entire system had been. He couldn't himself enter into it much, Henry confessed: "I can't be so theological, nor grant his extraordinary premises, nor [throw] myself into conceptions of heavens and hells . . . But I can enjoy greatly the spirit, the feeling and the manner of the whole thing." Henry had come to feel that Father, struggling on alone and lacking any worldly or literary ambition, was yet a great writer.

In *Notes of a Son and Brother*, nearly forty years later, Henry devoted a lengthy section to a retrospective meditation on his father. For the elder James's intellectual accomplishment and "theologic passion," he referred the reader to William's compilation, addressing himself rather to the father's method of discourse, his way of setting forth the large religious issues. It was essentially a *literary* critique, both considerate and hard-headed.

The heaven of his father's imagining, Henry wrote, was too sparsely populated for his taste, and compared unfavorably with the "social and material crowdedness" of the heavenly cities spoken of by others. His father's style had been too devoid of images, and Henry recalled longing for a greater diversity of expression when his father read aloud from his latest work: "Variety, variety—*that* sweet ideal, *that* straight contradiction of any dialectic, hummed for me all the while as a direct, if perverse and most unedified, effect of the parental concentration." Above all, there were for Henry no *stories* in his father's ideas; only a network of bodiless relations. The one genuine story provided by the elder James had been the experience at Windsor and afterward. "The *real* right thing for me," the novelist thought, "would have been the hurrying drama of the original rush, the interview with the admirable Mrs. Chichester, the sweet legend of his and my mother's charmed impression of whom had lingered with us—I admired her very name, there seeming none other among us at all like it."

Still, there had been no absence of the actual in the father's range of vision as it exercised itself in the family circle. It was a vision which perceived an "absolute expression of a resident Divinity" in every slightest fiber of shared humanity; and this being so, the father's attention could be seized by any singularity of character, any "spontaneity of life." This made for a palpable intensity of presence; but for all that intensity, Henry said, the father had never imposed his ideas or his way of seeing things upon the children. Henry, we can remember, had always found the elder James's convictions about filial upbringing more to his liking than had William or Alice. What he now felt was that their father "treated us most of all on the whole, as he in fact treated everything, by his saving imagination." And this, Henry concluded happily, "set us . . . the example of living as much as we might in some such light of our own."

No discussion of his father's nature, Henry went on to say, could even be attempted without reference to the central influence upon it: that of Mary James. Henry's language at this stage took on an oddly familiar note: the harmonious atmosphere of the family household, he wrote, was "for nine-tenths of it our sense of [Mother's] gathered life in us, and of her having no other." All the others in the family, he said carefully, "simply lived by her, in proportion as we lived spontaneously." The image returned to Henry's mind of his mother listening intently, her sewing on her lap, while Father read to her pages from a new article, pages "that were to show her how he had this time at last done it." The maternal posture at such moments represented for Henry a "smoothness of surrender that was like an array of all the perceptions." The children experienced the same totality of surrender, each of them and time after time; and indeed, Henry wrote, their mother "lived in ourselves so exclusively, with such a want of use for anything in her consciousness that was not about us and for us" that it could come as a surprise when she was proud of them. It was rather like their being proud of themselves.

The Mary James here envisaged, one comes to realize, is the feminine counterpart of that clearly masculine godhead we have heard described by Henry James, Sr. This is a being, at once divine and emphatically human, that lives exclusively *in* its progeny; that, in the

[358

phrase quoted by William from *Society the Redeemed Form of Man*, "is incapable of *realizing himself except in others*." It is a being from whom the progeny take their vital nourishment ("We simply lived by her"); and one whose "gathered life in us" created a social harmony out of the separate and implicitly self-asserting individuals. One may translate these formulations into domestically familiar terms—Mary James, for example, as the quintessential Victorian mother or maternal ideal—but what is apparent is that Henry James was providing his mother with an identifiably James-family mode of apotheosis.

Henry's supreme tribute to his father was contained in his novel *The Bostonians*, which began to appear in the *Century* in February 1885, only weeks after William's tribute in the *Literary Remains* came into print. He had begun to sketch out the narrative in the immediate wake of the elder James's death. Writing in his Mount Vernon Street rooms on April 8, 1883, Henry transcribed into his notebook a letter he had sent his publisher, J. R. Osgood, detailing the plot. The scene would be Boston, and the chief characters were an attractive young woman with a natural talent for public speaking (Verena Tarrant in the novel); another young woman (Olive Chancellor), wealthy and dedicated to the liberation of her sex, who conceives a "passionate admiration" for the other girl and believes that working together they can spur on the revolution; and a young man (the Mississippi-born Basil Ransom) who falls in love with the younger friend and attempts to woo her away from the feminist cause. The struggle ends, Henry said, with the young girl "breaking forever with her friend, in a terrible final interview, and giving herself up to her lover." He added, addressing himself (and, on some level perhaps, his brother William), that the whole thing was to be "as American as possible," and represented an effort "to show that I *can* write an American story."

The movement for the social rights of women, as a national phenomenon, has its sizable place in *The Bostonians*, and much can and has been made of Henry James's ambivalent treatment of it. But as a fictional element, it is subordinated to and colored by a larger and controlling theme: that of some tremendous loss, some kind of huge withdrawal that has resulted in a terrible, even fatal, deterioration on the human, cultural, social, sexual, and even physical American landscape. It is here that the effect of Henry Senior's departure from the scene is most evident. In delineating the pattern of loss, Henry James is giving narrative form and texture to his own sense of deprivation ("The house is so *empty*," he wrote William, and to a friend Henry said, "He seems immensely absent"); and even more to Mrs. Alice's

crisper way of putting it. "The world looks strange without him," she
had written her husband, "as if a piece of itself had vanished." In the
same spirit, the New York *Sun* informed its readers (Henry would have
seen the clipping): "One of the most interesting minds ever known
among Americans disappeared at Boston yesterday."

The theme as developed is drenched in the personal and familial
to a degree that can only be hinted at. The fateful shrinkage of religious
concern, for example, is imaged in the view from Olive Chancellor's
windows across the Charles River and toward Cambridge (the route
followed by Henry of an evening in the winter of 1882), where the
"sordid tubes" of factories mingle indiscriminately with the steeples
of churches. Writ larger than that is the militant program for the emancipation of women, which, at least as envisaged by Olive, comes to
seem a parody of the recently concluded Civil War.

At a meeting of reformers, Olive tells herself that she had been
born to lead a crusade, and that the cause of women's deliverance
"must exact from the other, the brutal, blood-stained, ravening race,
the last particle of expiation . . . and the names of those who helped
show the way and lead the squadrons would be the brightest in the
tables of fame." Twenty chapters later we come upon a different set
of honored names, different notions of triumph and defeat, the leaders
of other and earlier squadrons. This is when Basil Ransom escorts
Verena Tarrant through Harvard's Memorial Hall, and they linger
before the white tablets ranged around the walls of the great vestibule,
each inscribed with the name of a Harvard graduate fallen in the war.
"The effect of the place," the narrator writes, "is singularly noble and
solemn . . . It stands there for duty and honor, it speaks of sacrifice
and example." James, we surmise, was recalling his own visit to Memorial Hall, at some time after its inauguration in September 1874.
He would have seen there the names of his brother Wilky's fellow
officers, Robert Gould Shaw and Cabot Jackson Russell, killed at Fort
Wagner on July 18, 1863.*

The current style of the reformers, with its occasional shrillness
and its jostling for public attention, appears as no less a grievous decline
from that of its own precursors, the prewar Abolitionists represented
by the aging Miss Birdseye. She is the rumpled survivor of the old
heroic age of high thinking and moral passion, of Concord and Ralph

* Also inscribed were the names of cousins William James Temple, who died at
Chancellorsville on May 1, 1863, and "Gus" Barker, whose death is dated September
18, 1863, with no battle indicated (family tradition gave it as Antietam), and Charles
Russell Lowell, who was shot from his horse at Cedar Creek on October 26, 1864.

Waldo Emerson; the age, in short, of which Emerson's friend Henry James, Sr., was a vital product. No personality could seem more remote from the elder James than Miss Birdseye who, when we first meet her, is depicted with unsparing wit (an inconsequent old woman with "no more outline than a bundle of hay," and so on). Yet in her selfless and tireless humanity, in all the qualities that lead Olive to say of her that she is "our heroine . . . our saint," she belongs in Henry Senior's company. Thinking back to the father's socialistic ideas, Henry Junior remarked that they contained nothing of the violent; that the elder James indeed looked at the American social order "as lamentably, and yet . . . as amusingly and illustratively wrong— wrong, that is, with a blundering helpless human salience that kept criticism humorous, kept it so to speak, sociable and almost 'sympathetic.' "

These panoramas of loss and declension are the context for, and perhaps metaphors of, the evolving relationship in the novel between the two young women, Olive Chancellor and Verena Tarrant. A word on that, however, will come more appropriately in the chapter following.

Alice James, who had been taken to Beverly on the day after the father's funeral by Katharine Loring, returned to the Mount Vernon Street house in early January, and settled in there with Henry. "Our dear home is gone from us now," she wrote Anna Barker (Mrs. Samuel) Ward on January 7, "& a new leaf will have to be turned by us, but how blessed is our lot with its priceless memories! & I have no fear but that the burthen of loneliness, so heavy now, will be lightened for us by that Help which comes to all who really need it." She was adapting her rhetoric to the severe religious piety of her correspondent, and at the same time deploying it to suppress her own most personal feelings. Her repeated insistence that she felt no fear for the future, in fact, hid a deepening terror which would come to the surface some months later, as we shall see, when, with Henry back in London and Katharine away, Alice for the first time was altogether alone.

By her own evidence, Alice was not able to recognize fully what the loss of her parents meant to her until some seven years after Father's death. In January 1890, there was delivered to Alice, herself now living in England, her old desk from the Cambridge and Boston homes. Looking through it, she came upon letters written to her in years past, among them a bundle from Father and Mother. Reading these later, she said in her diary, was an intense and profoundly interesting experience. Her prose struggles a little here, but she seems to be saying that in the time since their deaths her parents had been unchangingly *present* in her consciousness—until now: when at last she really felt the loss of them, and so simultaneously could find them again as they had been in themselves and in their "responsive love" for her. The journal passage for January 29 moves toward the memory—which Alice could now face up to and shed purifying tears over—of the terrible years 1882–83, during the first of which she sought desperately to care for her widowed father.

The opening allusion to "ghost microbes" relates to a previous comment about the influenza germs that were causing an epidemic in England.

My being, however, has been stirred to its depths by what I might call ghost microbes imported in my Davenport which came from home ten days ago. In it were my old letters. I fell upon Father and Mother's and could not tear myself away from them for two days. One of the most intense, exquisite and profoundly interesting experiences I ever had. I think if I try a little and give it form its vague intensity will take limits to itself, and the 'divine anguish' of the myriad memories stirred grow less. Altho' they were as the breath of life to me as the years have passed they have always been as present as they were at first and [will be for] the rest of my numbered days, with their little definite portion of friction and serenity, so short a span, until we three were blended together again, if such should be our spiritual necessity. But as I read it seemed as if I had opened up a post-script of the past and that I had had, in order to find them *truly*, really to lose them. It seems now incredible to me that I should have drunk, as a matter of course, at that ever springing fountain of responsive love and bathed all unconscious in that flood of human tenderness. The letters are made of the daily events of their pure simple lives, with souls unruffled by the ways of men, like special creatures, spiritualized and remote from coarser clay. Father ringing the changes upon the Mother's perfections, he not being of the order of "charming man who hangs up his fiddle outside his own front door," for his fireside inspired his sweetest music. And Mother's words breathing her extraordinary selfless devotion as if she simply embodied the unconscious essence of wife and motherhood. What a beautiful picture do they make for the thoughts of their children to dwell upon! How the emotions of those two dreadful years, when I was wrenching myself away from them, surge thro' me!—The first haunted by the terror that I should fail him as I watched the poor old man fade day by day—"his fine fibre," William said, "wearing and burning itself out at things too heavy for it"—until the longing cry of his soul was answered and the dear old shrunken body was "lying beside Mary on the hilltop in Cambridge."—Mother died Sunday evening, January 29th, 1882, Father on Monday midday, December 19th, 1882, and now I am shedding the tears I didn't shed then!

CHAPTER ELEVEN

Alice James:
The Remaking of a Life

THE TWO ALICES

In the days following the death of Henry Senior, William's Alice, writing from Cambridge to her husband in London, spoke guardedly of her feelings about sister Alice and the latter's relationship with Katharine Loring. She had already admitted to staying away from the Mount Vernon Street home for a day or so "for fear of worrying Alice who hates to be broken in upon when Miss Loring is with her"; and earlier had observed that "poor Alice" was "keeping up bravely with Katharine always at her side." But in the distress and disarray of the family household following the funeral, Mrs. Alice's control of herself with regard to her sister-in-law began to give way.

Aunt Kate had come back from the cemetery, with Bob James and a few others, to spend the rest of the day at Mount Vernon Street. Sister Alice, closed in her room with Katharine, did not or could not even greet her. "Alice has used [Aunt Kate] very ill," wrote Mrs. William, "and almost broken her heart." This led to a groping appraisal:

To Alice I think I shall never again mete out judgment. Her laws are not ours, and her suffering should make us merciful. I don't think it possible that she herself can know how hard she has been, and Katharine adds to the complication. She is painfully prominent in the family, but no one is perfect and she means well, I am sure.

"I'm anxious to hear more of the dark hints you breathe about Alice having broken Aunt Kate's heart," William wrote back.

Part of Mrs. Alice's anguish was a fear that she had made a mistake in not cabling London sooner about Henry Senior's dying condition. But as to that, she said defensively in a letter of December 22, it was sister Alice who had argued against cabling. In fact, it was Alice who had "decided everything. I think she rules Katharine as well as everybody else, and Katharine has caught much of Alice's imperativeness of speech and manner . . . She is faithful to Alice and that means that she too is a lonely woman."

What Mrs. William was trying to say, to herself and her husband, began to edge through these strained evasions. She went on: "I am finally sure of this: she is not made as other women—our ways of feeling are not hers so we have no right to decide." This was Mrs. Alice's way of expressing her belief that her sister-in-law and Katharine Loring were engaged in a lesbian relationship. It was in this respect that sister Alice was not made as other—supply "normal"—women, and that, in her fidelity to Alice, Katharine "too" was a very lonely woman.

Passages like the above explain that part of the family folklore—passed down from family members to biographers—that attributed to Alice Howe James a conviction about the "perverse" character of the other Alice. But what has not been sufficiently remarked is the married Alice's staunch troubled attempt to cope with the discovery, to withhold judgment ("we have no right to decide"), to resist estrangement from her husband's sister. (The absent William was not being much help: "I am entirely unable to understand [Alice]," he confessed in a mid-January letter.) She expressed a resolve to try to be available to Alice as a sister, and on New Year's Eve she wrote that Alice might possibly be feeling "a step closer to me than before," and vowed to try even harder.

The day of New Year's Eve was cheered, at the Gibbens home on Garden Street, by the presence at lunch of Josiah Royce, the young intellectual who, at William's instigation, had taken over William's courses at Harvard for the year. Mrs. Alice thought Royce's wife was a "poor blundering young thing" because she refused to have a servant and forced her husband to do all the housework; but she was entertained by the fresh-faced and red-headed Royce himself, and at lunch that day was charmed by him. While they were still at table Henry stopped by. He had just walked out to the cemetery and his father's grave (where, though Mrs. Alice did not know it, he had read aloud William's farewell letter). Henry stood in the living room for some minutes staring down in silent surmise at three-year-old Harry, who stared back up at his corpulent uncle and finally shouted "Boo!"

Over much of January, Mrs. Alice was drawn into a fraternal dispute about the timing of William's return from Europe. On January 11, 1883 (which, as it happened, was William's forty-first birthday), there arrived a letter from William stating his intention of coming back within the month. The news brought Henry hastening out from Boston, almost (as he would say to his brother) with tears in his eyes. "He is really distressed at the idea," Mrs. Alice said to William, "he is sure you will repent and thinks it is such an open avowal of failure." She was disposed to agree, though she could not share Henry's severities, in letters to William, about the discomfort of being squeezed into a corner of the Garden Street house (the place on Appian Way having been leased through the summer), or the depiction of Cambridge, under a foot of snow, as "a barren scene . . . *nudified* and staring." But Henry was probably right, Mrs. Alice thought, in the high value he put upon "the advantages of London." She had tentatively suggested some time before that she might come over to England with the children to join William in "some Miss Austen spot"; but she now declared that proposal was "not worth seriously thinking about . . . Let us stand steadfast by the long separation which will bring its good fruit."

William, writing on a "caligraph" (a form of typewriter he had acquired in Paris and on which he composed erratically at the rate of twenty-five minutes per page), replied that her letter was a balm to him, wounded as he was "by the extremely and even fiercely dissuading voice of a letter from Harry which came in the same mail." Harry, said William, seemed to think that a return now would be a "disgraceful confession of instability of purpose, and of failure. A most ridiculous idea."

To Henry himself, William wrote with a certain rancor. His brother's attitude, he said in his most philosophizing manner, "flows from a great misconception of all the premises that are operative in the case." He specified: "The horror you seem to feel at Cambridge is something with which I have no sympathy, preferring it as I do to any place in the known world. Quite as little do I feel the infinite blessing of simply being in London, or in Europe *überhaupt*." He went on, softening a little, to express his understanding that each of them spoke "from the point of view of his own work; the place where a man's work is best done seems and ought to seem the place of places for him." He could not resist adding, even so, that Henry's view seemed to suppose that he, William, were a bachelor and, like Henry, one who suffered from "the skinniness and aridity of America."

The wifely Alice continued to rehearse the alternatives. Henry, she felt, was right—"as he looks at life"; for him, "this side," America and Cambridge, really was crude and distracting; she remarked perceptively that Henry was "sadly conscious of life here as exile." Speaking for herself, she acknowledged (on January 22) that "every plan which offers reunion with you draws me to itself with magnetic force. I sometimes wonder if I really loved you in the old engagement days, the torrent of my affection has grown so mighty. Some days I am half benumbed the time is so long without you." But she knew how restive William was likely to be, and how, as she put it, "my presence condemns you to settlement and a certain monotony." So she was still casting her vote for the longer stay in Europe.

Accompanying these reflections was a series of apologies on her part for mistakes (not cabling soon enough) and inadequacies ("I know my letters are unsatisfactory"), and promises to do better. She was determined, she said, her New England temperament showing never more clearly, to begin improving in her treatment of William. "For one thing I'll not *fuss* around you so much." She would try to stop interrupting him at work, and to cease pressing him when he was attempting to settle some plan or other. Meanwhile, she held up the children, metaphorically, for their father's attention. "In the twilight," she wrote one January evening, "I drew Harry round the room on his sled, baby in front of him, and as the firelight fell on the two bright little faces I thought it the prettiest picture in the world." Harry, she announced, was growing "into a consciousness of you . . . He said the other day that when his papa came back he should grow into a man. You mean a power with which his little nature seeks to ally itself."

Henry kept up the transatlantic debate for a while, but toward the end of January he drew himself together and expressed regret for having sounded "hasty or ill-tempered," and for having been "meddlesome." It was only that he regarded William's obvious improvement in health and spirits as evidence of the beneficent effects of Europe. In fact, William was complaining at just this time that he had never in his life felt seedier than during these weeks in London. But a visit with the William Darwins in Southampton had done some good, and on his forty-first birthday he confessed to feeling "quite hearty." He weighed 157 pounds, far more than his average weight in recent years of 140. The *Psychology* had made a "short incipient flight." He decided, after all, to stay on in Europe—but shifting over to Paris—through the winter, and booked passage from Liverpool on March 17.

A by-product of the meetings and talks in Cambridge was the developing relationship between Henry and William's Alice. After one extended exchange about what William should or should not do, Alice sent her husband a dispirited letter, to say next morning that she had been feeling dismal when she wrote but was now in a happier mood. It had been, she explained, "the after effect of Henry who is to me like a strange performance, very pleasant but leaving a curious lassitude behind. And he is so good!" A fortnight later she returned to the phenomenon of her brother-in-law, advancing a series of puzzled, affectionate, elliptical judgments:

I begin to feel less strange with him, and you know I always liked him. If I liked him less I should not mind his tremendous shield of reserve which so unfailingly intervenes between us. I am sure he does not mean it,—he is made so. My respect for him grows. I wish he were less middle-aged. It is strange that unimaginative me should take so curious an impression of him. His wraith bears a burden of *prose* which I only half explain by reflecting on the fact that he makes himself no illusions. Harry is great friends with him.

"Wraith" was a family word, or at least a "William" word, that carried a homemade connotation of inward spirit or psyche. Alice evidently felt that her thirty-nine-year-old brother by marriage had aged beyond his years through having divested himself, early on, of all youthful romantic hopefulness. It is a clouded portrait, but in its way as accurate a sketch of Henry James at this stage as would be done.

William countered with his own more critical analysis. "Yes, Harry is a queer boy, so good, and yet so limited, as if he had taken an oath not to let himself out to more than half of his humanhood, in order to keep the other half from suffering." After thinking for a moment, he added: ". . . Really, it is not an oath or resolve, but helplessness."

As the year 1883 set in, Mrs. Alice claimed to be in a good frame of mind about the other Alice. They were coming steadily closer, she wrote William, and she was grateful that she had kept quiet about the sister's unkindness to Aunt Kate. Miss Loring, too, was once again the easy, discreet person of earlier days. But on a visit to Mount Vernon Street on a cold and snowy January afternoon, Mrs. Alice's moral courage forsook her.

A fire was burning brightly on the hearth downstairs. The evening lamp had been lighted, and the table was almost ready for dinner; it would be served when Henry returned. In a bedroom upstairs, Alice James was lying on the bed; she had undergone a nervous spell during the week, so Mrs. Alice understood. Katharine Loring was moving about the room, straightening papers on the table, keeping an eye on her patient. It was a peaceful scene; but "the feeling of *strangeness*" pervaded the atmosphere, Mrs. Alice told William. "I was afraid," she wrote, that Katharine "would see in my eyes how painful the sight of her was to them—just then and there; so I scampered away. Of course it must be so, Alice has a deep right to arrange her life to suit her own wants."

Mrs. Alice would strive henceforth to keep her private counsel about her misgivings over the Alice–Katharine relationship, and would in time overcome them. A few days after the visit just described, she wrote William that his sister was quite cheerful and comfortable, and took pleasure in passing along Henry's information that Alice would remain in the Mount Vernon Street house and could easily afford to do so.

WILKY PEGS OUT

Alice James's material condition, as her sister-in-law implied, was a generally satisfactory one. The elder James's estate was valued at about $95,000. Of this, Alice, by the father's will, received a separate share amounting to some $20,000 in property and holdings, the share including the house on Mount Vernon Street and Burlington Railway bonds purchased with the proceeds from the sale of the Quincy Street home. The balance of $75,000 was divided equally among William, Henry, and Bob; it consisted of properties in Syracuse which yielded, at the moment, $5,250 a year, with optimistic predictions about increases in value.

Wilky was left out of the will entirely, on the grounds that he had received substantial sums from his father over the years from the Florida time onward, and had recently been given $5,000 to stave off a financial crisis. On learning of this, Wilky wrote Bob, nearby, in a sick frenzy of anger that his exclusion had been "unjust and damnable." It was "a base cowardly act of father's," and "a death stab" to a son "who dared to fight through the war for the defense of the family."

In a calmer mood two weeks later, Wilky could tell Fanny Morse that he was glad to think that his father had been "relieved of the burden of his lonely life." By this time he was probably aware that Henry, whom his father had unexpectedly named executor of the estate, was taking steps toward a redivision of the inheritance, whereby Wilky would receive a share more or less equal to the others. Alice warmly approved this plan; she had been unhappy about the original will to begin with. William jibbed a little at the suggestion that he give up a portion of his legacy, writing from London that with his growing family he had financial obligations that Henry and Alice seemed unable to understand, and that Father's testamentary wishes should not be so lightly set aside. But it was not long before his good fraternal feelings brought him round.

Bob's assent could be taken for granted; he had already loaned Wilky $1,500, and now offered to carve a share for Wilky entirely out of his own bequest. Bob was usually the most solvent of the children. He was by and large a frugal person, and his wife's father, Edward Holton, was a dependable resource at least for Mary Holton James. Henry was able to inform William in late January that the Bob Jameses, with Holton's approval, had invested $7,000 of Mary's money to buy a country home about five miles from Milwaukee and two from Holton's rural residence. It was "a small but solid brick house, with a Grecian portico, and a really very charming domain of thirty five acres."

The letter was written from Syracuse, New York, where Henry had come to inspect the family property (he could see some of it from the window of his room in the fashionable midtown hotel, even as he wrote), after a four-day visit with the younger brothers in Milwaukee. The report on Bob was hopeful, especially since he and Mary were back together for the moment. But Wilky was in wretched circumstances: "a sadly broken and changed person," Henry wrote. "I am afraid he is pretty well finished, for his spirits have gone a good deal, as well as his health, though all his old gentleness and softness remain."

Wilky's ailments included chronic disease of the kidney (Bright's disease), which affected his heart, and agonizing rheumatic aches in his right leg and war-wounded foot. (On hearing that Alice had "rheumatic gout" the previous December, Wilky had written Katharine Loring that the younger Jameses seemed "all to be afflicted with the same disease"; Bob had rheumatic trouble in his hands.) Henry thought that Wilky might hang on for a while, if only he or his wife, Carrie, had any notion of how he could be taken care of. "But they have absolutely none . . . and Carrie's imbecility is especially deplorable." All the more did Henry think it urgently desirable to arrange for the subdivision (which was shortly concluded). Henry ended by saying that the local agent, Munroe, had, that icy afternoon, driven him "along *James Street*, the 5th Avenue of Syracuse"; one of the handsomest American streets he had ever seen, and "named after our poor Grandfather!"

Henry's visit did a good deal to bolster Wilky's morale. Writing his brother in early February—and remarking that the day after Henry's departure the temperature in Milwaukee dropped to thirty-six below zero, with thirty inches of snow—Wilky said that Henry's tenderness and kindness and his loving and wise counsel had disarmed him "of all the fancied abuses and isolations under which my existence labored." The visit had the effect, Wilky said, of "shaking off in a day, almost all the evil omens" which he had been imagining; more from disease and discouragement, he now realized, than from real provocation. Invoking a key theme of his father's, Wilky added that the experience of fraternal union had left him "almost a redeemed man in mind and body."

Alice James had joined Henry in a letter from Boston urging Wilky to come to them, and under their care, for a few months. The invitation filled Wilky's heart with gratitude and love, as he wrote, but he offered reasons for not making such a trip for the moment. He no longer had a job to keep him in Milwaukee; ill health had forced him to abandon his position in the Internal Revenue office in March of 1882, but his finances were in grave disarray and needed some attending to. He was still in debt to several friends who had come to his aid during moments of crisis on the plantation and had paid his "laborers" what was owing to them. On top of that, his business failure in Milwaukee had been colossal: some $80,000 in indebtedness "scattered far and wide among a great many people."

The figure cited was provided by Wilky himself for Henry's and the family's information, and it may have been exaggerated. There was almost a note of pride in the stark announcement, as though Wilky was saying that if he had failed he had done so on a grand scale. He had obviously made one unwise investment after another, seeking to display his special acumen (his bid for Jamesian recognition) in ever more hopeless situations. But he was now willing to give up, and had declared himself legally bankrupt, being thereby (as he pointed out) protected by law against mercantile claims.

But there were other debts of honor on which he felt bound to take action, and he listed them with pitiful precision. There was the $1,500 loan from Bob; repayment would permit Bob to make necessary repairs on his newly bought house and to buy himself a horse. He owed about $2,000 to his Florida friends, and there were some smaller items. All told, he needed about $5,000 to salvage the worst of the mess, and it was his thought to sell a portion of his inherited Syracuse property to secure the amount. After that he would gladly come East and seek a job in some countinghouse or office in Boston. He was sure he would recover his health there.

A month later he reported on his condition to Fanny Morse, explaining that he was lying on his left side in bed as he wrote, with his head raised. He was still rheumatic and had a bad cough; on his doctor's advice he was planning to go South for five or six weeks to his old Florida plantation. Wilky was not able to make that journey; his physical state deteriorated steadily through the summer. On September 25 (1883), he wrote William listing his afflictions and speaking of his lack of appetite and loss of strength. "So that it looks," he concluded, "as if it would not be long before I shall peg out."

His wife, Carrie, to whom Wilky dictated the short letter, wired William ten days later to say that her husband was dying. William hurried out to Milwaukee, but had only a moment's visit with his younger brother before the doctor turned him out, Wilky being made too excited by his presence. Henry, who had been receiving regular bulletins, wrote Lizzie Boott from London that all the last news about Wilky had been "a record of unmitigated suffering." He had before him, on his desk, the pencil drawing William had made of Wilky in 1863, after he had been brought home from Fort Wagner. "Peace be to his spirit—one of the gentlest and kindest I have ever known!"

Wilky died on November 15, at the age of thirty-eight. His obituary in the Milwaukee *Sentinel*, obviously written by someone who had been fond of Wilky and had known him intimately, said that Mr. James "was eminently social in his nature. He was a delightful companion, gentle, unpretending, genuine." He was "kindly and without guile." His life and character reminded the writer of Wordsworth's 1802 poem about six-year-old Hartley Coleridge, the lines revised slightly to suit the occasion: "Pain was his guest, / Lord of his house and hospitality"; but nature had preserved for him "a young lamb's heart amid the fullgrown flock."

Carrie James insisted that Wilky be buried in Milwaukee, rather than in the family plot in Cambridge. Henry was arriving at a better opinion of his sister-in-law. She wrote Henry out of deep despondency, during the winter of 1884, that it would be a "glorious thing" if she and her children could simply lie down together and die. She was "desolate, feeble in health, and poor," Henry told Grace Norton; "but during the trials of her last six months has shown great courage, feeling and discretion; 'come out' more than I expected her to."

ENGLISH SOJOURNS

Alice James had made a brave show of independence through the winter months of 1883, presenting herself intermittently as strong enough to take charge of the household life on Mount Vernon Street, and even to preside over a few social gatherings. But in the first days of May, as another nervous crisis seemed about to strike, she took the initiative of entering the Adams Nervine Asylum, recently opened on a Jamaica Plains estate outside Boston. Katharine Loring's father was the treasurer, and one of the consulting physicians was William's astute friend James Jackson Putnam. The resident physician, Dr. Frank Page, was an able student of psychically troubled women who had come to believe that elements "incident to domestic afflictions"—that is, worry and care, with resulting sleeplessness, rather than simple and normal overwork—were the main causes of nervous unsettlement in women. The treatment he prescribed, not unlike that of the already eminent Dr. S. Weir Mitchell of Philadelphia (whom William admired), was rest and quiet, with an "Electrical Machine" to tone up the muscles.

Alice put in three months at the Nervine Asylum, and at the end of her stay, in August, Henry found her to be better, but there had been "no miraculous cure." Henry had written comfortably to his English publisher that he and his sister had made "an harmonious little *ménage*," and that "I feel a good deal as if I were married"; but he had also quite enjoyed having the Mount Vernon Street house to himself in Alice's absence, and spoke of lying about in it without any clothes in the hot summer weather, taking ten baths a day, and consuming quantities of lemonade and ice cream. But he knew it was time to return to England, where Frederick Macmillan was preparing a uniform pocket-size edition of his work (the first of its kind, and with the author listed as Henry James, without the Junior); and where, as he put it, he could lead a more "suggestive life." Alice saw him off to England on August 22, and went immediately to Beverly and Katharine Loring.

The visit, though protracted through the fall, was not a satisfactory one. Katharine's mercurial younger sister Louisa was having one of her spells of ill health—she suffered from a tubercular condition and from occasional fits of "nerves," though she would live to a fine old age—and kept Katharine pretty constantly on call. Toward the end of November, Alice yielded the terrain to Louisa and came back once again to Mount Vernon Street.

She was now, for the first time, alone in her own house; as it sometimes seemed to her, alone in the world. William was in Cambridge, scarcely five miles away; he had returned from Europe at the end of March to squeeze himself into the Garden Street house, but he was excessively busy with his work and his family concerns. He had given several lectures at the Concord Summer School of Philosophy, developing those notions he had put forward at the Scratch Eight in London about the difference between feeling and thought, and about feeling as "the germ and starting-point of cognition": notions that had their origin in the courtship experience. He had been away with his family in Keene Valley for the month of August; and in the autumn, while resuming his teaching duties at Harvard, was hard at work converting the summer lectures into a long article for the English periodical *Mind*. And his wife, Alice, by the end of November, was seven months pregnant with their third child.

Henry was across the sea. Wilky had just died. Bob was within visiting distance, having separated yet again from his wife and come East to take lodgings in Concord, do a spot of painting, and read aloud to William while his brother rested his eyes. But Alice had no wish for Bob's company; her settled aversion to him was signified by her sending him no word of their father's condition until the day of Henry Senior's death. Aunt Kate indicated her willingness to come up and live with her niece, but Alice quickly declined the offer. "She has always liked to be alone," Aunt Kate explained to Mary Holton James, "and sought to be so a good deal." To have someone else in the house, the aunt observed, "disturbs her life."

It was true that, in the absence of her older brothers and of Katharine Loring, Alice was excited and upset by the mere possibility of anyone else under the same roof day in and day out. At the same time, her inner desolation was becoming unbearable. It had begun to affect her as though it were a palpable and terrible presence, a nightmare visitation like that of the father's damnèd shape and William's epileptic idiot. She thus recalled it years afterward in her English diary:

In those ghastly days, when I was by myself in the little house in Mt. Vernon Street, how I longed to flee to the firemen next door and escape from the

"Alone, Alone!" that echoed thro' the house, rustled down the stairs, whispered from the walls, and confronted me, like a material presence, as I sat waiting, counting the moments as they turned themselves from today into tomorrow; for "Time does not work until we have ceased to watch him."

In February 1884, when Katharine Loring took Louisa to Europe for a travel cure, Alice, perhaps feeling that the rustling and whispering would overwhelm her, went down to New York and put herself into the hands of another nerve specialist, Dr. William Basil Neftel. The visit (she stayed in lodgings on East Fifty-sixth Street) had the merit of requickening the sardonic part of her temper. Dr. Neftel was Russian-born, and of a flirtatious and playful nature: "the Slavic flavour of our intercourse," Alice confessed to Sara Darwin, was a little racy for her puritan taste, and she felt it degrading to be examined closely by "a creature with the moral substance of a monkey." She was willing to admit, though, that however quackish his demeanor and large his fees, Dr. Neftel's treatment had done her good. Taking the opposite tack from Dr. Page, the New York specialist prescribed exercise rather than rest (Alice consequently walked so much in the city that she came down with "a long indigestion"), but he also went in for electrotherapy. "His electricity . . . has the starching properties of the longest Puritan descent," she told her sometimes lackluster friend Sara Darwin. "And I wish very much that you would try it some of these days."

New York seemed to her detestable, a "wilderness of Jews and ash-barrels," with no civic virtues; she rejoiced at being back in Boston, at 131 Mount Vernon Street, at the end of April. She was of a mind to stay there for the foreseeable future. A newspaper item announced the imminent departure of Alice James for England, and two friends called to say goodbye. But Alice had proved to her great satisfaction that she was capable of making a home for herself and declared herself as having at the moment no intention of moving.

She passed part of the summer at Pomfret, Connecticut, where she could recall contented summer weeks with her parents and William. It may be that the memory was too much for her. Out of her abruptly intensified loneliness, she wrote a beseeching letter to Katharine Loring. By September 10, Katharine, having left her sister and father in England to their own devices for a period, was in Mount Vernon Street, making ready to accompany Alice to England. Alice rented the Boston house and the Manchester cottage, and sailed with

Katharine for Liverpool, aboard the *Pavonia*, on November 1. She was never again to return to her native country.

Henry would be waiting for her on the Liverpool dock. Grace Norton had written Henry in October to voice an immensity of concern over Alice's impending arrival, as it were, on her brother's London doorstep. Between Grace Norton and Alice James, indistinctly jealous of one another, there was scant affection; Alice could refer to the older woman as "the ancient houri of Kirkland Street" and speak of her "mouthing ineptitudes, her 3 century old anecdotes and her snobbish pretentiousness"; and Miss Norton contributed to the opinion of some of her Cambridge friends that Miss James was a chilly and self-centered individual. Henry perhaps bore this in mind when he replied thanking Grace for her letter and saying he understood perfectly "the emotion that prompted it." But he felt no alarm whatever. Alice was "not coming in any special sense, at all, 'to me,' " and there was no question of her living with him. "She is unspeakably un-dependent and independent, she *clings* no more than a bowsprit, has her own plans, purposes, preferences, practices, pursuits, more than any one I know." Henry was convinced that after six months "in European conditions" Alice would have mended physically to the point of being no further preoccupation to him. In all this, Henry showed himself a better analyst of character than a prophet.

On the Atlantic crossing, Alice traveled in the company of both Katharine Loring and Katharine's quiet-spoken friend Mattie Whitney. It was a windswept voyage with a great deal of tossing and churning, and Alice, in her words, suffered "perpetual and violent indigestion"; during one siege of wrenching nausea, Mattie hurried to hold Alice's head, with Katharine uttering commiserating sounds from her own sick bunk. Alice was to realize later that the constant jarring of the ship had had a seriously damaging effect upon her back and legs. In Liverpool, with Henry on hand to supervise, Alice was carried ashore in the arms of two sailors, elbowing their way through the crowd of passengers. She rested for several days at the Adelphi Hotel in town and was then transported by train through the dark of an autumnal evening to London, where Henry engaged rooms for her at 40 Clarges Street, Piccadilly, around the corner from his Bolton Street lodgings. Clarges Street and Half Moon Street, Henry had remarked to Francis Boott, were *full* of available apartments—though the one chosen for Alice, by her account, consisted of no more than a "little parlor and a tomb-like closet for a bedroom."

[376

Tomb-like it may well have seemed, especially since Alice was largely confined to it for the first two months after her arrival, battered to exhaustion by sometimes excruciating pains; and once came close (as she thought) to dying in it. The personal maid Henry had taken on for his sister, Campbell by name, would tell her comfortingly: "Your illness is a very pleasant one, Miss, with some ladies it isn't pleasant at all"; but Alice was visited by attacks of what she called gout of the stomach, which gave her paroxysms, and her legs hurt so badly that she could do no more than hobble around her tiny room occasionally. She had frightful headaches. Attempting to relieve a headache one late December evening, Alice applied an electric battery to the base of her neck, just above her spine; and that treatment, according to Dr. Garrod, the specialist speedily summoned, brought on something like a paralytic stroke. It led to such terrifying throbs around the heart that Alice was sure she was on the point of death.

Earlier in the month, following up a suggestion by the family's Boston physician, Dr. Beach, Alice had called in the renowned English specialist in gout, Dr. Alfred Baring Garrod. Her first visit from this genial plump elderly gentleman Alice pronounced "the most affable hour of my life," though Garrod withheld any medical opinion. In the wake of the nerve-shattering experience with the electric battery, however, Alice spoke of him as "a *fiasco*," and "an unprincipled one too." Yes, he had said after examination, the pain and extreme weakness in her legs were probably produced by gout, though total paralysis was not, on the whole, to be anticipated. But gout was, in any case, only the smaller part of her problem, "it being complicated with an excessive nervous sensibility." With this, Garrod took his departure, leaving Alice with the sense—her language about it had a nice duplicity—that he was allowing her metaphorically to drown, or possibly that he had eluded her amorous advances: "He slipped thro' my cramped & clinging grasp as skilfully as if his physical conformation had been that of an eel."

Henry came by twice each day for a few minutes, and on the morning after New Year's, 1885, he brought with him a copy of *The Literary Remains of Henry James*, edited and with an introduction by William. Alice was only able to hold it in her hands for a moment or two, but as she did so she burst into tears, exclaiming: "How beautiful it is that William should have done it! isn't it, isn't it beautiful? And how good William is, how good, how good!" There were other less emotional moments, as when Mary Wilkinson came to call and both amused and wearied Alice by leaning close to ask a series of intent questions: "Are you fond of history, Alice?" "Do your brothers live anywhere near you in America, Alice?"

"Henry and Kath.," Alice told Aunt Kate, were her "only anchorages." But Katharine Loring was again forced to abandon her when, at the end of November, she went to Bournemouth to take up the care of her languishing sister. In mid-January, Alice followed her friend down to the coastal village. The train journey—four hours, and about one hundred miles southwest through Winchester and Southampton to the Channel—was enough to reduce Alice to virtual immobility. She did not leave her boardinghouse bed for many weeks. Katharine came in every day to tend to her, and Alice could sit up and look out at the passing carriage traffic. Her fear was that Louisa Loring would take it into her head to move on elsewhere, and indeed, in mid-April, the Loring sisters transferred themselves to London. Alice thereupon appealed to her other anchorage. Henry came down at once and engaged rooms in St. Alban's Cliff, as he told his English publisher, to "look after my sister, who is very feeble but tending to improve."

Henry was in fine literary form. He had experienced, for him, something of a dry season through 1882 and well into 1883, berating himself in his notebook for the paucity of his production and his lack of focus. As his fortieth birthday approached (it would occur in April 1883), he declared it an absolute necessity that he "make some great efforts during the next few years . . . if I wish not to have been on the whole a failure. I shall have been a failure unless I do something *great*." Larger and smaller efforts followed upon this recommitment, and by mid-1884 Henry was in full swing. "Lady Barberina," which reversed a familiar situation by having an English daughter of the aristocracy marry a wealthy American (a New York physician), ran in the *Century* from May through July. "The Author of Beltraffio," James's most remarkable treatment of the clash between puritanic moralism and the aesthetic personality, appeared in England during the summer. In September, *Longman's Magazine* published "The Art of Fiction," James's major statement about his own métier and the elements that went into it. And in February 1885, not long before Henry joined his sister in Bournemouth, *The Bostonians* began its yearlong run in the *Century*.

The Bournemouth life held several attractions for Henry. He worked in the morning on the thickening manuscript of his new novel, *The Princess Casamassima*. He walked along the cliffs and through the pine woods. Each morning and afternoon, he went to spend twenty minutes with Alice. "She has had a wretched winter," he wrote Grace Norton, "and is in a very weak and poor state now; though much better since I came." Meanwhile, he added, he had "a great resource, for the evening, in the presence here of Robert Louis Stevenson, who is an old acquaintance of mine, ripening now into a friend."

The ripening process is reflected in the changing forms by which Henry James addressed Stevenson in letters: from "My dear Robert Louis Stevenson" in December 1884 (replying amiably to his correspondent's not less amiable public dispute with "The Art of Fiction") to "My dear Robert Louis" and "Dear Stevenson" a year later and "My dear Louis" by August 1886 and thereafter. When Henry called on the Scottish-born writer at his home in Bournemouth, facing the sea, Stevenson was thirty-five years old and the author two years earlier of what James called "the adorable tale of 'Treasure Island.' " Stevenson was also, as Henry reported, "deadly consumptive," and had "not for two years been out of the house." He was married to a "Californian divorcée" (Mrs. Osborne), and wore on his emaciated person old sealskin garments belonging to his wife. "But his face, his talk, his nature, his behaviour, are delightful, and I go to see him every night." Stevenson was the British writer for whom Henry James had the most unequivocal admiration and affection; qualities that survived Stevenson's departure from England in 1887, for the United States and then for Samoa, where he died in 1894.

The relative tranquillity of the Bournemouth days came to an end in early May, when Alice underwent one of her worst attacks of "palpitations," and Henry, at his sister's urging, sent to London for Katharine Loring. Katharine came down with *her* ailing sister, and scurried back and forth between the two patients. Louisa, Henry wrote Aunt Kate with a sort of exasperated amusement, was having "nervous fits in one house, produced by her impatience to get away," and Alice, "in a state of great prostration, was having nervous fits in another (aggravated by a knowledge of Louisa's)." He predicted, accurately this time, that after Katharine had settled her sister on the Continent she would return to stay with Alice more or less permanently. He expressed his belief that Miss Loring did not expect Alice to live very long.

In other letters to Aunt Kate and to William at this hectic time, Henry attempted to reach his own judgment on the relation between Alice and Katharine Loring. The evidence was confusing. Alice often took a turn for the worse when Katharine went off to nurse Louisa; the jealousy and resentment on this score were so obvious that Henry hardly bothered to mention them. But equally Alice became bedridden anew the moment Katharine rejoined her, as though snuggling down to be the central object of her friend's attention. "As soon as they get together, Alice takes to her bed," Henry wrote William; and it was because of this that Henry wondered whether Katharine's presence might not be doing Alice "more harm than good." That presence, he was nonetheless convinced, was indispensable to Alice.

A devotion so perfect and generous as K.L.'s is a gift of providence. Moreover, there is about as much possibility of Alice's giving Katharine up on the ground I speak of as of her giving her legs to be sawed off. She said to me a few days ago that she believed if she could have Katharine *quietly & uninterruptedly*, for a year, "to relieve her of all responsibility!", she would get well.

The image of Alice giving up her legs had a macabre appropriateness, as referring to a woman whose father *had* had a leg sawed off; and for whom, with the near-paralysis of her limbs, Katharine Loring might be said to *be* her legs.

It is not easy to make out if Henry saw the relation, psychologically and sexually, as his sister-in-law Mrs. Alice was inclined to do; but if so, he ended with a similar stance toward it. As to Alice's prospects, he said to Aunt Kate, "She will get well, or she won't but, either way, it lies between themselves. I shall devote my best energies to taking the whole situation less hard in the future than I have done hitherto."

We may derive a hint about Henry James's view of Katharine Loring herself from *The Bostonians*, which, as had been said, was appearing in the *Century* at this same moment. It has almost been taken for granted, in some quarters, that the inconclusively lesbian friendship in that novel between Olive Chancellor and Verena Tarrant represented Henry James's fictive version of the intimacy between Alice James and Katharine Loring. But this doesn't work at all if you try to match up the real and the fictional females. Neither Olive nor Verena has Alice's coiling wit, her informed and sometimes abrasive intelligence, her special kind of courage, or her wracking illness. Nor does either Olive or Verena have anything to speak of in common with Katharine Loring. Miss Loring is unmistakably and even unforgettably in the novel; not, however, as either of the two women pointed to in the title (which had to do, Henry told William firmly *only* with those two, and not with anyone else in the story), but as Dr. Prance, the competent and self-contained young practitioner who takes over the care of Miss Birdseye.

Here really was a portrait to the life: "a plain, spare young woman, with short hair and an eyeglass"—Henry might have been studying Katharine Loring's photograph. She is "spare, dry, hard, without a curve, an inflection or a grace." She "seemed to ask no odds in the battle of life and to be prepared to give none"; so Alice had been heard to say of her friend, especially after the Adirondacks adventure. Dr. Prance is a prime example of the blurring of sexual identity, one of those several losses of definiteness which everywhere characterizes the novel's world. "She looked like a boy, and not even like a good boy," Basil Ransom thinks, and elaborates on the fancy. "If she had been a boy she might have borne some relation to a girl, whereas Dr. Prance appeared to bear none whatever." But Basil, though like Henry James he preferred curves and inflections and graces in women who set out to be women, is quite drawn to Dr. Prance from the start; he enjoys her dry conversation and her clarity of spirit. During the Cape Cod sequence, he comes to savor her wisdom and steadfastness as the care-taker of the dying saint. So, we may suppose, did Henry James come to appreciate the caretaker of his physically doomed sister.

With the coming of summer, it seemed advisable to move Alice back to London and settle her somewhere within Henry's neighbor-hood. Alice herself had grown weary of the Bournemouth confinement, though she could by now walk about her bedroom for a few minutes at a time. After some searching, Henry found a diminutive cottage on Hampstead Heath, high enough, he wrote William, for the atmosphere to be "exceedingly fresh and tonic." On July 13, Alice was conveyed on a litter, by train and carriage, to the cottage, accompanied by Katharine Loring and two nurses. There was the predictable if rela-tively brief collapse. But the stay in Hampstead, which lasted through September, was a salutary one, thanks in part to a Bath chair supplied by Katharine, a mobile affair with bicycle wheels and rubber tires—"so that," Alice wrote, "there is absolutely no jar & one can lie out in it like a bed if necessary." She made a dozen excursions on the chair, propelled by Katharine, on summery mornings, her first times outside her bedroom since she had gone to Bournemouth six months before.

THE PASSING OF HUMSTER

While Alice was still in a state of collapse, Henry received word from William—a word he withheld from his sister for the time—of the death on July 9 of William and Mrs. Alice's infant son, Herman, not yet eighteen months old.

Alice had greeted the arrival of her new nephew, on January 31, 1884, with "a thousand congratulations" to his mother. She was only sorry, she said, that the baby had "chosen the inferior sex"; but she supposed that Mrs. Alice might feel better about having "brought forth an oppressor rather than one of the oppressed," and would not consequently "have to look forward to evenings spent in Lyceum Hall trembling lest he should not be engaged for the german or left dangling at supper time." After some discussion, the boy's parents decided to name him Herman, after a German colleague at Harvard admired by William. Uncle Henry, in London, warmly approved the choice.

The period of calamity began in March 1885, when Mrs. Alice came down with scarlet fever. The whole family was quarantined, and William was evidently kept separated from his wife. In June the infant Herman contracted whooping cough, and his mother caught it from him. William took the older boys, with Alice's sister Margaret, to southern New Hampshire, where he rented a farm in Pottersville.

It was a pleasant form of existence, with William and the children sporting together in the barn or across the fields, and William taking Harry on a climb up a high hill to scramble down the other side. But William grew depressed by the long separation: "4 months of estrangement" since the attack of scarlet fever, he wrote Alice in late June. William's periodic need to disconnect himself from wife and family had not lessened with the years. The previous December, as was his wont, he had spent Christmas away from home (with the family of Pearsall Smith in Philadelphia); but typically, he wrote a lyrical letter to his wife on Christmas Eve, evoking her eyes ("like 2 brown moons"), her "rich red smile," the "rich graciousness" of her manner, and "the faithfulness" of her heart. The "estrangement" through the spring of 1885, however, was hardly to be borne, especially, as William complained, since the two children needed so uncommonly much taking care of.

Alice and the baby moved into the Garden Street house, where Mrs. Gibbens could be in constant attendance. Humster, as William called him, seemed to be recovering. But the whooping cough eventually led to bronchopneumonia, and when William rushed back to Cambridge, he found the infant suffering from convulsions. Humster hung on for nine desperate days; but "at last," William said to his cousin Kitty Prince, "his valiant little soul left the body"—on the night of July 9. "He was a broad, generous, patient little nature, with a noble

head who would doubtless have done credit to his name had he lived."
The child was buried in the Cambridge cemetery, next to his grandparents Henry Senior and Mary James.*

The great part of the experience for him, William told his cousin,
had been "the sight of Alice's devotion." (Kitty Prince could well believe this: she had herself been the frequent object of Mrs. Alice's
thoughtful concern on visits to Mrs. Prince in Somerville after one of
the latter's crises of nerves or stays in the local asylum.) Alice had gone
without regular sleep for six weeks, and during the final nine days had
slept no more than three hours in twenty-four: "And yet bright and
fresh and ready for anything, as much on the last day as on the first."
His wife had "so essentially *mellow* a nature," William said, that he
foresaw no morbid after-effects.

The death of Herman markedly increased William James's curiosity about the whole phenomenon of the supernatural. His interest
in the matter was of course long-standing, and had been reflected as
early as 1869 (it may be recalled) in a review of a book about spiritualism and spiritualist practices. Here again William was following in
the paternal footsteps: Henry Senior had himself addressed the spiritualist question in articles of the 1850s. The death of his father had
brought William to ponder more closely the possibility of otherworldly
experience and the meeting of loved ones. ("More than ever at this
moment," William had said to his father in the farewell letter, "do I
feel that if that *were* true, all would be solved and justified.") And the
rereading, meditating, and writing about Henry Senior's mystical ideas
had immensely strengthened William's concern, indeed his involvement, with religious and supernatural issues.

At some time in the year 1885 (some months prior to the death
of Herman, as it would seem), William took it on himself to found an
American branch of the Society for Psychical Research, similar to the
London society and in fact serving to discuss and disseminate the
publications of the English group. Among those who joined William
James at informal talk sessions were G. Stanley Hall, Henry Bowditch,
Asa Gray, and Josiah Royce, keen-minded men but most of them
dubious about the new field of inquiry. William James himself was

---

* Whittier, in a letter of September 30 to Mrs. Alice James, said that, though he
could not fathom "the depth of a mother's grief at the loss of child," he did himself
know what it meant "to look my last upon mother, brother and sister." It was the death
of his sister Elizabeth that was the immediate source of Whittier's masterwork "Snow-
bound" of 1866, where he also invoked the personalities and the loss of his mother and
brother, and others in his family.

anything but credulous: after attending a "spiritualist camp meeting" near Saratoga in August 1884, he had denounced it to Alice as nauseating and depressing. "It is a field in which the sources of deception are extremely numerous," he wrote his German ally Carl Stumpf. "But I believe there is no source of deception in the investigation of nature which can compare with a fixed belief that certain kinds of phenomenon are *impossible*."

The experience of watching his infant son's long-drawn-out death throes touched some special chord in William's nature, and set him thinking in a more imaginative and personal way about the mystery involved. At dawn on a day in early August, after his wife had joined the other children and her sister in Jaffrey, New Hampshire, William wrote from the Garden Street house (where the death had occurred) that he had been "lying thinking of all that happened in this bed-room three weeks ago . . . To think of that little fat, placid unconscious soul, with his broad kindliness, having to go through that dark portal, & become that changed little form gasping for breath on this bed, as he did! and we not understand a word of it, or where or what he is." To Kitty Prince, he stated his conviction that a "still better chance" was somewhere reserved for Herman, and that "we shall in some way come into his presence again."

A few mornings later, William went out early and walked to the cemetery. The lot containing his parents and Herman looked peaceful enough, he wrote. "The pine tree has grown. The grass on the little mound is about dead, but elsewhere the rains have brought it up." In the last days of August, he wrote his "Dearest Weibchen" that "I went last night after ten o'clock to Appian Way and looked at our old empty house under the clouded moon. As I gazed up at the closed shutters of the room in which our little one began his career, and thought what a queer little fragment it was, how quickly over, and how near at hand his death-bed was, and his grave, an awful sense of compassion came over me, and of close drawing to you, as if we were indefeasably one through this little life having proceeded from us."

In the months following, Mrs. Gibbens began to make secret visits to a Boston medium, a Mrs. Leonora (William J.) Piper, who was reputed to effect communication with the dead. Her daughter Alice, along with the younger sisters, followed suit, and Alice in particular became a convert. Before the year was out, she had persuaded William to accompany her on a visit. William's extensive firsthand experience as a psychic researcher had begun.

COMING TO TERMS

In the fall of 1885, Alice James again changed her London lodgings, shifting this time into somewhat more spacious accommodations at 7 Bolton Row, a short slice of roadway that ran past the northern end of Bolton Street (it has since been absorbed into Curzon Street). Katharine was with her for a month or so, before leaving in the usual haste to give succor to Louisa. But Alice was pleased with her new English "keeper," Miss Ward, an impoverished gentlewoman with orderly habits whose only defect, one that Alice habitually deprecated, was an excessive zeal for churchgoing. Henry, "as good as good can be," came in regularly from his apartment five minutes away at the Piccadilly end of Bolton Street. But he, too, was preparing to move, having taken a "residential flat" at 33 De Vere Gardens in Kensington, on a long lease. It needed to be "finished and furnished," Henry told Grace Norton, and would not be ready for several months.

Alice's physical condition was improving markedly. What had been, physically and nervously, the worst year of her life—the year following her flight from America, a year of learning to live without her parents—was now behind her, and she was growing stronger by the month. She had fewer "attacks," and was less often in pain. Gradually, the nights ceased to be "the periods of terror" (her phrase, to Aunt Kate) that they had been for fifteen months, when a strange defect in her digestive system caused waves of evil sensations at the moment of falling asleep. In the Bolton Row suite she was able to come into the sitting room each day at noon and stay there till five or six in the evening, managing as well to amble around the room half a dozen times. "My sister," Henry wrote Godkin in February 1886, ". . . is much better than at any time since she came abroad. She is destined, I think, to get better still and be an ornament, yet, to society."

She was encouraged after hearing the diagnosis of her state by a Dr. Townsend, a specialist in whom Alice placed a good deal of faith ("I never came in contact with a more beautiful soul, manly, impersonal, intelligent, kind as a nursing mother"). His opinion, in fact, coincided with that of the discredited Dr. Garrod: in Alice's wording, "a gouty diathesis"—a permanent or constitutional inflammation of the joints—"complicated by an abnormally sensitive nervous organisation." The pain and intermittent paralysis in her legs were "brought about by anxiety and strain" and would be much relieved by time and by his medicines, very strong tonics which Alice quietly failed to take. Dr. Townsend repeated what others had told Alice: "that I should be much better at any rate, when I reached middle life"—that is, menopause; something Alice thought quite probable, since, as she said to William, she had had sixteen periods in the previous year of pain and distress. At the least, she was glad to be able to say "just what is the matter with me."

The difficulty was that her nervous organization seemed to be growing no less "abnormally sensitive." Alice explained to Aunt Kate that, as her physical state became stronger, her "nervous distress and susceptibility" increased with it. Even as she lay motionless on the sofa, she could feel "a tornado going on" inside her, in her mind and nerve centers. The violence of consciousness and imagery suggestively resembled that in her retrospective account of the nerve storm in 1868; and indeed one gains the impression that for a year and more after her arrival in England, Alice had been living on the edge of a familiar nightmare, of some psychic horror pressing on the edges of her vision. There was, as an example, the burst of hostility toward the initially paternal Dr. Garrod, reminiscent in its savagery of her impulse (in 1868) to murder her "benign pater." There was again the sensation of the parts of her body going interchangeably mad: "every joint in my body," she wrote William in January 1886, ". . . constantly pierced with rheumatic pains flying from my head to my feet, from my stomach to my hands."

During that time, as well, the recurring submission of her body to being probed and tested and pulled at had been a fearful ordeal; a challenge and an indignity to her sexual nature that she felt bound to resist with all her force. She wrote to William in the same January letter:

I must confess my spirit quails before any more gladitorial encounters. It requires the strength of a horse to survive the fatigue of waiting hour after hour for the great man and then the fierce struggle to recover one's self-respect after having been reduced to the mental level of Charlie Möring [a Cambridge lackwit known to William]. I think the difficulty is my inability to assume the receptive attitude, that cardinal virtue in woman, the absence of which has always made me so uncharming to and uncharmed by the male sex.

It was a metaphorical medley of the combative and the erotic (by way of a report on the medical); of onslaughts barely survived and sexual aggressions rebuffed; versions of the male-female relation that could appear in Alice's lively imagination as surrogates for each other. But as elsewhere, the very composition of the passage, its literary power, was an indication of psychic control and of distancing.

Another indication in these ongoing months was Alice's tendency to be less self-absorbed, less watchful of her every changing symptom, and more alert to the world outside her. An uneven stream of visitors to the Bolton Row sitting room brought that world to her; Alice's "ability to see people," Henry remarked to William in March (and we may take the word "see" in more than one sense), "has sextupled since a year ago." The weather was bitterly cold in that London winter, and visitors were likely to discover Alice, on a couch drawn to within three feet of the fire, wearing a flannel-lined wrapper over two suits of heavy underclothing, two warm shawls over her shoulders, and a heavy rug over her legs, with the addition at times of a quilt stuffed with eiderdown and a fur cloak. Alice had to stiffen herself, mentally, for these visiting sessions, which could go on for three hours at a stretch; and she would sometimes yield to tears of exhaustion afterward. But she was visibly enjoying her new social life, and with wry pleasure passed along to Aunt Kate two opposite views of her expressed by callers: "One 'so subtle, just like your brother,' the other '& above all so original.' "

She began to be responsive to public and private events. The suicide of "Clover Hooper" (Mrs. Henry Adams), which she learned of early in 1886, Alice described as "a dreadful shock." But the marriage of the forty-year-old family friend Lizzie Boott, in March, to her energetic painting teacher Frank Duveneck drew a more characteristic comment. Lizzie spoke of herself by letter as "calmly happy & sketching"; at which Alice said she would have preferred "a little delirious joy, at any rate, for a week or two, to blind her to the terrors of her situation." Many of these observations came in long gossipy letters to Aunt Kate; from the vantage point of London, Alice seems to have felt again the old gratitude and affection for her devoted kinswoman. Talking of Katharine Loring, in an April letter, she declared that Katharine's self-sacrifice was too often taken "as a matter of course. I wonder how much of courseness there would be about it if she happened to wear trousers! Oh, the goodness of women!! But you certainly don't need any instruction so I shall stop my chatter."

The Piccadilly riots in early February brought Alice James back into the rush of history. Some ten thousand persons had gathered in Trafalgar Square to protest the widespread unemployment. The police charged and dispersed the crowd, whereupon a good many individuals went chasing along the streets to Piccadilly, heaving missiles and looting shops. In the next days, Alice wrote her aunt, "London looked like a city that was besieged . . . all the shops shuttered and barricaded." She was sure that the violence was committed not by workingmen but by "roughs and thieves"—the same phrase was used by Henry in a dispatch to William—"who were evidently upon a lark . . . There were numberless poor ladies dragged from their carriages & robbed of their jewels & frightened to death"—Henry said "hustled, rifled, slapped or kissed"—"the footmen in many cases running away!!!"

Alice's interest in English social conditions quickened at once, and she cast about for information. One of her regular visitors, the wife of a defeated Radical candidate for office, quoted to her the opinion of an East End clergyman that "he had never known such destitution in his life, that thousands of families were living in one room who had tasted no food all winter but 'sop' which consists of crusts of bread wh. they get from the parish & wh. they soak in water."

The attitudes that would henceforth be the recognizable features of Alice's English years were starting to appear. "Nothing more absolutely elementary than the British feminine mind" could possibly be conceived of, she wrote in April. She deplored the literalness of that mind (literalness, we remember, had been an object of scorn in the household of Henry James, Sr.). "It rather arrests the flow of analytical & rhetorical gymnastics." She spoke on another occasion of a new acquaintance who "is perpetually trying to escape from the terrors of the sentence in hand, or rather on the tongue, to fly to those she knows not of." When a cockroach was descried in the bedroom, and Miss Ward could do no more than stand with her petticoats drawn up moaning with fear, Alice had to climb out of bed, get down on her "ricketty knees," and smother the creature. "A moribund Yankee," she said to William, was thus shown to be "worth twenty of the deadly, stupid, lazy, doughy lumps, when there is anything to be done." She went on, in increasing vehemence, to evoke what was becoming one of her favorite contrasts, that between the English and the Irish.

They make me feel, just the look of them sometimes, as if I must shriek & scream or be stifled, it is perpetually like running your head into a featherbed . . . They are absolutely without the Irish brain cell & they have consequently a structural inability to conceive of an Irishman as having the ordinary human attributes.

A certain pride of being was making itself felt. "My ill-health has been inconvenient & not aesthetically beautiful," Alice wrote her older brother in January, "but early in youth I discovered that there were certain ends to be attained in life, which were as independent of illness or of health, as they were of poverty or riches, so that by turning my attention to them, even *my* torpid career has not been without its triumphs to my consciousness & therefore not to be pitied for." This was a casting back two decades to the days when she would walk along the Newport cliffs, communing with herself; but she was voluble in rejecting any commiseration over the self of 1886.

In July, William wrote her that she was "visited in a way that few are ever called to bear, and I have no words of consolation that would not seem barren. Stifling slowly in a quagmire of disgust and pain and impotence!" Alice quoted the last sentence back to him, saying that she and Katharine had found it cause for laughter: "for I consider myself one of the most potent creations of my time, & though I may not have a group of Harvard students sitting at my feet drinking in psychic truth, I shall not tremble, I assure you, at the last trump." She grasped and resented William's implication, through his use of the word "impotence," that she was destitute of will, and could have no say about her manner of life. To counter it, she offered her landlady's remark: "You seem very comfortable, you are always 'appy within yourself, Miss."

The letter was written from Leamington, a health resort some eighty-five miles northwest of London. Katharine Loring, having left Louisa with their brother and his wife in Germany, had come back to Alice in May and escorted her to the spa. The journey wore Alice out, Henry told William, but she "suffered *less* than from any similar effort she has made since she came to England . . . Katharine, who had not seen her for seven months, finds her, in spite of the knock-up of the journey, wonderfully better."

Alice was not only better in her physical circumstances, she was better in relation to them. She had come to terms with her condition, and with her foreseeable future. "I have been considering & deciding upon my probable future for the next three or four years," she continued to William from Leamington, "& I see no chance of my being well enough for the journey"—back to America—"for a long time to come." In view of this, she wanted William and his Alice to go to the warehouse in Boston where she was storing the things from the Mount Vernon Street house and the Manchester cottage, and to take for themselves anything they found useful: furniture, rugs, beds, pictures. "You must not regard this as a favour to you, it will be one to me." But they were not to take the barrels of crockery, since she felt rather sentimental about that.

389]

34 DE VERE GARDENS

Henry had taken possession of his new flat on the third of March. It occupied the fourth and top floor of a house at the end of De Vere Gardens, a short wide street that ran south from Kensington Road and away from the green expanse of Kensington Gardens. Coming west-ward down Piccadilly, as Henry (who measured London distances by walking time) described it to Grace Norton, it lay just five minutes beyond Queen's Gate Road, where Grace had lived in 1869. For the first time since his expatriation to Europe in 1875, Henry could enjoy a genuinely residential situation. The apartment had a sitting room, a study, a larger room which would be made into a library, a bedroom and a guest room, and servants' quarters, these at the moment con-taining a colorless couple named Smith. The whole lofty place with its many windows, Henry told William, was "flooded with light like a photographer's studio." His desk faced an immense window through which, looking west, he had a beguiling view of London housetops and streets, and of beautiful sunsets; he could peer up everywhere at "the unobstructed sky."

After Alice had been taken to Leamington in May, Henry had visited her only once. It was her own wish that he did not come more often, Henry confided to William, adding, in an echo of his sister-in-law several years before, that with Katharine Loring looking after her at the spa, Alice seemed content. He could also have said that, in any event, he had little time to spare. He was working to maximum capacity every day, exerting all his energy to bring to a close his novel *The Princess Casamassima*. It had been running in *The Atlantic Monthly* since September 1885 and would be appearing there through the issue of October 1886: fourteen installments altogether, Henry James's most sizable work of fiction to date.

Henry had high hopes for it, especially since its predecessor, *The Bostonians*, had proved so dispiriting a chapter in his career. There had been a commotion back home over the presentation of Miss Birds-eye in the early numbers of that novel's serial (she was said to have been a slander on the reformist educator Elizabeth Palmer Peabody), and William had remonstrated worriedly on the matter. William had written a handsome retraction after reading the entire novel, and Henry, by way of gratified reply, had nodded his agreement with Wil-liam's more technical strictures, saying that there had indeed been too much "describing and explaining and expatiating" in the middle part. But what dismayed Henry was the total absence of reader's response to the work. "Not a word, echo or comment," he said, had come to him from any quarter after the initial to-do. "This deathly silence seems to indicate that it has fallen flat." It was the more disappointing since Henry had not received a penny for the serial and was smarting under what he considered financial misusage.*

London, the city and the society, is the overwhelming presence in *The Princess Casamassima*. The urban world—its twisting streets and overcast skies, its hurry and uproar, its bridges and shops and crowded pubs, its slum dwellings and Mayfair mansions, its Sundays, its people high-born and working-class, wealthy and wretched, its speech—is rendered with a teeming fullness unmatched in English-language city fiction; unmatched even by *Little Dorrit*, the Dickens novel of 1857 which James's work seems laggardly to follow in its structure and some of its sequences, not to mention its diminutive protagonist. Through that London, the protagonist, Hyacinth Robinson, wanders even as Henry remembered himself doing a decade earlier. "I had only to conceive his watching the same public show, the same innumerable appearances I had myself watched," Henry was to say, "and of watching very much as I had watched." No character in his fiction more fully exemplifies that part of Henry James which can be labeled "the novelist-as-observer" (prior, it must always be said, to the novelist-as-maker); and what he observed is the city for which Henry had such intricately mixed feelings, and about which he was shortly to compose an article for the *Century*.†

Hyacinth, a slight, slim youth in his twenties and a bookbinder by trade, is the offspring of a dissolute English aristocrat and a French seamstress; the latter murdered her lover in a fit of passion and ended her days miserably in London's Millbank Prison (where Henry had spent a December morning in 1885 making notes for a scene set in it). Informed of this heritage in late childhood, Hyacinth foresees his fate as being "split open by sympathies that pulled him in different

---

* The *Century* magazine, which ran the serial, had paid J. R. Osgood, who was to publish the book, $4,000 to be forwarded to Henry James. But in 1885, Osgood's firm failed and Henry was unable to collect the sum. The affair had a temporarily harmful effect upon Henry's finances; but with $350 per number about to come in from *The Atlantic*, and with other fees and royalties, Henry survived the crisis and, for example, could contribute his $1,000 share for repairs on the family's Syracuse property.

† The article "London" finally appeared in the *Century* in December 1888.

ways." In a subsequent formulation, "there was no peace for him between the two currents that flowed in his nature, the blood of his passionate plebeian mother, and that of his long-descended super-civilised sire."

To reduce James's most densely plotted novel to half a dozen sentences: the plebeian side of Hyacinth leads him into the revolutionary underworld of London and to the inner sanctum of the anarchist movement; here he pledges himself to the leader, on command, to carry out an act of assassination which will certainly mean his own death. The civilized side, already evident in the youth's instinctive love of beauty and his skill at the art of bookbinding, is further developed when he is taken up by the alluring Princess Casamassima, the same Christina Light who swept through *Roderick Hudson* in 1875, now separated from her Neapolitan husband and seeking to atone for her life of luxury by interesting herself in the London poor. When he receives a legacy of £37 (currently perhaps $1,800), Hyacinth fulfills his old dream by going for several weeks to Paris and then to Venice. The experience clarifies his outlook; in a long letter to the Princess from Venice, Hyacinth acknowledges his reverence for "the monuments and treasures of art, the great palaces and properties, the conquest of learning and taste," even though all of it may be based upon "the despotism, the cruelties, the exclusions, the monopolies and the rapacities of the past."

He does not, however, repudiate his pledge. The word arrives: he is to assassinate a certain duke at a garden party (it is to be one of many such acts which are supposed to convulse and ultimately to destroy the existing order). By this time, though, Hyacinth finds himself a psychological alien: he has grown too skeptical of the anarchist movement to take any part in its program; but he is also aware of having been betrayed or abandoned by those to whom he has given his personal affection and loyalty: the Princess; Paul Muniment, an ambitious young chemist of calculated radical beliefs; and Millicent Henning, Hyacinth's closest female companion in his own class. He commits suicide by turning the gun on himself.*

---

* The betrayals are registered by two moments of that favorite Jamesian device and trademark, the unobserved observer. In the first, Hyacinth, hovering in the darkness outside the Princess's house (with the Prince himself watching agitatedly alongside), observes the Princess and Paul Muniment entering together. In the second, Hyacinth, in the dress shop, espies Millicent displaying a garment for the covetous eyes of Captain Sholto. Both tableaus are, of course, perceived signals of sexual yielding, and in the management and juxtaposing of them, James's craftsmanship was at its finest.

Historically minded critics have long debated the extent of James's knowledge about radical conspiratorial movements in Victorian London. It is perhaps enough for our purpose to say that James had at the least the superlative artist's intuition into the hidden drift of things— the quality he did not hesitate to claim for himself in his preface to the novel in the New York Edition: "the sense of life and the penetrating imagination," armed with which, he said, "you are not really helpless . . . even before mysteries abysmal." But Henry James was as well the son of Henry Senior, and never more so than in the mid-1880s, when the older man, his death, and his vanished reputation were much on his mind ("the pathetic, tragic ineffectualness of poor Father's lifelong effort," as he put it to William in a letter of October 1885). He looked at and into English society with something of the father's apocalyptic eye, and described what he saw with something of the father's scathing rhetoric:

It's the old regime again, the rottenness and extravagance, bristling with every iniquity and every abuse, over which the French Revolution passed like a whirlwind; or perhaps even more a reproduction of the Roman world in its decadence, gouty, apoplectic, depraved, gorged and clogged with wealth and spoils, selfishness and skepticism, and waiting for the onset of the barbarians.

That, in fact, is the Princess Casamassima, discoursing with un-characteristic eloquence to the wide-eyed Hyacinth. But it is also Henry James, Jr., who deployed the identical analogies in an outburst to Charles Eliot Norton in December 1886, and alluding to the English upper class:

The condition of that body seems to me to be in many ways very much the same rotten and *collapsible* one as that of the French aristocracy before the revolution—minus cleverness and conversation. Or perhaps it's more like the heavy, congested and depraved Roman world upon which the barbarians came down. In England the Huns and Vandals will have to come *up*—from the black depths of the (in the people) enormous misery . . .

In the novel, as it happens, it is the French émigré Eustache Poupin, Hyacinth's mentor and surrogate father in the bookbinding shop, whose social and political temperament is made most to resemble that of Henry James, Sr. Our first glimpse of M. Poupin is a tender and smiling filial reminiscence: he was "an aggressive socialist" and "a constructive democrat," "a theorist and an optimist and a collectivist and a perfectionist and a visionary." He believed that "the day was to come when all the nations of the earth would abolish their frontiers and armies and custom-houses, and embrace on both cheeks and cover the globe with boulevards, radiating from Paris, where the human family would sit in little groups at little tables . . . drinking coffee . . . and listening to the music of the spheres."

But M. Poupin is by no means the only character in *The Princess Casamassima* with detectable Jamesian ties. The novel, indeed, for all its exhaustively realized and exclusively English milieu (it is as wholly British as *The Bostonians* is wholly American), performs on one major level as a kind of James family drama, or dance. Lionel Trilling has made the argument in a brilliant essay of 1957, attributing to the novel a "personal" and "familial" nature and finding in it elements of immediate importance to Henry James "in his own family situation." We need not accept Trilling's particular match-ups to agree with his thesis. It is not the Princess, for example, who is drawn from Alice James (as Trilling thinks), but rather Paul Muniment's "small, odd, crippled, chattering sister" Rosy. She has lost the use of her limbs and is permanently bedridden. She is a "hard, bright creature, polished, as it were, by pain," who never spoke of her privations. She is "so miserable, and yet so lively"; she is "up on everything"—and especially the wondrous carryings-on of the aristocracy. Here, to be sure, in making Rosy Muniment an admirer of the English upper class, Henry was turning the real-life original inside out. It was his private joke; and his radically inclined sister seems to have shared it with him. Alice had a special affection for the book, as it were an understanding with it. She took it, she said to William, as "one of those things apart that one rejoices in keeping & having to one's self," and was scornful of William for failing to appreciate it.*

Pressing his case, Trilling calls *The Princess Casamassima* "an intensely autobiographical book," in the sense that it constitutes for Henry James a personal act, another maneuver in an old family debate. In the novel's tightening tension between the values of art and of action we can see a version of the overt and covert conversation on the general theme that Henry and William had been conducting since the 1860s, with the father, via his essays, extolling and denouncing the role of art, supplying ammunition for both sides. Nor is there any difficulty in

---

* Hyacinth does not like Rosy Muniment, and it may be that the average reader does not either. James also seems not to have liked her; but what was more important, he *understood* her: understood, that is, not only her snobbishness but her essentially tyrannizing nature.

(Above) Daniel Gibbens, 1864
(Below) Alice Howe Gibbens, 1872

(Above) Robertson James in Milwaukee, 1872
(Below) Garth Wilkinson James in Milwaukee, 1873
(Opposite, top) Kitty Prince, about 1868
(Right) Mary Holton, 1870
(Bottom) Alice Howe James with firstborn, Harry, 1879–80

(*Opposite, top*) Henry Senior, portrait
y Frank Duveneck, 1880. (*Bottom*)
5 Irving Street, winter 1888. (*Above*)
Villiam James, April 1887. (*Right*)
Ienry James, March 1890

(*Opposite, top*) The William James home in Chocorua. (*Bottom*) William James and Margaret Mary (Peggy), March 1892. (*Right*) Robertson James in the early 1890s. (*Below*) William James in Keene Valley, 1890s

(Above) Alice James in her Kensington lodgings, 1891
(Below) Alice James and Katharine Loring in their Leamington lodgings, 1889–90

discerning aspects of William James, the former chemistry student, in the affably domineering and older-brotherly Paul Muniment; and of Henry James in Hyacinth, with his constant openness to impressions (he was, Henry says, quoting from himself in "The Art of Fiction," "a youth on whom nothing was lost"), and his staunchness—it is not snobbery, in context it is almost the opposite of snobbery—in declaring the irreducible importance of the great artistic achievements. In the climax, little Hyacinth is shown to be the most daring of the local conspirators, and seemingly more closely connected to the center of power than either Muniment or the Princess; and this Trilling reads as Henry's sly statement about the superior potency, or adventurousness, of the artist and his profession.

The narrative is too ambiguous in its later moments for so final an interpretation of the issue. But we can again remind ourselves that the issue itself—"art" versus "action" would be only a belated formulation of it—appeared in Henry James's earliest Civil War stories, and had turned up periodically ever since. It had been a binding theme in *The Bostonians*, where the old fraternal diversity took the form of a tangled opposition between public and private: a public career of platform exhortations, and a private life of human intimacies. The theme would be pluralized in *The Tragic Muse* of 1890, with politics, painting, the theatrical profession, diplomacy, and aestheticism all vying for primacy.

ITALIAN HOURS

With two vast novelistic constructs completed in a little more than three years (for six months, from September 1885 onward, *The Bostonians* and *The Princess Casamassima* were running side by side in the *Century* and *The Atlantic*), Henry, giving off audible sighs of relief in letters to friends and family, departed for Italy on the first of December 1886. On the night train from France, he read Howells's new novel, *The Minister's Charge*, admiring it greatly, as he told his old friend, and turning the pages with the aid of a reading lamp while the train roared through the St. Gotthard tunnel. In Milan the next day he strolled about in "the delicious Italian sun," quite overcome by "the sweet sense of being once more—after an interval of several years [nearly six years]—in the adorable country it illumines." By December 7, he was in Florence.

He had planned an Italian stay of a few months at most, being apprehensive about leaving the De Vere Gardens flat uninhabited for a longer period, and afraid that his "domestics," uneasy souls that they were, might be demoralized by their master's protracted absence. But at the turn of the year Alice was able to move into the apartment and take over the running of it. Through the fall and early winter she had been living in rooms found for her by Henry on Gloucester Road, one short block from De Vere Gardens. But that situation proved unsatisfactory, and Alice carried her belongings and herself over to her brother's ampler quarters with distinct pleasure. Henry now felt free to extend the Italian visit indefinitely.*

Henry spent ten weeks in Florence before going on to Venice, and it was his ripest experience of the place. For the balance of December, he had the use of an apartment in Villa Brichieri, a roomy mansion with a decaying Renaissance exterior on the hilltop of Bellosguardo (above the south side of the Arno), which he remembered from earlier days. The villa was leased to Henry's friend of several years, Constance Fenimore Woolson; she herself for the moment was staying in Villa Castellani nearby, as a guest of Francis Boott. The two of them, Henry and Fenimore (his usual name for her: Alice James called her Constance), had first met in Florence in 1879, and had seen something of each other, of late, in London. She was a forty-six-year-old spinster, a niece of James Fenimore Cooper, and a gifted writer, thus far of regional tales set near the Great Lakes and in the Carolinas, Tennessee, and Florida. She was becoming an addicted Florentine, and two of her best future stories ("Dorothy" and "A Florentine Experiment") were set in and near the city. Henry James, who would have no hesitation in addressing a laudatory essay to "Miss Woolson" in 1887, spoke of her in letters as his "amiable and distinguished friend," as a "*méticuleuse* old maid" who was also "an excellent and sympathetic being," even though "almost impracticably deaf." When Fenimore assumed her occupancy of Villa Brichieri, Henry installed himself in his old hotel fronting the river on Piazza Goldoni.

From the instant of his arrival on the Tuscan scene, Henry was plunged into a whirlwind of social activity. He was " 'going out' here a good deal," he said; he was being " 'lionized.' " The society, which he now had the opportunity to anatomize, was a "queer, promiscuous

* There is a comic rhythm to the siblings' urban displacements. Alice takes rooms in Bolton Row, around the corner from Henry, who very shortly shifts base across London to De Vere Gardens. Alice, after an interval, settles virtually next door to him, and Henry leaves for Italy. Whatever else, Henry's alternating desire to be close to and distant from his sister seems apparent.

polyglot affair"; bad French was the chief form of social exchange in the international set. But he was drawn to Adolf von Hildebrand (the name to be distinguished from Henry's earlier philosophical acquaintance, Karl Hillebrand), a German sculptor of power and possibly of genius, whose Villa San Francesco di Paola lay at the foot of the Bellosguardo hill; Henry regarded him as the most interesting male he met during the stay. He also struck up a lasting and valuable friendship with Dr. William Wilberforce Baldwin, an American physician in his late thirties who had been practicing in Florence for some years. And he at last came to know Janet Ross, the intimidating leader of the English community and an accomplished student of Florentine history: "an odd mixture," Henry told Sarah Wister, "of the British female and the dangerous woman."

"The most intelligent person" in Florence, Henry came to decide, was Violet Paget, who had adopted the name Vernon Lee in part to honor her half-brother Eugene Lee-Hamilton. Miss Lee "received" every day between four and seven at 5 Via Garibaldi, just off the Lungarno, where she looked after her brother (the latter, a former member of the British diplomatic corps, was suffering from complete paralysis, but would later recover the full use of his legs). Henry dropped by frequently, to join and listen to the conversation. "She is disputatious and paradoxical, but a really superior talker," he told Edmund Gosse. Henry was properly respectful of Vernon Lee's intellectually vivid studies of Renaissance and eighteenth-century Italy, but deplored her novel of 1884, *Miss Brown*, the more so since it was dedicated to him.

One January afternoon, there appeared at Via Garibaldi a striking and (in Henry's estimation) exceedingly amusing woman, Contessa Gamba, whose husband was the nephew of Teresa Guiccioli, Byron's beautiful Venetian mistress, his "last attachment." The Gambas had fallen heir to a number of letters written by Byron in Italian to "the Guiccioli," but they refused to let them be seen. They shed a bad light on Lord Byron, the Contessa said; and Henry recorded in his notebook with a shiver that "she had *burned* one of them." The sofa-bound Lee-Hamilton, hearing this, launched into an anecdote about a certain Captain Silsbee, a passionate admirer of Shelley.

Silsbee learned that Claire Clairmont, another mistress of Byron and the mother of his daughter Allegra, was living in Florence at the age of eighty, with her niece, a younger Miss Clairmont of perhaps fifty. The two women possessed letters by both Shelley and Byron; and Silsbee took lodgings with them in the aim of somehow getting hold of the papers. The old woman died while Silsbee was in residence; "and then," Henry wrote in his notebook, "he approached the younger one—the old maid of 50—on the subject of his desires. Her answer was—'I will give you all the letters if you marry me!' " Silsbee, Lee-Hamilton said, was still running.

Henry felt sure that there was "a little subject there," and he took it with him when he went on by train to Venice on February 22. It lay alongside two other ideas for stories jotted down in the same entry: one of them (suggested by a bit of London gossip from Alice) became "The Marriages," and the other "Louisa Pallant."

In Venice, Henry was housed by Mrs. Katherine De Kay Bronson, an American woman who had been living in the city for a decade (both Henry and William had visited her, separately). Her home, Palazzino—or Ca' for Casa—Alvisi, was on the Grand Canal, at its mouth, a step away from Piazza San Marco and directly across the canal from the big doors of the Church of Santa Maria della Salute. Mrs. Bronson was hospitality incarnate for incoming Anglo-Americans. Robert Browning stayed there for a month at a time, and Browning's son, Pen, had only just departed after a three-month visit. Henry was established in an annex to Ca'Alvisi, to the rear, called Casa Giustiniani-Recanati. He settled in and began to write.

For several weeks he worked away assiduously, strolled across the bridges and through the piazzas, sat at Florian's café and mingled with the flow of guests at Ca'Alvisi. But in mid-March he began to be afflicted with violent headaches, followed by an attack of jaundice— "a most loathsome malady"—with a fever. He was kept to his bed for sixteen days, "the *longest* illness I have had," he wrote William in April, "since I was laid up with typhoid fever, so many years ago, at Boulogne." Henry's new friend Dr. Baldwin diagnosed the case by letter from Florence; by early April, Alice, from De Vere Gardens, passed on to Mrs. Alice the good news the Henry was sitting up and, as a good convalescent, eating a mutton chop. Henry wanted to complete his recovery in the "salubrious" air of Bellosguardo, so back he went around the middle of the month, to take up the apartment in Villa Brichieri.

Florence from this vantage point assumed for Henry James the aspect of a revelation. There spread out before and below him, he said, the most beautiful view on earth. It was the whole of the city, set forth by the curving river and its bridges, shaped by visible vestiges of the old circuit of walls, punctuated by Duomo and Campanile, façades and jutting palace towers and orange-tiled roofs: all dun-colored beauty and history and personal associations. Henry walked down into the town almost every day for dinner, climbing up the steep hillside afterward (a strenuous exercise, be it noted) in the gentle spring evening. His surroundings were peaceful and spacious, he told William, and he was working very well, although—and this note of alarm would deepen—"my productions bury themselves—indefinitely apparently, in the *Century* and *Harper.*"

In Bellosguardo, Henry finished the novella *The Aspern Papers*, the story evolving out of Lee-Hamilton's anecdote. The narrative follows that anecdote in its essentials, with the narrator enacting the role of Silsbee, insinuating himself into the home of an old woman and her niece in the hope of getting his hands on letters written to her years before by a long-dead poet. But James transferred the action from Florence to Venice, and he transformed the aunt and niece, the Misses Bordereau, into faded old American women. The poet-lover became Jeffrey Aspern of New York, one of the first to show that great literature was possible in America. The city is not mentioned, but James tells us in a later preface that he was *thinking* New York when he projected Aspern: not his own New York of the 1850s, but the New York his grandmother Walsh and to an extent his mother and Aunt Kate could have reminisced about to him. This was what he meant, in the same preface, when he spoke of delighting in "a palpable imaginable *visitable* past"; something one could reach back to and inhabit through the memories of forebears.

The familial American past mingles with the contemporary Venetian setting, and both gain animation from other personal and authorial concerns and anxieties. Amid the ambiguities of relationship and moral posture, a main ambiguity—it is unresolved through the story's final sentence—is in the narrator's perception of the niece, Tina Bordereau. To his eyes, at a key moment, she almost changes into a beautiful woman, like the old crone in the Wife of Bath's tale. The flickering vision may (this has been suggested) reflect a kind of ambivalence on Henry James's part toward Fenimore Woolson, who was occupying rooms on the floor below Henry's in Villa Brichieri while he was writing *The Aspern Papers*. But Fenimore, deafness, shyness, and all, was a far more resolute being than poor Tina, and the literary connection is tenuous.

A more urgent concern, and this would become a passion in the years ahead, was the fate of personal letters, whether—in the case of "public" personalities—they should be published or withheld.* Larger still is James's communicated consciousness of himself as a literary artist of very considerable achievement and immense ambition; a modern-day Aspern, lionized and deferred to in Florence and Venice; an *American*, with genuine if sparse native literary precursors, pursuing his career and solidifying his identity amid the richness and decay of the Old World.

The Italian visit of 1886–87 ushered in the most productive period of James's career in the shorter fictional form; and what we notice about these tales is the number of them that have to do with art and the artist, with the relation between art and life, and not less with the way art can be seen as an analogy for all other modes of conduct. To mention only stories written during the Italian sojourn or soon after Henry's return to London, we have an item about the mother as artist ("Louisa Pallant," in which the mother bitterly regrets creating a daughter—"the work of my hand"—who has turned out to be a kind of monster); the prevaricator as artist ("The Liar," in which the delightful Colonel Capadose is seen by the narrator as lying not for personal gain but out of a devotion to art, "a love of beauty"); and the butler as artist ("Brooksmith," in which the habitués of a London salon discover that the butler, Brooksmith, is responsible for the supremely artful arrangements of the place—"Brooksmith . . . was the artist").

As April 1887 passed into May, Florence continued to beguile. The bells of the city (Henry remarked) talked to him from a distance all day long; and he enthused over a procession of Florentine nobles, dressed in the costumes of their medieval ancestors to celebrate the unveiling of the new façade of the Duomo. He took pleasure in the daily commerce with Fenimore Woolson, aware perhaps (as she had hinted) that with her increasing deafness she appreciated the clarity and resonance of his voice. He escorted her to churches and galleries, though not presumably to the Basilica of San Lorenzo where, on an earlier Florentine tour, the vigorous nudity of Michelangelo's reclining figures had shaken her composure.

But Venice was also making its call. At the start of summer, Henry

---

* To *The Aspern Papers*, in this regard, we may add a somber comedy called "The Abasement of the Northmores," in which a collection of uninterruptedly fatuous letters by a once-omnipresent public figure puts an end to his reputation; and a nice ghostly tale of the same era (1900), "The Real Right Thing," which gives us a dead writer who returns from the grave to haunt his would-be biographer away from his private papers once and for all. (See also Chapter Eighteen, on Henry James in 1910 destroying the letters written to him over decades.)

accepted an invitation from Daniel and Ariana Curtis to stay with them in their Palazzo Barbaro, on the Grand Canal next to the Accademia bridge (William had also come by here for a call). Henry spent five weeks in the palazzo, composing one longer tale and several shorter ones in the time. Musing over the first of these, *A London Life*, Henry recalled writing it in one of "the wonderful faded back rooms of an old Venetian palace"; a room with a Tiepolo ceiling and walls of slightly shredded pale-green damask. On warm mornings, the room "looked into the shade of a court where a high outer staircase, strikingly bold, yet strikingly relaxed, held together one scarce knew how." There were Gothic windows at irregular levels; and one could always hear, outside, "the strong Venetian voice . . . waking perpetual echos." All of it would be remembered—the staircase, the Gothic windows, the echoing voice—as the final gracious dimming enclosure of Milly Theale in *The Wings of the Dove*.

THE ROYAL SPA

Alice had been finding the apartment in De Vere Gardens like a scene from *The Arabian Nights*, after what she called "the squalor" of her last two years. She had also discovered that it was drafty—she was as always extremely vulnerable to chill—and said that the library was uninhabitable in the winter months. But it gave her a sense of private home, and she could busy herself in it of a morning writing down quotations of special meaning to her in a leatherbound copybook, a practice she began just before Christmas 1886. The quotations spoke of death (from the *Rubaiyat*: "The wine of life keeps oozing drop by drop"), the enhancing power of suffering (from Flaubert), the human relation (from Henry: "The nearness counts so as distance"; and from herself: "The frightful separateness of human experiences").*

She professed herself thrilled to learn by a postcard from William that Mrs. Alice had given birth to a baby girl in late March (1887). Upon hearing that her sister-in-law was pregnant again, she had issued congratulations conditional upon Mrs. Alice showing herself "able to produce one of the nobler sex," a creature moreover of "Gibbensian

---

* Jean Strouse (262–70) lists and discusses the quotations selected by Alice for the commonplace book, and surveys Alice's reading in this period: Montaigne, Zola, George Sand, Flaubert, Maupassant, Carlyle, Dickens, George Eliot (especially *The Mill on the Floss*), Tolstoy, Miss Woolson, "everything Henry wrote," and a great deal more.

softness," with none of that "Jamesian asperity which has led to sour spinsterhood in the one feminine bosom which the race rose to bringing forth." The same mixture of tone—spirited and bitter—was audible in the response to the birth itself. "That 'he is a girl' delights me," she wrote Mrs. Alice. The whole atmosphere of the house would be improved: "You & she will be two against three. Mother & I, however, maintained the fight more unequally still, two against five," and not, she thought, altogether successfully. She proposed naming the child Margaret, after Mrs. Alice's older sister. So it was to be, Margaret or, more often, Peggy, with the parents adding the middle name Mary after the younger sister.

In April, William wrote Alice a letter so rich in sympathy as to make her eyes water. One passage in it, though, she was inclined to protest: that "no matter how ill one is, 'This is life,' and consequently of value and to be clung to." Alice repeated a phrase she had copied into her book: "*Vivre c'est sentir la vie*," adding bleakly that if that were so "I never expect to be deader than I am now, not even after the worms have gorged themselves." Later in the spring, she came down with some kind of "bad little illness" and, with Katharine returned to her, felt ready to go up to Leamington again. She reported to William and his Alice that the doctor she had summoned had examined her heart, which was acting up a bit, queried the protuberance of her eyeballs, and assured her solemnly, "You won't die, but you will live, suffering to the end."

The proper name for Leamington (pronounced Lemmington) was Royal Leamington Spa. Its mineral waters had made it a popular watering place since the late eighteenth century; people, mostly of the fashionable breed, came there for the treatment of gout—Dr. Garrod, the gout specialist, was the one to recommend it to Alice James—as well as for neuritis, obesity, and skin disease (of the latter, as Alice was wont to note, she was entirely free). It abounded in gardens and tree-lined avenues. Alice was settled in rooms at 11 Hamilton Terrace, just off the Parade, the town's main thoroughfare. Her living room, she told Aunt Kate, was the most comfortable "in the way of temperature" of any she had had, even though, facing north, it was sunless. Her bedroom looked south, and she could get the sun all morning until she arose about twelve-thirty. With the passage of time, she was able to make cautious outings in a Bath chair propelled by a man named Bowles, who had a disposition to tippling. To Sara Darwin, with the coming of fall, she wrote that though it would be "densely dull"— Katharine Loring had commuted back to her sister—she would spend the winter in Leamington. In fact, she remained there for three years, and at the same address.

Life at Hamilton Terrace was not so dull as to be without its moment of alarm. On the floor below there boarded a young clergyman, one of a pair of clerics, who, on her first visit the previous September, had drunkenly—and probably by mistake—tried to enter Alice's apartment. Henry, beckoned for at once by telegram, recounted the affair to Lizzie Boott. "They pretended they had been 'discussing theology' together below, and had become excited by so doing; but what they had been discussing was of course whiskey." The incident, Henry said, "including the row and the mess after it, made her very ill"; and was, for both Henry and Alice, an illustration "of what horrible little cads and beasts there are in the church of England." It was, in truth, a wretchedly disturbing experience for a woman of Alice James's precarious nervous and sexual balance; but a year later she could look back on it with a species of graveyard humor. To Sara Darwin in early October:

I am haunted . . . by the fear that I may be suddenly taken ill unto death & that before Henry can arrive to protect [,] my little ecclesiastical will introduce the curate to my bedside. Imagine opening your eyes & seeing that bat-like object standing there! I am sure it would curdle my soul in its transit & at any rate entirely spoil my post-mortem expression of countenance.

"My little ecclesiastical," Alice's churchgoing nurse, was in actuality tall, paper-thin, healthy, and eager to pick up scraps of learning from her patient.

Serio-satiric allusions to her own death, or to the fending off of it, alternated in Alice's observations with notes about the deaths of others. She had no present plans, she said to Sara Darwin, for drowning herself in the river Leam—unlike a certain butler who, according to her chair man Bowles, did just that after his master died. " 'is Lordship died, & it was like unto this, Miss, thank you, Miss, thank you, the butler became un'appy in 'is mind & put 'imself into the Leam, Miss." (If correct, the anecdote curiously anticipates brother Henry's tale "Brooksmith," wherein the butler fades out of existence in the wake of *his* master's death.) A much stronger jolt to Alice's sensibility was the violent death in November 1887 of Ellen Gurney.

She had, Alice learned, been reduced to near-madness by the suicide of her sister Clover Adams in December 1885 and the lingering illness and death of her husband, the Harvard history professor

Ephraim Gurney, the following autumn. Mrs. Gurney slipped out of her sickroom, wandered along the railroad tracks in west Cambridge, and was struck by a freight train. Alice assumed it was a case of suicide out of uncontrollable grief. She spoke of Ellen's "hideous" and "ghastly" act; it took on for her the form of a mythic rape—she could not get beyond the image of "that poor wandering body violated by that hideous iron monster."

Her own condition in the Leamington of 1887 was changeable. She had attacks "of all descriptions" more frequently than ever, she informed Aunt Kate in November, but she recovered from them more quickly than before and felt stronger in the intervals between. To William she made the familiar complaint that, though she experienced less pain and was not so tired as in the worst days, she was more subject to agitation than she had been. But in the same letter she exclaimed: "It is a wonderful time to be living," and that she was in a ferment of excitement over historical events, from the portentous to the transient. She was, after all, in the French maxim she had rejected, "feeling life." She was even able to palpitate over the America's Cup race and the victories of the American sloop *Volunteer* over the Scotch cutter *Thistle*.

CHAPTER TWELVE

A Gathering of Siblings: Leamington, 1889

SUMMONS FROM A BALCONY

On July 18, 1889, Henry and William traveled together from London to Leamington, arriving in the late morning. William had reached London and De Vere Gardens the day before, after a luxurious journey in a first-class compartment on the night train from Edinburgh. He had been a fortnight in the British Isles, divided equally between Ireland, which enthralled and troubled him, and Scotland, the experience of which led him to say to his wife, in a newly acquired accent, "I am dead in love wi' Scotland both land and people." In Leamington, Henry went off to have lunch with Alice and to give her the news of the two months since he had been with her. He told William that he would let Alice finish her lunch before announcing the brother's presence. If she survived the shock, Henry said, he would tie his handkerchief to the balcony outside her room, as a signal for William to advance.

William, in the interval, walked out to Warwick Castle, explored that picturesque feudal residence, and took his own lunch nearby. By two o'clock, the deadline indicated by Henry, William was back at 11 Hamilton Terrace, pacing nervously up and down. Three-quarters of an hour passed. Then "Harry's portly form" (as William described it to his wife) appeared on the balcony, beckoning energetically. William rushed upstairs. He found Alice lying on the bed, panting, half fainting, white as a sheet. Her arms were outstretched, and William threw himself into them.

The three had not been together, and Alice had not seen William, for five years.

THE INTELLECTUAL
AS FARMER AND HUSBAND

Alice had, of course, been in constant touch with her older brother, even though communication between them sometimes failed. She could rejoice at the news, in the fall of 1886, that William had purchased a farm, with surrounding acreage, on the shore of Lake Chocorua, New Hampshire, in the foothills of the White Mountains. As she heard details of William's restoring and furnishing the place, she was pleased to know that the things she had invited Mrs. Alice to take from the Boston storage would now come in handy. She urged again that they make use of any blankets and linen they might find in the trunks.

William had discovered the property in September when, again feeling out of sorts and grumpy (two days later he begged his wife's pardon "for all my gracelessness"), he took off on a jaunt through New Hampshire and into Maine. He was looking for a site on which to establish a summer home for the family, and after searching in vain in the neighborhood of Portsmouth (Maine), he came down into the White Mountains, and at Chocorua he hit upon something, he informed Alice, "which we might do worse than buy." To Henry, he was less guarded. There were, he wrote, "75 acres of land, mountain 3500 feet high, exquisite lake a mile long, fine oak and pine woods, valuable mineral spring, two houses and a barn, all for 900 dollars or possibly less. Two thousand five hundred dollars will give us the place in fine order." Some weeks later, Alice inspected the place and, rather to William's surprise, approved the purchase. It was concluded soon afterward.

Early in the following April, William came to Chocorua to find four feet of snow and drifts up to eight feet; prowling about the property, he fell through a crust up to his hip. He had come to make measurements and draw up plans, and also to get away from a Cambridge household currently upside down with the arrival of a new baby. Alice had given birth to the infant girl on March 24. William wrote back cheerily about possible names, and was more than pleased when—

with sister Alice's help, as has been said— Margaret Mary was chosen, for Alice's two sisters. Meanwhile, William sat at his ease before the wood fire at Chocorua House, sketching the local elevations.

Throughout the summer and into the fall, William devoted much of his time to making the new home livable and productive. He boasted to Alice, in July, that "we farmers" were blessed by living close to the soil, and expressed pity for the poor city folk. He had that day spent the morning going about the countryside looking to swap his recently purchased horse Lucy for a superior mount, and deciding to stick with Lucy. (His son Henry would contend that William was not the shrewdest of horse traders.) He bought himself a wagon and gossiped enjoyably with "the natives." He then put in three hours digging holes, bringing manure, and planting and watering two dozen tomato plants.

He dutifully planted potatoes, ordered raspberry and gooseberry bushes, and put out $500 for an additional meadow. In late July, he and Alice switched places—he came away with a haunting image of Alice riding off in the rain atop Lucy—and William went back to Cambridge and his work. From Cambridge, he issued a steady stream of detailed instructions: about doors, windows, screens, locks; draining the ditches; how to measure the field and lawn by pacing; the planting of two "sweet bough" apple trees he had ordered—she was to dig holes three feet across and twenty inches deep on the open land toward the pond, cover them with two inches of manure, and that with two inches of earth. Alice stayed on through October, faithfully carrying out her husband's orders. Her "administration of the works" was wonderful, William wrote her; and though she secretly felt rather dismal and isolated, she wrote William letters of a "high, sanguine, joyous, successful note."

On a later tour of duty, however, Alice evidently let slip something of her New Hampshire state of mind. William, in response, said that he had just then realized that her feverish activity at Chocorua was "the expression of a desperate soul seeking to forget itself in outward work" and that he was obtuse not to have seen this sooner. He hastened up to join his wife for a month, an experience, he then wrote, that "entwined us singularly around each other." The interlude led to a basic question about their involvement with the summer place, which William posed in a manner characteristic of his philosophical outlook. Should they, he said, be "gentlemen farmers," or should they be mere spectators?

At summer's end, 1887, William sent Henry a sketch of the property: the ample James Wing running north and south, the Gibbens

Wing (for Alice's mother and sister Margaret) protruding to the west, kitchen and shed to the rear, a piazza running around two-thirds of the house, a vegetable garden close by, and, across the road, the barn; farther south, the lake. "The house is very prettily shaped," he wrote, ". . . and has eleven outside doors, so that the rooms are all independent of each other and individual and characteristic in shape." William obviously carried his belief in individuality even into the interior makeup of houses. To his sister, it might be said, William had exulted that the farmhouse had "14 doors all opening outside"—three had since been removed—and recalling this, Alice commented to her diary: "His brain isn't limited to 14, perhaps unfortunately."

William had given Henry other details earlier: the James Wing contained ten large rooms, two of them 24-by-24, and three small ones; a hearth four feet wide; and a woodpile "as large as an ordinary house." If Henry wanted some "real, roomy, rustic happiness," William said, "you had better come over and spend all your summers with us." He could see that the mere thought made Henry sick: "so I'll say no more about it, but my permanent vision of your future is that your pen will fail you as a means of support, and having laid up no income, you will return like a prodigal to my roof." Henry, in Bellosguardo under Fenimore Woolson's roof, referred to the letter as "long and delightful," and made no mention of the dark prophecy about himself. It was perhaps meant as no more than minimally serious, but one part of it (about literary income) would befall as William claimed to foresee.

For Henry's benefit as well, William supplied intermittent reports on the progress of his *Psychology*. In April 1885, he had written Henry with some glee that the work was now truly under way, and he hoped to finish it by the fall of 1886: "Then shall the star of your romances be eclipst." In fact, quite a few portions of the book were already in print by this date and needed only to be revised, rounded out, and fitted into the volume's structure. Much of the chapter on "Reasoning" had appeared in the *Journal of Speculative Philosophy* in July 1878, while William and Alice were on their Adirondacks honeymoon. Sizable parts of the chapters on "Association" and "Will" were published in the course of the year 1880, and a good deal of the chapter called "The Stream of Thought" came out in *Mind* in January 1884. It should be remembered, too, that William spent most of 1883 and half the year following compiling his father's *Literary Remains*, a work that has come powerfully into its own in our time, but whose reception and sales in 1885 were chillingly disappointing (a mindless and uninformed review in *The Nation* elicited from William one of the few losses of temper in his public, as opposed to his private, life).

A Gathering of Siblings: Leamington, 1889

Eye trouble and insomnia, the latter sometimes due to intellectual excitement, caused frequent delays. In the first days of 1886, William explained to Carl Stumpf why the book was going so slowly: "No sooner do I get interested than bang! goes my sleep, and I have to stop a week or ten days, during which my ideas get all cold again." A year later he was "still troubled with bad sleep," he wrote Stumpf, but few days went by "without a line at least." William regularly understated his accomplishment. The entire chapter on "The Perception of Time" had appeared in October 1886, and 1887 saw the publication of the sections on "Habit" (intact in *Popular Science Monthly*, an odd repository for that essay with its Emersonian peroration), "Instinct," and "The Perception of Space."

It was a decidedly impressive showing. But William kept a measuring eye on his brother's output and was fully aware that Henry had two immense novels running simultaneously in two journals for half a year in 1885–86. In March of the prolific 1887, William wrote Henry that he had reason to hope that the *Psychology* would be done in another year, and went on: "How you produce volume after volume the way you do is more than I can conceive, but you haven't forged every sentence in the teeth of irreconcileable and stubborn facts as I do." He struck the same combination of notes in subsequent letters.

His "immortal work," William declared in April, was "more than two thirds done. To you, who throw off two volumes a year, I must seem despicable for my slowness." The trouble, he averred, lay in the " 'science' " of psychology; it was "in such a confused and imperfect state that every paragraph presents some unforeseen snag, and I often spend many weeks on a point I didn't foresee as a difficulty at all." In September, he addressed Henry in a mood of jaunty combativeness. He really did expect to finish the work before the next winter was through. Henry would be amused by his slowness of pace: "But almost every page of this book of mine is written against a resistance which you know nothing of in your resistless air of romance, resistance of facts to begin with, each one of which must be bribed to be on one's side, and the resistance of other philosophers to end with"—Helmholtz and Spencer were cited—"each one of which must be slain."

"Resistance," as has often been seen, was a key factor in William's evaluation of valid human action and significant human life; and he seems to have persuaded himself that novels like *The Bostonians* and *The Princess Casamassima* got written against only the slightest amount of it. But there was something like a metaphysical notion at play here, as there was a conventional literary attitude. In his introduction to the

Literary Remains, William had remarked approvingly that "For Mr. James a mere resistless 'bang' is no creative process at all."* Juxtaposed to this, the comment to Henry just quoted suggests that, for William, what Henry was doing was not really creative. Creativity involved struggle, the battle against some nearly intractable opposition, like the stubborn facts of mental behavior; but Henry wrote fact-free "romances."

It is true that most of the romances visited upon the American public across the century gave the impression of having come into being after the slightest of efforts. But for one thing, Henry had insisted for some time that (in the old generic distinction) his fictional writings were novels rather than romances, and that, as novels, they should be regarded essentially as *histories*. For another thing, no novelist in his time was more emphatic about the strenuous act of making, the severe struggle, that the creation of fiction required. For the euphorically teasing William, however, he was the one who dealt with facts, and Henry only with the airy stuff of romance.

In mid-January 1888, young Billy had a recurrence of the asthma with which he was occasionally afflicted and which made him peevish. Alice took the two boys and their infant sister down to the warming climate of Aiken, South Carolina, accompanied by her mother, her sister Margaret, and a German *Fraülein*, recently taken on. Husband and wife were separated for four months, and in the course of his daily dispatches, William, as he had before, sought to elicit from Alice a greater candor of expression and intensity of feeling than she normally allowed herself.

He liked her letters from Chocorua, he had told her the previous October, but could wish for "more sentiment" in them. In an attempt to bestir such response, William risked a nearly overt sexual allusion. He hoped she would return to Cambridge soon: "God knows, dear girl, that I have use enough for you when you come—even if we do have another child, I'm willing." He hurried on: "I trust you are not offended by the perhaps somewhat too transparent sense of these remarks. They need not go into the archives if you wish it not." Alice, at that time, sent him suitably "tender words," as William acknowledged, saying that he was "indeed rather starved for the like of them." From South Carolina the following January, Alice wrote letters that William declared to be "more of love letters than almost any you ever

---

* The passage went on: "A *real* creation means nothing short of a real *bringing to life* of the essential nothingness, which is the eternal antithesis to God."

wrote me." He was "uplifted," and fell to thinking about their early marriage days.*

He simply fed on her words of affection, William wrote; her letters were truly *"impassioned."* But in February, Alice's tone changed. She seemed troubled. Was Aiken not working out satisfactorily? William asked. She should hold nothing back: "Let your letters reveal every cloud that blows across the beautiful surface of your soul, as mine do mine." In reply, Alice indicated her distress at William saying he would like to kiss their servant Lizzie goodbye. But he often wanted to kiss other females, William protested; why should he not? The exchange continued for a few days, until William remarked that it was absurd of Alice to discourse at such length, as she did, about his "philosophy of kissing." He did bestow a farewell kiss on Lizzie, telling her she was a good girl. Soon, in her letters, Alice—so William told her, re- joicing—expressed a self that was "so free, so passionate, so powerful, so proud."

On a Sunday afternoon in early March, William wrote Alice what he later called "the fattest & (from the sentimental point of view) the most important" letter he had ever addressed to her. He had gone up- stairs the night before, he said, driven by what impulse he could not say, and had extracted from "the mystical portfolio . . . a lot of letters to *Mrs. W. James."* He sat reading them till past midnight, and arose at six the next morning to take from the portfolio "the letters to Miss Alice Gib- bens, and read *them* through." It was a strange experience, he wrote, of which he could hardly give a clear account. More painful than pleasant, perhaps, but very instructive. He was glad he had done it.

A stranger, reading those letters alone, would think of a man morally utterly diseased. That you, having read them, should still have been willing to risk things with me, seems to me now most surprising. I have got out of that whole frame of mind, not by any acute change or act or discovery, but simply, grad- ually, and by living with you, and it now seems so far off as to belong not only to another person, but almost to another kind of person.

Knowing what he then did know about himself, and revering Alice as he did, William continued, he was

* William wished more than once, as he confessed, that he had not destroyed the letters of those days. He also spoke of preserving Alice's letters of 1887 and 1888 for "the family archives." Since they have not, in fact, survived, it may be guessed that it was Mrs. Alice who burned them—as she could not bring herself to do, evidently, with the letters from her husband.

right, right, right, to feel torn asunder . . . and perplexed in the extreme. The only wonder was that I got through it alive at all. My scruples were not fantastical. No decently feeling man can be a sinner and look with equanimity towards playing the part in the world's life of a sound member. And dearest, now that you know what you then didn't know, you too can see that the whole thing had its inward law and truer logic. Your answering trust too had its logic, its truest logic of all, which has wrought out through all these swamps and valleys of our pilgrimage now over, my transformation into the normal man and husband you have now, to whom all that chapter of expression is a thing for ever closed, but whom it has made wise morally in a way impossible by any less costly means. Oh! the reality of the moral life—that is what all those poor pages with their writhings and turnings back, and homages to you, confess. I doubt if there were ever a more *real* struggle enacted in this world. Darling, I bow my head in awe before the whole thing, and in praise before its practical solution. It has been solved not by theory but by act, by your active answering faith and benignity.

. . . One sweetest thing emerges from these letters, love, and that is *your* personal identity and continuity. They bring back the touch of the old A.H.G.; and those prostrations, and adorations, and superlatives are still the way in which I now feel I ought rightly to have taken you. Sacred, spotless, good, divine you were then, divine are you, dearest, now. You had of course the character of ethereality, and intangibility in my eyes, which you have exchanged for that of substantiality.

. . . But I can't put all this down on paper! How I *do* wish you were here, my own, own, sacred love and mistress of my being! Then, with you telling your half and I telling my half, we could straighten out the whole story and let the letters burn. No third eye ought ever to fall upon them. I came near burning them this morning, but regarding them as in some sort no longer mine, I locked them back in the portfolio, where they await your return.

Then, after some news of the Syracuse holdings (an offer of $45,000 had been made for a portion of it) and a word on travel plans, William signed himself with "Love unutterable."

The word "moral" in William James's vocabulary invariably had to do with the intelligent and forceful exercise of will; and behind the hyperbolic self-accusations—"a man morally utterly diseased"—one senses the older William convicting the younger of a nearly disastrous failure of will in the courtship days. (In the chapter called "Will" in *The Principles of Psychology*, the author would describe "the obstructed will" as one of the two chief forms of *unhealthiness* in the voluntary power.*) He was recalling the time when he had permitted his murky intellectual ambitions to befog his relationship with Alice Gibbens, and before that phase was over, we remember, he was excoriating himself for his "impotence."

But from the vantage point of eleven years later, William was sure that, though he had been grievously at fault in his performance, he had been entirely right to feel the issue as a rending one. What was at stake was nothing less than "the reality of the moral life"—the whole phenomenon, and career, of the individual will. Here, as almost always, William's configuration of philosophic ideas interacted with his emotional dilemmas; and we hear the quintessential William James, when he says that the tremendous struggle was "solved not by theory but by act"—the "active answering faith" of Alice Gibbens.

A week later, William was all agog, as he wrote, for Alice's response "to that thick letter" of the fourth. "I hope it will be *warm.*" A number of days, however, would elapse before a reply from Alice arrived. A winter of unusually heavy snowfalls and freezing cold came to its climax in the second week of March with a blizzard that brought all mail services to a halt. Cambridge and New England were in fact passing through what would be known historically as the "Blizzard of '88." It was not until March 18 that the mails were again opened and a batch of letters from Aiken reached William at Garden Street. The last of them, in William's paraphrase, said that Alice and he, in that long moment of trial, had "probed the depths of good and evil, and fear and trust, in a way that can't be forgotten"; and William agreed fervently. A follow-up letter from Alice was evidently couched in more warmly emotional language.

Her way of referring to 1878, William wrote back, thrilled him. His own style grew ardent again:

Methinks, my love, that we are growing more and more infatuated with each other by living apart. It is becoming a sort of second edition of that primal estrangement, where imagination took the place of deeds. But it *will* make us intimate when we come together again, won't it dear? I rejoice so tremendously in this accession of freedom and moral lustihood on your part, and hope it will never fade.

* This section of the chapter was published in *Scribner's Magazine* in February 1888, a few weeks before the letter to Alice here being quoted; it gained him more success (William told his wife on February 29) than all his previous articles taken together. See also, below, p. 440.

In May, while Alice was preparing to make her way back to Cambridge (Margaret and the boys having come on ahead of her), William was able to transmit a singularly poetic word of praise. He had been talking with Mrs. Royce, the wife of his departmental colleague, who confided that when she had first come to Cambridge she had fallen in love with Alice. She had said as much to Ephraim Gurney, who replied: "Yes, she has eyes like a prayer, and I should be in love with her myself, if I dared to." Underlining the phrase about Alice's eyes, William remarked: "That is just the expression I have been seeking all my life."

KINFOLK AND COLLEAGUES

William, in these months, kept his wife informed about other members of the Gibbens and James families. In January, he passed on the telegraphed announcement from Chicago that Alice's sister Mary, now Mrs. William Salter, had given birth to a baby girl to be named Eliza. William Mackintyre Salter—"Mack"—had entered the scene a few years earlier. He had spent part of the summer of 1885 in Keene Valley and on an afternoon stroll with William had acknowledged that he had "made a proposal to Mary." William was favorably impressed by him. "I should welcome him as a brother in law," he wrote Alice, "altho' a poor man because he is doing something worth trying to live for, and in which *some* success is certain, and failure is perhaps a good deal better than other successes." Salter was occupied with writing and lecturing for the Ethical Culture Society in Chicago, an intellectually philanthropic organization, so to say, and would before very long earn a fairly wide reputation.

William thought him unduly laggard as a lover, and advised him to get himself to Cambridge as soon as he could. The encounter drew from William a reflection, at once amused and defensive, about the phenomenon under view. Salter's "slow ignition," he wrote, "is apparently connected with a sort of philosophical sense of leisure rather than with a lack of power to feel. A woman can *never* understand a philosopher before marriage,—rarely after." Salter, age thirty-three, and Mary Gibbens, a year older, were married in December 1885. They settled in Chicago, where they were visited regularly by Mrs. Gibbens and Margaret, and they came East most summers to Cambridge and Chocorua.

In the same January week of Eliza Salter's birth, William recounted a visit to his cousin Kitty Prince in a Boston insane asylum: "Much improved, same old smile and beautiful manner." It was a heartening contrast to her appearance three months before, when William found her sitting with her face to the wall, her hair down her back, talking to herself steadily in a low voice and paying no attention to him. But even now she harbored the delusion that she was a Madame K. C. Telle, and that her late husband had been a lineal descendant of "King Guillaume Telle," and that he held conversations with her by means of inward speech. William found that delusion persisting when he took Kitty for a drive to the Cambridge cemetery in April. Kitty's actual husband, Dr. Prince, had died about a year earlier; it was the grief following his loss that had caused this particular mental collapse. Given the fact, William was of the opinion that chronic insanity was perhaps the best condition for his cousin. She was absolutely happy, very sweet, and physically strong.

There were moments that winter when William wondered whether his brother Bob might not himself be verging on insanity. Bob had been living in Concord with his wife, going up into New Hampshire for some painting occasionally, but more often drinking heavily, quarreling with Mary, and hurling incoherent charges at William: a fairly fixed pattern. On the evening of February 1, Bob stormed out of the house, spent the night in Boston, and returned next day in woeful condition. Summoned by Mary's telegram, William found his brother with cuts and bruises on his face and no recollection of where he had been. He "was in a most pathetic mood," William told Alice, "praying to be confined, saying he was really insane, etc." Edward Emerson, Bob's neighbor and old-time schoolmate, advised that Bob be placed in the local reformatory—that is, the prison—where he would be forced to work. That experience, William thought, would "legitimately drive Bob mad." His letter was written at 1:00 a.m. in the station at Hartford, Connecticut, where William had come to arrange for Bob's admission into the institution run by a Dr. Crothers.

William's diagnosis, sent on to Henry, was somber: "Of course cure is hopeless, I think, his brain is getting more set in these irascible grooves, but there are no delusions properly so called, and he isn't technically insane . . . The only manly and moral thing for a man in his plight is to kill himself; but Bob will ne'er do that." The remarks echoed those William had made to Henry the previous April. Bob's case was incurable, William said then, "because his drinking comes from his pathological mental condition which is part of his very nature. He has *no* affection. And yet in his crises he goes through the emotional expression of an angel . . . But I wish the poor wretch could die in one of his bad sprees—it would be so much future misery averted for him as well as for the family."

Bob's treatment of Mary had for many months been scandalous and brutal, in William's view, yet she stuck to him "like a burr." She was wholly devoted, "quite anchored to his fortunes, without hope of release." Luckily, the couple had $3,000 a year well invested, as William observed to both Alice and Henry; and Bob had long since signed a deed making Joseph Warner, the lawyer, and William trustees of his Syracuse property, parts of which he was frequently tempted to sell to support his private indulgences. "Poor dreary dreary boy," William said in summary to Alice. "Why some of us are doomed to such lives and others to such different ones, it is impossible to see on any just ground." As a statement about the mystery of human destiny, it had a sad relevance; but William James would perhaps have been better able "to see" had the particular case not been that of his own brother. William's personality and successes were obviously among the immediate causes of the churning discontent and sense of failure by which Bob James was bedeviled.

William and his family reassembled at Chocorua in the latter part of June. We may identify its members in the 1888 summer: William himself, at forty-six, stocky and sturdy and with a swift rhythmical way of moving, displaying a full beard, mustache, and sideburns, hair thinning on top, eyes singularly intent; Alice, thirty-nine, with her firm attractive features, her erect carriage and aura of New England reticence and composure; Harry, now nine years old; Billy, just six; and Margaret Mary—alternately called Peggy—barely sixteen months.

One July afternoon, William came downstairs in search of an envelope for a letter to Henry, and came upon a scene he could not resist picturing for his brother. Peering out onto a grassy plot in back, formed by the angle of the house and kitchen and shaded from the hot sun, he found Alice sitting on a mattress (taken out to be aired for an arriving guest), sewing a blue point dress. The infant Peggy was rolling about from mattress to grass, prattling to herself and gurgling at a hard cracker held in her fist, while her mother smiled down at her. A man was papering and painting in one of the parlors, and a carpenter putting up a mantelpiece in another. He, William, was about to cross the lake by boat to post and collect mail. Harry, he supposed, would be taking a ride along the shore on a pony Aunt Kate had given him. Heaven knew where Billy and his German governess were. "Returning, I shall have a bath either in lake or brook"—William especially liked the brook, with its little pool of ice-cold water splashing over a natural dam—"doesn't it sound nice?"

Chocorua—Tamworth Iron Works was the post-office address, as

A Gathering of Siblings: Leamington, 1889

William was loath to admit—was altogether a family home. When William felt the need of solitude or the company of masculine friends, he usually went to the Putnam shanty in Keene Valley. But to the New Hampshire farm, with its woods and apple trees and horseback riding, William was now beginning to bring the family for the summer months. Alice, however diligent with the endless household and farming chores, did not conceal her deepening sense that, as she put it to William, the place was "essentially foreign to us." William, after ten days of physical exertion there, however, felt a rejuvenation of body and spirit, and scolded his wife a little for her attitude. He took to opening up the surrounding landscape with a zest, clearing away bushes and cutting down trees. "I have bought a house and am now creating a site around it, lowering the level of the landscape," he told his siblings in England. On drives around the area, William would head for some high hill where the family could picnic while overlooking a valley or gazing across at mountain peaks, and he even brought along axes so that (with permission) he could hack away at any trees that might impede the view.

Gradually, despite fits of impatience and bad temper, and abrupt imperious departures from home, William was becoming a family man, a father as well as a husband. He had anticipated this development with a sort of dark humor when he told Alice, not long after Billy's second birthday, that "I feel with terror that I am becoming more and more wedded to my children." When the latter were away in South Carolina, William, typically and familiarly, grew closer to them than he had yet been. His letters were sprightly. "Beloved Heinrich," he wrote. "You lazy old scoundrel, why don't you write a letter to your old Dad?" He told Harry a fable about a donkey who tried to act like a lapdog to win his mistress's love, and only succeeded in scaring her and having himself beaten by the servants. "Moral: It's no use to try to be anything but a donkey if you are one. But neither you nor Billy are one."

To "Beloved Heinrich" on March 27, after urging him to work hard on his books: "The best of all of us is your mother, though." William signed himself "Your loving Dad. W.J." but submitted to being called Popsy. To Billy at the end of April: "Beloved Williamson,—This is Sunday, the sabbath of the Lord, and it has been very hot for two days. I think of you and Harry with such longing, and of that infant whom I know so little." He told about some "learned seals" he had seen in a big tank of water in Boston: "They play the guitar and banjo and organ, and one of them saves the life of a child who tumbles in the water, catching him by the collar with its teeth, and swimming him ashore." Lest this account alarm Billy, his father added, "They are both, child and seal, trained to do it."

With the coming of fall, William resumed his duties at Harvard. He was offering a new lecture course, Philosophy 4, for forty students, on ethics and the philosophy of religion, the latter being a field of study that was beginning to attract him. He found himself reading Plato— Jowett's translation of the *Republic*—Aristotle, Adam Smith, and Spinoza for the first time. "It does one good to read classic books," he observed to Henry. But with the abundant reading for Philosophy 4 and two other courses, he was certain he would do "no writing to speak of this year," and expected to enjoy the time off hugely.

The opening of the college year was often anticlimactic for William James. "To prepare for the men is always rather inspiring," he wrote to Alice, in Chocorua, as the term began; but "to meet them is dejecting—they always look so haphazard and finite and inferior." At another moment, he spoke of "the loutish passive faces" staring up at him in the first days of a course, and at the year's end, he grew weary of students coming to him one after another to fight about their grades. Yet Professor James was the most responsive and pedagogically cordial and patient of teachers.

Striding across the Harvard campus, he could greet any student encountered by name; and it became a common thing to see the professor and an undergraduate walking along together, warmly debating some thesis William had advanced in class. He encouraged and enjoyed the strongest intellectual resistance; and at the conclusion of a course, he would make the then unheard-of proposal that students write down their criticisms of it, with suggestions for improvement. William received these various rebuttals with flattering attention and invariable good humor; and students, forgetting themselves amid the smiling professorial tolerance, could become strident and ill-mannered in their excitement.

William showed comparably mixed reactions toward his university colleagues. By the fall of 1888, he had been a full professor for two and a half years, and he took pleasure in telling Alice what he frankly thought about his peers. He had just been to see "the myriad-minded Royce," he wrote her in late September, having already confided his view that Royce was "by far the biggest mind I have ever known." One of the several reasons William disliked George Herbert Palmer was the chairman's prissy attitude toward Royce's inability to live within his income. Referring to this one day, Palmer informed William: "Our sins are here to be extirpated" and Royce had better begin immediately to exert his will and conscience. "I'll kill that man some day, he exasperates me so," William said, passing on the anecdote to his wife. William had a due regard for Palmer's cerebral qualities, and sometimes softened in his judgment because of them—only to be reminded again that Palmer could be "such an insulting brute." Some years after this, in fact, James and Palmer arrived at a certain mutuality of understanding and intellectual trust, indicated by Palmer's judiciously admiring memoir of his former associate.

After attending a lecture by Charles Eliot Norton, William let loose a diatribe. "Why can't one speak truth sometimes," he expostulated to Alice, "and call [Norton] publicly and without apology the infernal old sinner and sham that he is. There isn't a genuine word in him." It was perhaps Norton's European type of mind, steeped in Dante and medieval art, that put William off; but it is to be noticed that each of the James siblings tended to be chary toward the favorites of any of the others, and William had been hearing his brother Henry speak warmly about Charles Norton for twenty years. Meanwhile, though, another and more distinctly European personality began to be mentioned in William's letters.

"This A.M. came an essay by Santayana," William had written Alice in April. "The whole thing quite characteristic. Very exquisite but too much like a poem." George Santayana, half American and (via his father) half Spanish, was Catholic by upbringing and Continental in taste and temperament. He and William James would not seem to have been made for one another intellectually, and indeed they got off to a poor start when Professor James tried to dissuade young Santayana, as a freshman in 1883, from the study of philosophy. But time would show that the two had much in common in most fundamental ways, including a shared contempt for the professional academic philosophers, "our bald-headed young Ph.D.'s," as James would put it to Santayana, "boring each other at seminaries."* Santayana's doctoral examination was held in the Jameses' library at Garden Street on the

---

* See John McCormick's searching discussion of the relation between the two figures in *George Santayana: A Biography* (1987). McCormick also tells of the belated first meeting between Santayana and *Henry* James, in Logan Pearsall Smith's London home in September 1915; and he quotes Santayana as saying that he felt "more at home and better understood" with Henry than he ever had with William James. "Henry was calm," Santayana wrote in *The Middle Span* (1945); "he liked to see things as they are, and be free afterwards to imagine how they might have been. We talked about different countries as places of residence. He was of course subtle and bland, appreciative of all points of view, and amused at their limitations."

evening of May 23, 1889. The candidate was promptly granted the degree at the end of it. Santayana's thesis, which had preceded the interrogation, was "simply an exquisite production," William told Alice.

Uppermost in William's mind in that same spring of 1889 was the big new house he was having built for the family on Irving Street in Cambridge. It was not far from the old Quincy Street home, in a section known as Norton's Woods. He calculated, in mid-May, that the entire cost of the enterprise would not be less than $15,000; the thought made him sick with anxiety and cost him several sleepless nights. He managed, with considerable effort, to work things out in a fairly hopeful way; and at the same time he learned that Aunt Kate, who had died in March in consequence of a bad fall suffered a month or so earlier, had left him $10,000 in her will.

With this prospective sum to draw upon, William determined to give himself another vacation abroad. "I have been feeling so dead-tired all this spring," he wrote Henry, "that I believe a long break from my usual scenes is necessary. It is like the fagged state that drove me abroad the last two times." The trip would give him as well "the long-wished opportunity of seeing you and Alice."

William sailed aboard the *Cephalonia*, bound for Queenstown, on June 22, his last glimpse before departing being of his wife's "beloved tear-stained face." At sea, he read Henry's short novel *A London Life*, which he thought "extremely good," and Edward Emerson's book about his father, which he found curiously cool. During a week in Ireland, he grew far more alert than before to the complexities of "the Irish question," which he began to understand was "properly a religious movement on the part of the people." Near Killarney, he visited with Mrs. Keane, the mother of the Jameses' housemaid Ellen, who had emigrated to America with her sister. Mrs. Keane spoke of her daughter's reaction on first being confronted, in the household, by Andrew, the young black whom William had taken on the year before. "She fell into a dead wakeness when she first saw the black," so William quoted Mrs. Keane's brogue, "and wished to run away to her sister entirely." William offered no comment on this reversal of that earlier encounter between Irish and American black so often dwelt upon by Henry Senior in the New York winter afternoons.

After a day in Dublin and at Trinity College, William went through heavy rain to Belfast and crossed the Irish Sea to Glasgow. He made a daylong round-trip to Oban, by rail, steamboat, and coach, and thought the landscape like an Inness painting. He came on to Edinburgh ("that divinest of cities"), already "dead in love wi' Scotland." ("I had just begun to talk pretty easily like an Irishman," he wrote Alice, "and now comes the Scotch and puts me all out. I can't help imitating the accent, wherever I am.") By July 17, he was in London, at 34 De Vere Gardens, admiring Henry's apartment with its floods of light and beautifully shaped and furnished rooms. He was feeling extraordinarily well. "Scotland is the place for a man to go to," he said.

The next day the brothers traveled to Leamington, and a reunion with their sister.

HENRY: THE VIEW FROM GENEVA

It was during a short visit to Chocorua in the early fall of 1888 that William had written Henry about reading the "classic books" of Plato and Aristotle and foreseeing no work on the *Psychology* during the academic year ahead. He spoke of feeling "uncommonly hearty," lavishly praised his wife's prowess as a farming lady, and evoked the children's excitement in the country life. Henry, in reply, called the letter "beautiful and delightful," and said he had sent it on to Alice: "on whom it will confer equal beatitude: not only because so copious, but because so 'cheerful in tone' and appearing to show that the essentials of health and happiness are with you."

Henry wrote from Geneva, at the Hôtel de l'Écu, sitting in "our old family *salon*" in the same apartment where the Jameses had spent the winter of 1859–60: "in sociable converse with family ghosts— father and mother and Aunt Kate and our juvenile selves." From his window he looked out onto a scene "full of autumn colour as vivid as yours at Chocorua," with the Mont Blanc range hanging "day by day, over the blue lake." Geneva seemed both duller and smarter; the old academy was now the university and occupied a large, winged building in an old public garden; "but all the old smells and tastes are here, and the sensation is pleasant." Fenimore Woolson was also in Geneva, writing away at a hotel a mile distant (Henry was in Geneva flirting with Fenimore, in Alice's version). His own health was excellent, except for the recurring danger of stoutness—"portentous corpulence," Henry had dubbed it; in London he had engaged a fencing master to give him weight-reducing lessons twice a week in the art of thrust and, parry.

He had left "stale dingy London" for Switzerland three weeks before, after not having been out of the city, to speak of, for fifteen months, not since his return from Italy in July 1887. The intervening period had been a mixed one in Henry's fortunes and state of mind. The journey back had been enlivened by a stopover, at Stresa on Lake Maggiore, with Fanny Kemble, the elderly actress in whom he had taken social and literary pleasure for many a year. He then crossed the Simplon on foot: "a rapture of wild flowers and mountain streams," he told William; providing all the out-of-doors exercise he needed; let William have his Chocorua life.

Back in De Vere Gardens, Henry had reviewed his situation, as was his custom. His housing needs were well satisfied by the London apartment. Far from requiring a large openness of surrounding, in-doors and out, as William did, Henry wanted no more than "elbow-room for the exercise, as it were, of my art. I hope during the next ten years," he continued to William, "to do some things of a certain im-portance; if I don't, it won't be that I haven't tried hard or that I am wanting in an extreme ambition." He was being notably productive, having just sent off the eighth or ninth work of fiction (he had lost precise count) written over the previous ten months. But the problem he had cited for William the year before was getting worse: in late 1887, magazine editors were still failing to bring these writings into print.

Henry put the case dramatically to Howells, in a letter of January 2, 1888, that has been much quoted and sometimes misinterpreted. "I have entered upon evil days," he said. He was "still staggering a good deal under the mysterious and (to me) inexplicable injury wrought—apparently—upon my situation by my last two novels, the *Bostonians* and the *Princess*, from which I expected so much and derived so little. They have reduced the desire, and the demand, for my productions to zero—as I judge from the fact that though I have for a good while past been writing a number of good short things, I remain irremediably unpublished. Editors keep them back, for months and years, as if they were ashamed of them." However, Henry insisted with all his old staunchness, "I don't despair, for I think I am now really in better form for work than I have ever been in my life, and I propose yet to do many things. Very likely too some day all my buried prose will kick off its various tombstones at once."

This was exactly what began almost immediately to happen; the delays Henry found so disturbing were due mainly to technical and scheduling problems.* Over the next twelve months, eight short stories and novellas by Henry James, among them *The Aspern Papers* and *A London Life*, were published in seven different American and English periodicals. Alice, surveying the output in November 1888, remarked to William that Henry seemed "to have broken out all over stories." Her personal favorite was "The Modern Warning." "I feel as if *I* were the heroine," she said about the story, which deals with an American woman, Agatha Grice, who has Irish blood in her veins, is for that reason ill at ease with the English, and is caught between two much loved men, one of whom detests America and writes a book to say so, while the other loathes England and never fails to denounce it.† William, for his part, was especially struck by *The Reverberator*, a rather relaxed narrative that tells in part of the invasion of an old Franco-American family in Paris by a gossip-mongering newspaperman. He had "quite squealed through it," William said; it was "masterly and exquisite" and "the household has amazingly enjoyed it."

Frederick Macmillan brought out two new collections of Henry James's shorter work in this period. In March 1888, Henry consented to the request of Aldrich, at *The Atlantic*, to undertake a twelve-part serial for 1889; it would interweave two stories he had in mind and would probably be called *The Tragic Muse*. Before 1888 was over, Macmillan had also published *Partial Portraits*—Henry enthused a little over the adjective as meaning both "limited" and "favorable"—which contained ten essays on writers, plus "The Art of Fiction." Most of the essays had been written since 1883, and three of them—on Stevenson, Fenimore Woolson (peculiarly happy, according to William), and Daudet—within the year. Other essays and reviews were finding their outlet. No American writer of stature, it may be ventured, has ever been more productive or more published within a comparable space of time.

Sitting and ruminating in the salon of his suite in the Hôtel de l'Écu, Henry turned to his brother's inquiries about Alice. In Henry's view, she was not really nostalgic for America; indeed, she seemed to him "stimulated" and "healthily irritated" by her English environment. "I don't think she *likes* England or the English very much—the

* See Edel, *Henry James Letters*, III, p. 210. Here and in his biography of James, Edel has sought to correct the continuing misinterpretation of James's reference to his "buried prose" kicking off "its various tombstones" as a prophecy of some sort of "posthumous 'revival.' "

† See Ruth Yeazell's comment on the story in *The Death and Letters of Alice James*.

people, their mind, their tone, their 'hypocrisy' etc." This was partly owing to the confined life she was leading, Henry surmised, and the "fragmentary, unreacting way" in which she saw people, especially since she saw only women: "no men at all." But chiefly, he thought, it was because Alice, living in a country not her own, tended to confuse her mature and general opinions on human nature with a judgment on the particular (alien) land she inhabited: bending her profoundly ironic and critical disposition on the English in a contrast of international manners and morals—so ran the implication—with the Americans and the Irish.

A literary theme of sizable importance sprang from this fraternal meditation. For himself, Henry went on, "I am deadly weary of the whole 'international' state of mind—so that I *ache*, at times, with fatigue at the way it is constantly forced upon one as a sort of virtue or obligation." He dissociated his mode of appraisal from his sister's: "I can't look at the English and American worlds, or feel about them, any more, save as a big Anglo-Saxon total"; and to dwell on their differences, he felt, was becoming "more and more idle and pedantic." Looking out, as it were, from the neutral ground of Switzerland and with only the friendly Jamesian ghosts as his companions, Henry declared himself in a way that put him beyond the literary convention he had helped to establish. "I aspire to write in such a way that it would be impossible to an outsider to say whether I am, at a given moment, an American writing about England or an Englishman writing about America." It may be said that Henry James never did write in the manner aspired to, for which one may be grateful. But equally, he never returned to "the international theme" properly speaking.

After a few weeks in Monte Carlo and a month in Paris—which he described to Charles Eliot Norton as charming and civilized and "even interesting"—Henry was back in London by Christmas Eve. The wintry city as he re-entered it looked to him "like a big black inferno of fog, mud, drunkenness and pauperism." That impression was soon balanced by others, but Henry was far more conscious than in former days of "the vast miseries and meannesses of London," the London known to his Hyacinth Robinson.

He spent the week between Christmas and New Year's, 1889, with Alice in Leamington. She was stronger than when he had last seen her, and passionately attentive to what Henry called "the everlasting Irish question." Stirred by his sister's concern, Henry found it hard "not to put a little passion" into his own attitudes in the matter, especially his belief that Home Rule was the only feasible political solution. In the spring of 1889, and perhaps sitting in for Alice, Henry went several times to the court where the Special Commission was considering evidence that allegedly linked Parnell with the Phoenix Park murders in Dublin.* They were "two or three of the most interesting days I ever passed," Henry wrote Robert Louis Stevenson, now in the South Seas.

But the greater part of his energy was being given to *The Tragic Muse*, which had begun to appear in the January 1889 issue of *The Atlantic*. His immersion in it brought him to think afresh about the sinuous relations between art and reality. Writing to Norton in late March, he distinguished between the kind of literary realism he most esteemed and the "large allegorical designs" currently being painted by his friend Edward Burne-Jones. The latter's powers of imagination, Henry held, were moving in the wrong direction: "more and more away from the open air of the world and the lovely study of the aspects and appearances of things." *That* was the kind of openness that Henry James sought to reside in: the open air in the country of the fictive. To that world he would address himself for a dozen years, until he moved through and beyond it, too, if not to the allegorical, at least to the fabulous: to the dark expansive fables of the 1900s.

The Tragic Muse, meanwhile, kept him busy into the summer of 1889 and to the anxiously awaited appearance of his brother William.

ALICE: CAUSES FOR TAKING ON

Alice was in lively form in the later months of 1888, chattering away in letters to William about local incidents and the varied social and political spectacle. She was getting out in her Bath chair at Leamington fairly often, though on one excursion the attendant Bowles was very drunk and lurched and staggered so much as he propelled her that her stomach began to heave wildly. She continued to follow public events closely and wondered why no one back home ever mentioned the forthcoming American national election. After the election, when President Grover Cleveland, while winning a popular majority, was ousted by Benjamin Harrison in what has been called the most corrupt national contest in our history, Alice spent the night in tears.

William urged her not to "take on so about the election," to which Alice replied that it would be better all round "if there were a little

* See below, pp. 451–52.

more 'taking on,' " and that she would take on till she had drawn her last breath. She saw herself as a most contradictory being: "a wretched, shriveled alien enclosed within four walls, with such an extraordinary disproportion between what is *felt* & what is heard & seen by her [i.e., *of* her]—an emotional volcano within, with the outward reverberation of a mouse & the physical significance of a chip of lead-pencil."

There was a temporary estrangement from her brother and sister-in-law in mid-autumn. When William and Alice, acting on her invitation, had taken some of her furniture and other things to Chocorua, they had also moved the remaining items from Boston to a Cambridge warehouse near them and had been paying the storage charges themselves. Alice was outraged, both at the cavalier handling of her belongings and at the implication that she was too poor to pay the warehouse costs. She wrote on November 4, underscoring heavily: "*I have no words to express my extreme annoyance at yr. having paid the storage.* You doubtless meant to be kind, but you know that kindness imposed upon an unwilling recipient—and that I *was* an unwilling recipient you can't have had a *shadow of a doubt*—is likely to go astray & receive small gratitude in return."

Alice, at forty years old, exiled and bedridden, had little enough to call her own; her possessions, however remote, were dear to her, and this treatment of them was wounding and humiliating. William wrote back in a flood of apologies and explanations, entirely exculpating his wife and begging for forgiveness. This Alice speedily granted, but she could not refrain from remarking to Mrs. Alice that William illustrated something she had read recently: "The constructive, without the imaginative, sometimes leads to the destructive."

Death, far off or near at hand, penetrated Alice's consciousness more than ever. Lizzie Boott had died in Bellosguardo in March of 1888. The certified cause was pneumonia, but Alice, alluding to her "having so violently discontinued herself," seemed to be hinting that Lizzie had been a suicide. (The badly stricken Henry took the position, not that Lizzie had killed herself, but that his cherished friend of twenty years had simply been drained of strength by her family responsibilities.) The death in London of Edmund Gurney, William's friend and fellow psychic researcher (not related to the Boston Gurneys), was unquestionably a suicide. Alice knew that William would feel the loss, but was frank in thinking that Gurney, however strapping a figure physically, was slight-spirited almost to extinction, and that—unlike herself, she seemed to be saying—he had a very feeble "hold on life."

The worst event of Alice's stay in Leamington was the death of a newborn infant on the floor above at Hamilton Terrace during the Christmas season of 1888. To Aunt Kate, Alice told of hearing Christmas rejoicings through the wall on one side and the groans of the woman in labor in the room overhead. ("How my heart burned within me at the cruelty of men!" Alice interpolated. "I have been haunted by the thought of Alice & all child-bearing women since.") The mother was said to be glad the child had died, and Alice in a follow-up letter to William alluded to "a deed of darkness . . . we *know* that a little human soul was *left* to die." The father had drunk himself sodden with brandy and soda. Such a couple could easily get away with infanticide, Alice said in sudden anger, while a slum woman who killed a disease-ridden baby would be sent to penal servitude.

At the start of 1889, Aunt Kate, who had already begun to fail mentally, had some sort of fall in her home on West Forty-fourth Street in New York. Alice pictured her "as usual lying with folded hands fostering her own aches and pains." She died on March 6, at the age (presumably) of seventy-seven. Writing to William at the end of the month, Alice commented on her aunt's life with a sorrowing shrewdness: the failed potential, the thwarted longings, the "betrayal" that she, Alice, had visited upon her at a certain stage.

Poor Aunt Kate's life on looking back to it with the new distinctness which the completion always gives, must seem to our point of view such a failure, a person so apparently meant for independence & a "position" to have been so unable to have worked her way to them & instead to have voluntarily relegated herself to the contrary. But the truth was, as her long life showed, that she had but one *motif*, the intense longing to absorb herself in a few individuals, how she missed this & how much the individuals resisted her, was, thank Heaven! but faintly suspected by her. My failing her, after Mother's & Father's death, must have seemed to her a great & ungrateful betrayal; my inability to explain myself & hers to understand, in any way, the situation made it all the sadder & more ugly.

The passage was, in its way, a painful act of expiation. But Alice wrote in a different vein when she learned that Aunt Kate, in her will, had left her niece no more than a life interest in various objects. She instantly renounced the temporary legacy of a set of silver. But she paused over one item, a life interest in a shawl "with reversion to a *male* heir," which Alice found "so extraordinary & ludicrous a bequest that I can hardly think it could have been seriously meant." She declared she would accept it if William promised to wear the shawl at her funeral, and elaborated for some lines on that fancy. Aunt Kate may, in some dim way, have been indicating her unhappiness at Alice's conduct in 1883, even as she bequeathed $10,000 to William and left the balance of her estate to four Walsh cousins in Stamford, Connecticut. Alice did not resent William's good fortune, sensing that he had need of it, and knowing that from his youngest days William had been with some reason Aunt Kate's favorite among the children.

Alice had greeted the new year with a collapse which produced "a whirring heart & panting breath," while Henry watched beside her couch "like an angel" for a week. But the crisis passed. "I am sorry to have to tell you," she wrote William in her customary vein, "that you have again missed being released from me." The arrival of an exceptionally beautiful spring saw her in much improved condition. In June, she allowed herself cautiously to be pushed—by a new chair man, a fat person with clean hands—as far as the village of Lillington, a mile or so above Leamington: "where stands a manor house," as she said to Mrs. Morse, "an over grown farm house, a delicious little church in its graveyard—a microcosm of England." Given the chance, Alice would appreciate the physical aspects and arrangements of her adopted country, if only rarely its citizens.

Alice's diary account of "the somewhat devastating episode of July 18th" began with Henry taking lunch with her in her Hamilton Terrace rooms. As they were talking together afterward, Henry said suddenly "with a queer look upon his face, 'I must tell you something!' 'You're not going to be married!' shrieked I. 'No, but William is here, he has been lunching upon Warwick Castle and is waiting now in the Holly Walk for the news to be broken to you and if you survive, I'm to tie my handkerch[ief] to the balcony.' " Alice managed not to faint, and Henry went to fetch their brother.

THE GATHERING

The siblings spent more than three hours together. Alice's agitation continued for a time; she kept panting and trembling, and gasping out to William: "You understand, don't you, it's all my body, it's all physical, I can't help it." Gradually she quieted down. Henry had grown pale with apprehension, in Alice's own description, "as to which 'going off' in my large repertory would 'come on' but with the assistance of 200 grains of Bromides I think I behaved with extreme propriety."

William did not look to her much changed after five years' separation; what was mainly to be said of him was "that he is simply himself, a creature who speaks in another language as H. says from the rest of mankind and who would lend life and charm to a treadmill."

As the three of them sat and talked, as they exchanged memories and opinions, the afternoon became for Alice a soul-quickening experience wherein the family itself seemed to come richly back into being, a revived and reintegrated presence. Her isolation was overcome for the moment by the sense of being once again a surrounded and nourished member of that family. "What a strange experience it was," she wrote, "to have what had seemed so dead and gone all these years suddenly bloom before one, a flowing oasis in this alien desert, redolent with the exquisite *family* perfume of the days gone by, made of the allusions, the memories and the point of view in common, so that my floating-particle sense was lost for an hour or so in the illusion that what is forever shattered had sprung up anew, and existed outside of our memories—where it is forever green!"

To William, Alice, too, seemed surprisingly little changed. Her hands were thinner, but they were very elegant and graceful of gesture. She talked and laughed, he wrote his wife, "in a perfectly charming way," and it made him ashamed of the "dull ponderous moral" manner he had been taking with Alice from afar in the last years. She was witty, animated, and curious about everything. What especially struck him was that the note of invective and sarcasm, which in her letters had sounded shrill to him, was "uttered in the softest most laughing way in the world," and gave "an entirely different impression."

It was clear that Harry got on perfectly with his sister, ignoring all uncomfortable subjects and keeping up an easy humorous tone. William wound up his report: "Suffice it for now that the electric current is closed between myself and sister, and that the non-conducting obstruction is melted away."

The brothers went back to London. William remained in England for the rest of July, making a visit down to Brighton for an evening with his associates in psychic research, Henry Sidgwick and F.W.H. Myers. On the return journey to London, he stopped off at Haslemere for an evening and a morning with Logan Pearsall Smith, the witty and cultivated young American, now expatriated, who had been in one of William's classes a few years before.

William communicated to his Alice, in Chocorua, his impression of Henry after six years: "Harry is as nice and simple and amiable as he can be. He has covered himself, like some marine crustacean, with all sorts of material growths, rich sea-weeds and rigid barnacles and things, and lives hidden in the midst of his strange heavy alien manners and customs; but these are all but 'protective resemblances,' under which the same dear old, good, innocent and at bottom very powerless-feeling Harry remains, caring for little but his writing, and full of dutifulness and affection for all gentle things."

It was one of William's most memorable interminglings of the penetrating, the imaginative, and the misjudging. The portrait of Henry's real self hidden behind acquired English manners and habits of speech (as his face, under the balding dome, was covered by thick beard, mustache, and sideburns), conveyed in clustering marine and jungle imagery: this has a force of poetic and psychological insight that perhaps only a William James could arrive at. Even to speak of Henry as "innocent" has a genuine, if marginal, validity; one could long debate it, constantly redefining one's terms. But to attribute to his brother a feeling of powerlessness was only to perpetuate William's conviction that the life devoted to writing—Henry cared "for little but his writing"—was a life sadly deprived of power, or of the effective exercise of will. To Henry, the personal creative act had from an early literary age seemed potently and palpably otherwise.

On the same day (July 29), William wrote his sister in Leamington about Henry. "I have enjoyed being with Harry very much, but of London itself I'm thoroughly sated, and never care to see its yellow-brownness and stale spaciousness again." The profoundly Jamesian nature of the Leamington meeting had affected William not less than Alice, and his next reverberant remarks derived from it. ". . . Harry has been delightful,—easier and freer than when I was here before, and beneath all the accretions of years and the world, he is still the same dear innocent old Harry of our youth. His anglicisms are but 'protective resemblances'—and he's really, I won't say a yankee, but a native of the James family, and has no other country."

William crossed the Channel and passed through Boulogne-sur-Mer (where he could further recall the "Harry of our youth") to Paris. Here he attended a five-day session of the International Congress of Physiological Psychology. Professor "Will-yam Jammes," as a distinguished foreign visitor, was asked to preside at the opening meeting. William came away from the congress feeling encouraged about his field of study. In a comment to *Mind*, he stressed the "inspiration which came to everyone from seeing before them in flesh and blood so large a portion of that little army of fellow students from whom and for whom all contemporary psychology exists." To Carl Stumpf he wrote: "The sight of 120 men all actively interested in psychology has made me feel much less lonely in the world."

On August 14, after a few more days at De Vere Gardens, William, accompanied by Henry, traveled to Liverpool, where he was to embark for America. On the way, the brothers paused in Leamington. William gave Alice a spirited account of the Paris congress, but exhibited impatience to get back to Cambridge, the family, the new house a-building. Alice's next word of him was a letter, written on his arrival in Cambridge, "full of plans for his return"—to Europe—"*plus* wife and infants." He was "just like a blob of mercury," Alice said in her diary, "you can't put a mental finger upon him." She and Harry laughed together over William's quicksilver temperament, and in-dulged in another round of family recollections, back to the earliest days, marveling the while at the odd likeness between Father and William.

"Tho' the results are the same," Alice wrote, "they seem to come from such a different nature in the two; in W., an entire inability or indifference to 'stick to a thing for the sake of sticking,' as some one said of him once; whilst Father, the delicious infant! couldn't submit even to the thralldom of his own whim; and then the dear being was such a prey to the demon homesickness." Henry, mentioning places on the Continent which always brought back old scenes for him, sum-moned up the youthful past. In Alice's transcription: "Father's sudden return at the end of 36 hours, having left to be gone a fortnight, with Mother beside him holding his hand and we five children pressing close round him 'as if he had just been saved from drowning,' and he pouring out, as he alone could, the agonies of desolation thro' which he had come."

THE ABSENT SIBLING

Bob James spent some seven months in the Hartford asylum in 1888. During the first part of his time there, he fired off letters to William wildly denouncing his wife, Mary. William, who thought these missives perfectly lunatic, notified Dr. Crothers, the asylum director, with a request for a close watch on his brother.

Not long after Bob's release, in mid-September, William encoun-tered him en route to Concord, where he was to talk with Mary about taking up their life together. Physically, Bob looked better than William had seen him in perhaps ten years. He vowed he hadn't touched a drop of liquor since the February debacle, and was determined that Mary would not again drive him back to drinking. He then launched into a furious assault upon Mary as the cause of all his troubles, alcoholic and emotional. He was hopelessly deluded about her, William wrote Alice, "and made on me the impression of a person more impossible than ever to live with. The fact is that he hates her, I think, and she ought to be willing to let him go, instead of sticking to him in this absurdly ideal way."

By the following spring, the Robertson James ménage in Concord appeared to have settled down to a cautious tranquillity. Bob dropped in on his brother in Cambridge, looking and talking well; he wrote William cordial notes, and joined the Jameses for a few days in Chocorua. William could say no more about him on these occasions than that he was "interesting"; with an air of gladly accepting that quality in exchange for the rage and madness of the earlier period. But Bob, though William did not realize it, was entering into one of his extended religious phases; he was allowing his behavior to be guided by the felt presence of his father, and had grown conscious of an impending redemption.

To William Dean Howells, he opened his heart in a way he felt restrained from doing to any member of his family. "Since father died, who was the only being on earth I ever cared for deeply," Bob wrote Howells, "that loss has built up in me out of the ignominy of drink and debauchery what seems to me of late to be becoming one long day in which I see nothing but the faces of Seraphs smiling . . . There are moments in which my heart is wrung, as if with a sort of pain of bliss—a pain at the thought of all the glory which God will give to them who will wait, and *will not* surrender to the passing darkness. Forgive this burst, but for the most part my lips are mute."

That undated letter was probably written in the summer of 1889, at about the time his brothers and sister were forgathering at Leamington and while Bob was rereading his father's volumes of Swedenborg. He and Mary were seeing something of Howells and his wife, and the association led Bob, in the autumn, to read Howells's novel of 1881, *A Modern Instance*. He was intrigued by the figure of Marcia Gaylord in the story: the neurotically puritanical young woman whose marriage to the journalist Bartley Hubbard disintegrates because of Hubbard's financial, sexual, and alcoholic misconduct. The Hubbards' marital troubles perhaps struck a sympathetic chord in Bob, but from the novel as a whole he drew rather a paternal message. Praising

Howells for celebrating the obscure lives of ordinary people, Bob spoke, in echo of Henry Senior's prophetic sayings, of "the common lot with its warming loves and passions which are slowly but grimly and sweetly attaining to a final harmony."

Over the autumn months as well, Bob read the successive installments, in *The Atlantic*, of Howells's novel *A Hazard of New Fortunes*. He singled out as especially admirable the banquet scene, in which the millionaire Dryfoos comes under attack, and the deaths during the streetcar strike of Dryfoos's son Conrad and the German socialist Lindau. Thinking about Dryfoos, a one-time farmer who made a fortune out of natural gas, Bob indulged in an autobiographical excursion for Howells's benefit. It is one of the more remarkable documents in the James family saga.

Some day I would like to tell you of the true inwardness of a great Western Railway for which I worked for fifteen years. It was a great (and is) tomb to which young men go down and in which the many bury and have to bury every emotion and desire which can glorify life. I was the confidential clerk for a long while of one of the most successful and unscrupulous Railway Barons this continent has ever seen—the Manager of the St. Paul Railway. I knew all his inner history and his outer—(He is now dead). I can tell you chapter and verse of every business motive which enabled a poor New Hampshire stable boy to go West and die forty years later worth five million of dollars on a salary which could never have enabled him to *save* more than $100,000.

When we parted after fifteen years of intimacy, it was because not even penniless ill-health and self-contempt which association with him and his kind had brought me to could be bought by them any longer. I had never been requested *to do* the felonious things this management fattened on, but I was obliged *to know it* and keep still.

What we have here is a small concentrated work of fiction that conveys in disguised form a deeply hated personal experience. The fictionalizing becomes evident when we glance across the Wisconsin years. Bob James, to begin with, was never with *any* railway, or indeed with any other employer, for fifteen years. He may be credited with six years' employment by the Milwaukee and St. Paul Railway, in Milwaukee and Prairie du Chien; but far from being the confidential clerk of its manager and privy to his imaginably felonious doings, Bob was simply a bookkeeper, one of the clerks in the office of the railroad's auditor. Later on, Bob did another yearlong railroad stint with the

Milwaukee, Lake Shore and Western, and after that was never again gainfully employed.

The condition of "penniless ill-health" is another piece of fiction. From the time of his marriage in 1872 to the daughter of Edward Holton, Bob had no real financial anxieties. Nor is there any record of a single day's sickness during the Wisconsin epoch; for all his dissipation, in fact, Bob was the most robust of the James children. The entire scene of the sick and destitute young man refusing to serve any longer under a dishonest magnate is an imaginary one. What is Bob James seeking to perpetrate?

He is depicting his life as the son-in-law of Edward Holton, in the guise of a long servitude as private secretary to a railroad baron. It is Holton whose life is being traced in the persona of the unscrupulous manager: Holton who grew up as a New Hampshire farmboy, though not a poor one, and Holton who went West to amass great wealth in Milwaukee. He was not yet dead in 1889—that was a bit of wishful thinking on Bob's part. Holton would die in 1892, his estate then reckoned at between one and two million dollars. The ignoble and even criminal traits of Bob's fictive railway manager (Holton had had no formal connection with the railway since the 1860s) are a transposition of his father-in-law's pomposity, maddening self-assurance, hectoring, money-grubbing, and temperance preaching. Under that heavy and demoralizing shadow, Bob had served for more than a dozen years, until he quit and moved away to Massachusetts. By the time of the 1889 letter to his favorite American novelist, Howells, the whole experience was so hateful a memory that it could only be rendered as fiction or parable.

But if the imagery of young men destroying themselves in railway jobs had little relevance to Bob, it fitted his brother Wilky with unhappy accuracy. "Penniless ill-health" was just the state to which Wilky was reduced in his final years. At the same time, in his vigorous hostility to the conquest of society and morality by the forces of capitalism— the extinguishing power of "the Fate of Dollars," as he put it in the same letter to Howells—Bob was plainly following the lead of his socialist father. Drawing upon these personal and family ingredients and weaving them together into a kind of moral tale, Bob displayed a narrative potential reminiscent of some early story by his brother Henry. Bob, too, after all, and even at his most fantasy-ridden, was a native of the James family.

CHAPTER THIRTEEN

Fraternal Principles:
Psychology and Drama

''A LITERARY SUBJECT, LIKE AUTOBIOGRAPHY''

In the time after his return from England, William passed through a moment of sadness and marital tension and on to a stage of immense achievement and gratification. In early October, he wrote his Alice that his intellectual life had come to a standstill and that he had nothing on his mind "but house and you and the coming one." "House" was the new home at 95 Irving Street, in Cambridge; William had just spent his first night in it. It was a well-built three-story affair with a rather handsome exterior within the domestic architectural style of the New England day; quite roomy, and providing a large library with fireplace for William on the ground floor. For contrast, William prowled through the "ghost-haunted" old home on Quincy Street, now for let, and thought it shabby and tasteless: "This house is worth two of it in every respect."

As to "you and the coming one," Alice, as William remarked to her, was "embarking on this heavy journey for the fifth time." The forty-year-old Alice was six or seven weeks pregnant when, around the middle of October, she suffered a miscarriage. There followed the inevitable period of depression, in the course of which Alice's dark feelings turned outward against her husband. After one (as it seems) accusatory letter, William replied: "Be patient, and hate me as little as you can. I'm sure I never less deserved to be hated"; but if the emotion helped her, she should indulge it. He suggested that perhaps she should not write at all "till the cloud goes away," and confessed that he dreaded the thought of her coming back to Cambridge. But by the first days of November, Alice was overcoming her despondency, and William could delight in the "sun-breaking-through-the-clouds-like-tone" of her last letter.

William's intellectual life picked up again, and the book on psychology began to move toward completion with accelerated speed. He was often up at four, he told Henry, writing and rewriting; and sometimes wrote all day until six, sustained only by coffee. On May 17, 1890, he exclaimed to "Beloved Alice": "The job is done!" He labored over the voluminous proofs through most of the summer, with Alice—by now five months along in a new pregnancy—assisting him in the last phases. *The Principles of Psychology*, in two volumes, was published at the end of September.

A week after his joyous announcement to Alice, William came back from his afternoon lectures pleasantly weary, lit a fire in his study, and sank back for two hours of thinking, remembering and planning in the wake of "the big *étape* of my life which is behind me." He thought almost tearfully of his "child-friend-wife who threw in her lot with me so many years ago"; whose confidence in him, however sorely tried, had continued and increased "as one baby after another appeared, then the country place, then this noble house, and now at last the *book*, which proclaims me really an efficient man."

What pleased him most about the book, he said, was that it showed he did not "live *wholly* in projects, aspirations, and phrases . . . The joke of it is that I, who have always considered myself a thing of glimpses, of discontinuity, of *aperçus*, with no power of doing a big job, suddenly realize at the *end* of this task that it is the biggest book on psychology in any language except Wundt's, Rosmini's and Daniel Greenleaf Thompson's!" Even William James could scarcely realize that *The Principles of Psychology* was one of the biggest books by any intellectual and literary measure ever written by an American.

The immediate reception for the most part was decidedly enthusiastic. Stanley Hall, in a review, called it "on the whole and after all the best work in any language"; and Shadworth Hodgson wrote from England that he had found it "the most valuable and instructive book on the subject that I ever came across." James's inconsistency on one central subject, or perhaps his dialectical cunning, was reflected in one commentator's regret that no "transcendental agency" was mentioned in the account of the mind's motions, while another was puzzled by the author's *"penchant* for spiritualism in the new sense."

Charles Sanders Peirce, William James's old philosophic comrade, seemed to be addressing this matter when he wrote in *The Nation* that the author of *The Principles* was "materialistic to the core." With a sort of creative contempt for conventional meanings (William had spoken to Henry about Peirce's "paradoxical and obscure statements"), Peirce went on to attribute William's "materialism" to his father's Swedenborgianism, which, Peirce said quirkily, "is materialism driven deep and clinched on the inside." The work was undoubtedly important in its way, Peirce acknowledged, but it suffered throughout from "idiosyncracies of diction and tricks of language such as usually spring up in households of great talent."

The most eloquently accurate identification of the *Principles*, for our purpose and any other, was offered by George Santayana some thirty years later. At the time, Santayana praised the book warmly in *The Atlantic Monthly*, among other things calling its personal and individual flavor "a safeguard against pretension and hollowness." Then, in *Character and Opinion in the United States* in 1921, James's former student and colleague had this to say:

This is a work of the imagination; and the subject as [James] conceived it, which is the flux of immediate experience in men in general, requires imagination to read it at all. It is a literary subject, like autobiography or psychological fiction, and can be treated only poetically.

It is exactly *as* a literary subject—for all its diagrams and whirligig figures, its tabulations and scholarly thickenings—and in particular as autobiography and even psychological fiction, that *The Principles of Psychology* takes its immense place in the James family saga.

Other members of William's talented household hover in the pages. Henry Senior is recalled, not only in the occasional invocation of the horsecar, but in the citation of S. Weir Mitchell's case history (in "Sensation") of the patient who had lost a leg at the age of eleven and who, long after walking with an artificial limb, still underwent delusions about the missing foot. In a rather perfunctory chapter on "Imagination," William seems to follow Henry's way of opposing the simple faculty of reproducing impressions literally and passively to the capacity to "make new wholes." It is only in the latter case, William writes in a fraternal echo, that "we have acts of imagination properly so called."* Alice James provided some of the data for her brother's conjectures about "hysteric disease" and the "split-off consciousness." But William's own experience—as an individual, as teacher, traveler, husband, father, psychic researcher—is the main source of live evidence in the text. He tells about his sensations while lying in his berth at sea, and in his bed on a cold morning at home; about his mix of feelings while revisiting Paris in the 1860s; about the infant Harry unconcernedly fondling a frog at age six months, and being too frightened to touch one of the species a year later; about Peggy's sudden terror of the family pet pug dog; about fraudulent mediums. William's practice, begun so many years before, of taking himself as a chief object of psychological and physiological study here reaps its reward. "The more closely I scrutinize my states," he writes in a characteristic passage in "Emotion," where he is arguing that emotions are caused by (rather than lead to) physical stirrings, "the more persuaded I become that whatever moods, affections, and passions I have are in very truth . . . made up of those bodily changes which we ordinarily call their expression." And in "The Perception of Space," he rejects the Kantian categories of space and time as "mythological" on the ground (which other introspective minds might dispute) that "I am conscious of no such Kantian machine-shop in my mind . . . I have no introspective experience of mentally producing or creating space."

The personal element is at work more powerfully, if more covertly, when, in "The Perception of Things," he discusses hallucinations; and while insisting that *"in hallucination there is no objective stimulus at all,"* nonetheless, *"an hallucination is a strictly sensational form of consciousness, as good and true a sensation as if there was a real object there."* (All italics within quotations in this section are William James's.) The formidable reality for William's psychic life of the epileptic idiot envisioned in 1870 is thus reaffirmed.

There can be little doubt that in his analysis of the sexual impulse in the chapter on "Instinct," William James is exploiting his private memory as well as his professional knowledge. "Of all propensities," he begins there, "the sexual impulses bear on their face the most obvious signs of being instinctive, in the sense of blind, automatic, and untaught." But the facts, he goes on at once to contend, are just the reverse: "The sexual instinct is particularly liable to be checked and modified," especially by "contrary impulses" like shyness and "what

* It is in this chapter that William declares himself to be "a good draftsman"—as his diagrams show—but "an extremely poor visualizer."

Fraternal Principles: Psychology and Drama

might be called the *anti-sexual* instinct." The latter derives from a mode of "repulsiveness" in the mere idea "of intimate contact with most of the persons we meet." This is sensible enough; but to an extent, one cannot but feel, James is remembering his erotic flinch during the time of his courtship; and he is doing so again when he writes: "This strongest passion of all, so far from being the most 'irresistible,' may, on the contrary, be the hardest one to give rein to."*

As we examine *The Principles* in the personal perspective, we gradually make out in it a large autobiographical re-enactment, a replaying of William James's private life from the 1860s into the 1880s. Howells, the family friend and the fiction writer William most admired, remarked in *Harper's Magazine* that Professor James in his new work "writes with a poetic sense of his facts, and with an artistic pleasure in their presentation"; and both the pleasure and the poetry are apparent as William brings the autobiographical drama into being. It surfaces, so to say, in a series of interweaving passages from "Habit" early in Volume I through "The Perception of Reality" partway through Volume II to "Will," which, except for a brief epilogue, concluded the 1891 abridged edition of the text.

In the chapter on habit, William takes cognizance of the danger—his father had so earnestly warned him and Henry about this—of a premature choice of vocation: "Already at the age of twenty-five you see the professional settling down on the young commercial traveler, on the young doctor, on the young minister, on the young counsellor-at-law." But the opposite condition, for which he perhaps held his father partly responsible, could still cause William reminiscent anguish: "There is no more miserable being than one in whom nothing is habitual but indecision." And again, painfully recalling what he had for a time feared he might become: "There is no more contemptible type than that of the nerveless sentimentalist and dreamer, who spends his time in a weltering sea of insensibility and emotion, but who never does a manly deed."

What was at issue, as William had learned and relearned, was the

* After some fairly forthright observations about the total decay of chastity in certain human types (prostitutes, for example) and "the fondness of the ancients and modern Orientals" for modes of "unnatural vice" which he believes would horrify the Western man, James concludes: "These details are a little unpleasant to discuss, but they show so beautifully the correctness of the general principles"—about the phenomenon of instinct—"in the light of which our review has been made, that it was impossible to pass them over unremarked." Gerald E. Myers, in his invaluable *William James: His Life and Thought* (1986), has an exceedingly judicious discussion (212–13) of William James's philosophical views about sex.

439]

energizing of the individual will. And for William James, the will was not separable from belief. *"Will and Belief,"* he argued with maximum emphasis in "The Perception of Reality," *". . . are two names for one and the same* PSYCHOLOGICAL *phenomenon."* What inhibits the willed belief, and hence forestalls any action or manly deed that might follow, was the pernicious tendency to question everything; the habit of indulging in what William in the pivotal 1870 journal passage had described as "mere speculation and contemplative *Grübelei,"* his fatal addiction. He draws on the same verbal root when, in arguing that "doubt and inquiry" are the true opposites of belief, he speaks of "the pathological state" that "has been called the questioning mania (*Grübelsucht*) by the Germans." He rounds out this phase of the discourse by quoting from his own self-bracing article of 1882, which asked: What moral creed might fully *enlist* the individual belief? "The impulse to take life strivingly," William had written, "is indestructible in the race." Consequently, the kind of moral creed that speaks to that impulse will always be successful, however inconsistent and vague in expression.

The general theme is picked up five chapters later when William confronts the phenomenon of "the obstructed will"; and thereby confronts the William James of the 1870s, the uncertain academic and the vacillating lover. The discursive sequence has cumulative poetry. "The healthy state of the will," William says, "requires . . . both that vision should be right, and that action should obey its lead. But in the morbid condition . . . the vision may be wholly unaffected, and the intellect clear, and yet the act either fails to follow or follows in some other way." The tone deepens: "The moral tragedy of human life comes almost wholly from the fact that the link is ruptured which normally should hold between vision of truth and action." And a little later: "The consciousness of inward hollowness that accrues from habitually seeing the better only to do the worse, is one of the saddest feelings one can bear with him through this vale of tears."

William then posits an ideal impulse in some sort which will overcome "obstructive conditions" and issue in moral action consonant in power with the resistance it meets. But William has now passed beyond argumentation; and he takes flight in a passage of extraordinary rhetorical energy. It is the climax of the chapter, the climax of the book, and the climax of his intellectual and imaginative life to this moment.

If the "searching of our heart and reins" be the purpose of this human drama, then what is sought seems to be what effort we can make. He who can make

[440

none is but a shadow; he who can make much is a hero . . . When a dreadful object is presented, or when life as a whole turns up its darkest abysses to our view, then the worthless ones among us lose their hold on the situation altogether, and either escape from its difficulties by averting their attention, or if they cannot do that, collapse into yielding masses of plaintiveness and fear . . . But the heroic mind does differently. To it, too, objects are sinister and dreadful, unwelcome, incompatible with wished-for things. But it can face them if necessary, without for that losing its hold upon the rest of life. The world thus finds in the heroic man its worthy match and mate . . . He can *stand* this Universe. He can meet it and keep up his faith in it in presence of those same features which lay his weaker brethren low . . . And thereby he becomes one of the masters and the lords of life. He must be counted with henceforth; he forms part of the human destiny. Neither in the theoretic or in the practical sphere do we care for, or go for help to, those who have no head for risks, or sense for living on the perilous edge . . . We draw new life from the heroic example.

With this paean to the heroic mind (it repays reading slowly and savoringly), William James celebrated his victory over those former shadow-selves: the one who held back during the war, while his brother faced the battlefield horror and emerged a hero; and perhaps even more important, the self incapable of sustained action in the aftertime. He had become the champion of arduous effort, the apostle of risk-taking and of life at the perilous edge; the heroic image here portrayed is not other than a projection of his ideal self. There would be reprises in later years, two of which have been mentioned: an experience that led to the essay "What Makes a Life Significant," and the astonishing last lecture in *Pragmatism*, with its imagined challenge to mental heroism from the highest authority.

The long passage has a dazzling literary force, and in good part it is woven out of the literary past. The phrase "the lords of life" probably comes from the motto-poem at the head of Emerson's essay "Experience": "The lords of life, the lords of life,— / I saw them pass / In their own guise." Emerson is cited twice in the text (once with regard to the "abrupt epithets" used by the great poets), and the Emersonian *tone*, rhapsodic and galvanizing, is audible in the lines just quoted, as it is elsewhere. The experiential Emerson, so to name him, would not be fully felt until the early 1900s, when William began to flesh out his pragmatic theory of knowledge and experience.

Shakespeare enters the passage in "Will" with the phrase "When a dreadful object is presented . . ." Brutus's little soliloquy in Act II of *Julius Caesar* is indeed a precursor imaging of William James's meditation on will and action:

> *Between the acting of a dreadful thing*
> *And the first motion, all the interim is*
> *Like a phantasm, or a hideous dream . . .*

And T. S. Eliot merged the Shakespearean lines with the language and the psychological insight of William James in his classic poem about the obstructed will, "The Hollow Men" of 1925:

> *Between the idea*
> *And the reality*
> *Between the motion*
> *And the act*
> *Falls the Shadow.*

"The link is ruptured . . . between vision of truth and action," writes James, and this "consciousness of inward hollowness" is one of the saddest of human feelings.

But the mention of T. S. Eliot brings one to realize, with a certain surprise, that William James had arguably a greater literary influence than Henry James: that is, influence upon literary practitioners, poets and novelists, rather than critics and theorists. Robert Frost came to Harvard as a special student in 1897, at age twenty-three, to read classical literature, but even more to study under William James, whose volume of essays *The Will to Believe*, published the previous April, had impressed him enormously. In fact, when he signed up for Professor James's course in psychology, he discovered that James had taken sick leave for the year; but under the guidance of Hugo Munsterberg, young Frost made his way carefully through the abridged version of *The Principles of Psychology*, and he later used that text in his own course in psychology, in a Massachusetts high school. We hear James's voice unmistakably in Frost's later definition of a poem, any good poem: "an epitome of the great predicament; a figure of the will braving alien entanglements." We see the Jamesian drama of the will played out in a Frostian poem like "The Onset," where the speaker faces the alien entanglements of night, the dark woods, the first falling snow, and almost surrenders:

Fraternal Principles: Psychology and Drama

> *I almost stumble looking up and round,*
> *As one who overtaken by the end*
> *Gives up his errand, and lets death descend*
> *Upon him where he is . . .*

Robert Penn Warren has remarked that "Frost's basic view of poetry can be regarded as an extension of James's philosophy of pragmatism, of the interplay of will and uncertified possibility in the pluralistic universe, of the interplay of courage and the tragic contingencies."* Warren goes on to say about Gertrude Stein, one of James's favorite students at Harvard, that her theory and practice of writing were conditioned by James's ideas about the nature of consciousness; and suggests that Gertrude Stein might herself have been "the nexus between James and Hemingway, who, in a certain sense, was the embodiment in action of James's theories." The "drama of 'risk,' " Warren writes, "is at the center of the Hemingway story, as at the center of James's philosophy"; and for both writers, in this context, " 'style' . . . is a moral value, a redemptive truth."

The words come with special force from the writer in our time who, all things considered, has best turned the philosophy and rhetoric of William James to his own masterfully original imaginative ends. One could invoke many a Warren text in support of the statement: the psychic career of Jack Burden in *All the King's Men*, for example; the solicitation of risk in *Wilderness*; individual poems over forty-five years. We might allow the poem "Dragon Country" of 1956 to stand as a kind of shorthand in the matter. A mythical Beast prowls the Kentucky countryside; he is the source of violent death and destruction, but in the Jamesian phrase, he *makes life significant.* For—

> *If the Beast were withdrawn now, life might dwindle again*
> *To the ennui, the pleasure, and the night sweat, known in the time before*
> *Necessity of truth had trodden the land, and our hearts, to pain,*
> *And left, in darkness, the fearful glimmer of joy, like a spoor.*

RHYTHMS OF CONSCIOUSNESS

What rapidly became the best-known section of *The Principles of Psychology* is the ninth chapter of Volume I, "The Stream of Thought";

---

* Warren here (*American Literature: The Makers and the Making*, Volume C) is partly paraphrasing the acute comments by Jay Martin in *Harvests of Change* (1967).

in the abridged version and in the phrase that caught on, "The Stream of Consciousness." This, needless to say, was the chapter that would have an epochal and enduring influence on the world of letters, and especially on the novelists within it. It is here, too, that we come upon particularly suggestive affinities between William and Henry: the former's theory, the latter's practice.

The first cardinal point about thought, or thinking, William deposes, is that it is altogether *personal*. Individual minds are entirely apart one from another: "There is no giving or bartering between them." The condition is incorrigible: "absolute insulation," William holds, ". . . is the law"—as though to say that, in the mental life, every man is after all an island. A comparable conviction had long provided a recurring and often poignant motif in the fiction of Henry James, for whom, as one critic has well remarked, "the central adversity of the human condition . . . rises from the 'otherness' of every individual from every other individual. It is aliens who make every commerce there is, and every intimacy."*

Inspecting the personal consciousness, as to its nature and form of life, William rejects the old thesis of "clear and distinct ideas." In fact, he argues, "the definite images of traditional psychology form but the very smallest part of our minds as they actually live." Any definite image that the mind may entertain (William by policy uses the words "image" and "idea" more or less interchangeably) is suffused by the felt presence of swarming relations. Indeed, the very value of the image "is all in this halo or penumbra that surrounds and escorts it—or rather is fused into one with it." In a later passage, he offers *"psychic overtone, suffusion, or fringe"* to designate "the influence of a faint brain process upon our thought," as that process makes the thought aware of "relations and objects dimly perceived." What he was anxious to press upon the reader's attention, William said, was "the reinstatement of the vague to its proper place in our mental life." Virginia Woolf would carry forward from the Jamesian discussion and speak for a generation of "stream-of-consciousness" writers when she wrote, in an essay of 1925, that "Life"—and, again, she meant the mental life—"is not a series of gig-lamps symmetrically arranged; but a luminous halo, a semi-transparent envelope surrounding us from the beginning of consciousness to the end."

Given William's view of the mind, it is more than a little puzzling that he seemed unable to appreciate, or anyhow to honor, the mode

* R. P. Blackmur, introduction to the Laurel edition of *The Wings of the Dove* (1958).

of Henry's literary accomplishment. For it had been exactly Henry's intention to show the thoughts or images in his characters' minds as haloed and shadowed by shifting awarenesses; to introduce the vague into fiction writing. In his essay "The Art of Fiction" in 1884, Henry had established the basis for his novelistic practice by his definition of "experience," that entity out of which every author was enjoined to write:

Experience is never limited, and it is never complete; it is an immense sensibility, a kind of huge spider-web of the finest silken threads suspended in the chamber of consciousness, and catching every airborne particle in its tissue. It is the very atmosphere of the mind.

But as psychological analyst and fictional tactician, William and Henry were even closer to one another than has so far been suggested. To show how this could be, we must take a step backward in the career of Henry James.

It was in the spring of 1889 that Henry made the decision to try his fortune on the English stage. To this end, he accepted the invitation of Edward Compton, a young English actor-manager, to do a play version of *The American*. His basic motive, he told himself, was economic need. "Of art or fame *il est maintenant fort peu question*," he wrote in his notebook on May 12, 1889. "I simply *must* try, and try seriously, to produce half a dozen—a dozen, five dozen—plays for the sake of my pocket, my material future. Of how little money the novel makes for me I needn't discourse here." The two big novels of the late 1880s had not earned back their advance, and Macmillan had consequently proposed no more than £70 for the English edition of *The Tragic Muse*. When Henry James declared he would rather not be published in England than accept such a fee, Macmillan apparently raised it a little, but the signs were discouraging. Since Henry's payments from the Syracuse properties were still going to Alice (who did not spend them), his literary income was all Henry had for his generally comfortable style of existence, and it was no longer enough.

Writing to Alice from Palazzo Barbaro in Venice, in June 1890, Henry daydreamed about unending financial triumphs: maybe £350 a month ($17,000 a year) from the long London run of *The American*, larger profits from a New York production, money flowing in from road companies in the United States and Australia. With these heady anticipations, Henry settled down at last to the job, and completed it in relatively short order. There were long and, for Henry, inexplicable and exasperating delays until the play went into rehearsal in the fall of 1890. Edward Compton, the troupe leader, tall, slender, and elegant, with a tendency to lounge about hands in pocket (in emulation of a typical William James posture, according to the author), played a mustachioed Christopher Newman. His wife, the American-born Virginia Bateman, who first drew her husband's attention to *The American* as a possible play, had the part of Claire de Cintré.

"Our absorbing interest just now," Alice wrote her sister-in-law in late November, "is of course Harry's dramatic debut at the end of next month . . . I have been on tenterhooks about it for a year and half now." *The American* opened at the Winter Garden Theatre in Southport, Lancashire (a little to the north of Liverpool and providing, so Alice claimed, "the best provincial audience"), on the night of January 3, 1891. Henry, too nervous to eat dinner, went over to the theater ahead of time and walked about on the stage, dusting off the mantelpiece and setting some of the props straight. The performance succeeded well enough with its Lancashire playgoers, eliciting a good deal of laughter and applause. Henry's telegraphed report to Alice next day gave vent to forgivable hyperbole: UNQUALIFIED TRIUMPHANT MAGNIFICENT SUCCESS UNIVERSAL CONGRATULATIONS GREAT OVATION FOR AUTHOR. A week later, in London, Henry wrote Robert Louis Stevenson that he was still blushing over the play's enthusiastic reception, and struck an apologetic pose: "Don't be hard on me—simplifying and chastening necessity has laid its brutal hand on me and I have had to try to make somehow or other the money I don't make by literature." A few days after that, announcing that he had been out of town on "a base theatrical errand"—he was following *The American* around the provinces—he referred to the play as his "tribute to the vulgarest of the muses."

In another letter to Stevenson, Henry insisted that his zeal in the dramatic undertaking was matched only by his indifference. But he was beginning to confess to a profound literary gratification. "I feel," he said, "as if I had at last *found* my form—my real one—that for which pale fiction is an ineffectual substitute." He used almost identical words to William about the inadequacy of the "pale" art of fiction, remarking that he had always "innermostly" known that *drama* was his "more characteristic form," and that he had held back from it because of his partly exaggerated sense of what was difficult and disagreeable in the theater. There was considerable truth to this: Henry James's literary art had always veered toward the dramatic; an imaginative tendency starting in adolescence, bolstered by playgoing in New York and in the Paris of the 1870s, and by his recent fictional investigation of the theater and theatrical performers in his novel *The Tragic Muse*.

The well-known paradox remains. The inhering dramatic quality that Henry James never managed to achieve in his stage plays, neither in *The American* nor in anything else, was exactly the hallmark of his best fiction from 1890 onward. It was never better exemplified than in his story "The Pupil," written during the same months when Henry was dramatizing *The American*.*

Writing about "The Pupil," along with two other narratives of the 1890s, *What Maisie Knew* and "In the Cage," Henry James described them as "little constituted dramas," each embodying an *action*. They were organized along a series of scenes; they displayed on reperusal a thoroughly admirable "scenic consistency." Going over them again for the immediate purpose (the New York Edition in the 1900s) had, at all events, been for him "quite to watch the scenic system at play." He explained that system as an alternation of two key structural ingredients: "The treatment by 'scene,' regularly, quite rhythmically recurs; the intervals between, the massing of the elements to a different effect and by a quite other law, remain, in this fashion, all preparative, just as the scenic occasions in themselves become, at a given moment, illustrative."

Such was the fundamental vocabulary of what might be taken as Henry James's principles of dramatic action. In *The Principles of Psychology*, William James, exploring "the wonderful stream of consciousness," charts the differing pace of its parts, in the figure of a bird in flight.

Like a bird's life, it seems to be made of an alternation of flights and perchings . . . The resting places are usually occupied by sensorial imaginations of some sort, whose peculiarity is that they can be held before the mind for an indefinite time, and contemplated without changing: the places of flight are filled with thoughts of relations, static or dynamic, that for the most part obtain between the matters contemplated in the periods of comparative rest.

Let us call the resting places the "substantive parts," and the places of flight the "transitive parts" of the stream of thought.

* On the stage career of *The American*, and Henry James's other writings for the theater, see Chapter Fourteen.

A bit further along, after discoursing (in sentences quoted earlier) on the role of halo or penumbra in the coloration of thought, William writes in summary: "The only images *intrinsically* important are the halting places, the substantive conclusions, provisional or final, of the thoughts. Throughout all the rest of the stream, the feelings of relations are everything, and the terms related almost naught."

Between William's flights-and-perchings and Henry's intervals-and-scenes, we can posit, not an equation (which would be badly misleading), but a proportion. Thus: Henry's interval relates to his scene *as* William's flight does to his perching. Or, giving the elements the different Jamesian nomenclatures, we can say that William's transitive leads to his substantive in a manner similar to Henry's sequence from preparative to illustrative.

"The Pupil" is a capital case in point, and it has the added interest of its James family origin. It looks back, as was said, from 1890 to the period of the Jameses' wanderings in Europe in the 1850s, the time when Henry was content in the galleries and museums to serve as the pupil of his older brother, and the moment when the fifteen-year-old Henry underwent an attack of fever which almost bore him off—as, in the tale, the fifteen-year-old Morgan Moreen suffers a heart attack and dies.

The scenic system works to a kind of perfection. Part II, for instance, is an adroitly composed interval: it covers a stretched-out period of weeks and months in Nice, during which the young American, Pemberton, gropes his way into his situation as tutor to the frail and sensitive Morgan Moreen, the youngest member of the odd, untrustworthy Moreen clan. It consists of typical or recurring actions; in French, the narrative would be cast in the imperfect tense—"they *used to*" do this or that. Here, as in the places of flight in William James's tracing of consciousness, the thickening sense of relation is everything: the literal and the psychic relations of the Moreens to one another (they communicated, Pemberton notices, "in an ingenious dialect of their own"), of the other Moreens to Morgan, of Pemberton and his pupil.

Part III that follows is a scene pure and intact, and begins suitably with a dramatic shift to the emphasized particular and to the perfect tense: "At Nice, once, towards evening . . . Morgan said suddenly to his companion: 'Do you like it—you know, being with us all in this intimate way?' " It is quite literally a resting place: the pair, James tells us, "sat resting in the open air after a walk, looking over the sea at the pink western lights." The substantive element (in William's language), the image that comes to them and is contemplated in the brief time of perching, is contained in an intense but silent exchange of understanding—presumably of a shy, shared affection—that causes each to turn red.

The fraternal analogy at this stage is so striking that one has to wonder whether or to what extent Henry James in "The Pupil" was actually "applying" his brother's mobile diagram of consciousness. For Henry's subject, too—what he was dramatizing—was the movement of individual consciousness; as he would put it, "little Morgan's troubled vision" of the family, as reflected in the vision, "also troubled enough," of his tutor. And the recounted physical movements of the Moreens, their dashings and scramblings about Europe from lodging to temporary lodging, are themselves all plainly a series of flights and perchings.

There would not have been time for Henry to have read the chapter on "the stream of thought" in the *Principles* before writing this tale. But he did read an early version of it in the January 1884 issue of *Mind*, with another 1884 article in the same periodical that was enlarged into the chapter on "the emotions." "I have attacked your two *Mind* articles, with admiration," Henry wrote William in April 1884, "but been defeated. I can't give them just now the necessary time." But Henry often liked to disclaim any ability to cope with philosophic theory, his father's, his brother's, or anyone else's; and he did so with special emphasis if he was about to make fictional use of it. Some concatenation of perceptions and figurative phrases seems to have seeped into his mind, and there, it might be hazarded, it fused with that part of his imagination that was congenitally dramatistic.

The vivid little scene in Part III modulates into another interval in "The Pupil," with the group fleeing to Paris, where Pemberton and Morgan "took a hundred remunerative rambles" and "learned to know their Paris." Henry James is far from adhering to a rigid scheme, whereby one numbered section is a scene and its successor an interval; this would be false to the irregular pace of consciousness and boring to the aesthetic sense. Part IV, after carrying us through winter days at the Louvre and summer mornings along the Paris quais, comes to its own sharp scenic climax. Pemberton has confronted Mr. and Mrs. Moreen about his unpaid salary, and they have managed to dodge the issue. Going back to his ugly little room upstairs, Pemberton is seized with the most important "sensorial imagination" (William's phrase) in the entire tale, and he holds it before his dismayed mind for long minutes. "He had simply given himself away to a band of adventurers . . . The Moreens were adventurers not merely because they didn't pay their debts, because they lived on society, but because their whole view of life, dim and confused and instinctive, like that of clever colour-blind animals, was speculative and rapacious and mean."

So the process continues. In Part VII, we pass through another summer, this one spent amid a flurry of social events in Venice; until the narrative reaches a particular "sad November day, [when] the wind roared round the old palace and the rain lashed the lagoon"; and the Moreens are faced with a financial crisis so acute that Pemberton is forced to leave, to take employment with a rich youth in England. He is summoned back before long, at the start of the eighth and final part, where Paris again provides the setting. This second interval of "wan-derings and maunderings, [and] potterings on the quays" leads into the final scene, which takes place on "one winter afternoon—it was a Sunday," with the worst financial storm yet brewing up.

The parents declare their sacrificial willingness to let Pemberton take Morgan off their hands permanently. But the image that thereupon takes hold of Morgan's mind and by which he is instantly stricken is that of his tutor's instinctive recoil from the responsibility. Morgan turns white, clutches at his side, falls back in his chair; and his heart stops beating. Nowhere in Henry James's fiction does the scenic system, the pace of the dramatized consciousness, arrive at a more touching or a more absolute halting place.

CHAPTER FOURTEEN

Records of an Invalid:
1889-92

THE IRISH QUESTION

Thinking about her older brother a few weeks after the Leamington reunion, Alice remarked in her diary that William seemed "sound eno' on Home Rule, but how could a child of Father's be anything else!!" She also appreciated William's comments on the extraordinary way in which a "jovial, sociable, witty, intelligent race" could be seen coming out of the misery and squalor of the living conditions; and William may have said to her, as he did to his wife, that the gross social inequities visible in Ireland were enough to make anyone a revolutionist. Henry, too, as she knew, stood in favor of Home Rule for Ireland, though in an ambiguous and grudging manner. But in her James generation, Alice was by far the most passionately pro-Irish, and as Henry would acknowledge, the most unmistakable descendant of her County Cavan forebears.

"She was really an Irishwoman!" Henry was to exclaim to William with an air of belated discovery. The Irish political struggle aroused in her "a tremendous emotion" that was "inexplicable in any other way— but perfectly explicable by 'atavism.' "

"It is a horrible moment politically," Alice had written William in April 1887. The reference was to the new turn in the drama of Charles Stewart Parnell, the beleaguered and magnetic champion of the Irish cause and leader of the Irish party in the British Parliament.

The (London) *Times* had begun a series of articles called "Parnellism and Crime," and on April 18 published a letter allegedly written by Parnell which condoned the murder in Phoenix Park, Dublin, five years before, of England's chief secretary for Ireland. At that time, 1882, Parnell had wholly dissociated himself from the event, denouncing it publicly as cowardly and unprovoked, and more damaging to Ireland than any action in half a century. But now, according to the *Times* letter, it seemed that Parnell had privately endorsed the killings, particularly that of the under secretary, who "got no more than his deserts."

Alice was violently partisan. Nearly all her London friends, she told William, were opposed to Home Rule, or, as she put it, were "imbecile Unionist abortions." Their "hideous, patronizing, doctrinaire, all-for-Ireland's-good, little measured out globules of remedies," she said, "make my blood boil so I never speak on the subject." As to the charges being mounted against Parnell—conspiring to stir up "agrarian agitation" as well as the business of the Dublin killings—Parliament, after a delay, appointed a Special Commission of three judges to investigate them. The commission was able to settle the most sensational issue in a matter of months, establishing the fact that the *Times* letter was the forgery of a shady journalist named Richard Pigott, who confessed and then shot himself.

Henry, after attending the crowded hearings, supplied Alice with the text of a major speech by Parnell's defense counsel, the redoubtable Lord Charles Russell; Alice declared it "thrilling to read." When the judges issued their final report in February 1890, they exonerated Parnell of all charges of treason and incitement to crime, though finding him vaguely guilty in the matter of agrarian unrest. Russell made another speech at this time, extolling Parnell's historic services to Ireland and hence to the Empire. Alice thought it so moving that she pasted the key portion of it into her journal.

But at that same victorious instant, another part of the drama was beginning to unfold. In December 1889, Captain William O'Shea, Parnell's sometime emissary, filed divorce proceedings against his wife, Kitty, on the grounds of adultery with Parnell, who was named co-respondent. Alice lapsed into sympathetic brogue on reading the news: "Capt. O'Shea has laid a *nate* trap for Parnell, with his Divorce suit, just at this moment." She had nothing but contempt for "the hyper-refined Unionists" and the "choice allies" they had working for them: "Pigott and this vile O'Shea who uses his wife's dishonour to destroy his foe." From what she could hear, though, she supposed that Parnell was done for. She foresaw dire complications for the "Liberals," the pro-Irish wing of that divided party headed by Gladstone. But in a sentence she inscribed in her diary and wrote in a letter to her sister-in-law, she affirmed her belief that "Irish Home Rule like 'Emancipation' is one of the immutable moralities," and would triumph in spite of all setbacks and delays.

Henry James, taking note of the venomous disagreements in the British political world, wondered at times whether armed hostilities might not actually be in the offing. But he responded as a novelist and an incipient dramatist, and displayed little of the compelling historical awareness evident in the remark of Alice's just quoted.

The analogy between the battle for independence in Ireland and the long fight to free the black slaves in America was a potent one in Alice James's mind (as in that of others, then and since). The journal entry which contained the passage from Russell's speech, for example, was immediately preceded by her counter-comments on some profoundly wrong-headed statements, as she thought, about the American Civil War. One, in the *Pall Mall Gazette*, alluded to it as "the most savage war of modern times," with thousands of prisoners starving to death on one side and wounded men "shot in cold blood on the other." "Dost think," Alice silently asked the writer, "that the war was waged with no object save as a vent for savagery? or is the freeing of millions of human beings from bondage a cause unworthy to lift up the hearts of wives to send forth their husbands and mothers their sons to battle?"

Another onlooker, comparing "Russian despotism" with "American despotism" in the 1860s, said that the comparison was unfair to the Russian ruler: "For whilst Alexander Romanoff breaks the chains of his slaves Abraham Lincoln only breaks the chains of his enemies' slaves." Alice found this exceedingly bizarre. "The impression given . . . of that embodied benignancy, poor old, tragic Lincoln, freeing slaves only, *qua enemy's* slaves with a preserve, perhaps, of his own in the background at the White House shows the marvellous possibilities of non-apprehension."

But within that larger historical analogy, a more personal one was astir in Alice's consciousness. Her disquisitions on the Irish question tend to interweave in her diary, and especially in 1889–90, with accounts of her changing physical and psychological condition. What can be discovered just below the surface of the text is a felt intimate relation between Alice's struggle to live, for all her physical wretchedness, as a mentally alert and expressive individual and woman and the Irish contest for self-rule and national identity in the face of their own material miseries.

In a reflection of March 30, 1890, Alice was able to say that after three years at 11 Hamilton Terrace in Leamington, she was possessed by a feeling of at-homeness, even in the two rented rooms. She had as well become ever friendlier with the natural surroundings of the place, getting out in her Bath chair with some regularity on the coming of sufficiently clement weather; she celebrated July 4, 1889, by announcing "the glorious fact" that she had "been out already 15 times." She would be wheeled into a meadow where she could lie back in the sun while nurse and chair man picked flowers for her, a cuckoo audible in the distance and swallows circling overhead. Once, she was pushed into a hayfield amid the haymakers, and later through a flock of drifting sheep.

The immersion in nature could be exhausting: she remarked in her journal once that she hadn't been receiving visitors for the last days because "confronting the landscape in the a.m. leaves me without further resistance and then an afternoon of prattle! after that divine contemplation would be too much of an anticlimax." Not that her aesthetic judgment had grown sentimental. The English landscape, she wrote acutely (for what she knew of it), even when most "soaked in beauty," was an "arranged respectable expectedness," which might irritate those who preferred spontaneities in nature. It was, though, to her personal taste.

As autumn 1889 passed into winter, the old sense of solitude began to set in again. Katharine Loring, who had been with Alice in Leamington for several months, sailed for Boston on November 9. Recording the event, Alice found imaginative new language with which to praise her friend: even with "the burden of three invalids upon her soul" (Katharine's sister and father as well as Alice James), she retained her good humor and calm temper, and appeared to Alice as "an embodiment of the stretchable, a purely transatlantic and modern possibility." Henry was away, too, however, for a long stay in Paris, and Alice likened herself to a creature who, after a season of fresh air, was once more shut down, closed in, to the sound of "a hopeless and all too familiar click." She strove anew to adjust to the condition and, with the help of a quotation from Flaubert about the soul enlarging itself through suffering, tried to believe she could do so. But she confessed with bleak clarity that she could never allow it to be "anything else than a cruel and unnatural fate for a woman to live alone, to have no one to care and 'do for' daily is not only a sorrow, but a sterilizing process."

Alice kept going through the spring and into the summer of 1890 by a self-enlivening interest in the world around her—the vicissitudes of the Irish question, a revolution in Brazil, peculiar notes in the London news, further examples (as she saw it) of British pharisaism, the death of Robert Browning and Henry's obituary of the poet, the debate over a Channel tunnel to link England and France (a discussion which Alice thought reached peaks of absurdity).

In mid-July, she underwent a hideous attack in which clenching stomach sensations combined with an ulcerated tooth and a strained neck muscle to give her "shivering whacks of crude pain." Having taken a dose of morphia, she could, as she said, *experience* these onslaughts as from a distance in a hallucinatory way that was almost exhilarating. Then, on August 2, a Saturday, she "went under" in what was recognized as a nearly total collapse. In retrospect, one sees it as the last physical turning point of her life.

A telegram was at once dispatched to Henry in Italy. Three months before, Henry, having completed the dramatization of *The American*, and with *The Tragic Muse* having made its two-volume appearance in England, departed as per custom for a visit to Italy. As though reliving 1886, he read Howells on the rocketing night train from Victoria, the second volume of *A Hazard of New Fortunes*. In unwitting agreement with his brother Bob, Henry described the novel to its author as "simply prodigious," the best and most rounded of Howells's fictions, with a larger human variety than Zola. There was a fortnight with the Curtises at Palazzo Barbaro in Venice, and then a journey by carriage with his host and hostess up through the Dolomites to Oberammergau and attendance at the Passion Play—which Henry, generous with adjectives, characterized as curious, tedious, touching, and intensely respectable and German.

On his way back south, Henry made a stopover at Innsbruck— "all these Tyrolean countries are beyond praise"—and came down through Bolzano and Bassano to Venice and ultimately to Florence. He went up for an hour to Bellosguardo, sadly feeling the absence of Fenimore Woolson, who had given up Villa Brichieri and was now living in Cheltenham, in Gloucester, near enough to Leamington for an occasional visit. In Florence, Henry was the guest of Dr. Baldwin, and the two of them, with an Italian friend of the doctor's named Taccini (James took the name for use in *The Wings of the Dove*), made a four-day hiking trip through some lesser known corners of Tuscany.

Alice's telegram found Henry ensconced in an inn called Paradisino, properly so, Henry thought, in the village of Vallombrosa, a thousand meters above the Tuscan valley. The inn, on a pedestal of rock, hung over the abyss, in Henry's image, like the prow of a ship. He was altogether enchanted: "The place is extraordinarily beautiful and 'sympathetic,' " he wrote William in late July, "and the most romantic mountains and most admirable woods." With Milton's line from *Paradise Lost* echoing in his ear—"Thick as autumnal leaves that strew the brooks / In Vallombrosa"—Henry walked and wandered, in a manner he had not done for twenty years, through birch and chestnut groves and the dusky pine forest and lay, book in hand, on the warm, breezy hillside. It gave him a feeling of summer, he told his brother, that he had somehow lost in all the London Julys; gave indeed "almost the summer of one's childhood back again."

Even so, he responded immediately to Alice's appeal and was back in England in a matter of days. After inspecting the situation, he cabled Katharine Loring. She received his word in Beverly on August 6, and left by the first boat for Liverpool. By the second of September, Katharine and Henry, between them, succeeded in moving Alice from her Leamington lodgings back to London, and installed her in the South Kensington Hotel on Queen's Gate Terrace, a short street only a few hundred yards from De Vere Gardens.

In these new and comfortable quarters, Alice was, as she felt, "close to the excellent Henry whose anxious and affect[ionate] mind is gratified by keeping a daily eye upon the fading flower." There was little doubt that she *was* fading, though at an indeterminate pace. "There seems a faint hope that I may fizzle out," Alice informed her diary on September 12, and claimed to be pleased by the comment of Dr. Baldwin, who had come over from Florence and was staying with Henry. When asked by Henry and Katharine whether Alice could die, Dr. Baldwin answered: "They sometimes do." "This is most cheering to all parties," Alice wrote. It is from this time, in fact, that one can date Alice's most forthright, if usually self-mocking expressions of an effort to bring her life to a close. The only variety in her day, she wrote Mrs. William on November 26, was in the degree of discomfort: "And I find much entertainment therein. I am working away as hard as I can to get dead as soon as possible so as to release Katharine."

But as her diary and letters testify, there was no slackening in energy of curiosity, about either her personal state or the ironies of history. "Katharine is a most sustaining optimist," Alice remarked briskly in a January 1891 entry which was dictated to the person in question. "She proposed writing for me this morning. I said 'Why, you won't have time.' 'Oh, yes, I'm not going until twelve, and by that time you are always back again in bed, fainted.' " But the single most important matter in the world outside continued for Alice to be the Irish question.

Things on that front were coming to a head in the waning autumn of 1890. Gladstone let it be known in a published letter that, great as Parnell's contributions had been, "his continuance at the present moment in the leadership would be disastrous in the highest degree to the cause of Ireland." Parnell was urged to resign his seat in Parliament and his control of the Irish constituency. He angrily refused, countering with a manifesto, "To the People of Ireland," which accused Gladstone and the Liberals of systematically seeking to destroy the Irish party and, by innuendo, of betraying the cause of Irish freedom. This, coming after the revelation of Parnell's scarcely concealed and full-scale adultery, was too much for Alice James.

She was not unaware of Gladstone's calculated political maneuvering, but she was even more alert to the classical pattern of Parnell's story. To this, she devoted most of the journal entry for November 30, 1890, showing therein her own Jamesian flair for redoing history by lending artistic shape to facts and events:

Could there be a more dramatic irony? Parnell after his years of desperate struggle, within a few months, more or less, of a superb victory, escaping from the huge paraphernalia of the Commission built up so laboriously to crush him, smirched and of necessity to be eclipsed only for a short time by the loathsome divorce-suit, pushed on by relentless fate not only to ruin himself in the present but by a few strokes of his pen to brand himself as infamous for all history. What a heart sickening day was yesterday and how I wept over Parnell's Manifesto with its portent of the possible death and burial of Home Rule, for if tomorrow the Irish pronounce for him one's ear must turn itself, one's heart close itself against the woes of that tragic land. No cause is sacred eno' to be fought with such a base tool, the betrayer of his friend, the betrayer of his allies, the betrayer of his country!

The Irish, it may be recalled, did not "pronounce for him." At a meeting of the seventy-one Irish Members of Parliament, forty-five walked quietly out of the room as a way of signaling the end of Parnell's leadership. Parnell died the following year.

Alice's attitude—that if Ireland stood behind Parnell, it would forfeit its hold on her compassion—did not arise out of sentimental moralism, a quality that, as she knew, her father would have scoffed at. Her stance was uncompromising, but what she revered in Ireland above all else was its devotion to an ideal of freedom, dignity, self-respect; what she made out as its spirituality of nature. Applauding William for his image of the Irish, amid their penury, "living *entirely* upon an ideal," she added: "Oh, the tragedy of it! when you think of the dauntless creatures flinging themselves and their ideal for seven centuries against the dense wall of British brutality, as incapable of an ideal inspiration or an imaginative movement as the beasts of the field." It was this ideal, in Alice's sense of it, that further support of Charles Parnell under the circumstances would belie.

Her love and admiration for Ireland, as will have been evident, fed an almost unmodified severity toward England. As her months of residence passed, England became for Alice the home not only of the cruel repression of Irish hopes but, as causes of it, the hypocritically respectable, the humorless, the unimaginative, and of everything that she caught up in the word "pharisaism." This quality, she wrote in a February 1890 passage of developing intensity and thickening specificity, was something all pervasive in

the British constitution of things. You don't feel it at first and you can't put your finger upon it in your friends, but as the days go by you unfold it with your *Standard*, in the morn. It rises dense from the *P.M.G.* [*Pall Mall Gazette*] in the evening, it creeps thro' the cracks in the window frames like the fog and envelopes you thro' the day.

She ranged through the aspects of English social behavior that repelled her in a manner reminiscent of Henry's litany (in his book on Hawthorne in 1879) of what was deplorably absent from the American social scene:

It's woven of a multiplicity of minute details and incidents which elude you in the telling but which seem to exist in the texture of things and leave a dent in the mind as they file past. A monarchy to which they bow down in its tinsel capacity only, denying to it a manly movement of any sort; a boneless Church broadening itself out, up to date; the hysterical legislation over a dog with a broken leg whilst Society is engaged making bags of 4,000 pheasants, etc. etc., or gloating over foxes torn to pieces by a pack of hounds; the docility with which the classes enslave themselves to respectability or non-respectability as the "good-form" of the moment may be; the "sense of their betters" in the masses; the passivity with which the working man allows himself to be patted and legislated out of all independence; thus the profound ineradicables in the bone and sinew conviction that outlying regions are their preserves, that they alone of human races massacre savages out of pure virtue. It would ill-become an American to reflect upon the treatment of aboriginal races; but I never heard it suggested that our hideous dealings with the Indians was brotherly love masquerading under the disguise of pure cussedness.

Alice viewed the ongoing Irish struggle in the light of a religious drama, as no few Irish writers were to do, and as William had done when he wrote his wife from Killarney that "the 'Irish Question' . . . is properly a religious movement on the part of the people and is unconquerable." In this regard, brother and sister were equally the children of Henry Senior; but Alice, at least, paid scant heed to the burning practical issue that lay at the heart of the conflict. This was agrarian reform: the concerted attempts by Parnell and his cohorts to put an end, in effect, to the landlord system in Ireland and the whole business of ruinous rentals. It was for these efforts that his English judges found Parnell guilty as charged, though not in a way that could lead to prosecution. And it was under this system that Alice James's Bailieborough ancestors had labored and suffered, and because of which her grandfather William had left Ireland for America and Albany.

For all the pleasure Alice took in the fact of her Irish connections, she seems not to have known that, in 1890, there was accessible in Bailieborough an Irish cousin, the middle-aged son of the young man who had greeted her father in 1837. This was Robert James, the fourth of that name, known in the Bailieborough community as Bobby. He had been born in 1840, and would live until 1932.

Bobby James occupied a house halfway down the main street, possibly the same house originally purchased by his uncle, the physician Robert; and could be seen, characteristically standing outside the front door, chatting amiably with passing friends. Two more farms in outlying districts had been added to the Curkish holdings, but Bobby showed little practical interest in them, being content to live as a townsman off the income they brought, and to serve as the local justice of the peace. He was a courteous, gregarious man, mildly eccentric and much liked.

When he died at ninety-two, events were in train which would soon lead his Ireland to declare itself (his cousin Alice would have

459]

exulted) a sovereign democratic state, cutting all ties with the Commonwealth. Bobby was the last of the Bailieborough Jameses in direct descent from the Curkish townlander. His only son, Henry, studied in Dublin and later settled in Cheshire, England, where he practiced medicine. This Henry seems to have felt that with his own departure some long epoch had come to a close: for in the wake of his father's death, Henry, with his sister Helen, saw to the installation of a memorial stained-glass window in the Bailieborough church, at the foot of the main street. It was inscribed to the glory of God and in memory of the four successive overseers of the Jameses' farming land, with their wives: William, Robert, Henry, Robert.

THE TWO INVALIDS

Because of the incessant tinkering, revising, and what a later generation would call play-doctoring of *The American*, preparatory for its London opening in September 1891, Henry had taken to calling the play "the other invalid." The first invalid, Alice, was in fact somewhat sustained through the summer of the year by her keen interest in the fate of the play, but it was by this time known that she was a dying woman. She had been growing perceptibly feebler for a number of months; even taking her breakfast in bed, with every assistance, seemed now to wear her out, though she could occasionally move from her bed to the sofa for a six o'clock dinner. At the end of May, in view of her continuing decline, Henry called in Sir Andrew Clark, a distinguished physician and a cancer expert, and after a thorough examination, the great man, in Alice's gratified summary, pronounced that "a lump that I have had in one of my breasts for three months, which has given me a great deal of pain, is a tumour, that nothing can be done for me but to alleviate pain, that it is only a question of time, etc."

Sir Andrew's uncompromising verdict, Alice said, gave her an enormous sense of relief. For years she had been longing "for some palpable disease," only to be told time and again that her variety of pains and paralyses were the result of "subjective sensations" for which she was herself responsible. The British specialist did find her to be a "most distressing case of nervous hyperaesthesia" (*his* words, apparently), but his chief finding was the breast tumor. "One would naturally not choose such an ugly and gruesome method of progression down the dark Valley of the Shadow of Death," Alice wrote on June 1, "and of course many of the moral sinews will snap by the way, but we shall gird up our loins and the blessed peace of the end will have no shadow cast upon it."

There had been another change of living quarters in March. Katharine and Alice decided that they needed a house to themselves; and Katharine discovered and made ready a four-story house at 41 Argyll Road in the Campden Hill section of Kensington, in a block of houses halfway up the quiet slope. It was farther from De Vere Gardens than the hotel had been, but an easy walk for the attentive Henry, who reported to Isabella Gardner that it was "a very nice house to be very ill in." Alice had spacious rooms for herself, and, in addition to Katharine Loring—who had indicated to Henry the previous autumn that she would stay with Alice to the end—there were accommodations for the faithful and brightly talkative little nurse, for a housemaid imported from Leamington, and for a cook. From her sitting room, Alice could look out into a tiny garden at the back, where Katharine was industriously planting flowers.

Henry's friend Dr. Baldwin, passing through England, paid a series of diagnostic visits to Argyll Road in the later part of July. He was the one to declare without equivocation that the lump in Alice's breast was cancerous, probably transferring (or "metastasizing") from a malignancy originally in her liver. To diminish the pain over the foreseeably brief future, he prescribed morphia.

Katharine, with Alice's permission, disclosed the finding of the tumor to William. On July 6, William, from Chocorua, wrote Alice a long letter. Both it and Alice's reply, written on July 30, after Dr. Baldwin's visits, need to be quoted virtually in full.

[William to Alice]

So far from being shocked I am, although made more compassionate, yet (strange to say) rather relieved than shaken by this more tangible and immediately menacing source of woe. Katharine describes you as being so too; and I don't wonder. Vague nervousness has a character of ill about it that is all its own, and in comparison with which any organic disease has a good side. Of course, if the tumour should turn out to be cancerous, that means, as all men know, a finite length of days; and then, good-bye to neurasthenia and neuralgia and headache, and weariness and palpitation and disgust all at one stroke—I should think you would be reconciled to the prospect with all its pluses and minuses! I know you've never cared for life, and to me, now at the age of nearly fifty, life and death seem singularly close together in all of us—

and life a mere farce of frustration in all, so far as the realization of the innermost ideals go to which we are made respectively capable of feeling an affinity and responding. Your frustrations are only rather more flagrant than the rule; and you've been saved many forms of self-dissatisfaction and misery which appertain to such a multiplication of responsible relations to different people as I, for instance, have got into. Your fortitude, good spirits and un-sentimentality have been simply unexampled in the midst of your physical woes; and when you're relieved from your post, just *that* bright note will remain behind, together with the inscrutable and mysterious character of the doom of nervous weakness which has chained you down for all these years. As for that, there's more in it than has ever been told to so-called science. These inhibitions, these split-up selves, all these new facts that are gradually coming to light about our organization, these enlargements of the self in trance, etc., are bringing me to turn for light in the direction of all sorts of despised spir-itualistic and unscientific ideas. Father would find in me today a much more receptive listener—all *that* philosophy has got to be brought in. And what a queer contradiction comes to the ordinary scientific argument against im-mortality (based on body being mind's condition and mind going *out* when body is gone), when one must believe (as now, in these neurotic cases) that some infernality in the body *prevents* really existing parts of the mind from coming to their effective rights at all, suppresses them, and blots them out from participation in this world's experiences, although they are *there* all the time. When that which is *you* passes out of the body, I am sure that there will be an explosion of liberated force and life till then eclipsed and kept down. I can hardly imagine *your* transition without a great oscillation of both "worlds" as they regain their new equilibrium after the change! Everyone will feel the shock, but you yourself will be more surprised than anybody else.

It may seem odd for me to talk to you in this cool way about your end; but, my dear little sister, if one has things present to one's mind, and I know they are present enough to *your* mind, why not speak them out? I am sure you appreciate that best. How many times I have thought, in the past year, when my days were so full of strong and varied impression and activities, of the long unchanging hours in bed which those days stood for with you, and wondered how you bore the slow-paced monotony at all, as you did! You can't tell how I've pitied you. But you *shall* come to your rights erelong. Meanwhile take things gently. Look for the little good in each day as if life were to last a hundred years. Above all things, save yourself from bodily pain, if it can be done. You've had too much of that. Take all the morphia (or other forms of opium if that disagrees) you want, and don't be afraid of becoming an opium-drunkard. What was opium created for except for such times as this? Beg the good Katharine (to whom *our* debt can never be extinguished) to write me a line every week, just to keep the currents flowing, and so farewell until I write again. Your ever loving,

W.J.

[Alice to William]

My dearest William,

A thousand thanks for your beautiful and fraternal letter, which came, I know not when, owing to Katharine's iron despotism. Of course I could have wanted nothing else and should have felt, notwithstanding my "unsentimentality" very much wounded & *incomprise* had you walked round and not up to my demise.

It is the most supremely interesting moment in life, the only one in fact, when living seems life, and I count it as the greatest good fortune to have these few months so full of interest and instruction in the knowledge of my approaching death. It is as simple in one's own person as any fact of nature, the fall of a leaf or the blooming of a rose, and I have a delicious consciousness, ever present, of wide spaces close at hand, and whisperings of release in the air.

Your philosophy of the transition is entirely mine and at this remoteness I will venture upon the impertinence of congratulating you upon having arrived "at nearly fifty" at the point at which I started at fifteen! 'Twas always thus of old, but in time you usually, as now, caught up.

But you must believe that you greatly exaggerate the tragic element in my commonplace little journey; and so far from ever having thought that "my frustrations were more flagrant than the rule" I have always simmered complacently in my complete immunity therefrom. As from early days the elusive nature of concrete hopes shone forth, I always rejoiced that my temperament had set for my task the attainment of the simplest rudimentary ideal, which I could carry about in my pocket and work away upon equally in shower as in sunshine, in complete security from the grotesque obstructions supposed to be *life*, which have indeed only strengthened the sinews to whatever imperfect accomplishment I may have attained.

You must also remember that a woman, by nature, needs much less to feed upon than a man, a few emotions and she is satisfied; so when I am gone, pray don't think of me simply as a creature who might have been something else, had neurotic science been born. Notwithstanding the poverty of my outside experience, I have always had a significance for myself—every chance to stumble along my straight and narrow little path, and to worship at the feet of my Deity, and what more can a human soul ask for?

This year has been one of the happiest I have ever known, surrounded by such affection and devotion, but I won't enter into details, as I see the blush mantle the elderly cheek of my scribe . . .

Give much love to Alice and to all the household, great and small . . .

Your always loving and grateful sister,

Alice James

William's letter, of a kind with his farewell message to Henry Senior, was forwarded to the younger Henry in Ireland. "Alice must have greatly appreciated your beautiful and interesting long letter," Henry wrote his brother, "—as *I* did. You do not exaggerate her *force d'âme*—which is extraordinary; and cannot, without seeing it, appreciate the serenity of her present attitude, which strikes me, strange as it may appear to you, as a condition of greater *comfort* than she has known for years, or probably *ever* known. The 'nervousness' engendered by (or engendering) her intense horror of life and contempt for it is practically falling away from her in view of her future becoming thus a definite and not long—a rapidly *shrinking*, term . . . Don't, therefore, be too much *haunted* with her: I am less so now than I have been for years."

Thus the three Jamesian analyses: the medically direct but compassionate, with a touch of the paternally mystical; the alertly self-inquiring with a renewed insistence on the *un*frustrated mode of being; the fiction writer's probing of the psychic sources of a contempt for life, even a horror of it.

William came over to England in mid-September 1891 for a last visit with Alice and to see the opening of Henry's play in London.

The previous December 22, Mrs. Alice had given birth to another baby. Despite Henry's voluble protests, William named the infant Francis Tweedy: the first name for the estimable Francis J. Child, the second for the aging Newport family friend. They turned out to be poor choices. The name Tweedy refused to stick and was dropped after a few years; Francis was changed to Alexander. The psychic damage to the boy in question of these shifting identities can only be guessed at.

William spent most of the summer of 1891 preparing an abridged version of the *Principles* for classroom use. The new text was simply called *Psychology*; at Harvard, it was known as "Jimmy," to distinguish it from the full-length text called "James." To Henry Holt, the author gave a jocular account of the abridgment: he had added "some twaddle about the senses," had left out "all polemics and history, all bibliog-

raphy and experimental details," had excised "all metaphysical subtleties and digressions, all quotations, all humor and pathos, all *interest*
in short," and had produced a tome "which will enrich both you and
me, if not the student's mind." *Psychology*, with its blackened paragraph heads, its briskness of procedure and no-nonsense authorial
tone, is a teaching manual, and as such would be phenomenally successful in universities across the land for years to come. It is decidedly
a text by William James, but it is not the literary achievement that the
Principles had been and remains.

In August, William allowed himself a vacation in the western
reaches of North Carolina, passing through Linville, which William
was charmed by, and on up to Blowing Rock in the midst of the
Smokies. The air on those richly colorful, densely wooded slopes was
"round-edged and balmy," he told his sister, who always enjoyed William's atmospheric adjectives. One morning he rode on horseback to
the top of Grandfather Mountain, one of the highest and handsomest
peaks in the state.

On September 12, he departed from Hoboken on the *Eider*, "a
gentlemanly" vessel. From Southampton, William went straight to
London, and after depositing his luggage in Harry's apartment, made
his way to Argyll Road. Alice had turned faint at the news of his arrival,
but William found her calm and almost unchanged in the face, though
her voice was weak and she could lie only in one position, on her back.
She spoke constantly of her approaching end, asking William playfully
whether it was the "mortuary attraction" that had brought him across
the Atlantic, or the opening of Harry's play. He ran his hand over the
breast tumor, at Alice's request. William did not entirely hold with the
theory about the initial liver cancer, but hoped fervently in any case
that heart weakness would carry his sister away before the tumor came
to the surface and began "its loathsome course." To his wife: "Poor
strange and wonderful being that she is!"

William visited with Alice three more times over the next days,
remarking to his wife how hard it was to believe, from his sister's
animation, that she would not last long, though protracted life was
exactly what was to be dreaded. "She talks death incessantly," he wrote.
"It seems to fill her with positive glee." William went down to the
Pearsall Smiths' in Haslemere, and was back in London for the opening night of *The American*. The next morning he canceled a ten-day
stay in Paris and took the first sailing available, going up immediately
to Chocorua. With the irrevocable coming loss, he felt an intense need,
as he indicated, to be back again, and close, with his wife and children.

But he wrote Alice from New Hampshire that seeing her "so well-*minded* has colored all my imagings of you with a cheerful tinge."

The first night of *The American*, in the refurbished Opera Comique Theatre in the Strand, was a gala occasion, with a good sprinkling of affluent visitors from overseas in the audience. Constance Fenimore Woolson, who was on hand, reported to a friend that the house was packed and the applause great. After the performance ended, she said, "There arose loud cries of 'Author, author!' After some delays, Henry James appeared before the curtain and acknowledged the applause. He looked very well—quiet and dignified, yet pleasant; he only stayed a moment."

The reviews were mixed, generally respectful of the playwright but dubious about the play. The latter, by the time it got to the boards, was, in fact, a rather soft, blurred affair which today makes somewhat embarrassing reading. Its tone may be suggested by the denouement, which has Claire recovered from the convent and brought back to Newman; according to the final stage direction, he puts an arm around her and gives her a long kiss, after which "Exeunt rapidly." (At a later moment, James even rewrote the last act in a desperate effort to make it more appealing. In this version, Valentin does not die after all; the doctor rushes onstage to exclaim: "Great news! He's better!") *The American* nonetheless survived a series of crises and confusions, and though Henry came to regard it as a failure and thought his friends were avoiding him in the hour of his "disgrace," it hung on till the start of the winter. "*The American* died an honourable death, on the 76th night," Alice noted in her diary on December 30.

She found reasons external to the play itself for the disappointingly short run—it had been a disastrous season for all London theaters, and the players were inexperienced—but she had to thank "the beautiful play for all the interest and expectancy with which it has filled the last two years." There had been moments of great anxiety, but also moments of high comedy when she and her brother "grew fat with laughter." And throughout, Harry had been "so manly, generous and unirritated by all the little petty incidents and exhibitions, so entirely occupied with the instructive side, that one has had infinite satisfaction in him."

Henry's dream of large financial returns from this foray onto the stage was shattered: *The American*, when all the returns were in, earned him next to nothing. But while still entertaining these hopes, he had composed several more plays, with others yet in mind. Among these was a work based on his own short story "The Solution," about a diplomat who fears he may have compromised a young woman. It had been asked for by the American producer Augustin Daly, and went through various changes of title—*Mrs. Jasper, Disengaged* (an aptly clever but perhaps not inviting label) and *Mrs. Jasper's Way*—before Daly lost all faith and interest in it. An earlier effort, *Mrs. Vibert*, had been written just before Christmas 1890, while Henry was awaiting the provincial debut of *The American.* This one, involving adulterous intrigue and squabbling half brothers, had been taken by the English impresario Sir John Hare. The latter, Alice learned, called the plan a "masterpiece of dramatic movement," and Henry felt that the second act was "pure movement"; but it ran into casting difficulties and was set aside.

Half a year after the Southport opening, Alice took stock of Henry's theatrical and literary accomplishments over the year past, juxtaposed them to that of William, and, in an incisive act of self-measurement, placed herself alongside. "Within the last year [Harry] has published *The Tragic Muse*, brought out *The American*, and written a play, *Mrs. Vibert* (which Hare has accepted) and his admirable comedy; combined with William's *Psychology*, not a bad show for one family! especially if I get myself dead, the hardest job of all."*

THE DIARY

Alice James began her diary in her Leamington lodgings on the last day of May 1889. Her confessed aim was both consolation and psychological release. "I think that if I get into the habit of writing a bit about what happens, or rather doesn't happen"—such were the opening words—"I may lose a little of the sense of loneliness and desolation which abides with me." Restricted for the moment to brief exchanges with the nurse, she felt that "a written monologue by that most interesting being, *myself*, may have its yet to be discovered consolations." The monologue would provide a kind of company—regularly, in the journal, Alice would be addressing some other being, or another part of herself—and might serve an additional purpose: "as an outlet to that geyser of emotions, sensations, speculations and reflections which ferments perpetually within my poor old carcass for its sins."

There was as well a less articulated but more pressing and more

* The comedy referred to is *The Album*, a play Henry had committed to Edward Compton. For an account of all of Henry James's theatrical endeavors, plus texts, see Leon Edel, ed., *The Complete Plays of Henry James* (1949).

recognizably Jamesian intention: that of composing and perhaps even transforming the self. We get a hint of this when, four days after the initial entry, Alice remarked that all experience, one's reading included, was "only of interest and value in proportion as we find ourselves therein, form given to what was vague, what slumbered stirred to life." A year later, still in Leamington, Alice wrote that on those days when she could settle herself on the sofa and keep busy there for several hours, the very act of scribbling her diary notes and of reading her books worked to "clarify the density and shape the formless mass within," and that then life seemed to her "inconceivably rich."

At another moment, a quoted passage from a contemporary French philosopher suggested to her that among the lessons of continual suffering was "*la résignation dans l'effort*": by which was meant an effortful resistance to evil along with the patiently resigned awareness that evil was invulnerable. The humblest existences, so conducted (said the unnamed sage), could become "*des oeuvres d'art bien supérieures aux plus belles symphonies et aus plus beaux poèmes.*" Alice affected, on this occasion, to be modestly unsure whether hers might be called resignation with or without effort; but she glowed with the thought that her life—her actual life when given form, identity, meaning by the journal writing on the sofa (her life as *made* by her diary) —might take on something of a poetic or spiritual quality.

Alice James maintained her diary, with sizable interludes, for some two years and nine months, until the night before her death on March 6, 1892 (Katharine Loring described her whispering corrections in the final entry on that last Saturday night). We have drawn upon the diary a good many times in the course of our narrative, and those earlier passages and paraphrases may be kept in mind as we come to a more formal consideration of this, Alice's one sustained literary undertaking. There was her gossip about the several Irish forebears, and her attentiveness to the current Irish drama; with interpolated acerbities about the English. There were sprinkled reminiscences, both happy and somber—walking with Mademoiselle through the gray dusk of St. John's Wood in the winter of 1856; Harry, age thirteen, sitting on a swing amid the "desolate expanse" of Boulogne-sur-Mer, suddenly saying to her: "This might certainly be called pleasure under difficulties!"; the bleak Newport winter of 1863, the psychic falling apart in 1868, the "hideous summer" of 1878, the malevolent voice in the emptied Mount Vernon Street home whispering "Alone, Alone!"

We can remember, too, Alice's version of the reunion at Leamington; her portrait of Katharine Loring as a "purely transatlantic and modern possibility"; her chronicle of Henry's adventures on the stage; her response to the death verdicts pronounced by Sir Andrew Clarke and Dr. Baldwin.

A distinctive feature of the diary was the periodic wave of compassion for the wretchedly poor of Leamington and London. The sentiment was deep and real; at the same time, the expression of it was Alice's way of getting outside her own misery by concentrating on the woes of others. Her personal condition seemed bearable, she implied in early January 1890, when she thought of the helplessness and powerlessness she could see around her: persons with "no acrid strain to stiffen the sinews, creatures dropped out in the race and left all limp by the wayside," decorating their squalor "with pathetic tags of laces and pitiful ruffles."

In March 1890, she pasted in her book a clipping about a family in Hebburn visited by a police officer. The mother was in rags, not enough to cover her nakedness; the house contained two chairs, one backless, and two beds, one in ruins; the boy slept in the chimney, the girls in the bottom of a cupboard. The father, who was found making tea, in fact earned twenty-five shillings a week; he and his wife were sentenced to two months' hard labor for criminal neglect of the children. Another clipping in May told of a man named Vaille who fell dead in the street from starvation. The mother, it was learned, was in a lunatic asylum, "suffering from melancholia brought on through starvation"; four boys, "a set of wan, dirty little fellows, though intelligent," lived in the house with its "putrid atmosphere," its windows without glass and grate without fire.

Alice's sympathy for the English lower class was sometimes mixed with impatience; and in a less tender mood she could inveigh against its members' unquestioning acceptance of their "place" in society and its willingness, like a "cringing dog . . . to lick the hand that chastises." But she usually responded to the individual human instance, and was touched by the behavior of a couple named Bachelor who lived near her in Leamington. Their total income was three and six a week, a pension from a military band Bachelor used to play for before his eyes went bad; but he gave Miss James a brass pin tray for Christmas costing threepence, and always sent her his love.

The self being realized in the diary takes in a great deal from the father and the two brothers; they are never absent for very long from the pages. She was especially grateful to Father and William, Alice wrote in July 1889, for their perpetual gift of laughter. She had been thinking how "the entire want of humour cripples the mind," and this brought her to wonder if she would ever enjoy "convulsive laughs" again. "Ah, me! I fear me not. I had such a feast for 34 years that I can't complain." But she regarded it as a "curious extreme" for someone "to have grown up with Father and William" and then to be reduced to Nurse and her landlady, Miss Clarke, "for humourous daily fodder."*

Father, Alice recalled in a lighthearted moment reaching back to 1865, once met Mr. Alcott in the street and said to him: " 'They are reading *Dumps* at home with great interest.' '*Dumps?*' queried Mr. A. 'Yes, *Dumps*, your daughter's novel!' " The allusion was to *Moods*, Louisa May Alcott's first published novel. Henry Junior, in fact, reviewed it for the *North American Review* in July 1865, finding it quite remarkably silly in its plot and its ignorance of human nature, but clever and imaginative in marginal ways. Other of Alice's evocations of her father conveyed a similar fond amusement; but what most entered into her being as a paternal legacy, along with a love of laughter and the sense of Irishness, was her father's view of deity.

She was never more daughterly, so to say, than when, in December 1890 (and in a passage quoted much earlier), she expressed her contempt for the Protestant English modes of worship she saw or intuited about her: "a worship propped up by tortuous verbosity and emasculate evasions. Imagine," she went on, quickening her father's commercial tropes, "a religion imposed from without, a virtue taught, not as a measure of self respect, but as a means of propitiating a repulsive, vainglorious, grasping deity, and purchasing from him, at a varying scale of prices, a certain moderation of temperature through the dark mystery of the future."

She returned to the theme some months later in a still closer approximation of her father's God-centered vision. Nothing more hateful, she wrote, than "a religion subscribed to in conformity to an outward standard of respectability, not the spontaneous inspiration of the aspiring soul. A God with fixed and rigid outlines to be worshipped within a prescribed and strictly formal ritual, not a Deity that shapes himself from moment to moment to the need of the votary whose bosom glows with the living, ever clearer knowledge of divine things."

---

* A week before, Alice had written with surprising harshness about the third volume of George Eliot's letters and journals, mainly because of their lack of humor. "What a monument of ponderous dreariness is the book! . . . Not one burst of joy, not one ray of humour, not one living breath in one of her letters or journals." This may to a degree be another instance of jealousy, in this case toward a female literary figure her brother Henry had so largely, if not uncritically, admired.

But if Alice's religious disposition, with its accompanying rhetoric, came from Father, when it was a question of human conduct she took her lessons from William. She cherished spontaneity in the individual relation to God, but, following William, she regarded the factor of will as the key determinant in human actions. Finding herself (in a February 1890 entry) referring without qualification to "the superior weight of voluntary virtue over spontaneous," she hurriedly added an appeal: "Shade of my Father, visit me not if that heresy fall upon thine ear!" Borrowing William's terms, she equated "moral" with "voluntary" (or will-exercising), and recalled that it was because of her "relentlessly moral organisation" in girlhood that Henry Senior would say to her: "How hard you are!" And when a family friend assured Emerson of Alice James's highly moral nature, it may be remembered, Emerson asked, smiling, how in the world her father got on with her.

She treasured some of William's imaginative expressions, as when he referred to her normal condition as "bottled lightning." Browsing through *The Principles of Psychology* in the winter of 1891, she came upon his assertion that "genius, in truth, is little more than the faculty of perceiving in an unhabitual way." Here William, having eloquently espoused the element of habit in Chapter IV, was now observing in Chapter XIX that "most of us" become enslaved to "stock conceptions" and refuse to take account of anything that violates them; hence the exceptional nature of *un*habitual perception. To Alice's "sisterly mind," William's definition of genius was "more felicitous than the long-accustomed 'infinite capacity for taking pains' "; and she went on to apply it to modes of speech.

The Englishman, she wrote, tended to confine his "fancies" to "a dozen or so locutions, as if there were a certain absence of decency in playing with verbal subtleties." But the Yankee was never happier "than when he has made the next man 'sit up' by some start into the open, linguistic or ideal." The principle of analysis is admirable, and would have been approved by her psychologist brother, who was also a theorist of language. But one can only regret again, with Henry, the extreme narrowness of Alice's English acquaintance; the unchangeably conventional discourse she seems almost exclusively to have listened to; the varieties of linguistically inventive London folk she had no contact with.

Henry James, for his sister, was more than anything a wonderful and wonderfully human presence. "He is just back from Paris," she wrote on December 12, 1889, "as amusing as ever about his experiences, seeing things that no one else does." She relished Henry as the most absorbing commentator on the passing show that she had ever known; but it was for Henry's special mode of sympathy that she felt a kind of daily gratitude. In his relation to Alice, Henry evinced a rare capacity for sympathy or compassion in their root meaning of suffering *with*; even empathy, or suffering into. In a March 1890 entry, Alice described this quality with a nearly textbook precision. (Henry had come up to Leamington for the day on March 10.)

Henry the patient, I should call him. Five years ago in November, I crossed the water and suspended myself like an old woman of the sea round his neck where to all appearances I shall remain for all time. I have given him endless care and anxiety but notwithstanding this and the fantastic nature of my troubles I have never seen an impatient look upon his face or heard an unsympathetic or misunderstanding sound cross his lips. He comes at my slightest sign and hangs on to whatever organ may be in eruption and gives me calm and solace by assuring me that my nerves are his nerves and my stomach his stomach—this last a pitch of brotherly devotion never before approached by the race. He has never remotely hinted that he expected me to be well at any given moment, that burden which fond friend and relative so inevitably impose upon the cherished invalid. But he has always been the same since I can remember and has almost as strongly as Father that personal susceptibility—what can one call it, it seems as if it were a matter of the scarfskin, as if they perceived thro' that your mood and were saved thereby from rubbing you raw with their theory of it, or blindness to it.

In January of the same year, after Henry had visited with her, Alice wrote that it had been "as always a happy day with him. I should cry hard for two hours, after he goes, if I could allow myself such luxuries." Fourteen months after that, writing in the Argyll Road house—and in the wake of the wholesale collapse the previous August which made everyone, Alice not least, aware that death was at last in the offing—Alice recorded her strange sense of fulfillment and how much of it owed to Henry and Katharine Loring.

This winter has been rich beyond compare, the heart all aglow with the affectionate demonstration of friend and brother, the mind deeply stirred by most varied and interesting events, public and private, the spirit broadened and strengthened, let me hope, by a clearer perception of the significance of experience, whilst from the whole has flowed perpetually those succulent juices which exude at the slightest pressure from the human comedy.

Records of an Invalid: 1889–92

A literary consciousness is waywardly at work in Alice James's diary. The ongoing discourse, to be sure, is often quite random: ideas, perceptions, memories, snippets of conversation passing helter-skelter through Alice's mind and onto the page. Alice could be relaxed, trivial, gossipy, and some of the finest moments indeed seem occasioned by pure chance, as when an English friend came up one spring evening to announce with shining eyes and glowing cheeks that she was going to America the next day.

What a tide of homesickness swept me under for a moment! What a longing to see a shaft of sunshine shimmering thro' the pines, breathe in the resinous air and throw my withered body down upon my mother earth, bury my face in the coarse grass, worshipping all that the ugly, raw emptiness of the blessed land stands for—the embodiment of a Huge Chance for hemmed in Humanity! Its flexible conditions stretching and lending themselves to all sizes of man; pallid and naked of necessity; undraped by the illusions and mystery of a moss-grown, cobwebby past, but overflowing with a divine good-humour and benignancy—a helping hand for the faltering, an indulgent thought for the discredited, a heart of hope for every outcast of tradition!

It is an exemplary passage. The poignant and sensuous evocation of her onetime home in Manchester, Massachusetts, rises through the image of her native land's "raw emptiness" to what that emptiness *stands for*: a divinely blessed spiritual democracy, with space and place for everyone, and with help and hope for the faltering and the outcast; and the whole in contrast to the English circumstance, burdened by time and an overworshipped past. What began with a chance encounter enlarges into a rich thematic pattern: which itself, by verbal echo, joins in a broader design with other patterns relating to Lincoln and emancipation, the Irish effort, and her personal analogy to both.

So it is throughout the diary. The personal note is always fundamental and seminal; and what seems to be constantly taking place is a re-formation of the self through the arrangement, half-planned, half-instinctive, of its recorded thoughts and feelings. There is nothing like conventional form in those arrangements, nor should there be. But there is a sort of gathering coherence: a coherence of individual posture, an increasingly recognizable if effectively changing voice, a way with language that is the Jamesian-Irish way made distinctively her own, and a completeness, a total exhalation of breath, in the major passages.

We notice, too, a certain rhythm of reference and recollection after the 1890 summer, something animated by the awareness of dying and, intermittently, by the desire to die. Alice's alertness to suicide grew sharper than ever. In September, she entered a newspaper story about the thirty-three-year-old Amy Cullen, who took poison after her fiancé, John Aston, broke off their engagement. She left a letter of farewell which told "Jack" that he had done right to let her know the truth, but that she could not live without him. "What a beautiful sincerity and dignity!" Alice exclaimed. "How happy and wise to go in the illusion of her sorrow and never learn that 'Jack' is a figment of her fancy."* In October, Alice noted that a man committed suicide in the Cathedral of St. Paul's, and in January, she jotted down the news that the Duke of Bedford had killed himself. Over all these acts of self-extinction, and others Alice had mentioned earlier, there hovered the memory, as she put it, of "that month when Father lay dying, refused to eat."

Her personal reminiscences grew darker in the final eighteen months. There was, as before, a mixture of the grievous and the amused—that mixture would continue virtually to the end—but it was during this period that Alice's mind went back to the collapse of 1868, to those nights when she would cry out to her parents to ask what would become of her when they were gone, to "that hideous summer of '78, when I went down to the deep sea, its dark waters closed over me and I knew neither hope nor peace." This was written on February 2, 1892, less than five weeks before her death.

After they had read their sister's diary, each in his own copy, two years later, William and Henry exchanged reactions to it. On William, it made "a unique and tragic impression of personal power venting itself on no opportunity. And such really *deep* humor!" He felt the document should be published. "I am proud of it as a leaf in the family laurel crown, and your memory will be embalmed in a new way by her references to your person." Henry was dismayed at first, even "scared and disconcerted," at the thought of the diary coming into print with "so many private names and allusions," for a host of which he had been responsible; and as for the references to him, "they fill me with tears and cover me with blushes." Nonetheless, he said, "I have been immensely impressed with the thing as a revelation of a moral and personal picture. It is heroic in its individuality, its independence—its face-to-face with the universe for and by herself—and

* In the same journal entry, Alice inscribed the first stanza of Christina Rossetti's "song": "When I am dead, my dearest/Sing no sad songs for me . . ."

the beauty and eloquence with which she often expresses this, let alone the rich irony and humour, constitute (I wholly agree with you) a new claim for the family renown."

THE MOMENT

Alice wrote William on December 2, 1891, that "the grand mortuary moment" was "near at hand." She was deriving an almost physical pleasure from the word "mortuary" by this time and gave voice to it wherever possible. She would, in fact, live three more months, aided perhaps by some hypnotic treatments suggested by William, who also recommended Dr. Charles Lloyd Tucker, an English pioneer in hypnotic therapy, to administer them. These "pawings of an amiable necromancer," as Alice labeled them to Fanny Morse, did succeed in diminishing the acute pain; but when Tucker assured her in early February 1892 that she would "live a good bit still," she was honestly taken aback and let this be known to him—of which she was glad later, since the incident had tested "the sincerity of my mortuary inclinations. I have always *thought* that I wanted to die, but I felt quite uncertain as to what my muscular demonstrations might be at the moment of transition."

But as Henry observed to an English friend, Alice had long since entered into an "intermittent but perfectly inexorable decline." With the turn of the year, she noticed with mild interest that she never read a newspaper or a book any longer and that it had been months since she had even lain on the sofa. "This long slow dying is no doubt instructive," she remarked in her diary, "but it is disappointingly free from excitements." On March 4, a Friday, she dictated her last entry: "I am being ground slowly on the grim grindstone of physical pain, and on two nights I had almost asked for K.'s lethal dose, but one steps hesitantly along such unaccustomed ways and endures from second to second." She longed for the "divine *cessation*"—from agony and consciousness—that she had briefly experienced under Katharine's gentle rhythmic massaging.

Henry came to Argyll Road on Saturday morning, in answer to Katharine's hurried call. He found Alice in a condition of "supreme deathlike emaciation," a great change from forty-eight hours earlier. But she was "perfectly clear and humourous," he wrote William, though she had trouble breathing. Between little choking fits, she whispered a request to Henry, that he cable William her last message:

"Tenderest love to all. Farewell. Am going soon." She died at exactly four o'clock on Sunday afternoon, Henry informed his brother, noting that this was the same hour of the same day that their mother had died ten years before. In the last seconds, her face seemed to Henry "in a strange and touching way" to become clearer. Henry sat on alone for many hours in the still, little room, gazing steadily at the bed on which Alice lay, "as the very perfection of the image of what she had longed for years, and at the last with pathetic intensity, to be." Henry thought she looked "most beautiful and noble—with *all* of the august expression that you can imagine."

On Wednesday morning, Henry and three others accompanied the casket on the train from Waterloo Station to Woking, twenty-five miles southwest of London, to the crematorium there. With Katharine's help, Alice had set about arranging for the disposition of her body two years before. She wanted to be cremated, and Katharine, upon inquiry, found that the process cost only six guineas, plus one for a parson. On the trip to Woking, the hearse and horses were carried in another van. At the crematorium chapel, on the sleety, snowy March morning, an inoffensive young clergyman read a short simple service, the most Alice had agreed to put up with. Present with Henry and Katharine were Annie Ashburner Richards, Alice's friend from Cambridge days and recently in London, and the nurse; the four sat in a waiting room during the hour and a quarter it took to complete the cremation. All were back in London by the end of the afternoon, with Alice's ashes in an urn carried by Katharine.

There had been a ceremonial signing of Alice James's will in February 1890. The American consul in Birmingham was required to be a witness; Jim Putnam's sister Elizabeth happened to be staying nearby and agreed to take part as well. Their arrival in the Leamington rooms caused Alice to "go off" immediately, and she had to be put to bed. She lay there in a semi-faint, while through the mist she "vaguely saw five black figures file into my little bower, headed by the most extraordinary little man [the consul], all gesticulation and grimace." "It was so curious to me," Alice wrote, "just like a nightmare effect"; she felt as though she were listening to the actual reading of her will, after her death, "surrounded by the greedy relatives, as in novels."

The account can remind one of Emily Dickinson's poem "I Heard a Fly Buzz When I Died," in which the speaker, after death, recalls that at the instant of death she had been watching a similar gathering of relatives and distribution of legacies:

> *I willed my Keepsakes—Signed away*
> *What portion of me be*
> *Assignable—*

and then it was that the buzzing fly interposed itself and sight failed. Alice James, of course, had not at that time read any of Emily Dickinson's poetry. It was only in January 1892 that a volume of her work, edited by Thomas W. Higginson (whose taste and intelligence Alice darkly distrusted), came into her hands. She was pleased that English critics declared Emily Dickinson to be fifth-rate: "They have such a capacity for missing quality." The poem Alice seized on was the one beginning "I'm Nobody! Who are you? Are you—Nobody—Too?" "What tomes of philosophy," she asked, "*resumes* the cheap farce or expresses the highest point of view of the aspiring soul more completely than the following—

> *"How dreary to be somebody*
> *How public, like a frog*
> *To tell your name the livelong day*
> *To an admiring bog!"**

It was an artful gesture by the dying Alice James, to voice her contempt for celebrity, no doubt especially literary celebrity, by associating herself with a recluse woman poet of genius.

Alice's estate, including the property at Manchester, amounted to something more than $80,000. Katharine, William, and Henry each received about $20,000. Bob was left $10,000, Henry and Alice agreeing that some account should be taken (in Henry's words to William) of the "very substantial wealth of Bob's children's grandfather" Edward Holton. Bob's daughter, Mary, in addition, was given $2,500; and Alice had recently sent Mary Holton James $1,000 for young Ned's education, even though she had learned that he was thinking about becoming an Episcopalian clergyman, which she regarded as absurd. Wilky's daughter Alice and William's Peggy received $2,500 apiece; $1,000 went to Alice's cousin Lila Walsh, and the same to Professor Child's daughter Henrietta and Katharine Loring's admirable cousin Alice Gray, who had just then earned a job in the Boston Art Museum.

---

* Alice inscribed this stanza as Higginson presented it, after removing Emily Dickinson's dashes and characteristically dimming the third line, which rightly reads: "To tell one's name—the livelong June—."

William was given permanent possession of the furniture he and his Alice had been using for some years; the English furniture, pictures, and china went to Henry (a gift that would figure peripherally in his novel *The Spoils of Poynton*). All Alice's other effects were deeded to Katharine, who was to do with them as she wished.

William wrote from Cambridge on March 7: "I can't believe that imperious will and piercing judgment are snuffed out with the breath. Now that her outwardly so frustrated life is over, one sees that in the deepest sense it was a triumph." Elaborating on this, William arrived at a most Williamesque phrase. "In her relations to her disease, her mind did not succumb. She never whined or complained or did anything but spurn it. She thus kept it from invading the tone of her soul."

Bob James, from Concord, addressed his thoughts to Fanny Morse. Alice's death had carried him back to the childhood and nursery days he had shared with her in the Fourteenth Street home, and the compacts of marriage they had made, taking the roles of their father and their mother: "compacts which lasted their hours of innocence, but which after thirty-seven years come back to me today as the only innocent and living facts of life." He meant: in his own sorry life; but as to Alice's, he also saw an element of victory in it. It "didn't seem beautiful, but doubt not that it was interiorly beautiful. There is nothing beautiful in a life that has nothing to overcome. And she overcame more than any of us can ever know." Bob grew mystical. "Of course you and I do not know where she has gone. All that I *feel* is that she has gone where love is."

To Francis Boott, Henry wrote that, while he was deeply aware that death for Alice was a liberation from endless and complicated suffering, for him personally it was a great sorrow. "Because, even with everything that made life an unspeakable weariness to her, she contributed constantly, infinitely to the interest, the consolation, as it were, in disappointment and depression, of my own existence . . . Her talk, her company, her association and admirable acute mind and large spirit were so much the best thing I have, of late years, known here. But for her it is only blessed and bountiful."

Katharine Loring closed up the Argyll Road house and, after passing through Leamington and lingering over some of the places Alice had been fond of there, made her way to Liverpool, where Henry saw her off on the *Etruria* in the second week of April. She carried with her the two small leather-bound volumes of Alice's diary and a little box containing white ash. The box was placed beside the graves of

Henry Senior and Mary in the Cambridge cemetery. A year afterward, in Florence, William designed an urn to mark the grave and had inscribed on it lines from Dante's *Paradiso* X (128–29):

> *ed essa da martiro*
> *e da essilio venne a questa pace.*

Henry would say that the quotation took him at the throat "by its penetrating *rightness*": from martyrdom and exile she came to this peace. It was indeed extraordinarily apt, but Alice may be imagined resisting the suggestion that she had in any way been a martyr.

PART IV

Parts of a Unity

CHAPTER FIFTEEN

Ghostly Transactions

HENRY

In December 1893, twenty-one months after the death of Alice James, and responding to a particularly affectionate letter from Henry, William wrote: "As the ranks grow thinner, the survivors draw nearer, and I confess now that I 'realise' you in your loneliness, having reached the equilibrium in which you will probably remain for the rest of your days. I feel as if we formed a part of a unity more than I ever have before."

It was an immense fraternal insight, if not altogether cogent as prophecy; and it can serve as the controlling rubric for the balance of this narrative. The family story, that is, compresses hereafter largely and inevitably to the ongoing relationship between William and Henry and that relationship is primarily intellectual and literary. The brothers can be seen periodically in each other's presence in Europe and America through the 1890s and up to the day of William's death in 1910. Their mutual watchfulness and admiration, affection and enjoyment, anxiety and misunderstanding continued unabated in these years—the survivors did draw nearer, and they also on occasion drew agitatedly apart. Bob James, of course, moved on the edges of the story, erratically and sometimes tellingly; and the younger James generation, chiefly the four children of William and Alice, gave father and uncle much to comment on and inquire about. But the brothers can be seen even more clearly moving ahead in their professional lives, along separate but intermittently parallel paths, and toward a distinct and peculiarly Jamesian kind of unity.

The parts of that unity can be recognized in the nearly simultaneous publication in 1902 of William's *The Varieties of Religious Experience* and Henry's *The Wings of the Dove*, the novel of his maturity most permeated with a religious consciousness; and in 1907 of Henry's *The American Scene* and William's *Pragmatism*, the text that more than any other established a definitive American mode of philosophic thought. And more immediately, in the present chapter, we may consider the coincidence during the decade of the nineties of William's most active involvement with psychic research and the contested supernatural and Henry's most prolific period in the writing of ghost stories.

On March 26, 1892, one week after the ritual at the Woking Crematorium, Henry James, at his desk in the De Vere Gardens apartment, jotted down his ideas for two ghost stories. One of these would be called "Owen Wingrave" and it arose from the image of the "haunting, apparitional presence" of a soldierly ancestor "in the life and consciousness of a descendant." The ancestor became Colonel Wingrave, a formidable figure in the time of George II, who had killed one of his own children by a furious blow to the head. The descendant is his great-great-grandson, Owen Wingrave, a young man who refuses to follow his forebears into the military life and prefers to sit in the park reading Goethe (Henry James had observed just such an individual once in Kensington Gardens).

Owen is summoned to the family estate at Paramore, and there challenged to a test of courage: to spend the night in the room where the old colonel, following his child's death, had been found lying dead on the floor. Owen accepts the challenge, and next morning he, too, is found dead on the same spot. "He was all the young soldier on the gained field." The closing words suggest that Owen, by his courageous act, had become a soldier and a victorious one; and had hence won a place in his soldiering family.* But amid the ambiguities of this expert tale, there is also the ironic insinuation that Owen had won a *grave*, a place in the family graveyard. It is the Wingrave family that has killed Owen, the family tradition and values and military atmosphere; and

---

* Henry's notebook identifies the haunted room as Owen's "own battle-field." At some remove, Henry may have been pondering *his* "own battle-field," and William's; the field neither arrived at in the Civil War. The San Francisco earthquake, I will say in a later chapter, was William's belated battlefield.

in destroying Owen, the family has destroyed itself. He is the last of his line.

Henry James's own family was imaginatively implicated in the narrative. There are several thematic teasings of brother William, as when the amiable youth Lechmere, Owen's friend, lays it down—in plumlike tones, one fancies—that the military temperament is "the finest temperament in the world, and that there's nothing so splendid as pluck and heroism." And when Mrs. Coyle, the wife of Owen's mentor, asks, shrieking, whether the house is known to have "a proved ghost," she is using the technical phrase for an apparition that had been authenticated by psychic research: in 1892, by William James's Society for Psychic Research.

But beneath such fooling, there is throughout and climactically the deep sense of the death of the family: that is, of the old family, the one Henry and William and Alice had been born into and helped to forge; what William meant when he spoke of Henry as being "a native of the James family." "Owen Wingrave" reflects the feeling that, with the death of Alice, that family had come to an end. It seems to convey as well Henry's awareness that what had ended was an entity of fairly long duration.

James family deaths were no less discernibly on Henry's mind in the other story he began on March 26: "Sir Dominick Ferrand," about a poor young man of literary ambition, Peter Baron, who comes by chance upon a cache of private letters. They had been written years before by the distinguished public figure and unhappily married Sir Dominick Ferrand, addressed to the woman he loved and by whom he begot an illegitimate child. That child is the young widow Mrs. Ryves, with whom Peter is smitten and from whom he withholds the fact of the paternal correspondence. What is of interest is the discovered location of the letters: behind a sliding panel in a small mahogany desk known as a davenport, which Peter spotted in a secondhand shop on the King's Road.

Henry is here making nice literary profit of the episode in January 1890 when there was delivered to Alice James in her rooms at the South Kensington Hotel her old desk—her "Davenport," as she capitalized it—from her Cambridge and Boston homes. In it, Alice wrote, "were my old letters," and most movingly for her, letters from *her* parents, Henry Senior and Mary James. Alice read the letters steadily for two days, reliving her parents' relationship and their unfailingly loving remarks about one another, through to the end of their lives. "Mother died Sunday evening, January 29th, 1882, Father on Monday, midday, December 19th, 1882, and now I am shedding the tears I didn't shed then!"

Henry James published two other ghost stories in the year 1892: "Nona Vincent," in which the leading female character in a young dramatist's first play seems to come to actual life, and "The Private Life," an eerily comic tale about two radically contradictory person-alities—one of whom confines his real self to the privacy of his study, while the other literally does not exist in solitude but only when publicly performing.

All told, of the eighteen "stories of the supernatural" (to borrow Leon Edel's valid title*) that he published in his literary lifetime, Henry James wrote no less than twelve between 1891 and 1900, the four tales of 1892 among them. Prior to 1891, James had not written a ghost story for fifteen years. If the death of Alice and what figured for Henry as the death of the family account in part for the sudden proliferation of fictional phantoms, especially when they are familial or domestic (as in "Owen Wingrave," "Sir Dominick Ferrand," *The Turn of the Screw*, and "Maud-Evelyn"), there were also other sources and other deaths. Of the latter, there was a darkening succession: Wolcott Bal-estier ("poor dear big-spirited, only-by-death-quenchable Wolcott," Henry wrote in December 1891 about his capable young American friend), James Russell Lowell (from Ireland, Henry wrote Lowell, dying of cancer in London, to convey his sense of "how little we can interfere with the doom of our friends to *endure*"), Robert Louis Stevenson (to William, Henry spoke of Stevenson's "ghostly extinction"), Constance Fenimore Woolson.

"He numbered them, he named them, he grouped them—it was the silent roll-call of his Dead." The consciousness enacting itself there, and to an extent representing Henry James, is that of George Stransom in "The Altar of the Dead," published in 1895 in the volume suitably called *Terminations*. It tells of an Englishman, fifty-five when we first meet him, who has a laudable and finally all-consuming piety toward his personal dead (Henry felt that as a general thing the English were all too casual on this count). Stransom erects an altar in a London church and lights a thickening number of candles to his dear departed; until, at the end, a candle in *his* memory brings the ritual to a close. The last candle is lit by a grieving woman who comes to the church to pray for the man she has loved and whose betrayal of her she has

---

* *Henry James: Stories of the Supernatural*, edited by Leon Edel (1974).

forgiven. This sad, bereft, nameless woman is taken from Constance Fenimore Woolson, who had died in Venice in January 1894: an event, James told Dr. Baldwin, that caused him "ghastly amazement and distress." When he learned that Fenimore might well have committed suicide by throwing herself from the second-story window of her Casa Semitecolo, James declared himself to have utterly collapsed in horror and pity.

The artfully dim and drifting narrative of "The Altar of the Dead" quite likely reflects a portion of Henry James's feeling of having somehow failed, if he had not betrayed, Fenimore Woolson. His suppressed remorse would be given unforgettable treatment in "The Beast in the Jungle" in 1903. But for Henry James in the 1890s, it could appear, as it did to George Stransom, that he was entering "that dark defile of our earthly descent in which some one dies every day."

As the decade went forward, there may have been less easily determinable psychic sources—Edel speculates about this—for the obsession with the spectral: apprehensions, perhaps, of some sort of literary stoppage or death; combined with the image (as in "The Great Good Place") of some kind of ghostly rescue. But given the remarkable *variety* of these stories—there are dreadful occurrences and brightly humorous episodes, appalled envisionings and witty observings, frightful endings and happy endings—no single personal basis, no motif from the private experience, can be effectively adduced to explain them. An overall *literary* explanation is more persuasive.

For one thing, in the early 1890s, James was too busy with his stage fortunes to begin work on another full-length novel; there would be none such between *The Tragic Muse* in 1890 and *The Spoils of Poynton* coupled with *What Maisie Knew* in 1897. He gave himself over for the time to shorter pieces: "I must hammer away at the effort to do, successfully and triumphantly, a large number of very short things," he told his notebook in the summer of 1891. Within this breed, the ghost story has always had a broad appeal for the English-language readership; Henry James quite naturally applied his talent to the genre, and soon could realize his exhilarating command of it. But as always there was a deeper impulse in action. Henry James, by the instinct of his art, was moving beyond the realistic fiction which, for himself, he had pretty well exhausted in *The Bostonians* and *The Princess Casamassima*. In retrospect, he can be seen moving toward the dramatized fables, or passionate allegories, of his major phase: *The Ambassadors* and its successors. On the imaginative and experimental journey to that plateau, the ghost story was an indispensable way station.

THE JAMESES

WILLIAM

William's response to the death, or anyhow the severe shrinkage, of the family ("the ranks grow thinner") was to seek a new mode of proximity with Henry, and, at the same time, to address himself more actively to the younger generation of the family in his own household. To this latter end, he took his family abroad in late May 1892, sailing on the S.S. *Friesland* and going to Switzerland for the summer. His intentions were of the best, but within six weeks he was in a state of nerve-racked frenzy.

The family were occupying rooms in a small house in the village of Gryon, above Lausanne, and in conditions that drove William to distraction. He described the situation to Grace Ashburner, the Cambridge friend, in a rhetorical volley that made mockery of the program and premise of the year: "To combine novel anxieties of the most agonizing kind about your children's education, nocturnal and diurnal contact of the most intimate sort with their shrieks, their quarrels, their questions, their rollings-about and tears, in short with all their emotional, intellectual and bodily functions, in what practically in these close quarters amounts to one room—to combine these things (I say) with a *holiday* for *oneself* is an idea worthy to emanate from a lunatic asylum."

The family, in fact, had two bedrooms. William shared one with Billy, now ten years old, and Peg, now five; Alice bunked with Harry, who was thirteen, and the infant Francis Tweedy. After William subjected Harry to a storm of ill temper and paternal rebuke, he blamed the sorry display upon the closeness of their quarters. Matters improved a little in July, when William moved the family to a *pension* at Vers-chez-les-Blancs outside Lausanne, settled Harry with a pastor in Vevey, and dispatched Billy to study and take his meals with another pastor in town. But William was still feeling badly out of sorts.

Henry arrived for a visit on the twenty-eighth of the month, and William almost instantly took off for an extensive walking tour, eastward through Brig and Andermatt to Disentis, then circling southward to Chamonix. He needed desperately to regain his "nervous *tone*," he wrote Alice from Brig; the mountains and solitude were just right for the purpose. Henry, who had come in a family frame of mind and "intently occupied in realising I am an uncle," as he said to Isabella Gardner (his recent hostess in Venice), was quite taken aback by William's abrupt disappearance. He thought his nephews were charming, "and the little girl a *bellezza*"; but William was still off on his medicinal wanderings when Henry gave up and returned to London.

William escorted the brood to Florence in early October, for a six-month stay. They lodged in an apartment on the vast tree-dotted Piazza dell'Indipendenza, at No. 16; it had more than enough rooms for a family of six and was nicely furnished. To Grace Ashburner, the recipient of his lamentation from Gryon, William exclaimed that "Florence is delicious." He disliked the general air of debility in the city's atmosphere. "But the charming sunny manners, the old-world picturesqueness wherever you cast your eye, and above all, the magnificent remains of art, redeem it all." He could understand people, especially "northern loungers," deciding to spend the rest of their days in Florence.

A fortnight later, having self-confessedly fallen into wretched spirits, William departed for a week in Padua and Venice. Padua won his heart. "Florence can't hold a candle to it," he told his wife. "She has her galleries, her palaces and her bridges, but the rest is encumbrance. Here it is the entire town that speaks to one." Others have felt the same about the quietly perfect little city. Moving on to Venice, however, William struck a pose of moral revulsion. "Venice is rotten through and through," so ran his report. It "reeks of vice and sin as no other place on earth seems to . . . A wicked place!" Alice may have realized that, for her husband, wickedness was not the least desirable attribute of an environment; it was preferable anyhow to sinless serenity, as the record would show.

The relationship between William and Alice, during the Florentine months, passed through another phase of intense strain and renewed, enlarged attachment. William's *scappatine* were occasioned by bouts of irascibility, and he often left in a flurry of ill-chosen words, to apologize abjectly from the first stopping place. From Munich, in February 1893, replying to Alice's comment about enjoying the quiet of their apartment-home, William said gloomily that it was *his* absence that provided the quiet, and wished he had not been so fretful and "agaçant" (irritating) in recent weeks.

Alice wrote back by return mail: "Don't ever say that it is your absence that makes the quiet—it hurts my feelings, as Peggy says. You will never know the way I miss you, the want of you all day long and always recurring every time I come in and have no William to interrupt and talk to." William's absence brought Alice, as it had periodically over the years, to a mood of repentance and a determination to reform.

"I seem myself to have grown so hard to live with, but William darling don't despair of me for I can change with time and trying." She repeated an old vow: "I mean to contradict you no longer when you come back."

These protestations had their point, for Alice Howe James was anything but a submissive helpmate. Her son Harry in after years would recall from this era his mother doing battle with his father in a way that seemed earth-shaking to the teenage boy. Father "would pass from surprise to bewilderment, to excitement, to desperation," his nervous agitation increasing until he would explode in charges and recriminations. "There was Mother, holding her ground in the face of thunder, lightning and universal disintegration, her face flushed, tears finally rolling down her cheeks." His mother never flinched, Harry said, until or unless she became convinced of being in the wrong; "and she was often victorious." In the older son's opinion, his parents never in their long years together bored each other for half an hour.

There was a modest swirl of sociability in Florence, with a flow of Jamesian connections through the city. Bob's wife, Mary, arrived with her mother, recently widowed by the death of Edward Holton, and her daughter Mary Holton James. Carrie James showed up with her two children, but they all behaved so disagreeably, Mrs. Alice said, that "I never again shall feel the slightest responsibility toward them." Katharine Loring was in town, and with sister Alice no longer a distancing element, Mrs. William found herself warming toward her. "She is really kind. I am grateful too when people like me a little." Both William and Alice enjoyed a few visits with Mrs. Mary Costelloe. For William, she was of interest as being the sister of his young friend Logan Pearsall Smith. Neither James, presumably, knew of the developing liaison between Mary Costelloe and another of William's students, the thirty-eight-year-old Harvard graduate and art critic Bernhard Berenson; the two were living a few doors apart on Lungarno Acciaiolo. More than half a century later, Berenson would remember seeing William James frequently that winter. He recalled taking walks with James on the steep roads leading to Fiesole, and William "rebelling against walls along these lanes shutting out the view."*

On August 24, the Jameses sailed from London on the *Cephalonia*. On the pier at Boston in early September, they made a party of nine,

---

* *Sunset and Twilight*, Berenson's diaries of 1947–58. The diaries are salted with remembered comments of William James. "William James used to say," Berenson remarks typically on March 19, 1948, "that every gush of feeling should be followed by adequate action, or (he implied) the feeling turned to poison."

with three Swiss serving women. They brought with them, in addition to abundant personal luggage containing new clothes for everybody, some furniture, rugs, curtains, and an English bicycle for Harry. To the customs official, Alice, her face aglow with rectitude, explained that all these items had been used for more than one year and thus were free of duty.

Soon after the family's resettlement at Irving Street, there appeared the English psychic researcher F.W.H. Myers (William had run into him on his summer 1892 jaunt across Switzerland: a strange, intense person, he told his wife, imperious and egocentric). Myers brought with him Richard Hodgson, the secretary of the American Society for Psychical Research, and Mrs. Leonora Piper, the medium in whom William placed the greatest trust. Alice called on Mrs. Piper to hold a séance in the library. It was conducted there forthwith and, as the assembly noted, under the portrait of Henry James, Sr., hanging above the mantelpiece. Nothing could have been more proper: for it was exactly the mystical and the spiritualistic legacy of the elder James that his children and his daughter-in-law were drawing upon in their distinctively different transactions with the supernatural during the 1890s and later.

William had kept watch on Mrs. Piper with some regularity since his first meetings with her in 1885. In 1886, he wrote an account of those meetings for the newly formed American SPR, remarking on the numerous members of the same family who attended them (presumably Mrs. Alice, her mother, her sisters Margaret and Mary, Mary's husband, Mack Salter, and William himself). "The medium showed a most startling intimacy with this family's affairs," William said, "talking of many matters known to no one outside, and which *gossip* could not possibly have conveyed to her ears."

A few years later, in the fall of 1890, William compiled another report on Mrs. Piper, this time for the British SPR: "Certain Phenomena of Trance." His brother Henry was invited to read it at the October 31 meeting in the Westminster Town Hall. Henry declared himself "alien" to the whole spiritualist business (though a story like "Nona Vincent" shows he was not entirely so), but announced to William that he had read him "with great éclat." He had been introduced by Pearsall Smith as "a Bostonian of Bostonians"; but despite the familiar old misprision, Henry said, "You were very easy and interesting to read, and were altogether the 'feature' of the entertainment." " 'Tis the most beautiful and devoted brotherly act I ever knew," William observed between laughter and gratitude.

The report held items of family history which interested Henry as he read along to the London audience: the citation by the medium of a letter from Aunt Kate to Mrs. Alice, events in the William James family nursery, certain tantrums of young Billy, the crib creaking at night, Alice hearing footsteps on the stair. These murmured allusions served to deepen Alice's emotional belief in Mrs. Piper; William remained skeptical, open-minded, persuadable.

During the academic year following the return from Europe, William subjected Mrs. Piper to a continuing series of tests. As before, he tried to enlist his colleagues in the enterprise; their lack of interest, especially Royce's, enraged him. He was the more pleased when Charles Eliot Norton, at the Saturday Club, confessed himself convinced by Mrs. Piper's genuineness. William was prepared to take a better view than previously of the older man; but he himself found the medium's self-dissolving performance to a degree pathetic.

The poor innocent little woman [he wrote in late May]—she has to stamp her foot and shake her head occasionally, to make believe she has any individuality left. It does seem to me to be all smoothing out into a sheet of tissue paper.

But she is pure in heart, William concluded, which was "after all a good thing."

William's tentative findings in the matter of psychic investigation were contained in the essay "What Psychical Research Has Accomplished" in *The Will to Believe* in 1897. The essay tends to be circular and repetitious (it is a composite of three talks), but it contains a major statement by William James, in his mid-fifties, about two opposed modes of thinking, two ways of appraising reality and experience. "To no one type of mind is it given to discern the totality of truth," James declares at the outset. "Something escapes the best of us . . . The scientific-academic mind and the feminine-mystical mind shy from each other's facts, just as they fly from each other's temper and spirit." And near the end, in an extended peroration, he expands on the basic contrast: essentially, between the "scientific" and the "personal" view of life.

Although in its essence science only stands for a method and for no fixed belief, yet as habitually taken, both by its votaries and outsiders, it is identified with a certain fixed belief—the belief that the hidden order of nature is mechanical exclusively, and that non-mechanical categories are irrational ways of conceiving even such things as human life. Now, this mechanical rationalism, as one may call it, makes, if it becomes one's only way of thinking, a violent breach of the ways of thinking that have played the greatest part in human history. Religious thinking, ethical thinking, poetical thinking, teleological, emotional, sentimental thinking, what one might call the personal view of life, to distinguish it from the impersonal and mechanical, and the romantic view of life to distinguish it from the rationalistic view, have been, and even still are, outside of the well-drilled scientific circles, the dominant forms of thought.

It was another ringing manifesto, and as always infused with a personal ardor. Given the intolerance and contempt of the scientific community for the inquiries carried on by the Society for Psychical Research, William said, that society was engaged of necessity in a *humanizing* mission. William, in addition, was committed to a filial mission: to establish continuity between his father's mystical thought and the hardening scientific postures at the close of the century.

In the course of his discussion, William traced the history of the SPR since its English beginning in 1882, and described its chief participants: Edmund Gurney (whose suicide in 1886 touched off thoughts about that act in the mind of William's sister, Alice), F.W.H. Myers, and Henry Sidgwick, absolving them in a swift run of phrasing from the "soft-headedness . . . idiotic credulity . . . and general wonder-sickness" with which they had been charged by newspapers and social gossip. Theirs, he asserted, was the first systematic attempt he had ever heard of "to *weigh* the evidence for the supernatural."

The weighing thus far had been largely though not entirely inconclusive. Edmund Gurney in particular, borrowing from the studies of Pierre Janet and others, had demonstrated the existence of an "extra-consciousness" in the individual, something alongside the normal consciousness and upon which the supernatural might work its effect. (The idea of the extra-consciousness would loom centrally in *The Varieties of Religious Experience* five years later.) Apparitions of persons at or near the moment of death *to* other persons affected by those deaths: these seemed to James and his SPR colleagues to be beyond dispute. In a mysterious arithmetical calculation, James held that "the cases where the apparition of a person is seen on the day of his death are four hundred and forty times too numerous to be ascribed to chance." (This very phenomenon was the subject of Henry James's phantom-story of 1896, "The Friends of the Friends.")

Turning to mediums, James considered the so-called physical mediums, those who performed physical actions, wrote on slates, moved furniture, and so on; here James felt that the evidence collected was "destructive of the claims of all the mediums examined." The famous Russian performer Madame Blavatsky was among those named as fraudulent; it did nothing to impair her flourishing reputation.

But in the case of at least one "trance medium," the situation was strikingly different. James drew upon a familiar logical figure to make his point: "If you wish to upset the law that all crows are black, you must not seek to show that no crows are; it is enough if you prove one single crow to be white. My own white crow is Mrs. Piper." Her manifestations of knowledge during séances provided, indeed, the "thunderbolt of fact" which James thought necessary to sweep away mere presumings and counterpresumings. "In the trances of this medium," he remarked, "I cannot resist the conviction that knowledge appears which she has never gained by the ordinary waking use of her eyes and ears and wits. What the source of this knowledge may be, I know not, and have not the glimmer of an explanatory suggestion to make; but from admitting the fact of such knowledge I can see no escape."

William James's white crow, he then added, made it possible for him to examine the *other* evidence about supernatural doings, "ghosts and all," liberated a little from "the irreversible negative bias of the 'rigorously scientific' mind." But William remained loath to credit accounts of actual spectral visitations—he called them "ghost stories," as though to belittle his brother's fictional versions, and said they were dull and without point. What he found undeniable was some form of thought transference, from persons absent to persons present, even if the absent ones had departed this life.

AND OTHERS

That manner of transference was precisely what Alice James despised. In 1891, as she was approaching and thinking about her death, Alice expressed in her diary the fervent hope that "the dreadful Mrs. Piper won't be let loose upon my defenseless soul," after her death.

I suppose the thing "medium" has done more to degrade spiritual conception than the grossest forms of materialism or idolatry: was there ever anything transmitted but the pettiest, meanest, coarsest facts and details: anything rising above the squalid intestines of human affairs?

Ghostly Transactions

For Alice James, persistingly her father's daughter, supernatural negotiation meant a direct relation to divinity; human efforts to pillage the dead aroused in her a fury of disgust.

Communication with the dead and, most importantly, the family dead, was the major tenet of Bob James's spiritualistic beliefs. In the early 1890s, Bob was living alone in the Boston suburb of Arlington Heights (his wife, Mary, after a quarrel, had again gone off to Europe with her mother and her daughter); dabbling in painting, not all of it negligible, and making sporadic trials of mediums. On December 28, 1893, after a long session with Mrs. Piper, Bob drew up the most extensive and the most curious of his several reports about discourse with the departed. It has the air of being sworn testimony and bears the title "Record of a sitting with Mrs. Piper held yesterday." Apparently, a friend or neighbor named William Anderson was in attendance and supplied some of the notes for Bob's narrative.

"At this sitting," the document begins, "Father Mother Alice and Wilkie were said to be present." The dead ones spoke through Mrs. Piper's control, Phinuit, a Creole doctor. Alice said that "they are all in trouble about me [Bob] and that if they could take me out of my surroundings they would but that this they cannot do." Alice also wanted to know "if my resentment about her still exists to which I assure her it does not." She then spoke about Mary Holton James: "You may tell Mary for me . . . that she is going to grow into the right and that all things will be right in the end." At this point, according to Phinuit, Alice gives a cancerous cough. Father now wants to talk to his youngest son directly. Doing so, he says:

Bob, I command you Bob my son, I command you to make no change. You are in the right place. Then the medium very much agitated gropes with her hand and I give her pencil and paper and Phinuit says Father will write. The medium's hand then writes I am your father Henry James. Bob all will be well. I will watch over you always and call for me and I will come. I am your father H.J.

Bob asks Alice how it could be that when she and others were on earth they "threw discredit upon spiritualism," and thought it impossible or unwise for the dead to talk with the living, but now she is engaged in such talk. Alice's reply: "We all think differently now. You must not (with emphasis) think of us as we were but as we are." Father, Mother, Wilky, and she were together, she mostly with Wilky, Mother and Father never separated. Wilky's traits of character, she adds, "the ones which endeared him to people on earth are even more pronounced here."

Father, through Phinuit, assures Bob that he will never be called upon to bear any intolerable burden, and that he, Father, will take care of everything. After a brief and unexpected appearance by Emanuel Swedenborg, the record concludes with some vague prophetic glimpses: a new house with trees; a place by the water; an actual and distinct visit by Father at some future date; Bob with his Ned "in some tropical country."

The recitation amounts to a sort of ghostly family reunion, though the maternal presence is notably slight; Mother's disapproval of Bob's behavior over many years may be thought of as still rankling. For the rest, the emotions at work in the rambling document are not hard to make out: Bob's need for reassurance about his condition in life ("make no change"); the desire that his wife study to improve her character and conduct; the wish to be close to his sister, Alice, in affection and understanding as he had been in their childhood. Above all, of course, there is the profound longing to feel loved and valued and guarded by his father; to believe that the burden of his earthly existence could be shifted to his father's spectral strength. All that remained of the serious in Bob James's emotional life was contained in the sound of the older James commanding him, from beyond the grave, to make no change. And yet the impression one gets from watching Bob James in these mediumistic moments is akin to William's at a later occasion: "What a caricature of father he is beginning to be; and how father would writhe at the spectacle."

What actually happened at that séance in Arlington Heights on December 28, 1893? A fair guess is that certain messages of comfort and hope were given voice to by the medium, as from the sitter's sister and father, and that Bob James then went back to his lodgings and got slowly and broodingly and thoroughly drunk. The document is unmistakably influenced by liquor as well as by emotion. The handwriting is legible, but the punctuation is heedless. Alice James would have been chagrined at the awkward syntax and sentence structuring attributed to her in the afterlife, and Henry Senior seems half tongue-tied. But in the narrative Bob boozily put together, his greatest yearnings were dramatized as the imperatives of his dead kinfolk, dream-wishes coming out as paternal and sisterly prayers.

As yet there might perhaps be a measure of wisdom in keeping a William Jamesian stance about the reported conversation. We may recall William's remarks to his German associate in 1886 when, in the wake of his son Herman's death, William was becoming interested in psychical research: "It is a field in which the sources of deception are extremely numerous. But I believe there is no source of deception in the investigation of nature which can compare with a fixed belief that certain kinds of phenomena are *impossible*."

If Mary James hovered silently in the background of Bob James's 1893 experience, she was the moving figure in a transaction with the spirit world a dozen-odd years later. This episode, too—toward the end of 1905 in Boston—hinged on a sitting with Mrs. Piper. Present were Mrs. Alice James, the most passionate believer of all the clan in (as she put it) keeping the path open to "the spirits of the departed"; and her son Billy, twenty-four years old and just now turning from psychological and medical studies to a career in painting.

Mrs. Piper's control this time was named Hector. Twice during the séance, Hector spoke of a communication from "Mary"; the second time, he said: "Mary repeats her message to Henry. He must be anxious no more for the end shall be as he desires." As mother and son made their way back to Cambridge, Billy remarked thoughtfully, "I don't believe Uncle Henry will make much of that message." William, on being told of the event, cautioned against writing Henry about it; it would be hard for him to accept it as genuine, and given his devotion to his mother's memory, it would only upset him.

After some weeks' hesitation, Alice wrote her brother-in-law a straightforward, unemphatic report of the ghostly sentence. She wrote from Palo Alto, California, where she had joined her husband in February 1906, he having gone on ahead to begin his duties as visiting lecturer at Stanford University.

Henry responded from Lamb House on March 14 at excited length. "I am more touched than I can say by your report of Mrs. Piper's so striking—to me very wonderful—echo of Mother. Her manner of mention of me, and message, as it were, to me (dear Mother's own) makes indeed an immense impression on me and for a reason of direct and marked *relevance*, of the most startling kind." What it came to, Henry continued, was a situation of worry "over a matter known *to no one in the world but myself*." During two months of living with this never specified worry, he had constantly said to himself: "What wouldn't I give" for "some outside word . . . some mystic or revealed guarantee that 'anxiety' *is* superfluous." That mystic outside word was exactly what Alice had transmitted to him—"Henry . . . must be anxious no more for the end shall be as he desires." The message was "dear Mother's unextinguished consciousness breaking through the interposing vastness of the universe and *pouncing* upon the first occasion helpfully to get at me."*

In Henry's formulation, the incident was extraordinary and ineffable: "The measure of the value of an instance like this is one's own incommunicable consciousness and I have been hugely affected and emotionné by what you tell me." As he meditated "Mother's still sentient presence in the mystery of things," he realized another remarkable element in the matter. Only a little while before the sitting in Boston, the mother of John Singer Sargent, the painter, had died in London. Henry was moved to write Sargent's sister Emily:

I wrote, frankly, that the loss of one's mother is a loss that abides with one always, and how, after 25 years, I still feel that of my own, and what the wound was at the time; also that other sorrows in life repeat themselves, only that one—it is the one poor thing to be said for it—that one alone *never*.

Henry's letter followed Mrs. Alice to Los Angeles, where, at a hotel advertising "polo, automobiling and golf the year round," she and William were spending part of the spring holiday. "You were dear and generous to tell me that the message *did* reach its mark," she wrote in answer. "It is a solemn experience for me, that great grave voice reaching us across the immensities." She agreed with Henry that it was "the intensified consciousness" of his mother that "made this communication possible. If the spirits of the departed are to reach us, 'tis we somehow who must keep the path open."

After reading his wife's letter, William added a paragraph on the last page:

The episode of the message so exactly hitting your mental condition is very queer. There is *something* back there that shows that minds communicate, even those of the dead with those of the living, but the costume, so to speak, and the accessories of fact, are all symbolic and due to the medium's stock of automatisms—what it all means, I don't know, but it means at any rate that

* The months-long "anxiety" may have had to do with the negotiations and exchanges about the New York Edition of Henry James's fiction. His entire literary life and standing were caught up in this enterprise, and its relative failure upon the publication of the first volumes in 1910 brought him to the verge of suicide.

the world our "normal" consciousness makes use of is only a fraction of the whole world in which we have our being.

All things considered, the beautifully balanced statement constitutes the most searching commentary on the whole little affair. And in it, William laid out for the children of Henry James, Sr., Mrs. Alice among them, the ground they could share in common (whatever their individual doubts or fantasies) as they interrogated the supernatural.

CHAPTER SIXTEEN

Religious Variations:
1898-1902

WILLIAM

In mid-June 1898, at the end of an arduous academic year and feeling deadly tired after administering his last exam, William James took off for the Adirondacks. On July 8, at 7:00 a.m., he left the Adirondacks Lodge—he was much refreshed and relaxed by his stay there—and, after a five-hour climb, reached the top of Mount Marcy, at 5,344 feet the highest peak in the state of New York. William carried an eighteen-pound pack; his guide carried an equal weight. At four in the afternoon, the sound of an ax was heard from below; William made his way down to Panther Lodge Camp, an hour's descent, and there found a group of young people, among them a Columbia graduate student named Pauline Goldmark and her brother Charles. When William first met Pauline, in the Adirondacks in 1895, she had been a senior at Bryn Mawr; she was, he enthused to Alice, "a perfect little serious rosebud."

During the night, while the others slept in the cabin where a fire had been built, William wandered about outside communing with nature. He wrote Alice next day: "The sky swept itself clear of every trace of cloud or vapor, the wind entirely ceased, so that the fire-smoke rose straight up to heaven . . . The moon rose and hung above the scene before midnight, leaving only a few of the larger stars visible, and I got into a state of spiritual alertness of the most vital description." It was an all-absorbing vision: "the influences of Nature, the wholesomeness of the people round me, especially the good Pauline, the thought of you and the children, dear Harry on the wave [to England to visit Uncle Henry], the problem of the Edinburgh lectures, all fermented within me until it became a regular Walpurgis Nacht."

William passed most of the night in the woods, "where the streaming moonlight lit up things in a magical checkered play, and it seemed as if the Gods of all the nature-mythologies were holding an indescribable meeting in my breast with the moral Gods of the inner life. The two kinds of Gods have nothing in common—the Edinburgh lectures made quite a hitch ahead."

He groped for language to convey the "intense significance" of the scene: the "human remoteness of its inner life, and yet the intense *appeal* of it; its everlasting freshness and its immemorial antiquity and decay; its utter Americanism, and every sort of patriotic suggestiveness, and you, and my relation to you part and parcel of it all, and beaten up with it, so that memory and sensation all whirled inexplicably together." He now understood what a poet was: "a person who can feel the immense complexity of influences that I felt, and make some partial tracks in them for verbal statement." For himself, he confessed, "I can't find a single word for all that significance, and don't know what it was significant of, so there it remains, a mere boulder of *impression.* Doubtless in more ways than one, though, things in the Edinburgh lectures will be traceable to it."

The Edinburgh lectures recurringly mentioned were to be the Gifford Lectures on Natural Religion at Edinburgh University. In April 1897, William James had received an invitation to deliver the series, and after some negotiations and postponements a date was set for 1901 and 1902. At the moment, the invitation had seemed to be a diversion from William's intellectual pursuits, but in fact it was almost miraculously appropriate.

As early as February 1897, William had told a Massachusetts correspondent (Henry W. Rankin) that "religion is the great interest of my life," even though he was "hopelessly non-evangelical," and took the whole matter "too impersonally." Throughout the 1890s, indeed, William had been moving away from psychology of the laboratory sort that had dominated the *Principles* and into the area of religious biography and religious thought. At the same time, alongside of and overlapping with his psychical researches, William, in seminars and lectures, was exploring what he designated as "abnormal or exceptional mental life." In the fall of 1896, Professor James delivered the annual

Lowell lectures in Boston, his subject being "Exceptional Mental States," and his topics including such matters, familiar to SPR associates, as "Automatisms" and "Demoniacal Possession."

The continuing intention of the talks was to show that what had long been regarded as morbid or pathological in the mental life—the two adjectives coming respectively from the Latin and the Greek word for *disease*—should rather be attributed to a secondary intelligence or consciousness, healthy enough in its own way and acting quite apart from ordinary consciousness. James's favorite phrase for this phenomenon in the Lowell lectures was "subliminal consciousness," which he borrowed from his SPR colleague F.W.H. Myers, and which he used in its exact and primary meaning of *below the threshold*.

Not until *The Varieties of Religious Experience* did James begin to employ the later and more common wording of "the subconscious self." But Eugene Taylor has effectively charted the progress of William James's thinking in this whole realm: "James's earlier formulation of the fringe or halo of consciousness"—in the *Principles*—was "developed in the Exceptional State lectures into his summary of the sublimina . . ." and this in turn James "then incorporated into the *Varieties*" in his discussion of "the subconscious as a doorway to religious awakening."*

While still engaged in giving the first series of the Edinburgh lectures in June 1901, William James summed up for a correspondent his basic position in the talks: "The mother sea and fountain-head of all religions lie in the mystical experiences of the individual." William's mystical Walpurgisnacht on Mount Marcy was, as he wrote his wife, "one of the most memorable of all my memorable experiences." The Edinburgh lectures did indeed make "quite a hitch ahead"; and he was thereafter far more personally caught up in the religious question than he had previously declared himself to be. But the night vision on Mount Marcy was not the only such with William James. There had been the swift, exhilarating seizure in the Swiss summer of 1880, and a comparable experience during a performance of Offenbach's operetta *La Grande-Duchesse de Gérolstein* in the Boston summer of 1894. He felt a "good amount of cosmic emotion," William wrote Alice on this occasion; but he arrived at the "perception that my own real circumstances were richer and fuller of cosmic elements than any play I

---

* "Historical Introduction" to *William James on Exceptional Mental States* (1982); the Lowell lectures fully reconstructed from James's notes, lecture outlines, annotations in other texts, and newspaper reports by Eugene Taylor. This is an extraordinary feat of scholarship.

know." He elaborated: "The lucid scene spread roundabout our house at Chocorua, the living you in your rarity and love within . . . the incomparable Tweedy and his brethren, the unique mother-in-law . . . all of it came shining in upon me at once . . ."

At six on the morning after Walpurgisnacht, William shouldered his pack and climbed back up to the top of Mount Marcy. The rest of the party joined him there, and together they began the return journey: "10½ hours of the solidest walking I ever made, and I, I think, more fatigued than I have been after any walk." They plunged down Mount Marcy, then climbed Basin Mountain (4,825 feet), down Basin and then across and up Gothic Mountain (4,734 feet), with "a third down-and-up over an intermediate spur . . . The girls kept up splendidly, and were all fresher than I." William staggered up to the Putnam shanty at 8:00 p.m.

What William did not say was that on the long and arduous return trek he was carrying a double load, having taken over the pack his guide was supposed to carry, so that the guide in turn could relieve the girls of *their* burdens. It was a calamitous chivalric gesture on William's part; from the overexertion, he suffered a valvular lesion and what turned out to be irreparable damage to his heart. Two weeks later, he wrote Professor George Howison, who was arranging for him to give a series of lectures at the University of California: "My heart has been kicking about terribly of late, stopping, and hurrying and aching and so forth, but I do not propose to give up to it too much."

Before another year was out, he found himself on the verge of a total breakdown and forced to give up to it.*

HENRY

Henry James was staying in Rome in early May 1899, lodged in a hotel near the Spanish Steps, when he received from William a letter confiding for the first time the heart-straining experience of the sum-

---

* His son Henry added a note to William's letter of July 9, 1898, saying: "This adventure was what first strained W.J.'s heart," and explaining the business of the double pack load. He concluded: "My mother, who was anyhow unable to find Pauline Goldmark sympathetic, could never forgive her" for allowing the thing to happen. Pauline Goldmark went on to an admirable career in public service in New York City and throughout the state. William James kept in touch with her over the years, even though she was an intermittent source of friction between William and Alice.

mer before. It had been diagnosed by William's medical friend Jim Putnam as "a slight valvular lesion," and William assured his brother that it was not alarming. Mrs. Alice indicated to Henry on the side that William's case was extremely alarming, and that in the Irving Street household every effort was made not to distress further William's "irritable heart." Fortunately, William was due for a sabbatical leave for 1899–1900, and they would be coming abroad to try the curative powers at Bad Nauheim in Germany. Henry wrote back fervently to William, about the latter's "revealed delicacy," that "every scrap of your plan and every articulation of your news preoccupies, interests, animates me." The De Vere Gardens apartment was theirs from July 5 onward; or they were more than welcome to stay with him at Lamb House. It was a "heartbreakingly beautiful and loving letter," William said. "And I, who through all these years have 'claimed' that the Jameses were deficient in simple family affection, and that Celtic doubleness of nature and XIXth century 'critical spirit' had warped us far from these anchorages." The survivors had never drawn nearer.

The Italian visit—Henry had had a fortnight in Paris with his Emmet cousins and a week at Hyères with Paul and Minnie Bourget—was Henry's first exodus from England in more than four years. The stimulus as before was the appearance of a new large-scale novel, *The Awkward Age*: a "running (galloping, leaping, bounding) serial," so Henry put it to H. G. Wells, in *Harper's* from October 1898 to January 1899. It was work that manipulated a large and busily interactive cast of English characters, and one which deployed what Henry called his "scenic method" to the furthest imaginable extreme. As such it was the final vindication for Henry James of the terrible stage experience of four years before.

The story of the opening night of *Guy Domville* on January 5, 1895, in St. James's Theatre in London, has been told many times. The play presents a sensitive young Englishman who is about to enter a Benedictine monastery when he learns that, through the unexpected death of his kinsman, he, Guy, is suddenly the last of the Domvilles, with responsibilities toward the impoverished estate and the perpetuation of his line. He thinks of marrying his attractive cousin, but instead helps her elope with a naval officer; and after discovering himself, as he feels, surrounded by deceit and betrayal, he again changes direction and departs for the monastic life. *Guy Domville* contains several effective scenes, and is, in fact, far superior to *The American*. But a combination of things, including some grotesque costuming, caused mirth in the gallery, and further Cockney contempt was elicited when an unengaging story led to a non-happy ending. The popular actor-manager George Alexander, who played the lead, received his customary ovation after the curtain fall, but when he led the author onstage, Henry James was greeted with an outburst of hisses and jeers.

The hostile noise was countered by waves of applause from other parts of the audience, and for a quarter of an hour, in Henry's account of January 9 to his brother, "all the forces of civilization in the house waged a battle of the most gallant, prolonged and sustained applause with the hoots and jeers and catcalls of the roughs." The entire audience was more receptive the second night, and the play endured for four more weeks. But Henry knew that his trial of the London stage was at an end.

What was by no means finished, and of this Henry began quickly to assure himself, was his capacity for dramatic composition. The watchful William displayed a partial awareness of the matter when he commented to Alice: "It is indeed a pathetic and tragic thing that such critical intelligence of the techniques of playwriting should not avail a man to *make* a play." What it did avail Henry for—that is, critical intelligence allied with imaginative narrative power—was, of course, a special brand of histrionic fiction.

"I take up my *own* old pen again," Henry wrote on January 23, "—the pen of all my old unforgettable efforts and sacred struggles"; struggles, that is, in the art of fiction. ". . . It is now indeed that I may do the work of my life." Three weeks later, meditating the theme of what would become *The Golden Bowl* (a father and a daughter marrying at the same time), he spoke of doing a "full scenario" of it. And at the utterance of the word "scenario," something seemed "to open out before me"; he saw "compensations" for all the recent bitterness that, he said, had otherwise seemed "a mere sickening, unflavoured draught." The great compensation lay in the lesson of the theatrical experience: namely, the singular value *"for a narrative plan too* of the . . . divine principle of the Scenario."

The application of that principle, or "the scenic method," as he alternately called it, in a series of works over the ensuing five years— *The Spoils of Poynton, What Maisie Knew,* and *The Awkward Age,* with the novella *In the Cage*—was what rescued Henry from the despair brought on by the stage failure. "The *scenic* method is my absolute, my imperative, my *only* salvation," he wrote in December 1896, speaking of *What Maisie Knew.* It was a literary salvation: it showed him how, technically, to bring to a close his tale of the young girl who forms an extraordinary link between the two betrayed and abandoned second spouses of her divorced parents. But just as the original humiliation had been caused by a kind of literary defeat, so a newly recovered psychic balance would follow upon creative success.

In the later retrospect, Henry would realize that he had been practicing the scenic method to great effect since at least "The Pupil" in 1890. But for the moment he was conscious mainly of enacting a cultural revenge. Thinking again about the movement of *What Maisie Knew*, he made reference to the *"acts* of my little drama," and went on: "Ah, this *divine* conception of one's little masses and periods in the scenic light—as rounded ACTS; this patient, pious, nobly 'vindictive' application of the scenic philosophy and method." Henry let the adjective "vindictive" stand; it was wholly appropriate, but he put an asterisk against it, and in a footnote wrote the word originally intended: "vindicating." The great achievement of Henry James's dramatically organized novels in the later 1890s was a soul-satisfying vindication of the stage debacle of the earlier years. But it was in its way a vindictive accomplishment: Henry was striking back.

And of this process, to repeat, *The Awkward Age* of 1899 was the culmination: characters seen entirely from without, persons entering and exiting what are visualizable stage sets on cue, scene following scene, and the immensely complicated social intrigue (designed precisely for such scenic presentation) moving forward without losing a histrionic beat. It remained only for Henry James to carry the scenic method beyond the social and stagily comic realm of *The Awkward Age* for him to arrive at the larger and ultimately the religious vision that characterized his major phase.

Back in England at the end of July, Henry broached to William a "material matter" which had just then arisen and on which he sought William's counsel. Circumstances had made available for purchase Lamb House in Rye, Sussex, where Henry had been living for a year and which he had known and coveted since he first laid eyes on it in the spring of 1896. The house, dating from about 1705, was situated within the "little old, cobblestoned grass-grown, red-roofed town" of Rye, at the top of the hill climbing up from the main street. It had a delightful little parlor, a bedroom named for George II, and a garden house ideally suited for a study. The asking price, though, was £2,000, and he simply did not have it at his disposal. What did William suggest?

William, with Alice and Peggy, was at Bad Nauheim, where he was taking the baths to no obvious curative effect. The three were comfortably lodged, and William enjoyed sitting at the out-of-doors tables of the restaurant and listening to the band. But to Pauline Gold-mark, he complained of the "moral repulsiveness of this *Curort* life. Everybody fairly revelling in disease," and " 'heart,' 'heart,' 'heart,' the sole topic of attention and conversation." Within this mood and atmosphere, William received Henry's plea for help with a sort of cavalier impatience. The idea of buying Lamb House was ill founded, he implied, and anyhow the price was too high. He had consulted with Henry's physician friend, Dr. Baldwin (himself at Bad Nauheim), and quoted Baldwin as holding that £2,000 was a "very extravagant price." Henry should consult with a "wary" English businessman.

To this, Henry sent back by the next post a long outcry of wound-edness, anger, resentment, defensiveness, gloom, and finally exhausted calm. He begged William to believe that he, Henry, did know what he was about; and that he had grown "intently, piously *fond*" of Lamb House, "—so fond that to own it will be a direct operative good, a source of nourishing and fertilizing pleasure to me." Baldwin's judg-ment was worthless; his pronouncement that £2,000 was extravagant "would be grotesque if it were not perfectly ignorant." But his joy in the possible transaction, he confessed miserably, had "shrivelled" un-der William's warning. As a man "of imagination (and 'nerves') all compact," he suffered the more as he grew older from susceptibility to any suggestion given with assurance and emphasis; and doing so, he felt launched "on a sea—a torment—of sickening nervosity," and work, sleep, and peace all perished for the time.

William in instant reply was all contrition. He was sorry that his advice had "rubbed you the wrong way"; he and Baldwin had quite failed to understand the full state of things. In a subtler appeal, he explained the wretched condition he was in and the recent cause of it. "In June," he wrote, "I got lost in the Adirondacks and converted what was to have been a 'walk' into a 13-hour scramble without food and with anxiety." It had been a second mountain misadventure, and with-out doubt a grave and endangering episode. Coming down from Mount Marcy and entering the John Brooks Valley, William had stumbled for hours along the wrong path in the dark, and had fainted twice; he had no jacket, no matches, no food. To Henry, inviting compassion and absolution, William said that the result of this experience was "a very much worse condition of the cardiac organ, with entirely new symp-toms."

This missive crossed one from Henry, who had achieved a pre-carious balance. He looked upon Lamb House, he said, as "the 'last long home' . . . My whole being cries out aloud for something that I can call my own." When he looked about him at the splendid homes of literary friends like the Bourgets and the Howellses, and then discovered that *he*, "at fifty-six, with my long labour and my genius" was regarded as reckless and presumptuous "in curling up . . . in a poor little $10,000 shelter—once for all and for all time"; then, Henry ended, "I do feel the bitterness of humiliation . . . and (I blush to confess it) I *weep*!"

But enough, he said; he saw his way clearly enough to the purchase. He was "touched to tears (you will think me very lachrymose)" by Mrs. Alice's offer to turn over to him a recent $2,000 inheritance and make available $5,000 worth of stock, but he really did not need monetary assistance. He imagined them saying, "Why the deuce then did you write to us in an—as it were—*appealing*, consultative way at *all*?" Henry's answer consolidated a lifetime of strained-for brotherhood: "It was the impulse to *fraternize*—put it that way—with you, over the pleasure of my purchase, and to see you glow with pride in *my* pride of possession."

"Your long and heartmelting letter of the 9th arrives this evening," William wrote back on the eleventh, "making us feel better, for the tears were not all on your side." Alice had wept, thinking Henry looked upon her as an officious meddler. They had rapturously *wanted* Henry to have Lamb House, and were now relishing the image of their brother becoming "a sort of English squire."

The Varieties of Religious Experience

The Jameses—William and Alice, with twenty-two-year-old Harry (two years out of Harvard, and temporarily involved with forestry conservation)—entrained for Edinburgh in a first-class compartment on the thirteenth of May 1901. After a few days at the stiffly respectable Roxburghe Hotel, they moved into lodgings on cheerful Charlotte Square: several large rooms with lofty ceilings, and other smaller rooms on the floor above; meals provided by their landlady cook. "It augurs great peace and well-being," William wrote Henry.

Before the first lecture, Professor James met in the Senate Room with half a dozen professors of the university and the principal. They robed themselves and, preceded by a beadle, traversed the court to the lecture hall; here nearly a hundred students had been singing and stamping expectantly, while Alice and Harry looked on. To a total audience of 250, the American visitor was introduced in some quavering comments by the principal, and he then read his first lecture, "Religion and Neurology."

The series was a decided success from the outset. William had been warned that the audience would shrink after the first meeting, but it actually increased; its members followed the presentations closely and appreciatively and gave "solid and protracted applause" at the end of each talk. (William lent part of his manuscript to an Edinburgh newspaper reporter, who quoted paragraphs from it which, in fact, William had skipped, adding "applause" at appropriate moments.) The university folk displayed a charming friendliness to the Jameses, though not pressing for social gatherings, the word having spread that the professor was in need of rest and quiet. The family drove about the city a little—"Edinburgh is magnificent," William thought, "the noblest looking city in the world"—and did some modest sightseeing.

William was coming back to life. "The plunge is made," he told Henry, "the chill over and the warm reaction set in." He took a tremendous pleasure at feeling there come over him once more "the old sensation of excitement and action . . . after two years of the dull twilight of vegetative existence."

It had in all truth been a dreadful period; a "death-bound segment of life," in William's words to Fanny Morse, and to a demoralizing degree repeating the long crisis of 1869–70. William and Alice, sometimes with Peggy, wandered desolately from Bad Nauheim to England, for longer or shorter stays at Lamb House and in the De Vere Gardens apartment; to southern France for five months, back to Bad Nauheim (William alone here for a time), for another five months in Rome (at the Primavera on Via Veneto), and to England again. When William and Alice were together, they seemed to Alice, writing young Billy, "like two strange way-worn birds perching in a strange dark forest"; when they were apart, William fumed and lamented and changed his plans every other day. Henry recalled it as a haunted period; William admitted a total loss of mental energy—"My *intellectual* vitality seems for the first time to have given out," he wrote from Rome. But it was in Rome, too, that, as the 1901 winter waned, he began "to *warm*" to his task "as in old times," working every morning till noon. He had the first series in hand, ten lectures through the talks on "Conversion," by the time he was due in Edinburgh.

The Varieties of Religious Experience began with a circumscription and definition of the series topic. His inquiry, William James said flatly, was psychological, so that "not religious institutions, but rather reli-

gious feelings and religious impulses must be its subject." He took off
on the scoffers at religious emotions, particularly those whom he called
practitioners of medical materialism: a technique which (the speaker's
medical knowledge permitted him to formulate it to a nicety) dismissed
Saint Paul "by calling his vision on the road to Damascus a discharging
lesion of the occipital cortex, he being an epileptic"; and so arrived at
what he would mean by the term "religion." The italics are his:

Religion, therefore, as I now ask you arbitrarily to take it, shall mean for us
*the feelings, acts and experiences of individual men in their solitude, so far as
they apprehend themselves to stand in relation to whatever they may consider
the divine.*

(Since the cast of paradigmatically religious characters in the text includes Saint Teresa of Avila, Saint Catherine of Genoa, and the blessed
Margaret Mary Alacoque, the word "men" in that definition obviously
is intended to mean "human beings.") The process by which the individual may be brought "to stand in relation to . . . the divine" has
its start, William holds, in a deepening uneasiness. He demonstrates
as much throughout the lectures, and posits it in the conclusion as
simply as may be. "There is a certain uniform deliverance" in all
religions, he says there, despite their "warring gods and formulas." It
consists of two parts: "1. An uneasiness; and 2. its solution." As to the
uneasiness, it is in simplest terms "a sense that there is *something
wrong about us* as we naturally stand."

The story fleshed out in the Edinburgh lectures is the spiritual
journey from the place where humans, in their unease, *naturally* stand,
toward the redeemed condition in which, as might be said, they *divinely*
stand. Proceeding through this story, William gives his listeners accumulated evidence of "the reality of the unseen," examines the phenomenon of healthy-mindedness (his mother, Whitman, liberal
Christianity, and the mind-cure movement provide materials for this
lecture), and, in Lectures VI and VII, comes to what would be the most
famous section of the *Varieties*, the profile of the sick soul. Here, in a
survey of differing species of melancholy, William moves from the
simple incapacity for happiness to the sense, illustrated by Tolstoy's
My Confession, that life has no meaning, to the type of "religious
melancholy" reflected in John Bunyan's autobiography (a "case of
psychopathic temperament, sensitive of conscience to a diseased degree") and on to what he deems the worst kind of soul-sickness, "that
which takes the form of panic fear."

Religious Variations: 1898–1902

William's single example of panic fear, disguised (we remember) as the experience of a French correspondent, is his own vastation in the winter of 1870, when he was visited without warning by "a horrible fear of my own existence," and by the image of an epileptic idiot. "This image and my fear entered into a species of combination with each other," William's Frenchman writes. *"That shape am I,* I felt, potentially."

The way out of this frightful state of being is what William proposes to call "conversion." In 1870, by his own recorded understanding, William had lifted himself from the depths by his own act of will: "My first act of free will shall be to believe in free will." But this bold action was just what William of late had found it impossible to do. In the 1900 summer, writing despondently from Bad Nauheim to Alice (herself at Lamb House), William said he had *"no strength at all,"* and though he had tried to summon up a "will to believe . . . it is no go. The Will to Believe won't work." The Edinburgh lecturer acknowledges, similarly, how pointless it is to urge the melancholy person to "give up his anxiety . . . 'The will to believe' cannot be stretched as far as that."

William James was now inclined to locate the source of psychic renewal, not in a conscious act of will, but much rather in the activities of the subconscious. The psychic researching and the lectures on "exceptional mental states" coalesce; and if *The Principles of Psychology* can be seen as William James's autobiography into the 1880s and the hard-won victory over the "obstructed will," the *Varieties* carries the personal story through the breakdown of energy at the turn of the century and the new alertness to the under-consciousness. "The most important step forward that has occurred in psychology since I have been a student of that science," William said in the second lecture on conversion, "is the discovery that there is not only the consciousness of the ordinary field . . . but an addition thereto in the shape of a set of memories, thoughts and feelings which are extra-marginal and outside of the primary consciousness altogether." As before, he praised F.W.H. Myers's term "subliminal" for this additional consciousness, and remarked on the "wonderful explorations of Binet, Janet, Breuer, Freud, Mason, Prince and others, of the subliminal consciousness of patients with hysteria."

The application of all this to a course of lectures on religious experience was spelled out in the final talk, "Conclusion." The object or reality with which the converted spirit is united—what in established religions is called God—is identified by William James as "a MORE."

511   ]

The basic question, then, is the mode of the human union with this "more." Professor James at this moment delivered to his audience what was perhaps the most important and certainly the most beautifully tuned passage in the series:

Let me then propose, as an hypothesis, that whatever it may be on its *farther* side, the "more" with which in religious experience we feel ourselves connected is on its *hither* side the subconscious continuation of our conscious life.

If we start with such a recognized psychological fact as our basis, James went on, we preserve a contact with "science" which the ordinary theologian lacks. At the same time (the next italics are added)—

the theologian's contention that the religious man is moved by an *external power* is vindicated, for it is one of the peculiarities of invasions from the subconscious region to take on objective appearances, and to suggest to the subject an external *control*.

In religious experience, the analysis continues, this control is felt as something "higher"; but since it is the higher faculties of our own mind—according to the stated hypothesis—which are controlling, "the sense of 'union' with the power beyond is a sense of something, not merely apparently, but literally true."

The dialectic there may seem unduly elastic, but Gerald E. Myers summarizes it deftly: William James manages at once to express his belief that "the subconscious can revitalise one's energies," *and* to make evident his concordant conviction that to regain energy in the midst of pathological apathy seemed like nothing less than "a gift from heaven."

Mystical experience, James goes on eventually to say, is the most profound form of union with the "more." It is also exemplary, and in Lecture XVI James offers as undeniable the fact that "personal religious experience has its root and center in mystical states of consciousness." Some of the most striking instances he knew of, he observes, had taken place out of doors. He quotes one correspondent: "I remember the night, and almost the very spot on the hilltop, when my soul opened out, as it were, into the infinite, and there was a rushing together of the two worlds, the inner and the outer." Another tells of looking down from the summit of a high mountain and feeling himself in communion "with the divine." The mystical adventure on Mount Marcy is being relived at these moments, and William's account of it to Alice recalled; as it is when William speaks of the mystical experience as ineffable—"it defies expression . . . no adequate report of its contents can be given in words"; but it leads to "states of insight into depths of truth unplumbed by the discursive intellect," to "illuminations" and "revelations."

William attached the mystical consciousness, as he told a correspondent (while still in Edinburgh), to the "subliminal self, with a thin partition through which messages make irruption." But the messages were true; the experience was no illusion. In the "Postscript" to the lectures, William put it thus, climactically and poetically, with the help of a phrase from the *Paradiso*: "We can experience union with *something* larger than ourselves and in that union find our greatest peace." This was also, on William's part, an announcement of reunion with his father, especially when he remarks that such an expression of supernatural belief ran counter to "the current of thought in academic circles" and would be "shocking to the reigning intellectual tastes." In his memorial of Henry Senior in 1885, William had located his father in a similarly unfashionable spot.

Henry James, Sr., is specifically mentioned only in a footnote to the reminiscence of "panic fear": "For another case of fear equally sudden, see Henry James: *Society the Redeemed Form of Man*, Boston (1879, pp. 43 ff.)" But the paternal presence is palpable when William, alluding to a rationalistic theological text, describes the God in it as one whose typical function was to keep an eye out for forged bank checks; and again when he inveighs against "the worship of material luxury and wealth": of the current age which was making for "effeminacy and unmanliness." Most of all, Father may be recognized as the "self-surrender type" in distinction from the "volitional type," in the process of conversion, and in William's sketch of the "saintly character," one of whose prominent features is "an immense elation and freedom, as the outlines of the confining selfhood melt down."

William left Edinburgh with new heart in him because of the success of his lectures and looking toward the future (in his words to Charles Eliot Norton) with "aggressive and hopeful eyes." During the fall term at Harvard, with the connivance of departmental chairman Palmer and President Eliot, Professor James taught only one course, a seminar taken from the Gifford series. Through May 1902 and into June, William delivered the second set of ten lectures in Edinburgh; and came back to his native country on the *Ivernia*, observing it as potently symbolic that, after days of heavy sea and fog, the sun, one day out of Boston, had "risen upon American weather, a strong west wind like champagne, blowing out of a saturated blue sky."

The Varieties of Religious Experience was published in early June, and won a reception so rapid, widespread, and enthusiastic that William was positively startled. Eleven thousand five hundred copies were sold in the first year; letters of praise, along with some expressing disagreement, flowed in, and invitations to lecture. "If I go on at this rate, they'll make me a bishop," William commented to Munsterberg. Henry James, amid a houseful of cousins at Rye, wrote: "I am reading the *Varieties of Religious Experience* with such rapturous deliberation as so many Emmets in the air . . . permit." During the long stages of the series' preparation, Henry had dug up and dispatched to William, on the Continent, volumes of religious autobiography and the like, and had seen to the typing of the manuscript; he took a personal interest in the undertaking. In response to the fraternal message, William informed Henry that the *Varieties* represented the end of his religious career.

Three months later, as though in the wake of a protracted struggle, William told Henry that he had read *The Wings of the Dove*, for a copy of which novel he thanked his brother. "But what shall I say of a book constructed on a method which so belies everything that *I* acknowledge as law? You've reversed every traditional canon of story-telling (especially the fundamental one of *telling* the story, which you carefully avoid) and have created a new *genre littéraire* which I can't help thinking perverse, but in which you nevertheless *succeed*." William was willing to say that the work was "very *distingué* in its way . . . but it's a 'rum' way"; and he wondered if it was inevitable with Henry, or something he could put off and on. But he admitted in closing that he had gone "fizzing about" while reading it, exclaiming aloud in wonder. "So pray send along everything else you do, whether in this line or not, and it will add great solace to our lives."

The Wings of the Dove was published in the latter part of August 1902, about eleven weeks after *The Varieties of Religious Experience*. Henry James began to dictate the novel on July 9, 1901, at which moment William, having completed the first set of Gifford lectures, was on his way via Germany to Cambridge. The work went forward well, despite interruptions, other literary demands, and domestic crises at Lamb House. It was finished in mid-February 1902. Henry, in short, was bringing his story to an end—the death and the beatific intervention of Milly Theale—in the very days when William was composing his final lecture with its proposition (the whole passage has been quoted) that "the 'more' with which in religious experience we feel ourselves connected is on its *hither* side the subconscious continuation of our conscious life." In their gestations and birth dates, the two epochal texts are virtually twins; and on a certain rarified level of vision, they were remarkably akin—which is precisely what may have sent William fizzing about and exclaiming, whatever his mistrust of the literary manner.

The Wings of the Dove

The first year of the new century found Henry James in full creative stride. In July, he had completed *The Sacred Fount*, the most sugges-tively teasing of his novels: the tale, as it may be, of double vampirism peered at and puzzled over by an unnamed narrator during a house-party weekend. In one situation, a married woman grows younger at the seeming expense of her youthful husband, who (to the narrator) visibly ages; in another, an obtuse young man becomes unexpectedly brilliant, possibly by draining off to himself the mental abilities of a female associate.

The Sacred Fount was mostly dismissed by English reviewers, who called it "brilliantly stupid" (in one instance) and an absurd waste of time and effort (in others), but later readers have been as captivated by it as they have been baffled. Within our present context, we may look upon it as Henry's equivalent of William's Lowell lectures: a fictional exploration of exceptional intellectual, sexual, and aesthetic states. It offers as well a peculiarly quirky instance of the unobserved observer, that narrative agent whom Henry introduced as early as "A Most Extraordinary Case"; and, in fact, that phrase is used by the narrator with regard to the inexplicable wit and wisdom of Gilbert Long. Henry James omitted *The Sacred Fount* from the New York Edition (which he would begin putting together in half a dozen years); but in several important ways, it led directly to *The Ambassadors*, which James in the same edition named "as, frankly, quite the best 'all round,'" of my productions," and which he would start writing in December (1900).

Late August in the same busy year saw the publication of *The Soft Side*, a collection that included three tales of the supernatural: "The Great Good Place," "The Real Right Thing," and "Maud-Evelyn." (Mrs. Alice read the latter study of fantastic obsession aloud to her husband, who thought it was exquisite but lacking in realism.) Solicited by Howells, Henry James made a start on a ghost story with an international aspect, to be called *The Sense of the Past*. Setting it aside as unworkable (it would be published posthumously and incomplete in 1917), Henry spoke to Howells on August 9 of "a neat little *human*— and not the less international." The little human was *The Ambassadors*. A document signed by Henry James and dated September 1, 1900, provided Harper & Brothers with a 20,000-word scenario for the new novel, complete as to characters, plot development, motivations, dramatic structure, climax, and denouement. (The staff member at Harper's, after misreading the scenario with lordly assurance, concluded his report by saying, "I do not advise acceptance. We ought to do better.")

Henry was fairly well along on the actual writing—more accurately, the dictating—of *The Ambassadors* when Peggy James arrived to spend Christmas with him at Lamb House. The thirteen-year-old girl "tempered the solitude," so her uncle said. The two walked together through the white December mist out to the Rye golf course, and on Christmas Eve enjoyed a tête-à-tête over a huge turkey; after which Henry ascended to his study to write letters, leaving Peggy immersed in Scott's *Redgauntlet*. Henry continued work on *The Ambassadors* through the winter and spring of 1901, and finished it in July—though because of various delays and a twelve-month serialization, the book was not published until the fall of 1903, more than a year after its successor composition, *The Wings of the Dove*.

With *The Ambassadors*, Henry James's novel-making imagination moved into a new dimension. It carries forward from *The Sacred Fount* and *The Awkward Age* of one and two years before; but it moved beyond their themes and strategies to inaugurate what critics since F. O. Matthiessen have designated as Henry James's "major phase." Lambert Strether, the middle-aged American who comes over from Woollett, Massachusetts, to Paris at the start of the narrative, is the supreme observer in James's fiction. He is more intelligent, humane, and vulnerable than the voyeuristic inquirer in *The Sacred Fount*, but his undertaking is essentially the same: to pry out erotic and emotional entanglements, in particular that of Chad Newsome, whose wealthy widowed mother has dispatched Strether to Paris to rescue Chad from whatever French clutches he has fallen into. Through self-deception and the protective lying of other members of the American coterie in Paris, Strether is led to believe that Chad has formed a "virtuous attachment" to young Mlle Jeanne de Vionnet, whose charming mother, Mme de Vionnet, is evidently responsible for the astonishing improvement in Chad's personality.

No novel of Henry James yields less easily to plot summary than *The Ambassadors*; situations or seeming situations change or seem to change at a pace which defies description, the constant thread being Strether's tutelage in the meaning of life and of love. Suffice it that he is soon ready to approve Chad's involvement with Mlle Jeanne, and to urge him to stay on in Paris and live the good life with her. He then discovers that Chad has, in fact, all along been engaged in a sexual relationship with the older woman, Mme de Vionnet. Strether is so far advanced in his own sentimental education and so warmly admiring of Mme de Vionnet that he is willing to support this liaison, too. But Chad, showing his true colors, indicates boredom with the Paris scene and prepares to return to Woollett, the family's lucrative business, and an American wife.

Strether has in a way succeeded in his mission, but amid such ironies that he refuses to profit from the outcome, even, in the novel's closing scene, rejecting the companionship offered by his attractive confidante, Maria Gostrey: his "only logic," he tells her, is "not, out of the whole affair, to have got anything for myself." It is a high-minded gesture, if perhaps a bit chilling; and it signals Strether's choice of the detached life. He will remain the solitary observer, however well disposed toward those he looks out upon. Strether is thus the latest as he is the most memorable in the long line of unreliable surrogates in James's fiction. We may put it like this: if Colonel Mason in "A Most Extraordinary Case" in 1868 represented the passive looker-on at life that Henry James feared he might become as a "mere" writer of fiction, Lambert Strether in *The Ambassadors* of 1901 represented what he might—at best—*have* become if he had taken his literary mission as a less active enterprise.

In his preface to the novel, James rejoiced quite extravagantly in that active aspect, in the risk-taking, the adventure, the excitement of the shaping and extractive process; in what he recalled as "the suspense and the thrill of a game of difficulty breathlessly played." It was once more the game of dramatistics, of executing the novel as a form of drama, achieving therein a "scenic consistency" by an alternation (the language differs a little from that employed for "The Pupil") between "the parts that prepare" and "the scenes that justify and crown the preparation." The special difficulty all breathlessly surmounted in *The Ambassadors* was a new maneuvering of the elements. James now so commanded the dramatistic technique that he could render as a highly charged scene what would normally be a preparation or interval; and shroud with telling preparations what would normally be a scene. The dramaturgy is loosening; the novel form is being made ready for a new vision.

The Ambassadors, meanwhile, is a glowing, glittering novel: glowing with the actualities of Paris in spring and summer, "the vast bright Babylon," as Strether responds to it—the Louvre, a delicious lunch at a Left Bank restaurant, the views from balconies; and glittering at every turn with the verbal and compositional performance of a master. Among it all, two moments have proven unforgettable for most readers. The first, in the garden of the painter Gloriani, is Strether's outburst to the amicable Little Bilham, a message arising from the newly opened corridors of Strether's being: "Live all you can; it's a mistake not to. It doesn't so much matter what you do in particular, so long as you have your life. If you haven't had that what *have* you had?" And considerably more, about Strether's sense of having failed to live, to a final appeal: "Do what you like so long as you don't make *my* mistake. For it was a mistake. Live!"*

The second moment occurs much later, on a summer afternoon, when Strether has made an excursion into the French countryside, an hour away from Paris. Gazing out peacefully from the little pavilion of an inn onto the narrow river that curves away in front of him, and feeling relaxed and confident at last about his mission, Strether espies a couple in a boat approaching the landing place. It is Chad and Mme de Vionnet. For an instant, before Mme de Vionnet recognizes him, Strether stands frozen in the role of the Jamesian unobserved observer and, like Isabel Archer and Hyacinth Robinson, made privy to extramarital sexual attachment. It is clear that the two had spent the previous night together at the inn and had planned to stay there the coming night. Over supper, they are profuse with explanations and excuses, but Strether is wearily aware only of "fiction and fable . . . in the air." He finds, in fact, reflecting on the incident later, that its two main features were "the quantity of make-believe involved" and "the deep deep truth of the intimacy revealed."

The Ambassadors is a comedy of sorts, but in its inner dynamics of appearance and reality, it eventually leaves comedy behind. It becomes a dramatized probing to the depth of what it might mean to

* The outburst is a rewording of the speech Howells reportedly made in real life to Henry's young friend Jonathan Sturgis. It was the germ of *The Ambassadors*, as Henry explained at length, and it presumably struck him with uncommon force as a fresh formulation of his father's doctrine about the imperative to *be* rather than to *do*.

live. Lambert Strether is the attentive student of the question, but Mme de Vionnet is the one who suffers the most from the lesson arrived at. She is, at the end, a tragic and terrified woman, a person of remarkable spiritual beauty about to be deserted and destroyed by her profanely callous young lover. In giving us that last sight of her, Henry James brings us to the threshold of his privately imagined religious realm: the place where beatitude and blasphemy are again accessible in purely human affairs.

Henry sent the manuscript of *The Ambassadors* to his New York agent on July 10, 1901. Within a few days, he was notifying his English editor at Constable that he was well launched on the new novel and that its title would be *The Wings of the Dove*. "It fits happily enough— is 'pretty'—and I think will do generally," Henry wrote, not pausing to explain that the title came from a line in the Fifty-fifth Psalm which in the very sequence and fall of its phrasing fitted exactly the final stages of the novel's heroine: "Oh that I had wings like a dove! for then would I fly away, and be at rest."

William was wrong, in his October 1902 letter, to maintain with his fine air of bemusement that Henry had deliberately failed to tell a story in *The Wings of the Dove*. Not only is the emergent story clear and firm enough, once one gets habituated to the verbal swirlings; it is also in its essentials a story of the rankest mystery-melodrama variety. What we have in effect is a plot about plotting. The two young Londoners, Merton Densher and Kate Croy, are in love and secretly engaged. But they are impoverished, though Kate has been taken up by her wealthy, imperious aunt, Maud Massingham Lowder of Lancaster Gate; and Kate at least is determined not to marry without money. There then enters their lives an inordinately rich American heiress, Milly Theale, who has come to London with her companion Susan Stringham, and who is drawn into Maud Massingham's social milieu.

Kate happens to discover that Milly, whom she accompanies on a visit to the great physician, Sir Luke Strett, is fatally ill, though of a disease not pronounced; and also that the American girl has fallen secretly in love with Merton Densher. Her plan slowly emerges: Densher is to pay court to Milly; is, finally, to marry her, so that after Milly's foredoomed death Densher will be a rich man and endow a second marriage with Kate Croy. In the event, Densher cannot go through with the marital scheme; but on her deathbed in Venice, Milly, though now aware of the plot, bequeaths an enormous legacy to Densher, which we are given to understand he will not accept. To such

519]

a "yellow romance," in the Continental phrase, Henry James gave the richest imaginative texture of any novel he ever wrote.*

Milly Theale, of course, has her origin in Minny Temple, in Henry's sense of his cousin's extraordinary gift for spontaneity, her passionate desire to live, her dreadful apprehension of death. In telling the story of Milly Theale, Henry, as he was to say, was seeking to lay the ghost of Minny's tragedy "by wrapping it . . . in the beauty and dignity of art." Those words come from the preface to *The Wings of the Dove* in the New York Edition. At the time of writing, Henry talked not about personal origins but about compositional problems and (as he thought) structural flaws. He complained to Mary Cadwalader Jones, for example, that all the early part was much too long and the last part too foreshortened. But if we trace the story's seasonal rhythm rather than the length of its sections, we make out a structure of nearly incalculable significance.

We begin in early winter, a "dark December afternoon," in London. By the start of Book III, we have arrived, with Milly and Mrs. Stringham, at "the early high-climbing spring" in Switzerland; and in Book V, we are exposed to "the splendid midsummer glow" at the country estate of Matcham. It is on an October morning that, midway through Book VI, we find Milly in her Venetian palazzo; a number of weeks and pages later, "the first sea-storm of the autumn" turns Venice ugly, and Densher walks through a wind-and-rain-swept Piazza San Marco that seems to him an omen of moral catastrophe. Back in London in Book X, Densher and Kate Croy meet again in the December dusk, and the story reaches its climax on Christmas Day.

Encountering Maud Massingham that morning and learning from her that Milly has died—"Our dear dove . . . has folded her wonderful wings"—Densher says untruthfully that he is on his way to church. As

---

* Kate Croy's basic scheme is much the same as that of Jacqueline de Belfort in Agatha Christie's *Death on the Nile* (1938). There are indeed so many major and minor similarities between the two stories that it is hard to believe, improbable as it must seem, that Agatha Christie did not have *The Wings of the Dove* actually in mind.

In the arresting case of Ruth Rendell's *The House of Stairs*, however, not only the author but the narrator have explicitly in mind *The Wings of the Dove*. Elizabeth Vetch, the London-based narrator of this very well crafted and skillfully ill-lit mystery novel of 1988, is a devoted Jamesian, in part no doubt because she bears a surname borrowed from the central female figure, Fleda Vetch, in *The Spoils of Poynton*. Becoming involved in the frustrated love affair between a young couple of her acquaintance, Elizabeth, as she recalls, recommends that the two of them "do what the conspirators in *The Wings of the Dove* do"—i.e., that the young man should marry a wealthy and supposedly dying woman. One needs some sense of the Jamesian precursor fully to understand and to appreciate the complex plotting of *The House of Stairs*.

he moves on, he feels impelled to make good his word: but "to what church was he going, to what church . . . *could* he go?" He chooses the nearby Oratory on Brompton Road, and as, entering, he observes the splendid crowded Christmas service and the blaze of altar lights, he has an intuition of something "consecrated."

The Wings of the Dove enacts a steady controlled sea swell toward the realm of the consecrated. The literal dimension of the story is striking enough: London—opulent Lancaster Gate, grubby Chirk Street, depressing Chelsea, the National Gallery, Regent's Park; the great historic house of Matcham; Venice, the Grand Canal, the bridges, Florian's, the palazzo, San Marco. But these sites, when you look closely at them, are bundles of impressions, unparticularized. They are, so to say, the quasi–stage sets of *The Awkward Age* dissolving into sheer atmospheres of meaning.

Periodically, as the narrative goes forward, places, actions, and whole scenes give way to a sort of ineffable totality, an everything. "Papa has done something wicked," Kate confides to Densher; and when he asks what it is, Kate replies: "He has done everything." When Milly leaves Sir Luke, bearing with her his diagnosis of a grave illness and an exhortation to *live*, she knows that for the moment she wants only the human everything for her company: "Her company must be the human face at large, present all round her, but inspiringly impersonal." (It is a telling version of Henry Senior's idea that only in an organic relation with the whole of humanity can an individual stand redeemed.)

The yielding of the literal is a pervasive melting action. Social distinctions were disappearing, Lord Mark suggests, in a "senseless shifting tumble, like that of some great greasy sea in mid-channel, of an overwhelming melted mixture." Lord Mark, as Densher says of him, is the inevitable ass; he is also a villain of diabolic proportions; but he is allowed to contribute to the imagistic development. At Matcham, Milly Theale experiences a delectable fusion—the halls of armor, the cabinets, the murmurous welcome, her illustrious host and hostess; these elements "melted together" and, the narrator says, seasoned her metaphoric draught. Then later, standing before the Bronzino portrait of an elegant lady (it is Lucrezia Panciatichi), she feels that "once more things melted together—the beauty and the history and the facility and the splendid midsummer glow: it was a sort of magnificent maximum, the pink dawn of an apotheosis . . ."

Milly is being possessed by that "cosmic consciousness" which William James described in the *Varieties* and that he himself had undergone. It fills her with a joy past understanding; and looking at the beautiful but joyless face in the portrait, she exclaims softly, "I shall never be better than this." It is, fatedly, the moment of perfection for Milly; the next day she has her first session with Sir Luke, and as summer passes into autumn and the scene changes from London to Venice, Milly begins her slow decline into death. But the apotheosis— the transformation into the divine—that she had intuited at Matcham now occurs, within the consciousness of another, as touching Milly herself.

Looking back on his last hour with Milly in Venice, Densher at Lancaster Gate takes in the scene again as from the pages of a book. "He saw a young man, far off, in a relation inconceivable, saw him hushed, passive, staying his breath, but half understanding, yet dimly conscious of something immense and holding himself, not to lose it, painfully together." It was his own face, we are told, that Densher had recognized in that vision, and he knew "that something had happened to him too beautiful and too sacred to describe. He had been, to his recovered sense, forgiven, dedicated, blessed."

Kate Croy, incurably and even admirably secular, insists, when given an inkling of Densher's final Venetian experience, that he has simply fallen in love with Milly, or anyhow with her memory. But this is immeasurably less than the "relation inconceivable" that he has become aware of. Merton Densher has realized what William James in the *Varieties* portrays as a mystically felt union with the "*more*." This was the event "too sacred to describe," and it was by this deific "more," in the person of the dying and beneficent Milly Theale, that he has been forgiven and dedicated and blessed; and forever changed.

Biblical names, allusions, painted scenes, half-heard phrases bestir the pages of the novel, but they refuse to come together in anything like a doctrinal or even a Christian pattern; Henry James's shaping energy is working quite otherwise. It succeeds almost uncannily in begetting a mystic consciousness and a religious experience out of the irredeemably human and earthbound modern Anglo-American world. But it cannot and will not cast the narrative into a traditional theological frame. Henry James joins his brother as natives of the churchless James family. *The Wings of the Dove* contains within itself the visionary conviction espoused by William in the "Postscript" to the *Varieties*: that religious experience, as he had studied it, was far from supporting the traditional or sectarian images of God; and that "the only thing that it unequivocally testifies to is that we can experience union with *something* larger than ourselves, and in that union find our greatest peace."

CHAPTER SEVENTEEN

Homecomings: 1904-7

HENRY'S RETURN

As he neared what he called the "awful fact" of his sixtieth birthday in April 1903, Henry James began to talk about coming home for a period, perhaps six months or more. To William, he spoke of wanting to look into the state of his literary bookkeeping; and more, about a book of impressions of America, well funded by Harper's, which would cover the expenses of the trip and would lead him to see stretches of his native country never previously known to him. But he foresaw enormous practical difficulties, from arranging the care of his dog Max (a rose-red Dachshund, recently acquired) at Lamb House to the imaginable need to fend for himself in Western cities and strange hotels.

William sought at once to dissuade his brother from the venture, piling up ominous allusions to the grating voices of their countrymen and the loathsome manner in which American travelers handled their inevitable boiled eggs in dining cars. Henry joined on cue in the old antiphonal to say that William had quite failed to grasp his motive. The proposed American visit represented a last chance for a genuinely new travel experience; and as for the ugly aspects of American life, they were exactly what he wanted to see. "I want to see everything." William once again rounded out the edgy comedy of their fraternal days. Taking it in now that "a new lease of artistic life" was the aim of the visit, "all my stingy doubts wither and are replaced by enthusiasm that you are still so young-feeling, receptive and hungry for raw material and experience."

Henry was all of that, and he was the prey as well in the early 1900s of other literary and personal considerations—simultaneously reaching out toward the literary new and (partly by consequence) appraising and seeking reunion with the personal old. He carefully took the measure of his younger English contemporaries: Kipling (he was full of praise for *Kim*); Joseph Conrad ("I read you as I listen to rare music," he wrote the author of *Lord Jim*); G. K. Chesterton (despite the latter's habit of "putting of everything *à rebours*"). His most unstinted admiration was for H. G. Wells, whom he first met in 1898. After successively saluting *The Time Machine, Mankind in the Making, A Modern Utopia*, and Wells's novel of 1905, *Kipps*, Henry was willing to say flatly: "You are, for me, more than ever, the most interesting 'literary man' of your generation."*

His self-appraisal was taking the form of a collected edition of his fiction, something he began to ponder in mid-1904. *The Wings of the Dove* and *The Ambassadors* had appeared within the past twenty-four months; proofs of *The Golden Bowl* were waiting for its author upon his arrival in New York. No one was more aware than Henry James of his almost unparalleled fictional accomplishments in this opening phase of the new century. Unregarding of critical response, he was disposed to voice his lofty estimate of the recent writings, to himself and to others. He had become the Master, and happily agreed to be addressed as such (especially in French: *"Cher Maître"*). It was time to survey the entire career: to reread and reconsider everything he had written over forty years, to select those texts he thought worthy of being given a permanent place in a collected edition, and to revise as necessary.

Both the homecoming and the edition were elements in a still larger development, a multilayered act of autobiography that concluded with James's actual memoirs in 1913–16. As a prelude to that enterprise, there was Henry James's only excursion into biography, *William Wetmore Story and His Friends*—a work which Henry Adams, after digesting it in the autumn of 1903, declared to its author to be "not Story's life, but your own and mine—pure autobiography." Adams, in his extremist way, meant that Story as treated was a paradigm for the generation of prewar Bostonians who embarked on their profes-

---

* William James found *Mankind in the Making*—so he told Alice—good in parts, but basically crude and "bounder-like."

sions—sculptor, statesman, philosopher—in perfect ignorance of the difficulties to be met. But to a degree *William Wetmore Story* was literally a first run-through of Henry's autobiography.

Story was born in Salem, Massachusetts, in 1819, the son of the distinguished and influential Justice Joseph Story. After Harvard and a trial of law, Story turned to the world of art, to sculpture and poetry, went to Italy to learn the sculpturing trade, and settled in Rome in 1856. He died there in 1895, leaving behind a number of imposing, heavily draped figures from history and legend: Cleopatra (which reappears as the work of Kenyon, the American sculptor in Rome, in Hawthorne's *The Marble Faun*), Medea, Judith, the Lydian Sibyl (Henry James's personal favorite), and statues of eminent Americans. To James's view, there was no real plot to this successful and contented life, no interior strained unfolding worthy of a fiction writer's attention (Henry had taken on the job at the request of Story's children and for an inviting sum of money). So he filled out the biographical space with letters to and from notable friends, in particular James Russell Lowell, Charles Sumner, the fiery anti-slavery congressman, and Robert and Elizabeth Barrett Browning. Even more, the space is given life and color and a gathering shape by the memoirs of Henry James.

Mention of Story's bronze image of Joseph Henry, the electronics genius who had been Henry Senior's mentor in Albany, leads Henry to speak of "the connection, remembered, cherished, anecdotic on the paternal part, of grateful pupil with benignant tutor." A passing reference to the actress Charlotte Cushman sparks the memory of a New York winter night when the elder James drove back in a rush from the theater to snatch up William and carry him off to watch the remainder of Miss Cushman's performance in *Henry VIII*, leaving seven-year-old Henry to continue his lessons by lamplight and meditate upon "parental discrimination." In a winning passage, Henry James's mind leaps back to the moment in the Paris spring of 1856 when news arrived of the savage attack upon Charles Sumner by a South Carolina congressman. "I recollect from far away," James writes, "the terrace of a little ancient house in Paris" on the Champs-Elysées, ". . . with the Jardin d'Hiver opposite," and with "a beautiful young Empress to be watched for over the railing of the terrace," being driven in a gilded coach, the Prince Imperial by her side—and then, with the belatedly arriving American newspapers:

the reverberation in parental breasts, in talk, passion, prophecy, in the very aspect of arriving compatriots, of the news [about the attack on Sumner] which may be thought of today, through the perspective of history, as making the famous first cannon-sound at Fort Sumter but the *second* shot of the war.

The reminiscing grows more inward and questioning as Henry comes to the matter of Story's expatriation. Story was upward of thirty, Henry observes, when he left Boston to go to Rome for good; much the age of Henry James, it can be reflected, when he made *his* decision to try his fortunes in Europe. Looking back, Henry could not but sympathize with his former self and with Story, with anyone who had "bitten deep into the apple of 'Europe.' " But the phrase implies a mode of biblical "fall"; and in 1903, thinking of his native land and his planned return there, thinking of the literary career he had forged in Europe, of what he had given up as well as what he had gained, he could lay it down that "a man always pays, in one way or another, for expatriation, for detachment from his plain primary heritage."

Story had *paid* particularly, James felt, underlining the verb, in his poetic compositions: long Browningesque monologues on Italianate subjects, written in an atmosphere that provided too little of the resistance necessary for valid artistic achievement. Story's Roman career appeared to James, all told, as "a sort of beautiful sacrifice to a noble mistake."

How urgently the issue of expatriation and its calculable cost were on Henry's mind may be seen in his remarks to Edith Wharton not long before making a start on the biography. He was fulsome in his praise of Mrs. Wharton's first novel *The Valley of Decision*, set in eighteenth-century Italy, but he could not withhold his admonition that she abandon the European "in favour of the *American Subject.*" He enjoined her to profit from his own "awful example of exile and ignorance," and went on: "You will say that *j'en parle à mon aise*— but I shall have paid for my ease, and I don't want you to pay (as much) for yours."

As *William Wetmore Story* moves ahead, the two biographies, that of the subject and that of the author, overlap. Story's lively acquaintances become James's conjurable ghosts—like the Englishwoman Mrs. Anne Benson Procter, the venerable gossip who had known all the great English poets from the days of Byron and Keats. Story met her in 1850, James in 1879; in 1888, James rode to her funeral in the same carriage with Story's friend Robert Browning. The merging continues to the closing scene in Vallombrosa, three thousand feet above the Arno in eastern Tuscany. Here Story's wife, Emelyn, died in 1894, and Story himself a year later. Henry James delicately intrudes his

own "most intimate recollection of a summer spent some years ago"—
it was in 1890, shortly before Henry was summoned posthaste to England by his stricken sister—"at this admirable altitude." And he
quotes, as though intoning in unison, Story's description of the westward view: "There, far away in the misty distances, can be seen the
vague towers and domes of Florence: and through the valley the Arno
and the Sieve wind like silver bands of light, through olive-colored
slopes and vineyards . . ."

Henry sailed for New York aboard the *Kaiser Wilhelm* on August
14, 1904. A little less than twelve months later, on July 5, 1905, he
departed from Boston for Liverpool on the Cunarder *Ivernia*.

From William and Alice's home in Chocorua, five days after landing in New York, Henry wrote his brother Bob: "I have come home at
last (after twenty-two years since my last visit), to stay seven or eight
months if possible." It would, he said, "minister greatly to the richness
of the family life, and the sense of reunion offered to my long-starved
spirit, to have you here. The Dead we cannot have, but I feel as if they
would be, will be, a little less dead if we three living can only for a
week or two close in together here."

Bob seems not to have responded to this appeal; "we three living"
never did congregate on this or any later occasion; but on a November
Sunday, Henry went out from Cambridge to Concord, and in between
communings with the resident spirits there, especially the family friend
and visitor Emerson ("the first, and the one really rare, American spirit
in letters," Henry was to say), he spent some time with Bob. Henry
thought him aged beyond his fifty-seven years, but still given to bursts
of animated conversation. In Florida, a few months after that, Henry
caught up with Bob's wife, Mary, and their daughter Mary, the latter
seeming "very mature and very agreeable," and, in her uncle's view,
even susceptible of cultural enlightenment. In Seattle, Washington, in
April, Henry managed a friendly little visit with Bob's older child Ned
(Edward Holton) James and his wife, the former Louisa Cushing.*

But it was William, not surprisingly, with whom the reunion was
most stirring, and William who first gave the homecoming form and

---

* Henry had given cautious avuncular criticism to a couple of short stories by Ned
James in the *Harvard Magazine* ("I find your prose full of good intentions"). Ned wrote
long afterward that Uncle Henry's conversation had been wonderful, though he was put
off by the Western American speech and the signs everywhere of big business. Henry
was to turn against Ned James because of the nephew's anti-(British) establishment
haranguing, and to find Louisa lacking in "magnetism." See Appendix B.

meaning. Henry stayed a fortnight in Chocorua, then came down to Cambridge and the Irving Street household presided over by Alice. William showed up toward the end of September, as Harvard classes were about to begin; and one afternoon, the two brothers walked out to Fresh Pond and back. The experience, Henry told his notebook (he was by this time, late March, in California), gave him the sense of an "added grace to life." He mulled further about the fraternal phenomenon: "Whenever one is with William one receives such an immense accession of suggestion and impression that the memory of the episode remains bathed for one in the very liquidity of his extraordinary play of mind."

It was in the Cambridge cemetery, late on another November afternoon, that, for Henry, the family reunion reached its completion, and the final meaning of his return was disclosed to him. He walked out alone to the cemetery and found the family graves: that of his father—Henry had stood there in the December cold twenty-two years before, reading aloud William's farewell letter from London; of his mother; of William and Alice's infant son; and of Alice his sister. In *The American Scene*, Henry referred only and obliquely to the "merciless memories" that bristled for him in the Cambridge cemetery; but in his California notebook, he said: "I seemed then to know why I had done this; I seemed then to know why I had *come*—and to feel how not to have come would have been miserably, horribly to miss it. It made everything right—it made everything priceless." He gazed down through tears at the passage from the *Paradiso* that William had had engraved on Alice's urn: *Ed essa da martiro e da essilio venne a questa pace*. It was as though—Leon Edel's image is too exact and poignant not to borrow—Henry "had sunk on his knees before the symbols of family past and family history." Henry felt an "anguish of gratitude" for this long-awaited moment of blessed ingathering. To his notebook record of the event, he affixed his symbol of filial status: Henry James, Jr.

The American Scene

In *The American Scene*, the book commissioned by Harper's which would appear in 1907 (numerous sections were published in various periodicals), the visit increasingly takes on the guise of an act of repossession, the recapturing by Henry James of his personal past. It begins quietly enough with an October afternoon drive from western

Massachusetts into New York State (Henry was a guest of Edith Wharton, and a mildly apprehensive fellow passenger in Mrs. Wharton's motorcar), for a view of the Hudson River. The whole place, Henry wrote, "seemed to stretch back . . . to the earliest outlook of my consciousness." It stretched back to the mid-1840s and the Jameses' commuting life between New York and Albany, between the Walshes on Washington Square and Grandmother Catherine Barber James in the old house of North Pearl Street; when Willy and Harry—the latter no more than five at the end of this period—grew accustomed to the overnight trip on the paddle-wheel steamboat up and down the great river. "Many matters had come and gone," Henry said, continuing the account, ". . . yet here, in the stir of the senses, a whole range of small forgotten things revived." They were "small sights and sounds and smells that made one, for an hour, *as* small—carried one up the rest of the river, the very river of life indeed, as a thrilled, roundabouted pilgrim, by primitive steamboat, to a mellow, mediaeval Albany."

Henry James makes his way back down the river of his life in artfully planned stages through much of *The American Scene*. In "New York Revisited," the first of three chapters devoted to his native city, Henry reports on his wanderings through "the precious stretch of space between Washington Square and Fourteenth Street," arriving thereby, in memory, at the early 1850s, aware once again of "the unquenchable intensity of the impressions received in childhood," and able to recognize all the houses he had come to know half a century before—he specifically names his "officious tenth year"—from the shabby red two-story house on Waverly Place which had been his first school to the bakery on the corner of Eighth Street and Sixth Avenue at which there had been a daily pause on the return from the schoolroom.

These remembered scenes are made the more idyllic by their placing in the design of the book. James was in New York during two different seasons, in December and January and then in May and June. However he may in fact have arranged his comings and goings in those various weeks, in the literary presentation of "New York Revisited," he reaches the childhood locale only with the coming of spring. After "the grim weeks of midwinter," mostly spent, he implies, amid uptown discomfort, there was a wondrous attraction to the Washington Square area, "a grace that grew large . . . with the approach of summer." It was only then that the childhood impressions declared their intensity to him.

Their appeal is made the greater by another tactical maneuver. James conducts us down to Fourteenth Street in the springtime, im-

529]

mediately, in the telling, after a visit to Ellis Island on "a morning of winter drizzle and mist"—to a blood-freezing scene of immigrants, in their "first harbour of refuge," being "marshalled, herded, divided, subdivided, sorted, sifted, searched, fumigated, for longer or shorter periods." The treatment of these wretched beings as animals or automatons was shocking enough; not less so, James was frank to say, was the sense, as he studied them, that it was "his American fate to share the sanctity of his American consciousness . . . with the inconceivable alien." He would come to a more profound and enlightened understanding of the matter, but at the first encounter he was shaken to the core: he somehow knew on the spot that the *alien* (Henry's inveterate word for the immigrant) would ever afterward be an ineradicable part of his native country—of that entity toward which he maintained his "supreme relation." The discovery figured for him as that of a "questionably privileged person who has had an apparition, seen a ghost in his supposedly safe old house."*

The excursions into the old family places are thereupon rendered for us as nothing other than "an artful evasion of the actual." The actual was the alien: "There was no escape from the ubiquitous alien into the future, or even into the present; there was an escape but into the past." Hence the singular pleasure in the "frequentation of that ancient end of Fifth Avenue," the scene to which his "earlier vibrations, a very far-away matter now, were attuned." But in one key respect, the flight to the old neighborhood proved a sad disappointment. Crossing over to Washington Place to examine the house in which he had been born, Henry found it had been torn down and replaced by "a high, square, impersonal structure, proclaiming its lack of interest"— that is, in him or in anything his—"with a crudity all its own." Contemplating the big new building that reared up thus to block his view of the past, he felt, Henry wrote, as if he had been "amputated of half my history."

He was seized with a comparable sense of violent deprivation in Boston, as he recounts in the chapter of that name. In his deftly distributed memoirs, Henry James at this juncture, just halfway through

* This image recurred to Henry James a year or so later, to be dramatically enlarged into the finest of his ghost stories, "The Jolly Corner," in which, precisely, Spencer Brydon, coming back to New York after many years, encounters an apparition in his supposedly safe old house. The story can be persuasively interpreted in a number of ways—the apparition is the ghost of the ruthless financier grandfather, it is a dark symbol of the imagination, it is an instance of the Freudian "uncanny," of Henry James's corruptible other self. But in addition, it may be seen as re-enacting James's *frisson*, with all the ambiguities that attended it, upon detecting the presence of the alien in his safe old New York.

the text of *The American Scene*, has come to the 1860s and the period when the Jameses lived at Ashburton Place, on Beacon Hill near the State House. Henry without difficulty located the old family home, one of a pair of ancient houses; and he could read into it "a short page of history that I had my own reasons for finding of supreme interest, the history of two years of far-away youth spent there at a period—the closing-time of the War—full both of public and of intimate vibrations."

The public vibrations themselves had an intimate tonality, as Henry obviously felt a little later when, on the main staircase of the Boston Public Library, he came upon the "admirable commemoration of the Civil War service of the two great Massachusetts Volunteer Regiments." In their more purely intimate aspect, the echoings were of the initial literary efforts of Henry James, Jr.: as he puts it, "of a young man's, a very young man's earliest fond confidence in a 'literary career.' " Altogether, the house on Ashburton Place appeared to Henry as "a conscious memento, with old secrets to keep and old stories to witness for." But when he returned after a month, it was to discover that both houses had been torn down, leaving only "a gaping void, the brutal effacement, at a stroke . . . of the whole precious past." It was, this time, "as if the bottom had fallen out of one's own biography."

A kind of unity was restored, however, when Henry's explorations took him to Mount Vernon Street, nearby. Here his father and his sister had lived in the last year, 1882, of Henry Senior's life, and here Henry had joined Alice after Father's death for a number of memorable months in 1883. In miraculous contrast with Ashburton Place, "The old charm of Mount Vernon Street . . . wandering up the hill, almost from the waterside, to the rear of the State House . . . —this ancient grace was not only still to be felt, but was charged, for depth of interest, with intenser ghostly presences." If Henry grows lyrical about Mount Vernon Street—he calls it "the happiest street-scene the country could show"—it is perhaps because, as he imaginatively climbed the familiar slope, he brought effectively to an end the repossession in *The American Scene* of his personal, his family, and his American history. When, in the summer of 1883, Henry left Mount Vernon Street and departed for England, it was not to return to America for more than two decades.

While Henry James was thus revisiting the known, and exulting or lamenting over it, he was at the same time scrutinizing and responding to the American unknown—not only the "inconceivable alien," but whole panoramas of provocative novelty.

An early example, for James at least, was the Berkshires in western

Massachusetts, where, in the Lenox home of Edith and Teddy Wharton, he passed the last two weeks of October. Edith Wharton was not herself a total novelty for James, though he was still warily taking her complex measure. After several false starts, the two had met at last in England in December 1903 and again in the spring of 1904. But their friendship, of first importance for each of them over a dozen years, may be dated from the Lenox fortnight together. Partially new as well was Mrs. Wharton's automobile, "the wonder-working motor-car," in Henry's phrase ("a little sputtering shrieking American motor," in its owner's deprecatory description): there were outings in it every afternoon, crisscrossing the local region with what James called its "mountain-and-valley, lake-and-river beauty," going over into Connecticut and once, as has been noted, into New York State for a view of the Hudson.

To friends, Henry spoke of the Whartons' home as "exquisite and marvelous," though he felt occasionally weighted down by the atmosphere of unreckonable wealth. Henry endeared himself to Edith Wharton by reading aloud, of an evening, from the volumes of poetry on her shelves. It was on one such evening that, after reverentially crooning long passages from Walt Whitman, his and her favorite American poet, James ended the session by exclaiming, with a stammer and a twinkle, "Oh, yes, a great genius; undoubtedly a great genius! Only one cannot help deploring his too-extensive acquaintance with the foreign languages."

Edith Wharton is not identified in *The American Scene*. She remains hidden among the vaguely designated residents of the area who murmured elliptically to Mr. James about certain dreadful practices being carried on in remote farmhouses and hillside cabins. Pondering these hints and applying the principle (as he would suggest in his preface to *The Turn of the Screw*) of thinking the worst that might be conceived, James arrived, as "quite the horridest," at the idea of incest and associated sexual violence. The rustic settings thereby assumed for him an unexpected dignity: "a shade of the darkness of Cenci-drama, of monstrous legend, of old Greek tragedy." The story-seeker in him, James admitted, was deeply gratified; as was, we can add, the recently developing inquirer into the erotically arcane.

New York City provided Henry James with no few of the most agitating experiences of newness and difference that he underwent in the American tour. He withheld his first proffered glimpse of the city, in *The American Scene*, until his view of it in late April 1905, when his Washington–Boston Pullman was being transported around the foot of Manhattan on barges: so that James, as never before, could enjoy "the remarkable adventure" of absorbing the whole harbor spectacle from the water. James sensed an onrush of awe and wonder; he found himself exhilarated, inspired, and he lavished upon the scene the handsomest prose passage in the book. The appeal of it all, he said,

is the appeal of a particular type of dauntless power.

The aspect the power wears then is indescribable; it is the power of the most extravagant of cities, rejoicing, as with the voice of the morning, in its might, its fortune, its unsurpassable conditions, and imparting to every object and element, to the motion and expression of every floating, hurrying, panting thing, to the throb of ferries and tugs, to the plash of waves and the play of winds and the glint of lights and the shrill of whistles . . . something of its sharp free accent.*

The drive of rhetoric continues unabated, but the tone modulates toward the somber as—the train-barge now skirting the Battery—Henry James's gaze falls upon the tall buildings of the city's skyline: buildings that reveal to him the *nature* of the urban power being confronted. "Crowned not only with no history, but with no credible possibility of time for history, and consecrated by no uses save the commercial at any cost," these skyscrapers, James writes "are simply the most piercing notes in that concert of the expensively provisional into which your supreme sense of New York resolves itself." Most discouraging of all for the essentially literary observer, these huge mercantile clusters seemed already inaccessible to the image-making imagination; seemed, with their "immense momentum," to have gotten beyond "any possibility of poetic, of dramatic capture." But even as he meditated in this wise, thinking wistfully of Emile Zola's poetic capturing of Paris, Henry James's imagination gave rise to a quietly prehensile image that belied his very thesis:

That conviction came to me most perhaps while I gazed across at the special sky-scraper that overhangs poor old Trinity to the north—a south face as high

---

* Recall the language of Henry Senior in his 1845 lecture, "What Constitutes a State," saluting as harbingers of progress "our steamboats, our railroads, our magnetic telegraphs" and, in their "gigantic throbbings," discerning the descent of the divine spirit. See Chapter Two, above.

and wide as the mountain-wall that drops the Alpine avalanche, from time to time, upon the village, and the village spire, at its foot.

Not long after that, James inspects another representation of the new America, when, fighting his way through the January sleet and scrambling across the street purportedly at the risk of his life, he enters the Waldorf-Astoria Hotel. Here, in the "prodigious public setting," organized and adorned with matchless skill, James claimed to have come upon a fully realized American ideal. Any vestige of the private life (wrote the author of a story by that name) or interest in it had vanished; the public and the gregarious aspect was altogether dominant, and James, surveying it in a fine fit of hyperbole, was tempted to ask "if the hotel-spirit may not just *be* the American spirit most seeking and most finding itself."

But at about this point in his exposition, James's critique of New York comes to a halt, and another voice, that of his other self, could be heard addressing him: "It's all very well to 'criticize,' but you distinctly take an interest and are the victim of your interest, be the grounds of your perversity what they will." Indeed, the voice insists, "You *care* for the terrible town"; and so James obviously and helplessly did. For all its traffic and noise and bulging money markets (and ferocious winter weather), New York had taken on for James the character of a "bold bad beauty," and one, the voice told him, "to whom everything is always forgiven." Ironic forgiveness and irreducible affection, as of a son or a lover, palpably invade all but the severest moments in Henry James's portrait of New York. For he was, after all, nothing if not a New Yorker.

It is in the second of the New York chapters in *The American Scene* that Henry James returns to consider at some length the subject of the "alien," first broached in the passage on Ellis Island. James was quicker than many another social commentator of the era to recognize that the most striking and challenging element in urban America was the immigrant population, with its cultural and racial mix. Among some readers, it has been virtually taken for granted that in this dimension of *The American Scene* Henry James shows himself a snob and a bigot; elitist is almost the least of the charges brought against him; but a thoughtful reading can lead to a different and less simplistic view. James does raise the pressing questions, though he does so, of course, from his own vantage point and in his own idiom. Picking up on his allusion to the alien becoming part of his American consciousness, he raises what he calls "the great 'ethnic' question": What was going to be meant by the phrase "American character"; "what type, as the result of such a prodigious amalgam, such a hotch-potch of racial ingredients, is to be conceived as shaping itself?" James does not pretend to have the shadow of an answer, and it can hardly be said that the great question has been satisfactorily and peacefully resolved within American society eight and more decades later. James, the grandson of the young Irishman from Bailieborough, does not fail to pose the concomitant query: "Who and what is an alien, when it comes to that, in a country peopled from the first . . . by migrations at once extremely recent, perfectly traceable and urgently required . . . Which is the American . . . which is *not* the alien?"

For Henry James, "the incurable man of letters," the most fascinating and troubling question embodied in the new element had to do with language. He broods on it, for the reader, as he brings to an end his account of a warm June evening spent in the New York ghetto on Rutgers Street, as the guest of a "brilliant personality" (unidentified, but possibly the playwright Jacob Gordin) who was "the most liberal of hosts and the most luminous of guides." The neighborhood scene was swarming with people from very young to very old; it fairly "hummed with the human presence" beyond anything James had ever known, and this in consequence, he felt, of the sheer intensity of the "Jewish aspect," the degree to which the individual Jew seemed "more of a concentrated person," more "savingly possessed of everything that is in him, than any other human." The accumulating force of these impressions lifted James to a biblical, an apocalyptic strain: "For what did it all really come to but that one had seen with one's eyes the New Jerusalem on earth? . . . There it was, there it is, and when I think of the dark, foul, stifling Ghettos of other remembered cities, I shall think by the same stroke of the city of redemption, and evoke in particular the rich Rutgers Street perspective."

It is in the context of these remarkable emanations that James comes to the issue of language. As he looked about him in the East Side café, at his companions at table and other diners at other tables, he thought to hear a manner of speech, an accent, an intonation truly foreign to the linguistic tradition he knew, and bound, he felt sure, someday to conquer it. He seemed to hear the "Accent of the Future," and he was willing to grant it everything except the quality of recognizability.

The accent of the very ultimate future, in the States, may be destined to become the most beautiful on the globe and the very music of humanity . . . but whatever we shall know it for, certainly, we shall not know it for English—in any sense for which there is an existing literary measure.

James's temporal phrase is "the very ultimate future," and for this the last years of the twentieth century may not qualify. But at this stage, Henry James's linguistic prophecy is far from fulfilling itself. What has happened is something more interesting than James foresaw. The Anglo-American "accent" has survived in a manner knowable as English, but as an English immeasurably enriched and vivified by the disparate energies within it of the racial voices. At the same time, racial vernacular languages, particularly African-American speech in its popular modality, have been coming into their own, bringing with them idioms, metaphors, modes of allusion, and humor that relate in a kind of grand cultural dialectic to the Anglo-American form.

At the start of February 1905, Henry made his first descent into the American South, doing so, as he would say, with every expectation of entering the land of romance. Throughout his earlier years, Europe had been the very domain of the romantic, the place where, for an American, life could be more fully lived and more keenly felt; but now, so he remarked to his old friend Sarah Wister in 1902, when he was starting to think about a homecoming journey, "my native land, in my old age," was becoming, "more and more, romantic to me." And it was with regard to the South that he hoped most fondly for stirring novelty, perhaps both beautiful and sad. To his consternation, his first unmistakable impression on his first stopover, in Richmond, Virginia, was of something "simply blank and void"; not merely with no palpable consciousness of the past, but with "no discernible consciousness, registered or unregistered, of anything."

Henry James thereupon "read into" that alleged surrounding void the import of his impression: "I was tasting, mystically, of the very essence of the old Southern idea—the hugest fallacy . . . for which hundreds of thousands of men had ever laid down their lives . . . the project, extravagant, fantastic, and to-day pathetic in its folly, of a vast Slave State."

There is a good deal more along this line: James was temporarily transfixed by his Northern-nurtured sense of the Southern desolation and (for him) its historical origins. In the Richmond Museum, as he moved from room to room, he felt that "it was impossible . . . to imagine a community of equal size, more disinherited of art or of letters . . .

The social revolution had begotten neither song nor story."* But it was in the museum, too, that he met a handsome young Virginia farmer who had come by for an hour to look at regimental insignia of the kind worn by his father in the Confederate Army, and who recounted for the Northern visitor a paternal adventure that included the smashing of a Union soldier's skull. The Virginian added with a smile that he would be ready to do the same thing himself. James was much taken with him, and reflected after they parted: "He was a fine contemporary young American, incapable, so to speak, of hurting a Northern fly—*as* Northern"; but then it came to him that though the Virginian "wouldn't have hurt a Northern fly, there were things (ah, we had touched on some of these!) that, all fair, engaging, smiling, as he stood there, he would have done to a Southern negro."

Henry James is carefully restrained during this phase of *The American Scene* in his comment on the Southern Negro. He took note, while waiting for his luggage in the Washington railway station, of some "tatterdemalion darkies" lounging and sunning themselves nearby; and after a Negro hotel porter in Charleston had dumped his suitcase in the mud in front of the awaiting omnibus, James had meditated "the apparently deep-seated inaptitude of the negro race at large for any alertness of personal service"—part of the blacks' heritage, he understood, from the age-long time of enslaved service. But he admonished himself and all Northerners to refrain from lecturing the South about how to deal with the black population. The non-resident, he said, should keep his silence in this regard; as so James mostly did.

After a week at Biltmore, the colossal estate in the North Carolina mountains of George Vanderbilt (about which he was expressively ambivalent), Henry came to Charleston. From the battery on the curving seafront, he looked across the bay to Fort Sumter and thought of the recent confession by his young friend, the novelist Owen Wister (Sarah Wister's son, and himself partly Southern in background). The remark counterpointed that of the young Virginian in the Richmond museum. However conscious he was in Charleston of the sadness of the South, Wister said, "I never . . . look out to the old betrayed Forts without feeling my heart harden again to steel."

---

* The verdict is, of course, unfair: a certain modest amount of genuine song and durable story came out of the war and the Reconstruction years in the South. But one may self-indulgently regret that Henry James did not live to observe, within a decade of his death, the first fruits of the Southern literary renaissance in Nashville, Tennessee. It would have been greatly to his liking.

For Henry, though, whatever his thoughts about the firing on Fort Sumter and the near-fatal wounding of Wilky James on nearby Morris Island two years afterward, any hardness of feeling tended to melt away in an impression of current emptiness. It was the felt *vacancy* of Charleston, he wrote, that gave him to wonder. He drove the point home by a literary allusion: "How can everything so have gone that the only 'Southern' book of any distinction published for many a year is *The Souls of Black Folk*, by that most accomplished of members of the negro race, Mr. W.E.B. Du Bois?"* Here, where the Civil War had taken its start, Henry James suggests by indirection that the long chapter of his relation to the great conflict, both sibling and imaginative, was drifting to a close.

The Southern tour ended with ten days in Florida: Jacksonville, Palm Beach, and St. Augustine; and to his astonishment, James found his romantic expectations belatedly being realized. He was at least, he said, much "nearer to some poetic, or say even to some romantic, effect in things, than I had hitherto been." It was the natural setting that gratified and beguiled him most, the "divinely soft air" and a "blandness in nature" (this latter phrase to Edmund Gosse). He attributed to Florida the secret of pleasing; and as though released from some inner tension and tightening, he permitted himself such adjectives as "exquisite," "irresistible," and even "adorable" to convey his feelings about the region. An inspection of the country's oldest city, St. Augustine, and a visit with his sister-in-law Mary James and her daughter rounded things out.

On his way North from Florida, looking out from the car window of his Pullman, Henry James gave vent to so fierce a monologue about American materialism and its desecration of the landscape that the pages were excluded from the New York Edition of *The American Scene*. He addressed all those responsible for the blighting of the visible environment. "If I were one of the painted savages you have dispossessed," he said to them, ". . . I should owe you my grudge for every disfigurement and every violence, for every wound with which you have caused the face of the land to bleed." As it was, he offered a different indictment; and it comes to us today with startling immediacy and power:

* William James had sent Henry *The Souls of Black Folk* (which was not exactly a " 'Southern' book") in the spring of 1903, soon after its publication, as of interest to Henry on his proposed trip to America. "I am sending you a decidedly moving book by a mulatto ex-student of mine, Du Bois, professor of history at Atlanta (Georgia) negro college [University]. Read Chapters VII and XI for local color etc."

You touch the great lonely land—as one feels it still to be—only to plant upon it some ugliness about which, never dreaming of the grace of apology or contrition, you then proceed to brag with a cynicism all your own. You convert the large and noble sanities that I see around me, you convert them one after the other to crudities, to invalidities, hideous and unashamed.

Nor did any one care about or even notice the spreading ugliness. No displeasure was registered, no countermovement (said Henry James in 1907) was in view.

The American Scene ended on that note. Henry's journeying, in fact, continued through a nearly eight-week tour of the Midwest and Far West, before he returned to the East for May and June; but as he would explain to William, the Western trip had been "too brief and breathless for an extended impression," and he gave up the plan for a second volume.

There was a good deal of lecturing in and around Chicago and in St. Louis during the middle weeks of March, Henry delivering before sizable and responsive audiences—and for noteworthy fees (he had $1,350 in his pocket when he left for California)—his talk on "The Lesson of Balzac." Balzac, whose entire enormous oeuvre Henry had reread and reviewed for *The Nation* in 1875, was identified as the father of all modern novelists; and it was as a deeply indebted fellow practitioner that Henry James spoke of the French writer. Balzac, he said, brought into play, not a world of *ideas* and of characters who embodied ideas, but rather "the packed and constituted, the palpable, provable world before him, by the study of which ideas would inevitably find themselves thrown up." It was another partial self-image, and Henry James rendered it in an assured, subtly flattering and often witty manner that captivated his listeners. William, just back from Europe at the start of the summer, told his brother that he had been hearing "the most extravagant opinions about the charms of your lectures," and added: "*There's* a new profession for you, any day, if you can stand it"—following in the footsteps, so to say, of their energetically lecturing father.

Henry spent three days and three nights on the Pullman from Chicago to Los Angeles: an experience William would have treasured, but which exhausted and sickened the already weary Henry. He went at once to the Hotel del Coronado on Coronado Beach, near San Diego, where "the charming sweetness and comfort" completely "bowled me over." He enthused further, to Mrs. Alice, about days "of heavenly beauty" and wild flowers, "which fairly *rage*, with radiance." He put in his time writing in his notebook a long retrospective on the American visit so far (it was quoted from earlier), and his plans for the book.

In Los Angeles, Henry gave the Balzac lecture, which he now professed to be bored by, to a women's club of 900 members. He devoted five mid-April days to San Francisco, where he talked reminiscently to the widow of Robert Louis Stevenson, and with an engaging young man of artistic gifts, Bruce Porter (designer of the Stevenson memorial in the city's Portsmouth Square), who would marry Peggy James in 1917. There was the visit with Ned and Louisa James in Seattle before the long train journey back through Chicago to New York.

Henry had fulfilled the ambition he set himself in his original planning of the American tour. When he insisted to William that "I want to see everything," he had specified "the Middle West and Far West and California and the South." He had come home to his family and to family places, come back to his old New York and New England, delighted and downcast by turns; and he had also traversed the whole expanse of his home country, observing it with whatever mix of enlightenment and prejudice. The expanded homeland would in the years remaining be part of his American consciousness not less than the immigrant population and the racial communities in New York.

WILLIAM: WANDERINGS AND EXCHANGES

William had preceded Henry in the exploration of the American South, in several sojourns in the Smokies of North Carolina. In January 1904, he extended his knowledge when a long comfortable train ride from Washington took him to Jacksonville in northeastern Florida. It was "a roaring centre," he told Alice, "like a western city, with elements of greatness," and he thought sadly of "poor Wilkie," who had "so much to do with it in its old mean estate" in the postwar years.

He allowed himself a week in Tallahassee, on the other side of the state, spending several rainy days sitting in front of the fire at his hotel and working on a review of *Humanism* by F.C.S. Schiller, an Oxford don of distinguished intellect with whom William was exchanging ideas that seeded the philosophy of pragmatism. (Schiller's book had come under attack. "Poor S.," William wrote his wife, "but Dewey, he, and I can easily slay our enemies.") Practicing the local accent, as was his wont, William confided a plan to look into "the white man's college hyer." The young president of the college introduced Professor James as the greatest philosopher in America.

Another day he was taken by a former student to the "negro Industrial School." It was *"much* the best thing I've seen in Tallahassee!" The chapel was a wonderful solid sight; but what caught and held him was "all those opaque black faces, hiding heaven knows what souls, girls on one side, men on the other, age about 18 or 19, really magnificent *singing.*" He was asked to say a word, and as he did so, eyeing his young audience, he grew ever more aware of "that great human fact with nothing but an interrogation point—?—ahead of it. *That* is the most *real* impression I've got from this trip so far."

A beautiful new Pullman (in his description) carried William north from Florida through Savannah and Charleston to Richmond. From his room in the Jefferson Hotel in Richmond, he peered out "over the blood soaked country . . . What a memory that war has been for these people—so much more than for us." A *presence*—of suffering and grief—rather than an absence of conscious connection (as with Henry) was what impressed him; and compassion rather than steeliness of heart arose in him. The statues of Lee and Stonewall Jackson, with the house of Jefferson Davis, brought the vast event home to him, he thought, as nothing had before.

Throughout the summer weeks, William visited with various relations, summarizing his reactions for Alice. At Stockbridge in June, he cast a clinical eye on his infant niece Rosamund Gregor, the daughter of Alice's sister Margaret and her husband (since 1899), Leigh Gregor. The latter was a professor at the University of Montreal; William regarded him as rather vapid, but was sure that three-year-old Rosamund had "too much inner reality" to become the same. In Salisbury, Connecticut, he consorted with his second cousins the Emmet girls, sitting for a portrait by Bay while the other two, Rosina and Leslie, looked on and chattered. (To William, his eyes, glaring out of the canvas, seemed very irascible.) The girls were enormously excited by the forthcoming arrival—in a matter of weeks—of Uncle Henry: "the absolutely *silliest* man that ever existed," Bay was quoted as saying in a rapture of praise.

On a fine late September morning in Chocorua, William recounted the James children's doings for the benefit of Alice, she being back in Irving Street. The afternoon before, Peggy—seventeen years old and just starting to think about a choice of college—had gone for a long walk in the rain with Anne Sherwin and Alice Runnells, the daughters of two neighboring families. A notation about this, made years later by Peggy's mother, identified the second-named: "married WJ Jr." Alice Runnells was the daughter of John Sumner Runnells— president and general counsel for the Pullman Car company, enough by itself to recommend him to W.J., Sr.—and Helen Rutherford Baker of Chicago. Billy and Alice (she would be the third of that name in the James family) were informally engaged by the time of William's death in 1910, and married in 1912.

In September 1904, Billy James, twenty-two, tall, slender, a fine athlete, and an engagingly openhearted young man, was moving toward a career in art. He had spent two years at Harvard—being a member of the freshman crew that beat Yale in 1901: "on such things is human contentment based," William said to Henry at the time— then put in a winter at Geneva studying with Theodore Flournoy, whom William had known and admired since 1892. Billy returned to Harvard, with the vague intention of following his father into the medical profession, and, after graduation, actually attended Harvard Medical School for a year. He had now wearied of medicine and was enrolled in the School of the Museum of Fine Arts in Boston. He was beginning to paint portraits, and in these very days, William announced, had sketched his father and his brother Aleck.

Aleck, the former Francis Tweedy (at age seven, he had been renamed for William's maternal grandfather, Alexander Robertson, the baptismal names failing to stick), was hard for his parents to make out. His father's phrase for him was "tall and taciturn," though he was, in fact, given to bursts of animated conversation with his mother. He did miserably in his school studies and was never able to gain admission to college; it was discovered very much later that he suffered from the reading disability which has become known as dyslexia. At his own pace, Aleck too would take up a career in painting; he would establish himself and his studio in Dublin, New Hampshire, and earn a considerable measure of success as a portrait painter—particularly of local community types.

The firstborn, Harry James, happened not to be on the scene: he was organizing himself to begin the practice of law in Boston. Harry had finished his undergraduate career at Harvard with a flourish, becoming president of the *Crimson*, the college newspaper, in his senior year. Harry's graduation in 1899 coincided with the onset of William's period of illness and despondency; and he devoted a good part of his time over the next couple of years—when he was not working in Washington, in the Forestry Division of the Department of the Interior, under Gifford Pinchot—to standing by his parents, accompanying them to

Edinburgh and Bad Nauheim, providing staunch moral and emotional support. He received his law degree from Harvard in the spring of 1904; a career of some distinction in law and even more as institutional administrator and trustee was in the offing for him.

Brother Henry the traveler was currently lodged on the top floor of the Irving Street home. "I am glad that Henry is at 95 and that he likes his quarters," William wrote Alice. "How beautiful your relation to him is!" So it had become, steadily more so since the uneasy unifying time after the death of Henry Senior in 1882.

The brothers had ten days together at Irving Street in February; after which Henry left on the first leg of his Western American tour and William boarded the S.S. *Romanic* for Italy. For the time being, the two were exchanging geographical loyalties, as they would exchange characteristic reactions. One senses in retrospect a certain fraternal push-and-pull in the matter: William being driven to explore "Henry's" Europe in retaliation for Henry investigating, even taking over, "William's" America. This phenomenon will be considered further.

In Naples, William walked through the old city, up hilly streets crowded with cave-like shops and swarming with the very poor, as well as with goats, donkeys, and chickens. It all seemed to William human and social reality at its most fundamental; and he had a message for the difficult Aleck: "Tell Aleck to drop his other studies, learn *Italian* (real Italian, not the awful gibberish I try to speak), cultivate his beautiful smile, learn a sentimental song or two, bring a tambourine or banjo, and come down here and fraternize with the common people along the coast—he can go far, and make friends, and be a social success."

William's primary goal on this European venture was Athens, which he reached on April 3 (Henry was relaxing at the Hotel del Coronado on that date), at the end of a voyage to the Piraeus and a carriage ride into the city. With his old Boston friend George Putnam, he strolled forth to examine the Acropolis. He was almost struck dumb by the Parthenon. "There is a mystery of *rightness* about that Parthenon that I cannot understand," he said to the family. "It sets a standard for other human things, showing that absolute rightness is not out of reach . . . I couldn't keep the tears from welling into my eyes." Soon afterward, he was addressing Alice as "sweet, kind, loving, lovely, truthful, hospitable, charitable, darling of a wife. Parthenon among the other wives of the world."

543]

He went somewhat aimlessly from museum to museum; then had, by his own account, a wonderful day at Mycenae and the treasure house of Atreus: the Homeric civilization, as William reminded his wife, uncovered by Schliemann. He was in Rome by Easter eve and went out to mingle with the throng in the vast piazza. He was impressed on the spot by "the essential *wrongness*" of St. Peter's in its "architectural conception" by comparison with the "absolute rightness" of the Parthenon. Even so, he said, "Rome is great, great," and he went on to respond to the Roman environment with every part of himself.*

A congress of psychologists was being held in Rome, and after some hesitation William decided to attend it. He went around to sign in, and when he gave his name, the lady receptionist (he reported) almost fainted, saying that "all Italy loved me, or words to that effect." He was flattered into giving an address, being assured that his name would be the meeting's great attraction.

Buoyed up by his good personal feelings, William never appreciated Europe more. Alice had forwarded Henry's letter from Coronado Beach, with its confession of having been completely bowled over by California. He was glad Henry felt that way, William commented; he, William, had loved California, too. "But how thin is American civilisation compared with this, and how *graceless*." " 'Europe' is a great 'place,' " he said a few days later, setting the key words off in quotation marks, in Henry's distancing and sanctifying manner. The fraternal voices, after listening to one another for so many years, seemed to have traded host bodies.

William gave a forty-minute talk written in his own French; Pierre Janet, in attendance, declared himself *stupefait* by the linguistic performance. The address, *"La Notion de Conscience,"* was a French version of the essay "Does 'Consciousness' Exist?" published in September 1904. James argued in that essay that the word "consciousness" did not stand for any existing entity, but only for a function, and "that function is *knowing*." There was but one primal stuff in the world, not two (e.g., knower and known); that stuff was something we may call "pure experience." "Knowing" was simply the name we give to a certain relation between two different portions of the same entity. "Does 'Consciousness' Exist?" was the first in a series of essays propounding a theory of "radical empiricism"; and it does not square very

---

* William James was by temperament far more attuned to Rome and *Romanitas* than to Greece and the Greek vision of life, truth, and beauty. This was particularly true on the intellectual level. Though he never quite remarked on it, William James's pragmatism—the philosophy he was now working toward—had its classical origins in Rome and the Ciceronian revisions and practical reductions of Greek metaphysical thought.

well with earlier elements in James's thought.* It seems indeed a departure from, if not an outright repudiation of, James's characteristic tendency to speak of consciousness not only as an existing entity but as a power, a maker. When James, in the interest of dialectical fairness, articulates one strong opposition to the new theory, we cannot but feel that the older part of him is here debating with the newer: "We . . . *know* that we are conscious," says the objector. "We *feel* our thought, flowing as a life within us, in absolute contrast with the objects which it so unremittingly escorts."

The most interesting and edifying aspect of the Rome visit, for William, was meeting and conversing with a little group of Florentine "pragmatists"—he put that word in quotes, too, in a letter to Santayana—led by the brilliant young Giovanni Papini. "Papini is a jewel!" William exclaimed to Schiller, after reading the Florentine's book *Crepuscolo dei Filosofi*; with the writings of Dewey and Schiller, he said, the book sounded the death knell of "intellectualism" in philosophy (its title means "Twilight of the Philosophers"), and the impending triumph of a new humanism.

There was, apparently, the briefest of stopovers in Florence and a conversational carriage ride with Bernhard Berenson, before William took the train via Pisa and Genoa to Cannes. Here he walked and talked with Charles Augustus Strong, an exceedingly able philosopher and psychologist (his first important book, *Why the Mind Has a Body*, appeared in 1903), twenty years younger than William James and a person for whom William entertained high intellectual hopes.

William had stayed more than once in the Lakewood, New Jersey, home of Charles Strong and his wife, the former Bessie Rockefeller, the oldest child of John D. Rockefeller. The multimillionaire oil king was on hand each time, and William was unabashedly fascinated by him. "A very *deep* human being," William wrote Alice in January 1904. The student of "the energies of men," and author of the essay bearing that title, felt that Rockefeller "gives me more impression of *urkraft* [primitive or original force] than anyone I ever met." After further observation, William expressed an opinion which would have astonished many among the American public: "Glorious old John D . . . [is] a most loveable person." He added to the portrait in the last noteworthy response by a member of the James family to the phenomenon of the American rich man: "so complex, subtle, oily, fierce, strongly bad and strongly good a human being."

Bessie Rockefeller Strong by 1905 was suffering from a strange

* See Gerald E. Myers, op. cit.

illness which made her childlike. Upon first seeing William James, she addressed him in the following French cadences:

M. James, cela me fait de joie de voir votre bonne figure, vous avez un coeur généreux comme mon papa. Nous sommes très riches maintenant. Mais Papa me donne tout ce que je lui demande pour le donner à ceux qui ont besoin. Moi aussi j'ai un bon coeur.*

"It was just like a fairy-tale," William said. Bessie Strong died in November 1906.

William came late in May to Paris, where, at the home of Rupert Norton (a son of Charles Eliot Norton), he rounded out his tour of philosophers in Europe by a meeting with the formidable French thinker Henri Bergson. The two had been corresponding since December 1902, when William wrote a lavish word of congratulations for Bergson's *Matière et Memoire*—"a work of exquisite genius," Copernican in its revolutionary treatment of the relation between object and subject in perception—and sent on his own *Varieties of Religious Experience*. "Visit from Beautiful Bergson," William wrote in his Paris diary. By Bergson's memory, Professor James opened the hour-and-a-half conversation by asking Bergson how he "envisaged the problem of religion." William regularly included Bergson's name among those with whose work he felt most sympathy, and he greeted *L'Évolution Créatrice* in 1907 as the act of a magician.

William sailed from Liverpool aboard the S.S. *Cedric* on June 4 and was met by his wife at the Boston dock on the eleventh. Henry, long since back from the Far West, was lecturing in Baltimore on the eleventh; he visited with Sarah Wister in Philadelphia, spent several days with Howells in Maine, and had another look at Newport before making his way to his brother's home in Cambridge on June 24. After no more than a weekend at Irving Street, Henry moved on to Lenox and a leisurely farewell visit with Edith Wharton. Henry was back in Cambridge on July 2, but by that time William was in Chicago, delivering a series of lectures at the university's summer school. From his room at the Quadrangle Club, William wrote Henry a bon voyage letter. Henry took ship for England on July 5.

* "Mr. James, it gives me joy to see your nice face, you have a generous heart like my papa. We are very rich now. But Papa gives me everything I ask him for, to give to those who are in need. I too have a good heart."

The two of them were not only moving in opposite directions; they were doing so in an almost programmatic manner. Indeed, something seems to have been badly amiss during these weeks, and a sign of it may be one of the strangest documents in the family archives: a letter written by William James on June 17 (1905) refusing election to the American Academy of Arts and Letters. The Academy was a body of distinguished figures, eventually to number fifty, just then being formed out of the larger National Institute of Arts and Letters, which had been created in 1898. Both Henry James and William James were members of the Institute. The election process for the new organization was a complicated affair. Seven Institute members managed to get themselves named as the initial Academicians, among them Howells, St. Gaudens, John La Farge, and Mark Twain. These seven, balloting among themselves in February, elected eight new individuals, of whom Henry James was the first; he was soon joined by Henry Adams, Charles Eliot Norton, the architect William McKim, and four others. In turn, these fifteen took in five more in April, Theodore Roosevelt and John Singer Sargent now entering the company.

It was this group of twenty, meeting on May 13 in club rooms on Fifth Avenue borrowed for the purpose, that elected William James, with Winslow Homer and eight more. Henry James, who had accepted election with warmest appreciation (in a letter from Richmond, Virginia, on February 1), duly attended the May meeting and cast his vote for his brother William.

William—who presumably knew little of these machinations, save that Henry had been named to the Academy at an earlier date—found waiting for him, on his return from England, a letter from Robert Underwood Johnson, secretary of the Academy, notifying him of his election. After considering the matter for a few days—with "terrible searchings of the heart"—he replied that he was unable to accept. He said he was opposed in general to honors, or "vanities," as he preferred to call them, of this kind, especially when conferred by academies that had not themselves any working function but seemed to exist mainly to enable certain individuals "to say to the world at large 'we are in and you are out.' " He added a personal note: "I am the more encouraged in this course by the fact that my younger and shallower and vainer brother is already in the Academy and that if I were there too, the other families represented might think the James influence too rank and too strong." He took the occasion to resign from the Institute as well, at the same time expressing the hope that Johnson would not think him "unfriendly or ungenial, but only a little cracked."

William's basic position was well grounded, though the stated objection to academic honors carries little plausibility (Edel and others have remarked on this) from one who had accepted no few of them from working and non-working institutions alike. (In a *curriculum vitae* that William James forwarded to the Institute in 1902, he took pains to indicate his membership in five academic bodies.) But it is, of course, the words about Henry that disconcert. Very likely, William thought he was being humorous; but any tinge of humor dissipates in the palpable little spurt of irritation and jealousy. We may perhaps construe William's attitude like this: that Henry had recently invaded and published sometimes demeaning commentaries on what had long been William's cultural territory and it was time to put him in his place. So the William who had sniped at Henry's early stories and accused his brother of losing touch with American speech now returned to say in effect that Henry's American travelogues were simply shallow. For William, it obviously made matters worse that the younger brother had been elected to the Academy two ballots and three months ahead of the older one. And in the letter's context, Henry was manifestly "vainer" than William, since he had accepted the academic vanity bestowed upon him.*

Something of this sort may be guessed at: as it were, a sudden boiling over of a buried resentment. Even to say so much, however, only adds to the mystery—or, should we say, the all-too-human revelation—that William James, at a height of international renown and acclaim, should harbor these feelings. In any event, a certain fraternal rancor may explain why William did not get around to reading Henry's

---

* William James's identification of the new Academy as an institution without a function was entirely accurate. Henry quite agreed. In June 1914, replying from London to a jubilant letter announcing the gift of a vast sum of money to create a permanent home for the Academy, Henry declared himself "far from . . . jubilant." "The Academy should to my sense have largely made good a promise and abounded in a performance before complacently accepting large money-gifts." Its acceptance of such gifts, he went on, "in the so striking absence of anything to 'show' . . . is an exhibition—well, giving one, to my mind, very gravely 'to think.' "

It was not until 1941 that the Academy and Institute inaugurated a full-scale program of cultural activity: presenting numerous and varied awards, purchasing works of art and mounting exhibitions, underwriting musical productions, conferring fellowships on writers. If elected today, William James would no doubt accept with alacrity.

In 1957, William's son Billy was given copies of his father's 1905 correspondence with the Academy. He detected, or claimed to detect, no sour note in them. "They are so characteristic and so charmingly expressed," he said, that he was sending them to the Houghton Library at Harvard.

novel *The Golden Bowl* until almost a year after its November 1904 publication, and why he spoke so critically when he did read it.

The work, William wrote Henry on October 22, 1905, left him "in a very puzzled state of mind." He didn't himself enjoy novels built around "problems," like that of "the adulterous relations between Charlotte and the Prince." He admired the book's "brilliancy and cleanness of effect" and its "high-toned social atmosphere." But he indicated his own preferences in fiction and his own recoil from virtually every aspect of *The Golden Bowl* when, adopting a piteous air, he begged Henry to "sit down and write a new book, with no twilight or mustiness in the plot, with great vigor and decisiveness in the action, no fencing in the dialogue, no psychological commentaries, and absolute straightness in the style. Publish it in my name, I will acknowledge it, and give you half the proceeds."

William with his usual acumen was pointing to a number of the novel's characteristics. There is a decidedly high-toned social atmosphere, created by the marriage between Maggie Verver, the daughter of the enormously wealthy American tycoon Adam Verver, and the Roman aristocrat Prince Amerigo. Fashionable London hovers in the background, and there is a glimpse of the elaborate country estate Matcham, first visited in *The Wings of the Dove*. The "problem" has to do with the Prince and Maggie's closest friend, Charlotte Stant; they had known each other before Amerigo's marriage, and the question is whether the two had been lovers, and more, after Charlotte's marriage to Adam Verver (a third of the way into the story), whether they have again become lovers. About this, there is no end of conversational "fencing," especially between the onlookers Colonel Bob Assingham and his wife, Fanny; in no novel of Henry James do dialoguing characters so often "hang fire," to borrow one of Henry's favorite turns. Gropings toward psychological understanding pervade the narrative; and a permanent twilight makes the plot-unfolding difficult to make out. The answer to the "problem" is, of course, that Amerigo and Charlotte had been and are again engaged in a sexual relation.

Henry James thought while he was writing it that *The Golden Bowl* was "the best book I have ever done," and a case can be made for its being so. It is perhaps the most *powerful* of James's novels—in several senses. There is the sheer power of imaginative begetting, something one feels in the choreography of personalities, the animated settings, the succession of histrionic scenes, and most especially in the meanings that are made to accrue, that are forced into being by authorial endeavor, within the old moral vocabulary. There is a power of historical suggestion, of what is happening to and between American and European societies as represented in the novel by the interplay of wealth and birth, of old preconceptions and new aggressions. Beyond that, *The Golden Bowl* is a dramatized inquiry into the very nature of power.

We are as before in the presence of money as power: "the power of the rich peoples," as the Prince reflects in the opening pages on a stroll through London. But deeper and far more sinister than financial power is the dire ability of one person to bend another to his or her will. We touch here upon the question of evil: for "evil" is invoked more than once in *The Golden Bowl*, as James again guides us, as he did in *The Wings of the Dove*, into a human realm where theological terms can recover vibrancy. "Evil" enters Maggie's mind when, pacing about outside the smoking room at Fawns and looking in to see the two lovers playing bridge as partners, with her father between them (needless to say, the archetypal unseen watcher), she feels

the horror of finding evil seated, all at its ease, where she had only dreamed of good; the horror of the thing hideously *behind*, behind so much trusted, so much pretended, nobleness, cleverness, tenderness . . . It had met her like some bad-faced stranger surprised in one of the thick-carpeted corridors of a house of quiet on a Sunday afternoon.

Henry James's special domestic phantom there (as in "The Jolly Corner") makes another appearance. But evil in the *texture* of this novel is not equated with adultery; it relates to sexuality in only a secondary manner. Consciously or not, Henry James was reconstituting the conception of evil put forth by his father, as a quality of self.

"The only evil known to the spiritual universe," Henry Senior had written, following Swedenborg, was "self-sufficiency"—or, as he called it elsewhere, selfhood, egotism, selfishness. Evil thus understood was a malign exercise of power, the manipulation of one person's being by another. This is the sin Charlotte and the Prince may be charged with, Charlotte a little the more in her deceitful arrogance toward Maggie (Section XXXIX in Book II). But Charlotte falls *victim* to evil, too: Adam Verver, in Maggie's appalled and appalling image, has looped an invisible silken halter around his wife's neck; and Maggie thinks to hear her father boasting: "Yes, you see—I lead her now by the neck, I lead her to her doom," to a tamed subservient life back in America.

If Maggie herself escapes an evil action, it is only barely, and at the end.

In reply to William's castigating, pleading letter, Henry (on November 23) promised "to try to produce some uncanny form of thing, in fiction that will gratify you, as Brother—but let me say, dear William, that I shall greatly be humiliated if you *do* like it, and thereby lump it, in your affections, with things, of the current age, that I have heard you express admiration for, and that I should sooner descend to a dishonoured grave than to have written." Growing more serious, he continued: "I'm always sorry when I hear of your reading anything of mine, and always hope you won't—you seem to me so constitutionally unable to 'enjoy' it." William habitually looked at a novel by Henry, the latter felt, in a manner irrelevant to the work or its origins or the discernible literary intentions. "It shows how far apart and to what different end we have had to work out (very naturally and properly) our respective intellectual lives." But Henry instantly modified that statement of distance: "And yet I can read *you* with rapture . . . Philosophically . . . I am 'with' you, almost completely."

WILLIAM'S EARTHQUAKE

The year 1906 began for William with a five-day journey to Los Angeles, starting on New Year's Day. There was a brief stop at the Grand Canyon in Arizona, and William was rendered nearly speechless by the sight. Moving cautiously about the rim and squinting down into the depths, he had the definite impression that the canyon was *alive*: "a wonderful, solemn, gorgeously colored individual Being."

Professor James had come to California to give a lecture course, an introduction to philosophy, at Leland Stanford University. It had been founded fourteen years before, William informed Theodore Flournoy, by two wealthy Californians as a memorial to their son, who had died at the age of fourteen. It covered innumerable square miles of land, had an endowment that brought in $750,000 a year, and buildings that had cost $5 million. There were 1,500 students of both sexes, who paid nothing for tuition. The landscape was classically beautiful, San Francisco was only an hour and a quarter away by train, and the climate was perfect. Everything was pleasing, William said, except the social insipidity (Henry had made a nearly identical remark about *Southern* California) and the terrible "historic vacuum and silence."

Close to 600 students, a third of them enrolled, came to hear Professor James's (for once) well-organized lectures. He was to receive $5,000 for the course, which was scheduled to run until May 27.

Alice joined him in the second week of February to share their second-floor apartment on Salvatine Row, a residential street on university land. Each had a bedroom, with a third all-purpose room, a kitchen and bathroom. They took some of their meals in a boarding-house across the way. "We shall have a sort of honeymoon picnic time," William said to Henry. For better than two months they did so. In early April, William gave Peggy a word portrait of her mother: Alice's face was "smooth as a young girl, and her voice, which lays down the law, communicating valuable information and advice to all, in a steady stream, is like clarified butter of a firm consistency . . . It is easy to *offend* her, in entirely unexpected ways, but she gets over it always in about 3 hours, and is then the sweetest, most innocent child imaginable." The letter, which William no doubt showed his wife before mailing it, wound up: "Suffice it that she is the most utterly delectable, devoted, wise, simple, fierce, dependent, sociable, kind-hearted, angry, forgiving, beautiful, helpful, radiant, affectionate treasure that ever a family clustered about." He especially cherished Alice's intent, appreciative face when she watched him lecturing.

Thus things were when, at five-thirty on the morning of April 18, William's bed began suddenly to shake. Sitting up in it, he was thrown on his face; bureau and chiffonier tumbled over in a crash. The shaking became rapid and vehement; a tremendous roaring noise filled the outer air. The San Francisco area was being visited by an earthquake. The event lasted forty-eight seconds.*

During those seconds, William, as he would say, was seized with overpowering emotions that blotted out anything like rational thought. His paramount emotion was sheer ecstatic excitement: "pure delight and welcome." He would also recall, to Fanny Morse and in a magazine article (*The Youth's Companion*, June 7, 1906), that he figured the earthquake to himself as a living being—he was again, as at the Grand Canyon, personifying the gigantic inanimate—that had been withholding its activity, but now entered his room and made directly for him. As it rattled the windows and shook the whole edifice, William imagined a snarling expression on its face. "It was impossible," he told Fanny Morse, "not to conceive it as animated by a will, so vicious was the temper displayed." William could hear it shouting, "Now, *go*

---

* The San Francisco earthquake of October 1989 lasted fifteen seconds.

it!" and he almost echoed the cry: "*Go* it . . . and go it stronger!"

William managed to climb onto the only train making the thirty-five-mile run into San Francisco, and was on the last train coming back. For nearly five hours he wandered through the ruined city, much of it in flames—"fires most beautiful," he said to Fanny—helping Miss Lillian Martin of the philosophy department locate her sister, and taking the measure of the fantastic natural spectacle and the behavior of the people. The entire population seemed to be out in the streets, carrying trunks and furniture, moving in a stubborn tide ahead of the advancing flames and explosions. Order was being created out of chaos with astonishing speed, and there was a sort of universal equanimity. William heard the words "awful" and "dreadful" frequently enough, but (to his personalizing imagination) with faces "that seemed to admire the vastness of the catastrophe" as much as they bewailed its destructiveness.

William had his own explanation for the rush of joy he experienced during the violence. As he phrased it to Fanny Morse, it sprang from "the vividness of the manner in which such an 'abstract idea' as 'earthquake' could verify itself into sensible reality." But there was more to it than that genuine, characteristically Jamesian, and indeed pragmatizing mode of philosophical delight. For William James, age sixty-four, the earthquake was the culmination of a nearly forty-five-year strain in his emotional and intellectual life. In simplest terms: on April 18, 1906, William at last underwent his personal battlefield experience.

The Civil War was again on his mind in these days. (It seems in all truth never to have been very far from the mind of that generation of Jameses.) On February 25, before the assembly of Stanford University, William delivered an address on "The Moral Equivalent of War" (that eventually famous essay was published in 1910). The talk began with references to "our war for the Union" and to "those ancestors, those efforts, those memories and legends" which were "the most ideal part of what we now own together." No one in the present day, William was sure, would seek to start another Civil War merely to engender further legends and memories. But a war-making party there was in the country, a party of virulent military patriotism responsible, among other evils, for "our squalid war with Spain."

William acknowledged an ineradicable part of human nature responsive to the martial virtues, and for which the war party exerted an appeal. In view of it, he proposed another way of developing those virtues: a substitute or moral equivalent for actual war. His idea was the conscription for three years of the entire youthful population of America into an army "enlisted against *Nature*."*

The earthquake, as imaginatively framed by him, was William James's personal moral equivalent for the war in which he had failed to take part. That failure, as we know, visibly stimulated a rising intellectual partiality to the phenomena of risk, of adventurousness and manliness, and a settling commitment to the daring life in its manifold guises. As an example: On a January evening in 1895, William came out of his Boston club after listening to boring and hollow talk there; and as he walked across the bridge in the starlight, he was put in mind of another winter evening, this one in the 1860s, during the war, when he emerged from a party at Tom Ward's and walked under the frosty stars with the John Brown song in his head:

He captured Harper's Ferry with his 19 men and true,
And he frightened old Virginny till she trembled through and through.

He told of this in a reminiscing letter to Alice which concluded: "And the contrast between the two kinds of life smote into me."

A larger sense of that fundamental contrast was borne in upon William James in the summer of 1896, during a week at Chautauqua, the vastly successful summer educational resort near Lake Erie in upstate New York. William gave and attended lectures before audiences of a thousand and more; heard disquisitions on bread-making, walking, and telling stories to children; and talked with scores of teachers and enthusiastic visitors. He summed up the mental equipment of these folk in one of his most pictorially suggestive metaphors: "It takes them ½ an hour to get from one idea to its immediately adjacent next neighbor, and that with infinite creaking and groaning. And when they've got to the next idea, they lie down on it with their whole weight and can go no farther, like a cow on a door mat, so that you can get neither in nor out with them."

Afterward, on the train going East, William wrote a series of spirited notations to Alice which were elaborated into the forceful diagnostic statement of "What Makes a Life Significant," the 1899 essay which takes its start in the Chautauqua experience. William recalls that on escaping from the place with its healthiness, model schools,

* More than one commentator has noted the resemblance to the proposed youth conscription, and the possible derivation from it, of the CCC of Franklin D. Roosevelt (known to be a reader of William James) and the Peace Corps of John F. Kennedy.

Henry James and William James at Lamb House, September 1900

(Above) Lamb House gathering, September 1900: Alice, Peggy, William, Henry
(Below) Lamb House and garden

(Above) Henry James and William James, 1904–5
(Below) Alice and William James in Farmington, Connecticut, 1904

(Above, left) Robertson James, about
1907. *(Above, right)* Henry James and
Edward Holton James, Lamb House,
1907. *(Right)* William James in the
garden at Lamb House, July 1908

(*Right*) William James in 1907.
(*Below*) William James's library and
study at 95 Irving Street

(Above) Henry James: portrait by Joh[n]
Singer Sargent, 1913. *(Left)* Alic[e]
Howe James and Henry James, Irvin[g]
Street, 1911. *(Opposite, top)* Alic[e]
Howe James: portrait by her son Wil[-]
liam James, 1921. *(Bottom)* Alic[e]
Howe James and the Porter famil[y]
San Francisco, 1921

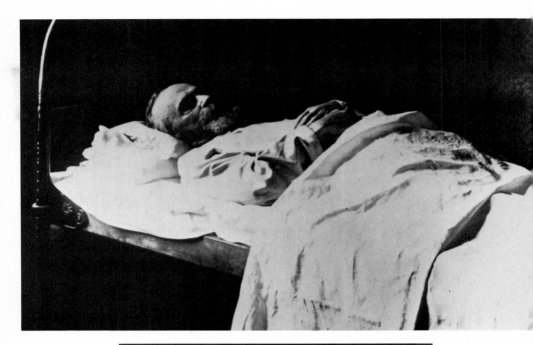

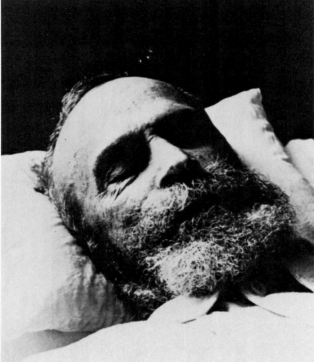

William James on his deathbed, August 26, 1910

and absence of crime, he found himself exclaiming, "Ouf! what a relief. Now for something primordial and savage . . . to set the balance straight again." The Chautauqua culture, which he regarded as second-rate, revealed an "atrocious harmlessness of all things," and he could not abide it. Analyzing so unrestrained a judgment, William asked himself what was lacking "in this Sabbatical city," and came up with the most forcefully worded description in his later years of the life worth living.

I soon recognized that it was the element that gives to the wicked outer world all its moral style, expressiveness and picturesqueness,—the element of precipitousness, so to call it, of strength and strenuousness, intensity and danger. What excites and interests the looker-on at life, what the romances and the statues celebrate and the grim civic monuments remind us of, is the everlasting battle of the powers of light with those of darkness; with heroism, reduced to its bare chance, yet ever and anon snatching victory from the jaws of death.

"The element of precipitousness." The image links up with the one invoked by William James to define the heroic mind in *The Principles of Psychology*, as one imbued by a sense "for living on the perilous edge." And from his train window as he sped toward Buffalo, leaving Chautauqua ever farther behind, William (he said in the essay) espied the perfect embodiment of his risk-taking ideal: "the sight of a workman doing something on the dizzy edge of a sky-scaling iron construction."*

William's exuberance over the earthquake—the savage shaking and rocking of his little house—arose from a subterranean recognition that here was *his* moment of "strength and strenuousness, intensity and danger." Here, in fact, was an equivalent of sorts for the grand historic danger he had not confronted. William can almost be heard giving voice to that uncontrollable glee felt by Wilky James as he charged down the hill at Kinston, North Carolina, amid a hail of bullets. In fact, as we read it, William associated the earthquake both with Wilky's Civil War exploits, particularly his role in the attack on Fort Wagner, and with the anxious waiting at home for news of the wounded brother. Writing to Henry, who had been cabling frantically from Rye for some word of William and Alice, William apologized for not letting Henry (and Billy, who was with him) know at once that all was well.

* All the more did William regret the Adirondacks incident that had produced in him, as he told Pauline Goldmark, a "precipice-disliking soul," and that caused him to creep so warily around the rim of the Grand Canyon.

"*All* the anguish was yours," he said; and the experience confirmed for him "what I have always known, that in battles, sieges and other great calamities, the pathos and agony is in general solely felt by those at a distance." He could well recall the pathos and agony felt by the family, himself among it, so far distant, in Newport, from Charleston harbor. But now he had taken part in his own battle, had survived his own siege.*

Stanford University closed down for the balance of the spring semester. William was paid in full, though he was able to complete only about three-fourths of his lecture course. He and Alice left for the East on April 27 and were back in Irving Street on May 3. " 'Home' looks extraordinarily pleasant," he wrote Henry, and added words of heartfelt praise for Henry's article on Boston in the *North American Review*.

Pragmatism

As the autumn 1906 semester at Harvard drew to its close, William wrote his daughter that his next Tuesday's lecture would be his last "before a class in Harvard University, so help me God amen!" At the completion of the lecture two days later, an undergraduate asked Professor James to autograph his notebook. The professor complied: "Wm. James. Good Bye Harvard! January 22, 1907." Alice James, seated at the rear of the hall, could witness the ovation that greeted William's concluding remarks and the silver cup given him by the students.

William James had finally succeeded in resigning from Harvard, after teaching there for thirty-five years (several earlier efforts had failed); Eliot at once awarded him a pension of $1,200 a year. But William's lecturing days were far from over. One week following his last class at Harvard, William was in New York giving the first of eight lectures on the philosophy of pragmatism at Columbia University, a repetition of the series he had delivered at the Lowell Institute in Boston the previous November and December. The lectures appeared in June as the volume called *Pragmatism*.

The New York visit, eleven days in all, proved unexpectedly ex-

* William's son Harry expressed a comparable yearning for battlefield experience—a familial and filial yearning, it would seem—when serving in the Verdun area in World War I. See Appendix B.

hilarating for William. The impact of the city itself was overwhelming. He stayed at the Harvard Club on Forty-fourth Street, and went up every weekday by subway to the Columbia campus at 115th, roaring back and forth between the two locations, as he put it. His usual impression of New York over two decades had been one of "repulsion at the clangor, disorder, and permanent earthquake conditions." But this time, installed at midtown "in the centre of the cyclone," he "caught the pulse of the machine, took up the rhythm, and vibrated *mit*, and found it simply magnificent."

He wondered that Henry had not been more enthusiastic about the city in the articles that had appeared in magazines, but hazarded the guess that "that superbly powerful and beautiful subway was not opened when you were there." (In fact, the first completed section of the New York subway, abuilding since 1900, was inaugurated in the winter of 1904 and cars were running during Henry's New York months. He seems to have taken no notice of them.) William, meanwhile, was excited by a New York altogether different from the town he and Henry had known fifty-odd years before. "It is an *entirely* new New York, in soul as well as in body, from the old one, which looks like a village in retrospect. The courage, the heaven-scaling audacity of it all, and the *lightness* withal, as if there was nothing that was not easy, and the great pulses and bounds of progress, so many in directions all simultaneous that the coordination is indefinitely future, give a kind of *drumming background* of life that I never felt before." He might have been competing with Henry for rhetorical mastery of the urban scene, the "heaven-scaling audacity" and the exuberantly indefinite *future* of his own cityscape contrasting with Henry's sense of the sheer "power of the most extravagant of cities," and something "crowned . . . with no credible possibility of history, and consecrated to no uses save the commercial at any cost."

William lectured to an audience that reached one thousand. There were four separate dinners in eight days at the Columbia Faculty Club, with John Dewey and other distinguished members of the university faculty, a number of them, like Dickinson Miller, former students of William James: "certainly the high tide of my existence," William told his brother and his son Billy, "so far as *energizing* and being 'recognized' were concerned."

Pragmatism was also the high tide of William's intellectual life, or so it seemed to him. In April, with the proofs of the book corrected and ready for the printer, William wrote Billy in a jubilant letter that *Pragmatism* was "the most important thing I've written yet, and bound,

I am sure, to stir up a lot of attention." A negative response from his colleague Munsterberg rather encouraged him than otherwise. After reading a chapter in manuscript, Munsterberg remarked that James seemed ignorant of Kant ever having written: "Kant having already said all that I say. I regard this as a very good symptom," James informed Flournoy. "The third stage of opinion about a new idea, already arrived: *1st*: absurd! *2nd*: trivial! *3rd: we* discovered it!"

William's good feelings about *Pragmatism* were not only due to his having promulgated therein "a new idea" (his subtitle, for all his derision of Munsterberg, was "A New Name for Some Old Ways of Thinking"). They were spawned, as one gathers, by an awareness that the most of him had come together in this single volume. The relatively short text (132 pages in a recent edition) was a kind of Jamesian *summa*, if not the one he sometimes planned or dreamed. It drew betimes upon his medical training, his psychological studies, his religious inquiries, and his literary culture (Goethe, Lessing, Wordsworth, Browning, Emerson, Whitman, and the Greek anthology are among those quoted from), as well as his philosophical interests. Within the latter, the discussion moves between philosophical methodology, moral philosophy, metaphysics, theories of knowledge and of truth, and religious ideas.

Stylistically, the lectures are William James at his most engaging. Like Henry holding forth publicly on Balzac, he could be artfully deferential to his listeners; and he adopted for their instructive pleasure a tone that could be by turns conversational, intellectually unremitting, witty, scornful, and poetic. He spoke of "the everlasting weather of our perceptions," and suggested that the unpredictable actual weather in Boston could serve as analogy for the helter-skelter flow of our thoughts. Alluding to the human habit of *adding* to sensible reality, he says: "We carve out groups of stars on the heavens, and call them constellations, and the stars patiently suffer us to do so." He is nowhere more eloquent than in taking on the rationalists. Objective truth for the rationalist, he observes, has nothing to do with *facts*, but "must be something non-utilitarian, haughty, refined, remote, august, exalted." The "Schiller-Dewey view of truth" had been "ferociously attacked by rationalistic philosophers" who "abominably misunderstand." For the rationalist, the whole pragmatic account of truth "describes a tramp and vagrant world, adrift in space, with neither elephant nor tortoise to plant the sole of its foot upon."

This series begins with a look at "the present dilemma in philosophy," as constituted by the two opposed camps of what William, in a now famous distinction, calls the "tender-minded" and the "tough-minded." The former are said, typically, to be rationalistic, idealistic, religious, free-willist, dogmatic, and so on; the latter empiricist, materialistic, irreligious, fatalistic, skeptical, and the rest. What was needed, for better philosophical health in the world, was an instrument of mediation; and William James's first big claim for pragmatism is that it can be exactly that—a method for resolving intellectual disputes.

Neither of the two contrasted mixtures, the lecturer concedes, is completely coherent; we have seen William James position himself at various points on both sides. He was empirical and skeptical, certainly, but he was hardly irreligious; materialistic is not the best term for his metaphysical view, and he was a free-willist of long persuasion. Addressing the issue of free will in the third lecture, William clarifies his stance as of 1907 by refusing it absolute rationalistic sanction while resting comfortably with the pragmatic definition of it. Free will pragmatically means *"novelties in the world"*; it means that "the future may not identically repeat the past." Earlier in the same talk he has said that philosophy in general is not entirely "retrospective," as Spencer would like; it is "prospective also," and asks the question "What does the world *promise?*" In the lecture's peroration, he warms to the theme: "From looking backwards on principles . . . pragmatism shifts the emphasis and looks forward into facts themselves. The really vital question for us all is, What is this world going to be? What is life eventually to make of itself?" Like William James's New York, his pragmatism's "coordination is indefinitely future."

It is in its rhythmic stress on the forward-looking act and its sense of the world's promise and possibility that *Pragmatism* bespeaks its American lineage. The lectures celebrate the achievements of John Dewey, F.C.S. Schiller, and Giovanni Papini; and James is careful to note that the term "pragmatism" itself—"from the Greek word *pragma*, meaning action"—was first introduced into philosophy by Charles Sanders Peirce in an article of 1878 which, after contending that "our beliefs are really rules for action," argued that "to develop a thought's meaning, we need only determine what conduct it is fitted to produce."* The book is dedicated "to the memory of John Stuart

* William James, in a talk at the University of California in 1898—sometimes taken as the first formal declaration of the pragmatic philosophy—acknowledged Peirce as the key precursor. Peirce's theory of "practicalism" (James's word)—"or pragmatism, as he called it, when I first heard him enunciate it at Cambridge in the early '70's"—gave him, James said, the direction he wanted to follow.

Mill from whom I first learned the pragmatic openness of mind." But the philosophical theory in *Pragmatism* is unfolded within an atmosphere deeply, pervasively informed by the nineteenth-century American philosophical spirit, and most especially by the spirit of Emerson.

William had reread Emerson's entire literary output four years before, in preparation for his talk at Concord for the Centenary of Ralph Waldo Emerson on May 25, 1903. The experience, he wrote Fanny Morse one day after the gathering, "has made me feel his real greatness" in a new way. The scene at the old Concord meetinghouse had been a delight: "the descendants of the grand old man in such profusion," and "the allusions to great thoughts and things, and the old-time New England rusticity and rurality." It all made a "matchless combination," William thought; it "took one back to one's childhood." William was assuredly taken back to his own childhood, to the family story of Emerson on his first appearance at the James family home in Washington Place being taken upstairs to give his blessing to the infant Willy, to Emerson's periodic visits to the house on West Fourteenth Street and the glimpses of him sitting between the elder Jameses, facing the fire in the back parlor. The re-encounter with Emerson, reverberating as it does in *Pragmatism*, was another and not the least important form of imaginative homecoming for William James.

Twice during the Concord talk William quoted the lines from Emerson's "Voluntaries" that had meant so much to the Jameses:

> *So nigh is Grandeur to our dust*
> *So near is God to man.*

The poem, we recall, was a chant for the 54th Black Massachusetts Regiment and their heroism at Fort Wagner. William takes the lines as illustrating Emerson's belief that "the effulgence of the Universal Reason" shines through the rudest individual fact; and that, in the same way, every individual human being, however lowly, can be illuminated by highest truth. So it is that William finds Emerson declaiming—and this, he says, is the "bugle-blast" which future critics will regard as "the soul of [Emerson's] message"—that "the present man is the aboriginal reality, the Institution is derivative, and the past man is irrelevant and obliterate for present issues." In a life at first hand and there only does there reside something of the sacred; this, William told his audience, is Emerson's recognizable note.

As to Emerson's optimism, William said it was wholly unsentimental and had "nothing in common with that indiscriminate hurrahing for the Universe with which Walt Whitman has made us familiar." The trope is enjoyable; but we come upon a soberer Jamesian estimate in a letter three weeks later to Henry Rankin, where William offered the following: "Rereading [Emerson] *in extenso*, almost *in toto*, lately, has made him loom larger than ever to me as a human being, but I feel the distinct lack in him of too little understanding of the morbid side of life." This was only a milder version of Henry's dictum that Emerson "had no great sense of wrong . . . no sense of the dark, the foul, the base"; that he had at best "a kind of hearsay, uninformed acquaintance with the disorders" of the human spirit.

Emerson's enabling presence can be felt at many moments in *Pragmatism*. The passage in the third lecture about philosophy being "prospective" as well as "retrospective" takes its origin in Emerson's pivotal essay of 1836, "Nature," which, beginning with the statement "Our age is retrospective. It builds the sepulchres of the father," concludes with the gleamingly hortatory section called "Prospects." The fourth talk opens with a fresh formulation of the same motif: "The pragmatic method . . . plunges forward into the river of experience." It is—to enlarge a little on the earlier summary—in the referring all things, all questions and ideas to *experience*, and in the locating of experience as invariably *lying ahead*, that *Pragmatism* earns the title, long granted to it, of *the* American mode of philosophy; and William James appears as a chief offspring of Emerson and those others among his contemporaries who have been collected historically into "the party of hope."

This is not to say, however, as it is being asserted in some current literary quarters, that Emerson is the exclusive source of everything worth keeping that has been written in America after him; or that William James descends without other ingredients from Emerson. But the issues here involved may await another day.

A bold and sinuous argument runs through the final three lectures. In a vast simplification: Lecture VI lays it down that truth *happens* to an idea; Lecture VII says that that happening is a human event—that truths are *made* by human beings; Lecture VIII argues that in that human activity there lies nothing less than the salvation of the world.

In Lecture VI, "Pragmatism's Conception of Truth," James advances a main thesis: "Truth *happens* to an idea. It *becomes* true, is *made* true by events. Its verity *is* in fact an event, a process: the process namely of its verifying itself, its veri-*fication*." To this, the lecturer hears the rationalist voice replying belligerently: "Truth is not made, it absolutely obtains." Truth has nothing to do with our experience. It is simply the agreement of our ideas with a reality that "stands complete and ready-made from all eternity."

James pushes forward. "*The true,*" he says, stressing hard, ". . . *is only the expedient in the way of our thinking, just as 'the right' is only the expedient in the way of our behaving.*" For expressing such a thought on other occasions, he and Schiller had been accused of the rankest relativism, of holding that for the pragmatist a person could say whatever he wanted to say and call it truth. "I leave it to you," James said, nodding (one fancies) to his audience, "to judge whether this be not an impudent slander." No one is more conscious than the pragmatist of standing between the "whole body of funded truths from the past" (James has already made much of this burden) and the coercions of the sensible world around him; hence of the enormous external pressures that control our thinking. "If any one imagines that this law is lax, let him keep its commandment for one day, says Emerson."

Drawing on Schiller's doctrine of "humanism" in Lecture VII, James proposes that "to an unascertainable extent our truths are man-made"—if they happen, it is because human beings are making them happen. He quotes from Schiller: "The world is essentially *ule* [matter or stuff], it is what we make it . . . The world is *plastic.*" A few minutes later, James arrives at his own stirring inference: "In our cognitive as well as in our active life we are creative. We *add*, both to the subject and to the predicate part of reality." For himself and his pragmatist associates, he said, this notion was inspiring; Signor Papini "grows fairly dithyrambic over the view that it opens of man's divinely-creative functions." And for William, the moment was a celebrational reunion with the intellectual self of thirty years before that had argued, against Spencer, that "the knower is not simply a mirror . . . passively reflecting an order that he comes upon"; the knower, on the contrary, "is an actor"; mental activities "help to *make* the truth which they declare."

The whole extent of the difference between pragmatism and rationalism, James then said, was now in sight (italics his):

The essential contrast is that *for rationalism reality is ready-made and complete from all eternity, while for pragmatism it is still in the making, and awaits part of its complexion from the future.* On the one side the universe is absolutely secure, on the other it is still pursuing its adventures.

In the closing lecture, William James enlarges on that last image of an adventurous universe. The grand issue arises of "the salvation of the world"; and as against the pessimists who declare it impossible and the optimists who think it inevitable, the pragmatist takes the view that the world's salvation is *possible*. The pragmatist, says James, believes that the world can be bettered, here and there, bit by bit, in patches—and this by the moral and intellectual actions of individual human beings. "Our acts, our turning-places, where we seem to ourselves to make ourselves and grow . . . why may they not be the actual turning-places and growing-places . . . *of the world* [italics added]— why not the workshop of being, where we catch fact in the making, so that nowhere may the world grow in any other kind of way than this?"

In content and image, the passage partakes of the intellectually breathtaking, manifestly the product of William James as of no other American thinker in his generation. But if it arises from the philosopher of risk, it does so not less from the son of Henry James the Elder. For the conception of human beings by their endeavors ultimately bringing about the salvation of the world: this is a version, however individualized, of Henry Senior's vision of human society as the redeemed form of man. In William's words about the paternal doctrine, it is human nature purified and illuminated that "will form the kingdom of heaven on earth, the regenerate social order which none of us yet know."* The author of that 1885 statement returns in 1907 to the theme of the "regenerate social order," or "the salvation of the world," and locates it once again in the actions of human beings.

But where the father never attempted to explain *how* the redemptive society might come into being, the son imagined a mighty human response to a clarion call to action. Suppose, he told his audience, that the world's author had said to them before the creation: "I am going to make a world not certain to be saved, a world the perfection of which shall be conditional merely, the condition being that each several agent does its own 'level best.' " The voice is heard making the challenge: "I offer you the chance of taking part in such a world. Its safety, you see, is unwarranted. It is a real adventure with real danger, yet it may win through . . . Will you trust yourself and trust the other agents enough to face the risk?"

The individuals who make up the human race are, in effect, being offered a non-Chautauqua manner of life; they are being summoned to a life made significant by "the element of precipitousness . . . of strength and strenuousness, intensity and danger," heroism reduced to its bare chance, as he wrote in the aftermath of the Chautauqua visit.

* See above, p. 355.

In response to the challenge from on high, William foresaw the morbid-minded and the sick in soul, mistrustful of the chanciness of life, surrendering themselves to "the everlasting arms" of divinity. The tough-minded are envisaged marching cheerfully forth to face the danger. The two reactions, as William inspects them, assume the form of the old paternal dialectic: religion and moralism, the subject of Henry Senior's first book in 1850. William James thereupon exerted himself, as though for one last time, to perform the task of mediation, as he had done most recently in the "Postscript" to *The Varieties of Religious Experience*. He takes his place between religious self-surrender and moralistic self-reliance, modulating each toward a possible accommodation with the other. His own instinct, he confesses (to the surprise of no listener or reader), is for risk-taking: "I find myself willing to take the universe to be really dangerous and adventurous, without therefore backing out and crying 'no play.' " But the religious way of appraising the universe is not discredited, and lest any one should think so, Professor James ends with a passage that might have been written to his father—the still flexible substance of his filial religious imagination:

I firmly disbelieve, myself, that our human experience is the highest form of experience extant in the universe. I believe rather that we stand in the same relation to the whole of the universe as our canine and feline pets do to the whole of human life. They inhabit our drawing-rooms and libraries. They take part in scenes of whose significance they have no inkling. They are merely tangent to the curves of history the beginnings and forms of which pass wholly beyond their ken. So we are tangent to the wider life of things.

CHAPTER EIGHTEEN

1910 and Later

BROTHER TO BROTHER

The last of the compelling fraternal dialogues was stimulated by the appearance in the spring of 1907 of *The American Scene* and *Pragmatism*, closely following one another in February and June respectively. Henry, settling back in Rye in October after two months with Edith Wharton (in Paris and touring southern France) and two months in Italy, tried to explain why he had not written William at once after reading *Pragmatism*. It was, he said, because he had simply sunk down "into such depths of submission and assimilation that *any* reaction . . . would have had almost the taint of dissent or escape." He likened himself to M. Jourdain, the vainglorious figure in Molière's *Le Bourgeois Gentilhomme* who discovered to his amazement that he had been talking prose all his life: "I was lost in the wonder of the extent to which all my life I have . . . unconsciously pragmatised."

It was a delving insight into an entire fiction-making career; for Henry James's characters—Isabel Archer, Hyacinth Robinson, Merton Densher—do not come at life with ready-made values; they arrive at such truth as experience enacts for them. Truth *"happens"* to their ideas, even as it does to the truths that may be attributed, in any given case, to the Jamesian novel itself. Henry's remark holds for the rich imaginative process that (we have suggested) produced the religious sensibility in *The Wings of the Dove* and the idea of "evil" in *The Golden Bowl.*

"You are immensely and universally *right,*" Henry concluded; and went on in the same paragraph to say how moved he had been by William's recent praise of *The American Scene.* "The tribute of your calling the whole thing '*Köstlich* [exquisite] stuff' and saying it will remain to *be* read so and really gauged, gives me more pleasure than I can say."

It was Henry's chapter on Florida—William had been reading it aloud to the locally visiting wife of Ambassador James Bryce—that William declared to be "*Köstlich.*" He had also been reading, to himself, fifty pages of the New England section, "melting with delight" over the description of Chocorua. It was a book that would last, William assured his brother, and bear reading again and again—"a few pages at a time, which is the right way for 'literature' fitly so called."

He had never paid Henry a handsomer compliment. William's first reaction to *The American Scene* some months earlier had, however, been wittily ambivalent. He there had contrasted his own stylistic impulse "to say a thing in one sentence as straight and explicit as it can be made" with that of Henry, which he identified in a self-perpetuating sentence that mimicked its object. Henry's tendency was "to avoid naming it straight, but by dint of breathing and sighing all round and round it, to arouse in the reader who may have had a similar perception already (Heaven help him if he hasn't!) the illusion of a solid object, made (like the 'ghost' at the Polytechnic) wholly out of impalpable materials, air, and the prismatic interferences of light, ingeniously focused by mirrors upon empty space. But you *do* it, that's the queerness!" "Breathing and sighing": it was an apt phrase for what might be called Henry James's respiratory method of creativity; and nothing more slyly felicitous than the poetico-scientific image of the *illusion* of an object caused by mirrors playing prisms of light upon an empty space.

Something about *The American Scene* both tantalized and beguiled William James. On the same day that he dispatched the above to Henry, William wrote Alice in a quite different tone about his brother's book. It "delivers its secret only to leisurely readings," he said, "with attention paid to every word . . . It bears reading, I am sure, many times over. A most extraordinary and exquisite thing." He advised Alice to read at breakfast the pages "on the absence of men from 'society' in America, and the role of the American women." (The pages referred to, in the chapter on Washington, assert that "the woman is two-thirds of the apparent life" in America, "—which means that she is absolutely all of the social"; and Henry points to many complexities and ironies in the "women-made" American social order.) He recommended as well—"for an almost rabelaisian expression of alienness, too good-humored almost to call 'antipathy' "—Henry's observations on the commercial types he met in the South.

Such rancor as was guardedly attributed to William earlier, at the manifestations in literary journals of Henry annexing the American world for himself, had plainly disappeared by the time in 1907 that William could examine the entire book of impressions.

Later on in the October 1907 letter, Henry took an avuncular look at the younger Jameses. Billy struck him as "essentially and intensely entire"—a good thing, Henry added in a dim echo of Henry Senior, "if it doesn't mean you're prematurely concluded," as Billy obviously was not. Of Harry, his uncle said he couldn't trust himself to speak. The emotion was due to Harry's astuteness in handling his uncle's finances, as he had been doing for some time, and notably increasing them. Henry was also glad to have received a "Delicious Letter" from Aleck, and one from Peg that made her sound thriving.

All this led Henry to speculate about Bob James. William and Alice had sent Henry a "happy impression" of the younger brother. "It brings tears to my eyes to think of him at last in quiet waters—if they *be* waters unadulterated. Heaven grant he be truly a spent volcano."

BOB JAMES:
SOURCES OF CONFINEMENT

The water image, of course, conveyed a weary hope that Bob James was no longer drinking himself toward extinction. As of the autumn of 1907, Bob had not, in fact, been dangerously or self-destructively drunk for some time. But he had gone through a long, grim stretch beginning about a dozen years before.

Edward Holton, Bob's father-in-law, had died in 1892, and Mary Holton James, Mrs. Bob, along with each of her two Milwaukee sisters, inherited something over half a million dollars. It was more than enough to fund Mary's frequent traveling to Europe and across the American continent, no expenses being spared, and usually accompanied by her widowed mother and her daughter Mamie. (In 1893, the three of them crossed the path of William and Alice James in Florence.) These excursions became part of the established routine in the Robertson James family, more often than not occurring after Bob had stormed out of the Concord home to set up a temporary household in Arlington Heights or Boston. Here he could enjoy an occasional drinking bout, a spiritualistic séance, and the proximity of a female companion referred to decorously by his older brother as Mrs. S. Bob more forthrightly spelled out her name: Schischkar.

In March 1897, after several weeks of alcoholic rage and violent speech, Bob left abruptly for England. He spent a day with Henry in Liverpool, and returned on the next boat to tell Mary that Henry strongly supported his plea for a divorce. Informed of this, Henry, from Rye, wrote that he would be amazed by Bob's report of his opinion, "could I, after all that has come and gone, be amazed at anything he says or does." At the end of the year, Bob was back in England and visiting with Henry; he performed in such a manner that, after his departure, Henry voiced genuine alarm for his sanity in a cable to William.

On the night of January 7, 1898, a Boston cabdriver assisted a hopelessly drunk Bob James onto the porch at Irving Street, explaining to Mrs. James that he had found his fare "knocking about" Bowdoin Square in town, had managed to elicit his Cambridge address from him, and so brought him out. William was dining at his club, but Billy James appeared and got his uncle up to bed. William and Alice, coming down to breakfast next morning, found Bob in the library, to their astonishment "perfectly sober," in Alice's account to Henry, "and strangely *sane.*"

Bob evidently felt that he had again crossed some invisible boundary. Around midmorning, he approached Alice and asked if she thought his mind might be failing. She could only reply that it *was* failing, "and that another six months of such racking of himself could have but one end." Bob agreed to being placed under some kind of restraint. A doctor was called in and papers were signed, according to which Bob, on William's order, could be committed at any time to the Foxboro, Massachusetts, asylum for inebriates. Foxboro, Alice explained to Henry with a shudder, was a "semi-penal institution," where the men, many of them "the very offscouring of the police courts," were "all locked in together in a common ward. Oh horrible!" Confronted by that threat, Bob seized upon the "mild alternative" of a stay in the Dansville Asylum, a health resort on forty acres of land overlooking the Genesee Valley near Buffalo, in western upstate New York, and able to accommodate two hundred patients.

Bob also cooperated in turning his money affairs over to William and in general, Alice thought, behaved in a docile and loving manner, all defiance gone. Exactly so had he seemed on the previous occasion in the winter of 1888, when Bob's carryings-on forced William to clap him into an asylum in Hartford, Connecticut. But now, as then, Bob's alcoholic wiliness had not deserted him. William accompanied his brother to Dansville, at the last moment acceding to Bob's pathetic request for a sum of money with which to buy a pair of shoes. Bob straightway went into the village and got drunk.

Drinking steadily for five hours a day, Bob managed to stay drunk for an entire week, at which point, he told Alice, "the beasts" in him departed, at least temporarily. Bob was again making a confidante of Mrs. Alice in these days. She was always anxiously affectionate toward him; and talking to her was perhaps a way of sliding around the un-settling presence of his ever more accomplished and authoritative brother. To Alice, Bob confided that Mrs. Schischkar was an important part of his "labyrinth." She wanted to be a good person, Bob said, but didn't know how. She lied a lot, and Bob lost his temper with her; but "her little lies were sweet against the lie of my whole life." There was also mention of a Miss Clark, apparently another sometime mistress, who had tried to get in touch with Alice. Bob spoke of his writing ambitions, and sent on some verses.

He also composed an autobiographical essay at Alice's request, and forwarded it to her in the last days of February. It began on a disheartened note. The lines in the palms of his hands, Bob wrote, signified that "Destiny of itself gave me bad fortune" (he could only have meant being born the younger brother of William and Henry), and he, in turn, "made that Destiny worse." His life story "would have to be the biography of broken fortunes." But happy memories surged to mind when he went back to the childhood days, "to 54 West 14th St. in N.Y." There was "Alice James and the nursery there . . . the Irish nurse whom I have never yet forgotten." He saw "a troop of figures" coming out of the shadows: Uncle William from Albany, throwing his nightgown and nightcap onto the steps from the omnibus window, crying out, "Tell Henry and Mary . . ." as the omnibus rum-bled on; Charles Dana, George Ripley, Bayard Taylor at dinners; Uncle Edward and Uncle Gus; "Grandma James—her silk dress—pepper-mints, lace mittens and gentle smile"; his mother walking down Sixth Avenue to Washington Market, while "I tagged after her, aged six years, and held to her shawl"; the procession to welcome General Kossuth; "Mr. Thackeray who carried me on his shoulder."

But then came Boulogne-sur-Mer "and the Collège Municipale

and its stone vaulted ceiling where Wilky and I went and failed to take prizes." This was the moment not to be forgotten, the climax and end of his reminiscence. "I see yet the fortunate scholars ascend the steps of [the Mayor's] throne, kneel at his feet, and receive crown or rosettes, or some symbol of merit which *we* did not get. The luck had begun to break early."*

He had much to say about his son Ned. "Literature in some form," he thought (correctly, as it happened), would be Ned's future; perhaps literature mixed with ideas of social reform. Ned had worked for a Populist paper in Milwaukee, and later was fired from the Milwaukee *Sentinel* for his socialistic pronouncements around the office. From Howells, in New York, Ned procured a letter of introduction to Henry Demarest Lloyd, the journalistic crusader against monopolies and the public spokesman for Eugene Debs and the men convicted after the Haymarket Riot: a man, Bob said, "on whose lips, as I found when I met him, live the accents of the emancipated American spirit."

During the winter of 1898, Ned James (twenty-four years old and two years out of Harvard), had, so his father learned, fallen in love with a young woman "of good family." This was Louisa Cushing, the daughter of Robert Maynard Cushing and the former Olivia Donaldson Dulany, wealthy and socially conspicuous Bostonians. Bob inspected his daughter-in-law-to-be in late October of the same year, and received the impression that she was "rather cold and statuesque." But she seemed strong enough to control Ned's worst propensities—"waywardness and duplicity" were the terms Bob used about his son, though insisting that these qualities were the result of his upbringing. Mr. Cushing gave Louisa $2,000 a year, and built a house for the young couple in the Boston area. Ned and Louisa were married at the end of December 1899.

Bob was a resident at Dansville for the better part of five years, with intermittent trips away from it, sometimes (as in the fall of 1900) for a period of months. At one moment he was seized with the idea of moving to New York City, to live in a "Catholic Club" there and engage in the Church's charitable work. Bob's enthusiasm for the Catholic Church was fed by the belief that it stood alone in the United States in opposing the annexation of the Philippines. Everyone else in the land, he wrote Alice in April 1900, was driven by pure greed, and a

* See above, p. 90.

pride in belonging to "the richest nation on earth . . . In no institution do I find that man has any shelter save in the divine democracy which lives in the Catholic Church." The local priest was heroically anti-imperialist, and Bob went to hear him preach every Sunday. Nothing came of the proposed New York venture, and despite family rumor Bob seems not to have converted to Catholicism.

By the fall of 1907, Bob had been back in Concord for several years. A certain peace seemed to have descended on him. He drank, now, rather for enjoyment than out of a rage of dissatisfaction. He and Mary were living together in relative harmony. By his own estimate, Mary had been "gentleness and sweetness itself" from the moment of their son's engagement; and if she continued to dash off to Milwaukee or California or Florida on pleasure jaunts, Bob spoke kindly of her "never-ending sight-seeing" and her letters home.

Mamie, who at one time had seemed destined to be the bride of an English baronet, was married in April 1907 to George Vaux, Jr., the son of George Vaux and Sarah Morris, Philadelphians both. The younger George was a lawyer with an interest in prison reform. Like the rest of his family, he was also a staunch Quaker; and Bob, in fact, made a point of not attending the wedding on obscurely stated religious grounds (perhaps vaguely recalling his father's scorn of religious establishments). But he soon apologized and sent love; the Philadelphia connection, he told Alice, regarded him as anathema, but "the saintly George . . . shows signs of regarding me as human." When a son George (the tenth of that name) was born in September 1908, Grandfather Bob quickly became devoted to the infant and renamed him Flub-Dub.

Ned and Louisa, meanwhile, after a spell in Fargo, North Dakota ("plank sidewalks" and "prairie mud," Bob imagined), were settled in Seattle, Washington. Louisa had given birth to three daughters. On an evening in early 1904, Bob and Mary went to dinner at the Cushings', Bob arriving more than a little the worse for wear. Mary was upset, but Bob chatted about it to Alice with easy good humor: Mr. Cushing was amiably empty-headed; Mrs. Cushing was philistine in her views (why had Henry James unpatriotically gone to England to write?) but likable all the same; the two butlers were intimidating.

Sometime in 1906, Bob suffered what appears to have been a heart attack. It quieted him down even more, and helped restore him to something of his old sweetness of temper. Thanking his niece Peggy in August 1907 for a necktie on his fifty-ninth birthday, Bob wrote: "Your Aunt Mary says I look very pretty in it—but I don't care so much what other people think, so long as I feel pretty—and I do that. Dear Peggy, it's all in the feeling. I've galloped through all kinds of feelings during my career, but the problem of getting a feeling to stay by you more than 24 hours, I am still hammering at."

WILLIAM GOES AHEAD

William came over to England, with Alice, in the spring of 1908 to give the Hibbert Lectures at Manchester College, Oxford, on "the present situation in philosophy." The seven lectures were delivered between May 4 and May 28 to the largest audiences that had ever attended lectures on philosophy at the university. Published in book form in 1909, they bore the superbly Jamesian (and quasi-oxymoronic) title of *A Pluralistic Universe*. The discussions ranged over nineteenth-century and more recent philosophical expression, touched on Hegel, Gustav Theodor Fechner (a German thinker, whose concept of cosmic consciousness William James had made his own), F. H. Bradley, Bergson, Josiah Royce, and others; and they explored ideas about the multipleness of reality, or, in William's word, the "eachness" of its parts, and the continuing change and growth—the incompleteness, if not the incompleteability—of the world. The talks have perhaps less literary lift and charm than *Pragmatism* and its predecessors, but they constitute a solid block in the philosophical arch of William James. And in the final lecture, which according to Alice held the audience "simply spellbound," William in his customary fashion drew his enterprise to a close by reflecting on religious matters: the sense of a self in touch with "a *more* . . . with a wider self from which saving experiences flow in"; and the metaphysically inescapable conclusion that that wider self, that "superhuman consciousness, however vast it may be," must itself have "an external environment, and consequently is finite."

Harry and Peggy joined their parents in the late spring, the former taking time off from his Boston law practice, the latter after finishing her sophomore year at Bryn Mawr. The four Jameses were in and out of Lamb House through the summer. Forgatherings were arranged with Logan Pearsall Smith, the matchlessly brilliant Greek scholar Gilbert Murray, the Bertrand Russells, and Lady Ottoline Morrell. Once, G. K. Chesterton was staying at an inn on the other side of the Lamb House garden wall, and William, eager to catch a glimpse of the portly writer, set a ladder against the wall and, according to legend, climbed up to peer over it. Henry is said to have been scandalized by

William's unmannerly American conduct and to have expostulated about it for some time afterward, while William had the look of a naughty child. (The anecdote is given us by H. G. Wells in his *Autobiography*, and seems to partake of the "comic portrait" which, as biographers discover, tends to grow up around well-known literary figures.) In early August, William spent an evening with Chesterton and "that singular being H[ilaire] Belloc," talking and listening until nearly midnight. Belloc held forth on military history, while "dear good Chesterton" merely "gurgled and giggled."

Mrs. Alice sounded a worrying note during the summer, when she wrote William from an inn in Lincoln: "Do be careful in your walks and don't go to steep or dizzy places." For more than a year, William had been suffering sharp attacks of pain in the heart—"angina" was his summary term for them. He was taking regular medication, and nothing prevented him from walking by the hour.

In October 1909, William admitted to his diary that he had experienced "dreadful angina on going to bed," and observed in himself "decided symptoms of nervous prostration." He remarked quietly to Theodore Flournoy: "It hasn't gone well with my health this summer, and beyond a little reading, I have done no work at all." The allusion to his physical condition was understated, but the comment on his work was familiarly misleading. William James was forging ahead at a daunting pace. He saw *A Pluralistic Universe* to press in April; and four months later, after an elaborate editorial effort, he brought out a collection of eighteen essays bearing the general title *The Meaning of Truth*. The substantial introduction was dated August 1909, the month the book appeared, and two new essays were written for the volume, one of them after the proofs were done. Nine of the entries had been composed during the previous two years.

The Meaning of Truth is complementary and supplementary to *Pragmatism*. Considered as a single discourse, the essays evolve out of the trenchant assertions in the sixth lecture of that series (they are quoted in the book's preface) that "Truth *happens* to an idea" and that "*The true is only the expedient in the way of our thinking.*" Nor does William James fail to pursue his personal corollary that human individuals not only make truths in their experiencings, they add to the making of the *world* and of its piecemeal salvation.

The volume offers a number of defenses, melancholy or impatient, against attacks on pragmatism and misstatements about it. At one point, William lays into those critics who have seen pragmatism as appealing to action on the lowest level, enunciating with dour exactness the notion of pragmatism as it was already beginning to deteriorate. The word "pragmatic" did come, he agreed, from the Greek word *pragma* for action; but to hear critics talk, you would think that the only action in question was money-making or "gain[ing] some similar practical advantage." So misconstrued, pragmatism was taken to be useful mainly to "engineers, doctors, financiers," and to people in need of some sort of "rough and ready *weltanschauung*." It was in this sense that pragmatism was looked on as "a characteristic American move-ment . . . excellently fitted for the man in the street." But if ideas did indeed work in the field of practical action, they also, William insisted, "work indefinitely inside of the mental world," and that was where it counted.

William James, then, was anything but inactive in his intellectual life as the first decade of the century went by. But he was increasingly limited—by health problems, but equally by too many communications, too many visitors, too many demands upon the most sought-after phi-losopher in the English-speaking world. Only those close to him were aware of his frequent spasms of discomfort. "He bore his ills without complaint and ordinarily without mention," his son Harry was to re-member, looking back from 1920. Harry recalled from this time a man who still walked with an elastic step and carried himself erect; who until the very end gave the appearance "of a much younger and stronger man than he really was." Filial piety is recognizable there, but all the other evidence supports the picture. William entered the year 1910, in fact, feeling unusually well and lively, firing off a series of sprightly letters to his former student John Jay Chapman, and openly delighted at having been elected to the Académie des Sciences Morales et Politiques in France (Bergson cabled him the news). On January 11, he told his diary: "68 years old today! Wrote. Good day."

HENRY: A CAREER RELIVED

Just before Christmas 1907, in an unbroken rush of a letter to A. E. Norris (a friend of a dozen years), Henry James expressed himself as engaged "in a perpetual adventure, the most thrilling and in every way the greatest of my life." It consisted, he said, in "having [for] more than four years entered into a state of health so altogether better than any I had ever known that my whole consciousness is transformed by the intense *alleviation* of it."

The passage emphasizes bodily health, implicitly after a long stretch of the opposite. But the language reflects something more comprehensive: a sense of *general* well-being, of high achievement realized, of goals successfully pursued, of anxiety far transcended. In his private utterances in this era, Henry James was more inclined than ever toward extravagant imprecisions. One need not press his arithmetic too hard to notice that a period of "more than four years" had produced *The Wings of the Dove, The Ambassadors*, and *The Golden Bowl*, followed by *The American Scene*; these plus the complicated labors on the New York Edition of "The Novels and Tales of Henry James." That accomplishment, one might well say, constituted the greatest adventure of Henry's life. And we may identify the implied preceding time of ill health as the years following the failure of *Guy Domville* and the wreckage of Henry's hopes for the theater.

Work on the New York Edition—work, that is, not only by Henry James but also by his agent, James B. Pinker, and by the publisher Charles Scribner—began effectively in the summer of 1904, as Henry was preparing for his homecoming trip. Delays were caused by James's earlier publishers. Macmillan of New York held out for a fee of £100, this being the sum they reckoned to have lost on *The Bostonians* and other titles. Houghton Mifflin of Boston, which had first made Henry James visible as a distinguished writer of fiction (with volumes through *The Portrait of a Lady*) and still felt bitter about losing him, tried to impose severe restrictions on printing style. But gradually, over 1905 and 1906, the collection took shape.

The edition expanded from sixteen volumes (not more, James was said to insist) in 1905, to twenty-three in 1906, even with a number of texts excluded, mostly for reasons not given: *Washington Square, Confidence, The Europeans, The Bostonians, The Sacred Fount.* Nine novels were included. Six of them, from *The Portrait* to *The Golden Bowl*, would require two volumes each; three—*Roderick Hudson, The American*, and *The Awkward Age*—could each be fitted into a single volume. There would be four volumes of novellas and four of short stories. The twenty-three-volume total happened to be the same as that of Balzac's *Comédie Humaine*. Henry James did draw from Balzac the inspiring image of a completed oeuvre, and he had been addressing audiences on the Balzacian example during the American tour. But it is doubtful that he was aiming at a numerical analogy between his edition and Balzac's *Comédie*; and in any event, with the author adding certain shorter writings faster than he deleted others—there were eventually fifty-eight of them—the New York Edition as published ran to a final figure of twenty-four.*

By May 1906, the demanding and scrupulous act of revision—chiefly of the early novels and tales—had been pretty much completed. *The American* was the one most thoroughly worked over, with James, as F. O. Matthiessen has suggested, seeking to edit out "the falsely romantic aspects of his denouement." *Roderick Hudson* was considerably touched up; in the preface to that novel, James spoke of only a "mild overhauling" to bring up some "buried secrets," but he crowded the margins of the manuscript with such illegible scrawls that the typesetters were hard put to cope. The emendations of *The Portrait of a Lady* were especially imaginative: innumerable changes of single words and phrases, but with several scenes—notably the final confrontation between Isabel Archer and Casper Goodwood—tightened and intensified to release more forcible dramatic and erotic charges.†

Turning next to the question of illustrations, Henry enlisted the services of Alvin Langdon Coburn, a twenty-eight-year-old American photographer of well-earned reputation (Bernard Shaw admired him). Coburn was sent on his travels with detailed instructions. For *In the Cage*, as an instance, he was to search out "a London corner . . . with a grocer's shop containing a postal-telegraph office." In Paris, he should photograph the outside of the Théâtre Français for *The Tragic Muse*, and the "classic colonnade" of the Odéon Theater for *The Ambassadors*. In Venice, he should take the vaporetto along the Grand Canal to the Stazione, and proceed from there to Rio Marin, where

---

* The edition was filled out after Henry James's death by the two unfinished works, *The Ivory Tower* and *The Sense of the Past*, bringing the total to twenty-six as of 1917. A "New and Complete" edition, published in 1921–23, was made up of thirty-five volumes.

See the article on the composition of the edition by Michael W. Anesko in the September 1983 issue of *The New England Quarterly*. The article was absorbed into Professor Anesko's *"Friction with the Market": Henry James and the Profession of Authorship* (1986).

† Opinion will continue to differ on the relative merits of the revised texts in the New York Edition as against their originals. This writer's view is, simply enough, that it varies from text to text. In that view, *The Portrait of a Lady* is decidedly improved, while *The Aspern Papers* and *The Turn of the Screw* are slightly marred. The Library of America, bravely committed to reprinting all or most of Henry James's fiction, has this to say at the back of the volume containing novels from 1871 to 1880: "Though James later made revisions in some of these novels, those revisions were made by a more experienced and sophisticated writer. This volume reprints the works of a young Henry James just beginning his long and productive career. The earlier versions offer the best opportunity to recapture that beginning."

he would hit upon the old palazzino known as Ca' (for Casa) Capello; he should take pictures of the exterior, of the garden behind it, and especially (if he secured permission) of "the big old Sala, the large central hall of the principal floor of the house"—all this for *The Aspern Papers*. Afterward, Coburn should position himself on the Accademia bridge and photograph the Palazzo Barbaro opposite, for *The Wings of the Dove*.

There remained the prefaces to the individual novels and groups of stories, eighteen such treatises in all, and comprising another extensive phase in the process of self-revisiting and reappraisal that was Henry's all-consuming activity of these years. In case after case, he gives us what he calls the *story* of the story. He evokes the Florentine Piazza Santa Maria Novella and the lodgings in which he wrote *Roderick Hudson*; the Paris of 1875, where he resurrected the idea, for *The American*, that first came to him in an American horsecar; the glow and the echoing voices of Venice, where he made exhilarating progress on *The Portrait of a Lady*. There is the teeming London of *The Princess Casamassima*; the anecdote, listened to by James in Florence, that led to *The Aspern Papers*; and in the same preface, the reference, made to a gathering around the fire in a grave old country house, of "a couple of small children . . . to whom the spirits of certain 'bad' servants, dead in the employ of the house, were believed to have appeared."

James was endlessly intrigued by the way tiny anecdotal seeds had been nurtured by his art to flower into something as relatively short as *The Turn of the Screw* or as long and dense as *The Ambassadors*. So he moved among his creations over nearly forty years, watching them in memory as they grew, watching himself as he braved stimulating dangers or skillfully dodged them, here nodding his head in admiration of a "scenic consistency," there pursing his lips over a faultiness of structure; and encasing the discussions from start to finish in a rich and ranging disquisition on the art of fictional composition.

All of his accumulated experience went into the prefaces, and Henry was inordinately pleased with them. In the October 1907 letter to William drawn from earlier, Henry nearly stammered as he explained that he was writing "Prefaces of the most brilliant character . . . The prefaces are very difficult to make *right*, absolutely and utterly, as they supremely have to be. But they are so right, so far, that the Scribners, pleased with them to the extent quite—for publishers—of giving themselves away—pronounce them 'absolutely unique!' " Little wonder that Henry, two months later, was experiencing the euphoria he described to A. E. Norris. A fortnight after that, on New Year's Eve, he acknowledged to Scribner's receipt of "the two beautiful first volumes of The New York Edition," *Roderick Hudson* and *The American*, exulting in them and "almost ridiculously proud" of the entire enterprise. "The whole is a perfect felicity, so let us go on rejoicing."

The euphoria continued until well along in 1908. In mid-August of that year, Henry wrote Howells to say about the prefaces that "they ought, collected together . . . to form a sort of comprehensive manual or *vademecum* for aspirants in our arduous profession." R. P. Blackmur, who did collect the prefaces in 1934, quotes this letter and says in agreement with it that the prefaces are "the most sustained and I think the most eloquent and original piece of literary criticism in existence."

It was a devastating blow when, in the early fall of 1908, Henry's first report from Scribner's about the sales of the edition notified him that he was owed little more than £40. The news was the more shocking, he wrote Pinker, after "the treasures of ingenuity and labour I have lavished on the amelioration of every page of the thing." Henry bore up as best he could under a weight of depression, but as the winter drew on, his nerve began to go and he feared he might have undergone a heart attack. In February, he consulted the famous heart specialist Sir James Mackenzie, who, after a thorough examination, was, Henry told William, "extraordinarily encouraging and reassuring." There was no "irregular action of the heart," and Henry was urged to take more exercise and lose weight.

The specialist was undoubtedly correct: Henry James's trouble was not a damaged heart. It was a wound to the self. The New York Edition was shaping up as a failure, and Henry, taking in the fact, experienced a kind of death. "I *have* had . . . a bad and worried and depressed and inconvenient winter," he told Edith Wharton in April 1909. It had been a "brush of the dark wing," which "leaves one never quite the same."

Henry rallied over the next seven or eight months, getting *Italian Hours* belatedly to print (the articles in that fine collection dating back, some of them, to the early 1870s) and writing several pieces of short fiction. The latter include "A Round of Visits," a brilliant tale about the paradoxes of suffering, set in the New York James had recently discovered; and *The Bench of Desolation*, the last of James's novellas and one of his best, similarly on the theme (it was *Henry's* theme for the time) of suffering and its perversities. He took pleasure in an enlarging group of younger male friends, some of the relationships being vaguely or more manifestly homoerotic: with the sculptor Hendrik Andersen, whose colossal statues (in James's language) of "divinely naked and intimately associated gentlemen and ladies, flaunting their bellies and bottoms," Henry tended to overrate out of love for the youth; Rupert Brooke, the almost excessively good-looking poet-in-the-making; and Hugh Walpole, transplanted New Zealander and aspiring novelist (*Mr. Perrin and Mr. Traill*, an excellent work, appeared in 1911), whom Henry after their first meeting enjoined to "hold me in your heart, even as I hold you in my arms," and permitted to address him as "my very dear Master (for the present)." He cooperated with Edith Wharton, while voicing much mock-incredulity, in deviously conveying to Morton Fullerton a sum of money sufficient to rescue him from the toils of a blackmailing former mistress.*

But severe depression took hold again in December 1909. At about this time, he made a "gigantic bonfire" on the Lamb House property, and therein—with thoughts of death in his mind, as he admitted—he burned almost all the letters written to him over the years. The motive for this drastic act, as he told Mrs. Annie Fields (who had visited him, with her friend Sarah Orne Jewett), was so as not to leave "personal and private documents"—after his "latter end"—"at the mercy of accidents or even of my executors." Henry did, certainly, attach a sacred value to privacy. There was also the implication that, if his life's work had been rejected by the reading public, he, as a final gesture, might dispose of his life's correspondence as well.

The year 1910 ushered in the blackest period Henry James had ever known. On January 21, by his own dating, Henry collapsed and took to his bed. One of his worst symptoms, as he put it to William, was that of "sickishly *loathing* food"; as a result, he blamed his condition on "Fletcherising" (a technique of chewing every morsel of food until it liquefied). William seems to have understood from the first that his brother's illness was psychological; he instantly dispatched Harry, who reached his uncle at Lamb House on February 24. Harry wrote home about sitting by Henry's bedside and holding his hand "while he panted and sobbed for two hours till the doctor came . . . He talked about Aunt Alice and his own end," Harry said, remarking with great astuteness, "and I knew him to be facing not only the frustration of all his hopes and ambitions, but the vision looming close and threatening to his weary eyes, of a lingering illness such as hers."

* See R.W.B. Lewis, *Edith Wharton*, pp. 263–64.

In March, Harry escorted his uncle to London and Garland's Hotel on Suffolk Street. Henry was examined by Sir William Osler, another distinguished physician who had once tended to William James. Osler found no organic trouble in the sixty-seven-year-old novelist; he was, in fact, "splendid for his age," and needed only to take better care of himself. William wrote from Cambridge that Henry was evidently in the throes of a nervous breakdown. Henry replied scoffingly that "my illness has no more to do with a 'nervous breakdown' than with Halley's comet." But Edith Wharton, hurrying over from Paris on March 18 to lend what aid she could, gave a portrait (to Morton Fullerton) of a man in an advanced state of suicidal melancholia:

I sat down beside the sofa and for a terrible hour looked into the black depths over which he is hanging—the super-imposed "abysses" of all his fiction. I, who have always seen him so serene, so completely the master of his wonderful emotional instrument—who thought of him when I described the man in "The Legend" as so sensitive to human contacts and yet so *secure* from them; I could hardly believe it was the same James who cried out to me his fear, his despair, his craving for the "cessation of consciousness," and all his unspeakable lone-liness and need of comfort, and inability to be comforted! "Not to wake—not to wake—" that was his refrain; "and then one *does* wake, and one looks again into the blackness of life, and everything ministers to it."*

In response to Harry's alarming cables, William and Alice left for England on March 29. Their ship passed the steamer carrying Harry back to America.

DARKNESS AT CHOCORUA

For Henry, William's arrival at Lamb House was an "unspeakable godsend"; he seems to have been too sunk in misery to notice his brother's failing strength. Alice, watching with hope and fear, described the two of them in her datebook: "William cannot walk, and Henry cannot smile." The suggestion was that, if William could no longer leap over stiles as on his previous visit, he still could smile; and we

* The story cited by Edith Wharton, "The Legend" (1910), tells of a writer of genius, a philosopher who grows so despondent at the failure of his "message" to be attended to, or even read, that he drops from sight and allows it to be believed that he is dead.

may imagine him doing so in the letters that continued to flow from his pen (for instance, a letter to Tom Perry commenting on Frank Harris's—in William's opinion—absurd and outrageous, yet cogent and entertaining book about Shakespeare). William was able to keep silent about his ailments, they being primarily physical and perfectly understandable to his medical mind. Henry, caught in a mental depression of the worst order, could talk of little else through the spring and early summer.

"I have been continuously and drearily ill," he wrote Jocelyn Persse on April 28; "I have been miserably and interminably ill these five months," he told Andersen on May 21, and used the same words to Howells a week later. On June 13 he reached a nadir, speaking to Edmund Gosse of "my damnable nervous state, chronic, but breaking out too in acute visitations . . . black depression—the blackness of darkness and the cruellest melancholia are my chronic enemy and curse." Henry could no longer deny that his condition was a terrible darkness of spirit, and not a grievous upset of stomach. The word "visitation," as always in the family vocabulary, hints at a nightmare invasion of the psyche of the sort father and brother had undergone.

The two brothers were in Bad Nauheim by this time. William had gone ahead to the German resort, pausing in Paris for a stay with Charles Strong and a call on Edith Wharton. ("A very pleasant visit," William wrote Alice, "in which the main conversation was H.J. We developed no clashes of opinion, and I found we formed a sympathetic combination."*) From Paris, he addressed the pair at Lamb House: "Alice, you triple extract of perfectionism, and Henry, triple extract of *aff*ection, I take my pen in hand . . ." At Bad Nauheim, the doctors declared him afflicted with heart failure (in the later usage), a chief sign of which was increased difficulty in breathing, or dyspnœa.

"H. and W. both silent," Alice observed, after the brothers were reunited in Germany in early June. The daily baths were debilitating for William; and seeing no gain for any one of them at the spa, he moved the family group on to Geneva on June 23. His dyspnœa was getting worse "at an accelerated rate," he reported to Flournoy on July 9. The next day he was too weak to get out of bed. The party made its way painfully back via Paris to Rye, and on August 12 they embarked for Quebec on a vessel of the Canadian Steamship Line. William was carried on board.

---

* William had no doubt been made privy to Edith Wharton's declared antipathy to him, based in part, one judges, on her resentment of Henry's devotion to his brother.

Henry, meanwhile, was gradually emerging from his own inward horror. "I eat, I walk, I *almost* sleep," he wrote Edith Wharton from Nauheim; and at the end of July, from Rye, he was willing to say that "I am definitely much better and on the road to be *well*." In his returning sanity, he could take querulous cognizance of William's condition. "He is painfully ill, weak and down, and the anxiety of it, with our voyage in view, is a great tension to me in my still quite *struggling* upward state."

A further and more ambiguous shadow was cast over the brothers by the word, received in Geneva, of the death of Robertson James on July 3. Bob died of heart failure, "smiling, in his sleep," so Peggy told her mother. He was alone in the Concord home, Mary having gone off to Europe with her granddaughter Vaux seven months before, when Bob started in on another drinking bout; the body was not discovered for two days. Mary James is said to have greeted the news with disbelief, muttering repeatedly: "Bob is dead. I can't believe that Bob is dead." William, in Geneva, murmured to Alice: "It fills me with a new respect for Bob, and how I should like to go as quickly." For Henry, Bob's had been "a painless, peaceful, enviable end to a stormy and unhappy career."

The Boston *Evening Transcript* on July 9 identified Robertson James as the "youngest brother of Henry and William James, with talents as brilliant as theirs, had they been as steadily exercised." The newspaper managed to locate Bob rather than Wilky at the 1863 attack on Fort Wagner, but it returned to firmer ground in saying that "he was by turns journalist, artist, man of leisure and occasional contributor to the magazines,—a charming talker, and in religion a constant seeker, without finding rest in any form of faith." Bob could not have sought for a better conclusion to his obituary. He was buried in the Sleepy Hollow Cemetery in Concord.

The Jameses arrived at Quebec in a pouring rain on August 18, and Harry was there to meet them. The following day, Friday, they endured a long, excruciating train trip to Intervale, New Hampshire, from where Billy drove them to Chocorua. By now William's whole body was affected by his ailing heart. "A terrible day of suffering," Alice recorded on the Wednesday. William whispered to her that she must "go to Henry when his time comes," and this she would do.

Around noon on Friday, August 26, Henry began a letter to Grace

Norton. Alice's two sisters had arrived, and Harry had been summoned back from New Brunswick. "My own fears are of the blackest," Henry wrote, ". . . and at the prospect of losing my wonderful beloved brother out of the world in which, from as far back as in dimmest childhood, I have so yearningly always counted on him, I feel nothing but the abject weakness of grief and even terror." He could not but observe a new and final version of a lifelong fraternal rhythm, the one brother recovering while the other declined. "*My* slowly recuperative process goes on despite all checks and shocks, while dear William's, in the full climax of his intrinsic powers and intellectual ambitions, meets this tragic, cruel arrest."

He opened the letter in mid-afternoon to add a postscript: "William passed unconsciously away an hour ago—without apparent pain or struggle. Think of us, dear Grace—think of us!" Alice's diary entry: "William died just before 2.30 in my arms. I was coming in with milk and saw the change. No pain at the last and no consciousness . . . Poor Henry, poor children."

Harry and Billy went into Boston to make funeral arrangements. On Tuesday the thirtieth, Alice and Henry accompanied the hearse to Conway, Mrs. Gibbens and Peg following by car. From Conway to Boston, the party traveled in a Pullman supplied by John Sumner Runnells. The coffin lay open at Irving Street until the four o'clock funeral service in Appleton Chapel on the Harvard campus. The honorary pallbearers included President Lowell of Harvard, Henry L. Higginson, James Putnam, George Palmer, Charles Strong, and Ralph Barton Perry (who would be William James's editor and biographer). The Reverend George A. Gordon of the New Old South Church in Boston said in tribute: "The scholar, thinker, teacher is merged at last in the human being. The man is the ultimate and everlasting value."

The Boston *Evening Transcript* published an array of eulogies, one of them, by H. Addington Bruce, holding that the death of William James was "the removal of the greatest of contemporary Americans." *Le Temps* in Paris called him "the most famous American philosopher since Emerson"; *The* (London) *Times* quibbled over this, acknowledging the greatness but tying it rather to William James's work as an "experimental psychologist." The journals argued with each other— they still do—over which phase of William James's many-tiered career most accurately displayed his genius and his lasting influence. As to this, William James was temperamentally disposed to regard whatever area of inquiry he was currently involved in as the most significant for him, putting each behind him as he moved on: psychology, religious thought, epistemology, metaphysics. He was invariably multiple and always growing, like the world itself in his vision of it.

"I sit heavily stricken and in darkness," Henry wrote his and William's old friend from the Newport days, Tom Perry, "—for from far back in dimmest childhood he had been my ideal Elder Brother, and I still, through all the years, saw in him, even as a small timorous boy yet, my protector, my backer, my authority and my pride." "My beloved brother's death has cut into me, deep down, even as an absolute mutilation," he said to Edith Wharton. "He did surely shed light to man, and *gave*, of his own great spirit and beautiful genius, with splendid generosity"—this to H. G. Wells, who had conveyed a singularly warm message of condolence.

The very eloquence of these letters, and the vigor of them, tell of an enormous experience grappled with and converted into language, with a consequent enlargement of being. Whether, as the surviving brother, Henry felt a measure of victory as well as the more familiar measure of guilt, it is impossible to say, though he would have been less than human if he was not assailed by some such mixture of emotions.* In any event, the more abundant language that resulted and the more settled and composed emotions that followed went into the long fraternal and filial chronicle on which Henry began work fourteen months later.

In the interval, Henry commuted between Massachusetts and New York. Mid-October 1910 found him in New York and dining, at the Hotel Belmont, with Edith Wharton, her lover, Morton Fullerton, and her favorite male companion and fellow traveler, Walter Berry—Edith weary enough, though resilient, after seeing her physically and mentally precarious husband, Teddy, off on a round-the-world tour. The encounter was cheering for Henry. Invoking the mock-heroic title he had bestowed upon Mrs. Wharton, he told Howard Sturgis that he had been called down from Cambridge by "the silver steam-whistle of the Devastating Angel . . . and, strange to say, the being devastated (in another way, from the one in which I have been) has done me perceptible good."

---

* Leon Edel, culling the elusive evidence (*Henry James*, Vol. I, Ch. 5), suggests that Henry James's dream of the Louvre might have taken place at about this very time. If so, and depending on one's interpretation of the dream, it might say something about Henry's suppressed reaction to his brother's death: a sense of rivalry overcome. The conditionals cluster thickly there, however. Henry's considered retrospective words are probably a more reliable guide.

He returned to New York in the spring of 1911, rediscovering in himself, as he said to Hugh Walpole, "a sneaking kindness for its pride and power . . . born of early associations and familiarities—of the ancient natal order." Henry spent much time in Cambridge with Alice and his nephews and niece, as the latter came and went; himself now, to an extent, the head of the family. In a certain real sense, he was now the entire family.

On July 30, he sailed for England aboard the *Mauretania*. At the end of September, in response to an invitation from Edith Wharton to join her and Berry on an Italian tour, Henry declared that he had only just "got Home . . . and got there with the most passionate determinations to stick fast for the rest of my life." He would never go outside of England again. "Home," however, was shortly to be London, at least in the winters: "The era of Rye hibernations is definitely closed," he informed Mrs. Wharton. In London, he stayed at the Reform Club, doing his work in two rooms provided by Miss Theodora Bosanquet (his secretary since October 1907, an exceptionally able young woman) and adjoining her flat on Lawrence Street.

Henry James was once again going about his literary business. There was a belated flurry of theatricals. *The Outcry*, a three-act comedy remade into a novel, had just been published in fictional form with no little success, and a stage production was in question. *The Other House*, another play turned into a novel and then turned back into a play, was being tinkered with. *The Saloon*, the play version of "Owen Wingrave," was being readied for what became a short London run. But by far the most demanding enterprise started upon in these days was the work to be known as Henry James's autobiography.

We first hear of it in late October (1911), when Henry speaks to Miss Bosanquet of "having got back to work and to a very particular job," and, a few days later, of the problem of "Letters to be copied or dictated"—the letters of William James. The undertaking began indeed as the story of the early years of Henry's older brother, as the first volume, *A Small Boy and Others*, indicates in its opening sentence: "In the attempt to place together some particulars of the early life of William James and present him in his setting, his immediate native and domestic air . . ." But as he meditated the task, the author said, connections and images began to swarm, memories to crowd in. "To knock at the door of the past was in a word to see it open to me quite wide—to see the world within begin to 'compose' with a grace of its own round the primary figure, see it people itself vividly and insistently."

585]

So the authorial eye drifts musingly back to "the world of our childhood," to "our infantile Albany," to "a softly-sighing widowed grandmother, Catherine Barber by birth." And hence on to "our father's father, William James, an Irishman and a Protestant born (of county Cavan) [who] had come to America, a very young man and then sole of his family, shortly after the Revolutionary War." Henry Senior is identified as "the second son of the third of the marriages to which the country of his adoption was liberally to help him." Maternal great-grandfathers are pointed to: Hugh Walsh, who came from County Down to Newburgh-on-the-Hudson in 1764; Alexander Robertson, who crossed the sea from "Polmont near Edinburgh" in mid-century to prosper in New York.

The story, as it flows onward, moves in rivulets between the generations, the memories, the cousins, the visitors (Emerson appears early on), the teachers, the clan lore. William remains the "primary figure" for a time, as "occupying a place in the world to which I couldn't at all aspire," and as being "always round the corner and out of sight." But gradually Henry enlarges beyond his brother and himself, and is embarked on nothing less than a narrative of the James family.

Its three volumes comprise what is perhaps Henry James's masterwork in non-fictional prose, though the travel writings provide formidable competition. *A Small Boy and Others*, ending in Boulogne-sur-Mer in 1858, with the fever-stricken fifteen-year-old Henry lapsing into unconsciousness, was published in 1913. The no less suitably titled second volume, *Notes of a Son and Brother*, which closes with the death of Minny Temple in 1870 and "the end of our youth," came out in 1914. A third volume, *The Middle Years*, carrying the story through the decision to settle in London and on into the later 1870s, was left uncompleted when Henry James died in his Chelsea lodgings on February 28, 1916, in the third year of the Great War.

The Strange Death
of Daniel Gibbens

The death of Daniel Gibbens in the fall of 1865 in Alabama was intimately connected with the cotton dealings there of his Boston friend T.C.A. (Thomas Coffin Amory) Dexter; these, in turn, formed part of a larger story, that of the confiscation of Confederate property by United States Treasury agents in the period following the end of the Civil War. And this story is itself only one element in the much vaster historical unfolding known as Reconstruction.

At particular issue in the episode that concerns us is the suspect disposition of cotton. Statistics vary widely as to the actual amount of the invaluable commodity remaining throughout the South—after deliberate burning and random looting—as of April 1865. Apart from not always decipherable court records, much of the information comes from anything but impartial sources: the report of a Ku Klux Klan committee in 1872, for example, which put the figure at 5 million bales—before 3 million were made away with by criminal Northerners. Whatever the amount, the Treasury Department created a network of agents to collect the cotton and see to its shipment North: supervising special agents, assistant special agents, collection agents, and the like. It seems probable, too, as Southern historians have long claimed, that after the four-year struggle and in the flush of victory, Union representatives took a special satisfaction in laying hands on what had been the centerpiece of the Southern economy and a symbol of the culture.

Owners who could demonstrate somehow that they had been "loyal" to the Union could sell their stores to collection agents, though at a one-third loss of value. In the first months, however, virtually every owner was identified as disloyal: a former Confederate soldier, or his widow or kin, or someone who had supported secession or who had sent supplies to the troops. All cotton belonging to these people was simply seized by the agents; and sometimes other items as well, corn, syrup, and even horses that had been used in service.

Theoretically, the confiscated cotton was sent North to a general agent acting on behalf of the federal government; one such was Simeon Draper, with an office in New York City. What happened, in fact, was what one Southern historian has called "a carnival of corruption." According to this source, there was no protection for the owner against a government agent:

> He claimed all cotton and, unless bribed, seized it. Thousands of bales were taken to which the government had not a shadow of a claim. In November, 1865, the *Times* correspondent (Truman) stated that nearly all the Treasury agents in Alabama had been filling their pockets with cotton money, and that $2,000,000 were unaccounted for. One agent took 2000 bales on a vessel and went to France.*

Those are strong scholarly words, but Secretary of the Treasury Hugh McCulloch, an honorable man and a Lincoln appointee, is quoted by the Northern journalist Whitelaw Reid, himself well versed in the postwar Southern scene, as saying: "I am sure I sent some honest agents South; but it sometimes seems very doubtful whether any of them remained honest very long." The network of agents swelled to include Southern cotton thieves, local informers, and inevitably corruptible owners; and the result seems indeed to have been a gigantic exercise in stealing.

Alabama had a larger stock of cotton on hand at the war's end than the adjoining states: perhaps 150,000 bales. Of these, as best one can ascertain, only about 20,000 bales finally made their way to a bona fide federal authority; and even these 20,000 were reduced in bulk on the journey North by felonious devices known as "tolling" and "plucking." As many as 130,000 bales appear to have found their way into private hands, by means of General Agent Draper—who, as it was observed, was destitute when he began his office and a millionaire when he finished. The price of cotton was artificially high in 1865, coming to $1.25 or more a pound in Alabama (and in Florida, as Wilky James was hearing, to as much as $2.50, before plummeting to 50 cents in 1867). A bale weighed between 200 and 500 pounds; a bale of cotton in 1865

---

* Walter L. Fleming in *Civil War and Reconstruction in Alabama* (1905), a revised version of a doctoral dissertation at Columbia University. This is the same source to which the Library of Congress authority drew the attention of William James's son Henry, when the latter was compiling information for the family archives about the death of his mother's father, Daniel Gibbens. Walter L. Fleming was professor of history at Louisiana State University from 1907 to 1917, and then at Vanderbilt University.

was worth on average $350–$400, to which the agent was able to add shipping costs and other expenses. One young agent is said to have cleared $80,000 in a single month through the sale and shipment of four hundred bales.

For purposes of collection, Alabama was divided into a number of agencies. T.C.A. Dexter was named supervising special agent of the Ninth Agency, which brought in cotton from eleven counties, among them Montgomery, Tuscaloosa, and Mobile. In May 1865, Daniel Gibbens came up from New Orleans to serve as assistant special agent under Dexter (though the younger Henry James, as we will see, would dispute the nature and title of Gibbens's appointment). At some moment after that, a certain T. J. Carver was also made assistant special agent. Thirty-six subagents scurried about the region doing the work of seizing and hauling.

At the end of October 1865, Dexter and Carver were brought before a federal court on a number of charges. The defendants challenged the jurisdiction of the court. A military tribunal was then convened, on November 13, with Brigadier General William B. Woods presiding. This time Dexter and Carver questioned the legality of a military court holding a trial in time of peace, but the case went forward. Dexter's arraignment held that he "did fraudulently remove and appropriate to his own use" various supplies of cotton across the state at specified times in the summer of 1865. They added up to 3,426 bales: a tiny fraction of the total amount, 130,000 bales, which appear to have been stolen overall, but enough to earn Dexter three-quarters of a million dollars. On a second charge, it was declared that Dexter "did feloniously trade, barter and sell the office of Special Agent" for $25,000 to Carver; or more accurately, did sell the office "to one John H. Garner for and on behalf of Thomas J. Carver." Carver, meanwhile, was accused of paying out a bribe to a government official and of engaging in cotton fraud.

On the morning of Sunday, December 3, with the military hearing still at an early stage, Daniel Gibbens committed suicide by cutting his throat with a razor. He was found by friends lying on the floor of his lodgings in his own blood, with the razor beside him. A surgeon was summoned, but Gibbens died within the hour. In the words of the New Orleans *Times* (December 5, under the heading "Melancholy Suicide in Mobile"), Gibbens's "body was immediately sent to the embalmer's to be prepared for sending to Boston." There was time for a hurried autopsy, which, according to the same newspaper, revealed that Gibbens "had been taking sulphuric ether" and presumably had killed himself in a deranged state of mind, after inhaling an overdose.

In March 1936, Henry James, William's legally trained son, set himself to examine the evidence, the documents, and the rumors relating to "the Death of Daniel Lewis Gibbens." He was inclined on balance to exonerate his maternal grandfather of any wrongdoing. Gibbens, he wrote, was working in Dexter's Mobile office only as assistant or secretary, and not as any kind of special agent. "Nobody suggested that DLG had any concern with the shipment and sale of cotton, or that he participated in any way in profits derived therefrom." It is true that the record, such as it is, shows no suggestion of that kind, by the military prosecutor or anyone else; it is also true that the New Orleans *Times* routinely referred to Gibbens as an assistant special agent.

In any event, the more dangerous allegation involved the $25,000 payment for T. J. Carver's appointment. Witnesses at the trial, Henry James took note, said that the sum of money was left lying in Dexter's office when Gibbens was alone there; and the prosecutor, after Gibbens's death, even alleged that Gibbens had pocketed it. His grandson was convinced that Gibbens had done no such thing, but it was possible, James admitted, that Gibbens had been a "conduit" in what he knew was a crooked arrangement. And this, James surmised, was why Gibbens had killed himself. He could not have testified, by this analysis, without ruining his reputation. The crisis came, moreover, when Gibbens was on the verge of rejoining his family after several years of separation. For Eliza Gibbens, "any suggestion of dishonesty would have been utterly repulsive . . . How could he ask the women in Weymouth to take back a husband and father whose honesty had just been publicly impugned?"

During the month after the first arraignment, Gibbens seemed to suffer a nervous collapse, in Henry's view. He cited his mother, Alice Howe James, who told him that her father took to drink again in this interval; and it was here that Henry disclosed Gibbens's suicidal impulses following drunken fits in his early married life. James also mentioned a family friend who said (confirming the newspaper story) that Gibbens had turned to drugs as well in his last days.

Returning to his inquiry two months later, in May, Henry James scrupulously confided the information that Gibbens left an estate of nearly $25,000. He added what his cousin Rosamund Gregor Marshall had found, that Gibbens earned $4,800 a year in his former job in New Orleans, from which (James thought) he could have saved a fair amount. There also might have been "legitimate odds and ends like notarial fees." In sum, James refused to deprive Gibbens "of the benefit of a large and reasonable doubt." It was a generous verdict, but it seems unquestionable from this distance that Gibbens had accepted some share of the loot, though apparently not a great deal. What was unfortunate for Gibbens and his wife and daughters was his association with an extremely rare instance—quite possibly the only important instance—when Alabama agents were brought to trial for cotton fraud.

T. J. Carver was convicted of fraud, fined $90,000, and sentenced to one-year imprisonment, but not to be released until the fine was paid. On February

The Strange Death of Daniel Gibbens

17, 1866, as related in a General Order issuing from the headquarters of the Department of Alabama, T.C.A. Dexter was convicted of fraud and sentenced to a fine of $250,000, "to be paid to the United States." He was to be "confined in a penitentiary for one year," but not to be released until the fine was paid. Neither man was able to pay the fine, and both remained in prison for an indeterminate number of years. What became of Carver is not known. Dexter's Boston friends worked hard for his release; they could not raise the requisite money, but they begged persistently for clemency, especially in view of the suffering and innocence of Dexter's New England wife and her family. Dexter was eventually set free, seemingly on the belated judgment that the military court should not have tried him in the first place. He returned to Boston and perhaps took up some of his financial interests. When he died in Boston in October 1890, at the age of seventy-three, he was identified by the newspaper as a "cotton broker," though it was observed that "he has been entirely out of active business for eight years."

The Later Jameses

When Henry James died in London in February 1916, it seemed to the world at large that the James family itself had passed away. Of the entity usually meant by that title, Henry had been the last survivor. To review the necrology: Henry James, Sr., had died in 1882, less than a year after the death of his wife. Of their five children, Wilky died in 1883 and Alice in 1892. William and Robertson died within weeks of each other in 1910. With Henry these five had comprised the domestic phenomenon William had in mind when he remarked that Henry was really neither an American nor an Englishman but "a native of the James family." And yet, as of February 1916, a number of individuals in direct descent from the elder Henry and mostly bearing the family name were carrying on their lives, pursuing their various fortunes, making their several marks. Alice Howe James (Mrs. William), Carrie James (Mrs. Wilky), and Mary Holton James (Mrs. Bob) could count between them eight children, ranging in age from forty-two to twenty-six years. Eight James grandchildren were on the scene in 1916, with five more to come.

Consideration of this progeny can begin with the first-born child of William and Alice James.

1

This younger Henry James—he was sometimes referred to as Henry 3 and sometimes signed himself Henry 5, but he was known personally as Harry and will be mostly so named hereafter—earned his law degree at Harvard in 1904, and immediately went to work for a law firm in Boston. By 1909 he was a partner in the office of Warren, Hague, James and Bigelow; but in 1912, at the age of thirty-three, he abandoned both his law practice and Boston and went down to New York to take up a position as manager of the Rockefeller Institute for Medical Research.

His new duties seemed strange to him at first, so he said later; one of them, encountered at once, was to put a stop, publicly, to false allegations about research practices—for example, that a certain physician had demonstrated on decapitated cats before a congress of surgeons in New York. Harry resigned from the institute in January 1917: "in order to give all my time to the war" (to his Harvard class secretary). He had, in fact, been involved in the European war almost from the outset; it galvanized some latent impulse in him. From November 1914 to March 1915, he toured Europe—Belgium, unoccupied France, Serbia—as a member of a Rockefeller commission to make plans for the relief of non-combatants. In January 1916, Harry was in London, this time to attend the deathbed of his Uncle Henry. The novelist's secretary, Theodora Bosanquet, described Harry James in her diary as "nearly white-haired, but still black-moustached," with "a tremendous chin" and "the most obstinate-looking jaw."

In June 1917, Harry married Olivia Cutting of Westbury, Long Island, the youngest of the four children of the late William Bayard Cutting, a New York lawyer of some renown, and Olivia Murray Cutting, a forceful woman, much occupied with philanthropic activities. (Their son, Bayard Cutting, Jr., had been a cherished friend of Edith Wharton and a young diplomat of promise before his death in 1914, and *his* daughter, under her married name of Iris Origo, would achieve distinction as a writer on Byron and Leopardi, and on a fifteenth-century Tuscan merchant.) It was a woefully ill-advised marriage, Olivia James revealing herself after a certain painful time to be by every inclination a full-fledged lesbian.

A desire to escape the marital discomfort combined with James's surging interest in the war led him, in May 1918, to enlist as a private in the United States Army. He was assigned to Company D of the 342nd Machine Gun Battalion of the 89th Division. The 89th, twenty thousand strong, was massed at Camp Mills, New York, preparing to embark for Europe, when Private James reported to the company commander, Captain Sandford Sellers, Jr. After examining his record and inspecting the man—James standing at attention in the pyramidal tent, in hobnail boots, wraparound puttees, and loose-fitting uniform—Sellers told him that, with his legal and administrative experience (not to mention his family connections), at his age (thirty-nine), married, fluent in French and German, he should apply at once for Officers' Training Camp, and that he owed it to the Allied cause to do so. To this James replied, by Sellers's much later account, that "he desired to see active service with the armed forces of Europe." That same afternoon, the divisional commander, Major General Leonard Wood, a peacetime acquaintance, made the same appeal to Private James; but the latter continued to plead that he "wanted to see action," and his wish to remain with the 89th was granted.

On June 3, James, crammed in with the other enlisted men below decks, sailed on the Cunard liner *Corona* to Liverpool, whence the division was ferried over to France. In early August, after two months of training in the village of Vesaignes, the battalion was moved into the forward area at Toul, southwest of Verdun, to serve in support of the French infantry crouched in the trenches opposite Montsec. There was periodic strafing by artillery and airplane, and skirmishing at night in the no-man's-land between Allied troops and German; one attack of cannon fire and poison gas cost another newly arrived American unit in the adjoining sector 800 casualties.

In early September, Company D received word that an attack was shortly to take place in the St.-Mihiel area. It was to be (unbeknownst to the 342nd) the first all-American action: some 600,000 troops were to take part, and it was to be launched at 5 a.m. on September 12. The immediate aim was the capture of Montsec, which the Germans had held for four years, and on which they had built massive fortifications. On the morning of the eleventh, there arrived at headquarters, quite unexpectedly, a telegram instructing Private Henry James to report forthwith to the Officers' Training Camp at Langres. James, summoned, read the telegram, standing at attention, then said (the language is probably Captain Sellers's): "But we are to start the attack at five in the morning. I would like to remain with the Company until this battle is concluded." Sellers, though sympathetic, replied that it was his duty to order James on his way. James said no more, but, Sellers recalled, "tears rolled down his face while he offered his hand in farewell."

It is not hard to interpret the tears. Not only was the son of William James being denied his own battle action, and a particularly challenging one; the nephew of Wilky James was at the last moment denied participation in an attack on a fortified area inevitably reminiscent of mountainous Fort Wagner. The casualties resulting from the St.-Mihiel fighting, it can be added, compared in scope with those suffered by the 54th Massachusetts Regiment and the others fifty-five years earlier.

James was commissioned second lieutenant in November 1918, ten days before the Armistice. He stayed on in France for another ten months, serving with the U.S. Reparations Committee at Versailles, and with an interallied study group making what Harry thought was a pointless if picturesque tour of the Danubian countries. He was back in New York by late summer 1919.

Harry's main preoccupation for a time was something that had been on his mind for quite a few years. In 1911, as a memorial to his father, young Henry brought out a volume of William James's uncollected essays, *Memories and Studies*. It is knowingly compiled, and an indispensable coda to the philosophical career; included in it are the Emerson Centenary Address of 1903, lectures on Louis Agassiz and Robert Gould Shaw, "Final Impressions of a Psychical Researcher," two key essays—"The Energies of Men" and "The Moral Equivalent of War"—and some witty, acerbic animadversions on the American university, "The Ph.D. Octopus" among them. At the same time, 1911, Henry set himself to gathering materials for what, in a class report, he called "a biographical selection from his father's correspondence." *The Letters of William James Edited by His Son Henry James* (no one was to suppose that this was somehow a posthumous achievement of the novelist Henry) appeared in two volumes just before Christmas 1920; the editor's mother was able to play some part in the selection process, and could read the published texts at her leisure (she died in September 1922).

Harry performed his immense task with more than creditable skill and discrimination. The letters to Alice Howe Gibbens as William's fiancée and then his wife were largely excluded, as how could they not be; and other especially private letters and portions of letters were omitted. But there are generous selections of letters to Henry and other members of the family, and to colleagues, intellectual associates, former students, and simple friends, and the unique William Jamesian personality is present on every page. The letters glisten with wit and insight; they are seeking, inquiring, joking, enthusing, caviling; they are a mine of information about the writer and about the history of thought in America between 1861 and 1910. Harry's biographical and editorial commentary has a discreet and cultivated elegance. The whole job was sufficiently well done that nearly seventy years would go by before another edition of William James's letters got under way.*

Over the next years, Harry busied himself, as he always did, with James family financial affairs and related matters: not always, as we shall see, in particular with his brother Aleck, to the unadulterated pleasure of his kin. (There was a certain lordliness to Harry James; as early as 1903, his then-sixteen-year-old sister Peggy, writing from Chocorua, remarked that Harry was arriving soon "to see that we haven't been naughty and set us right if we have.") He also took part in a group seeking to diminish the legal and political barriers that beset the Middle Atlantic area of New York, New Jersey, and Connecticut; less came of this than might have been hoped. In 1920 as well,

---

* A splendidly ambitious edition of the letters of William James, including a large number of letters *to* him, and currently projected for eleven volumes, is in the making under the general editorship of Ignas G. Skrupskelis, professor of philosophy at the University of South Carolina, and sponsored by the American Council of Learned Societies. Mention should also be made of the 600-page *Selected Unpublished Correspondence 1885–1910*, edited by Frederic J. D. Scott (1986).

The Later Jameses

James began a seven-year term as a member of the Harvard Board of Overseers, serving on committees that "visited" the Department of Philosophy and the Zoological Museum (an element in the legacy of his father's mentor Louis Agassiz). But his chief interest until its publication in 1923 was a biography of Richard Olney (1835–1917), Attorney General and then Secretary of State in the second presidential term of Grover Cleveland.

The biographical portrait is admirably candid. Olney's very aspect, wrote the recent war veteran, suggested a "ruthless being, like one of those modern war-tanks, which proceeds across the roughest ground, heedless of the opposition, deaf alike to messages from friends or cries from the foe." But that same roughshod quality in political action won James's approval, as with Olney's swift dispatch of federal troops in 1894 to break up a strike of Pullman car workers in Chicago; there might have been some few "injustices," James conceded, but the strike was "brutally oblivious of the interests of the nation." (It is perhaps worth noting that Harry's brother Billy James was the son-in-law of the president of the Pullman Company; see below.) In the same way, James supported the bellicose posture of Cleveland and Olney in the dispute with Great Britain in 1896–97 over the borders of Venezuela. Following a condescending note about the issue from the British Prime Minister, Cleveland, in a statement co-written by Olney, announced that after a certain point the United States would "resist by every means in its power, as a willful aggression upon its rights and interests"—and in an application of the Monroe Doctrine—any British attempt to appropriate lands on what America deemed the Venezuelan side of the border.

As Henry knew, his father had been vehemently opposed to the administration's position and its rhetoric. He had included in the *Letters* William's remark that Olney's obdurate style "makes of our Foreign Office a laughing stock." In *Richard Olney: A Life Service*, Henry James, scrupulous as always, cited various severe criticisms of Cleveland and Olney in the Venezuela controversy and drew special attention to William James's reflection, ending in the remark just quoted, on

> how near the surface in all of us, the old fighting instinct lies, and how slight an appeal will wake it up. Once *really* waked, there is no retreat. So the whole wisdom of government should be to avoid the direct appeals. Cleveland, in my opinion, by his explicit allusion to war, has committed the biggest political crime I have ever seen here.

The younger James, by way of reply to this, argued that the Cleveland–Olney policy had been successful in that it led quickly to a satisfactory settlement of the border quarrel, and that it "gave the United States a new standing in the eyes of other nations." The contention was undoubtedly correct, looking back to the late 1890s from the perspective of 1923 and the more recent display of American power and valor. For some readers today, it may have a disquietingly familiar ring.

Henry James's connection with Harvard grew apace. In 1927, he was elected by the alumni to a second seven-year term on the Board of Overseers, this time taking part in visiting committees for the Departments of Philosophy and Biology. In 1936, he was taken into the Corporation, a non-elective, self-perpetuating body consisting of the president of Harvard—James Bryant Conant in 1936—and five fellows serving until death or retirement. The Corporation was and is junior to the Board of Overseers by statute, but more authoritative in practice. As to James's contributions to the Corporation and its biweekly meetings, a New York newspaper editorial shortly after his death may be quoted. It would be hard to estimate the value of James's services on "this almost mythical board," it said, but exactly because "the mysteries which surround this smallest and most powerful of educational bodies are impenetrable to the ordinary eye."

At the start of his second term as an overseer, James set himself to write the life of Charles William Eliot, president of Harvard from 1869 to 1909 (he had recently died). The biography was published in two volumes in 1930, and won the Pulitzer Prize the following year. James tells his story with at least a modicum of the family's narrative flair, though of necessity he has to spend many a page on colorless institutional history, with maps and appendices; and for a later taste, he lets his subject do too much of his work for him by quoting at great length from too many not very arresting letters. But the story has a clarity of theme: the interaction over forty years between an able, tireless, and strong-minded individual and a provincial college capable of being transformed into a university of enormous and many-faceted stature.

A more inward part of the story is the process by which Eliot—a cold imperious figure, unpopular with both faculty and students for the first twenty years or so ("He was not loved," James says flatly)—learned gradually how "to come closer to people." By 1894, James writes, it was possible to "raise a cheer for him." The biographer's obvious pleasure in this development suggests that he saw something of himself in Eliot, as he had done in Olney. He was perhaps *expressing* himself in Eliot: a person of exceptional talent for acting within the combative elements of his own world, who yet found it difficult to elicit affection from those to whose welfare he was committed, but who might in time win some degree of warm feeling.

When he addresses Eliot's views on various social issues, James tends to agree with them, even when it meant diverging from his father's philosophico-political path. He quietly applauds a speech by which Eliot demolished a

proposal to admit women to Harvard. On the matter of disputes between labor
and capital, Eliot is shown as cheerfully oblivious to the reality of economic
hardship. In a speech to the alumni in June 1896, Eliot orotundly endorsed
his country's role in the Spanish-American War. "The educated youth who
loves his country," said the chief of the country's leading educational institution, "does not stop to consider in what precise cause his country has gone
to war"; the youth simply answers his government's call. The Harvard audience, James writes, thought this "the most impressive speech they had ever
heard," and James seems to be of the same opinion.

Henry James described himself in the *Who's Who in America* for 1936–
37 as "author and trustee," and trusteeship did become his most visible public
profession. He continued as trustee of the American Academy in Rome, and
took up comparable posts with the New York Public Library, the Rockefeller
Institute for Medical Research (of which he had once been the manager), and
the Carnegie Corporation. It was the latter connection that led to his appointment in 1932 as chairman of the board of the Teachers Insurance and Annuity
Association—TIAA—which the Carnegie Foundation had begun in 1918 to
provide retirement benefits for employees of American colleges and universities. James served as president and chairman until a month before his death.

Henry James was largely credited by the association for the increase of
policyholders during his tenure from 11,000 to 50,000, of participating institutions from 176 to 525, and of assets from \$35 million to \$220 million. In
no other enterprise was Henry James's financial acumen more valuably allied
to his own cultivation and his educational and cultural interests. He was in a
way the identifiable descendant of William of Albany, and the first member
of the family since that William to be a genuine man of business affairs. (The
novelist Henry, it can be recalled, rejoiced that since his grandfather's time
no member of the family for two generations had been guilty of a single stroke
of business.) Like the founding William, too, Harry James displayed a vein of
moral hardness, a severity of expectation.* But with the TIAA Henry exercised
his professional acuteness, his academic devotion, and his human generosity
in the same maneuver. This was no doubt why he gave his younger colleagues
in the uptown New York TIAA office such an impression of contentment. They
remember him as affable and unassuming, excellent company, though keeping
his privacy; quietly correcting their epistolary style (deploy shorter words and
simpler sentences); pausing at the door of a Friday, battered hat on his head,

---

* The image of Henry James as a latter-day William of Albany has been well
sketched by Alan D. Weathers in a Boston University master's thesis on Alexander James,
Harry's younger brother, in 1986.

to announce happily that he was off for a weekend of fishing and hunting in Vermont.

Henry was the most dedicated figure in his James generation in the collecting and preservation of family archives and biographical materials. It was he who first organized the extensive James archives, now resting in Houghton Library at Harvard; who meticulously corrected the genealogical records; and who added new documents as they came to hand. His cousin Edward Holton James (brother Robertson's son) reported in November 1933 that Harry was putting together masses of family materials. They may never mean much to our descendants, Harry was quoted as saying, but at Harvard they would be preserved for five hundred years—"for whatever good they may serve." When he received a letter during World War II from Captain William Cosby James of the Canadian Army Overseas, announcing himself as the grandson of Cartney James, nephew of William of Albany, and asking for further information about the family, Henry took pains to reply.

Harry went to Dublin in June 1931 to meet Helen James, then teaching music in a city school, to drive up with her to Bailieborough to have lunch with her ninety-one-year-old father, Robert James. This was the Bobby James of local fame and popularity, the grandson of William of Albany's older brother. His hearing was a bit impaired and he moved with some difficulty, but he was a solicitous host and Harry liked him very much. After lunch Bobby took his American kinsman to the cemetery to see the flat tombstones carrying the names of the departed Jameses back to the first or farming William: all named Robert, William, McCartney, or Jane, Harry noted. They walked over to the spot where Robert James's house had stood. The view was the same William of Albany had grown up with: the horizon line of the opposite hill a thousand yards away, and beyond it the tops of other hills making a far skyline; a scene everywhere of "green mowings, green grazings, green hedges."

A year and a half later, Helen James wrote to tell of the death of her father on November 21, 1932. He had been standing in the village bank, chatting with friends, when he collapsed and died. Helen and her brother, Henry, now practicing medicine in Cheshire, England, had decided to "break up the old home."

Henry's marriage to Olivia Cutting lasted for thirteen years, an endless source of torture for both wife and husband. In 1930, Henry stage-managed a divorce proceeding with himself as defendant, his sister-in-law Frederika James (Mrs. Aleck, who owed him a favor) testifying as to his cruelty and misbehavior. Harry remained single for eight years until, in 1938, he married Dorothea Draper, the widow of Linzee Blagdon, a New York lawyer and broker. She was an older sister of the gifted monologuist Ruth Draper and the aunt of the dancer and choreographer Paul Draper; Aunt Doro can be recalled taking one or another of her James nephews to see Paul Draper perform. She was an imposing woman, forty-seven when she became the second Mrs. Henry James, and soon to be elected president of the board at the Bellevue Hospital School of Nursing. She survived her husband by twenty years.

Harry James died of heart disease, the particular fatal affliction of the Jameses, in December 1947. In an editorial a few days later, the New York *Herald Tribune* spoke of "that most extraordinary of American families" from which James descended, with its genius "born of conflict and restraint." After surveying Henry's career as biographer, foundation executive, and Harvard Fellow, it concluded: "To wear a great name lightly yet proudly, to do a rich life's work amid devoted friends—what better grandson or son or nephew could the Jameses of the great past ask to pray for?"

2

In a recording he made in 1952, when he was seventy years old, William James's second son and namesake, commonly known as Billy, spoke in his grave, precise Cambridge voice and in slow, sculpted sentences about the early decades of his life. He told at one moment about a visit in September 1903 to his Uncle Henry at Lamb House in Rye, Sussex. He, Billy, had just acquired an Airedale terrier. Uncle Henry had himself recently come into possession of a rose-red thoroughbred dachshund, Max by name, and the joy of the novelist's heart; Billy was in no little trepidation about his terrier's welcome. But when the crate was opened and the puppy floated out onto the lawn, the portly Henry followed and danced around it, holding out the skirts of his coat to be snapped at. The Airedale's assigned name was Brawling Bagman, but upon its arrival in Massachusetts, Billy's teenage sister proposed calling him Ryelie, in honor of his place of origin. From afar in England, Uncle Henry demurred at the "incongruous Irish title" for a Yorkshire product—he was always ambivalent about his Irish antecedents—and urged the name be fore-shortened to Ri. But the relationship between uncle and nephew, rewarding for both, was solidly established.

Billy had stopped off at his uncle's at the end of a year's study in Europe, much of it with his father's philosophical friend Theodore Flournoy. The academic year 1902–3 was Billy's senior year at Harvard, and his decision to devote it to foreign study was as astonishing as it was commendable. Billy had been a member of the Harvard freshman crew that defeated Yale in 1900 ("On such things is human contentment based," his father said at the time); and in the summer of 1902, after leading the senior eight to another victory, Billy was elected captain for the following year. This experience he set aside in favor of going abroad.

During the year after his graduation, Billy made a loyal filial try at the Harvard Medical School, but then, reversing the paternal example, he abandoned medicine for art, and in the fall of 1904 he entered the school of the Boston Museum of Fine Arts. The museum had opened in a Gothic building on Copley Square in 1876, and the museum school began to receive students at the same time. For young William James in 1904, as for his fellow aspirants, the chief attractions of the school were Frank Benson and Edmund Tarbell, two of the painters who brought Boston somewhere near the forefront of painting in America between the late 1880s and the early 1900s.

Both had been students at the school, and the two of them began teaching there together in 1889. Benson and Tarbell, with several others, helped beget a movement—it never quite amounted to a "school" in the French manner—of American Impressionists, their own work deriving in part from the Impressionist paintings of Monet, Renoir, Manet, the American Mary Cassatt, and others which they had seen and studied in Paris. The Bostonians shared with the French a deployment of free rapid brushstrokes, an addiction to bright shimmering surfaces, and a softening of edges; but they remained rather more committed to form and the conventional look of things than did their Gallic precursors.

Benson and Tarbell were charter members of the influential group formed at the Players Club in New York in 1897 and calling itself The Ten. The group came into being, as such groups tend periodically to do, in protest against the formalism and traditionalism of the day. Eight of The Ten were actual or former Bostonians, others from that city including Willard C. Metcalf and Robert Reid, as well as the superb craftsman Childe Hassam, with the gifted New Yorkers John H. Twachtman and J. Alden Weir. (It might be noticed that Winslow Homer declined membership in The Ten and that Thomas Eakins and Albert Pinkham Ryder were not invited.) All things considered, there was a great deal of aesthetic urgency and very considerable achievement and promise in the American art world in the years surrounding the turn of the century; the work produced enjoys repeated recovery and acclaim. But the Boston segment of that world was perceptibly beginning to lose its impetus at just the moment Billy James made his entrance into it. His active years coincided with the era of relative decline in Boston's creative adventurousness. He may even, perhaps, be taken as a representative of that later and more modest stage.

After two years in the museum school, Billy James, as the custom was with young American painters, departed for Paris and eighteen months at the little school—three large crowded rooms and two smaller ones on the rue St.

Denis—run by a hefty Frenchman named Julien. It was a diverting experience, but not, Billy felt, a particularly liberating one; the Ecole Julien stood for the conservative branch of contemporary French art. More to Billy's taste were study-visits to the Louvre and other Paris art centers; and the high point of the long stay was a day in February 1907 spent by him copying a head drawn by Degas which, he said, "Miss Cassatt had lent me." The report was contained in a letter to his father, replying to one in which William had told of his days in New York when he was giving the lectures on pragmatism at Columbia.

Billy put in three more years at the museum school, accompanying it in 1909 to its new location in a vast Beaux Arts building on the Fenway. He was painting steadily, portraits for the most part: of his grandmother Eliza Gibbens, of his mother and father, of his siblings. His younger brother, Aleck, was also showing an interest in art, something quickened after a visit by the seventeen-year-old to the home in Dublin, New Hampshire, of the painter Abbot Thayer. Billy further kindled his brother's new excitement, and the two occasionally would work at their painting side by side. In early 1911, Billy completed a portrait from photographs of his Uncle Henry, an Olympian forbidding countenance in the outcome; he donated it to Isabella Stewart Gardner, his uncle's old friend, to be hung in her home, Fenway Court. Mrs. Gardner professed herself nearly speechless at the gift: "It *is* Henry James—wonderful!"

A frequent sitter for Billy during summer weeks at Chocorua was Alice Runnells, whose family had owned a home near the lake for some time. In September 1911, the engagement was announced of Alice Runnells and William James; they were married in Chicago in January 1912.

Chicago was the Runnellses' main place of residence, but both the father and the mother came from venerable New Hampshire stock. There had been Runnells farming folk in the area over several generations. One ancestor fought at Bunker Hill, and at the age of 106, as the battle's only survivor, he came over from New Hampshire to Boston to take part in a Bunker Hill celebration. Alice Runnells's grandfather John Runnells came to Chocorua in 1852 with his wife and two children, and as Elder Runnells ministered to the Baptist church there for thirty-five years: a well-esteemed man, sweet-natured, narrow in his views and unremittingly melancholy ("49 years old today," he wrote in his diary on March 9, 1866, "—verging on the grave, sun setting, probation ending").

His son John Sumner Runnells, Alice's father, was of a far livelier and more assertive disposition. He studied law after graduating from Amherst College (in 1865), and was taken on as private secretary to Governor Merrill of Iowa, himself originally from New Hampshire. In Des Moines, he met and married Helen Baker, whose father had been governor of New Hampshire before coming to Iowa during the Civil War as attorney general for the territory. In 1887, John Runnells gave a talk at a city ceremony in Chicago that so impressed George Pullman, in the audience, that the railroad chieftain offered him the job of general counsel for the Pullman Company. Runnells remained with the company in Chicago for the rest of his long life. In 1911, when his daughter and Billy James were getting engaged, he succeeded the rigidly conservative Robert Todd Lincoln, the oldest of Abraham Lincoln's sons, as president. John Runnells, addressed as Sumner by his intimates, was a large, well-proportioned man with an air of being at ease with great power and wealth. He also gave an impression of benevolence, which was not misleading, but he was capable of violent bursts of temper. Alice was the youngest of his three daughters; there was a younger brother as well.

The honeymoon couple booked a bedroom on the Twentieth Century Limited from Chicago to New York. In the 1952 recording, Billy recalled that the bride so managed things that they arrived at the LaSalle Street station many minutes after the train was to leave. Needless to say, the famous trans-continental express was held until Mr. Pullman's daughter and son-in-law had taken their places. From New York they crossed to England and a months-long stay with Henry James in Rye. The novelist, a more avidly watchful family man with every passing year, had taken to Alice Runnells from the start. "I can't thank you enough," he wrote her when she told him of their marriage plans and future hopes, "for talking to me with an exquisite young confidence and treating me as the fond and faithful and intensely participating old Uncle that I want to be."

Two children were born of the marriage in rapid succession: another William, to be known as Billy, in 1913; and a second son, John Sumner Runnells, in 1914. Alice Runnells James was a tall, good-looking woman; in her outward seeming, vigorous, smiling, and spirited; one who enjoyed social gatherings to the last guest's departure and who made of 95 Irving Street in Cambridge and the summer home in Chocorua inviting social and literary centers for four decades. But she suffered from ailments, most of them real (there was a thyroid deficiency), though some imaginary, all her adult life, and had to remove herself regularly for rest and convalescence. Writing to his daughter Peggy in October 1907, William James spoke of Alice Runnells's "invalidism" and how it had "wrought refinement in her inwardly." The re-finement grew stronger with time: it was hardly a secret among the James kinfolk that Alice had little taste for the sexual aspect of marriage, whereas her husband had an exceptionally energetic sexual nature. Affairs with graceful female models and perhaps others, on Billy's part, were an inevitable conse-quence; and it appears that in the 1940s, after thirty years of marriage, Billy grew so edgy that he prepared to move out once and for all.

The Later Jameses

A form of nervous discontent, even a subdued fierceness, was indeed becoming perceptible in those years, though perceptible only to a close and concerned observer. If the discontent was in part marital, it was also surely in part aesthetic. Billy James began teaching at the Boston Museum School in 1913, as successor to Frank Benson, who, with Edmund Tarbell, had summarily quit the school in a policy dispute. With various interruptions—in late 1918 and early 1919, for example, Billy was in France, working with the drafting division of the United States Air Service—Billy taught at the school for twenty-five years, and was associated with it administratively into the 1950s. In his fiftieth-anniversary report to the secretary of the Harvard Class of 1903, Billy wrote that ever since graduation he had been occupied "in (1) trying to find out how to paint a better portrait; and (2) how to organise a better art school." As to the art school, one hostile commentator, a disaffected painter, held that it was the administration of William James that led to the museum school's decline. This seems not to be the general opinion; or rather, it is one among a conflict of art-historical opinions; but the school clearly had little of the excitement and sense of direction it had enjoyed in an earlier day. As to portrait painting, both Billy's achievement and his self-regard were at a low ebb in the late 1930s and for some years afterward.

Billy's best work, one might say overtidily, was done in the 1920s and the 1950s. The portrait of his mother in 1921 is almost disturbingly brilliant; what one visitor described as Alice Howe James's "great dark luminous eyes"—her daughter called them "enormous"—shine in it never more darkly and piercingly. But dissatisfaction set in at mid-career. To his brother Aleck, who was contemplating a change in his artistic course following a day at the Prado in Madrid, Billy wrote in 1930: "You and I are both trying to writhe away from something we don't like in our work." Billy was writhing away from photographic naturalism, in his own phrase, and in emulation of the Renaissance masters was seeking to contrive or find symbols that might convey his vision of things. It was not a very well-conceived search. As late as October 1956, he was exclaiming to his friend E. E. Cummings, "Are you a poet? Yes! Am I a painter? No!" But the very zest of the denial suggests its opposite, and in fact, by the 1950s Billy James was again a painter of genuine merit. The portraits of his lifetime friend, the art curator Longdon Warner, of Charles Copeland, and most especially of Lewis Perry, headmaster of Phillips Exeter Academy, attest to this.

Yet having said so, one must add one's sense of a final lack of fulfillment in Billy James. John H. Finley, Jr., the classical scholar and eminent Master of Eliot House at Harvard, has put the case (in a 1988 memoir) as winningly as can be. Billy James, he said, was really interested in experience itself, for its own sake. "Which may be to say that, reasonably fit vehicle though painting was for one who saw the light and shade of human faces and of the minds behind them, it was secondary. He was less a painter than a listener, a watcher for ideas and feeling, one who waited to catch meanings."

Finley was one of a number of accomplished literary scholars who enriched the Harvard scene in the years immediately after the Second World War, and who could be found on occasion at Irving Street. Billy met more than once with F. O. Matthiessen, when the latter was completing his masterful volume *The James Family* (1947). (Hearing of this in San Francisco, and of the excellent reception being given Matthiessen's book, Peggy James wrote her brother: "What one wouldn't give if Uncle Henry could have sat at the centre of all this appreciation of him!") Theodore Spencer, tall, lounging, friendly, urbane, was also on hand, until his untimely death in 1949; Harry Levin, writing his seminal book on James Joyce; "Jack" Sweeney of the Fogg Museum; the English literary theorist I. A. Richards; and at a much later date, for a term, Edmund Wilson ("I like him, decidedly," Billy remarked, "but I don't always agree"). Billy James used to claim that E. E. Cummings and the actress-photographer Marion Morehouse owed their marriage to having met in the Irving Street living room; their friendship elicited from Billy a series of witty and exuberant letters between 1940 and 1961, with running and often acute commentary on such artists as Abbot Thayer, Sargent, Eakins, John Butler Yeats (the poet's father, then living in Greenwich Village), and Rodin. There was smiling-eyed admiration for Cummings's poetry. "Dylan Thomas says you are the best poet in these states," Billy wrote his friend in June 1950. "All those in favor—"

But what must yet be reckoned with amid all this is the feeling of belatedness that anyone bearing the name William James and coming to maturity in the early twentieth century could scarcely have escaped. Billy's wife, Alice, alternately reveled in the Jamesian legacy and wearied of it. She apparently read every word of Henry James, and took pleasure in her role as heiress apparent and social arbiter in her James generation, but she could also say abruptly, "I'm getting goddam tired of the James know-it-all," after listening to an intellectual debate between Billy and their son Bill. Billy himself seems to have enjoyed his position as crown prince, at least within the Cambridge community, but he likewise felt the weight of the name, as John Finley remembers. And he was conscious, so Finley suggests, of a local environment that offered less to resist or challenge, where there was somewhat less room to create, than in his father's time. Perhaps being a listener, a catcher of meanings, was what the cultural condition called for.

Alice Runnells James died of a stroke in April 1957. In November 1959, Billy James married for the second time, to Mary Brush Pierce, the daughter of George De Forest Brush, a painter known for his American Indian subjects and for a sequence of madonna-and-child portraits, grave and appealing, and based on a careful study of Italian Renaissance models. (Both Billy and Aleck James painted pictures of him.) Mary was a fine painter herself, Billy told Cummings; she had been widowed for twenty years, and had lived a good deal in Italy. The seventy-seven-year-old Billy boasted by innuendo to Cummings that the first week of their marriage had been a sexual whirlwind. And indeed, at the end of the week, Mary James confided to one of Billy's nephews: "I thought I was marrying a very old man. But . . . I'm . . . exhausted."

Billy James died in 1961. His father's biographer, Gay Wilson Allen, dedicated *William James* to him in 1967.

The son Bill, already mentioned, attended Exeter for a year, but bypassed college to put in the years 1934–37 at the Boston Museum school. Doing so, he was not only following in his father's footsteps, he was studying in an institution where his father was a key administrative and pedagogical figure— a chancy situation, as no few in the teaching profession can attest. Father and son survived to become an amicable pair, arguing together pleasurably, exchanging views on life and art. In December 1950, Bill helped his father hang the paintings for an exhibition. (Singling out for special praise three portraits of the brain surgeon Harvey Cushing, the Boston *Globe* commentator said that the paternal "talent for psychology had passed on into painting.")

In 1938, Bill bought an 80-acre farm spread across a Vermont hillside, near Woodstock, complete with barn and a 1790 Greek revival house, all for $1,900; a farming neighbor told him laconically that he had been cheated, he could have had the lot for a thousand. Here he farmed and painted through the years of the war. It is from this time that there dates his definitive portrait of his father, aristocratically lean-faced, pensive, seeming on the very verge of talk or action. Bill was turned down twice by the Draft Board because of defective vision in one eye, and served instead in the Vermont National Guard, which was keeping an eye on matters of internal security. Near the war's end, he married Juliana Holden of Bennington, Vermont; she had been a member of the first class to graduate from Bennington College and had two young sons from a former marriage.

Bill and Julie James moved to Aspen, Colorado, in the late 1950s, and here Bill, in a variety of landscapes, did some of his best work. By 1969, the Jameses, with three grown children, were in Santa Fe. Further trouble with the defective eye caused Bill James to give up painting. His family had presented him with a violin for Christmas—one of the things he inherited from his mother was a profound and knowledgeable love of music—and the next thing anyone knew, Bill had set himself to making and repairing violins. Recently, he has been able to return to painting, and keeps at it when not busy fixing up a new home in Santa Fe.

609   ]

The children are married, the parents all told of six scattered across the country. Nathaniel, born in 1946, lives in Colorado and works with film crews. Sarah, born in 1947, lives in California with her husband of French descent. Jemima, born in 1948, makes her home in Tarrytown, New York; her child carries the name William, attached to the surname Mason, into the seventh American generation.

Bill James, an uncommonly *simpatico* individual to begin with, has accumulated a large store of Jamesiana and is generous in making it available, even to searching his own memory in telephone conversations. It is said about his offspring, however, that they display hardly a flicker of interest in their James background. But this, an outsider may be inclined to feel, is not altogether a bad thing.

John Sumner Runnells James turned out to be as formidable in some physical and psychological ways as was his syllabically sonorous name. When he reached his full growth he stood six feet four and weighed up to 270 pounds. At Harvard, from which he graduated in the class of 1937, he was an athlete of no small prowess and earned a reputation as a young man invincibly sure of his ideas about practically everything. Soon after the outbreak of the war in Europe, he came abroad with the American Field Service in a unit attached to the French Army. Back in America, after failing to be taken by the American military, he made his way to Montreal and enlisted in the Canadian Army. He was eventually commissioned second lieutenant (his father liked to spell the first part of the title "Left") in the 17th Duke of York Royal Canadian Hussars. He spent a long, restless year in England with the Canadian Third Division, and in June 1944, on D-day plus 10, he crossed the Channel and clambered ashore at Caen. During a night reconnaissance a few days after that, he stepped on a land mine. As late as April of the following year, he was writing his parents that physical sensation was only just then beginning to return to his leg and foot.

He would say that the whole experience with the Canadian Army, with all its danger and violence, was the most satisfying period in his life; and so it undoubtedly was, as in different military connections it was for so many of his age. But, as with those others, the war's end—in his case, after a year as military governor of a town in Holland—left him with the sense of an occupation gone. The recently formed CIA, offshoot of the OSS, came to his rescue by recruiting him in 1950. After an extensive briefing in Balkan and eastern Mediterranean history and politics, he was sent to Istanbul.

In 1947, John had married Margaret Stackpole Parker, the mother of two daughters by a previous match, and a distinctly beautiful woman, tall, lissome, dark-haired; she was a favorite subject of her portrait-painting father-in-law.

The Later Jameses

A male child was born dead in 1948; Margaret collapsed and had to be institutionalized. She underwent shock treatment and was given drugs: to which she became all too familiarly addicted, as she became wily in acquiring them. Intermittently thereafter, while retaining her beauty and her charm, she seemed to live in a private dream. A daughter, Margaret Alice, was born in 1949: Maggie James, the curator of many James family archives, memorabilia, photographs, paintings, and books. She inhabits a two-story white farmhouse in western Pennsylvania, where her son Matthew comes to stay during vacations from Northeastern University. By her own testimony (given to this writer over the telephone, when arrangements were being made to meet in the Pittsburgh airport), she is five feet three and a strawberry blonde. She is also a vital and quick-minded woman; no one cherishes the Jamesian saga more.

Growing up in a family presided (and towered) over by John S. R. James, Maggie can tell you, was mysterious, romantic, and terrible. John put in three years in Turkey, and then had a stretch in Sofia. In 1954, after a stint in Washington, he was sent back to Istanbul; informing E. E. Cummings of this, Billy James, who was finding John hard to deal with, remarked that he "must be useful to somebody." There followed four or five years in Italy, in Genoa and then in Fiesole, where the family lived comfortably in a converted monastery. The household, wherever situated, grew accustomed to John James disappearing for days at a time; and Maggie remembers a stranger once sidling up to her and asking her in bad English to pass on a note to her father. By 1962, John, it seems, had become too well known, with his height and bulk and swaggering manner, to be serviceable to the agency any longer.

His private behavior was exacerbated by alcohol and drugs: a good deal of social drinking ("4 happy alcoholic days with John and Peggy in Washington," Billy wrote Cummings in March 1958), and bouts of solitary belligerent drinking; as well as drugs to go along with those being used by his wife. There were ferocious bursts of temper, in the course of which he might batter his daughter, Maggie, unmercifully. (It has been surmised that John's father gave *him* a whack from time to time in his childhood and maybe later.) Margaret James died of throat cancer in March 1965. In July, John married Jessica Holiday (Holly) Philbin-Clark, said to be his first wife's closest friend.

The ensuing domestic scene was one of permanent commotion. There was drinking and quarreling, and great gusts of laughter; there was extravagant love, renewed fighting, and very lively talk. One evening, as Maggie James distinctly remembers, father and stepmother climbed up into the attic and rummaged among the relics William James had brought back from the Louis Agassiz expedition to Brazil in 1865. These they proceeded to destroy amid much boozy merriment. When John began to be afflicted with a kidney disease, he and Holly retired to her large estate in Massachusetts. The Irving Street house—the family home since 1889, inherited by John through Billy—was sold by John for $250,000 to Harvard, where it is now the home of a faculty member.

In the spring of 1969, John was seized by a heart attack and dropped dead in front of the polar bear cage at the Haverford (Pennsylvania) Zoo. He was fifty-five years old. Holly James died in 1989, though not before seeing to the deposit of a valuable little packet of James documents in Houghton Library.

3

During the months from the fall of 1899 to the spring of 1901, while William James, with his wife, wandered from place to place in Europe seeking relief from his physical and mental anguish (the period that ended with the Edinburgh lectures on religious experience), his daughter, Peggy, was at school in England. For Peggy, just entering her adolescence, it was both a fearful and a maturing time. She was lodged with the family of Joseph Thatcher Clarke (an American historian of ancient architecture and a friend of William's), on the edge of Harrow, to the west of London; and the first of her troubles was the four Clarke children. The parents were kindly enough, but the children harried and hectored their house guest; the oldest of them, Rebecca, accused her of lying, cheating, vulgarity, and other sins. Rebecca also punched and kicked her mother in retaliation for an accidental pinprick, according to Peggy, who described the household atmosphere, when the father was away, as "a weird nightmare." Peggy had been placed in a neighborhood school called Northlands; but what with homesickness, discontent, and the sense of having been abandoned, she found the place intolerable, and by mid-January 1900, at her own beseeching, she had been transferred to Hampstead High School.

Anxiety for her sorely afflicted father was another factor in her unease. Letters to her parents—in Bad Nauheim, in southern France, in Rome—were punctuated by prayers for William's recovery; he must have "courage and faith," she wrote him on one occasion, "and you will surely get better." William, encased in his own wretchedness, was not able to appreciate these messages. In the summer of 1899, when he and Alice were making plans for Peggy's upcoming school year, William wrote her fussy, admonishing letters, exhorting her to practice good posture by throwing her arms up in the air three times daily, and telling her that "a new and more responsible period is now beginning to open" in her life. He instructed the twelve-year-old that she must learn to rely on herself, and to "bottle up your feelings, and not expect pity or sympathy from parents, aunts or grandmothers."

The advice was ill-timed. In the winter and spring of 1900, Peggy fell victim to a severe bout of depression, the first of several such in the recorded history of her early decades. It took the form of intense self-deprecation. "I am fighting hard to overcome my faults which I find are *very* many," she wrote her father on April 3. "Sullenness, impatience, dirtiness, lazyness, selfishness and slouchiness. But I will fight over them harder than ever." She had begun to menstruate the previous month, and she took note that she had been particularly disagreeable when she had what she called her "turn." William's response to this and similar unhappy and revealing letters was a form of moral chastisement. "The bad thing," he said, "is to pour out the *contents* of one's bad spirits on others," and this is what Peggy had done. Her parents were alarmed: "for your shrieks of anguish were so excessive, and so unexplained by anything you told us in the way of facts, that we didn't know but what you had suddenly gone crazy."

In the clinical diagnosis of Peggy's state of being that William then provided, he was, one realizes in retrospect, visiting upon his daughter a portion of his own autobiography. He was describing what he was going through in this haunted period (the phrase was Henry's), and even more what he bleakly remembered from the dark epoch of the late 1860s. "There will be waves of terrible sadness," he wrote, "which last sometimes for days; and dissatisfaction with one's self, and irritation at others, and anger at circumstances and stony insensibility, etc., etc., which taken together form a melancholy." He concluded with a sentence that echoed a remark he had made to Wendell Holmes from Berlin in 1867: "The disease makes you think of *yourself* all the time; and the way out of it is to keep as busy as we can thinking of *things* and of *other people*."

Peggy no doubt caught the "we" in those last phrases, and understood that her father was addressing her within a shared mental misery. As a result, she could even tell her mother that "Papa's letter was a beautiful one; it cheered me immensely." She was determined, she went on, to act upon Papa's advice; and "with God's help I think I shall be a better girl." But even as she sought to adopt the paternal precepts, she was showing herself to be more than ever her mother's daughter. We hear the New England conscience of Alice Howe James at work when Peggy deplores her faults of character and vows to do better.

The other major event for Peggy James in these months, and one that would have a lasting effect upon her, was a growing closeness to her Uncle Henry. After spending Christmas 1899 at Lamb House, she wrote her brother Harry that she found her uncle "very nice" but rather too "fashionable and critical." Over the course of the year 1900, her tone warmed audibly, and Henry responded in kind. "May studies, spirits, sports, leap and march and stride together in right military step," he exclaimed in a September letter. ". . . I greatly miss you, dearest Peggot, and my small dashes down into High Street are solitary and sad." At the same time, he begged her to send on more copies of the photograph she had taken of him at Rye that summer, and had developed herself: "Myself with my hands in my pockets and my head and eyes twisted a bit up to one side, standing in a corner of the garden." He thought it one of the best pictures ever made of him.

He arranged for Peggy to watch the funeral procession of Queen Victoria in January 1901, escorted her with several classmates to see *Twelfth Night*, and brought her up to London for a viewing of the Cinematograph, early examples of moving pictures; and hoped in a follow-up note that the "rather horrid figures and sounds that passed before us . . . didn't haunt your dreams." He commiserated with her when she had mumps in November, recalling that he, too, had come down with them at a young age. He tried in vain, meanwhile, to persuade his brother and sister-in-law to place Peggy in an educational milieu more beneficial for her, one dedicated to " 'social' and aesthetic" rather than "moral and spiritual" ideas. "Uncle Henry is most awfully nice to me," she told her parents, after Henry had showered her with letters, five in all, about her forthcoming Christmas 1900 visit with him.

Back in Cambridge, Peggy settled into a routine of school and teenage social activity. In November 1901, she was present at the Harvard–Yale game with her brother Billy: "Billy shouted and I shouted and everybody shouted all the way through," she wrote her uncle. (Harvard won 22 to 6.) A dance she attended in the winter of 1904—she was seventeen by this time—was not "rapturous," she confessed to her mother, though she did meet "various boys." A coasting party scheduled for the following week was more to her liking. In other letters she rattled on about an assortment of clothes she hoped to buy. In the winter of 1906, she "came out," the event marked by stylish new gowns and a large tea party, but no dance.

The previous September, Mrs. William had taken Peggy to Bryn Mawr College for interviews and a tour of inspection. "We are basking in the reflected glory of you and Papa," Peggy told Henry. Her uncle had given his lecture on Balzac at Bryn Mawr early in the year, and had enjoyed the experience so much that he accepted an invitation to speak at commencement. (The second talk was "The Question of Our Speech.") As to William, his writings, especially *The Principles of Psychology*, were key texts in the undergraduate curriculum. At the end of the visit, Peggy was admitted to Bryn Mawr in the class of 1909, but perhaps wanting to let a year elapse between her uncle's campus appearance and her own arrival, she deferred entrance until September 1906. Thinking about all this, as the year drew to an end, she remarked to Uncle Henry: "I like your books even if Papa sometimes fails to grasp them."

Peggy was given an attractive room in Pembroke West. Her roommate, Mary Worthington, was the niece of the president of Bryn Mawr, Martha Carey Thomas (she rarely used her first name), who had been associated with the college since it held its first classes in 1885 and was emerging as one of the most powerful and influential figures in the country for the education of women. The president's niece was a brilliant and promising girl; she had spent nine years in England, Peggy reported to Billy, and talked beautifully; she was pink-cheeked, had long yellow hair, and was if anything too sweet-tempered. (Mary Worthington's promise was cut short when she died in 1912, two years after graduation.) In the same newsletter, she said she was taking three courses, each with five lectures a week, was having trouble with French, and had submitted to a silly and tedious hazing by a bunch of sophomores.

Two days later, she lamented to her parents that she had been so homesick she "couldn't see straight." One thing that upset her was a junior dropping by to inform her she was known around campus as "Jimmy Psych," and that it was common knowledge that her father had written of her to the dean that she was "a sweet child but uninteresting." Paying scant attention to this, William James, busy preparing his lectures on pragmatism, suggested that she "cultivate repose and dullness" and all would be well. Christmas at home was a relief, with a series of parties arranged by her mother; but in early January, Peggy had a falling-out with her roommate. She wrote an agitated account back home. The issue was another freshman, Ethel. Peggy portrayed her as drinking, smoking, and reading bad books; Mary thought they should try to reform her; to which Peggy (invoking a paternal phrase) said, "She is a sick soul and unreformable by us." Mary countered by accusing Peggy of being cold and hard, but, Peggy insisted, "she doesn't care for people at all in the way I do."

Partway through the second term, Peggy suffered a mild breakdown and had to be brought home for a convalescent period. She was able to return in March, but only under the strictest orders from her doctor and her father. She must lie down twice each day, be in bed by nine each evening, and engage in no athletic games. Otherwise, William warned, "nervous invalidism lies ahead." One event that helped her recovery was a blossoming friendship with a sophomore named Marianne Moore.

Marianna, as Peggy came to call her, was from Carlisle, Pennsylvania (though born in a suburb of St. Louis). There was an older brother, Warner, at Yale, and at home a strong-minded mother, Mary Warner Moore. It was an unusually close-knit family, and Marianne wrote home almost daily. The future poet was, at twenty years old, immensely interested in and responsive to the world immediately around her, especially her fellow students. From April 1907 onward, no name appeared in her letters more often than Peggy James's, and no one was studied and meditated on more persistently. Marianne, a devotee of Henry James's short stories and a diligent reader of William James's *The Will to Believe*, was at once fascinated and baffled by this female offspring of (as she put it) the famous James family. She thought Peggy was decidedly lovely, with her dark hair and dark eyes, and found her essentially innocent and even childlike, for all her air of almost frightening intellectuality. What Marianne could not make out, and said so in letter after letter back home, was whether Peggy James was as truly drawn to her as she was to Peggy.

A letter from Peggy in the summer of 1907 seemed to give an affirmative answer. Writing from Chocorua, Peggy said that she had cried all the way home, on the night train to Boston, at the thought of "all you dear people" she had left behind. She enclosed a poem she had written the previous autumn, "because you said once that you wanted to see something of mine and that you would *never* show it to any one . . . It is not poetry at all, I see now," Peggy continued, "—just a queer little gust of my own feelings at the time." This was a fair estimate of the eight-stanza poem that began:

> *The hills wave on in undulating line,*
> *Smiling and green and pleasant to the eye.*
> *The faint autumnal breezes sway the pine*
> *And fleecy clouds are clustered in the sky.*

The first hint of autumn brings with it sad thoughts of mortality; but the melancholy is assuaged in the last stanza by an expression of loving friendship, and this is perhaps what the act of forwarding the poem meant to convey.

> *Then take my hand and walk on yonder hill,*
> *Look down on nature's beauty round displayed.*
> *We too are standing on life's window-sill.*
> *Look and be glad and feel no more dismayed.*

She added that she had been reading Emerson's essays—"very wonderful and satisfying"—and ended: "I love you very much, as you know. And am your affectionate friend Peggy James."

From Marianne Moore's point of view, the relationship reached its peak of intensity during the fall of 1907, the first term of Peggy's sophomore year. Marianne spoke of Peggy, frequently for pages on end, in not less than sixteen letters during the month, saying at one moment that she knew no one more winning than Peggy and at another that Peggy was impossibly temperamental and made her furious. She was, for the time, obsessed with the James girl, and virtually admitted as much. Peggy James had in fact not only seized Marianne Moore's curiosity and affection; she had entered her creative imagination.

In the course of her Bryn Mawr years, Marianne Moore published eight stories and eight poems in the college literary magazine, *Typin O'Bob*, known as *Typ*. (Her first collection of verse, *Poems* in 1921, contained revised versions of several poems from this period.*) Of these various products, the most accomplished, by general reckoning, was the short story "Pym," written in October 1907 and published in January 1908. In late October, Marianne informed the family that she had "written what I like better than anything I have ever writ before," something perhaps to be called "Pym." It consists of five journal entries by young Alexander Pym—"I'm so glad you call him Alexander," Peggy said on reading it, "I have a brother Alexander"—who is torn between a literary career and a life in society. What it amounted to, in Marianne's words to the family, was "what [Henry] James calls the record of 'a generation of nervous moods.' " It ends on a nicely ambiguous note, with Pym returning to his socialite uncle and guardian but not quite abandoning his artistic hopes.†

A central emblem in the story is the "portrait of an unknown lady" that hangs in Pym's lodgings, a work based on a painting by John White Alexander that Marianne had seen in a Philadelphia museum. Marianne confided to Peggy that in the story the painting was related to her. The main mention of it seems clearly to suggest the quality of Marianne's absorption in her younger friend. Pym writes:

> I rest my eye fixedly upon my portrait of the unknown lady in the green dress. I watch an occasional diagonal of fire-light splash across her dark slippery hair, across the zig-zag light parts in her dress, and over her hands.

Just so had the attentive Marianne described Peggy, to her mother, in imagery of lights flashing and subsiding. "I like that slippery hair," Peggy said; "is it all yours?" When at the end, Pym prepares to leave his present surroundings, he writes: "The portrait and the dark blue rug . . . I shall take with me. All else I abjure."

Marianne's report of October 17 was notable for its changes of emotional direction. Her mother had been issuing stern instructions about not becoming too involved with Peggy James; Marianne said she would heed the advice, and that the friends one loved were troublesome, weren't they? She told of a meeting of the college English club, where a talk on Henry James was given by an American journalist named Morton Fullerton. He was the brother of Katherine Fullerton, Marianne explained, Miss Fullerton being a young En-

---

* For this and other information drawn on in this section, I am indebted to Charles Molesworth, *Marianne Moore: A Literary Life* (1990).

† See Patricia Willis, "MM on the Literary Life, 1907," in *Marianne Moore Newsletter*, Vol. V., No. 1, Spring 1981. This intriguing article (which Ms. Willis kindly sent me) contains the five-page story "Pym."

glish instructor whom Marianne liked and took tea with.* In Marianne's view, the talk had been pretentious and obscure, but Peggy James was radiant at the meeting. When asked if her father was not present, though, Peggy said, "My dad? . . . No, he isn't here. I wish he were"—and gave what Marianne thought was a strange, somber laugh. Pondering this, Marianne declared abruptly that she did not care in the least for Peggy; only to add that when Peggy was made much of, after the talk, she was no more affected than an adored baby.

So the relationship continued through the fall and the winter following, with Marianne changing her opinion from letter to letter and even paragraph to paragraph. In one passage, she quoted Peggy as saying it was wrong for girls to be "rabid" about one another; elsewhere, she expressed the belief that Peggy really cared only for her parents and her brothers. Through it all we can watch the recognizable Marianne Moore in the making, as she praises Peggy James for her eccentricities and independence, as of qualities shared, and takes pleasure in Peggy's quirky manner of speech. Marianne was particularly delighted with Peggy's casual comment (February 1908): "Yes, I care for Hamlet a great deal." It could almost be a low-keyed line in a later Moore poem.

Meanwhile, the second year went better, in most ways, than its predecessor. Peggy, studying hard, did well in philosophy, though poorly in psychology (that was all right, said William, "one psycholog is enuf in one family"). She wrote essays on Dickens and other literary figures (on a February evening, Peggy and Marianne walked and talked about Dickens and Meredith), and she performed the lead role of John ("Jack") Worthing, alias Ernest, in the Class of 1910 production of Oscar Wilde's *The Importance of Being Earnest*. She was wonderful, Marianne wrote home, even if she didn't really act; she simply gestured and bowed and smiled as she did in actual life.

Even so, by mid-term in the spring of 1908, it had been decided that Peggy would not return to Bryn Mawr for a third year. Her mother wrote a long, apologetic letter to President Thomas, thanking her for the kindness shown to "the child," but saying that she and Mr. James felt it wise that she

---

* Peggy James, Marianne Moore, and the others were all unwittingly, on this occasion, in the vicinity of an unfolding romantic drama. Morton Fullerton had come to America armed with a letter urging him to call upon Edith Wharton. He would shortly visit the Wharton home in Lenox, Massachusetts, and there then began what developed into the single passionate extramarital relationship in Edith Wharton's life. At the same time, one main reason for Fullerton's visit to Bryn Mawr was to propose marriage to Katherine Fullerton. The latter had grown up believing herself to be Morton's sister, but had learned a few years before this meeting that she was in fact his first cousin. She accepted Morton's proposal. See R.W.B. Lewis, *Edith Wharton*, 183–84 and 200–2.

should live at home for the time being. "While she can have her father and her brothers, it seems fitting that she should be sharing their very interesting life. The years will come when she can revert to books." If it was an odd proposition to be voiced by the wife of a Harvard professor, it was a conventional maternal attitude, in its time, as regards the educational welfare of daughters.

Peggy wrote Marianne Moore from Cambridge in June that it was "ghastly to leave that wonderful B.M. and I cannot realize that it is for good or I should be sorer and sadder still." But by the end of the month, she was in England with her mother and father, her Uncle Henry, and her brother Harry; and there was plainly no other place she would have preferred to be. From Lamb House in July, she wrote her brother Billy that her father and uncle had "very funny discussions on every subject under the sun, he chaffing Uncle Henry about his 'mondain' views, and the latter fuming gently and fussing about." It was in this letter that Peggy spoke of G. K. Chesterton living next door to Lamb House, on the other side of the wall. "I have spent many hours on the top of the ladder," she said, "trying to see him but he never comes." If William, too, climbed the ladder to peer over the wall, Peggy never mentioned it.

She wrote Marianne Moore from Sussex as well, to thank her for the handkerchief Marianne had made for her and enclosed in a letter to the ship ("I shall . . . think of you whenever I look at it"), and to recount her London doings. The four Jameses had been to see *Cyrano de Bergerac* with the great comic actor Coquelin in the title part. Peggy found it utterly "melting," but Uncle Henry enraged her by saying coolly, "It's too melodramatic, isn't it?" "I just gritted my teeth and preserved my composure." The London days also included attendance at Bernard Shaw's *Getting Married* (it was good, and *true*, Peggy thought) and a lunch with Roger Fry, the art critic, whom Peggy identified as "the long-haired artist."

Through the two years following, Peggy marked time, helping run the Irving Street home, visiting cousins in New York, and once journeying as far as St. Paul, Minnesota, for a month-long stay with some remote Walsh cousins. In November 1908, she returned to Bryn Mawr to play the male lead in the Class of 1910 play, an antic American comedy of manners; Marianne again remarked that she simply played herself (especially as to casting soulful glances about her) and was most attractive. Seven months later, she came down for another short visit; this time, after a long evening walk with her, Marianne felt that the two of them had less in common than she had remembered.

William and Alice went to England in April 1910 to look after the nerve-racked Henry, and Peggy took sole charge of the household. "You seem to be leading a very humdrum and domestic life," her father wrote from Bad Nauheim, where he had gone because of his own rapidly deteriorating condition. Peggy was at Chocorua in August when her dying father arrived, tended by Mrs. Alice, Harry, and Billy. With the others she took part in the funeral service for William James at Harvard.

It was toward the end of that year that Peggy entered the longest period of depression she had yet known. In July 1911, Henry James, speaking from recent experience, tried to assure her that the "evil episode will pass." The news of Billy's engagement to Alice Runnells in September seems to have brought on a worsening of her condition; their marriage in January did not improve it. It was not until mid-April 1912 that Uncle Henry could rejoice in the "so thoroughly recovered health and happiness" expressed in her letter to him. Throughout this episode, Peggy strikes one as strangely re-enacting the behavior of her Aunt Alice in the late 1870s, as though smitten to immobility by a comparable sense of loss. In Peggy's case: her father had died; her brother Harry had left Irving Street to take lodgings in Boston—"one more step in the disintegration of the family," William had written her glumly at the time; Billy was married and away on a protracted honeymoon; Aleck was nominally at home, but much of the time was off in New Hampshire studying with the painter Abbot Thayer; Uncle Henry was in England. She felt bereft (it seems) both of family and of private purpose.

The letter that spoke to her uncle about recovered health was written from Fort Myers, Florida, where Peggy was a houseguest of Mr. and Mrs. Thomas Alva Edison. Peggy had become friendly, at Bryn Mawr, with their daughter Madeleine, and the famous inventor, on a visit to the college, was much taken with her. (Henry James, sailing to England on the *Mauretania* in August 1911, had discovered that "the great bland simple deaf street-boy-faced Edison" was on board. "He has asked very kindly and sympathetically about Peggy," Henry told Mrs. William. "I thought he had known William a little, and he said " 'No, but I know his charming daughter.' ") In February, the Edisons invited Peggy James and another classmate, Rosalind Romeyn, to go South with Madeleine to the family's Florida home, Seminole Lodge. The Edisons themselves, with the twelve-year-old Theodore (an "enfant terrible," as Peggy remembered him), followed a few days later. Mrs. Edison had spoken of "camping" and the need for rough clothes, but upon arrival at Seminole Lodge, Peggy found "two large low white painted houses with red roofs and wide verandas and French windows." The bedrooms, Peggy went on (to Mrs. Billy), were "pink or blue bowers with their own bathrooms." There was a bevy of delightful English servants and a French chef, and the family and guests dressed for dinner every night.

Peggy's long letters from Fort Myers, to her mother and her sister-in-law, are among the most richly descriptive she ever wrote. "The vegetation and flowers," she said, "almost destroy one's reason . . . Great orange, grapefruit, lemon, citron, lime, mango, guava, coconut, palm trees and bamboo thickets

. . . Exquisite roses, hibiscus, camellia, bougainvillea and a tree of lilac flowers looking like orchids." Later in the month, the company enjoyed a five-day cruise on the Edisons' sixty-foot boat, with its captain and crew of five. They made their way up the Caloosahatchee River, and after the first hour the river narrowed so one could almost touch either bank with an oar. There were "tall palms and live oaks with brilliant orchids growing on them, all tangled like a jungle growth." Peggy caught sight of half a dozen alligators "looking wickedly out of their narrow eyes at us."

They passed the town of La Belle and came onto Lake Okeechobee, where they spent two days fishing (Peggy caught two bass, three and four pounds). They anchored at the mouth of the lake; at night there was a crescent moon, and the sound of "whippoorwills and herons and bitterns and owls calling." The boat then carried the group across the lake and into Hillsboro Canal, for a forty-mile run through the Everglades. Here Peggy could marvel at "the infinite number and variety of the birds. Hawks, eagles, buzzards, limpkins, ducks, herons, curlews, cranes, egrets . . . It was beautiful to see them circling with the great sweep of wings and rising from the reeds quite near by."

Peggy was as eloquent about the human beings at Seminole Lodge as about the natural settings. She thought Madeleine Edison ravishing in her dress with white lace ruffles and her hair down in corkscrew curls. Rosalind she regarded as "a walking platitude," blue-eyed and pretty but given to endless hilarity, "always roaring over something she has said" that was not in the slightest amusing. As to Mr. Edison, Peggy was aware that since the phonograph and the other achievements in the 1870s, he was generally considered the greatest of American inventors. He sat mostly in silence, occupied with his own thoughts; but Peggy said she liked "the feeling of a big brain and intelligence in the house." She took note of his forgetting to shave, removing his shoes in the sitting room, and chewing tobacco. On the first evening, not knowing of that latter habit, Peggy sat between Mr. Edison "and the object of his aim, and was frightened out of a year's growth by suddenly having him fire a long distance spit at it over my head." Mrs. Edison confided to her guest that her husband had become "vain and self-conscious" after all the honors and awards heaped upon him in recent years. She added "that she'd like to be admired and asked about for herself alone and not merely because she was Mrs. Edison."

In the summer of 1914, Peggy came to England with her brother Aleck, and was drawn by Uncle Henry into the very midst of the English social and literary world. Over luncheons, at the Russian ballet, at a house party in Buckinghamshire, she was introduced to Hugh Walpole, Mrs. Belloc Lowndes, Mrs. Humphry Ward, the historian George Macaulay Trevelyan (Mrs. Ward's son-in-law), the drama critic Desmond MacCarthy ("so very Irish"), the civil servant and poetry connoisseur "Eddie" Marsh, the scholarly writer Vernon Lee ("a holy terror"), Rupert Brooke—"a beautiful young poet," Peggy wrote her mother, "charming, simple and unspoiled."

Through all of these affairs, in his niece's words, Uncle Henry never failed to talk brilliantly, even while keeping a careful eye on Peggy's welfare. By the end of July, Peggy had fallen in love with England and had made up her mind to marry an Englishman and settle down in her adopted country. "I have never been so happy as I am here." Of course, she said, she did not "expect this wonderful time to continue," and proposed a modest and quiet life, with a job of some sort and perhaps a little writing.

The wonderful time did not continue, needless to say. Eleven days after the letter just quoted, England and France were at war with Germany, and there had begun what Henry James, in near-collapse at Rye, called "the funeral spell of our murdered civilization." Looking back at that moment seventeen months later, Peggy, again in London, recalled it as a strange mixture of the frightful and the romantic. The awful havoc of war had started, she said, but at the same time her brother Aleck "was engaging himself"—a secret undertaking to which only Peggy was privy. The fiancée was Frederika Paine, the daughter of an American naval officer whom Aleck had met at the museum school in Boston. She, too, was in London in the 1914 summer. Aleck squired her about town, feeling freer to do so, one judges, when Uncle Henry was in Rye since Henry was openly if inexplicably hostile to the young woman.

Henry James was felled by a stroke on December 2, 1915; a second one followed. Alice Howe James went over at once on receiving the cabled news, and Peggy, for whom her uncle had particularly asked, sailed on Christmas Eve. In the Cheyne Walk flat, she sat by the bedside listening to Henry's murmurings. "I hope your father will be in soon," Henry said to her on one occasion—"he is the one person in all Rome I want to see." She took down portions of his fragmented talk: "Individual souls, great of . . . on which great perfections . . ." "The magnificent brain" was "no longer in command," she told Billy, and it wrung her heart. And she went on: "To me he is a poet, as well as all the splendid things that he is, and it seems at times as if I cannot let him go and face the empty savorless world without him." Henry died on February 28, 1916. At the funeral in the little Chelsea church, Peggy sat in the front pew with her mother, John Singer Sargent, and Sargent's sister Emily.

One December afternoon, in a lucid interval, Henry began to reminisce with Alice about his 1905 California visit. Mrs. William and Peggy, as Henry knew, had spent the previous June in San Francisco as guests of Mrs. J. D. Hooker, a wealthy friend of Alice Gibbens from the far-off days of the late

1850s, when Alice and her sister had been taken by their parents to the Santa Clara valley for a three-year effort at ranching. Referring to this, Alice said: "You remember Bruce Porter in San Francisco. He and Peggy have made fast friends on the basis of their love of you." This was no more than the truth. Writing her uncle from San Francisco on June 29 (1915), Peggy had spoken of "your friend and admirer Mr. Bruce Porter," who had designed the Hooker house on Pacific Avenue where daughter and mother were staying. Peggy described herself as liking everything about San Francisco except a certain naïveté in the people. Her uncle's friend was an exception: "Your Mr. Porter is completely sophisticated." The fast friendship led before very long to marriage. Peggy James and Bruce Porter were married at Irving Street in Cambridge on October 6, 1917. The bride was thirty years old. The husband was fifty-two: old enough, one cannot but observe, to be her uncle.

Bruce Porter was an accomplished and engaging presence within a San Francisco artistic community that had been flowering since the mid-1890s. He was a professional muralist and designer of stained-glass windows, and a cultivated amateur in architecture, landscape gardening, and literature. After studying in Paris, London, and Venice in his twenties, he returned to San Francisco to design the leaded windows of the Swedenborgian church in the city (he himself was a Swedenborgian and would persuade Peggy to explore that creed a little). He was responsible for the windows in the San Diego Children's Home. It was Bruce Porter who, in 1897, executed the granite plinth for the Robert Louis Stevenson memorial in San Francisco's Portsmouth Square: this being the basis for the cordial meeting in April 1905 between Porter and Henry James, when, the novelist said, Porter showed him such great kindness.

Porter was a founding member of the loose assembly of artists and writers, the Bay Area Bohemians, who called themselves *les jeunes* and who established the magazine *The Lark*, which published insouciant poems, sketches, and drawings for the two years of its life, 1895–97. It was in *The Lark* that Gelett Burgess, the co-editor with Porter, printed his little poem:

> *I never saw a purple cow,*
> *I never hope to see one.*
> *But I can tell you, anyhow,*
> *I'd rather see than be one.*

The poem quickly became the most popular bit of verse in America.

With twenty-four others in the Association of American Painters and Sculptors, Porter was an active sponsor of the Armory Show in New York in 1913, commonly regarded as the most influential exhibition of modern art ever held in the country. For all his achievement and local renown, Porter was an exceedingly personable human being: slender, with a range of expression, easy-tempered, voluble (his own word for himself), a warm sense of humor, and generosity of spirit.

There seems no doubt that, in an old-fashioned phrase, it was a marriage of love (her wedding day, Peggy said on its first anniversary, was "the happiest for me that ever was"), yet Peggy James Porter had barely settled into her San Francisco home before she was brought down by a paralyzing depression. Family legend or fable declares that Bruce Porter was ready at need. He escorted his bride down to Santa Clara and the foot of Mount Hamilton, and then coaxed and prodded her into climbing the 4,200-foot slope; he exhilarated and exhausted her, showed her the wonders of the landscape, and so put an end once and for all to what her father had described as her "bad state of spirits." The family legend pronounces this a California cure for a New England psychological illness.

A son, Robert Bruce, was born to Peggy and Bruce Porter in 1918; and in 1921, a daughter, Catharine, soon to be renamed Jimsie. A 1937 Bryn Mawr questionnaire asked the question: "Do you administer the household?" To this, Peggy Porter, ex-1910, replied "Yes." It then asked: "Is it your chief occupation?" and Peggy wrote down an emphasized "No." In fact, though hers was a busy and varied life through the later decades, there seems to have been no single central continuing activity. She was the best of citizens in San Francisco, working with the civil rights group and helping to organize a visit from Roger Baldwin in the 1940s; supporting the Community Chest operations and heading up the Ladies' Protection and Relief; giving her time, after 1939, to British War Relief. She was a staunch Democrat and reported with feigned disbelief in 1948 that a friend had voted for Dewey. On the social side, there was no end of teas and supper parties: this darkly handsome, deep-voiced, thoughtfully spoken woman was much in demand. Nor was there any discernible letup in her appearances at concerts and the theater and literary readings (she was in the audience for W.E.B. Du Bois in 1945).

Family, both Porters and Jameses, was perhaps her steadiest concern. She read the novels of her Uncle Henry aloud to her patient husband, devoting one entire winter to *The Golden Bowl*. She wrote decisively to Billy, in 1949, about the disposition of her mother's letters: they should be "placed beside Dad's and H.J.'s in Houghton Library." Her mother was their mainstay, and a "part of their story," as well as "a person of character and accomplishment" in her own right. (Most, though not all, of Alice Howe James's letters are now in Houghton.) She yearned to be in closer touch with her Eastern relatives; she treasured her only tour of them in 1933, and Billy's visit with her and Bruce Porter in 1943. She regarded her brother Harry as "the head of my clan," gratefully accepted his help in preparing her tax returns (and money, secured from the Syracuse property, to pay the amount due), and took his side in a falling-out with Aleck. During the Second World War, she lived for news of Aleck's three sons, and high points were the arrival in the San Francisco harbor of vessels carrying one or the other of them.

Peggy Porter fell gravely ill in the fall of 1950. Billy went out at once, to find his sister already "beyond communication." She died on December 10.

Robert Bruce Porter (Robin) interrupted his undergraduate career at Berkeley in 1943 to marry Paula Rossi, of a well-to-do San Francisco family; his mother sighed a little over the extreme youth of the couple. They had two children, Arnold and Frances; the family eventually moved to San Antonio. Jimsie Porter made a pass at a secretarial career in New York in the early 1940s, though she mostly gave herself up to moviegoing and the theater. By late 1944, she was in Los Angeles working as a welder in the wartime industry of Marinship; and left this employment to marry the stepson of her working mate Kaye Short (later with the Office of War Information and a target of right-wing allegations).

The marriage with Bill (William Hathaway) Short produced two children, Douglas and Margaret, before the parents agreed peacefully to a divorce. Billy James, after several days with Jimsie and her two "charming gentle children," in the ranch house at Tiburon, across the bay from San Francisco, described her to Cummings as "a trump" who "understands everything." This is exactly the verdict of the many friends who contributed to a collection of memoirs about Jimsie after her death in April 1990. A quick and original sense of humor was mentioned by almost everybody, a talent for aphoristic wit and political satire, a ready ring of laughter. More than one friend observed that Jimsie Short was vaguely uneasy about her Jamesian background; it aroused the wrong sort of expectations, she said, and she sometimes adopted a quite misleading anti-intellectual pose. But the editor of the collection, Jimsie's old friend Nan Sparrow, thought it appropriate to close with the farewell letter written by Jimsie's grandfather William James, to *his* father Henry James, Sr., in 1882, as a model message to a parent who is gone.

4

The youngest child of William and Alice James was named Francis Tweedy upon his birth in December 1890, his father combining for him the first name of a colleague and the surname of a kin. William addressed the boy as Tweedy, his mother as Francis: until it became evident that the boy himself squirmed under both names. For an indeterminate time he was called John in the family household. Then William, following Henry's suggestion, renamed the seven-year-old Alexander Robertson, in honor of his, William's, maternal grandfather, the Scotsman who came to America in 1850 and flourished as a merchant in New York City. William thereafter employed the name Aleck; Mrs. William and sister Peggy kept up Francis for another three years. After he passed his majority, Aleck dropped the middle name altogether.

The effect of these changes can only be conjectured. But the record shows Aleck alternating between openhearted boisterousness and taciturnity, festive sociability and sullen withdrawal, during his first two decades; and the theme of his life, certainly of his life as a painter, was that of identity, the search for the real self and the expression of that self. There were, meanwhile, other factors in the shaping and the troubling of his personality. He was an almost hopelessly slow learner at school, and it was not realized until long afterward that he suffered from dyslexia, a severe reading disability that was not even identified—that is, as a visual rather than a mental incapacity—until the mid-1920s, and the scope of it not fully recognized—and a term for it agreed upon—until the 1960s. William may be forgiven for not understanding the nature of Aleck's problem, but his shortness of temper with the boy's wretched school performance only added to Aleck's acknowledged feelings of shame and embarrassment.

When William and Alice went to Europe in 1899 for what turned out to be two years, they left Aleck behind, to be taken care of by his grandmother Gibbens in Cambridge in the winter, and his Aunt Mary and Uncle Mack Salter in Chocorua in the summer. It was probably a sensible arrangement under the circumstances, given William's bad state of health and Alice's need to devote herself to him entirely. But the long experience left its scar. Aleck, just arriving at his tenth birthday, felt that he had been abandoned; or so he would think, and say to his own children, looking back.

Before his school days were over, Aleck had managed to fail the entrance examinations for Harvard five times. This was the less discouraging, however, since from the time of his sixteenth summer Aleck's gathering intention had been to skip college and take up the study and practice of painting. In the summer of 1907, Aleck spent some days in Dublin, New Hampshire, at the home of Abbot Henderson Thayer, the well-known but semi-recluse painter who had come there from New York to live and work a few years earlier. Aleck was a friend of the painter's son Gerald; it was a fine, stirring visit that included a good deal of commotion with the local police, and Aleck came back from it, his father said (writing to Billy), "happier and more exultant than I've ever seen him." It was a great step in the boy's life, William felt: "Aleck . . . is aflame with plans for being an artist."

Abbot Thayer had achieved a standing as a painter of ethereal madonnas, energetic virgins, and girls with angel's wings, a body of work that would be generally dismissed as sentimental. But even skeptical art historians have praised the strong sculptural quality of some of his female figures; and his

The Later Jameses

New Hampshire landscapes could be exquisite: as an example, *Monadnock* of 1911, painted from his own garden, all shimmering pale blues and whites and shadows, and tall spare trees thrusting against the mountains.

Aleck worked under Thayer's direction intermittently for half a dozen years. The apprenticeship began in effect after the death of William. A number of months before that, in December 1909, when William seemed bent on pressing Aleck to make yet one more try for Harvard, Thayer wrote to intervene: "To me you are doing for Aleck the same as if one were to lash the magnetic needle . . . to an approved northerly direction." Would not Professor James "let Aleck spend a few months here now (to our great joy for we love him), testing his art faculty?" The testing began in the late summer of 1910, and that fall Aleck followed his brother Billy to the Boston Museum school and put himself under the guidance of Frank Benson and Edmund Tarbell.

It was at the museum school in 1912 that Aleck met Frederika Paine, a seventeen-year-old girl of singular loveliness, the daughter of a naval officer stationed at Newport, Rhode Island. The courtship that ensued went on for four years—with a secret engagement arrived at, as we have seen, during the tumultuous English summer of 1914—before a marriage was grudgingly consented to by Aleck's mother. Aleck had usually been on easier and more intimate terms with his mother than with his father; typically, coming back to the Irving Street house after an outing, Aleck would enter in a rush, letting the door slam behind him, and yell out "Ma-a?" before leaping upstairs to pour out his day's doings for her indulgent listening. But for reasons undisclosed, Mrs. Alice took a dislike to Frederika Paine. It may have been due to the girl's youth; but it can be observed that a chilling severity crept into Alice James's being following her husband's death (something not uncommon with the widows of men of authority and distinction) and expressed itself now and again. The marriage took place in 1916. The next year, Aleck and Frederika moved to Santa Barbara, California, for an unsuccessful attempt to live and make do in new surroundings. Their first child, Alexander Robertson, Jr., was born there in 1918. Aleck put in a year teaching at the Corcoran Art School in Washington, D.C., where Edmund Tarbell was now in charge. In 1921, the Jameses were in Dublin, New Hampshire; with one interruption, it would be their permanent location. A second son, Daniel, was born in Dublin in 1921; a third son, Michael, in 1923.

Alexander James was a portrait painter first and last; and the story of his artistic career is the development from the relatively straightforward and academic portraits through the 1920s—of his wife, Frederika, of his remembered father, of the art curator Langdon Warner—to the far more probing and revealing portrayals of the 1930s and 1940s. The turn came, apparently, during

627]

a year in France, 1929–30, and particularly several months in the French fishing village of Saint-Jean-de-Luz in the Pyrenees (now a major tourist attraction). The peasants on his walks—big and rangy, with high cheekbones and prominent noses, pinched eyebrows, and dark, deep-seeing eyes—seemed to Aleck exactly the kind of richly human subject he had been half-consciously looking for. And yet, he wrote Billy, the difference may have been in himself even more than in the people he was living among and studying. He made the point more forcefully a few years later, again writing to Billy (an unfailing source of encouragement), when he distinguished between artists who did work of "incredible ability" which left the spectator at once admiring and cold, and others, like himself, "who suffer and are appalled at what they see or realise beneath the surface." He went on: "These men suffer because they become so easily almost the thing itself—. And these fellows when they paint are aiming at an expression of this realisation which is therefore *an expression of themselves.*"

No better statement of intention and belief could be asked for. In 1930, Aleck brought the family back to New Hampshire and the Dublin home; but he set himself up in a barn in the village of Richmond, twenty-five miles to the southwest. There, as would be said of him by a perceptive reporter, "he farmed and painted and reflected and worked out a manner of painting." The family—the oldest boy, Sandy, was thirteen in 1931; the youngest, Mickey, was eight—was reunited on weekends and during vacations. Aleck continued to do portraits of Frederika and the children, as well as of his brother Harry and his fellow artist, Mrs. Dean Acheson. But he was making his enduring mark with sketches of local characters, each of whom to a later viewer might be imagined as taking part in a cluster of small-town stories, like *Winesburg, Ohio*; or better, and closer in every way, in Thornton Wilder's play of 1938, *Our Town*, which unfolds in the village of Grover's Corner, New Hampshire.

Aleck James's subject-characters over the last sixteen years of his life included the local carpenter, the tax collector, a group of selectmen, a man who lived alone with six cats (*A Solitary*), Sammy, the young black who worked around the house, an old hunter, a frame maker caught in the act of tuning his violin for a square dance (*Choose Your Partners*), a group of neighbors drinking together, a rugged-faced farmer hunched over a typewriter working out the town's accounts (*Embattled Farmer* of 1939, one of the artist's most powerful and communicative works), and Luther Smith, the town cobbler and socialistic philosopher who inhabited a desolate one-room cabin. About the latter, Thornton Wilder wrote that it "grows more searching, beautiful and true the more one looks at it." Wilder insisted on the "deep truth" of the picture, but added: "How sovereignly it avoids the thing which the painter's father warned his students against: the merely abject truth."

Aleck James's unrelaxing commitment to his work—what Wilder called his *ostinato rigore*—was rewarded by two exhibitions in the Walker Galleries in New York City, in January 1937 and January 1941; each won gratifying reviews but few sales. About the earlier show, Rockwell Kent, a reasonably reliable witness, wrote that one saw "not merely pictures painted in oils on canvas, but human personalities recreated and intensified." The remark suggested that Aleck James had fulfilled his ambition. His preoccupation as a painter, he told a female client, was with the sitter's "personality and character"; he aimed at an *"inner* portrait," and admitted that not every woman would care to sit for one. "You've taken my clothes off," one sitter told him in dismay and admiration in 1941. Not long after that, his New York agent, commenting on Aleck's portrait of a young New York society girl, said: "You've done a remarkable thing from the point of view of painting and psychology—but a hopeless one from the point of view of a successful commission." Aleck had shown prophetically what the girl would be like in fifteen years, and what mother would welcome that?

Aleck was stricken with a heart attack in September 1943. He recovered sufficiently to return to work, and drove himself as never before. His last years were especially productive and successful, and included such peak achievements as *Choose Your Partners* and a portrait of novelist and neighbor John P. Marquand. He had just moved into a new studio, something he had created out of a deserted farmhouse in Richmond, when he died in February 1946. A memorial exhibition of his work was held in Manchester, New Hampshire, in the summer of 1947, in the Boston Museum of Fine Arts later that year, and in the Corcoran Gallery in Washington through the winter of 1948. The reporter for *The Christian Science Monitor*, Dorothy Adlow, reviewing the show, risked the opinion that Alexander James "came closest to being a New England Eakins." The claim was not wholly exaggerated. Thomas Eakins, who died the year Aleck James and Frederika Paine were married, was himself essentially a realist who painted portraits of his family, friends, and neighbors, and the natural scenery around him in Philadelphia and its suburbs; and though his work displayed decidedly more substance, more well-staged scenes, more scope and finish, than that of Alexander James, Eakins shared with James the fiction writer's sense of the subtle ways in which character declared itself and could be rendered.

The review wound up: "He was not a colorist, though he used his pigments well, he was not abstract, nor surrealistic, nor expressionistic. His was not an art of labels, but an art allied with human experience." His uncle Henry James, addressing a summer school on "the novel" in Deerfield, Massachusetts, in 1889, laid it down that a novel must always be written from a particular point of view; but, and more important: "Any point of view is interesting that is a

629]

direct impression of life." Alexander James might have applied that language to the art of painting and, giving equal emphasis to the two words in the definition, would have energetically concurred.

After attending the funeral in Dublin, Harry James wrote his brother Billy a long letter reminiscing about Aleck's life and saying in a musing tone that "temperamentally, Aleck was more like Dad than any of us." He seems to have meant by this that Aleck, too, combined an intuitive human sympathy with the quality of tact; and not less that Aleck, like his father, kept at his chosen task to the end, never letting up despite grievous physical suffering.

It was a generous judgment, considering the recurring estrangement between the brothers. From the time of Aleck's return from France to New Hampshire, Harry James had been a chief source of financial support; and this, perhaps inevitably, led to friction and misunderstanding. It could be said, oversimply, that Harry James *made* money, Billy married money, and Aleck's family struggled to live on his meager artistic earnings. From time to time, Harry paid the school bills of Aleck's children (in 1934, for example, Harry forwarded $1,000 for Sandy James's tuition, accepting which Aleck did not deny that he would welcome another comparable contribution). Some of the money was a fraternal gift, some of it came from Harry's final sales of the dwindling James family property in Syracuse. In either case, Harry let it be known that the only return he looked for was superior academic performance by Aleck's boys. A typical bad moment came in 1940, when Mickey James, his uncle's particular beneficiary at the time, compiled a deplorable series of grades at the Pomfret School. The seventeen-year-old Mickey had, in fact, inherited his father's dyslexia; and though, as events proved, he had a first-class brain, something persistently interfered with his accurate reading of words on a page or a blackboard. Harry, uncomprehending, reviewed the record and raised a chiding and protesting voice. Among the flurry of letters that followed was one from Aleck to the headmaster of the Connecticut school:

> What Henry James does not know, due to some regrettable dead spot in his imagination, is that his financial backing of Mickey's schooling has not been simply and blessedly just that. His self-appointment to the post of the one qualified and final judge in every question relating to the boy has imposed the unhappiest weight on all concerned.

Peggy James Porter, receiving news of such matters in San Francisco, sided entirely with her brother Harry. She had no sympathy with the financial difficulties of Aleck and Frederika, as described in a letter from Freddie, she wrote her daughter in April 1945; they had only to appeal once again to Harry for the needed money and he would supply it as he always had. Henry, his

[630

sister said, was not to be taken lightly in his financial capacity, but he was a tower of strength. When, in July 1945, Peggy learned that Harry and Dorothea were told by Freddie not to come to Dublin for a visit as planned, that Aleck was too busy to see them, she was horrified. "If it killed one, one would welcome a brother."

The three boys survived what Aleck called their "school anxiety," to confront the larger dangers of the world war. Daniel was in the Merchant Marine, on board a Matson Line ship, on December 7, 1941; two days later his ship was sunk, and Danny spent ten days on a raft in the open sea before being picked up. Aleck wrote Harry about the fearful ordeal undergone by the family back home during the stretch of time, and Harry, answering, virtually echoed his father's comment after the 1906 earthquake: "I'm not sure that the vicarious sharing in experiences like Danny's may not be in some ways harder than direct experience." Danny was given leave before he returned to duty; meeting him in Cambridge, Uncle Billy found him "humorous, cheerful, affectionate, interested," and prepared to meet anything.

After the war, Danny studied political science at Colorado College, and then entered the field of social work in Boulder: an astute and vigorous concern for the welfare of others was, by all the testimony, his most salient quality. In 1946, he married Edith Felix; their son Christopher is a well-regarded photographer who has taught in the Harvard Art Department. Danny had two children by a second marriage to Jeanne Bishop. He died of heart disease in 1955, at the age of thirty-three.

Sandy James, Alexander Junior, like his brother Daniel, saw strenuous action in the Pacific during the Second World War. He enlisted in the Marines and took part in the series of attacks on the heavily defended islands, culminating in the violent struggle for Iwo Jima in early 1945. He was commissioned second lieutenant just before that invasion, and received the Purple Heart after an incident that cracked his eardrums. In March of that year, he wrote his Uncle Bruce and Aunt Peggy casually that everything had quieted down on Iwo Jima and that it was now "a safe place for Americans." But he advised them never to come "to this least appealing of Pacific Islands"; it had no vegetation of any kind.

After the war, Sandy studied architecture at Harvard on the G.I. Bill, then grew disaffected with a department dominated by the theories and practice of Walter Gropius and transferred to Yale. His first employment was as a draftsman in a San Francisco architect's office—on the waterfront, Peggy told the family, high up by the end of the Bay Bridge. He was now married (in late 1946) to Rosemary Puddington, a young Nevada-born woman. Their first child,

born in San Francisco, was given the name Cartney, in honor of the Bailieborough land agent whom William of Albany had known as a boy. Five more
children were born to Alexander and Rosemary James over the next decades;
they carry such familiar clan names as Susan, Frederika, Rosemary, Henry,
and Robertson (the latter two are twins).

In the 1950s, Sandy James brought the family back to Dublin and pursued
his architectural profession there for twenty years. He dealt exclusively with
the designing or remodeling of private homes in the state of New Hampshire,
and former clients report that he did stunning work. Then, at a certain moment,
Sandy retired to County Cork in the south of Ireland; he now lives there in a
shapely rural home overlooking the sea and the fishing village of Glendore.
Sandy James is the official custodian of the James family archives, as many a
scholar has gratefully acknowledged.

In a letter of late March 1945 (to her daughter, and enclosing Sandy's
letter from Iwo Jima), Peggy Porter described a visit from Mickey James, who
had turned up unexpectedly at the Pacific Avenue home the evening before.
His ship had put in for repairs that afternoon. "He has a becoming black
moustache," Peggy noted; and she thought him very good-looking. They began
at once on family talk, and only later did Mickey tell of some of his experiences
with the Navy. He had enlisted as a seaman and had made his way up to petty
officer first class; he had toured the Pacific for nearly four years from New
Hebrides to Tokyo Bay, his job being that of a weatherman or, in the naval
language, aerographer. "He came home this time," Peggy reported, "because
their ship, which is an airplane carrier, was badly mauled in the typhoon which
wrecked some of the older vessels entirely. As it was, they lost every single
plane and had two decks on fire."

After being discharged, Mickey James studied art history on the G.I. Bill,
giving up graduate school in 1949 to accept an appointment with the Byzantine
Institute. The job took him to Istanbul and the church of Hagia Sophia, where
he worked with a team restoring the ancient mosaics. Returned to America
and Dublin, New Hampshire, he made a try at painting. But soon, in his own
phrase, he "discovered junk": he discovered the sculptural uses to which junk—
rusty pitchforks, old nails, hinges—could be put. Beginning in the spring of
1951, successive exhibitions were mounted, from New York City to Des
Moines, Iowa. It was strikingly original and engaging work, and rated a profusely illustrated review in *Life* magazine. What the exhibition made apparent
was the strong religious bent of Michael James's imagination, religious in a
more direct and articulated way than any member of the family since the elder
Henry James.

Mickey continued with his sculpture as the years passed, though it did not in his opinion—others, kinfolk and outsiders, do not agree—grow as it should have done. He shifted course to novel-writing, six novels in all, no one of which he felt fit for publishing. Today, Mickey James lives in the Back Bay area of Boston and cultivates a farm in Massachusetts. In his later sixties, he is the member of the James clan most in touch with all the others, most well-disposed, most observant and tolerant; and, all things considered, the most Irish.

5

Immeasurably less is known about the descendants of Wilky James than about those of his older or his younger brother. When Wilky died in Milwaukee in 1883, he left a widow, Caroline Cary James, and two young children. Carrie outlived her husband by almost fifty years, and outlived the children as well, dying in a nursing home, likewise in Milwaukee, in 1931 in her eighty-seventh year. She was by this time an extremely wealthy woman, having inherited estates, one after the other, from her three unmarried Cary brothers. The younger child, Alice, was thirty-five when, in 1910, she married David Alexander Edgar, originally from Hamilton, Ontario, who migrated to Milwaukee and there established an eventually flourishing investment firm. There was something touchingly incomplete, unrealized, about Alice Edgar, so her Uncle Henry felt when he first met her in London in 1913, though he thought her appealing as well; her Aunt Alice, Mrs. William, agreed on both counts. Alice Edgar died of heart disease in 1923. There were no children.

Her older brother, Joseph Cary, known by his second name, had a conventionally successful career in Milwaukee, a career aided both by the esteem and affection in which his father, the late Captain James, was held in the city, and by his marriage in 1907 to Antoinette Pierpont, who was described in the county memoirs as coming from an old and prominent Milwaukee (and, it could have added, American) family. Cary directed a notably profitable sand-and-cement business, and operated as a real-estate broker. Cary and Antoinette appear to have been in the forefront of the younger Milwaukee social set. Their only child, Garth Pierpont, was born in 1909. Cary James died at the age of fifty in 1925.

The life of Garth James, for the chronicler, remains blurred in outline. A former Milwaukee schoolmate remembers him as pleasant but unpredictable. He served in World War II, evidently; then moved to St. Thomas in the Virgin Islands, where he may have held some sort of official, perhaps consular, position for a while. He married in St. Thomas and became the father of three children; and died there around 1970.

What Garth James seems to have chiefly accomplished was to squander the enormous fortune he inherited from his grandmother Carrie James and his parents. It is reckoned by some to have amounted at one time to a million dollars a year; Garth was certainly the wealthiest member of the family since the death of William of Albany. Lavish and innumerable island parties took care of much of the inheritance; another large portion came into the hands of his wife, by way of alimony, after the divorce.

His son, David, served with the U.S. Marines in the Vietnam War, thereby representing the fourth generation of Jameses in an American military enterprise. No James in any generation, not even Wilky at Fort Wagner, underwent a more harrowing experience than David James. He was gravely wounded, taken prisoner by the North Vietnamese, held by them for two years, and persistently and savagely maltreated. At a later date, David studied architecture at the University of Arizona, and started practice in Walnut Creek, California, near Oakland. He was married by now, with one son; the family was encountered on occasion (this was in the early 1980s) by Henry James Vaux, David's first cousin twice removed, and a professor of forestry at Berkeley.

There followed a few years in Massachusetts, after which David moved back to St. Thomas, where he now resides. His two sisters, Leslie and Antoinette, are also thought to be island residents. David James, not improperly, is the custodian of many of his great-grandfather Wilky's letters and documents.

6

Unlike Wilky, Bob James, who died in 1910, lived to see his children fully grown and married, and himself a grandfather. Mary Holton James, his widow, lived another twelve years; she collapsed in a Boston trolley car one day in November 1922 and died instantly. (Her last notebook entry recorded the death two months before of her sister-in-law Alice Howe James.) The older child of Mary and Bob, Edward Holton James, "Ned" in his younger years, offers the spectacle of the most wayward career in the family story, yet one that is unmistakably if sometimes antically Jamesian.

Ned James graduated from Harvard in 1896, worked successively on two Milwaukee papers (absorbing the potent socialistic atmosphere of one of them), and in December 1899 married Louisa Cushing, the daughter of Robert Maynard and Olivia Cushing, socially visible and well-to-do Bostonians. Heading West, the couple paused in Fargo, North Dakota, before moving on to Seattle and a hilltop home with a view of Puget Sound and, far off to the south, Mount Rainier. Here Edward set himself up in the practice of law, and here Louisa presented him with three daughters in five years: Olivia in 1900, Mary in 1902, and Louisa in 1905.

Edward became famous in the Seattle community as the result of a now legendary legal foray, about which one cannot do better than to quote a recent narration of it by Henry James Vaux, Edward's nephew (the son of his sister Mary). It was in Seattle, Professor Vaux writes, that Edward James

> undertook the first of the series of Quixotic enterprises that would occupy most of his life. Seattle was a boom town, the principal continental base for the Alaska Gold Rush. As such it had a lively and extensive red light district. Edward perceived this as gross violation of law and undertook to close down all the houses of prostitution in town. For two weeks he was eminently successful—so much so that he had to have a personal bodyguard whenever he went out, a function performed by a friend, one White, who was the brother of Stanford White.

In January 1907, Ned was summoned from Seattle to London by his wife, who had been visiting with her father when the latter met his end. Robert Cushing was struck by a hansom cab in a London street and thrown face downward onto the ground, where the grit and grime entering a gash in his face brought on blood poisoning. It was a "dismal death," as Henry James remarked; but Louisa's sister Olivia was with her, and Henry, coming up from Rye, found them both calm and controlled. He also disclosed (to nephew Billy) that Cushing had left Louisa $12,000 a year; on which, he said, Ned and his wife could "easily float." Ned came down to Lamb House later in the month; and after two days and nights of him, Henry pronounced Edward "as charmless as he is harmless." To judge from a picture of the two of them in the garden at Lamb House (see following p. 554), Edward was simply intimidated— perhaps reduced to stiff-backed silence—by his imposing uncle.

Another of Edward's crusading activities at a later date struck Henry James as anything but harmless. After a season in London, Edward escorted the family to France and a house in St.-Germain-en-Laye, outside of Paris. From this base, he began publishing an English-language monthly called *The Liberator*, identified by its editor as "a journal devoted to the international republic." In the course of his readings and conversations, Ned came upon the story, going back a good many years, of the alleged morganatic marriage of the then Prince of Wales, the future King George V. As a confirmed socialist, Ned was adamantly opposed to the institution of monarchy, and hence could not rest until he could lay the newly discovered "facts" before the British public. Copies of *The Liberator* carrying the story were circulated in England (Professor Vaux is again our source); the English distributor was clapped into prison for libeling royalty, and Edward Holton James was informed that he, too, would be jailed if he ever again set foot in England. His uncle took such offense at the episode that in a codicil to his will he withdrew the small gift he had intended for Edward.

During these same Paris years, Edward began a tangled line of inquiry into the historical figure of Jesus, an inquiry which would have bored or baffled his uncle, but located him clearly in the Jamesian line from the elder Henry. In 1934, he published a review of his researches over a quarter of a century, a book titled *Jesus for Jews* (*A History*), printed by his own press in his Concord, Massachusetts, home. Jesus emerges from the rambling but sporadically thought-provoking discussion as a figure existing and acting quite apart from institutions and theologizing; in effect, the supreme religious socialist: the exemplar for all time of the persona Henry James, Sr., aspired to. We hear a garbled echo of Henry Senior when Edward speaks of "mak[ing] ourselves one with the Eternal Greatness"; and of the "welding [of] all peoples into one people" as the way to that union, or indeed as itself the incarnation of the union.

When war broke out in Europe in 1914, Edward happened to be in Berlin, attending an international gathering of socialists. A number of the delegates were rounded up by the German authorities, among them Rosa Luxemburg, "*rote Rosa*," the Polish-born activist. Herr James was escorted across the border into Holland and told that he would be imprisoned for the duration of the war if he came back. Edward, not one to permit any government to say what he could or could not do, promptly crossed back into Germany, was instantly arrested, and placed in the Moabit Prison, where he remained until the Armistice in 1918. "Interned in Germany throughout the World War as a political prisoner": this was Edward's laconic summary of the affair for *Who's Who* in 1937.

It was not long before Edward James found another cause to ally himself with. This was the case of Nicola Sacco and Bartolomeo Vanzetti, the two Italian immigrants who were arrested in May 1920 on the charge of murdering a paymaster in Bridgewater County, Massachusetts. Sacco and Vanzetti were convicted of murder in 1921, and it was then that a legion of protesters went into action to have the verdict set aside on demonstrable grounds of bias by the presiding judge. Motions for retrial were made and rejected over a six-year period; the pair were executed on August 27, 1927.

Edward James was a vociferous supporter of Sacco and Vanzetti, tirelessly seeking evidence of what he was convinced was their innocence. With others, he made stormy speeches on the Boston Common denouncing the Massachusetts judiciary and was jailed for disturbing the peace, his front teeth being knocked out by the cop who arrested him. He took Sacco's son Angelo into his Concord home for a lengthy and protective stay. But Edward was also among the relatively few who continued to work for the exoneration of Sacco and Vanzetti even after their execution. Hearing that an associate of theirs, one who might have crucial information, had gone back to Italy and been locked up by Mussolini as a dangerous radical, Edward betook himself to Italy to look for the witness. James family memory deposes that Edward traveled without a passport, declaring that he refused to make the oath of allegiance—necessary for procuring a U.S. passport—to a government responsible for so disgraceful a miscarriage of justice. How he managed to depart without a passport is not established, but in Italy he was welcomed as an American champion of two native sons, though it was stipulated that, on visiting any new town, he should spend the first night in prison. Mussolini gave Signor James permission to visit the witness in question, who was at last discovered in a dungeon in the Italian Alps. The adventure seems to have ended inconclusively.

In the early 1930s, Edward Holton James, incessant traveler that he was, made a long tour of India, the result of which was *I'll Tell Everything: The Brown Man's Burden*. (In addition to *Jesus for Jews*, Edward's other writings include *The Trial Before Pilate*, essentially a gloss on the sources, published in a limited edition in 1909, and *Crossroads in Europe* in 1929.) It is a fast-moving piece of work, journalistic in manner and of some abiding interest. Edward James here directs his wrath against England, not for their treatment of the Irish, as his Aunt Alice had done, but for their treatment of the Indians. The British monarchy and aristocracy come in for severe and repeated indictment, and the sacred shrines of India are warmly defended against British allegations that their walls portray nothing but unbridled sexuality. In a brief interview with Gandhi, Edward elicits the Mahatma's praise of Thoreau and Emerson, and especially of Thoreau's essay on civil disobedience; and after criticizing Gandhi for vanity, slyness, and inconsistency, Edward declares it impossible not to love the man.

It is in this text that Edward James's politico-religious sentiments get their best formulation. The political problems of India, he says, cannot be separated from the religious, and the Indian people would not achieve self-government "without some kind of general religious unity and purpose." Shifting his sight then to biblical Capernaum, James asserts that from the crucifixion of Christ there came "the greatest movement of civil disobedience which the world had ever known." Following the example of Jesus, Edward continues, hundreds and then thousands "refused to cooperate with Caesar" and were put to death. Non-coöperation "is a principle which history has made sacred," and the potential glory of India lay in its rediscovery by Gandhi and those he inspired. "The authority of the cross," he concludes, meaning by "the cross" the symbol and rallying point for religiously grounded civil disobedience, ". . . is with and for the Indians today, if they will take it . . . No nation, no religion, no continent has any patent to it."

Some of his later actions reflect an individual of misdirected or simply undirected energies. He flirted with a Fascist coterie in New England (Edward loathed and despised Hitler, but like no few others felt friendly toward Mussolini); and he was again sent to jail in the 1940s for making speeches in Boston accusing Franklin Roosevelt of treason. Eccentric to the end, he used to walk the streets of Concord, in his last years, leading a pet squirrel on a leash. He built a separate home for himself in a corner of the Concord property; it had a number of low-ceilinged rooms and straddled a little brook which Edward diverted so that it ran through the basement over a waterfall. He played the violin atrociously, in the memory of his son-in-law Alexander Calder, but played it unceasingly, to the accompaniment of a gramophone record controlled by a foot brake. For all that, he was a person of great warmth and sweetness, so his cousins recall, and a gracious host. Edward Holton James was widowed in 1948, and died in Concord in 1954.

The three daughters of Edward and Louisa James moved variously into new areas of American art and letters. Olivia, the oldest, married Chanler Armstrong Chapman, the only child of the writer John Jay Chapman and Elizabeth Chanler. The older Chapman was a brilliant literary essayist (on Emerson and others) as well as an intense individual; he had been a student at Harvard of Olivia's great-uncle William James and, in his collection *Memories and Milestones* of 1915, left one of the most telling portraits of his teacher ever written. Elizabeth Chanler came from a modestly distinguished old New York family, and was the sister of Winthrop Chanler, sportsman and socialite. Chanler Chapman inherited both a maternal and a paternal country place in Barrytown, New York, on the Hudson River, both of them locally famous; he and Olivia lived in one, after John Jay's death in 1933, while the other was rented. Chapman was for many years editor and publisher of the Barrytown *Explorer*. The marriage with Olivia, however, did not last beyond the 1930s.

Mary James, a painter of talent and a connoisseur of the modernistically beautiful, was a woman of poise and presence undeterred by a nearly total deafness resulting from a childhood accident. In the mid-1930s, she married William Slater Brown, author (at least one novel), critic, and wit: Bill Brown, among his friends; Slater Brown on the title page and in literary reference. He was the original of the character B., the author's friend and the cause of all his woe in E. E. Cummings's *The Enormous Room* of 1922. In his home in Patterson, New York, and with his first wife, Sue Jenkins, Slater Brown had been an advisor and host of Hart Crane; with Mary James Brown in their Massachusetts home, he has been a literary companion for many decades of Kenneth Burke, Malcolm Cowley, and other New York and Eastern writers.

Louisa James ventured on a career in the theater in her early twenties, joining Walter Hampden's stock company and playing ingenue roles in several productions. In the spring of 1929, her father took her with him to Europe to introduce her to a different cultural environment. In June they sailed back to

The Later Jameses

New York on the *De Grasse*, and on the first day out they encountered the thirty-three-year-old sculptor Alexander Calder. The latter tells us in his memoirs that he was walking the deck when he observed "an elderly man and a young lady."

> Upon coming abreast of them the next time around, I said "Good evening!" And the man said to his daughter, "There is one of them already!"
> It was Edward Holton James, my future father-in-law.
> She was Louisa.
> Her father had just taken her to Europe to mix with the young intellectual elite. All she met were concierges, doormen, cab drivers—and finally me.

Calder was the grandson of Alexander Milne Calder, who had overseen the execution of several hundred sculpted figures (including that of William Penn) for the Philadelphia City Hall in the late nineteenth century, and the son of Alexander Stirling Calder, perhaps best known for his two huge groups—of "nations," east and west—for the Panama–Pacific Exposition in San Francisco in 1915. The third Alexander Calder, Sandy, had by 1929 earned a measure of fame and popularity for his wood-and-wire toys and animals, and finally his complete sets of circus figures—animals, clowns, tumblers, and trapeze artists—which he set going for the entertainment of guests at parties. In December 1929, he put on a show for the stage designer Mrs. Aline Bernstein and her friends. Louisa, who now accompanied him everywhere, came with him to the Park Avenue apartment. Calder was unaware, he later said, that Thomas Wolfe "was present at my circus performance," but, Calder added, the writer made "some nasty remarks" about it "in a long-winded book." The reference is to "The Party at Jack's" in *You Can't Go Home Again*.

Sandy and Louisa met in Paris by arrangement in the fall of 1930, and they were married in January 1931. For the wedding party at the James home in Concord, the bridegroom conducted a circus show. The couple lived in Paris for the next few years, in the thirteenth *arrondissement*; and it was in Paris that Marcel Duchamp, inspecting Calder's motor-driven and wind-driven objects, suggested the name "mobile."

As for Louisa, "she took all my new objects and my work without demur," Calder was to say: but to say, as it were, within his wife's hearing and imaginably with a sidelong glance. The two were very close, as spouses, as parents, as planners of life—and as dance partners (they are still remembered by Connecticut residents for their passionate enjoyment of dancing). They traveled much of the globe together: Europe, Russia, the Middle East, India, South America, mostly to allow Calder to complete some new commission. On one of their European trips, they bought an old mill near the village of Saché in the Touraine, and here they lived on and off for many years. In America they divided their time between New York and the family home in Roxbury, Connecticut.

A daughter, Sandra James, was born in 1935; in the mid-1950s, she married Jean Davidson, the son of the sculptor Jo Davidson but born and brought up in France, a cultivated journalist who served as the American correspondent for a French newspaper. A second daughter, Mary James, is married to Howard Rower. Alexander Calder died in November 1976.

7

The younger child of Bob and Mary Holton James, Edward's sister, was named for her maternal grandmother, Mary Walsh James. She traveled a good deal with her mother in her young womanhood and grew used to sudden departures from home after a parental explosion. There was talk for a time of her marrying a British baronet, but in April 1907, the younger Mary became the wife of George Vaux, a Philadelphia lawyer with an interest in social reform, and went to live in his native city.

George Vaux was the ninth of that name, and came from a lineage even more lengthily traceable than that of the American Jameses. Remote Vaux ancestors left France in the seventeenth century, crossed to England, and settled in Sussex. One of the George Vauxes was a London physician whose son Richard came to America as a young man and died there in 1790 at the age of thirty-nine. The strong Quaker component in the family began with Richard's son Roberts, a businessman and philanthropist who directed considerable energy toward the bettering of prison conditions in Philadelphia. His older son, George Vaux VIII, social-minded like his predecessors, married Sarah Morris of Wynnewood, Pennsylvania; and it was their son, George Vaux IX, born in 1863, who joined in marriage with Mary Walsh James.

George IX busied himself admirably with what a later day would call minority rights: particularly those of black Americans, with special attention to the question of education, and those of American Indians. For twenty years (1907–27), he headed the United States Board of Indian Commissioners, a group entrusted by the President with the task of keeping an eye on the United States Bureau of Indian Affairs and its treatment of the Indians in its charge. He spent one month in every year on one or another Indian reservation in the West.

Mary James Vaux adopted her husband's Quaker credo and vision, and added his social consciousness to her own. She was an ardent suffragette, did what she could to alleviate racial tensions in her neighborhood, and helped form the League of Women Voters in Pennsylvania. After the death of George Vaux in 1927, Mary allowed the Jamesian side of her to become more active.

She had always spoken with uncritical fondness of her father Robertson, and was now expressing the view that the younger siblings of William and Henry James were taken too little account of in discussions of the family. It was Mary who procured the handwritten volumes of Alice James's diary from the blind and aged but still devoted Katharine Loring; and Mary who found a Philadelphia writer, Anne Robeson Burr, to edit the manuscript within a work to be called *A Gathering of the Family*. Mary's brother Edward, when he read the diary in the fall of 1933, said it was "possessed of that peculiarly captivating charm which was the capacity of that generation of Jameses to put into their work." He wondered, though, whether Mrs. Burr or anyone else had the understanding necessary for dealing with "such complex people."*

George IX and Mary Vaux had two children. The older, George X, married the former Anne Hawks; now widowed and retired from business, he lives in Bryn Mawr and is receptive to James-seeking visitors. The younger son, Henry James Vaux ("James" has been reduced to "J." in his signature), was named, according to his mother, not for the novelist Henry but for Henry James, Sr., for whom she retained great admiration. Henry Vaux has completed a long and distinguished service, beginning in 1948, in the School of Forestry at the University of California in Berkeley; he was Dean of the School from 1965 to 1975. For a number of years he was chairman of the California Board of Forestry (appointed thereto by Governor Jerry Brown), a body that devises policy for the legislature in matters of fire protection and logging practices in state and private forests.

Henry Vaux is the curator of James family materials descending from Robertson James, joining his cousins Bill, Sandy, and Mickey James, and his niece Maggie in the preservation and, as need be, the circulation of the archives. He is married to Jean Macduff, formerly of Chicago. Their daughter, Alice James Vaux, who is married to Edward Hall and lives in Portland, Oregon, is the keeper of Alice James's diary. Their son, Henry James Vaux, Jr., professor of economics at the University of California in Riverside, is married to Prindle Sue Anders. With their two children, Robert and Katharine, born in 1972 and 1974 respectively, a sixth generation in direct descent from William James of Ireland and Albany is approaching its majority.

---

* Anne Robeson Burr's book, not very happily titled *Alice James: Her Brothers—Her Journal*, appeared in 1934. It was well received in the American press, but it is unsatisfactory on several counts. Alice James's diary was later (1964) and properly edited by Leon Edel.

PICTURE NOTES AND CREDITS

Endpapers

Front: The city of Albany, in a sketch of 1798. From 1813 to 1832, the home of William James was on North Pearl Street. From *The History of the City of Albany* by Arthur James Weiser, M.A., 1884. (Courtesy the Yale University Library)

New York City, in a map of 1885. The James family lived on Washington Place, east of Washington Square, in 1842–43; and on Fourteenth Street between Fifth and Sixth Avenues from 1848 to 1855. The Walsh home was on Washington Square. (Courtesy map collection, Yale University Library)

Back: Newport, Rhode Island, in a map of 1883. The Jameses lived on Kay Street in 1858–59 and at No. 13 in 1860–62. From 1862 to 1866, they lived on Spring Street, at the corner of Lee; just off this map, to the lower left. (Courtesy map collection, Yale University Library)

Cambridge, Massachusetts, in a map of 1878. The family home was on Quincy Street from 1866 to 1882. (Courtesy map collection, Yale University Library)

Frontispiece

The family members in Newport, sketched by William in a letter from Cambridge, in early November 1861: Alice, Mother, Father, Henry, Aunt Kate, Bob. William introduced the sketch by speaking of "the lustre of far-off shining Newport all silver and blue, and this heavenly group below." See

p. 121 and note. (By permission of the Houghton Library, Harvard University, and Alexander R. James)

Pictures following page 74

William James of Albany in the 1820s. The photograph was taken from a copy, owned by the philosopher William James, of a portrait by an unknown artist in Paris. (By permission of the Houghton Library, Harvard University, and Alexander R. James)

Catharine Barber James, about 1830. From a portrait, owned by William James, by an unknown artist. (By permission of the Houghton Library, Harvard University, and Alexander R. James)

Henry James, Sr., as a young man, by an unknown artist. (By permission of the Houghton Library, Harvard University, and Alexander R. James)

Alice James about 1854. (By permission of the Houghton Library, Harvard University, and Alexander R. James)

Henry James, Sr., and Henry Junior, 1854. By Mathew Brady. In *A Small Boy and Others*, section VII, Henry speaks of sitting for this daguerreotype in "the great Broadway establishment of Mr. Brady, supreme in that then beautiful art"; and of "the little sheath-like jacket" he wore for the occasion, "tight to the body, closed at the neck and adorned in front with a single row of brass buttons." Thackeray happened to visit the family at about this time, and Henry never forgot the novelist, catching sight of him, calling out: "Come here, little boy, and show me your extraordinary jacket." (By permission of the Houghton Library, Harvard University, and Alexander R. James)

Henry James, age seventeen. (By permission of the Houghton Library, Harvard University, and Alexander R. James)

William James in 1858. (By permission of the Houghton Library, Harvard University, and Alexander R. James)

Henry James in 1862, painted in Newport by John La Farge. Henry devoted many pages in *A Small Boy and Others* to John La Farge and the James brothers' deepening acquaintance with him, in the Newport of the early 1860s. He himself, said Henry, often served "as an abundantly idle young out-of-doors model" for La Farge. This picture hangs in the Century Club on West Forty-third Street, New York City (Courtesy Jonathan Harding and the Century Association). See also *American Art at the Century* by A. Hyatt Mayor and Mark Davis, 1977.

Mary Walsh James, about 1865. (Courtesy Henry J. Vaux)

Henry James, Sr., about 1865. (By permission of the Houghton Library, Harvard University, and Alexander R. James)

Catharine Walsh, "Aunt Kate," about 1860. (Courtesy Henry J. Vaux)

Picture Notes and Credits

Pictures following page 234

William James, age nineteen. (By permission of the Houghton Library, Harvard University, and Alexander R. James)

William James in Newport, about 1863. (By permission of the Houghton Library, Harvard University, and Alexander R. James)

William James, about 1862. (By permission of the Houghton Library, Harvard University, and Alexander R. James)

"The Wizard." Pencil sketch by William James. Inscription: *Done by Billy James for Frank Tweedy 1859.* Howard M. Feinstein, in *Becoming William James* (1984), was the first to make available this and two dozen other similar sketches made by William between 1859 and 1873. As Professor Feinstein maintains, the sketches are deeply revealing of William's changeable state of mind and his varied apprehensions (in this instance, the fear of being overwhelmed by his father) during those troubled years. (By permission of the Houghton Library, Harvard University, and Alexander R. James)

Here I and Sorrow Sit. Pencil drawing by William James, probably early 1860s. See preceding note. (By permission of the Houghton Library, Harvard University, and Alexander R. James)

William at the P.O. Sketches by William in a letter to his mother of September 16, 1861, depicting himself as he approaches the Cambridge Post Office desperately sure there will be no letter for him, and then as he emerges letter in hand. See page 120. (By permission of the Houghton Library, Harvard University, and Alexander R. James)

"The Foreboding Meeting." First page of a playlet by William James (probably in 1864) about running into Emerson at a Cambridge boot-black stand. As the "drama" continues, Emerson requests that his "immortal boots" be polished, and then inquires about a learned young friend of William's, John Bancroft. (By permission of the Houghton Library, Harvard University, and Alexander R. James)

Garth Wilkinson James, September 1862. "His plump corpusculous looks as always," William told the family in a November 1861 letter, after a visit from Wilky. (Courtesy Henry J. Vaux)

Garth Wilkinson James in uniform, 1863. (Courtesy Henry J. Vaux)

Robertson James in Newport, April 1862. (Courtesy Henry J. Vaux)

Adjutant Garth W. James and Lieutenant-Colonel Hallowell, July 1863. See page 138. (By permission of the Houghton Library, Harvard University, and Alexander R. James)

Wilky James in Newport, late summer 1863, recovering from the wounds suffered at Fort Wagner. Pencil sketch by William James. (By permission of the Houghton Library, Harvard University, and Alexander R. James)

645]

William James in Brazil, June 1865. See page 174. On the Agassiz expedition, in Rio de Janeiro, William came down with what was at first diagnosed as smallpox but later identified by Agassiz as varioloid, a lesser disease that resembles smallpox. William's eyes were so inflamed that he feared losing his sight. (By permission of the Houghton Library, Harvard University, and Alexander R. James)

Alice James in 1870. (By permission of the Houghton Library, Harvard University, and Alexander R. James)

Alice James in a sketch by Henry James. The sketch was contained in a letter from Henry to his mother, written in Queen Hotel, Chester, England, May 23, 1872. "The above is a feeble sketch of the position and circumstance of your exiled daughter. She sits before a great bow window, looking out into an elegant and verdurous garden. The ivy crawls and clambers in along the edges of the casement." See also Edel, *Letters of Henry James*, I, 285. (By permission of the Houghton Library, Harvard University, and Alexander R. James)

Minny Temple, 1869. (By permission of the Houghton Library, Harvard University, and Alexander R. James)

Henry James, 1863–64. (By permission of the Houghton Library, Harvard University, and Alexander R. James)

William James in 1869. (By permission of the Houghton Library, Harvard University, and Alexander R. James)

Pictures following page 394

Daniel Lewis Gibbens. Photograph contained in a letter from him to his daughter Alice, written in New Orleans, 1864. (By permission of the Houghton Library, Harvard University, and Alexander R. James)

Alice Howe Gibbens, 1872. (By permission of the Houghton Library, Harvard University, and Alexander R. James)

Robertson James in Milwaukee, 1872. (Courtesy Henry J. Vaux)

Garth Wilkinson James in Milwaukee, 1873. (Courtesy Henry J. Vaux)

Katharine James Prince, about 1868. Kitty Prince was William James's first cousin, the daughter of Henry Senior's half-brother William. See page 170. (By permission of the Houghton Library, Harvard University, and Alexander R. James)

Mary Holton, 1870. (Courtesy Henry J. Vaux)

Alice Howe James "with H.J."—i.e., Harry, the firstborn, who later wrote the caption: *1879–80*. (By permission of the Houghton Library, Harvard University, and Alexander R. James)

Henry Senior, portrait by Frank Duveneck, 1880. This portrait hung over the mantelpiece in the Irving Street home. See page 491. (By permission of the Houghton Library, Harvard University, and Alexander R. James)

Picture Notes and Credits

95 Irving Street, Cambridge, winter 1888. (By permission of the Houghton Library, Harvard University, and Alexander R. James)

William James, signed by him: *April 1887.* (By permission of the Houghton Library, Harvard University, and Alexander R. James)

Henry James, March 1890, according to a notation in his hand. (By permission of the Houghton Library, Harvard University, and Alexander R. James)

The William James summer home in Chocorua, New Hampshire. Sketch by D.D.L. McGrew, a neighbor, in September 1903. (By permission of the Houghton Library, Harvard University, and Alexander R. James)

William James and his daughter Margaret Mary (Peggy), March 1892. (By permission of the Houghton Library, Harvard University, and Alexander R. James)

Robertson James in the early 1890s. (Courtesy Henry J. Vaux)

William James at the Shanty in Keene Valley, the Adirondacks, 1890s. (By permission of the Houghton Library, Harvard University, and Alexander R. James)

Alice James in her lodgings at 41 Argyll Road, Kensington, London, in September 1891. (By permission of the Houghton Library, Harvard University, and Alexander R. James)

Alice James and Katharine Loring, in the sitting room of their lodgings at the Royal Leamington Spa, 1889–90. (By permission of the Houghton Library, Harvard University, and Alexander R. James)

Pictures following page 554

Henry James and William James at Lamb House, September 1900. (By permission of the Houghton Library, Harvard University, and Alexander R. James)

A gathering at Lamb House, September 1900: Alice Howe James, Peggy James, William James, Henry James. (By permission of the Houghton Library, Harvard University, and Alexander R. James)

Lamb House and garden. (By permission of the Houghton Library, Harvard University, and Alexander R. James)

Henry James and William James: picture taken in 1904 or 1905, probably in Cambridge, during Henry's American tour. (By permission of the Houghton Library, Harvard University, and Alexander R. James)

Alice and William James, in Farmington, Connecticut, 1904. (By permission of the Houghton Library, Harvard University, and Alexander R. James)

Robertson James, about 1907. (By permission of the Houghton Library, Harvard University, and Alexander R. James)

Henry James and Edward Holton James in the garden at Lamb House, January 1907. See page 635. (By permission of the Houghton Library, Harvard University, and Alexander R. James)

William James in the garden at Lamb House, July 1908. G. K. Chesterton's
lodging adjoined Lamb House at this time, and his little garden was on
the other side of the wall. Peggy James spent hours on the top of a ladder
set against the wall, in the vain hope of catching a glimpse of Chesterton.
Despite an old legend, William almost certainly did not climb the ladder.
See pp. 572–73 and 619. (By permission of the Houghton Library, Harvard
University, and Alexander R. James)

William James in 1907. (By permission of the Houghton Library, Harvard
University, and Alexander R. James)

William James's library and study at 95 Irving Street. (By permission of the
Houghton Library, Harvard University, and Alexander R. James)

Henry James: portrait by John Singer Sargent, completed in June 1913. Henry,
who admired the painting unreservedly, described it to his nephew Billy:
"One is almost full-face, with one's arm over the corner of one's chair-
back . . . Of course, I'm sitting a little askance in the chair. The canvas
comes down to just where my watch-chain (such as it is, poor thing) is
hung across the waistcoat." To Rhoda Broughton, he said that he was "all
large and luscious rotundity" in the portrait, "—by which you may see
how true a thing it is." The portrait hangs in the National Gallery in
London. (Courtesy the National Gallery)

Alice Howe James and Henry James, seated on the couch at 95 Irving Street,
probably in early 1911. (By permission of the Houghton Library, Harvard
University, and Alexander R. James)

Alice Howe James, portrait by her son William James, painted in Cambridge,
winter 1921. This painting hung for forty years on the stairway landing
at 95 Irving Street. (By permission of the Houghton Library, Harvard
University, and Alexander R. James)

Family members in the San Francisco home, at 944 Chestnut Street, of Peggy
and Bruce Porter, July 1921. Alice Howe James, Julia Porter (Bruce's
sister) holding the recently born Catharine (Jimsie), Bruce holding the
three-year-old Robert Bruce, Peggy. (By permission of the Houghton Library, Harvard University, and Alexander R. James)

William James on his deathbed. William James died at the Chocorua home
at 2:30 p.m. on August 26, 1910. That same afternoon, Alice James called
in a local photographer, a Mr. Holmes, to take photographs of her deceased
husband. It may be conjectured that she wished to have at hand a picture
of the being with whom she would subsequently seek to communicate.
She is reported to have made such an effort in a séance some years later,
but to no avail. (By permission of Alexander R. James, and the kindness
of Michael James)

NOTES

The principal aims of the annotation following are simplicity and usefulness. The vast majority of the passages quoted from letters and journals in my text are from documents in Houghton Library at Harvard University. Whenever possible, however, I have indicated the most available published text where the quotations can be found. Where quotations are sufficiently dated in the narrative, I have not redated them in the notes.

Code Letters

Jameses

AHJ	Alice Howe (Gibbens) James
AJ	Alice James
AJ D	*The Diary of Alice James.* Edited, with an introduction, by Leon Edel, 1964
AJ Lt	*The Death and Letters of Alice James.* Selected correspondence, edited, with a biographical essay, by Ruth Yeazell, 1981
GWJ	Garth Wilkinson James
HJ	Henry James
HJ Au	*Henry James: Autobiography.* Edited, with an introduction, by Frederick W. Dupee, 1956 (paperback, 1983)
HJ Lt	*Henry James Letters.* Edited by Leon Edel. 4 vols. 1974–84
HJ Nb	*The Notebooks of Henry James.* Edited by F. O. Matthiessen and Kenneth B. Murdock, 1947
HSr	Henry James Senior

MJ   Mary Walsh James
RJ   Robertson James
WJ   William James
WJ Lt   *The Letters of William James.* Edited by his son Henry James. 2 vols. 1920

Biographies and Studies
GWA   Gay Wilson Allen, *William James*, 1967
LE   Leon Edel, *Henry James.* 5 vols. 1953–72
GG   Giles Gunn (ed.), *Henry James Senior, A Selection of His Writings*, 1974
JM   Jane Maher, *Biography of Broken Fortunes: Wilky and Bob, Brothers of William, Henry and Alice James*, 1986
FOM   F. O. Matthiessen, *The James Family*, 1948
JS   Jean Strouse, *Alice James: A Biography*, 1980

Library
HL   Houghton Library, Harvard University

One. William James of Ireland and Albany

page
  3 "a very small sum of money": WJ Lt, I, 2.
  7 "for the reception of country produce": Quoted by Katharine Hastings in *William James of Albany and His Descendants*, reprinted from the *New York Genealogical and Biographical Record*, LIV (1924), 101.
  7 "very advantageous": John J. McEneny, *Albany, Capital City on the Hudson* (1981), 83.
10 "withdrawn from the superintendence": Joel Munsell, *The Annals of Albany* (1869), Vol. 3, 137. The fire on the Albany pier referred to in the next paragraph is recorded on p. 161 of this volume.
11 William of Albany's will: See p. 34 below.
11 "to make an owl weep": Franklin P. Chase, *Syracuse and Environs and History* (1924), 23.
11 For the transactions involving the acreage bought by William James and its division into lots, see also Dwight K. Bruce, ed., *Memorial History of Syracuse, New York* (1891).
12 "When old Billy James": WJ Lt, I, 4.
12 "Near the close of the second day": Harold A. Larrabee, "The Elder James and Union College," *Henry James, Sr.*, in the Union Worthies Series, Union College, Schenectady, NY; No. 18 (1963), 7–8.
13 "The rupture with my grandfather's tradition": HJ Au, 109.

13 "I cannot conceive": from Henry Senior's "autobiography," properly called *Immortal Life* (see Chapter Two: "The Trouble with Seminaries"); in FOM, 24.

14 "a grasping deity": AJ D, 160.

15 "I have nothing to say": FOM, 20. The quotations following in this paragraph are in FOM, 20, 21, 30, 36.

16 "collectively, so genially interested": HJ Au, 36.

17 "I cannot recollect": FOM, 18.

17 "freedom itself": Ibid., 20.

17 William of Albany's forgetfulness: WJ Lt, I, 3.

17 "I was never so happy": FOM, 37.

17 "I lived": Ibid., 34.

18 "morbid process in the bone": Ibid., 18.

18 "Instead of progressing": Jennet James to Marcia Ames James (wife of Reverend William James), Albany, November 16, 1827, HL, included in packet of letters to Reverend William James.

18 "an exalted sense of his affection": FOM, 18.

20 "I consider you": Austin Warren, *The Elder Henry James* (1934), 16.

21 "so debased himself": Ibid.

21–22 The account of the Literature Lottery and the life and career of Eliphalet Nott may be found in Codman Hislop, *Eliphalet Nott* (1971).

22 "My ambition is awakened": Warren, 19.

22 "I have been introduced": Ibid., 20.

23 "a great revulsion of spirit": HJ Au, 303.

24 William Bayard's speech: Joel Munsell, *Collections on the History of Albany* (1867), II, 442–43.

24 William James's speech: Ibid., 443–48.

25 *Daily Advertiser*'s transcript of William James's 1825 speech: Ibid., 460–67.

26 Obituary of William James: Joel Munsell, *Annals*, 259–60.

26–30 The last will and testament of William James of Albany, with its many restrictive clauses, is contained in the Records Room of the Surrogate's Office, in the County Courthouse of Albany. The documents include the successive applications by the trustees for further time to complete the inventory.

The second phase of this story, the suit to set aside the restrictive clauses of the will, and what became of it, may be found in HL, in a bound volume bearing the title "In Chancery: Before the Chancellor." (HL likewise has a copy of the original will.) Here we have eight appeals to the Court for the Trial of Impeachments and the Correction of Errors, and the court's final decision.

30 "Leisured for life": Warren, 21; also Larrabee, 9.

34 The letters cited to Joseph Henry, with letters *to* him from Henry James, Sr., are in *The Papers of Joseph Henry* (1979), Vol. 3, 344–499 passim. On Billy Taylor, see letter to A. D. Bache, June 19, 1837.

34 "in the winter afternoon firelight": HJ Au, 396 ff.

Two. Henry James, Sr.: The Endangering Self

39 "unconscious hypocrisy": GG, 17; from "the editor's" introduction to *Immortal Life*.

Note: some of the passages from Henry Senior's writings quoted in this chapter may be found in FOM, 136–89, William James's introduction to *The Literary Remains of the Late Henry James* (1884). Others may be found in the text indicated above: Giles Gunn, *Henry James Senior: A Selection of His Writings* (1974).

40 "He only cared for virtue": HJ Au, 123.

40 "The whole New Testament": HSr's unsigned preface to his edition of Sandeman's *Letters on Therson and Aspasia* (1838).

41 "Merchant": HJ Au, 6.

42 "Great-grandfather Walsh": AJ D, 81.

43 "The flesh said": FOM, 6 (from Emerson's journals).

43 "who has thought all his life": AJ D, 217.

45 "shapely maid": FOM, 23.

46 "active enmity": Ibid., 24.

46 "the spectral eye of God": Ibid.

46 "some wanton ungenerous word": Ibid., 29.

47 "The more I strove": Ibid., 159 (from *Substance and Shadow*, 1866).

47 "mystical or symbolic record": Ibid., 160.

47 "to talk familiarly": Ibid., 39 ("Letters to Emerson").

47 "to admire": HJ Au, 7.

48 "the best apple on the tree": Gay Wilson Allen, *Waldo Emerson* (1981), 401.

48 "Here I am": FOM, 42.

48 "How long I shall stay": HL.

48–49 "Take them all in all": *Substance and Shadow*, 324 (quoted in part in GWA, 14).

49 "the very best interpreter": FOM, 43.

49 "You don't look upon Calvinism": Ibid.

49 "James is a very good fellow": *The Correspondence of Emerson and Carlyle*, edited by Joseph Slater (1964), 352.

49 HSr to MJ: HL.

50 "a not insignificant mite": FOM, 160.

Notes

51 "I remember": Ibid., 160–61 (from *Society the Redeemed Form of Man*, 1879).

53 " 'It is, then' ": Ibid., 163.

53 "all the contemporary philosophy of England": "Swedenborg" in *Representative Men* (1850, original lectures 1845–46).

54 "influence was seen everywhere": Sidney Ahlstrom, *A Religious History of the American People* (1975 edition), I, 584.

54 "the main philosophical obligation": GG, 65.

55 "self-sufficiency": Ibid., 151.

55 "moral or voluntary power": FOM, 165.

55 "When I sat down": Ibid., 166.

57 "Such, as I have been able to apprehend it": GG, 74.

57 "The sect of the *soi-disant* New Jerusalem": FOM, 181.

58 "four stout boys": Ibid., 45.

59 "initiation into History": HJ Au, 33.

59–60 The lecture "What Constitutes a State" is contained in *Lectures and Miscellanies* (1852).

60 MJ to Mme de Gammon: HL.

60 "There is nothing": FOM, 44.

61 "into an army": Ibid., 47.

61 The lecture "Socialism and Civilisation" is contained in GG.

62 "at the door of the carriage": HJ Au, 355.

63 "immense temperament": FOM, 168.

63n HSr on Margaret Fuller: to Edmund Tweedy, February 24, 1852; HL.

64 *Re* Thoreau: FOM, 43.

64 *Re* Alcott: Ibid., 44.

64 "that I may": Gay Wilson Allen, *Waldo Emerson*, 534.

64 "elegantly slim": HJ Au, 358–59.

64–65 HSr to Tweedy: HL.

65–66 The exchange between Andrews and Henry James, with much interesting comment, is contained in Stephen Pearl Andrews, ed., *Love, Marriage and Divorce and the Sovereignty of the Individual. A discussion by Henry James, Horace Greeley and Stephen Pearl Andrews* (1853).

66 *"which one suffers"*: GG, 149.

67 "so far as I can": HJ Au, 38–40.

67–68 On Helen Wyckoff: Ibid., 71.

Three. Overschooled Childhoods

71 HSr to Samuel Gray Ward: HL.

71 "America is 'the lost Paradise' ": to Edmund Tweedy, July 24, 1860; HL.

72 "bonne Lorraine": HJ Au, 160.

72 "absurdly cushioned state": Ibid., 160–61.

73 "There's nothing like it": HSr to his mother; HL.

73 "a poor and arid and lamentable time": HJ Au, 170.

73 "It was just the fact": Ibid., 170–71.

74 "green shirred silk": AJ D, 46. Other London references: same page.

74n "a capital tutor": HSr to his mother, November 30, 1855; HL.

75 "a sort of sub-antagonism": HL.

75 "an intense longing": AJ Lt, 162 (to WJ, March 22, 1889).

76 "finally 'give out' ": HSr to Edmund Tweedy; HL.

76 "frightful mistake": HSr to Emerson, June 18, 1855; HL.

77 "There is no nobler ingredient": HSr to Edmund Tweedy, May 23, 1856; HL.

78 "They do not lie": HSr to Edmund Tweedy, September 14, 1856; HL.

78 "John had an enormous social instinct": same letter.

79 "l'ingénieux petit Robertson": HJ Au, 185.

80 "with no account at all": Ibid., 43.

80 "the agonies of the desolation": AJ D, 58.

80 "We have had": AJ Lt, 49.

80 "He reacted": HJ Au, 43.

81 "a miserable home-bred": WJ Lt, I, 20.

81 "Willy is very devoted": HSr to his mother, October 15, 1857; HL.

82 "What enrichment of mind": November 4, 1888; AJ Lt, 148.

82 "the anguish greater": AJ D, 128.

83 "just to *be* somewhere": HJ Au, 17.

83 "the only form": Ibid., 16.

83 "in the streets": Ibid., 17.

83 "since one was all eyes": Ibid., 166.

84 "as if he had gained": Ibid., 147.

84 "in the grateful . . . position": Ibid., 162.

84 "more heart than head": HSr to his mother, October 15, 1857; HL.

84 "one way of taking life": HJ Au, 164.

85 The Louvre and the Galerie d'Apollon: Ibid., 195–99.

86 "the gravest illness": Ibid., 224.

86 "trembled more than once": HSr to his mother, October 15, 1857; HL.

87 "Was anything clearer": HSr to (brother) William, October 25, 1856; HL.

87 "away into the country": MJ to Catharine Barber James, August 25, 1856; HL.

89 "the strange sense": HJ Au, 236.

89n "Crinoline?": Ibid., 52.

90 "fictive evocation": Ibid., 107.

90 "very clever and promising": HSr to his mother, October 15, 1857; HL.

90 "receive crown or rosettes": RJ's autobiographical letter to AHJ, February 24, 1898 (it begins "You speak of an autobiography. Would that I could write one"), FOM, 270–71.

91 "We are settled very comfortably": HSr to Mrs. Charles Dana, August 15, 1858; HL.

91 "a thousand delicate secret places": HJ Au, 300.

92 "as if he had found": FOM, 88–89.

93 "I have grown so discouraged": HSr to Samuel Gray Ward, September 18, 1858; HL.

93 "Newport and the Newporters": HJ Lt, I, 6.

93 "had simply said": HJ Au, 241.

93n See LE, I, 137–39. Also HJ to Tom Perry: HL.

94 "an obscure . . . failure": HJ Au, 241.

94 "some poetical-looking manuscripts": LE, I, 150.

94 "To no style": Ibid., 151–52.

94 "Whatever he played with": HJ Au, 247.

94–95 "Mother does nothing": WJ to HSr; HL.

95 WJ's "sonnate": JS, 53.

96 "Willy felt": HSr to Edmund Tweedy, July 24, 1860; HL.

97 "of liking for us": HJ Au, 240.

98 "Alice at the window": WJ to his parents, August 12, 1860; HL.

99 "I wish you would": WJ to HSr, August 15, 1860; HJ Au, 265.

99 "Having such a father": Ibid.

99 "the gush of God's life": FOM, 93.

99 "father's artistico-metaphysical opinions": HL.

100 "this estrangement": HJ to Tom Perry, July 18, 1860; HJ Lt, I, 22.

100 "should somehow": HJ Au, 274.

Four. The Home Front

103 "new fellow": GWA, 53.

104 "in all the elevated thoughts": JS, 62.

105 "I buried": HJ Au, 368–69.

106 "And what sort of a girl": AJ D, 193.

106–7 "The adipose and affectionate Wilky": E. W. Emerson, *The Early Years of the Saturday Club*, 328.

107 "quite the most emphasised": HJ Au, 323.

108 "shone with the vividest lustre": Ibid., 282–83.

108 "dissecting": HSr to Edmund Tweedy, October 1, 1860; HL.

109 "Do as you feel": Helen Mary Knowlton, *Art-Life of William Morris Hunt* (1899).

111 "so forced was I": HJ Au, 293.

111 "whether I am suited": WJ Lt, I, 23.

112 "dispensed with any suggestion": HJ Au, 268.

113 "flexibility and resilience": FOM, 100.

114 "The Social Significance of Our Institutions" is contained in FOM, 59 ff.

117 "the soft spring of '61": HJ's account of his "obscure hurt" is in HJ Au, 414 ff. Leon Edel's reconstruction of the event is in LE, I, 173 ff.

119 "the best time": JS, 73.

120 "I don't believe": WJ Lt, I, 35.

120 "I haven't for one minute": GWA, 78.

120 "no well-stored pantry": WJ Lt, I, 34.

121 "Many times": HJ Au, 316.

121 "babbling confidingness": WJ Lt, I, 41.

122 "His plump corpusculous": Ibid., 33.

122 "electrified": GWA, 83.

122 "The radiance of H.'s visit": HJ Au, 327.

122 "tell Alice": JS, 67.

122 "the palpitating Alice": HSr to Emerson, December 22, 1861; JS, 67.

123 "Charmante jeune fille": HJ Au, 320.

123 "Est-ce-que tu songes": Ibid.

124 "*Gulielmo*" (WJ's spelling): Ibid., 319.

124 "The way I excuse": LE, I, 171–72.

125 "to part with one so young": JM, 24.

Five. The Younger Brothers in War and Peace

126 "To me, in my boyish fancy": the entire text of Wilky's speech was carried in the Milwaukee *Sentinel* on Sunday morning, December 2, 1883.

126–30 Wilky's letters from North Carolina are in HJ Au, 462–67.

130–33 Most of the information about the formation of black regiments— including newspaper editorials, Frederick Douglass speeches, and T. W. Higginson's diary entry—may be found in Dudley Taylor Cornish, *The Sable Arm* (1956).

133 "in this new negro-soldier venture": WJ's address on Robert Gould Shaw; see note to p. 141 below.

133 "many sharp rebukes": JM, 31–32.

134 "state of juniority": HJ Au, 456.

135–40 Quotations regarding the 54th Regiment are taken from *A Brave Black Regiment: History of the Fifty-Fourth Regiment of Massachusetts Volunteer Infantry 1863–1865* by Luis F. Emilio (author and text are identified on p. 137n). See also *Massachusetts in the Rebellion*, on the various Massachusetts regiments, by P. C. Headley (1866).

Notes

141–42 WJ's talk on Shaw is in *Memories and Studies* (posthumous, 1911).

142n "Tonight news comes": *The Journal of Charlotte Forten*, edited, with an introduction and notes, by Ray Allen Billington (1961), 214.

145 "as some object": HJ Au, 383.

146 "How I recall": AJ D, 45.

147 "Ah, father": JM, 49–50.

148 "He is vastly attached": HSr to Caroline Sturgis Tappan; HJ Au, 382.

148n Louisa May Alcott's poem is quoted intact in the Milwaukee *Sentinel*, November 17, 1883, in an obituary of Garth W. James.

149 "Wilky is improving daily": WJ to Kitty Prince; WJ Lt, I, 44.

149–52 Bob James's letters home and Henry Senior's letters to him, which are in HL, are generously quoted from in JM. JM includes part of the "darling Bobbins" letter quoted on my p. 151. The letter on my p. 152, beginning "It was when," is also in HJ Au, 458.

152–56 Wilky's letters home in 1864–65, which are in HL, are quoted from in JM, 54 ff. and in HJ Au, 467 ff.

157 "The whole situation": HJ Au, 457.

158 "restlessly strolling": Ibid., 423.

158 "facing us out": Ibid., 384.

158 "the single sense": Ibid., 460.

161 "the freeing of millions": AJ D, 97.

161 "the divinely pompous": HSr to Annie Fields, May 11, 1866; HL.

161 "because I am tired of the place": GWA, 97.

162 "I feel myself": JS, 91.

163–67 Letters from Florida: in JM, 77–108. On the postwar history of Northerners attempting to run Southern plantations, see *New Masters: Northern Planters during the Civil War and Reconstruction* by Lawrence N. Powell (1980).

165–66 On John Murray Forbes, see Henry Greenleaf Pearson, *An American Railroad Builder, John Murray Forbes* (1911).

Six. William James and the Moral Business

168–77 WJ Lt, I, 45–69.

168–69 WJ on Wyman: *Memories and Studies*.

170 "Everybody in New York": HL, in group of documents assembled by Henry James III.

171 "higher nature": WJ to MJ; HL.

176 Agassiz quoted: *Memories and Studies*.

176n "give up our pet theories": WJ to parents, April 2, 1865; GWA, 103.

177–78 "by far the nicest girl": WJ to GWJ, February 25, 1866; HL.

178 "Northern triumph" and quotations following: HJ Au, 492.

178 "interesting pair": Ibid., 508.

179 "miserably stricken": HJ Nb, 320.

179 "I am less quiet": WJ Lt, I, 77.

180 "It comes to me": HJ Au, 498.

180–83 JS, 98–116.

183 "the humdrumness": WJ to AJ, February 18, 1867; HL.

183 "There is no wisdom": JS, 110.

183–94 WJ Lt, I, 99–128.

188 "a certain neatness": GWA, 143.

191 "You mean I don't explain it": Ibid., 138.

192 "wholly skeptical": WJ to HSr, September 26, 1867; HL.

194 "unspeakable disgust": FOM, 210.

194 "He *is* a perfect born *collector*": HL.

195 "I am coming home": WJ to Tom Ward, October 29, 1867; HL.

195 "delicate": JS, 123.

196 "total absence": Ibid., 124.

196 "It is a case": Ibid., 123.

197–98 "altho' I have never": AJ D, 149–50.

199 "poky banality": Quoted by Van Wyck Brooks, *From the Shadows of the Mountains* (1961), 45.

199 "mental labor": HL.

200 HSr and WJ *re* President Eliot: GWA, 156.

200 "I thoroughly agree": HL.

201 "Nature and life": GWA, 163.

201 "Today, I about touched bottom": FOM, 216.

202–3 "Whilst in this state": *Varieties of Religious Experience*, Lectures VI–VII.

204–5 "I think that yesterday": FOM, 218.

206 "The knower is not simply": Ibid., 211. The entire article is in *Collected Essays and Reviews* (1920).

Seven. Henry James in the Early 1870s

207–30 HJ Lt, I, 90–292.

207 "abjectly, fatally homesick": HJ to MJ; HL.

210 "Your letter last evening": MJ to HJ, July 24, 1869; HL.

217 "He is one of the very few people": HJ Au, 511.

217 "Death, at the last": Ibid., 544.

221 "a great symphony": FOM, 319.

224 "*funk*": AJ D, 47.

225 "displayed more gaiety": JS, 149.

225 "Let your mind go to sleep": Ibid., 152.

Notes

225 "It makes some difference": Ibid., 154.

226 "with unabated elasticity": Ibid., 157.

230 "The most fearful thing": HL.

230–34 WJ Lt, I, 161–79.

232 "resolved to fight it out" and quotations following: GWA, 181–83.

233 "dear courageous": MJ to HJ, September 6, 1869; HL.

233 "drinking their tea": HJ Lt, I, 385.

234 "I had to make up": Ibid., 399.

235 "First—of the angel": LE, II, 147.

235 "the 3rd generation": GWA, 189.

235–40 HJ Lt, I, 410–84.

237 "When we entered": WJ to HSr, November 30, 1873; HL.

238 "I'm in a permanent path": GWA, 171 (April 18, 1874).

243 "a robust young Briton": LE, II, 174.

247 "You would make dear Harry": HL.

248 "gone abroad again": LE, II, 199.

Eight. Marriage Ventures

251–68 All the passages quoted, with the few exceptions listed below, can be found in JM.

252 "consanguinous union": HL.

253 "painting the back": JS, 126.

259 "We both feel": AJ to MJ; HL.

263 "There is an awe & terror": Gay Wilson Allen, *Waldo Emerson*, 650.

269 The articles mentioned are in *Collected Essays and Reviews* (1920).

272 "the growing desire": Mary Elizabeth (Fiske) Sargent, ed., *Sketches and Reminiscences of the Radical Club*.

273 Whittier's letters to Alice Howe Gibbens are in HL.

274–85 WJ's letters to Alice Howe Gibbens during the courtship period are in HL.

281 "was sleepless and restless": GWA, 220.

281 "I, for one": Ibid., 225.

281 "all sentiments": review of Spencer's *Definition of the Mind* in *Collected Essays and Reviews*.

283 "a slight mention": HJ Lt, II, 174.

284 "is the greatest event": GWJ to Alice Howe Gibbens; HL.

284 "I can imagine": JS, 182n.

285 "a nervous breakdown": Ibid., 183.

285 "periods of depression": Ibid.

285 "on the verge": Ibid., 185.

286 "the great joy": AJ Lt, 76.

286 "poor, shabby, old thing": AJ D, 230.

287 "Quelques Considérations" and "The Sentiment of Rationality" are in *Collected Essays and Reviews*.

288 "they are both writing it": GWA, 238.

Nine. Henry James and les siens

289–310 HJ Lt, II, 9–314.

292 "living extravagantly": HL.

295 "Go to; I will try London": HJ Nb, 27.

299 "critical faculty": LE, II, 160.

299 "Of the people": Ibid., 41.

300 "agreeably speckle the columns": GWA, 177.

300 "Keep watch and ward": LE, II, 241.

304 "For one who takes it": HJ Nb, 28.

306–7 "the negative side": this passage from HJ's essay on Hawthorne is quoted intact in LE, II, 388.

310 "Florence was divine": HJ Nb, 29.

310–19 All the letters from WJ to AHJ are in HL.

312 "conjugal and domestic virtues": HL.

313 "We have had one good present": AJ Lt, 68.

313 "eminently social": Milwaukee *Sentinel*, November 18, 1883.

315 "descant upon his sensations": HJ Lt, II, 292.

316 "I think as he grows older": GWA, 234.

320 "Was there ever a more exquisite": HJ Lt, II, 230.

320 "half the time": JS, 185–86.

321 "My patience, courage & self-control": AJ Lt, 78.

322 "all about": HJ Lt, II, 172.

323 "nothing in the way of discomfort": AJ Lt, 80–82.

324 "I was a good deal": Ibid., 84.

325 "the same delightful kind creature": JS, 198.

325 "Delightful to me": HJ Nb, 36.

325 "Alice and Miss L.": HL.

325 "Here I am back in America": HJ Nb, 23.

325 "One wishes": HL.

326 "The view from my windows": HJ Nb, 31.

327 "The long interval of years": Ibid., 35.

329 "honest," "sturdy": "Francis Boott" in *Memories and Studies*.

Notes

Ten. Deaths in the Family, 1882

333 "An equal sum": JM, 139.

334 "William was successively": Jacques Barzun, *A Stroll with William James* (1983), 227.

334 "a princely gift": JM, 139.

334 "Every year of this western life": HL.

334 "our good little friends": HJ to Sir John Clark; HJ Lt, II, 366.

335 "We have all been educated": JM, 142.

335n "Mrs. Van Buren": October 16, 1882; HJ Lt, II, 386.

336 "William James": WJ Lt, I, 9.

336 "old wrinkled peasant women": September 24, 1882; HL.

336 "a beautiful illumined memory": AJ D, 221.

336 "You knew my mother": HJ Lt, II, 376.

336–37 "She was our life": HJ Nb, 40.

337 "I lose the regular correspondence": HL.

337 "on a deeper level of feeling": LE, III, 38.

338 "the long low bridge": HJ Nb, 44.

338 "to have brought new life": HL.

339 "She was not to me": FOM, 129.

340 "tyrannical selflessness": JS, 26.

340 "the little house": Ibid., 204.

341 "My love, my life, my bride": HL.

341–42 "a poetess, a magaziness": HL.

342 "I don't exactly understand": HL.

342 "My!—how cramped": WJ Lt, I, 209.

343–46 WJ to AHJ : HL.

346 "I can never be half the help": JS, 205.

347 "a very sweet good woman": HL.

347 "in charging ill will": HL.

347 "How long it will last": JS, 205.

347 "an extraordinary instance": FOM, 269.

347 "Father and I": JS, 206.

348 "The last seven months": AJ Lt, 86.

348 "so sweet and good-natured": to WJ; JM, 144.

348 "It is weary work": JS, 207 (quoting Grace Ashburner).

348 "She thought he was dying": JS, 208.

349 "That here is a man": Aunt Kate's version of the statement; LE, III, 58.

349 "He has distinctly made up his mind": HL.

349 "Never mind, Father": AJ D, 217.

349 "Darling father's weary longings": AJ Lt, 87.

350 "not only without a Christmas dinner": HJ Lt, II, 396.

350–51 WJ Lt, I, 218–20.

351 "which I am sure": HJ Lt, II, 398.

352–54 WJ to AHJ: HL.

354–57 WJ on his father's life and ideas: FOM, 138–87.

356–57 "deep and true insight": WJ Lt, I, 241.

357 "great filial and fraternal joy": HJ Lt, III, 61.

357–58 "theologic passion" and quotations following: HJ Au, 339–44.

359 "passionate admiration": HJ Nb, 47.

359 "The house is so *empty*": HJ Lt, II, 396.

359 "He seems immensely absent": to Helen De Kay Gilder; HJ Lt, II, 403.

361 "Our dear home": AJ Lt, 88.

362–63 "My being, however": AJ D, 78.

Eleven. Alice James: The Remaking of a Life

364–69 Letters between WJ and AHJ: HL.

366–67 Exchange between WJ and HJ: HL.

369 "unjust and damnable": JM, 150.

370 "a small but solid brick house": HJ Lt, II, 402.

370 "rheumatic gout": HL.

370 "But they have absolutely none": HJ Lt, II, 402.

371 "of all the fancied abuses": JM, 158.

371 "scattered far and wide": HL.

372 "So that it looks": HL.

372 "a record of unmitigated suffering": HJ Lt, III, 8.

372 "was eminently social": Milwaukee *Sentinel*, November 17, 1883.

372 "glorious thing": HJ Lt, III, 33.

373 "an harmonious little *ménage*": JS, 214.

374 "She has always liked": HL.

374–75 "In those ghastly days": AJ D, 45.

375 "the Slavic flavour": AJ Lt, 91–92.

376 "the ancient houri": Ibid., 135.

376 "the emotion that prompted it": HL.

376–78 AJ Lt, 96–101.

377 "How beautiful it is": HJ Lt, III, 62.

378 "Look after my sister": Ibid., 80.

378 "make some great efforts": HJ Nb, 40.

379 "She has had a wretched winter": HJ Lt, III, 82.

379 "the adorable tale": Ibid., 83.

379 "nervous fits in one house": JS, 240.

380 "As soon as they get together": HL.

380 "A devotion so perfect": JS, 241.

381 "exceedingly fresh and tonic": HJ Lt, III, 95.

381 "so that there is absolutely no jar": HL.

382 "a thousand congratulations": AJ Lt, 88.

382 WJ to AHJ: HL.

382 "at last his valiant little soul": GWA, 279.

383n "the depth of a mother's grief": HL.

384 "It is a field": WJ Lt, I, 248.

384 "lying thinking of all": HL.

384 "still better chance": GWA, 279.

384 "I went last night": HL.

385–89 AJ Lt, 104–19.

385 "finished and furnished": HL.

390–401 HJ Lt, III, 114–82.

394 "in his own family situation": Introduction to *The Princess Casamassima* (Macmillan, 2 vols., 1948).

397 "she had *burned* one of them": HJ Nb, 72.

401–4 AJ Lt, 118–40.

403 "They pretended": HJ Lt, III, 135.

Twelve. A Gathering of Siblings: Leamington, 1889

405–8 WJ to AHJ: HL.

406 "75 acres of land": HL.

408 "The house is very prettily shaped": HL.

408 "14 doors": AJ D, 68.

408–21 WJ Lt, I, 213–85.

409 "How you produce": HL.

409 "But almost every page": HL.

410–21 WJ to AHJ: HL.

415 WJ to HJ about brother Bob: HL.

417 "I have bought": HL.

419 "This A.M. came an essay": HL.

421–25 HJ Lt, III, 203–56.

423 "quite squealed through it": WJ Lt, I, 281.

426–28 AJ Lt, 144–70.

428 "the somewhat devastating episode": AJ D, 51.

429 "in a perfectly charming way": HL.

429–30 "Harry is as nice and simple": WJ Lt, I, 288.

430 "I have enjoyed": HL.

430–31 "inspiration which came to everyone": GWA, 310.

431 "The sight of 120 men": Ibid.

431 "Tho' the results are the same": AJ D, 57–58.

432 "and made on me": HL.

432 RJ to Howells: HL.

Thirteen. Fraternal Principles: Psychology and Drama

435–36 WJ to AHJ: HL.

436–37 Reviews of *The Principles of Psychology*: GWA, 323–25.

445 "Of art or fame": HJ Nb, 99.

446 "Our absorbing interest just now": AJ Lt, 184.

446 "UNQUALIFIED TRIUMPHANT": HJ Lt, III, 320.

446 Letters to Stevenson: Ibid., 326, 327, 336.

Fourteen. Records of an Invalid: 1889–92

Note: Most of the quotations in this chapter are from Alice James's diary. To simplify the annotation, the diary will be referred to as D and the reference in each case limited to the book-page number and the diary-page number where the quotation appears.

451 D, 54.

451 "She was really an Irishwoman": HJ Lt, III, 482.

451 "It is a horrible moment": AJ Lt, 127.

452 D, 37.

452 D, 73.

453 D, 73.

454 D, 97.

454 D, 42.

454 D, 37.

454 D, 47.

454 D, 56, 57.

454–55 D, 129.

455 "simply prodigious": HJ Lt, III, 281.

455 "all these Tyrolean countries": Ibid., 293.

456 "The place is extraordinarily beautiful": Ibid., 301.

456 "almost the summer": Ibid.

456 D, 135.

456 D, 164.

456 D, 164.

457–58 D, 158–59.

458 D, 54.

458–59 D, 87–88.

459 "the 'Irish Question' ": HL.

460 "the other invalid": HJ Lt, III, 358.

Notes

460 D, 207.

460–61 D, 207.

461 "a very nice house": HJ Lt, III, 342.

461–63 WJ's letter quoted intact in JS, 303–5.

463–64 AJ's response: AJ Lt, 185–88.

464 "Alice must have": HJ Lt, III, 349.

464–65 "some twaddle about the senses": WJ Lt, I, 314.

465 "round-edged": HL.

465 "a gentlemanly": HL.

465 WJ to AHJ: HL.

466 "so well-*minded*": HL.

466 "There arose loud cries": LE, III, 297.

466 D, 224.

467 D, 197.

467 D, 211.

467 D, 25.

468 D, 27.

468 D, 55.

468 D, 128.

468 D, 230.

468 D, 45.

469 D, 116.

469 D, 157.

470 D, 45.

470 D, 71.

470 D, 160.

470 D, 196.

470n D, 41.

471 D, 84.

471 D, 192.

471 D, 165.

471 WJ quoted: D, 165.

471 D, 64.

472 D, 104.

472 D, 74.

472 D, 183.

473 D, 119.

474 D, 141.

474 D, 125.

474 D, 230.

474 "a unique and tragic impression": JS, 319.

474 "scared and disconcerted": HJ Lt, III, 481.

475 "the grand mortuary moment": AJ Lt, 190.

475 "pawings": Ibid., 192.

475 D, 230.

475 "intermittent but perfectly inexorable decline": HJ Lt, III, 349.

475 D, 229.

475 D, 232.

475 "supreme deathlike emaciation": HJ Lt, III, 374.

476 "in a strange and touching way": Ibid., 376.

476 D, 89.

477 D, 227.

477 "very substantial wealth": HJ Lt, III, 380.

478 "I can't believe": HL.

478 "compacts which lasted": HL.

478 "Because, even with everything": HJ Lt, III, 381.

479 "by its penetrating *rightness*": HJ Nb, 321.

Fifteen. Ghostly Transactions

483 "As the ranks grow thinner": HL.

484n "own battle-field": HJ Nb, 120.

485 "Mother died Sunday evening": AJ D, 79.

486 "poor dear big-spirited": HJ Lt, III, 364.

486 "how little we can interfere": Ibid., 347.

486 "ghostly extinction": HL.

487 "ghastly amazement": HJ Lt, III, 457.

487 "I must hammer away": HJ Nb, 105.

488 "To combine novel anxieties": GWA, 351.

488 "nervous *tone*": HL.

488 "intently occupied": HJ Lt, III, 391.

489 "Florence is delicious": GWA, 351.

489 "Florence can't hold a candle to it": HL.

489 "Venice is rotten through and through": HL.

489–90 Exchange between WJ and AHJ: HL.

490 "would pass from surprise": the younger Henry James's memoir of AHJ and WJ; HL.

490 "I never again shall feel": HL.

491 "The medium showed": GWA, 284.

491 "You were very easy": HJ Lt, III, 305.

491 " 'Tis the most beautiful": GWA, 327.

492 "The poor innocent little woman": HL.

494 "the dreadful Mrs. Piper": AJ D, 231.

495 "Record of a sitting": HL.

496 "What a caricature": March 19, 1899; HL.

497 "It is a field": WJ Lt, II, 248.

497 "the spirits of the departed": HL.

497 "I am more touched": HL.

498 "You were dear and generous": HL.

Sixteen. Religious Variations: 1898–1902

500 "a perfect little serious rosebud": September 5, 1895; HL.

500 "The sky swept itself clear": WJ Lt, II, 76.

501 "religion is the great interest": Ibid., 58.

502 "The mother sea and fountain-head": Ibid., 149, to Henry W. Rankin.

502 "good amount of cosmic emotion": July 25, 1894; HL.

503 "10½ hours": WJ Lt, II, 77.

503 "My heart has been kicking": Ibid., 78.

504 "a slight valvular lesion": HL.

504 "irritable heart": GWA, 385.

504 "revealed delicacy": HL.

504 "heartbreakingly beautiful": HL.

504 "running . . . serial": HJ Lt, IV, 86.

505 "all the forces of civilization": HJ Lt, III, 508.

505 "It is indeed a pathetic and tragic thing": January 8, 1895; HL.

505 "I take up my own old pen": HJ Nb, 179.

505 "full scenario": Ibid., 188.

505 "The *scenic* method": Ibid., 263.

506 "*act* of my little drama": Ibid., 258.

506 "material matter": HL.

507 "moral repulsiveness": WJ Lt, II, 96.

507 "very extravagant price": August 2, 1899; HL.

507 "intently, piously *fond*": HL.

507 "rubbed you the wrong way": HL.

507 "the 'last long home' ": HJ Lt, IV, 113.

508 "Your long and heartmelting letter": HL.

509 WJ to HJ: HL.

509 "like two strange way-worn birds": GWA, 403.

512 "the subconscious can revitalise": Gerald E. Myers, *William James: His Life and Thought*, 472.

513 "aggressive and hopeful eyes": WJ Lt, II, 151.

514 "risen upon American weather": Ibid., 167, to Mrs. Henry Whitman.

514 "If I go on at this rate": GWA, 432.

514 "I am reading": HL.

514 "But what shall I say": October 25, 1902; FOM, 338.

516 "a neat little *human*": HJ Lt, IV, 159.

516 "I do not advise acceptance": HJ Nb, 372.

516 "tempered the solitude": HJ Lt, IV, 172.

519 "It fits happily enough": Ibid., 194, to William Meredith.

Seventeen. Homecomings: 1904–7

523 "I want to see everything": HJ Lt, IV, 273.

523 "a new lease of artistic life": WJ Lt, II, 195.

524 "I read you": HJ Lt, IV, 418.

524 "putting of everything *à rebours*": Ibid., 425.

524 "You are, for me": Ibid., 378.

524 "not Story's life, but your own": LE, V, 161.

526 "in favour of the *American subject*": HJ Lt, IV, 235.

527 "I have come home": Ibid., 320.

527 "the first, and the one": HJ, *The American Scene*, Chapter VIII, "Concord and Salem."

527n "I find your prose": HJ Lt, IV, 29.

528 "added grace to life": HJ Nb, 323.

528 "I seemed then to know": Ibid., 320.

528 "had sunk on his knees": LE, V, 261.

532 "exquisite and marvelous": To Howard Sturgis, October 17, 1904; HJ Lt, IV, 325.

532 "Oh, yes, a great genius": Edith Wharton, *A Backward Glance* (1934), 186.

536 "my native land, in my old age": HJ Lt, IV, 259.

539 "the most extravagant opinions": June 28, 1905; HL.

539 "the charming sweetness": HJ Lt, IV, 356.

540–45 WJ to AHJ: HL.

541 "the absolutely *silliest*": WJ to AHJ, August 20, 1904; HL.

542 "on such things": HL.

543 "Tell Aleck": GWA, 443.

543 "There is a mystery": WJ Lt, II, 224.

544 "all Italy loved me": GWA, 444.

545 "Papini is a jewel": WJ Lt, II, 245.

545 WJ to AHJ, about Rockefeller: HL.

546 "a work of exquisite genius": WJ Lt, II, 179.

547–48n WJ, HJ, and the American Academy of Arts and Letters: From documents at the American Academy and Institute of Arts and Letters in New York City.

549 "the adulterous relations": FOM, 339.

Notes

551 "to try to produce": HJ Lt, IV, 382.

551 "historic vacuum": HL.

552 "We shall have a sort of honeymoon": WJ Lt, II, 241.

552 "smooth as a young girl": HL.

552 "It was impossible": WJ Lt, II, 248.

554 "And the contrast": HL.

554 "It takes them ½ an hour": WJ to AHJ; HL.

554 "What Makes a Life Significant," in *Talks to Teachers* (1899), is also in FOM.

555n "precipice-disliking soul": WJ Lt, II, 239.

556 "*All* the anguish was yours": Ibid., 251.

556 " 'Home' looks extraordinarily pleasant": Ibid.

556 "before a class in Harvard": Ibid., 262.

556 "Wm James. Good Bye Harvard!": Gerald E. Myers, *William James*, 610.

557 "repulsion at the clangor": WJ Lt, II, 264.

557 "certainly the high tide": Ibid., 265.

557–58 "the most important thing": Ibid., 276.

558 "Kant having already said": Ibid., 267.

560 "has made me feel his real greatness": Ibid., 194.

561 "Rereading [Emerson] *in extenso*": Ibid., 197.

561 "no great sense of wrong": FOM, 452, 442.

Eighteen. 1910 and Later

565 "into such depths of submission": HJ Lt, IV, 466.

566 "*Köstlich* stuff": WJ Lt, II, 299.

566 "to say a thing": Ibid., 277.

566 "delivers its secret": HL.

567 "essentially and intensely entire": HJ Lt, IV, 464.

568 "could I, after all": HL.

568 "knocking about": AHJ to HJ; JM, 185–86.

569 RJ to AHJ: HL.

569 "Destiny of itself": FOM, 270–71.

571 "Your Aunt Mary": JM, 190.

572 Letters between WJ and AHJ: HL.

573 "dreadful angina": GWA, 469.

573 "It hasn't gone well": WJ Lt, II, 326.

574 "He bore his ills": Ibid., 283.

574 "in a perpetual adventure": HJ Lt, IV, 483.

576 "the falsely romantic aspects": F. O. Matthiessen, *Henry James: The Major Phase* (1944), 153.

576 HJ to Coburn: HJ Lt, IV, 424–27.

577 "Prefaces of the most brilliant character": Ibid., 467.

578 "the two beautiful first volumes": Ibid., 484.

578 "they ought, collected together": Quoted by R. P. Blackmur, *The Art of the Novel*, new ed., (1984), xvi.

578 "the treasures of ingenuity": HJ Lt, IV, 498.

578 "extraordinarily encouraging": Ibid., 516.

578 "I *have* had": Ibid., 518.

578 "divinely naked": Ibid., 405.

579 "hold me in your heart": Ibid., 520.

579 "gigantic bonfire": Ibid., 541.

579 "sickishly *loathing*": Ibid., 547.

579 "while he panted and sobbed": LE, V, 440.

580 "splendid for his age": Ibid., 441.

580 "my illness": HL.

580 "I sat down beside the sofa": *The Letters of Edith Wharton*, edited by R.W.B. Lewis and Nancy Lewis (1988), 202.

580 "William cannot walk": LE, V, 442.

581 "I have been continuously": HJ Lt, IV, 550.

581 "I have been miserably": Ibid., 553.

581 "my damnable nervous state": Ibid., 556.

581 WJ to AHJ: HL.

581 "H. and W. both silent": GWA, 483–84.

581 "at an accelerated rate": WJ Lt, II, 399.

582 "I eat. I walk": LE, V, 444.

582 "I am definitely much better": HJ Lt, IV, 557.

582 "smiling, in his sleep": JM, 192.

582 "Bob is dead": Ibid., 191.

582 "It fills me with a new respect": Ibid., 193.

582 "a painless, peaceful, enviable end": HJ Lt, IV, 557.

582 "youngest brother": JM, 193.

582 "A terrible day": GWA, 490.

582 "go to Henry": Ibid., 491.

583 "My own fears": HJ Lt, IV, 560.

583 "William died": GWA, 491.

584 HJ to Perry and Wells: HJ Lt, IV, 561–62.

584 HJ to Edith Wharton: LE, V, 448.

584 "the silver steam-whistle": Ibid., 450.

585 "a sneaking kindness": HJ Lt, IV, 577.

585 "got Home": Ibid., 582.

585 "having got back to work": Ibid., 589.

ACKNOWLEDGMENTS

To David Milch, I owe a very large and special debt of gratitude. This work began in fact as a collaborative venture with my former student, colleague, and office-sharer, the venture itself being an offshoot of a proposed television series on the James family. The series was first conceived by David Milch, and we worked it up together into twelve episodes. It fell by the wayside, however, and the collaborative biographical enterprise was eventually given up as impractical. But the book I went on to write, this book, contains—however transformed in definition and style of expression—many ideas, findings, and emphases originating in discussions and trial runs with David Milch. It is an enormous pleasure for me to record this debt, even as it is next to impossible for me to measure it.

Other biographers of the various Jameses have led the way invaluably. I have read and reread so persistently in Leon Edel's classic five-volume life of Henry James that I would not be surprised if some of my formulations are unintended echoes of his own; there are points at which Professor Edel's narrative is simply the way I have come to understand the matter in question. Gay Wilson Allen's biography of William James remains, after nearly thirty-five years, by far the chief source of knowledge about his subject's career. Jean Strouse's *Alice James* seems to me a model of its kind, and I am frank to say that it grows steadily in insight and magnitude the more I pore over it. And I enjoy realizing that Jane Maher's excellent double biography of the younger brothers Wilky and Bob James, *Biography of Broken Fortunes*, took its start as a term paper in a graduate seminar of mine at Yale. I am also beholden to

Gerald E. Myers for his book, *William James: His Life and Thought* (1986), and to Giles Gunn for *Henry James Senior: A Selection of His Writings* (1974), with the editor's introduction and commentary. I have spoken elsewhere of my admiration for the work that initiated it all, F. O. Matthiessen's *The James Family*, and for its author.

The great collection of James family archives is in the Houghton Library at Harvard University, established there in the 1930s by William James's son Henry. My gratitude to the Houghton Library staff for unfailing kindness and efficiency over a number of years and countless visits is immense and enduring: gratitude in particular to the director, Rodney Dennis; the curator, James Lewis; and to Susan Halpert, Jennie Rathbun, and Melanie Wisner.

I owe thanks to a number of other libraries where I have happily delved and studied: the Sterling, Beinecke, and Art Libraries of Yale University; the library of Union College, the University of Wisconsin at Madison, the University of North Carolina at Chapel Hill; the State Historical Society of Wisconsin, Milwaukee County Historical Society; the New York Public Library, the Milwaukee Public Library, the Albany Public Library, the Redwood Library in Newport, Rhode Island. I should also mention the helpfulness I experienced at the Albany County Courthouse (the Surrogate's Office) and the American Academy and Institute of Arts and Letters.

Appendix A. My inquiry into the "strange death of Daniel Gibbens" was virtually made possible by the expert guidance of Peter A. Coclanis, professor of history at the University of North Carolina in Chapel Hill.

Appendix B. Perhaps the most enjoyable phase of the work on this book occurred after I had more or less finished the book itself as originally envisaged. This was the tracing of "the later Jameses," an undertaking, begun in the summer of 1989, through which I came to know a number of contemporary Jameses. The process began when Alexander R. James, from Ireland and in answer to my appeal for help, directed me to his cousin Margaret James, "Maggie," with an address near Pittsburgh. During a memorably fruitful visit with Maggie James in February 1990 (my son Nat accompanying and taping), Maggie put me on to Michael James, "Mickey," and before long I was conversing with Mickey James in his Back Bay, Boston, home and experiencing his generosity of spirit, command of the family history, and finely etched judgments. On another occasion, we met in a Cambridge restaurant, where we were joined by Roberta Sheehan, an exceedingly learned Jamesian with a particular interest in William James's son Billy.

After that, one way and another, I came in touch, for phone conversations and exchanges of letters, with the present William James in Santa Fe (John and Pamela Blum helped in this connection), with Henry James Vaux, Robertson's grandson, in Berkeley (here Jean Strouse supplied information), and

[672

Acknowledgments

with two other Californians, Margaret Short Rogers and Nan Sparrow. Margaret Rogers is the granddaughter of Peggy James, William's daughter, and in an extraordinary act of trust she forwarded to me some 300 letters written by her grandmother (to father, Uncle Henry, brothers, daughter) dating from 1899 to 1949. Nan Sparrow, a close family friend, added further information and insights into the family relations.

Most of the Jameses just mentioned are described in the appendix, where I also try to indicate the special kind of help each gave me. What I offer here is a collective heartfelt word of gratitude.

Libraries again proved indispensable: the Pusey Library at Harvard, where the alumni archives are stored—I am indebted to the curator, Clark Elliott (and to Robert Shenton, Secretary of the Corporation, who courteously put me on to the archives); Sterling Library at Yale; Bancroft Library in the University of California at Berkeley; Bryn Mawr College Library, where the curator of the alumnae archives, Ms. Caroline Richardson, kindly supplied me with data on Peggy James's college years and letters between the senior Jameses and M. Carey Thomas. The diary of Peggy's roommate Mary Worthington has recently become available there, and at some future date I hope to examine it with an eye to writing about it. I should also make special mention of the Rosenbach Museum and Library in Philadelphia, with its vast Marianne Moore archives. I am thankful to Patricia Willis of the Beinecke Library at Yale for guiding me to this charming institution; and to Leslie Morris, the Curator of Books and Manuscripts, for making available the exchange of letters on deposit there between Peggy James and Marianne Moore.

Margaretta Lovell, then of the University of California at Berkeley, pillaged local archives for a mass of material about Bruce Porter; for this heroic feat, much thanks.

Jane Maher partook of information about Wilky James's descendants. Peter and Ebie Blume talked helpfully about the daughters of Edward Holton James and Louisa Cushing. Alexander Calder's autobiography, *Calder* (1966), was an attractive source; and Eleanor Clark reminisced with me about the Calder family. Nicholas Fox Weber, already helpful in other ways, put relevant volumes from his art library at my disposal. For the career of the painter Alexander James, I am indebted to the catalogue of the Memorial Exhibition of his work (1947–48), in which Thornton Wilder is quoted.

Other individual assistance

It is a pleasure to declare my gratitude to: Liam Kelly of Bailieborough, Ireland, our entertaining and knowledgeable guide through the area and two centuries of its history; Guido Calabresi for an explanation of a singular New York statute regarding property; the late Sidney Ahlstrom for instruction in the evening catechism of Calvinist families; Joel Pfister, then in the American Studies graduate program at Yale, for shedding light on certain social-theory debates in nineteenth-century America, including the writings of Stephen Pearl Andrews; George Abbot White, for so kindly making me free of the Matthiessen Room in Eliot House at Harvard, on my visits to Houghton Library.

Daniel Aaron took time off from the many demands on him to read the entire manuscript, and to bring it down, with voluminous notes and queries (all of which were acted on), for a daylong conference. Friendship, even of more than forty years' standing, can go no further. Bertram Wyatt-Brown read several of the chapters and, during our 1989–90 association at the National Humanities Center, gave expert advice stemming from his own labors on a biography of the Percy family, a book to be eagerly waited for.

Book-making

No aspect of the work on this book was more enjoyable and fruitful than the association with Roger Straus and Robert Giroux. The former gave light and zest to every meeting with him; the latter enriched the whole experience not only by his editorial skill and wisdom, but by discoursing out of his own literary lore about American writers past and present. Visits to the publishing offices on Union Square were something invariably to be treasured. Lynn Warshow, the copy editor at Farrar, Straus and Giroux, did an exceptionally painstaking and proficient job on a bulky manuscript that provided more challenges and questions than I like to admit. I have been the lucky beneficiary over half a dozen years of the typing and word-processing skills of Lorraine Estra and May Sansone at Yale, of Linda Morgan and Karen Carroll at the National Humanities Center, and in the later stages of Sue Berger in New York.

The index was prepared by the talented and knowledgeable Bonney MacDonald, author of *Henry James's Italian Hours* (1990).

The gifted Virginia Schendler was responsible for the photograph on the jacket, thereby admitting me to her enlarging gallery of individuals from the world of letters.

Prior publication

A version of Chapter One appeared in *The New Republic*, and most of Chapter Two in *American Literature, Culture and Ideology: Essays in Memory of Henry Nash Smith*, Beverly R. Voloshin, editor. Portions of Chapter Seven were combined in an article in *19th Century Fiction*. The second half of Chapter Eight came out in *The Yale Review*. Chapter Seventeen, more or less intact, appeared in the *South Atlantic Quarterly*.

Acknowledgments

Alexander R. James

The literary executor of the James family archives has been acknowledged more than once in this book's notations. Here let me express my very great thanks for his permission to quote from those archives wherever located.

Family

The assistance of the members of one's family is especially welcome with a work that itself has to do with family relations. Nathaniel Lewis, after reading the manuscript, made one key suggestion that was immediately acted upon; and I have benefited frequently from conversations with him about American cultural history and this portion of it, most memorably on a wintry trip to western Pennsylvania. Emma Lewis accompanied me to Ireland and to Bailieborough, took pictures of considerable later value, and has served as a memory resource about the region and about the "James family London," which we later explored. Emma and Sophie Lewis, meanwhile, have contributed more than they may know in their continuing interest, questions, comments. Nancy Lewis, as before, as always, was the sustaining presence. Erstwhile co-editor and permanent partner, she is, in the phrase of William James, one who makes a life significant.

In the front of this book, I have hinted at how much I cherish and I owe to Nancy Lewis's sister Judith McConnell and her cousin Sue Berger.

INDEX

List of abbreviations
AJ   Alice James
AHJ   Alice Howe Gibbens James
GWJ   Garth Wilkinson James (Wilky)
HSr   Henry James, Sr.
HJ   Henry James
MRJ   Mary Robertson Walsh James
RJ   Robertson James (Bob)
WofA   William James of Albany
WJ   William James
KPL   Katharine Peabody Loring
MT   Mary Temple (Minny)
AK   Catherine Walsh (Aunt Kate)

Index

693   ]

Index